DISCRIMINATORY CLUBS

Discriminatory Clubs

THE GEOPOLITICS OF
INTERNATIONAL ORGANIZATIONS

CHRISTINA L. DAVIS

PRINCETON UNIVERSITY PRESS
PRINCETON & OXFORD

Published by Princeton University Press
41 William Street, Princeton, New Jersey 08540
99 Banbury Road, Oxford OX2 6JX

press.princeton.edu

All Rights Reserved
ISBN 978-0-691-24779-3
ISBN (pbk.) 978-0-691-24778-6
ISBN (e-book) 978-0-691-24780-9

British Library Cataloging-in-Publication Data is available

Editorial: Bridget Flannery-McCoy and Alena Chekanov
Production Editorial: Jenny Wolkowicki
Cover design: Katie Osborne
Production: Lauren Reese
Publicity: William Pagdatoon
Copyeditor: Bhisham Bherwani

This book has been composed in Arno Pro

10 9 8 7 6 5 4 3 2 1

For my parents

CONTENTS

ILLUSTRATIONS

Figures

Tables

ACKNOWLEDGMENTS

MY FIRST two books on international cooperation focused on the negotiation and enforcement of rules, but I was often asked about selection bias. That criticism led me to think more about how states choose their partners. This book attempts to provide the answer to why some states agree to pursue shared governance through joining international organizations. The story of Japan's entry into the trade regime in 1955 revealed the importance of its alliance with the United States to open doors for a former enemy and mercantilist country in a decision that would lay the foundation for Japan's export-led growth miracle. As I looked further, I found this was more than just an exceptional case. Across organizations and governments, relations between countries seemed to matter as much as or more than compliance with rules. While writing about accession to the WTO and OECD in papers that provided the impetus for my research on enlargement processes, the events in Ukraine during the fall of 2013 highlighted broader currents of meaning that attach to decisions about membership. For Ukraine, the choice between association with Europe in the EU Eastern Partnership Policy or deepening integration with Russia in a proposed Eurasian Economic Union sparked a social movement that overthrew the government and led to the sequence of events toward war with Russia. Clearly the participants understood that membership was about more than adjusting tariff rates. But I felt that theories on international institutions were neglecting this relational dynamic. Explaining how countries choose sides forces one to recognize the club dynamics that underlie multilateral organizations.

Teaching international organization and global governance seminars at Princeton and Harvard has provided me with the opportunity to develop ideas in conversation with incredible students. As we debated the applications of Palestine or Taiwan to join international organizations or tried to understand Brexit, we discussed the many implications of membership for the identity of states and their people. The students challenged conventional views about market failures and power politics and shared stories about their experiences in student clubs and sports teams. My office at Princeton where I did much of the research for this book overlooked the eating clubs on Prospect Street where students gather for meals and socializing, with each club having its own arcane system to select members. The "bicker" and "sign-in" processes for joining a Princeton eating club, which I heard about when I was doing research on negotiations over accession to the trade regime, offered the background for the analogy that runs through the book. Exchanges with students proved fertile ground to explore different approaches to international relations.

My work with Meredith Wilf and Tyler Pratt began when they were students in my international organization Ph.D. seminar at Princeton, and led to co-authoring articles that greatly moved forward the research on this project. I could not have asked for better collaborators who brought creative ideas and statistical skills that made the research far better. I am grateful to them for letting me include their work as co-authored chapters 3 and 4, and I am deeply indebted to them for their input on the entire book.

Policymakers in Japan, Korea, Europe, and the United States helped ground this research with real-world perspectives. I am grateful to the many policymakers who agreed to be interviewed and were generous to share their time and knowledge so that this book could better reflect the practice of diplomacy. Although some requested to remain anonymous and provided information on a background basis, I would like to thank in particular the following individuals: Byung-il Choi, Naoshi Hirose, Douglas Yu-Tien Hsu, Jun-il Kim, Takeshi Komoto, Frank Lee, Rokuichirō Michii, Seiichirō Noboru, Myoung-ho Shin, Noriyuki Shikata, Jonathan Sun, and Akihiko Tamura. For research in chapter 5, I benefited from access to the archives of the OECD, and I am grateful to the assistance of Sandra Willmott, who made it possible to gather extensive materials in a short visit in 2014. Several officials of the OECD were kind to grant their time for interviews and to share data on participation in the institution. I thank Gita Kothari, Luiz de Mello, Andreas Schaal, Jeff Schaffer, and Jan Schuijer. My research on the Taiwan case benefited from a visit to Taiwan in December 2019 to speak at the Taiwan Political Science Association and at National Taiwan University. I thank Hans Tung for providing me this opportunity and making comments on my research. Hans and May Lin of TECO Boston arranged interviews for me to meet with officials in government and the private sector.

The chapters of this book were presented over the years at many conferences and seminars, where I received invaluable feedback with both sharp criticism and enough interest to encourage further work. I thank Inken von Borzyskowski, Lawrence Broz, Allison Carnegie, Jonathan Chu, Cecilia Corsini, Janina Dill, Axel Dreher, Marina Duque, Alison Duxbury, Andreas Fuchs, Judith Goldstein, Emilie Hafner-Burton, Marina Henke, Stephanie Hofmann, Yoram Hoftel, Liesbet Hooghe, Masahiro Kawai, Tsuyoshi Kawase, Keisuke Iida, Dan Keleman, Barbara Koremenos, Kyle Lascurettes, Phillip Lipscy, Tom Long, Ed Mansfield, Lisa Martin, Julia Morse, Megumi Naoi, Kalypso Nicolaïdis, Saadia Pekkanen, Jon Pevehouse, Mark Pollack, Paul Poast, Stephanie Rickard, Peter Rosendorff, Nita Rudra, Ken Scheve, Christina Schneider, Duncan Snidal, Mireya Solis, David Steinberg, Randall Stone, Mike Tomz, Felicity Vabulas, Lora Anne Viola, Erik Voeten, James Vreeland, Daniel Wajner, Oliver Westerwinter, and Boliang Zhu. I am surely leaving off some names, as this book has received countless rounds of feedback, and I am grateful to the helpful advice of all who have offered their questions and comments.

Conversations with colleagues at Princeton and Harvard have enriched my understanding of international relations and offered a sounding board for different parts of this book. I am especially grateful to Stephen Chaudoin, Sannoy Das, Jeffrey Frieden, Amaney Jamal, Iain Johnston, Robert Keohane, Josh Kertzer, Sophie Meunier, Christoph Mikulaschek, Helen Milner, Andrew Moravcsik, Susan Pharr, Dustin Tingley, Mark Wu, and Keren Yarhi-Milo. Joanne Gowa pushed me with tough questions that were softened by friendship and a willingness to always give more comments. Robert Keohane encouraged me to probe more deeply into why relationships matter and to look for broader patterns that shape cooperation.

I am grateful for institutional support from Princeton University for the starting years as I began research into the politics of membership and from Harvard University for the final years of the project. At Princeton, the Niehaus Center for Globalization and Governance provided rich intellectual exchange in the weekly seminars and in conferences around the world, and almost every chapter in this book was presented at these different venues. During the 2016–17 academic year, I hosted six scholars to visit Princeton for the Fung Global Fellows Program of the Princeton Institute for International and Regional Studies to research on international society and global governance. Lai-Ha Chan, Srividya Jandhyala, Anastassia V. Obydenkova, Jong Hee Park, Lena Rethel, and Vinícius Rodrigues Vieira contributed greatly to this manuscript through sharing their own research and providing me with feedback on the manuscript over the year. They joined Julia Gray, Anja Jetschke, and Krzysztof Pelc in a workshop for this manuscript in April 2017. The detailed comments on draft chapters at the book workshop offered important direction for finalizing the book, and I am so grateful for their careful reading and time spent reviewing each chapter. Julia Gray has been exceptionally kind to read multiple versions of many chapters over the years and exchange notes and reflections on everything from coding treaties to why all this matters.

At Harvard, the associates and speakers of the Program on U.S.-Japan Relations have offered an insider perspective on key issues that have helped me connect my academic research to both historical events and current policy debates. Two years as a Radcliffe Fellow provided me with release from teaching and an incredibly diverse community. Learning different perspectives on discrimination as it has been experienced and studied across cultures and disciplines helped me sharpen my ideas on the tensions between universal norms and discriminatory practices that coexist within multilateral institutions. I am grateful to Susan and Kenneth Wallach for their generous funding to support scholarship at the Radcliffe Institute for Advanced Studies.

For a book of this size, many research assistants deserve credit. Raymond Hicks provided extensive support for the development of the datasets analyzed in the book and spent countless hours delving into different sources to track down the charters of international organizations and any variable that could help improve my analysis. Max Calleo, Nina Coomes, Ashleigh Maciolek, and Emilee Martichenko worked as my faculty assistants to gather materials for case research and proofreading. Sophie Welsh handled everything from data coding to editing, as she learned more than she ever expected about international organizations. Many others have supported my research with critical input, and I am grateful to the following students: Idir Aitsahalia, Emmanuel Calivo, Brandon Chen, Mari Chen-Fiske, Ian Chong, Natalie Dabkowski, Nathan Eckstein, Cassandra Emmons, Noah Dasanaike, Tai Hirose, Armita Hosseini, Kaede Ishidate, Ali Jebari, Shirō Kuriwaki, James Lee, Jialu Li, Ruofan Ma, Kouta Ohyama, Alex Park, Yon Soo Park, Reshini Premaratne, Eli Soffer, Harry Sparks, Diana Stanescu, Shiyun Tang, Kento Yamada, Shun Yamaya, and Jason Weinreb.

I thank the University of Chicago Press and the Southern Political Science Association for permission to include an edited version of "Joining the Club? Accession to the GATT/WTO," which was published in the *Journal of Politics* as a co-authored article with Meredith Wilf (2017, 79:964–978). I also thank Springer Press for allowing me to reprint part of "The Forces of Attraction: How Security Interests Shape Membership in Economic Institutions," which was published in the *Review of International Organizations* as a co-authored article with Tyler Pratt (2021, 16:903–929). Portions of chapter 6 were previously published in "Japan: Interest Group Politics, Foreign Policy Linkages, and the TPP," a chapter in Benedict Kingsbury et al. *Megaregulation Contested: Global Economic Ordering After TPP,* (Oxford University Press, 2019: p. 573–591) and appear by permission of Oxford University Press.

At Princeton University Press, Bridget Flannery-McCoy guided the book from submission to completion, while Alena Chekanov and Jenny Wolkowicki helped with production and Heather Jones compiled the index. My copyeditor Bhisham Bherwani worked tirelessly to improve consistency and clarity throughout the manuscript. I am extremely grateful to the reviewers who saw promise in the ideas and urged clarification of key points to better explain my theory and contribution. Their detailed comments greatly improved the book.

Trying to complete a book during a pandemic presented its own challenges, but I had already finished my field work, and I am fortunate to have a supportive family. My teenage children Keiji and Misaki have such a positive attitude about their own studies that I could not be discouraged by the various setbacks that came up in my work. I am grateful for their willingness to listen and share ideas over family meals and on our many hikes together. My parents-in-law Takashi and Fumiko Imai hosted us in Tokyo when travel was possible and made time for calls when we could not visit. My husband Kosuke Imai has supported me through every twist and turn of writing this book while raising a family. He both made sure I had time to write and forced me to stop writing so we could have fun together. Choosing Kosuke as my partner for life was the best decision I ever made—by any evaluation criterion. I dedicate this book to my parents, Alton and Carole Davis. They inspired my love of reading and learning and encouraged me to pursue my dreams even when it has taken me far away to explore the world.

DISCRIMINATORY CLUBS

1

Membership and International Cooperation

MEMBER SELECTION forms one of the defining processes of social organization. Whether it be individuals joining a sports team or a social club or countries joining international organizations, the choice of membership imposes categories on who we are and what we do. Group membership determines status. Theories of socialization and institutional commitment depend on our understanding the full context of rules. Even the fundamental difference between types of government derives from the selection process for leaders. Without understanding who takes part in governance, one cannot understand the effectiveness of the organizations that we study. Certainly we know that few organizations are formed around a random sample of actors—self-selecting, screening for talent, and selling access to the highest bidder represent some of the many ways through which groups form.

How does member selection occur at the international level? The concern with selection bias has long confounded research on the effectiveness of international institutions because it is difficult to know whether the conditions leading to membership or the constraints of membership shape behavior. Few international organizations offer automatic admission. Even an organization like the United Nations that espouses universality encounters controversy over membership—North and South Korea were unable to join until 1991, Switzerland did not opt to join until 2002, and Palestine and Taiwan remain outsiders today. Nor do we see consistent enforcement of performance criteria with screening for quality. Indeed, some countries join organizations without making significant policy changes. How can we explain Turkey as a founding member of the Organisation for Economic Co-operation and Development

(OECD) in 1961 and communist Poland joining the General Agreement on Tariffs and Trade (GATT) in 1967? Even regional organizations constitute more than a geographic category, as seen by the British experience in joining the European Economic Community in 1973, 16 years after formation and its most recent decision to exit. Far from being automatic or technocratic, membership decisions are deeply political. States evaluate the benefits of joining the organization and their relationship with other members. Rather than treat biased entry into organizations as a nuisance for research on the effects of institutions, we must seek to understand the complex process by which states coalesce into groups that become members of an institution.

This book develops a theory about international organizations as discriminatory clubs of states. A core of like-minded states with common security interests choose to cooperate on other issues through joining together in international organizations. Their geopolitical alignment shapes who wants to join an organization, whether they are accepted into the club, and the price of entry. In contrast to theories that explain cooperation in terms of market failure within an issue area, my argument shows the channel by which security interests form the basis for cooperation and status. Geopolitical alignment generates the willingness to recognize the authority of another state as a rule-maker in global governance. Approving joint membership in international organizations allocates status. The empirical evidence highlights systematic biases in the patterns of states that enter international organizations. But this is not an argument about screening for compliance—states eschew the narrow selection criteria expected by a contractual approach in favor of discretionary selection as part of broad strategies of economic statecraft. Blackmail, side payments, and favoritism are rife in the accession politics of international organizations.

Despite the emphasis on public goods as the core problem for cooperation, many policy problems present impure public goods for which clubs can provide the benefits to a limited number while excluding others. Most international organizations include provisions for defining membership as a way to restrict cooperation to a subset of states. Moreover, international organizations are discriminatory because members care not only about provision of the cooperative good but also about the identity of other members. Rather than screening for states with the highest capacity, the process of joining international organizations often resembles entry into a social club that admits friends and excludes rivals. Where social clubs may rely on race or socioeconomic status as the basis for discrimination, states use geopolitical alignment as the basis for discrimination in decisions over organizational membership.

The discriminatory politics of membership embed within international society patterns of interaction. For example, not only NATO and other alliances, but also the European Union (EU), OECD, and international economic institutions like the GATT established boundaries of cooperation for a coalition of states that share a common security interest. The group of states commonly referred to as "the West" during the Cold War was defined by these overlapping memberships in institutions more than by a geographic location or liberal ideology. As a rising power, China pursues a strategy that first brings countries together under its umbrella for cooperation in institutions. From its co-leadership with Russia of the Shanghai Cooperation Organisation starting in 2002 to formation of the Asian Infrastructure Investment Bank in 2016, China unites like-minded states in institutions as a way to build a sphere of influence. Weaker states also use institutional agglomeration as a step toward unified action. The formal rules of membership draw lines to establish who is expected to act together, which is a critical component of social norms.

The argument places security first in the sequence of cooperation. Yet the security interests that motivate coalition-building through shared memberships in institutions are more diffuse than specific threats to survival. Joining organizations is a tool of soft power diplomacy—organizational membership represents an investment in relationships with other states. In some cases, states offer preferential entry to a potential cooperation partner as a reward and bribe intended to entice them toward closer relations. Here institutions broaden and deepen the ties among states that are not allies. In other cases, shared membership helps states to consolidate alliance ties through expanding the range of issues for cooperation beyond security. Finally, rivalry manifests itself through excluding enemies from organizations as a strategy to deny access to both material benefits and relational networks.

This sequential enlargement privileges early entry by allies and gradual enlargement to include others after the rules and membership coalition of allied states have already been consolidated. When allowed to enter, non-allied states may pay a higher price through larger reform commitments relative to the easy path to entry given to allies. Yet overexpansion may arise if too many join. The need to reconfigure which groups of states are willing to work together has become a factor driving the fragmentation of global governance across multiple overlapping international organizations.

The theory looks beyond great power politics. Major powers are at the forefront of establishing institutions and serving as gatekeepers over membership, but they are not the only ones to use this strategy. Coalitions form through a joint decision by states to form a group, and security interests shape not only the motives of powerful states who lead but also the willingness of others to participate. If anything, smaller states have greater need to use institutions as a way to expand ties and establish their position within the social hierarchy of the international system. For marginal states seeking to normalize relations after a rupture, entry into organizations signals commitment to joint actions and mutual recognition.

The question of whether to join or leave a major international organization goes to the highest levels of authority within a state—these are not decisions left to mid-level diplomats. The Brexit referendum on UK membership in the EU absorbed national politics for years. But even for less high-profile cases, the decisions are taken very seriously. The Mexican debate over joining the GATT offers an interesting example. Having declined to join the original GATT agreement in 1948—the Finance Minister denounced it as a threat to national industries—the government began talks about joining in 1979. Working party negotiations were going well, with GATT members agreeing to allow flexibility for Mexico to preserve many of its core developmental state policies. Alongside those negotiations, Mexican president José López Portillo conducted a domestic evaluation on the merits of GATT accession, with input from economic analysts and in consultation with industry and labor groups. The question was covered in front-page media commentary (Ortiz Mena, 2005, pp. 221–222). Critics portrayed accession as a move toward dependence on the United States as well as a threat to economic sovereignty and the development model writ large. The final vote of the cabinet in March 1980 opposed accession. López Portillo announced the postponement of GATT accession on the forty-second anniversary of Mexico's expropriation of U.S. oil companies, framing rejection of the GATT in terms of Mexican nationalism and anti-American policy (Story, 1982, p. 775).[1] Eventually the government did join the GATT in 1986, after relations with the United States had significantly improved and economic reform held new urgency (Davis and Wilf, 2015).

The foreign policy process at the domestic level reinforces the security framing of membership decisions. The executive leadership and foreign

---

1. Story (1982) contends that the desire to show independence from the United States perversely pushed López Portillo to decline joining after receiving strong pressure from the United States that it should become a member. López Portillo's relations with the Carter administration were poor at this time.

ministry prioritize security, and they are the lead actors who set the agenda to seek membership. Later, during ratification, other domestic actors must accept or decline membership as a package deal. Broad foreign policy identity augments the attractiveness of an organization that confers status by means of deepening association with other like-minded states. Or, as in the example of Mexico in the GATT, foreign policy tensions could reduce the appeal of joining. Actors who may have little understanding or interest in the details of the rules will pay attention to the high politics of joining an organization.

Outside the scope of specific policy reforms and institutional constraints, membership plays a role in defining how states fit within international society. When protests erupted in Ukraine in 2013 over the choice between joining a customs union with Russia or signing a trade agreement with Europe, the issue represented more than any terms contained in the agreement—it signaled the future direction of Ukraine: to be a European democracy or to remain within the sphere of Russia.[2] The brutal war to come saw its origins in this turning point. Further back in history, Japan joined the founders of the International Labour Organization in 1919 as part of its foreign policy goal to follow world trends and achieve major power status as a permanent member of the League of Nations, while the government expressed grave concerns about the possibility of foreign imposition of restrictions on labor policies. Neither the trade interests of Ukraine nor the labor policies of Japan would account for their membership choices. Through membership in international institutions, they sought to shape their association with other states. States join organizations as much for the benefit of status gained by their association with a particular group of states as for the need to cooperate on a particular set of policies.

Ending membership represents the ultimate sanction because it breaks all association with the other actor. Russia's invasion of Ukraine provoked proposals to exclude it from international organizations—in 2014, after the first invasion, accession talks for Russia to join the OECD were put on hold, and Russia was removed from the G8; the second invasion in 2022 led the OECD to terminate the Russian accession process, while the Council of Europe voted to end Russia's membership in the organization. An emergency session of the World Tourism Body was called to hear a proposal to expel Russia from its

---

2. Many inside and outside of Ukraine portrayed the decision as putting its reputation at stake even when the actual levels of economic integration would not have changed in significant ways. Rejection of the association agreement in September 2013 triggered street protests and shook investors' confidence in Ukrainian sovereign debt (Gray and Hicks, 2014, pp. 331–332).

membership, and some called for suspending its membership in the International Monetary Fund (IMF), World Bank, and World Trade Organization (WTO). These were unusual requests, as states rarely ask for and even more rarely succeed in expelling other states. In contrast, offering membership entry as a sign of solidarity happens more often. After years of deflecting Ukraine's wish to enter the EU, in response to Russian aggression the President of the European Commission Ursula von der Leyen proclaimed in February 2022 that "Ukraine is one of us and we want them in EU."[3] Seeking to enhance its ties to Europe, Georgia filed its application to join the EU days after the Russian invasion of its neighbor. In reality Georgia and Ukraine have years before membership, but just the act of applying offers a symbolic step to deepen the association with Europe.

Belonging to institutions has a significant impact on behavior. Empirical studies assess the importance of specific institutions in shaping outcomes within the issue area through comparison of policies of members and non-members.[4] Scholars examine how the number of memberships across international organizations more generally can shape trade or conflict (Russett and Oneal, 2001; Boehmer, Gartzke, and Nordstrom, 2004; Ingram, Robinson, and Busch, 2005). Bearce and Bondanella (2007) find there is significant convergence of interests among states that share common IGO membership.

Theories of international institutions explain demand for cooperation that arises from the interest in the issue area regulated. This suggests that membership rules would be clearly defined, whether by laying out eligibility for a universal organization or by establishing rigorous conditions for a restrictive organization. To maximize cooperation, accession would follow a review of whether a state meets the provisions in agreements. Members could conduct this review themselves or delegate to a committee or bureaucracy.

Therefore it is puzzling that the rules of membership are discretionary and flexible. In a comprehensive review of charter provisions in international organizations, I find that a surprising number of international organizations are quite vague about membership criteria. Founding members sign up without any review process, while those who join through enlargement may negotiate terms with members but typically do so absent formal guidelines. Club IGOs

---

3. Euronews, 28 February 2022, available at https://www.euronews.com/2022/02/27/ukraine-is-one-of-us-and-we-want-them-in-eu-ursula-von-der-leyen-tells-euronews, accessed 17 March 2022.

4. For example, see literature on WTO (Rose, 2004; Gowa and Kim, 2005; Goldstein, Rivers, and Tomz, 2007) or environmental policies (Young, 1999; Breitmeier, Underdal, and Young, 2011).

steer a middle course between universality and precise entry conditions. Choosing flexible membership rules supports discriminatory membership. Such institutional design provides maximal discretion to change the terms of membership as part of strategic bargains. Governments have opted to allow themselves discretion over membership in a wide range of institutions from NATO to the WTO. This discretion can be applied to lower the entry bar for some states and raise it for others. Within these organizations, geopolitical alignment strongly predicts membership patterns.

As a club IGO, the OECD illustrates wide discretion over membership. While the organization is often viewed as an exclusive grouping of rich industrial democracies that advocate liberal economic policies and business regulatory standards, the reality is more complex. The OECD counts Turkey as a founding member, welcomed Mexico in 1994 before it had either completed its democratization process or achieved high income status, and most recently admitted Colombia to become its thirty-seventh member. Close affinity with the United States and Europe matter as much as economic policies to explain such decisions. In contrast, since expressing interest in the organization in the mid-1990s, Russia's effort to join was first slowed by reviews of problems in its banking sector and corruption, and then halted in response to the invasion of Ukraine.

Charter provisions are even more sparse when it comes to expelling a member from the organization. One might expect that states would enforce compliance through provisions for suspending or even terminating membership of repeat offenders. Designing terms to end a contract in case of violation would strengthen the commitment device of joining the institution. But states do not adopt this strategy of conditional membership. Few international organizations have terms for expelling a member based on noncompliance. As EU negotiators confronted the Greek debt crisis in 2010, the concern about Greek exit missed the point that while Greece could vote itself out of the union, the other EU members could not vote to throw it out! States can act outside of treaty rules, of course, but they do so in order to ostracize a pariah state rather than to enforce rules. For example, the majority of members in the Universal Postal Union (UPU) voted to expel South Africa as an expression of opposition to Apartheid policies, and they did so despite objections that there were no rules in the organization for expulsion and no evidence that South Africa had acted contrary to IGO principles for postal service cooperation. The area most likely to witness suspension is democratic backsliding, not regulatory violations. And even then, democratic backsliding by strategic partners is usually not targeted (Borzyskowski and Vabulas, 2019a).

Individual country departures correspond to a geopolitical rift. The World Health Organization (WHO) has been the center of controversy in super-power rivalries on numerous occasions—the USSR left the World Health Assembly (WHA) in 1949 to protest what they said were unfair actions by the WHO to withhold medical supplies from Eastern Europe (Fee and Brown, 2016). President Trump dramatically announced he would exit the organization amidst a pandemic because he saw the organization as favoring China.[5] Cuba departed the IMF within five years of its revolution over a disagreement about repayment of loans by the Batista government that had just been over-thrown. Others have had disagreements with the IMF over loans, but without exiting, though geopolitical tensions may impede the willingness of governments to work through a deal.[6] In their analysis of 200 exit cases, Borzyskowski and Vabulas (2019b) show that foreign policy affinity among members reduces the likelihood of exit.

Viewing international institutions as clubs embedded within broader political relations among states explains the rarity of expulsion. Just as governments do not revoke citizenship as punishment for criminal actions, most IGOs do not include expulsion as a tool for enforcing compliance. Political selection to get into international organizations magnifies the significance of expulsion threats. Not only would it deny the benefits of cooperation, but expulsion would also constitute a rejection of continued association and removal of status within international society. States would not be willing to confront a threat of expulsion for failing to meet criteria that were not necessary for entry. Such provisions would be incompatible with the entire notion of joining a community.

This book will develop a theory to explain why states use club membership design for accession and how they take advantage of the discretion over conditionality and participation mandate to inject geopolitics into their membership decisions. The vague terms and room for exclusion at the time of entry represent a flexibility mechanism in the institutional design. Ad hoc criteria facilitate statecraft that uses IGO membership as carrot and stick to advance purposes beyond cooperation on the issues regulated by the rules.

5. The emergence of leaders seeking to end isolation brought the governments back. Nikita Khrushchev sought "peaceful co-existence" with the United States, and as part of this strategy returned to active engagement in WHO in 1955; President Joseph Biden terminated the process of U.S. withdrawal from the WHO.

6. The Castro government went on to repay the loans without rejoining the organization (Boughton, 2016, p. 5).

1.1 Defining IGO Membership

Membership politics are the process by which states set boundaries around a community of states for cooperation. At the level of self-governing villages, the first design principle of cooperation is setting boundaries for the group (Ostrom, 2000). Global governance also requires community. When going beyond the village, community cannot be taken for granted. Nationalism looms large in the community-building process to form state boundaries. Anderson (2016) established the paradigm to view *imagined communities* that develop when individuals become conscious of belonging with a particular political group. In Anderson's societal argument, the development of capitalism and the printed word opened horizontal ties of shared experience that facilitated identity aggregation.

At the international level, states must also set boundaries and build communities to facilitate governance. They do so through membership in international organizations. An international organization can serve as a forum to gather states together and a resource to facilitate cooperation. An IGO can become an actor that empowers transnational bureaucrats for independent action (Hurd, 2021). Through each of these processes, the IGO builds on relational ties among states and further deepens those ties. The gains of cooperation provide incentives for states to limit joint action to subgroups. Interactions among states create the coherence for shared identity that determines who is included within these boundaries.

The commitment to ongoing interaction differentiates membership from simple treaty commitments. Governments bind themselves together as a group and not just as independent actors agreeing to specific terms about behavior. Hooghe, Lenz, and Marks (2019, p. 15), in their theory of international organization, describe the nature of an evolving cooperation project among members as part of the sociality of incomplete contracting that occurs in international organizations. They emphasize that "participants are not merely making a bargain. They are also consenting to an iterated process of negotiation as circumstances change." The layering of new commitments will often occur at a lower level of approval, without a return to the same domestic ratification process.

This book examines formal intergovernmental organizations (IGOs). These are organizations that are established by three or more states and have a permanent headquarters, with regular meetings among member states. Their founding documents include membership criteria and obligations. The set of formal IGOs encompasses organizations with little institutional structure, such as the Association of Southeast Nations at its formation in 1967, and those with more of an institutional "footprint," such as the United Nations. It also includes organizations with a narrow focus on a single issue, such as OPEC, and those with a broader scope, such as the OECD.

International organizations sometimes include more complex structures to accomplish tasks, such as emanation organizations or subcommittees. These secondary levels of organizational structure are not the focus of analysis here. In most cases the membership in the primary organization corresponds directly to membership in the subordinate organization. Informal organizations also represent a critical arena for diplomacy that is subject to socializing effects (Vabulas and Snidal, 2013; Roger, 2021). But this lies outside the scope of this study. My focus lies in explaining the puzzle of informal practices that seep into formal structures.

What counts as membership? There are many forms of interaction with an IGO that can fall short of membership but nonetheless represent meaningful diplomacy. For example, observer status is widely used by the United Nations and the OECD. The GATT allowed a range of ad hoc roles that have been considered de facto membership in some studies (Goldstein, Rivers, and Tomz, 2007). This book will focus on formal membership, while considering the intervening steps that may precede a country's joining the organization. Informal participation can ebb and flow, with little observable indication to outsiders.[7] More importantly, there is a substantive difference in the commitment level of a country that chooses to attend meetings and its decision to formally commit to abide by all requirements of membership, including budgetary support and rule compliance. Formal membership brings voting rights and governance authority that implicates status as an equal actor.

There is a demand and a supply side to membership. First, a government must seek to join.[8] What motivates states to seek entry? There have been occasions of coercive pressure, such as Russian threats and bribes to induce former Soviet Republics to join the Commonwealth of Independent States. But at some level, sovereign states choose whether to seek membership. Not all are successful. An applicant must earn approval from other members.

---

7. See Gray (2018) for measures of this vitality of organizations that records emergence of zombies at the IGO level where activity wanes but the organization remains. It would be more challenging to document the change of engagement at the state level.

8. Others have given attention to expansion of access for nongovernmental organizations that in some cases become members of IGOs (Tallberg et al., 2013). This book focuses on state membership in intergovernmental IGOs.

This leads to the supply side of membership, whereby other states accept an applicant subject to conditions. What incentives shape entry conditions and approval? The conditions set by members can also influence outcomes. Some countries initiate membership talks but do not complete them. This book will examine the application and the approval stages for individual international organizations and country experiences. The more aggregate analysis of membership patterns, however, will examine the final membership outcome.

States can become a member either as a founder of the organization or by accession. While there are important differences in the bargaining dynamic experienced by founding states and accession states, this book will treat both forms of joining an IGO as membership. At formation, the demand and supply constraints occur in a simultaneous negotiation over the IGO itself. For accession, the late joining state has less ability to renegotiate the terms of the IGO and is more likely to face one-sided conditions for entry. Nonetheless, states whose participation is critical to the IGO may be in a position to bargain for better terms. Therefore even accession states may shape the rules.

There are three ways for membership to end—dissolution of the IGO, exit, and expulsion. This book focuses on the state-level decisions toward membership, which includes the latter exit and expulsion cases. Indirectly, these actions contribute to the broader trends in the evolution of the IGO population. The "death" of organizations can be seen as the cumulative exit decisions of members who have changing interests toward the issue or in their relations with each other. While geopolitical rivalry provides the core motivation for entry into the organization, rapprochement brings IGO dissolution (e.g., the Council for Mutual Economic Assistance at the end of the Cold War). For others, the emergence of geopolitical rivalry among members acts as catalyst for death, especially in the case of security IGOs (Eilstrup-Sangiovanni, 2020).

Finally, it is important to acknowledge that membership can imply different levels of activity and distribution of benefits. Some members lack influence or choose not to participate (Stone, 2011; Davis and Bermeo, 2009; Libman and Obydenkova, 2013; Hooghe et al., 2017). Research on the vitality of organizations suggests wide variation in the degree to which members engage with each other and deliver expected policy coordination (Gray, 2018). Viola (2020) shows that in many cases the expansion of participation accompanies restriction of rights through procedural rules that favor incumbents. A large swathe of empirical research examines the effectiveness of individual international organizations. Debates continue on whether the trade regime increases trade flows, multilateral aid promotes development, or human rights courts raise protection of rights. One could reasonably ask, why study membership if some states never attend meetings or change their policies? While there are certainly examples of meaningless membership, they are not the norm. At the outset at least, accepting formal rules brings an expectation of compliance (Franck, 1990; Hooghe et al., 2017). By exploring who comes to the table, this book lays an important foundation for understanding the role of international institutions.

1.2   Membership in International Relations Theory

International relations theory highlights power, material benefits, and social norms as motives for states to join institutions. Examining each in turn reveals the gaps that remain for understanding membership.

Hegemony and rule creation

Powerful states often take the lead role in establishment of IGOs. Writing the rules of international order promotes their interests in systemic stability and a political order that reinforces their own position (Krasner, 1976; Gilpin, 1981; Kindleberger, 1986).[9] Lake (2009) argues that a hierarchy among states arises from differential power and forms the basis for social contracts that establish an authority structure between dominant and subordinate states. Institutions connect these partners more closely to work together for common interests, and membership changes such as NATO enlargement broaden the reach of U.S. hierarchy (Lake, 2009, p. 134). Lascurettes (2020) highlights how excluding rivals through membership rules is necessary to support the depth of behavior rules among the subgroup of states that support the order.

What determines the threshold when the hegemon will value participation of other states more than the risk of losing control over the organization? Stone (2011) argues that informal influence allows the United States to balance competing goals for participation and control. He argues that institutions such as the IMF and the WTO induce the hegemon to follow the rules in normal times while allowing deviation over critical issues. This theory suggests IGOs will admit a broad membership on the assumption that there is differential application of the rules. Sponsoring allies and former colonies for

---

9. While power is the basis of hegemonic leadership over institutional creation, the specific orientation of the hegemon toward the ideas of liberal multilateralism shape their propensity to build institutions (Ikenberry, 2001).

membership represents an important side of informal politics exercised in the shadow of universalistic rules.

Small states also form and join IGOs. Democratizing states fit rules to their own needs in new organizations and join at higher rates than other states as a way to provide for public demands (Poast and Urpelainen, 2013, 2018). Outside of institutions they have the least influence and their capacity constraints often prevent their achieving important governance tasks. International cooperation offers a solution to their weakness—even if power asymmetry continues within a rule framework. Gruber (2000, p. 8) contends that large states use their "going it alone" capacity to force on smaller states terms that they would not prefer over the status quo, while setting new baselines such that joining a coercive institution is still better than "being completely shut out."

Even within the constraints of power, states retain the choice to join. At the multilateral level, participation arises from a national decision and a collective decision. This requires looking more carefully at how IGOs form a club with capacity to provide benefits to members and exclude benefits from nonmembers.

Designing Rules to Overcome Barriers to Collective Action

Demand for regimes arises when states would benefit from cooperation and an institution helps them overcome market failures that would prevent such cooperation. Keohane (1984) develops the core logic of functional demand for institutions based on their ability to lower transaction costs. His theory focuses on the collective action problems and asymmetric information that characterize cooperation for public goods. On the assumption that benefits are non-rival and non-excludable, institutions are necessary to provide information, monitor compliance, and link issues in ways that support cooperation among a large group. Membership itself is not a central question. For a pure public good, screening membership is ineffective because members and nonmembers alike can benefit from the cooperative output.

Nevertheless, limiting cooperation to a subset of states is widespread practice by international institutions. Using a club model of cooperation builds on common interests within a smaller group of states on a subset of issues— for example, the early years of the trade regime excluded illiberal states and kept narrow focus on trade policies at the border to facilitate easier bargaining over agreements (Keohane and Nye, 2001). Trade policies allow states to discriminate in provision of market access to members and nonmembers in the multilateral trade regime, and governments apply elaborate rules of origin to further differentiate trade among states with preferential trade agreements (e.g. Gowa and Kim, 2005; Mansfield and Milner, 2015). States rely on alliances to defend against shared threats, with careful selection of members to maximize security (Sandler, 1999). This reflects the fact that many cooperation problems constitute impure public goods where *exclusion is possible.*

Even in the area of climate change, which represents a classic public goods issue, Keohane and Victor (2011) argue that the environmental regime complex will function better when multiple institutions such as the G8 and EU compete to find solutions to problems among smaller clubs of leading governments. In order to transform environmental cooperation into a club good, Nordhaus (2015) recommends linking climate policies to trade. He proposes using tariffs as a punitive measure against states that do not join the climate change organization. The article highlights that the key to success for international cooperation lies in finding an effective exclusion mechanism. Yet few IGOs follow this solution to expand issue scope and coerce membership through punitive sanctions. Doing so relies on positive utility from enacting sanctions for current members, and this rarely attains credibility. Even in the trade mechanism suggested by Nordhaus (2015), economic theory and empirical trends in trade agreements both contradict his assumption that all states benefit from raising tariffs. More often, such as in the IAEA or climate change protocol, issue linkage uses various forms of aid as a carrot to entice membership. In both positive or negative sanctions in a universal group and reducing membership to smaller groups, these theories recommend changing the issue scope so that cooperation can be treated as a club good for provision by a subgroup of states rather than as universal cooperation for public good provision.

This leads to the question of how states design the exclusion mechanism for international institutions. To address fears of free riding and cheating, membership conditions should represent a significant hurdle such that those unwilling to comply with the rules will not become members (Koremenos, Lipson, and Snidal, 2001). Lower barriers to entry would be expected for coordination games like standard-setting, where wider participation generates more benefits. This leads to contradictory predictions for membership provisions when cooperation involves both distributional and enforcement challenges (Koremenos, Lipson, and Snidal, 2001, p. 796).

The trade-off between depth of rules and breadth of participation can be considerable in the face of diverse state interests. The optimal size of an IGO depends on the enforcement concerns and the distribution of gains from cooperation in an issue area as well as on the preferences of states (e.g. Martin, 1992; Drezner, 2007; Koremenos, 2016). A small group with similar preferences can more readily reach agreement for cooperation and faces fewer monitoring problems (Kahler, 1992; Downs and Rocke, 1995; Thompson and Verdier, 2014). This justifies rigorous screening based on performance capacity. In the context of public goods provision, however, a smaller group also means that other states can free ride as they choose not to contribute to cooperation at the high level demanded (Stone, Slantchev, and London, 2008). The substantive significance of "deep" agreements diminishes due to the limited number of participants. A larger membership gains from pooling resources and taking advantage of the economies of scale, which is the rationale for cooperation through formal organizations in the first place (Abbott and Snidal, 1998).

Where international relations theories highlight distributional conflict over accession, they build the expectation for international organizations to sort states into subgroups with similar preferences on the regulated issue. Downs, Rocke, and Barsoom (1998) suggest the optimal pathway for cooperation outcomes lies in *sequential liberalization*, whereby small groups set the rules and gradually expand to admit new members after their preferences have converged. Gray, Lindstädt, and Slapin (2017) model enlargement scenarios in which the location of the original group and applicants on a unidimensional space determine the probability for enlargement. Small and homogenous founding groups can achieve stable enlargement without changing the organization, whereas a more diverse set of founding states may find that misperceptions about applicants lead to enlargement that changes the level of ambition in agreements. Both of these theories focus on the unidimensional preferences of members in the issue regulated by the regime. Voeten (2021) contends that the differences among states lie within a low-dimensional space that can be defined in terms of support for the Western liberal order. Viola (2020) develops a theory of how states manage diversity through a strategy of *assimilative multilateralism*, with entry conditional on conformity within a specific range of issues. These theories follow the logic that similarity supports cooperation, but leave open the question of how states coalesce around similar interests within the regime issue area or broader world order.

The institutional design theories reviewed here highlight the importance of studying conditions for entry. Yet they cannot answer why so few IGOs apply rigorous screening. Letting in noncompliers lowers cooperation while adding to the burden of high cooperation states.

The Social Role of Organizations

States may look outside of the policies regulated by the regime when considering the benefits of collaboration with particular states. Association with other actors through organizational membership carries spillover effects. Joint membership forms an association that shapes investor perceptions and security coalitions (Gray, 2009; Brooks, Cunha, and Mosley, 2015; Henke, 2019). Following the foundational work of Bull (1977), I examine international society from a perspective that heeds both power and the dimensions that are based on a social process of interaction and shared community norms. Hooghe, Lenz, and Marks (2019, p. 2) make the critical point that "we need to consider how participants feel about being bound together in collective rule" through studying international governance as it serves functional and social purposes. They compare market traders to those bound in marriage to illustrate how the different perceptions of community could influence cooperation. This turns us to the question of group formation. Absent dating services, how do states form the right group with a sense of community? Membership decisions account for the probability of cooperation by the new entrant and the expected gains from establishing a closer association.

When members care about both the shared good and the attributes of other members, they may devise "discriminatory clubs" that select according to the desirability of the applicant and not just their expected contribution to cooperation outcomes (Cornes and Sandler, 1996, p. 385). As an example, members in a social club care not only about the entertainment activity itself but also about member composition. This changes the logic of cooperation. In most models of membership in institutions, the bargaining problem models anonymous states holding proportional contribution to cooperation based on their size and interests (e.g. Stone, Slantchev, and London, 2008). In discriminatory clubs, where the attributes of other actors are important to members, the utility of joining a club consists of two components—provision of goods by the club, and consumption of characteristics of other members (Cornes and Sandler, 1996, p. 385). When members care about *who* joins, there is "nonanonymous crowding" in the provision of the club good. The common example is a golf club, where members value association with those of high socioeconomic status as opposed to simply caring about the number of people using the course or their golf abilities. There are several reasons why governments should care about which states they form ties with through IGO membership.

First, membership defines legal status. Belonging to organizations forms the basis of a state's position in international society. Recognition by other states is necessary to establish international legal sovereignty, but there are no consistent rules guiding such recognition (Krasner, 1999, p. 15). Indeed, research on diplomatic recognition, which is the most basic status requirement, indicates that relational variables matter more than country attributes (Kinne, 2014; Duque, 2018).[10] In addition to diplomatic recognition by other states, membership in organizations such as the United Nations is one of the most visible forms of recognition. States that may otherwise not benefit from full rights of sovereignty in the sense of independent control of their territory may nonetheless gain equality through membership, such as the case of India being a member of the League of Nations and founding member of the United Nations while it remained a British colony. Diplomatic recognition reveals network effects in which states pattern their own decisions on those of other states that are seen as friends (Kinne, 2014, p. 248). Similar kinds of dependent decisions across IGOs occur, such as when membership in the United Nations forms a precondition for membership in many other organizations. Each additional membership can reinforce the extent to which a state enjoys recognition. As distinct from the specific benefits of the IGO, through supporting international legal sovereignty, IGO membership brings diffuse benefits that include both material and normative resources, such as prestige before domestic audiences from the appearance at international venues and reassurance to investors about certainty of contracts when dealing with a recognized state (Krasner, 1999, p. 16).

Second, membership creates peer groups. Through the activities of an organization, opportunities for interaction with other members increase and the norms of the organization shape behavior of members. States become identified with the organization such that the members' own reputation can be influenced by the reputation of fellow members of the organization. Both economic and security actors may respond to this reputation in ways that generate material consequences. Organizational membership can impact country risk ratings and bond yields. Dreher and Voigt (2011) find that independently of the quality of domestic institutions, membership in international organizations improves the country risk rating. Gray (2013) identifies peer effects in

---

10. Social identity theories may not readily apply to the formation of collective identity among states, but state recognition provides a first step in such a process. See the discussion by Greenhill (2008).

which a state joining an organization can be seen as a better or worse investment environment simply because of its association with a particular group of states through joint membership in a regional economic organization. She theorizes that investors use the IGO membership information to inform their risk assessment, and finds evidence that bond yields change in response to accession negotiations.

Third, membership establishes a forum for interaction. States build trust through social ties, which can occur irrespective of the issue area of cooperation and hold positive externalities for trade and security. The step to establishing closer relations through participation in a formal organization with joint governance creates opportunities for members both to learn more about each other and to form in-group identity. Indeed, Ingram, Robinson, and Busch (2005) find sociocultural IGOs promote trade as much as economic IGOs. Yet the quality and degree of interaction may vary depending on the institutional context and relative status of each additional tie for groups of states. Boehmer, Gartzke, and Nordstrom (2004) find that membership in structured IGOs with formal rules and procedures reduces the probability of conflict onset, while Hafner-Burton and Montgomery (2006) emphasize IGO membership holds pacifying effect conditional on how the IGO determines the social network position of a state. Taking a network approach to examine convergence of IGO membership, Kinne (2013a) shows that deepening ties across IGOs reduces the probability of militarized disputes. This could arise through states screening out conflict-prone states when making membership decisions (Donno, Metzger, and Russett, 2015). States that associate together in IGOs send informative signals about their type to both potential investors and disputants.

Across each of these dimensions, the attributes of other members shape the benefits of shared membership. States will want to be selective about whom they recognize as equal and associate with as a peer for greater interactions. They hold incentives to favor entry for states with desirable characteristics. Criteria for discrimination in social clubs range from income to race, but it is unclear what would be the equivalent criteria for desirable attributes of states within international society. Region, economic development, prestige, and security alliances all form potential bases for discrimination. Internal politics may elevate one dimension over another.

The promise of gains from status by association makes membership more attractive. A government could even decide to join an organization that offers few benefits from the provision of goods but yields large status gains from association with a particular group of states. Classifications within organizations take on larger significance because of their role of sorting states into groups.[11] At the same time, members may screen out those who offer less benefits from association even when they could otherwise meet performance conditions for compliance with rules. This can be seen from data on networks of diplomatic recognition, whereby states cue off of central states' decisions more than of those on the periphery (Kinne, 2014).

States have reason to fear that they will be branded according to joint association with other states. Johnson (2011) argues that there is a process of *guilt by association*, whereby unfavorable views toward one member can lead to overall skepticism toward the organization as a whole. The perception that the hostile state holds institutional or ideational influence gives rise to such negative feelings, which is supported by evidence from public opinion polls. Gray (2013) further demonstrates that the strength of association with other states can have unexpected spillover; membership in a regional organization will impact bond yields, as members gain better reputation from joining an organization with low risk countries and suffer when joining an organization with high risk countries.

Group membership is how international society allocates status across states. But rather than being a uniform and objective metric, status by association varies according to the criteria used as the exclusion mechanism in group formation. Dafoe, Renshon, and Huth (2014, p. 375) define the concept:

> 'Status' is an attribute of an individual or social role that refers to position vis-a-vis a comparison group; status informs patterns of deference and expectations of behavior, rights, and responsibilities. Status categories may be dichotomous (e.g. membership in a group) or rank based (e.g. position in a hierarchy). A change in an actor's status implies a change in at least one other actor's status, either because of a change in rank or because of a (perhaps slight) change in the meaning of membership in a group.

The connection to membership is clear—status is a function of community recognition, and joint membership in organizations is one visible signal of such recognition. While diplomatic recognition is the baseline of status, membership in organizations offers a more differentiated perspective. Paul, Larson,

---

11. In one such example, states seek to "graduate" from World Bank lending programs despite the prospect of less foreign aid, and undertake more political reforms for this goal (Carnegie and Samii, 2017).

and Wohlforth (2014, p. 7) define status as "beliefs about a state's ranking on valued attributes," such as wealth or diplomatic clout, and note that status manifests itself in international politics through "membership in a defined club of actors." Elite clubs like the G7 or the permanent five members of the UN Security Council are considered status markers.

The pursuit of status has long served as motivation of states. From Thucydides to contemporary scholarship, theories account for wars fought in the name of honor and prestige. Keohane (2010) advocates "esteem" as a source of incentives for governments to support climate change policies. Although there are different nuances across terms, one can reasonably aggregate honor, prestige, and esteem as forms of status. Furthermore, the rival nature of status can also be understood through its relative position. If all states are members of an organization, membership no longer confers status to one state relative to another. Finally, the status by association in IGO membership is differentiated by the quality of other members rather than simply by an attribute of one state.

Notably, status as a motivation for entry into organizations differs from both the socialization that occurs *after* joining and scripted behavior. Johnston (2001) argues that institutions represent a social context in which shaming and backpatting influence states toward compliance. This socialization process, however, depends on the state having first joined the organization. To the extent only pro-social states choose to join the organization and are allowed to accede by members, constructivist theory about socialization in IGOs is equally subject to the selection bias concerns that face functional theories of institutions. In his study of China's decision to engage with international institutions for security cooperation, Johnston (2007) argues that concerns about avoiding isolation and taking conformist positions were more important than the impact of proposed commitments on relative power. In his theory, the first step occurs as mimicking, when states follow the behavior of others, based on the assumption that if others are joining the institution it must present benefits. After entry, states are then socialized through interaction as they respond to social rewards and punishments and build their own internal organizations to support their work within the institution. A government that once was content to be isolated, through membership becomes attuned to its position within the group in ways that make it susceptible to social pressures and lock in a new direction of cooperative policies. But the theory does not answer the question about why states choose to mimic one group of states and not another.

Placing social interaction at the center of theories, constructivist international relations scholarship offers several insights related to membership in organizations. In constructivist theories, the historical context of relations among states and the decision processes within states exhibit path dependence and cognitive biases that differ from simple calculation of interests. Organizations may serve as an arena for rule-bound behavior that follows a logic of appropriateness (March and Olsen, 1998). From this perspective, states join organizations because that is what states do, irrespective of the costs and benefits of specific organizational membership decisions. Current members find themselves caught in their own rhetoric of inclusion and cooperation, and are unable to turn away applicants (Schimmelfennig, 2001). Variation in membership patterns could arise through channels of emulation, whereby states follow the IGO membership decisions of influential regional leaders.

When states join organizations as part of a script for modernity to follow the behavior of other states, membership in organizations takes on larger purpose than the simple provision of benefits. As described by March and Olsen (1998, p. 964), organizations like the OECD or European Union are "creators of meaning in general and more specifically of identities." Through joint membership, deep ties emerge that could influence state preferences. Constructivist theory emphasizes the possibility for states to set aside self-interest within a larger collective identity (Wendt, 1994). This collective identity emerges from repeated interaction. These theories of socialization acknowledge the importance of forming ties in an IGO. Next we consider how security underlies the choices about which states seek closer association—the choice of whom to mimic and what attributes to value in cooperation partners arises from geopolitical alignment.

1.3   Geopolitical Alignment as Basis for IGO Cooperation

States take sides within international politics. The shorthand term for this is *geopolitical alignment*, which refers to a like-minded approach to world affairs and especially to international security problems. The concept overlaps with alliance structures but can differ in important ways. States ranging from Switzerland to Israel fall within a sphere of common security interests with the United States while never having established alliance ties. The states of Southeast Asia have formed a like-minded approach to security that emphasizes non-intervention in domestic affairs even while their alliance affiliations differ. During the Cold War, the nonaligned movement countries engaged in security cooperation by the joint decision not to become allies with either the United States or USSR. The concept of geopolitical alignment differs from that of ideology because of the defining role of security. Whereas liberal ideology differentiates between democratic and authoritarian regimes or market and non-market economies, geopolitical alignment supports cooperation with any political regime type. Likewise, ideology prioritizes differences in economic policy orientation that are not significant from a security standpoint—partnering with states that uphold liberal markets or with those with more intervention for developmental or socialist policies may serve security interests despite vast differences in ideology.

Two features of geopolitical alignment make it the favored selection criterion in the politics of joining international organizations. First, alignment offers information about reliability. Second, it aggregates interests to support bargaining. The former reduces fears that a prospective cooperation partner will cheat while the latter encourages a broader view of the distributional gains from cooperation. Here I briefly take up each in turn.

As an information tool, geopolitical alignment provides a valuable cue about the quality of cooperation expected from another country. Selecting partners for cooperation requires an assurance about future behavior. States that change regulatory policies or pool resources expose themselves to risk if the others fail to comply. But since compliance types are difficult to judge ex ante, states must seek information from other sources. The accumulation of security cooperation reflected in activities ranging from alliances to military training exercises and joint foreign policy statements or voting in the United Nations provides many opportunities for states to learn about the geopolitical alignment of prospective partners. Their success coordinating on issues related to security builds trust to support subsequent cooperation on new challenges.

Equally importantly, geopolitical alignment expands the bargaining range to include more issues. States that share interests for foreign policy can more readily generate mutual gains from trade-offs between economic and security policies. More expansive cooperation is possible when linkages support sharing economic gains. This can facilitate bargaining even beyond the narrow sphere of allies and for cases where the economic exchange is asymmetric. States may tolerate cheating or unequal distributional outcomes within the confines of the regime in exchange for wider benefits across the relationship.

The role of shared security interests, to provide information and linkage channels, differs from the conventional view in the literature on cooperation. In his foundational theory of international regimes, Keohane (1984) focuses on the role of enforcement and issue linkages carried out *within* the regime jurisdiction as ways to overcome the information asymmetry that hinders cooperation. Instead, my argument highlights how political relations that exist prior to and *outside* of the regime provide information about expected compliance. When states let non-regime issues such as security determine membership choices, they open themselves to less effective regimes through overexpansion, as they let in unqualified applicants, or underprovision of cooperation, when they leave out otherwise qualified entrants.

In the leading realist perspective on overlapping security and economic interests, Gowa (1994) theorizes that the security externality of trade motivates allies to trade more with each other in order to share the income gains from economic exchange.[12] But this logic applies to the relationship between pairs of states where common security interests are certain, such as bilateral trade between allies during the Cold War. It cannot explain the surge of institutionalized cooperation after the end of the Cold War, when there is *less* certainty about which states will be allies or adversaries. The puzzle remains of why states would commit to multilateral cooperation when their security relationship could change. Indeed, within the context of the long-term commitment to repeated action in an IGO, a security externality could worsen the bargaining problem by increasing distributional stakes (Fearon, 1998).

The security linkage that underlies multilateral institutions offers an alternative logic to one based on principled beliefs. In his theory about ideology and multilateralism, Voeten (2021) argues that the United States uses multilateralism to advance its ideological principles. In order to move the status quo in the preferred policy direction, the United States coerces those joining institutions to follow regime rules as part of a strategy to diffuse liberal principles of free tade and democracy. Screening for shared beliefs at entry and upholding high compliance with policies would advance those goals. But security linkage has no such restrictions—patronage politics to favor allies could even motivate states to lower standards for entry and compliance. Indeed, U.S.

---

12. Gowa (1994) shows that trade gains form a positive security externality when allies trade, in contrast to the negative externality arising from trade between adversaries. The bipolar structure of an international system supports open markets more than a multipolar system because the security externality motivates altruism between allies in their trade relations (Gowa, 1989).

allies have been shown to undertake less economic reform when entering the
GATT or receiving IMF loans than their counterparts (Stone, 2008; Davis and
Wilf, 2017).

It is difficult to differentiate between the ideological and security logic.
Shared values and beliefs about the organization of society form a foundation
for cooperation on security, which contributes to the overlap between geopolitical alignment and ideology. During the Cold War this overlap occurred in
the bipolar division of competing alliances between communist and capitalist
sides. One might expect that the role of alliances in shaping entry into multilateralism would end after the Cold War, along with the decline of the ideological
basis for alliances. But it has not. States are still more likely to enter IGOs with
their allies. The security logic of geopolitical alignment to build a coalition
through multilateralism remains amidst the uncertainty of a changing order.

Joining international organizations together strengthens security coalitions.
In hierarchical relations of exchange, states reinforce their ties through offering side payments to support security cooperation (Lake, 2009). This process
is easier when states share membership in organizations so they can exchange
favors on priority issues (Henke, 2019). As fellow members in an IGO, states
can use patronage or bribery to gain leverage over critical swing states in a
broad security coalition. Research confirms that within multilateral economic
institutions, allied states lend more and trade more with each other than with
other members (Thacker, 1999; Gowa and Kim, 2005; Stone, 2008; Dreher
et al., 2013).

Policy coordination outside of defense policies also helps states to signal
intentions of goodwill and commitment to security partners (Morrow, 2000).
Henke (2019) shows that diplomatic embeddedness through the exchanges
that take place in multilateral fora support the formation and maintenance of
multilateral military coalitions. Linking economic and security cooperation
has also been shown to reduce conflict within alliances and increase alliance
performance (Powers, 2004; Poast, 2013). Joint association in an international
organization sends a message of solidarity.

At the same time, excluding rivals denies them the benefits of the organization. States have less leverage to punish a rival after it has joined a multilateral
organization. Indeed, according to Carnegie (2014), rivals receive a large boost
to their trade after entry into the trade regime. Multilateral norms do not prevent biased allocation within organizations, but they make it more difficult to
restrict access to a state than if it were a nonmember. Exclusion of rivals also
signals outsider status by isolating them from routine diplomatic exchanges.

The status benefits of IGO membership also engender cooperation among allies. From basic recognition of sovereignty to major power status, IGO membership converts relationships into a broader standing within international society. Reputation may generalize across members in the institution. This can deliver additional benefits as states improve their standing in the eyes of investors or gain credibility vis a vis hostile states. Keeping these benefits within a security community is optimal. The social interaction amplifies the preference for association with security partners. Choosing to form closer relations by joint membership arises from willingness to engage in close interaction and share cooperation benefits. Joint membership also informs all states about the social categories of which states work together. States will value status by association with security partners more than status by association with other states.

In the domestic politics of international cooperation, accession offers a window for security to take priority. Diplomats and top leaders take charge of treaty negotiations. Given their mandate over foreign policy, these actors have incentives to allocate significant attention to security stakes and diplomacy (Bueno de Mesquita and Smith, 2012; Milner and Tingley, 2015). As these negotiators coordinate with domestic actors over treaty ratification, they can emphasize geopolitical alignment with other states to build support outside of the direct constituencies for the agreement. Policies within the regulated issue areas confront stakeholders lobbying for gains and resisting costly adjustment. Issue linkage offers an effective tactic for breaking through divisions. In this case, joining organizations helps diplomats and leaders with strategic goals frame the broader stakes in cooperation and avoid zero-sum single-issue politics. The public may favor cooperation with allies independently of the specific issues in the treaty (Carnegie and Gaikwad, 2022). Adding potential gains from the security dimension makes entry more likely than if partners are seen as rivals or the IGO is evaluated only in terms of the issue area.

From a coalition-building view of IGO membership, states seek additional leverage in their relations with other states by broadening and deepening their sphere of connections through IGO membership ties. As a form of balancing, strategic use of IGO membership represents a useful tactic for both strong and weak states. It also remains relevant during periods of low certainty over alliance relationships, which calls for keeping options open on whom to be able to influence. This supports an expectation that many states will design IGOs as discriminatory clubs and use that flexibility to favor their security partners. There will be less variation by issue area or distribution of power than implied by competing explanations focused on cooperation problems and distribution of power.

To evaluate the argument, the book will test three core claims about how states discriminate over membership. The first hypothesis addresses the rules and decision-making procedures that form a background condition for discrimination. The second hypothesis looks at the nature of bias that shapes membership patterns. The third considers how the entry process allows for differential costs of entry.

Hypothesis 1, Discretionary Rules: States will design IGO accession rules to provide discretion over selection. More international organizations will follow the design of club models, with an exclusion mechanism based on voting rather than policy evaluation of rule compliance. At the design stage, it is difficult to define ex ante the in-group, and states want the flexibility to engage in discriminatory practices. Therefore, they leave the entry qualifications vague while assuring control over selecting who gets in. The selection could favor anything—security, culture, economic interests, or compliance—because the rules do not specify. The second hypothesis explains the geopolitical logic that drives the pattern of membership in IGOs and is the primary focus of the book.

Hypothesis 2, Geopolitical Discrimination: States with shared geopolitical alignment form organizations together and are more likely to join the same organizations. In this relational theory, states discriminate to favor others based on their preexisting security ties. Shared alliances and similar voting in the United Nations serve as proxies for measuring like-minded orientation to security issues. Alignment with other members and not just the largest power can support entry and continued membership. Yet non-allies and even rivals can and do join IGOs—the hypotheses are probabilistic and not deterministic. As states consider cooperation partners, non-security gains may outweigh the security factors. In the sequencing of member expansion, early entry by allies will consolidate the voting core and rules, while non-allies must wait longer and do more to win approval. The third hypothesis explains the conditions for entry.

Hypothesis 3, Favoring Friends: States with shared geopolitical alignment with other members will make fewer reforms as a condition of entry. This final hypothesis is nested within the first two because discretionary terms of membership allow variable conditions across applicants, and lowering the bar for friends facilitates early entry. Holding up non-allied states until they meet a higher threshold accommodates mixed incentives about who can join—as in societal discrimination where the out-group applicant must be twice as qualified on performance basis to overcome the bias against them.

The argument holds implications over the politics for ending membership as well. Geopolitical alignment supports ongoing membership after having joined an organization. The discretionary approach to accession extends to rules for exit and expulsion. States are not required to prove compliance in order to remain in the club.

Empirical analysis will compare the role of geopolitical alignment with the demand for membership based on interests within the issue area regulated by the IGO. The large body of literature on functional theories of institutions posits that the desire to achieve mutual gains in the face of market failure motivates cooperation in international institutions; this leads to the baseline expectation that interests, information, and policies within the issue area should explain who joins. Since geopolitical alignment and interests within the issue area overlap entirely in the area of security organizations, looking outside security organizations is necessary to test the hypotheses. In the area of economic organizations one can compare how economic interests contribute to expected benefits from membership relative to the impact of geopolitical alignment. Supporting evidence would include examples where states that have little engagement in international trade join the trade regime at the encouragement of an ally. Further evidence would include internal statements from diplomats and security hawks in support of joining the IGO, and lenient provisions to allow entry without requiring substantial economic policy reforms. Raising non-trade issues and extra concessions as a condition for membership to block entry by a rival state represents the exclusionary side of discrimination. In contrast, support for functional theories would include evidence that most of the variation in membership arises from differences in the trade interests of states. The domestic political interests would largely revolve around debate among different economic ministries and business groups, and accession negotiations would extract substantial concessions to ensure conformity with rules. There would also be divergent expectations about the conditions that would lead states to exit or be expelled from an organization. Whereas the discriminatory club model of IGO membership suggests exit would be largely independent of compliance with IGO rules, the functional model of institutions implies that exit and expulsion would occur after a period of noncompliance.

Although the argument implies that states expect to deepen cooperation with other states through shared membership, this book will not evaluate the effects of entry. Nevertheless, there is a dynamic where states are selecting based not simply on existing security but also on the security relationships they want to develop by means of shared membership. The politics of engagement with Eastern Europe or newly independent states during the Cold War stand out as such examples. At the two ends of the spectrum of geopolitical alignment, there are clear incentives to favor allies and exclude rivals. But for swing states there may be differences in approach, as diplomats are making bets on the future trajectory of a state and trying to shift that trajectory. The hypotheses above can only partially capture this strategic dynamic: flexible rules maximize discretion for borderline cases and on average those that are closer in geopolitical alignment will be more likely to join, with lower conditions. Many of the hardest cases to predict will be those where contextual factors will shape perceptions of whether geopolitical alignment of the state is in transition.

1.4   Chapter Overview

The book proceeds to further develop the logic of the argument and explore the patterns of membership politics. Moving from the general theory of international organizations as discriminatory clubs to applications in the context of specific international organizations and country experiences, I will balance conceptual approaches with the nuance of history and mixed motives. Where the aggregate analysis of international organizations uses proxies to measure geopolitical alignment, case studies will probe more deeply the various forms of in-group identity on security issues and the interaction between domestic politics and international cooperation. Although unable to leverage exogenous shocks or randomized experiments for rigorous identification of causal effects, the sum of descriptive inferences across mixed methods analysis supports the hypotheses and builds an agenda for future research.

The central research question of the book asks how states choose their cooperation partners. This introductory chapter has laid out the core claim that geopolitical alignment shapes multilateral cooperation on non-security issues through membership politics. When international organizations become discriminatory clubs, they set the boundaries for cooperation among a subset of states chosen for their affinity. Security forms the basis for affinity in this study, but the larger claim contends that like-minded states cooperate by means of biased membership decisions. Viewing membership as a choice of association within international society differs from the conventional expectation that international organizations represent contracts to uphold the interests of powerful states and coordinate common interests within an issue area.

International organizations are a heterogenous set of institutions that vary in size, rules, and issue mandate. The research design of the book takes different approaches to assess geopolitical alignment relative to other conditions when controlling for some of the features that differ among organizations. Chapter 2 compares the design of all IGO charters, looking at how discretion appears across IGOs in different issue areas and with different membership size. The empirical analysis of membership decisions in chapters 3–5 focuses on economic IGOs to evaluate whether security interests unrelated to the mandate of the organization emerge as a factor over membership alongside economic interests. Chapter 6 looks from a country perspective at membership decisions across all organizations over time. Then the book turns to IGOs with two different types of entry rules: chapter 7 focuses on organizations with a regional focus, while chapter 8 looks at those that explicitly embrace the principle of open eligibility for all states. Across this range of institutional settings, geopolitical alignment emerges as a consistent factor in membership. This is not limited to the domain of global institutions or those within Europe; organizations large and small and those across different regions heed the pull of geopolitical alignment when considering members. Yet other factors also matter, and statistical analyses with control variables and case studies with attention to different narratives reflect on these mixed motives.

Chapter 2 develops the theory of membership that makes IGOs form discriminatory clubs. States seek both gains from cooperation and status from association with other states. This dual purpose explains the form of membership provisions that are designed to promote cooperation among a community of states. The central importance of geopolitics motivates the prevalence of discretion over member approval. States retain control to choose with whom they cooperate.

The chapter goes on to test the hypothesis about discretionary design of membership provisions with a comprehensive analysis of IGO charters and their terms for membership selection. A typology of IGO membership provisions illustrates variation across the dimensions of participation mandate and conditionality terms. These concepts are mapped onto accession rules for 322 international organizations using a new dataset. For issues that represent global public goods, universalistic principles underlie membership with open eligibility for all states. Most join easily. Nevertheless, screening for entry into universal organizations determines who counts as a state within international society, and so even universal organizations include some selection. Attention is given to how design varies by issue area, but there are surprisingly consistent features across issues. For the majority of issues that constitute club goods where exclusion is possible, states design IGO membership provisions to select a smaller group of states. Surprisingly few organizations screen for compliance based on objective performance standards or policy review. Instead, vague eligibility terms, negotiable terms, and the requirement of member approval characterize club standards for membership. I argue that states choose this design structure in order to maximize their flexibility to have informal norms and geopolitical interests operate as de facto criteria for who joins. Alongside the discretionary approach to accepting new members, IGOs rarely terminate membership over noncompliance. This chapter explores why states refrain from following reciprocity strategies that would call for threatening to expel states that repeatedly reject IGO rules. Analysis of IGO charters examines which types of IGOs include provisions for expulsion and exit. The infrequency of member suspension for noncompliance upholds the logic that membership in an IGO confers a form of citizenship within society rather than a simple contract.

Chapter 3 evaluates the second hypothesis that geopolitics correlates with membership.[13] Looking at multilateral economic IGO membership offers a sharper test, since the substantive focus of the organization itself does not require coordination of security policies. We use data on alliances and UN voting similarity to measure geopolitical alignment, and compare the geopolitics hypothesis with the benchmark model that organization membership reflects economic interests measured by the trade ties between countries. Analyzing membership patterns for 231 multilateral economic organizations from 1949 to 2014, we use a finite mixture model to examine the relative importance of economic and security considerations, finding that geopolitical alignment accounts for nearly *half* of the membership decisions in economic institutions. The geopolitical origins of IGO membership represent an important mechanism connecting the security and economic behaviors of states.

---

13. This chapter is based on an article co-authored with Tyler Pratt, "The Forces of Attraction: How Security Interests Shape Membership in Economic Institutions," *Review of International Organizations* 2021.

Turning to focus on one international organization, chapter 4 looks at how the trade regime expanded from a small club to a nearly universal organization.[14] The trade regime is important for both its substantive significance and because archival records include information on all countries that have applied for membership, which is often not available for other organizations. This allows comprehensive research into the full accession process for all eligible countries over the period 1948 through 2014. Using a duration model to analyze when states apply and the negotiations for accession offers insight into the demand and supply sides of membership. Consistent with hypothesis 2, geopolitical alignment predicts who applies to join, and consistent with hypothesis 3, corresponds with lower cost of entry, as shown by shorter accession negotiations with fewer concessions. Our findings challenge the view that states liberalize first in order to join the regime. Instead, democracy and foreign policy similarity with members encourage states to join. Moreover, the level of tariff cuts and conditions for accession are higher for non-allied states. While now there is much attention to China's role as a challenger within the regime, from a historic and comparative perspective, China was late to join and made substantial concessions as a condition for entry.

The OECD exemplifies the discriminatory role of IGOs. Yet its exclusive nature is not as its nickname "rich country club" would suggest. Chapter 5 documents how this organization plays a key role in shaping international coordination of regulations on policies that range from taxation and investment to education and corruption, but also constitutes a quasi-alliance bringing together "the West." Scholars and commentators alike refer to OECD states without sufficient attention to the unifying principles that shape who can join this exclusive international club. The organization provides both public goods in the form of policy information and club goods in the form of status. Through a process of self-selection by applicants and screening by members, the organization has managed gradual expansion while preserving its value as an elite club of like-minded states. Informality of accession criteria has allowed flexibility to raise and lower the bar for entry. Statistical analysis highlights that democracy and geopolitics correlate with earlier entry into the OECD relative to other countries, while there are less clear patterns for the role of trade and financial openness. Case studies of Mexico, Korea, and the Czech Republic are used to examine how prospective OECD membership motivated reforms in

14. This chapter is based on an article co-authored with Meredith Wilf, "Joining the Club? Accession to the GATT/WTO," *Journal of Politics* 2017.

regulatory policies and trade. These countries sought the status of association with the advanced industrial democracies. On the basis of shared liberal orientation and geopolitical alignment, they were accepted into the club. At the same time, a case study of Brazil highlights how its initial reluctance to seek OECD membership reflected a political preference to remain distant from the advanced industrial nations even as its economy and policies had become highly integrated with these states. The analysis also examines how Brazil's effort to establish closer ties with the United States led it to recently apply to join the OECD.

In chapter 6, the book shifts from the IGO level to a country-level perspective. This chapter explores the experience of Japan from 1853, when it first opened to the West, through today, when it is member of more than 80 IGOs. With attention to domestic politics and the perception of allies and rivals, this chapter closely examines why international organizations are viewed as a way to shape the national position in international society. Tracing Japanese foreign policy through its approach to IGO membership highlights the role of status-seeking through association with allied countries. Whether it be Meiji Japan's effort to prove itself a sovereign state that could win itself free of the unequal treaties, or post-WWII Japan's effort to reenter international society after defeat in war, IGOs have long been about more than functional tools to provide specific goods. While foreign policy goals lay behind Japan's membership decisions, entry into organizations then formed key leverage points to bring about domestic reforms. The chapter documents how Japan's relations with the UK during the Anglo-Japanese alliance and with the United States during the post-war alliance shaped its entry and exit from organizations, and examines how changing diplomatic relations with China have influenced the Japanese position toward China's role in IGOs. The theory helps account for several surprising membership outcomes—such as the improbable entry of Japan into the ILO in 1919, when it did not allow union representation, and its refusal to join the Asian Infrastructure Investment Bank in 2016, even as the government increased spending for infrastructure in the region. The case research draws upon archival materials and testimony in the Japanese legislature for a range of perspectives on how foreign policy ties emerge as a prominent consideration in the discussion of IGO membership.

Regional boundaries are the most frequent criteria for international organizations that form subgroups of states. Yet the political construction of regions occurs when geography becomes a discretionary criterion for membership in regional organizations. Under the facade of common location, some regional organizations represent discriminatory clubs in disguise. Chapter 7 examines the role of foreign policy in determining membership in regional organizations relative to the importance of democracy, economic ties, and geographic location. Statistical analysis of 197 regional organizations shows evidence that security ties have as large an effect as distance and democracy in correlating with membership. Two case studies, of the EU and ASEAN, provide more detailed analysis of entry decisions. The chapter highlights exceptions to meritocratic review that occur even in the EU, which represents an ideal type of conditional entry based on democracy promotion—the 1963 French veto of British entry, mixed strategies in the Eastern enlargement, and resistance to Turkish membership. Brexit is discussed as an outlier case for theories of integration and for the argument of this book. While not a divorce over divergent security goals, foreign policy differences were one factor within the broader context of sovereignty concerns. In contrast to the EU, ASEAN never presumed to establish hard criteria for membership, and its enlargement occurred through gradual expansion across a set of governments that range widely in political and economic conditions. Formed to strengthen resistance to communist Vietnam, ASEAN would eventually embrace Vietnam as a member. In both the EU and ASEAN cases, foreign policy shifts were a critical antecedent to membership changes. Rather than constituting fixed standards for entry, both democracy and geography are selectively applied as conditions for membership in regional organizations alongside foreign policy criteria. Through the political process of selecting members in regional organizations, states shape the most fundamental parameters of regional identity.

In a hard test for the argument about IGOs as discriminatory clubs, chapter 8 focuses on those international organizations that embrace the goal of including all states. For cooperation to provide a true *public* good, universal IGOs have open eligibility for accession. Yet here, too, membership terms set limits on universality. The community of states relies upon membership in IGOs to define sovereignty, and this means debates over membership take heightened significance for contested territories such as Palestine or Taiwan. This chapter explores how entry into universal organizations relies on positive relations between states and not simply on the capacity to participate in the cooperative endeavor or on legal standing through diplomatic recognition. Statistical analysis of entry into 88 universal IGOs shows that security ties correspond to higher probability of entry, which indicates that even universal IGOs undertake discriminatory politics to favor allies. Four case studies examine membership for contested states. The longstanding controversy over membership in the United Nations for North and South Korea was only resolved with their simultaneous admission in 1991 at the end of the Cold War. Taiwan serves as the extreme example of a high-performing government that has been excluded on the basis of its sovereignty conflict with China rather than any concern about compliance. The case study examines how the United States and political leadership in Taiwan have influenced when and how the country joins international organizations. Taiwan's struggle to participate in the WHO takes on greater significance amidst the pandemic. The movement to expand recognition for Palestine in IGOs shows divisions along political lines irrespective of the qualifications of Palestine to join any individual organization. Identity and rivalry also play a central role in debates over termination of membership, which is explored in the case study of South Africa's expulsion from the UPU as a sanction against Apartheid. Variation across IGOs for these cases helps to illuminate the trade-offs between efficiency for cooperation and reconciliation of sovereignty conflicts.

The final chapter explores the implications of IGO member politics for our understanding of international institutions and cooperation. When institutions form discriminatory clubs, cooperation expands along familiar cleavages of security interests. Geopolitical rivalries also generate balancing in the sphere of multilateral governance. The conclusion focuses on three larger questions. First, to what extent do institutional ties reinforce or even aggravate geopolitical divisions? The chapter reflects on the role of membership selection to shift how we interpret studies about security cooperation. Second, does the practice of discriminatory membership promote international cooperation? On the one hand, unexpected joiners expand participation in cooperation, but on the other hand, they reduce the effectiveness of rules. This highlights the difficulty of accurately assessing the net gains for policy outcomes and the legitimacy of international organizations. Third, what are the dynamic trends for IGO membership patterns? Given an underlying demand to discriminate, expanding membership in IGOs will in turn generate new pressures for the proliferation of international organizations. States create new institutions as a tactic to continue the practice of discrimination and adapt to the problem of overexpansion. The answers to these questions open a broader agenda for research into how states use institutions to structure international society.

1.5 Conclusion

The book considers IGO membership from the perspective of security interests along with institutional design and effectiveness. The politics of joining organizations touch closely on concerns about consolidating relations with other states as well as on functional demands for cooperation in complex issue areas. Drawing on insights from economic theories of club goods and sociology theories of networks and status, the book offers new insights into how states choose the groups they belong to and why these decisions have far-reaching consequences.

At one level, the security logic of IGO membership challenges institutionalist theories by introducing a different source of demand for institutions. Nevertheless, this opens the possibility for more impact by the institution on behavior because entry is not simply derivative to the policy interest in the issue area. States that join for other reasons related to foreign policy bring upon themselves pressure to reform policies. Entry triggers domestic mobilization of interest groups, reputation incentives, and socialization. Institutional theories explain how these mechanisms support cooperation. The role played by foreign policy at the time of entry increases the scope for unexpected reforms brought by the institution that are distinct from what the state would otherwise have done outside the institution.

Furthermore, recognizing the foreign policy role of IGOs should moderate any assessment about institutional effects. When states form club-style IGOs that favor entry by friends, they lower the level of cooperation in the issue area relative to a meritocratic process with rigid conditions for reform as condition of entry. But it would be wrong to then conclude the institution is ineffective—states have chosen to prioritize other purposes related to status and economic statecraft over maximal gains from issue area cooperation. Evaluating outcomes based on policy reforms and gains observed within the issue area neglects the broader foreign policy benefits achieved by participating in the organization. At the same time, any pacifying effect attributed to IGO membership may arise from the earlier selection mechanism based on common geopolitical interests. Without attention to selection, researchers will miss larger effects of joining IGOs and may reach the wrong conclusion about the mechanism for the correlation between IGOs and peace.

As a result, geopolitical discrimination is inefficient from the narrow perspective of cooperation on the regulated issue, but can generate benefits for IGO cooperation through increasing the likelihood that states enjoy positive relations. The dysfunctional aspect of politicized entry into institutions is the risk of overexpansion. Logrolling to allow entry of friends before they have completed reforms contributes to broader expansion from what one state would choose as the optimal number of cooperation partners. Consequently, use of IGOs as a discriminatory club could yield mixed overall welfare effects.

This book explores why club-style IGOs are prevalent and what determines who joins the club. The geopolitical logic of IGO membership accounts for both unexpected reformers and inefficient expansion of IGO membership beyond clubs. Supporting evidence can be found in the evolution of membership in organizations and in country-level decisions.

2

Flexibility by Design: Rules for Accession

CLEAR BOUNDARY rules form the first design principle for cooperation. According to Ostrom (2000, p. 149), "using this principle enables participants to know who is in and who is out of a defined set of relationships and thus with whom to cooperate." Only after setting boundaries can a group allocate rights and obligations. Sometimes the process to differentiate between in-group and out-group is straightforward, but how can states in international society reach such an understanding? In her work on local communities, Ostrom notes, "Group boundaries are frequently marked by well-understood criteria, like everyone who lives in a particular community or has joined a specific local cooperative. Membership may also be marked by symbolic boundaries and involve complex rituals and beliefs that help solidify individual beliefs about the trustworthiness of others." To the extent that states form a small community with a long history of interaction, they establish regional associations or commodity cartels in a process not unlike that in villages. As collective actors, however, states also confront unique problems to sustain cooperation. Systemic competition for power prevents centralized governance, while repeated interactions necessitate policy coordination. States balance these contending forces through careful selection of partners for cooperation in international organizations.

When organizing an institution to provide a public good, the goal is to maximize participation for mutual gain. But many policy problems are impure public goods—they are neither fully public with common benefits shared by all, nor are they private with zero-sum rivalry over consumption. Instead, excludable benefits and congestion characterize club goods where a smaller group can share in the production and utilization of the good.[1] From golf clubs to cartels, exclusion mechanisms support joint contribution while limiting congestion.

Most international organizations are designed for the provision of club goods (e.g., Keohane and Nye, 2001; Greenhill and Lupu, 2017; Viola, 2020). They erect entry barriers and set approval processes to restrict membership. This book builds on this insight to portray how IGOs act as *discriminatory clubs* that select partners who have positive attributes on other dimensions distinct from criteria directly related to cooperation on the regulated policies. The process of joining international organizations often resembles entry into a social club that has the ability to deny entry based on informal decisions about who is the right type for the club. Members care about not only provision of the cooperative good but also the identity of other members of the club. Therefore, rather than screening for states with the highest capacity to share in the production of the cooperative good, states allow entry for those who share their values, regime type, and foreign policy, while excluding others. Flexible rules facilitate this process.

Much attention in international relations has shown that hierarchy and discrimination can remain within an order based on sovereign states. Powerful states establish rules to reinforce their authority, and these interests shape exchanges within international institutions and exclude some from joining the order (Gilpin, 1981; Lake, 2009; Lascurettes, 2020; Viola, 2020). By varying the level of delegation or pooling of authority, states can set bounds on the authority ceded to the international organization (Hooghe, Lenz, and Marks, 2019). Multilateral norms of nondiscrimination, however, restrain efforts to distort the allocation of benefits within an institution. Much of the authority of international institutions derives from their ability to appear legitimate and exert normative pressure over state behavior (Hurd, 1999). States have tried to reconcile these tensions between hierarchy and legitimacy through their design of international institutions. (Martin, 1992; Koremenos, Lipson, and Snidal, 2001).

Membership politics represents one of the foremost ways for states to embed discrimination within cooperation. Hurrell (2004, p. 41) writes, "Control over the membership norms of international society and the capacity to delegitimize certain sorts of players through the deployment of these norms represents a very important category of power." A critical decision to shape

---

1. See Buchanan (1965) and Cornes and Sandler (1996).

the organization, membership has not been delegated to bureaucrats within the organization.[2] The informal nature of discrimination over membership preserves the principle of multilateral cooperation that is the basis for legitimacy. After limiting who can join, states can more readily support multilateral norms within the organization.

This chapter explains the variation in the design of membership provisions for international organizations. My goal is to evaluate the hypothesis that states will design IGO accession rules to provide discretion over selection. I focus on two related questions. First, under what conditions do states pursue open multilateralism? To the extent that cooperation represents a public good, one would expect the prevailing form of membership to be open membership without restrictions. The frequency of selective IGOs suggests instead that many of the cooperation problems in international affairs represent club goods. This leads to my second question: when states restrict membership, how do they design the exclusion mechanism? Precise conditions for entry paired with provisions for suspension and expulsion could support deepening cooperation with high compliance. A third-party review committee could assess suitability for membership based on inspection of implementing legislation. But this kind of meritocratic screening is surprisingly rare. More often, the provisions for membership are vague about the terms of entry and rely on votes of approval. I argue that this discretion allows members the flexibility to exclude states for reasons outside of the formal scope of the institution. Just as social clubs do not write down the rules that would differentiate on the basis of race or ethnicity, IGOs do not formalize the criteria for entry.

The vague terms and room for exclusion at time of entry represent a flexibility mechanism in the institutional design. Ad hoc criteria facilitate statecraft that uses IGO membership as carrot and stick to advance purposes beyond cooperation on the issue at hand. Empirical analysis in subsequent chapters of the book demonstrates how states have used this flexibility to inject geopolitics into economic organizations like the OECD and WTO. Turkey found early entry into the OECD possible as a NATO ally. Iran's application to join the WTO in 1996 was blocked by the United States under the guise of its needing more time to review Iran's trade policies, even while Afghanistan's application in 2004 reached its conclusion despite major obstacles to effective

---

2. In their analysis of decision procedures for international organizations, Hooghe et al. (2017, p. 130) find the least delegation for accession and suspension relative to policy-making and budget areas.

compliance. One can imagine that different outcomes may have resulted from a meritocratic selection by a review commission assessing performance criteria. Yet even as legalization trends are characteristic of enforcement in the WTO and many other IGOs, few have delegated the decision over screening members to third-party assessment.

This chapter develops an argument about the design of membership provisions in section 2.1. It explains why membership criteria are deliberately vague and prone to discrimination. Section 2.3 introduces data from over 300 IGO charters on the design of accession rules. In section 2.4, I discuss the patterns for the design of IGO membership rules and consider dynamic questions related to the evolution of accession processes and use of informal practices.

2.1 IGO Accession as Club Membership

What we know about IGO membership has been developed within the context of studying cooperation problems in international relations. Theories address the question of why states choose to establish institutions and the conditions that influence compliance with rules. Empirical research provides extensive analysis of ratification patterns and the impact of treaties on behavior. These are related questions, but distinct from membership. On the one hand, membership politics are a subset of cooperation problems that arise around the decision to accept an agreement. The key variables of power and information asymmetry that underlie existing theories about cooperation also shape membership politics. On the other hand, membership politics represent a unique dynamic shaped by entering a formal organization with a particular group of states. Relational variables become important because the decision is not only about whether to cooperate on an issue but also about *who* should work together.

International organizations allow states to pool their authority through collective decision-making. We can observe wide variation in the degree to which members retain control, but an entrant into an organization accepts common participation in governance activities (Stone, 2011; Hooghe et al., 2017). Beyond the commitment to uphold the signed agreement, membership includes a promise of forward-looking engagement to enforce rules and deliberate about new policies. In this sense, the comparison of treaty ratification versus accession can be seen as the difference between firms making a contract for a single project and those forming a joint venture. Both agreements would commit actors to terms for pricing and activities, but the latter also allocates managerial authority. This dimension of shared authority makes selection of partners one of the most important parameters of cooperation within an international organization. The design of accession rules by the states that found the organization emerges out of their own choice of scope for cooperation with other states. Once enshrined in a founding charter, the membership provisions lock in this selection criteria—or defer the evaluation of what it takes to qualify for membership by *not* specifying selection criteria.

The conventional view in international relations theory addresses two types of IGO—universal organizations that aim to provide global public goods and smaller organizations representing a subset of states that share preferences for cooperation on the given issue. The presumption is that the former include all states while the latter engage in rigorous screening for expected compliance. Neither fits reality. Most IGOs fall into a form of club IGO, where membership is neither universal nor based on rigorous screening. These are *discriminatory clubs;* they evaluate members in terms of their ability to contribute to cooperation within the issue area and their attributes outside of the issue area (Cornes and Sandler, 1996, p. 385).

The discriminatory club model introduces a relational component to the membership equation. The value of association with another state makes others support its membership independently of its expected contribution to collective action for the cooperative outcome. Income, race, or other features could enhance the value of association. The point is that states may want to design a selection process such that they can choose their own criteria for membership. When the criteria are unrelated to the mandate of the organization, selection will become discriminatory. Instead of evaluating expected performance ability, actors inject their own preferences for whom to associate with through interaction in the club.

In a period of heightened attention to racial justice, we are increasingly aware of the ripple effect of racial discrimination in causing harm to individuals and society. These patterns of bias become embedded in institutions that perpetuate the gap in opportunity. On top of the moral objections to discrimination, one can also condemn its negative effect on welfare. Becker (1971) pointed out the economic inefficiency of racial discrimination, since hiring based on attributes unrelated to productivity would lower output. Applying the economic method to analyzing society, such behavior is rational for the individuals who practice it as long as one widens the assumption of preferences to include what Becker termed a "discrimination coefficient." This takes into account the possibility of prejudice, making race, gender, or other attributes influence employers and customers outside of the characteristics of goods and services provided. The framework encompasses discrimination to favor an individual based on non-market attributes.

In international affairs, the use of alternative criteria for selection outside of performance could also constitute a discrimination coefficient. As with employment discrimination, it would reduce the effectiveness of regime performance in the issue area but remain rational. The alternative criterion may achieve other goals. There can also be cases where discrimination advances moral causes, such as affirmative action policies, or excludes actors as a punishment. As we will see in a later chapter, one case of IGO discrimination arose over the expulsion of South Africa from the UPU as a sanction for the injustice of Apartheid. It is not my purpose to judge the morality of states when they diverge from a rigid performance evaluation. The analysis here focuses on why and how states discriminate and the features that make countries attractive for joint membership.

When states design international institutions, membership conditions range from inclusive to exclusive participation, and they also vary in the rigor of their requirements for entry. Four models characterize the types of membership design: meritocratic IGOs establish strict conditionality for compliance in order to prevent free riding (Downs, Rocke, and Barsoom, 1998), hierarchical IGOs allow variable commitments and authority based on capacity (Gilligan, 2004), club-style entry uses attraction and selection with flexibility for response to changing circumstances, and universal organizations welcome all who are acknowledged as members of a community. The first two conditionality models focus on performance within a single-issue dimension, whereas the latter offer more discretion, with flexibility for issue linkages to geopolitics that raise and lower the bar. Institutional theory and realist skeptics both presume the prevalence of conditionality or universal organizations, but a surprisingly large and diverse range of organizations follow the club model.

Figure 2.1 displays four ideal types based on the variation in participation mandate and conditionality terms. The participation mandate sets parameters for whether all states are in principle eligible for membership and establishes the expectation of whether the IGO aims to achieve narrow or broad membership. The conditionality terms establish criteria for the accession process, which can be precise benchmarks identified as objective measures or may be left to the discretion of members. Precise conditions effectively serve to limit participation, but they could simply codify a broad set of eligibility criteria that any state could meet. Furthermore, an organization could be selective,

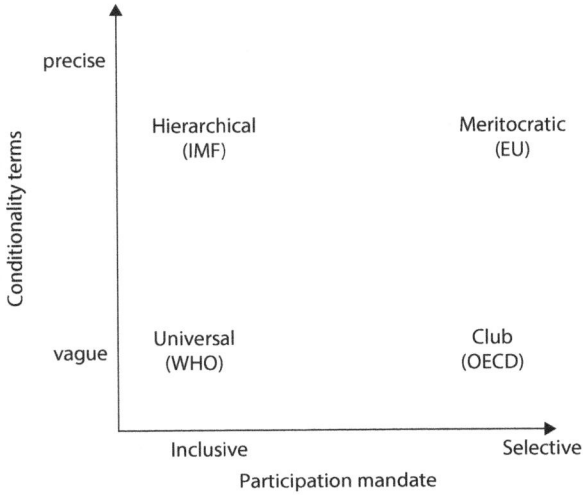

FIGURE 2.1. Four models of IGO accession process

without offering details on how it restricts membership, or it could be inclusive, while requiring steps necessary to gain entry. If one takes the analogy of the university admissions process, conditionality terms are more vague for Ivy League schools in the United States, which rely on a wide range of evaluation criteria, than for a national university in Japan, which relies on test scores, even though both are highly exclusive in limiting admissions. In the realm of extracurricular activities, a ballet troupe and a tap dance club may both have similar policies for club tryouts (precise entry terms), while the former is more exclusive in limiting membership to a small group, and the latter takes an inclusive approach, allowing participation by any who show up. The categories hold heuristic value to contrast alternative models. Yet even the IGOs given as examples of meritocratic or universal IGOs fail in practice to uphold such principles. Case studies in this book will reveal evidence of discrimination over membership within both the WHO and the EU.

A universal IGO claims to be open to all states. Global public goods issues such as health and the environment are leading areas for the univeral IGO structure. Climate change negotiations face the challenge that nonparticipation by large developing countries will prevent others from achieving their goal to stop the rise of global temperatures. The Covid-19 pandemic shows how diseases in any country could affect everyone, which makes it important for all states to share information with the WHO. Unable to exclude bene-fits or harm, states will favor open eligibility for a universal organization in the effort to support global public good provision. The legitimacy of these IGOs depends in part on the perception of their universal principles and fair procedures (Lenz and Viola, 2017; Tallberg, 2019). Nevertheless, the use of membership as an organizing concept implies distinguishing between insid-ers and outsiders. Welcoming all states still requires deciding what counts as a state. Sovereignty is a multifaceted concept without a single definition (Kras-ner, 1999). States may harbor intense disagreements over this question, such as those witnessed over applications by Palestine and Taiwan to the United Nations. The affirmative outcome of membership decisions of the universal IGOs offers recognition of sovereignty. Even universalism has its limits, which are all the more intense because the vague mandate of eligibility leaves open to members' discretion the decision to define what counts as statehood.

Hierarchical organizations are inclusive in mandate and limit membership benefits through conditions that determine influence over decision-making.[3] The IMF requires states to contribute a subscription share to support avail-able funds. The fee-based entry of the IMF goes beyond mere requirement to pay dues. Each member entering the IMF is assigned a quota based on its size in the global economy that determines the financial resources it shall commit and its voting share.[4] This formula offers a way for the institution to remain open, while weighting influence toward those with the greater share of duties. An alternative fee-based formula would rely on utilization rates, similar to a toll road. Remarkably few IGOs apply this particular form of variable mem-bership entry requirements. One example would be the Advisory Center on WTO Law, an organization that charges members dues to support the organi-zation and hourly fees for use of legal staff to support the government in WTO dispute settlement proceedings. While utilization fees such as those of the ACWL are unusual, budget dues are a common requirement of membership, with nonpayment constituting reason for suspension of membership privi-leges. Budgetary dues are typically allocated in proportion to income, which is, if anything, the reverse of utilization rate, given that governments of low-income states are more likely to rely on IGO services. The regular assessment

---

3. I thank Stephanie Rickard for clarification on this point. This category encompasses the heirarchical multilateralism and exclusive multilateralism described by Viola (2020, p. 85) as strategies by which states expand membership but limit access within the institution.

4. Although even the allocation of quota rights and decision authority is not as objective as it may first appear, and has been the source of contestation (Stone, 2011; Lipscy, 2015).

of dues is characteristic of all four entry types, and it is only when contributions generate differential categories of membership benefits that I consider it a form of selection.

The upper right quadrant of the figure shows the meritocratic IGO that is both exclusive and sets clear conditions for membership. The closest approximation can be found in the EU enlargement process following the principles established at the 1993 Copenhagen meeting of the European Council. The participation mandate restricts eligibility by both region and regime type. The accession negotiations involve European Commission officials undertaking a detailed review of compliance with each of the 35 chapters of the *acquis* that represents the body of EU legislation. This type of membership design presents many advantages for cooperation—an exclusive mandate lowers collective action problems by focusing on a smaller number of states, based on common traits. Precise entry conditions make explicit the practice of screening for compliance at the start of membership. The process itself becomes more bureaucratic with delegation to IGO officials. To maximize the depth of cooperation achieved within an issue area, one would expect states to pursue this form of membership design. It is therefore surprising to observe that very few IGOs adopt this design in their membership provisions. Even the EU deviates when it holds some countries in the waiting room after having started accession talks, or jumps forward Ukraine as an eligible country in a gesture of solidarity during war after years of insisting its policies fell short of EU standards. There are elements of discrimination that seep into the most meritocratic process.

The final category includes club organizations that are exclusive but set only vague conditions for entry. Social organizations such as a fraternity clubs or elite groups like the Council on Foreign Relations do not specify the qualifications for membership. This does not mean that there is not a review process that can involve hazing rituals and reference letters to assess applicants. The OECD stands out as an example of an international organization that follows club-style entry provisions, with the OECD charter Article 16 stating: "The Council may decide to invite any Government prepared to assume the obligations of membership to accede to this Convention. Such decisions shall be unanimous." In the case of the OECD, countries' policies are carefully examined. Nevertheless, decisions about whom to invite to enter accession negotiations reflect a complex calculation about whether a state is "like-minded" and a "significant player," and not simply the conformity of policies with the many OECD conventions. Other organizations dispense entirely with any review process to assess compliance with terms of the agreement; the deposit of a treaty protocol means commitment in principle but not proof of adherence. For club-entry IGOs, the organization charter provisions on accession typically require acceptance of the organization principles and approval of members, without offering any restrictions based on review of policies. The addition of membership approval allows for the possibility that a state could meet all terms of the organization agreements, but still be denied membership for other reasons. The majority of IGOs fall within this range of moderate selectivity and vague conditionality. In short, the process to enter most IGOs is much closer to getting into a social club than trying out for a sports team.

The advantages of club-style accession processes are twofold. First, members maximize their discretion over enlargement. Without any need to write down new rules, states can extend preferences to former colonies or allies across a range of issue areas through selective membership. Discretion allows states to change the criteria over time, such as shifting to consider democracy or other conditions that may not have been important at formation of the regime. Using their discretion over entry criteria, members can adjust across multiple criteria rather than holding to a single rigid standard. A state that meets one standard could fail on another. Second, members retain their bargaining advantage through not being transparent about the accession process. Uncertainty over what must be done to join the organization can be used to extract more concessions during accession negotiations (Schneider and Urpelainen, 2012).

There are also advantages to the applicants. First, the approval or rejection of an application carries information for the applicant about their social position in the international system because the process allows room for favoritism and discrimination. Amidst the uncertainty of anarchic international relations, institutions establish affiliations through mutual cooperation for governance. Common institutions form the basis of an international society and can become a tool in the maintenance of hierarchy (Bull, 1977; Lake, 2009; Viola, 2020). Joining organizations forms one kind of signal that states have a working relationship based on mutual recognition. Conversely, rejection implies that other states do not view the candidate as a valuable partner. For states seeking information about their threat environment and the hospitality of the international system, such signals of approval or rejection carry weight beyond the business of the organization.

Second, entry will signal status more effectively when membership is not simply a rubberstamping of objective conditions. Entering into an organization is equivalent to choosing a social category for belonging to a group. Not only are states accepting specific commitments, they are also choosing to associate with a particular group of states. Indeed, the social context lends more power to the norms of compliance, as individuals receive utility from conforming to group expectations (Akerlof and Kranton, 2010). This same process is posited to operate at the level of states as they interact within an organization (Johnston, 2001). The two-sided nature of membership reveals both that the state seeks this deeper association and that other states accept its entry into their community.

As a choice of partners with whom to associate, IGO membership shapes the views of others about foreign policy, economic risk, and regime transition. Most directly, the IGO membership portfolio of a state identifies its foreign policy orientation. New choices can signal shifts in foreign policy direction. Kinne (2013a, p. 664) argues that IGO-based signaling reduces conflict between two states as they perceive entry as a meaningful step for cooperation even if the organization has nothing to do with security policies. The states of Eastern Europe and former Soviet republics had to navigate their transition to a new foreign policy identity closer to the West, and expanding their IGO memberships to include more European-centered organizations was a critical part of this process—for a state like Georgia, these steps were "deliberate Georgian efforts to signal an interest in cooperation with the West." Boehmer, Gartzke, and Nordstrom (2004) find that membership in structured IGOs with formal rules and procedures reduces the probability of conflict onset. They posit information transmission improves the bargaining environment so that states can avoid conflict. The most pertinent information conveyed by IGO membership is the voluntary decision by a group of states to establish closer relations through their participation in a formal organization.

Association with other states also conveys information to domestic and international audiences about the direction of regime transition—just as democratizing states may signal their intentions through joining IGOs with strong democracies, non-democracies participate more in IGOs with other non-democracies (Mansfield and Pevehouse, 2006; Libman and Obydenkova, 2013).[5] Finally, joint membership conveys information to markets. Gray (2013) finds that peer effects from association in an IGO have substantial impact on how financial markets perceive the risk of a country, beyond the

---

5. Not all states are allowed to join—Poast and Urpelainen (2013) highlight that democratizing states often have to form IGOs when unable to join existing ones.

objective policy measures of risk characteristics. Investors looking for cues are quick to classify states into groups, and membership forms one such benchmark (Brooks, Cunha, and Mosley, 2015). The aspirational desire for peer effects and self-binding to the norms of a particular group of states contribute to demand for entry into club IGOs. In contrast, universal or meritocratic processes carry less information about a state's social position.

IGO membership forms the tool for allocation of status within international society. The dual basis for membership based on performance and association value makes it a more meaningful status indicator than if membership were only based on one vector. Performance alone does not require separate validation. The relational component is based on prior ties well known to both sides. Clearing both thresholds marks a high level of approval for the position of a state relative to others who are not members. Performance and relational ties evaluated at the group level produce membership outcomes that contribute to status at the international level.

2.2   International Society and Ending IGO Membership

Exit and expulsion represent the other side of membership politics. The right to exit reflects the voluntary nature of cooperation in anarchy. Just as few states are coerced into joining an organization, as sovereign actors they retain the right to leave. Similar processes to those that shape entry into an organization also arise for ending membership—losing interest in the issues at stake within the organization or shifting away from shared values and geopolitical alignment. As preferences diverge, a state will judge the gains of membership are no longer worth the cost of compliance or budget fees, and either exit or lapse into noncompliance. Several theories about international institutions emphasize the willingness of states to exit as a critical constraint on cooperation (Stone, 2011; Johns, 2015). In the case when deviation leads to noncompliance rather than exit, current members face the question of whether to suspend or expel the state to eliminate free-riding and to uphold the cohesion of the community. Expulsion is more difficult as a collective decision of members to reject continued cooperation with a state. This section examines how the club logic of IGOs appears in the domain of exit and expulsion.

Some stickiness of membership is to be expected—path dependence and sunk costs endow institutions with an inertia that helps them outlast the configuration of interests at their formation (Krasner, 1983; Jupille, Mattli, and Snidal, 2013). Indeed, some organizations remain in operation long after they cease to deliver major gains from cooperation—Gray (2018) shows that these zombie organizations account for a substantial share of international organizations. Even in a context of sticky institutions, however, one would expect some attrition. On the demand side, shifting preferences and power balances can diminish the gains from participation for members. On the supply side, members should exclude those that routinely violate rules. How do the rules over membership address this potential for exit and expulsion?

Agreeing on the terms over exit as part of the IGO charter assures other states that they will receive notification of any change. Cooperation occurs through the mutual adjustment of policies, so when one side ends cooperation, others will want to adjust. A universal organization that asks little of states to enter may still request prior notification of exit. Most recently, this was seen in the case of the U.S. declaration that it would leave the WHO. President Trump first announced his intentions to leave in May, and then in July 2020 the government issued the formal notification to the WHO. Rules for a one-year transition period meant that the U.S. exit would have taken effect a year later, in July 2021. Given the reversal of the decision by the Biden administration, however, the United States never actually exited the organization. In the case of the United Nations Educational, Scientific and Cultural Organization (UNESCO), the United States has exited the organization twice; it withdrew in 1984, criticizing poor administration as well as pro-Moscow and anti-Israel leanings on policy, only to reenter in 2002 when building international support for the war on terror. The Trump administration announced plans to exit in October 2017, with formal membership ending in December 2018. This second exit episode was the culmination of opposition to UNESCO membership for Palestine, and has yet to be reversed (see chapter 8). The provisions on exit are discretionary for the state choosing to leave without a vote by IGO members.

The threat to end cooperation by expulsion marks a stronger form of conditionality. In bargaining models, a grim trigger strategy describes the termination of all cooperation as a response to defection by another actor. For membership organizations, this would take the form of expulsion. Looking at local cooperation based on gradation of sanctions for noncompliance, Ostrom (2000, p. 151) notes that "the capability to escalate sanctions enables such a regime to warn members that if they do not conform they will have to pay ever-higher sanctions and may eventually be forced to leave the community." The possibility looms over interactions in a group even if it is not frequently used or written in the treaty. Nevertheless, to the extent states seek credible commitments that signal future behavior, one would expect formalization of terms for expulsion. Expulsion could complement precise entry conditions or serve as a substitute. On the one hand, an organization with precise entry conditions and limited eligibility could gain leverage to enforce those provisions through parallel terms for ending membership when violated. On the other hand, an organization with open entry rules could review member policies and expel low performers to uphold compliance. From a contractual perspective, expulsion terms should feature prominently in IGO charters, and it is surprising to note their relative infrequency.

States largely treat the question of ending membership as a separate matter from compliance. This is reflected in both the design of IGO rules and the behavior of states. In a pattern that more closely resembles citizenship than a contractual relationship, few choose to exit and even fewer find their violations of rules and principles sanctioned by expulsion. Despite the low threshold for exit, it rarely occurs. In a study of IGO treaty withdrawals from 1945 to 2014, Borzyskowski and Vabulas (2019b, p. 339) document 200 instances, which represent only 0.04 percent of IGO-member-years. The most frequent exiters—the United States and Canada—have only withdrawn ten and nine times respectively. Even more stark is the absence of expulsion terms in agreements. Surprisingly few IGOs include specific provisions for expelling states from membership, and when present, such provisions are rarely acted upon. This is readily apparent for some human rights organizations, where the inclusion of states with terrible records for abuses attracts scorn, but supports the belief in universal norms. When exit and expulsion do occur in international organizations, it rarely is about compliance. The most prominent cases of ending membership seem to be less about contract enforcement than a divorce in the relationship, such as the Brexit departure from the EU. An extreme cases, the expulsion of South Africa from the UPU, represented anti-Apartheid foreign policy sanctions rather than enforcement of postal rules.[6]

In part, the dearth of expulsion for noncompliance reflects the use of alternative punishments. Members exercise specific reciprocity or peer pressure to influence behavior from within an organizational context rather than expelling

---

6. As part of the international pressure applied on South Africa to end Apartheid, the members of the Universal Postal Union voted to expel it from the organization in 1964, despite objections from some who noted that expulsion was supposed to be limited to states shown to violate UPU regulations ("Universal Postal Union," 1966, p. 834). This case is examined in chapter 8.

noncompliant states. Partial responses occur in the kind of graduated sanctions expected by Ostrom (2000). One such measure is the temporary suspension of voting rights, such as the OAS's actions against Cuba. Yet even this action requires a strong consensus among members; in their comparison of IGO charter rules, Hooghe et al. (2017, p. 125) find that IGOs have the least amount of pooling for decision-making related to suspension. Another response to noncompliance is the withdrawal of benefits proportional to the degree of violation, such as in WTO dispute settlement. Differential levels of benefits allocated among members can reward some and punish others (Stone, 2011; Vreeland and Dreher, 2014). As Europe debates democratic backsliding in Poland and Hungary, conditional subsidies have emerged as one leverage point. Finally, the continuity of state membership masks other forms of dynamism in who cooperates that arise by changing recognition of a government. The dissolution of the USSR and its replacement by Russia occurred without a new accession process. According to Landau-Wells (2018, p. 103), civil wars often bring a change of recognition that precedes victory on the battlefield. Others may refuse to acknowledge a ruling government, as in the controversy over representation of Afghanistan and Myanmar in the United Nations that prevents the ruling government from participation in meetings.[7] This flexibility supports ongoing membership, although nonrecognition may form de facto expulsion. These lower-level enforcement actions play an important role as states monitor and sanction noncompliance.

But more generally, the restraint about using membership as a tool to punish noncompliance reflects the nature of organizations as institutions that build on community. When ties go deeper than policy coordination, they are not used for enforcement. From the perspective of IGOs as discriminatory clubs, ending membership is also about the relationship among countries. The frequent analogy of Brexit as a divorce highlights the notion that positive or negative relations motivate exit. In order to become members in a discriminatory club, actors value joint association as well as the collective effort for provision of public goods. Factors that diminish the value of association can strain perceptions about continued cooperation in the IGO. For individuals, income, race, or religion may form indicators of shared status. A fall from fortune or change in social norms toward in-group identification may shift individuals to lower attractiveness as fellow members in a club.

7. Gladstone, Rick. "U.N. Seats Denied, for Now, to Afghanistan's Taliban and Myanmar's Junta," *The New York Times*, 1 December 2021.

For governments, peer status as like-minded countries hinges upon ideology, regime, or geopolitical alignment. When a regime has a revolution or breaks alliance ties, this changes the calculus for assessing the value of association with that country. A turn inward toward isolationism corresponds to retreat from international organizations. When others come to view a state as a pariah unfit for peer association, this can build momentum for the collective decision to expel it from membership.

The relational value of membership in a discriminatory club offsets the attention to policy. On the one hand, this could reduce the need to include expulsion terms for noncompliance in the charter. When other states receive reputational spillover from association with other members, it weakens the link between compliance and membership. They can continue to cooperate with a noncompliant state that remains in good standing in terms of political relationships just as they may choose to terminate cooperation with a fully compliant state because it has violated community norms. On the other hand, the discriminatory club may expel members when association with a member takes on negative value. Vague entry rules facilitate formation of a club of like-minded actors along multiple dimensions, including some unrelated to cooperation, and vague rules on expulsion also support the termination of cooperation without due cause so long as the membership votes one out of the group. Omission of rules on expulsion leaves such actions at the complete discretion of members. Charters with vague or missing terms for expulsion are consistent with a club model of IGO membership.

The threshold of conflict that could lead to ending IGO membership is quite high as a result of collective decision-making processes that favor the status quo. With the need for a supermajority of members to vote for suspension or expulsion, broader ties across the entire membership matter. A state may witness criticism and deterioration of relations with some states but not yet trigger opposition from sufficient states to warrant expulsion. As each state fears itself being the next target for such votes, they may not readily join a coalition to expel another. In some institutional contexts, smaller states can exert a surprising degree of influence through their blocking power— multilateral institutions are inherently prone to this problem of multiple veto players that block policy changes (Tsebelis, 2002). This is widely evident within the European Union. The nature of EU decision-making rules has shifted the relative influence of states such that a country that may not have power in the traditional sense could nevertheless shape decisions through its outlier preferences on policy (Garrett and Tsebelis, 1996; Scharpf, 2006;

Schneider, 2009). Enlargement adds to the challenge of decision-making by creating even greater preference heterogeneity. Yet when states become dissatisfied with open noncompliance, other members can block reforms, including those related to membership. In the most sensitive issues of suspension over democratic backsliding, veto players have largely protected Poland and Hungary. One may only appear to be a promising cooperation partner to join, while a state behavior must be extremely negative to draw calls for expulsion.

The low incidence of expulsion carries implications for membership politics. In effect, states have created an obsolescing bargain, whereby once entry is granted, other members have less influence over behavior than they did at the time of accession.[8] This places greater importance on the need to carefully screen entry into the organization.

States establish formal membership provisions, which they can modify with additional practices that will condition outcomes. The particular historical experience within a region and examples from other organizations can lead to different combinations of institutional design rather than a singular template (Alter, 2014; Jetschke, 2017). Other studies document how enforcement provisions vary widely across institutions, and we see similar variety in the design of membership rules. Evaluating the range of design choices will help to test the prevalence of the club model. Attention to rules for entry and exit offers insight into how states do and do not condition membership.

2.3   Data on IGO Accession Rules

This section uses descriptive statistics about the rules of accession to evaluate the first hypothesis underlying my theory about IGOs as discriminatory clubs: states will design IGO accession rules to provide discretion over selection. Further, I shed light on the two motivating questions of the chapter: when are IGOs universal, and how do restrictive IGOs screen for membership? Following the typology of four models of the IGO accession process (Figure 2.1), I categorize the means of exclusion mechanisms in terms of participation and conditionality. As a preview, the evidence presents an overall picture of discretionary rules that maximize the flexibility for members to choose how they screen members and documents the prevalence of the club model.

---

8. See Carnegie (2015), who models membership in international institutions as a constraint on the exercise of coercive diplomacy.

I also compare the pattern of accession rules for IGOs in different issue areas. The logic of discrimination in my theory arises across issue areas, but much of the literature on institutional design suggests that states adapt provisions to guide behavior appropriate for the kind of cooperation problem of an issue area (e.g. Martin, 1992; Koremenos, Lipson, and Snidal, 2001; Hooghe and Marks, 2015). In the environmental policy issue area, the cooperation problem is more likely to resemble provision of a public good where exclusion is not feasible. In the social issue area the distributional stakes may be lower such that exclusion would be unnecessary. This could be a limiting scope condition for IGOs to form a discriminatory club. The expectation from this literature holds that policies to regulate the environment and social issues would have a higher frequency of universal IGOs relative to economic and security issues. Examining whether discretionary rules and selective membership occur across issue areas is important for understanding the generalizability of my argument.

2.3.1   Founding Charter Documents

In order to research the design of institutional rules, I restrict my inquiry to those IGOs for which a formal document specifies the rules governing the institution. These documents are referred to by different names, including constitution, treaty, convention, agreement, statute, and charter. I will refer to them collectively as "charter," which reflects that the text describes the basic rules and principles for the organization irrespective of its legal status. My analysis focuses on the design of membership provisions as written in the charter documents. Informal IGOs that lack a public record of a charter fall outside the scope of the analysis presented here.

The population of IGOs for analysis draws upon the Correlates of War (COW) International Organizations Dataset version 3.0 (Pevehouse, Nordstrom, and Warnke, 2004). Starting from the 534 IGOs listed in the COW data for the period from 1815 to 2014, I coded accession provisions for 322 IGOs for which I could locate a charter document establishing governance rules of the IGO. The search for IGO charter included identification in the UN Treaty Series, the IGO website when available, and the volumes on International Governmental Organizations by Peaslee that are referenced as a source for the IGO database (Peaslee and Peaslee Xydis, 1979).[9] The oldest available charter

---

9. I thank Raymond Hicks for this extensive search to assemble the complete charters for analysis. I have omitted IGOs that were entirely subsidiary to another IGO, such as the

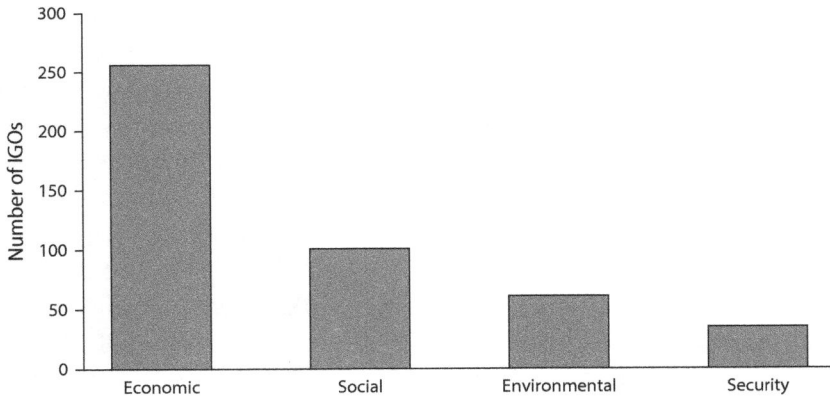

FIGURE 2.2. *IGOs by issue area*: The figure shows the number of IGOs by the issue areas that represent part of the core mission. Note that IGOs may be classified under multiple issue areas.

forms the basis of coding membership provisions. My question of interest is about the institutional design decision of founders. Moreover, research into the changes of charter provisions over time for these organizations suggests that states rarely modify the membership provisions.[10] The informal practices of how states evaluate candidates shift more than the legal constraints.

The data describes the issue area of the IGO based on the aims expressed in the preamble of the charter and information from the Yearbook of International Organizations regarding the fundamental aims and subject area for all organizations.[11] Some organizations with a broad mandate will address several issue areas, while others are more narrowly focused. Figure 2.2 presents the

Inter-American Defense Board that operates within the Organization of American States. In this data, IGOs that have a substantial change of legal status are treated as new IGOs, i.e., the GATT and WTO appear as two IGOs. Two additional organizations that fit the criteria of an IGO according to COW guidelines were added: Eurasian Development Bank and the Global Green Growth Institute.

10. In their detailed history of 76 organizations for the period 1950–2010, Hooghe et al. (2017) found only 14 that changed provisions for accession (variable ACC17), with all but two of those changes simply moving from a status of "no documentation" to coding that there is no requirement for member ratification. The substantively meaningful change was the EU addition of a requirement that members must ratify an agreement for the accession of new members.

11. The Yearbook of International Organizations is a compendium of information on over 66,000 international organizations produced by the Union of International Associations. Coding relies on two categories of information: the goals of each organization ("aims") and

distribution of the IGOs across four issue areas. Looking at the categories of economic, security, environmental, and social issues for the 322 IGOs in the sample, 80 percent refer to economic topics as a core aim. This in part reflects the broad definition of the category, which includes not only the WTO but also the UPU. Furthermore, there is a tendency for IGOs to link their purpose with economic development—the Global Environment Fund is classified as both an environmental IGO and an economic IGO. Only 11 percent of the IGOs fall within the category of security issues. Many alliances do not take the form of an international organization—NATO enters the sample while the U.S.-Japan security alliance does not. Nineteen percent of the IGOs incorporate environmental goals as a priority, with many holding this as their core purpose, such as the International Whaling Commission (IWC), and others, such as the African Union (AU), that uphold environmental sustainability as one of several goals. Social issues are highlighted for IGOs that may serve general purposes of regional integration, such as ASEAN, or for IGOs where they constitute the central focus, such as UNESCO and the International Organization for Migration.

The overall size of the IGOs varies from small organizations, with a few members, to the United Nations, with 193 members. This range is apparent across issue areas. When facing the trade-offs between larger or smaller membership size, it is not evident that the nature of the issue plays a determinative role. The median organizational size is 20 members, which is similar to that of economic, social, and security organizations.[12] Environmental organizations have a lower median size of nine members, which reflects the regional focus of several that address a specific river basin or fisheries area. Figure 2.3 presents the data for the total number of members in IGOs disaggregated into the issue areas.

2.3.2   Participation Mandate

There are three ways in which IGO design of the charter can restrict membership. First, the charter can establish a broad category of eligibility rules. These

---

the issue area listed for the organization ("subject"). Text scraping software parses these descriptions for keywords. For example, keywords such as "commerce," "development," or "finance," which indicate a focus on economic activity, would categorize the IGO to fall within an economic issue area. This text coding is supplemented by the descriptive coding of the IGO charter.

12. This focuses on the largest size achieved by the organization, whereas looking at the average size of an organization over its existence would show a smaller figure of 15 members as the modal size of organizations.

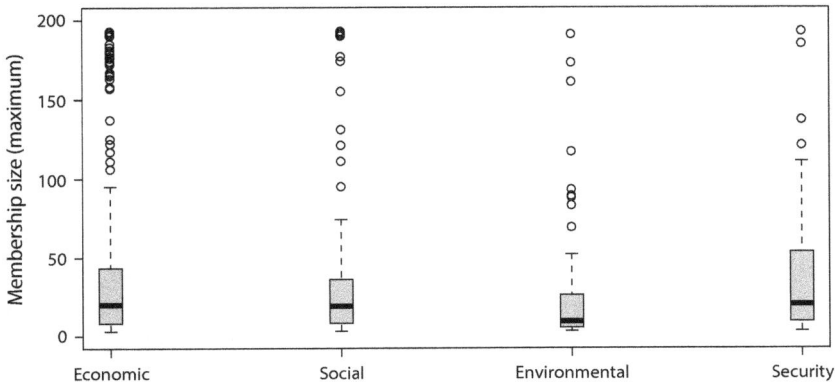

FIGURE 2.3. *IGO size by issue area*: The figure shows the number of members in each IGO at the maximum size observed during its existence. Note that IGOs may be classified under multiple issue areas.

serve ex ante to limit the set of countries that would seek membership. Second, negotiable terms of membership allow for evaluation of policies as well as demands for additional reforms to make it easier or harder for a country to join the organization. Powerful states are likely to favor the use of negotiable terms that allow them to use bargaining leverage and informal influence to shape who can join and to determine the price of entry. Third, a requirement for member approval in the form of a vote ensures support for new members. Rules vary in terms of the size of majority vote required, and some call for unanimity. The requirement for an invitation to apply adds another layer of member approval. Negotiations and approval requirements offer members more discretion than do eligibility rules. IGOs may use a combination of these steps to restrict participation.

Universal IGOs are open on all three dimensions of participation. For example, the WHO in Article 3 of its 1948 Constitution of the World Health Organization declares that "membership in the Organization shall be open to all States." Even the IGOs with open eligibility often contain some restriction, such as the WHO requirement that the Health Assembly vote by majority to approve membership in the case of states that are not already members of the United Nations (UN members may simply deposit the signed agreement without vote approval).[13] In the sample of 322 IGOs, only 40 fall in

13. The significance of restricting entry for recognized states is further developed in chapter 8. An important exception is actors that are not UN members. These often must receive approval by a majority, or in some cases a supermajority, of members.

the category of universal organizations, including those such as the International Telecommunication Union (ITU), UPU, International Labour Organization (ILO), and WHO. The vast majority of IGOs take measures to limit participation.

Restricted eligibility. Eligibility rules form the most frequent restriction. Sixty percent of organizations have some regional focus within their mandate, although not all restrict membership to those within a geographic region.[14] When regional IGOs restrict membership to the region, they often do not define the scope of the region in objective terms. For example, ASEAN declares that the "Association is open for participation to all States in the South East Asian Region" without specifying the borders of the region. Chapter 7 will analyze how discretionary rules allow geopolitics to play a role alongside geography when selecting members. The next most common form of exclusive eligibility is a charter restriction that refers to membership in another IGO—69 of the IGOs refer to another IGO such as the UN or a regional organization.[15] A small group of 23 organizations such as OPEC regulate prices and related policies for commodity trade and restrict membership to those that are producers of the commodity. Yet even among the commodity organizations, a few, such as the IWC, lack such a restriction.

It is equally important to note what kinds of exclusive eligibility restrictions are *not* present in IGO charters. Rules generally have not mandated a particular political regime as a condition for entry. The EU stands out for its requirement that member state governments be founded on the principles of democracy (Article F of the Treaty on European Union), but most organizations do not specify such a requirement, even when the members consist almost entirely of democratic regimes. For example, as discussed in chapter 5, the OECD has come to treat democracy as a priority in review of accession applicants, but non-democracies were among the founding members, and the formal charter provisions for membership do not specify any restriction by

14. Of the 322 organizations, 196 are treated as regional organizations because the organization title and/or charter specifically refer to a region, and 117 have a membership provision that restricts eligibility to countries in the region.

15. The dataset excludes organizations that are completely subsidiary to another IGO. Some eligibility restrictions are relaxed with a provision for a secondary track for accession, whereby a non-regional applicant or state not recognized as a member of the UN could become a member through a higher review process that often requires a two-third vote approval, while states in the main category of accession countries face an easier accession process.

political system. Neither do IGO rules specify alliances as a precondition of membership.[16] The practice of favoring fellow democracies and allies occurs almost entirely in the shadow of membership rules as informal discrimination to favor these states.

Negotiable terms. The more flexible forms of membership restriction arise in the requirements for members to negotiate terms with an applicant for their accession. All but four of the 56 negotiable IGOs include economic topics. Negotiations at the time of accession specify the level of commitments in ways that allow for variation across members and within specific issues. For example, the WTO charter simply notes that "any State or separate customs territory possessing full autonomy in the conduct of its external commercial relations and of the other matters provided for in this Agreement and the Multilateral Trade Agreements may accede to this Agreement, on terms to be agreed between it and the WTO." Accession negotiations have become lengthy sessions of bargaining over tariff schedules and periods to phase-in policy changes. A country such as China was led to make changes that exceed current member commitments in some areas while falling short of member commitments in other areas.[17] In contrast, environmental topics are less likely to refer to negotiable terms of entry for accession—only five of the 59 IGOs that address topics related to the environment include negotiable accession terms. The original bargaining at IGO formation and for revision of the agreement is certainly negotiable, but the effort to include wide participation has inhibited use of negotiation at the time of accession.

Member approval. A requirement for approval by members forms a general way to screen applicants without the need to specify criteria for admission. For example, the OECD Convention in Article 16 states: "The Council may decide to invite any Government prepared to assume the obligations of membership to accede to this Convention. Such decisions shall be unanimous." This accession rule is quite open in its terms of eligibility, but restrictive to require invitation and unanimous approval by members. Thirty-eight percent of the IGOs require member approval by a vote, with some calling for a majority, supermajority, or consensus. By issue area, security IGOs are significantly

16. The exceptions are a subset of the security IGOs that form a security alliance, such as NATO and the Warsaw Treaty Organization.

17. See Yamaoka (2013) for details on WTO-plus and WTO-minus commitments in the Chinese accession protocol.

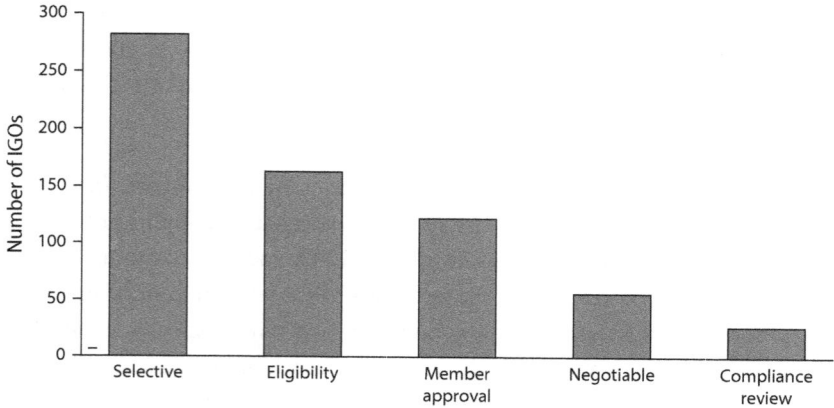

FIGURE 2.4. *Restrictions on participation mandate*: The figure shows the number of IGOs by the type of membership restriction present in the charter. Note that any single IGO may include multiple types of restrictions.

more likely than others to require member approval, with 54 percent having this requirement. But there is not as significant a difference across the other issue areas, where about a third of the organizations include a requirement for member approval. Thirty-eight percent of economic IGOs relative to 30 percent of environmental IGOs call for member approval.[18]

IGOs vary in the threshold of member approval specified in the charter document. Among the 122 IGOs with a member approval requirement, only 22 of them accept a simple majority vote. More common is a stringent approval requirement, which calls for a supermajority or unanimous consent of existing member states to admit new members (100 IGOs). These stringent approval IGOs have the same average membership as the full sample and are distributed across the issue areas. They form about one-third of regional IGOs (57 of 196) and also form about one-third of open IGOs that do not have any restrictions on eligibility (29 of 88).

Selective IGOs. Restrictions on eligibility, negotiable terms, and member approval together differentiate *selective* IGOs from *inclusive* organizations. Figure 2.4 shows in the first column the number of IGOs that are selective

18. Only eight of the 61 IGOs with environmental mandate include an approval requirement. Thirty-five of the 101 social topic IGOs include an approval requirement. A comparison of means test shows that the only significant difference from population average is in security IGOs.

on at least one of the three dimensions of restricted participation. With 282 of the 322 IGOs including some form of participation restriction, selective IGOs are the overwhelming majority (88 percent of the sample). In a hypothesis test for the IGOs in each issue area, only economic IGOs show a significant difference in their high use of selection relative to other IGOs.[19] But this does *not* mean that the social and environmental issues are largely addressed within inclusive organizations—many selective organizations include a mandate for addressing social and environmental issues.

The figure shows the distribution across each of the three types of participation restrictions examined separately, showing the most frequent use of eligibility restrictions, followed by member approval and negotiation. This pattern is similar across issue areas, with the one exception that security IGOs are more likely to rely on member approval than eligibility. For comparative perspective, the final column of Figure 2.4 shows that the use of compliance review as a form of conditionality to limit entry is much less frequent than the use of participation restrictions.

2.3.3   Conditionality Terms

Conditionality arises through two processes. First, states can specify the review of policies as part of the accession process. As distinct from negotiating the terms of entry, precision about conditionality represents a formal process to assess whether the country has changed its policies to comply with the treaty when it deposits the ratification instrument to become a member. Second, suspension and expulsion in the case of noncompliance forms the flip side of requiring compliance at the time of entry. The resolution of disputes over individual policy questions may go forward without implications for membership status, but conditionality terms set the expectation that some level of noncompliance could revoke membership.

Meritocratic IGOs use conditionality to ensure that all states pass the required benchmarks for compliance. The Treaty on European Union signed in Maastricht in 1992 provides for accession in Article O:

> Any European State may apply to become a Member of the Union. It shall address its application to the Council, which shall act unanimously after

19. Among 256 economic IGOs, 230 are selective (90 percent) while among the 61 environment IGOs, 51 are selective (84 percent); among the 101 social IGOs, 88 are selective (87 percent); and, finally, among the 35 security IGOs, 31 are selective (89 percent).

consulting the Commission and after receiving the assent of the European Parliament, which shall act by an absolute majority of its component members. The conditions of admission and the adjustments to the Treaties on which the Union is founded which such admission entails shall be the subject of an agreement between the Member States and the applicant State. This agreement shall be submitted for ratification by all the contracting States in accordance with their respective constitutional requirements.

The conditions of admission and adjustments to the treaties are separately acknowledged because the former include negotiable terms not formally laid out in the treaties while the latter affirms that policies are in full accordance with the treaties at time of admission. The treaty does not include provisions for expulsion from membership for noncompliance. The IAEA implies the threat of suspension in Article XIX as a form of conditionality:

A member which has persistently violated the provisions of this Statute or of any agreement entered into by it pursuant to this Statute may be suspended from the exercise of the privileges and rights of membership by the General Conference acting by a two-thirds majority of the members present and voting upon recommendation by the Board of Governors.

The models of IGOs represent an ideal type, and individual cases may fall between categories, with an IGO design that contains elements of multiple policy restrictions. For example, the EU holds weighted voting for hierarchy and imposes meritocratic conditionality as well as more discretionary member approval.

Accession review process. Few IGOs specify the need for a compliance review process as a condition for accession at the charter level. The European Union treaty refers to the need for an agreement between members and the applicant detailing the "adjustments to the treaty." Some will include reference to an assessment of intentions, but fall short of requiring a review of policies to confirm adherence to the treaty. In this category, one finds IGOs like the IAEA, which states: "In recommending and approving a State for membership, the Board of Governors and the General Conference shall determine that the State is able and willing to carry out the obligations of membership in the Agency, giving due consideration to its ability and willingness to act in accordance with the purposes and principles of the Charter of the United Nations." But most IGOs simply require that the applicant deposit an instrument of ratification, and do not mandate a compliance review.

The lack of conditionality within the terms of IGO charters does not mean that states disregard compliance. Members may determine through informal assessment that a state is far from compliance and vote against its membership, or they may use the negotiation of terms for entry as the means to impose conditionality. For example, the WTO establishes a working party of member states that reviews a document prepared by accession candidates on their trade policies and drafts an accession protocol that is brought to the full membership for approval. These procedures for reviewing applicants for admission typically lie outside of charter provisions. Including the formal requirement for review of policy conformity for membership represents a higher threshold of conditionality.

Expulsion terms. We also observe conditionality through provisions for the suspension of membership in cases of noncompliance. For example, the West African Monetary Union charter in Article 4 declares that, "subject to automatic debarment from the Union, the States signatories shall undertake to honour the provisions of this Treaty and of enactments adopted for its implementation. . . . The Conference of Heads of State of the Union, by unanimous decision of the Heads of State of the other members of the Union, shall confirm the withdrawal therefrom of a State which has not honoured the above commitments." Thirty-one percent of the IGOs (100 of 322) include a suspension clause; among these, 66 refer to nonpayment of dues as grounds for suspension, and 42 refer to noncompliance with the rules and norms of the organization. For suspension, states may lose the right to attend meetings and receive benefits of the organization on a temporary basis. In a more extreme provision, 62 organizations call for expulsion from the organization with terms to remove membership status. This often follows a period of suspension and requires a vote of the membership.

The decision to include such rules is a sensitive matter. Emmons (2022) looks at the OAS deliberation over the amendment of institution rules in 1992 to add a Washington Protocol that included terms for suspension of governments that reversed on the organization commitment to democratic representation. States that had experienced *external* intervention feared that IGO terms for suspension could cover for another round of coercive moves by regional powers against their sovereignty, which led them to favor a high threshold for adoption, and led many to reject the protocol with a reservation. This example illustrates the problem with using the charter as a contract to enforce compliance. Expulsion provisions could safeguard against backsliding, and would be most valuable amongst a heterogenous group of countries. But the diverse preferences and potential for disagreement in such a group will also make states reluctant to establish such terms.

Calls for expulsion often meet the reality that the rules set too high a bar. The Russian invasion of Ukraine prompted many governments to urge rejection of its membership in international organizations. The Council of Europe, which has provisions for suspension and termination of membership for actions that violate its core commitment to rule of law and human rights, voted 15 March 2022 to expel Russia.[20] In other organizations, this was more difficult. When the United States and its allies sought to suspend Russian membership in the International Criminal Police Commission, the secretariat office responded that there were no rules for ending membership and such decisions would require agreement of 195 members.[21] As part of economic sanctions, governments sought to expel Russia from multilateral economic organizations, which also met with difficulty. The U.S. House approved legislation urging the USTR to "consider further steps with the view to suspend the Russian Federation's participation in the WTO" and the European Commission president declared that "we will also work to suspend Russia's membership rights in leading multilateral financial institutions, including the International Monetary Fund and the World Bank."[22] Since the WTO is among those organizations lacking any provision for expelling members, WTO experts supportive of expelling Russia explained that the path forward would be for two thirds of members to vote for an amendment to the WTO rules, creating a provision for expelling Russia.[23] It was much easier for states to undertake actions to halt the WTO accession negotiations of Belarus for its support of the Russian invasion than to expel Russia. The IMF charter provides for expulsion of a member, but limits this to follow after members vote for a period of suspension and find "the member persists in its failure to

20. Council of Europe Newsroom, "The Russian Federation is excluded from the Council of Europe," https://www.coe.int/en/web/portal/-/the-russian-federation-is-excluded-from-the-council-of-europe. Accessed 19 March 2022.

21. Darryl Coote, "Intel Alliance Asks Interpol to Suspend Russia as Kyiv Wants Moscow Isolated," *UPI*, March 7, 2022.

22. House Committee on Ways and Means GOP, "Brady, Neal Introduce Bill to Further Punish Putin: Legislation Suspends Normal Trade Relations with Russia and Belarus," March 17, 2022; European Commission, "Statement by President von der Leyen on the Fourth Package of Restrictive Measures against Russia," 11 March 2022.

23. Bacchus, James, "Boot Russia from the WTO," *The Wall Street Journal*, 28 February 2022.

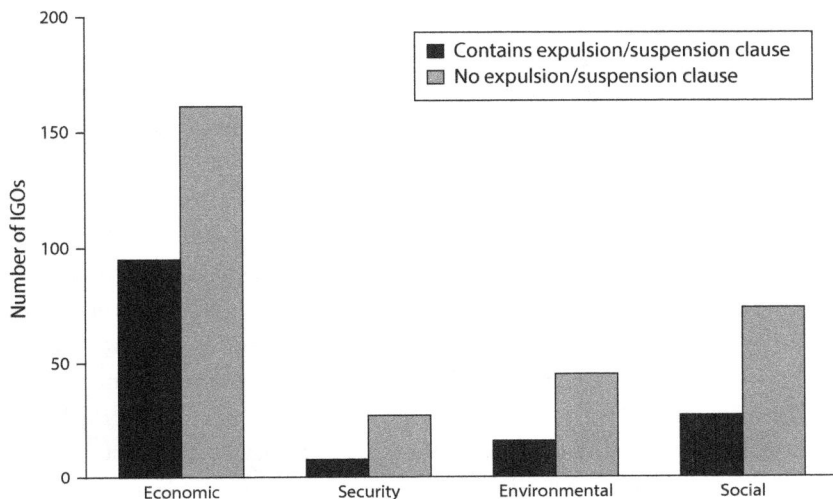

FIGURE 2.5. *Membership suspension and expulsion*: The figure shows the number of IGOs that include provisions in the charter for the suspension or removal of membership status. IGOs are grouped by issue area with the potential for an IGO to appear in more than one category.

fulfill any of its obligations under this Agreement." Membership termination requires approval by an 88 percent voting share of the Board of Governors. That threshold requires support not only of the United States, but also China. An EU official acknowledged the challenge of expelling Russia from the IMF, noting, "The consensus legal reading is that it cannot be done. Even for members guilty of genocide it was not done, because it would require proof of a legal breach of the IMF agreement, so it [is] very unlikely."[24]

One might expect some variation by the nature of the issue. Koremenos (2005) finds that states set shorter terms to treaties in some issue areas as a way to ex ante limit their commitment. A similar logic could extend to provisions for exit and suspension, but that is not what I find. Figure 2.5 shows by issue area the use of conditional membership through expulsion and suspension provisions in the charter, with comparison of the relative frequency of such provisions within the IGOs of each issue area. In none of the issue areas does the use of expulsion/suspension reveal a significantly higher or lower prevalence in comparison with the full population.

24. Reuters, "Exclusive: EU May Curb Russia's Rights in IMF," 4 March 2022.

Exit from IGOs is relatively rare, and most of these cases occur as voluntary exit rather than expulsion. Seventy-seven percent of the IGOs include a provision for exit from membership. Nevertheless, even these organizations average only four exit cases over the lifespan of the organization's existence.

Hierarchical decision-making. Hierarchical IGOs establish two or more classes of membership to uphold conditionality while having differential expectations of members. The provisions in the charter on membership are not restrictive on eligibility per se, although they may include more approval steps than the truly universal IGOs. Rather, in the allocation of decision-making authority within the IGO, the charter establishes differential influence. Many of the international financial institutions, including the IMF, World Bank, and Bank for International Settlements, adopt weighted voting based on the share of the funds contributed. Some commodity organizations allow for membership by both exporters and importers, but establish voting rules that distinguish between them. For example, the International Cocoa Organization fixes the total weight of voting rights available to exporters as a group relative to importers, and within these groups allocates weighted voting by share of exports/imports. The United Nations provides for a fixed hierarchy in the Security Council, which arises from the distinction between permanent members with a veto right and nonpermanent members elected from the full membership.

As seen in Figure 2.6, economic IGOs are the most likely to implement weighted voting, and development banks stand out within this population. When an issue area confronts multiple institutions, weighted voting offers flexibility to accommodate asymmetric and changing power relationships (Lipscy, 2017). But the weights achieve control for contributors rather than serving as a tax on utilization. The differentiated membership supports broader participation by allowing those who pay more funds to exercise influence while lightening the burden on other states that will be drawing on the services of the IGO most heavily.

Having examined each component of charter design that restricts participation and imposes conditions, we can revisit the four conceptual models of IGO accession presented in Figure 2.1 at the beginning of the chapter. The pie chart in Figure 2.7 shows the breakdown when classifying each of the 322 IGOs into one model based on their charter provisions for membership. The universal IGOs, which are in principle open to any state, do not restrict eligibility on region, commodity production, or other criteria, hold a

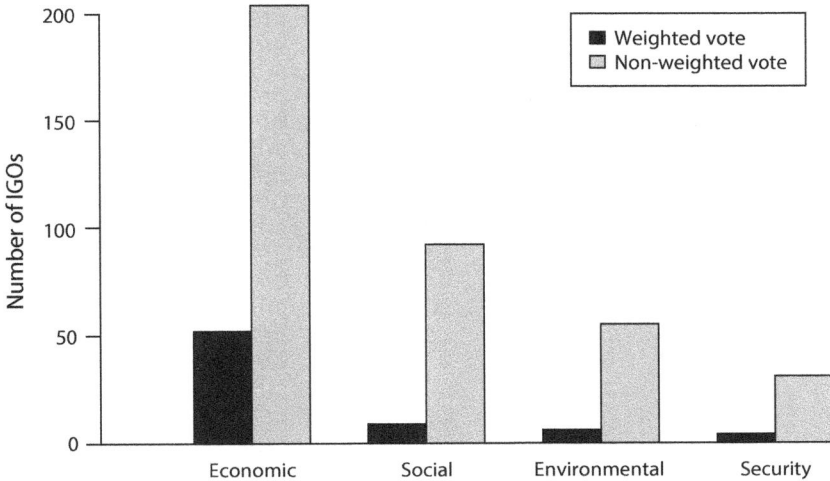

FIGURE 2.6. *Weighted voting:* The figure shows the number of IGOs with weighted voting by issue area.

low threshold of member approval, and do not impose conditions to screen compliance or differentiate among members with weighted voting. In the hierarchical model, weighted voting differentiates among members, and there may also be a member approval requirement. Meritocratic IGOs are highly selective as they make membership conditional on inspecting that states implement rules. The club model is also selective through limiting eligibility and/or requiring member approval but does not require review of policies as a condition of membership. The dominant design choice for accession in IGO charters is selective participation and vague conditionality, with nearly 80 percent of the IGOs falling into the category of the club model accession process.

Accession also includes informal practices. The OECD, WTO, and Asian Development Bank (ADB) do not refer to compliance review in their charter, but lay out a rigorous accession review process with detailed information available on their website. Yet, expanding the compliance review to include practices mentioned on the IGO's websites, and shifting these IGO's classification from club to meritocratic, would expand the share of meritocratic IGOs from seven to only 19, and remain a minority practice. While other IGOs may conduct screening, they choose not to make the compliance review explicit as a condition for entry either through the charter or website. Such choices let members raise or lower the entry conditions as they see fit. The charter

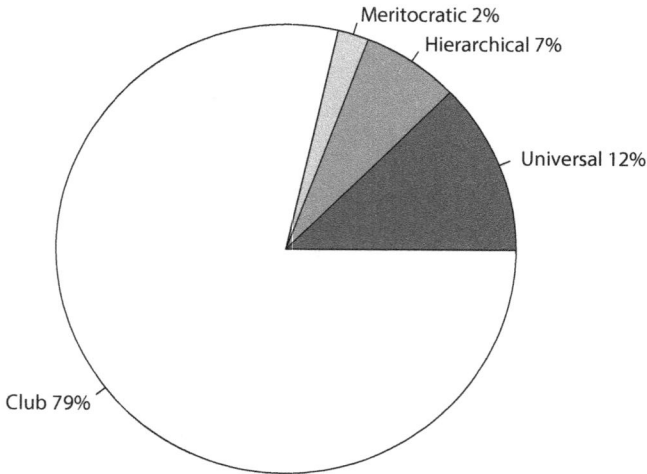

FIGURE 2.7. *Accession patterns*: The figure shows the share of IGOs according to their category of accession process.

design reveals state preferences for a club model that provides wide discretion to determine which states qualify to join.

2.4   Toward a Broader Understanding of Accession

This survey of the design of membership provisions contained in IGO charters shows two clear patterns. First, universal IGOs are a small share of the IGO population. Most IGOs restrict membership. Second, when limiting entry, they rely more on participation rules than conditionality. Neither the formal review of policy compliance nor the threat of expulsion for noncompliance are commonly used.

The exclusion mechanisms uphold discretion for members to change their criteria for screening members. Member approval and negotiable terms leave the widest flexibility for raising and lowering the entry bar. Yet even exclusive eligibility rules appear to be vague in their categories rather than rigid performance criteria or fixed categories of states. The most limiting category of regional integration itself has been flexible through fluid definitions of region and allowance for participation by states outside of the region for some regional organizations.

The IGOs that address environmental topics that come closest to public goods are more likely to have inclusive participation rules and are less likely to impose conditionality. Yet it is not true that they are all large in membership and uphold a universal accession process. Indeed, the average size of environmental IGOs is smaller than that of others. Economic IGOs show a strong pattern for restrictive membership and stand out for use of exclusive eligibility, negotiable terms, and weighted voting. On dimensions of member approval and use of expulsion/suspension provisions, the economic IGOs resemble those in other issue areas. These could be limiting factors that facilitate discriminatory practices for economic IGOs and reduce the room for discrimination in environmental IGOs. But the differences would be a matter of degree. Broadly speaking, the analysis of charters reveals that deference to states to select members occurs across issue areas.

There are several caveats with which we must view the analysis of IGO charters. These documents are open to change. Few have revised their rules on membership, but this is an area for future research into the evolution of membership rules. More challenging is the role of administrative procedures and informal practices that shape accession processes outside of the strictures of the founding documents. States have chosen to leave this area of IGO rules vague in their constituting documents. Instead of setting ex ante conditions for entry, they establish decision rules at a lower level and fill in gaps with informal practices.

2.5 Conclusion

This chapter has explained the prevalence of club-style design of international organizations. As states seek to maximize both the value of association with particular states and the gains of cooperation on important policy issues, they have prioritized flexibility over membership decisions. The evidence from analysis of IGO charters strongly supports the hypothesis for discretionary rules. This lays the baseline institutional context for geopolitical discrimination. Because IGO membership rules are more often discretionary than rigid, members can inject alternative criteria into their decisions to select members. If the OECD mandated democratic governance, or if the organization engaged in rigorous performance review of member compliance with all its codes and conventions, states such as Turkey and Mexico may have had more difficulty in becoming members. If the WTO were truly universal, the long negotiations with China or exclusion of Iran over foreign policy objectives unrelated to trade would not have held up the accession of those countries. Instead, flexibility in the exclusion mechanism applied within IGO charters has allowed unexpected entrants and the denial of unwanted applicants.

The advantage of the club model for selective but discretionary design of accession lies in its flexibility. This both allows members to discriminate and applicants to differentiate themselves as belonging to a special group. Yet such discretion comes at a cost as states eschew forming a rigid contract that defines terms for entry and expulsion as leverage to achieve higher levels of compliance. States have been willing to accept this trade-off across a large number of IGOs. Although environmental IGOs are more likely to adopt a universal scope and economic IGOs are more likely to adopt selective entry, the use of club design holds across all issue areas. Moreover, the mechanism of selection is voting approval. Compliance reviews are rare, and, when taken, exist as an informal procedure adopted outside of the formal charter rules for membership. The extensive reviews of policy changes to impose conditionality on EU applicants for the Eastern enlargement represent an unusually rigorous accession process, and such meritocratic evaluation is far from the norm. Yet neither do IGOs allow any applicant to join. In the gray zone between universality and compliance evaluation lies discrimination—choosing to cooperate with those states that form a community. Next we turn to examine the unwritten criteria for membership and explain how and why security interests impact global governance through the politics of IGO membership.

3

Membership Patterns in Economic Institutions

Christina L. Davis and Tyler Pratt[1]

DURING THE formation and enlargement of international organizations, membership depends on states' specific attributes relevant to the regulated issue as well as their broader political relations. The main theme of the book engages the idea that *geopolitical discrimination* occurs when states selectively allow those who share their foreign policy interests to enter international organizations. This chapter measures the timing and weight allocated to geopolitics in the membership choices for multilateral economic organizations. We demonstrate that geopolitical discrimination has been a prevalent practice across a broad swathe of economic organizations for over 60 years. In this role, shared security interests form a foundation for economic cooperation.

This builds upon a wide range of research into the interaction between states' economic and security interests (e.g. Gowa and Mansfield, 1993; Mansfield and Bronson, 1997; Mansfield and Pollins, 2003; Lake, 2009). During the Cold War, states allocated aid according to the military importance of recipients, and new strategic needs shape development policies today (e.g., Meernik, Krueger, and Poe, 1998; Bearce and Tirone, 2010; Boutton and Carter, 2014; Bermeo, 2018). Like aid, trade flows tend to follow the flag (e.g., Pollins, 1989; Keshk, Reuveny and Pollins, 2004; Pandya, 2016). The income gains from trade spillover into military power, motivating states to trade with allies

1. This chapter is based on the article Davis, Christina L. and Tyler Pratt. 2021. "The Forces of Attraction: How Security Interests Shape Membership in Economic Institutions." *The Review of International Organizations* 16:903–929.

(Gowa, 1989; Gowa and Mansfield, 1993; Gowa, 1994; Mansfield and Bronson, 1997; Long and Leeds, 2006). Other sources of influence can skew trade toward states with good relations (Berger et al., 2013; Fuchs and Klann, 2013). We look beyond bilateral exchanges of trade and aid during the Cold War to examine how security linkages shape multilateral economic governance.

The use of geopolitical discrimination when states join multilateral economic institutions resolves a dilemma for states. On the one hand, the principle of nondiscrimination and practice of collective decision-making render multilateral institutions inefficient as tools of economic statecraft. It is much easier for states to manipulate bilateral aid and trade policies where national governments wield control. On the other hand, multilateral institutions govern a large amount of economic activity, and states have incentives to exploit these gains for geopolitical advantage. Discrimination over membership allows states to steer benefits under the guise of multilateralism. Through this practice, powerful states build their geopolitical coalitions and weaker states minimize the reforms needed to gain entry.

Section 3.1 connects the theory about geopolitical discrimination to the empirical test on multilateral economic organizations. We specify observable implications to assess the theory's predictions for patterns of membership. In section 3.2, we introduce our data on economic IGOs and present the results of our empirical analysis of membership. The chapter examines a sample of potential memberships in 231 multilateral economic organizations for cases when existing members have discretion over new members. We develop a relational measure of geopolitical alignment based on alliance ties and UN voting similarity between potential members and other states in the organization. Trade flows between new states and other members serve as a proxy for the functional theory that economic interdependence explains demand for institutionalized cooperation on economic issues. We find that measures of geopolitical alignment between countries are strongly predictive of membership even when controlling for trade ties. Where earlier work focused only on enlargement, our evidence reveals that geopolitical discrimination occurs during the formation and enlargement of economic organizations. After confirming that both geopolitical alignment and economic interdependence drive membership, we use a finite mixture model to estimate the relative weight accorded to security versus trade ties. This model specification allows us to estimate *how much* states care about security ties when making membership decisions, while recognizing that economic interests also play an important role. We find that geopolitical alignment motivates 44 percent of the membership decisions in our sample of

231 multilateral economic organizations over the period 1949–2014. Far from being the exception, security ties are a prominent factor that shapes who joins and remains in multilateral economic organizations.

3.1   Geopolitics and Economic Cooperation

Economic interdependence generates potential mutual gains, and states have incentives for cooperation to harness these benefits. Functional theories emphasize the ability of institutions to overcome market failures that hinder cooperation (Keohane and Nye, 1977; Keohane, 1984; Farrell and Newman, 2015; Koremenos, 2016). The long-term gains from setting economic policies in cooperation are supported by commitment and enforcement mechanisms in multilateral economic organizations that raise the cost of unilateral policies that might otherwise tempt states to capture short-term gains. Eighty percent of IGOs with formal charters include economic cooperation within their mandate. Economic interests are a prime driver of membership in these organizations.

As a baseline expectation, membership selection should privilege those with the economic profile conducive to cooperation in the issue area regulated by the institution. A performance evaluation would focus on the many available economic indicators. For example, development banks might review financial accounts to evaluate the need for a country to receive development assistance and its ability to repay creditors, or to assess the potential of a government to serve as a donor. Trade volume could indicate the potential value in accepting a state into a trade organization, alongside reviews of market-based economic regulations. The specific economic criteria could be tailored to the mandate of each organization.

Discretion over membership, however, allows states to politicize institutional outcomes and choose members based on noneconomic criteria. When IGOs become discriminatory clubs, membership reflects both the ability to contribute to the joint project and an intrinsic value to the group. From this perspective, the appeal of joining an IGO depends on the composition of its members and not just mutual interests on a narrow issue.

While states could choose among many criteria when discriminating, the geopolitical discrimination hypothesis posits that security interests form a common source of discrimination in IGO membership. Both *security externalities* and *security linkages* undergird the logic. The security externality mechanism focuses on the inherent connection between economic and military power. Efficiency gains from economic cooperation can be channeled into military power (Gowa, 1989; Gowa and Mansfield, 1993; Gowa, 1994). States recognize these spillovers and respond strategically, steering the benefits of multilateral economic cooperation toward allies and away from adversaries.

Whereas the security externality arises as an indirect byproduct of economic exchange, a security linkage represents a joint decision that brings economic and security interests together. In this strategy, membership becomes a bargaining chip for states to expand their geopolitical coalitions. Different preferences for security and economic cooperation create the opportunity for a mutually profitable exchange (Tollison and Willett, 1979; Davis, 2004; Poast, 2013). Some states may be more motivated by the prospective economic gains from membership, while others seek enhanced leverage on security matters. The institutional context strengthens the linkage by providing an exclusion mechanism that restricts cooperation to the subset of members and increases the credibility of promised benefits to recipients.

We recognize that state preferences may arise from both functional demand for gains from regime cooperation and geostrategic goals. States must balance the desire to exploit selection of members for geopolitical gain with the functional trade-offs. The key task is differentiating their relative impact on outcomes.

3.1.1   Testable Implications for Membership Patterns

The empirical analysis examines whether states are more likely to join international organizations when they share geopolitical alignment with current members. This examines the second hypothesis presented in chapter 1: *States with shared geopolitical alignment form organizations together and are more likely to join the same organizations.* Our research design uses observational data about state behavior, making it hard to identify causal effects. To reduce the risk of a spurious finding, we use multiple measures of geopolitical alignment, explore alternative model specifications, and exploit dynamic breaks in alignment to more closely identify the mechanism.

We compare geopolitical alignment with economic interdependence as two forces that influence the demand for membership. Since geopolitical alignment and interests within the issue area overlap entirely in the area of security organizations, looking at economic organizations provides a better test. Our argument contends that security interests shape membership even in multilateral economic organizations, while the functional perspective would suggest a smaller role. We use shared alliances as our primary operationalization of geopolitical alignment, and we analyze similarity of alliance portfolios and UN voting patterns as two alternative measures. Trade ties between states control for the underlying interdependence that contributes to functional demand for cooperation on economic policies.

We also examine conditions that influence the importance of security interests. First, we distinguish between geopolitical alignment with all members of international organizations versus the most powerful member states. In principle, any existing member state can link accession of potential members to shared security interests. Below, we measure a state's geopolitical ties with all IGO members to assess how comprehensively the state shares foreign policy interests with existing members. Then we separately measure a state's ties with powerful states, who are the most likely to engage in linkage strategies as they cement relationships with strategic partners (Schneider and Urpelainen, 2012). Our relational measures of alignment differ from the monadic approach of current studies. For example, Kaoutzanis, Poast, and Urpelainen (2016) focus on the regime type of new entrants and Donno, Metzger, and Russett (2015) examine their conflict history.

Second, we analyze whether the role of geopolitical alignment differs over the lifespan of an IGO. Establishing an IGO raises transaction costs, as states negotiate the IGO charter and set up a headquarters and financial base. While states may use security linkages to overcome the initial cooperation challenges, they could focus strictly on policy when establishing the rules of the game and only later politicize membership. Prior work on screening members has been limited to enlargement (Kydd, 2001; Schneider, 2009; Stone, 2011; Donno, Metzger, and Russett, 2015). Through separate analysis of each stage, we test how geopolitics shapes membership at founding and enlargement.

3.2 Empirical Analysis of IGO Membership Patterns

Our empirical tests have two primary objectives. First, we estimate the effect of geopolitical alignment on the probability of IGO membership in a series of regression models, controlling for functional economic interests. Second, we estimate the relative weight given to geopolitical and functional considerations. We use a finite mixture model to assess which observations are more consistent with geopolitics or economic interdependence, and to show the conditions under which states privilege one over the other.[2]

3.2.1 Data on Membership in Multilateral Economic Organizations

We analyze a sample of 231 economic IGOs for the period from 1949 to 2014.[3] Starting with the IGO membership data introduced in chapter 2, we subset to those IGOs with an economic focus.[4] We conduct our analysis at the level of the state-IGO-year (Poast and Urpelainen, 2013; Donno, Metzger, and Russett, 2015). This unit of observation reflects the decision process we seek to model: when a state elects to form or join an IGO, it considers a specific group of other states. Because we are interested in how states exploit discretion over membership, we limit our sample to "potential but not automatic" IGO memberships. This entails two exclusions from the set of all possible state-IGO-year pairings in the period 1949–2014.[5] First, we exclude universal IGOs, where existing members have less discretion to select new entrants.[6] This removes organizations where membership is functionally automatic for states that seek entry, like the UPU or International Maritime Organization (IMO). Second, we exclude state-IGO pairings for regional organizations where the state resides outside the regional scope of the IGO.[7] As a result, the sample does not include memberships with little chance of being instantiated

2. See the supplemental materials in Davis and Pratt (2021) for tables including robustness checks.

3. Economic topics are broadly construed to include aid, finance, trade, and more general management of resources, travel, and standards relevant for economic exchange. Our coding of organizations draws on the Yearbook of International Organizations' description of the aims and subject of each organization along with information contained in the IGO charter documents.

4. The main dataset draws upon the Correlates of War (COW) International Organizations Dataset (Pevehouse, Nordstrom, and Warnke, 2004), with additional filtering based on coding of the organizations with a formal IGO charter document. Results are not contingent on our exclusion of IGOs without charter documents.

5. Our empirical results are robust to the inclusion of these observations.

6. Chapter 8 applies the theory to open eligibility organizations, including the universal IGOs. The analysis of this chapter has also been applied to the full sample of all IGOs; see appendix tables in Davis and Pratt (2021).

7. See chapter 7 for separate analysis of regional IGO membership, including non-regional states as potential entrants.

(e.g., Swedish membership in the AU). This generates 570,695 state-IGO-year observations.[8]

The dependent variable, *IGO Membership$_{ijt}$*, is a dichotomous measure of whether state i is a member of organization j in year t. *IGO Membership* is equal to 1 in 36.9% of observations. In the tests below, we also subset this sample to assess whether geopolitical alignment has different effects on joining as a founding member, joining later by accession, or exiting the organization. Our theory suggests security externalities and linkage will shape incentives for both founding members and those joining later, so our main sample pools these two paths to membership. Yet, to account for potential differences in these underlying decision processes and address alternative approaches in the literature, we also test our argument separately within each subset.[9]

Formal alliances are our primary measure of geopolitical alignment.[10] The variable *Average Alliances$_{ijt}$* measures the proportion of IGO j's member states with which state i shares a formal alliance in a given year. In the sample, it ranges from 0 (49.7% of observations) to 1 (4.5% of observations), with a mean value of 0.15. Second, *Lead State Alliance$_{ijt}$* indicates whether state i shares an alliance with the leading economic power among member states of IGO j during year t, with economic power measured annually by gross domestic product (GDP). In our sample, states are allied with an IGO's most powerful member state in 23% of state-IGO-years.

We also analyze two alternative measures of geopolitical alignment. *S-scores* is a continuous measure of similarity across states' entire portfolio of alliances; it reaches its maximum (1) when two states have identical alliance portfolios.[11] *UN Ideal Point Similarity* is a continuous variable that increases as the UN voting records of two states converge (Bailey, Strezhnev, and Voeten, 2017).

---

8. IGOs enter the dataset in the year in which they are founded and continue until 2014 or the year that the organization ends. We include all states listed in the COW state system for which we have data on covariates. Covariate coverage primarily excludes small states (e.g., Grenada) or those for which data is unavailable (North Korea). We follow the COW coding for the start and end of IGO existence.

9. Donno, Metzger, and Russett (2015) focus their analysis of IGO accession on the enlargement phase, and Poast and Urpelainen (2013) demonstrate that the politics of forming new IGOs differs from that of joining existing IGOs.

10. Data on alliances, which include defense pacts and neutrality or nonaggression pacts, come from version 4.1 of the COW Formal Alliances dataset (Gibler, 2009).

11. S-scores are calculated using the COW formal alliance dataset.

This measure offers a broader perspective on the foreign policy orientation of states across a range of topics on the international agenda, and it has been widely used in the literature to measure geopolitical alignment (e.g., Bearce and Bondanella, 2007; Vreeland and Dreher, 2014). Each alternative measure is operationalized to create both an "average" and "lead state" variable.

Trade with IGO members and trade with the IGO lead state measure the impact of shared economic ties.[12] We include monadic variables for *income* (GDP per capita, logged), *market size* (GDP, logged), and *trade openness* (total trade / GDP).[13] Conditioning on these economic variables addresses the possibility that economic flows and security interests are jointly determined.

We control for additional variables that influence the demand to join IGOs and the willingness of members to grant entry. *Polity scores* capture the tendency of democratic states to join and form IGOs with higher frequency (Russett and Oneal, 2001; Poast and Urpelainen, 2015). We account for the screening out of conflict-prone states (Donno, Metzger, and Russett, 2015) by including a variable measuring the number of fatal interstate militarized disputes (*MIDs*) between state i and members of IGO j.[14] To address potential diffusion effects, the variable *Total IGO Membership* is a count of members in each IGO, which could exert positive attraction for other states to enter. Since neighbors may exert stronger influence over states, we also include a variable for *Members from Region*, indicating the number of states residing in state i's geographic region that are members of IGO j. Separate control variables measure shared colonial history as well as a state's average geographic distance from IGO j's member states.[15]

Finally, the design of the IGO influences its openness to new members. An indicator for *Stringent Approval* identifies organizations that require a supermajority or unanimous consent of existing member states to admit new

12. Bilateral trade data is from the IMF Direction of Trade dataset. The "trade with members" variable measures average (logged) volume of merchandise imports and exports between state i and each member of IGO j. The "trade with lead state" variable measures (logged) trade volume with the lead state. We add 1 before taking the log to ensure values of zero trade are not excluded due to the mathematical transformation.

13. We use the natural log of GDP and GDP per capita in constant 1967 U.S. dollars. Data through 2004 are from Goldstein, Rivers, and Tomz (2007); we use adjusted World Bank GDP estimates to fill in subsequent years.

14. MIDs data are from the dyadic version of the COW Militarized Interstate Disputes Dataset.

15. Data on geographic distance and colonial linkages are from CEPII.

members, according to the founding charter.[16] We include an indicator for regional organizations and follow Carter and Signorino (2010) in modeling time dependence with a cubic polynomial for t in all models. A Cold War indicator (1947–1991) adjusts for baseline differences in membership rates during the bipolar era.

3.2.2   Logistic Regression Analysis of Membership

We first use a logistic regression model to predict the dichotomous outcome variable, IGO membership. Independent variables are lagged by one year, and standard errors are clustered at the country level. We estimate the following model of IGO membership for state i in IGO j and year t:

$$\Pr(\text{IGO membership}_{ijt} = 1) = logit^{-1}(\alpha + \beta_1 \text{Alliances}_{ijt-1} + \beta_2 X_{ijt-1}).$$

The model predicts IGO membership using our primary operationalization of geopolitical alignment, formal alliances. All models include a set of control variables X_{ijt}, which are measured at the level of the state-IGO-year (e.g., Trade and fatal MIDs with IGO Members); state-year (Trade Openness, GDP, GDP per capita, Polity); and IGO (Stringent Accession, Regional IGO).

We begin using the *Average Alliances* measure of geopolitical alignment. Table 3.1 displays results for a reduced form specification (Model 1) and a full model with all control variables (Model 2). In these first specifications, we assess membership in the broadest sense, including a state's entry into an IGO and each year of continued membership.[17] The results support our primary hypothesis: as states share more alliances with an IGO's member states, they are significantly more likely to join the organization. In the full model, a one standard deviation increase in the *Average Alliances* measure increases the probability of membership, on average, from 35% to 41%. The relationship holds when controlling for functional economic interests (measured by trade with IGO members), which also has a positive and significant association with IGO membership.[18]

---

16. We also include IGOs that require potential members to receive approval from a specific committee. Approximately a third of the IGOs in our sample (75) have stringent approval procedures.

17. This is consistent with Stone (2011), who theorizes participation in IGOs as an ongoing process of decisions to enter and continue cooperation.

18. States' alliance and trade ties are positively correlated in our sample (0.18), consistent with existing work demonstrating that allies are more likely to trade with each other (Gowa and

Dependent variable: IGO Membership

	(1) Baseline	(2) Full	(3) Entry	(4) Formation	(5) Enlargement	(6) Exit	(7) State-IGO FE	(8) Diff-in-diff
Average Alliances	1.321***	1.949***	1.123***	1.296***	1.038***	−0.300	3.104***	0.335***
	(0.113)	(0.171)	(0.050)	(0.145)	(0.083)	(0.262)	(0.114)	(0.027)
Trade with Members	0.196***	0.296***	0.120***	0.168***	0.107***	−0.002	0.082***	0.012***
	(0.010)	(0.033)	(0.006)	(0.017)	(0.009)	(0.037)	(0.009)	(0.001)
Polity	0.001	0.011*	0.029***	0.019***	0.033***	−0.014	0.040***	0.002***
	(0.004)	(0.006)	(0.002)	(0.004)	(0.003)	(0.010)	(0.004)	(0.001)
GDP	−0.098***	0.053	0.025**	−0.060**	0.034**	0.030	−0.485***	0.022***
	(0.018)	(0.062)	(0.011)	(0.030)	(0.015)	(0.060)	(0.106)	(0.006)
GDP per capita		−0.245***	−0.159***	−0.225***	−0.141***	−0.189***	0.401***	−0.015***
		(0.043)	(0.015)	(0.034)	(0.020)	(0.069)	(0.101)	(0.005)
Trade Openness		−0.014***	−0.019***	−0.036	−0.019***	−0.005	−0.017***	−0.0005**
		(0.005)	(0.006)	(0.036)	(0.006)	(0.017)	(0.006)	(0.0002)
Stringent Approval		0.069	−0.105***	−0.514***	0.066*	−0.240*		0.012**
		(0.049)	(0.029)	(0.048)	(0.039)	(0.135)		(0.005)
Regional IGO		0.325***	0.109***	0.121*	0.041	−0.817***	−2.164***	0.040***
		(0.102)	(0.037)	(0.069)	(0.058)	(0.199)	(0.185)	(0.012)
Cold War		−0.038	−0.704***	−0.340***	−0.815***	−1.066***	−0.707***	
		(0.039)	(0.062)	(0.098)	(0.088)	(0.280)	(0.074)	
Observations	570,695	570,695	364,822	10,590	354,232	211,039	364,822	570,695
# IGOs	231	231	231	193	231	227	231	231
# States	164	164	164	164	164	164	164	164

TABLE 3.1. *Effect of alliances on IGO membership*: Results of logit models estimating the effect of alliances on membership in economic IGOs. Coefficient estimates are displayed with robust standard errors in parentheses. Models 2–6 include the following controls (not shown): *Fatal MIDs with Members, Members from Region, State-IGO Same Region, IGO Membership Size, Total State Memberships, Former Colony, Common Colonial History*, and a time polynomial. Models 3, 5, 6, and 7 utilize rare events logit. Statistical significance is denoted by: * p<0.1; ** p<0.05; *** p<0.01.

Model 3 restricts the sample to examine state entry into IGOs, including those who join in the founding year and those who join later by accession. This sample omits the years after a state has joined an organization, acknowledging that they rarely reevaluate membership decisions in any given year.[19] Both geopolitical alignment and trade ties have a strong, positive association with entry.

Models 4–6 analyze how security interests shape IGO membership at different stages in the evolution of a regime. Model 4 examines state entry as a founding member in the year of IGO *formation*.[20] Model 5 considers entry by accession during the subsequent years of IGO *enlargement*.[21] In periods of both formation and enlargement, geopolitical alignment has a significant association with entry. Model 6 reverses the membership question to analyze exit from IGOs; shared alliances do not significantly affect the likelihood of a state's exiting IGOs.[22]

Model 7 adds fixed effects at the state and IGO levels to the state entry sample in Model 3, addressing unobserved heterogeneity unique to each state and organization that influences the likelihood of membership. The effect of geopolitical alignment is even stronger. Trade with IGO members also significantly increases IGO membership. In the cross-section analysis (Models 2–6), high income correlates with lower average probability of membership, but when looking at the relationship within a given country we observe that states are more likely to join as their incomes grow. Finally, a difference-in-differences specification (Model 8) examines how changes in geopolitical

---

Mansfield, 1993). Our estimates for the effect of alliances are therefore likely to be conservative: by controlling for trade ties, we omit one potential causal pathway (*alliances → trade → IGO membership*) in which alliances encourage IGO membership.

19. This "entry" sample is equivalent to a model of membership onset. Following McGrath (2015), we treat continued membership as missing for this model. This sample has a much lower probability of membership at .003 (relative to .37 for samples in Models 1 and 2), given that it drops current members while retaining observations for all nonmembers. This attenuates the effect size substantively.

20. The sample in Model 4 only includes the year of formation for each IGO, yielding a smaller sample. Thirty-eight IGOs created before 1950 drop from the sample.

21. The sample in Model 5 excludes the year of formation for each IGO, examining state entry in subsequent years. As in Model 3, we exclude continued membership after a state has joined an IGO.

22. The dependent variable in this model is a dichotomous measure of exit, equal to 1 when existing members leave an IGO. We use rare events logit because exit is very infrequent (0.12% of observations).

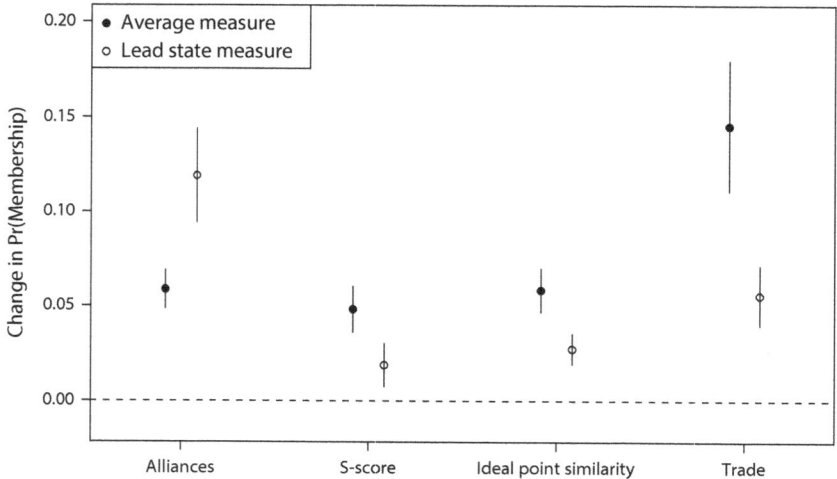

FIGURE 3.1. *Substantive effect of geopolitical alignment*: The figure displays the change in the predicted probability of membership when shifting the independent variable listed on the x-axis. Continuous variables are increased by one standard deviation above the sample mean; dichotomous variables are shifted from 0 to 1. All other covariates are held at their observed values. Predicted probabilities and confidence intervals are generated via 1,000 quasi-Bayesian Monte Carlo simulations of the full model (Model 2).

alignment influence shifts in IGO membership among state-IGO pairs.[23] The coefficient estimates suggest a strong effect of geopolitical alignment: a one standard deviation shift in *Average Alliances* increases the probability of membership by 9.05%.

In Figure 3.1, we compare the effect of *Average Alliances* with the effect of holding an alliance with the lead state of an IGO.[24] Geopolitical alignment with an IGO's most powerful member state measured by GDP has a significantly larger effect. Shifting the *Average Alliances* variable by one standard deviation above the mean (from .149 to .419) increases the probability of IGO membership, on average, by 5.9 percentage points. Moving the *Lead State Alliance* variable from 0 to 1 increases the probability of membership by 12.0

23. Here, we revert to the full sample used in Model 2. Following Lechner (2011), we use a linear probability model for the difference-in-differences specification. We remove the "Cold War" indicator in this specification, since the model includes year fixed effects.

24. For Figure 3.1 and subsequent empirical tests, we use the pooled sample of state-IGO-year observations from Model 2 above. Results are consistent with replication in the entry-only sample.

percentage points, equivalent to adding an alliance with more than 50% of other IGO members. These are substantial effects, given a baseline membership rate of 36.9%. The figure shows consistent results for the alternative measures (*S-scores* and *UN Ideal Point similarity*).[25] Trade with IGO members shows the expected positive effect. In contrast to alliance ties, trade ties influence membership patterns more strongly through the pull of the average state than the lead state.

Over the evolution of the organization, states join by different paths to entry. Other studies of membership have limited their scope to countries joining an existing organization through accession (e.g., Donno, Metzger, and Russett, 2015; Kaoutzanis, Poast, and Urpelainen, 2016). By including the full set of membership observations, we are able to highlight the significance of geopolitics for both formation and enlargement. When looking at effects in separate sub-samples, we find that the effect of geopolitical alignment has larger magnitude at formation than enlargement. For overcoming high transaction costs to initiate cooperation, prior relations outside the area of cooperation exercise considerable influence.

Expanding our scope of analysis to a broader sample of IGOs, we compare the effect of geopolitical alignment across issue areas (Figure 3.2). The same analysis is conducted separately for the IGOs disaggregated by their topic.[26] As expected, security-oriented IGOs feature the strongest association between alliance patterns and institutional membership. Compared to economic IGOs, the effect of a one standard deviation increase in the average alliance measure is more than twice as large in security organizations. Geopolitical alignment exhibits the smallest pull in decisions to join environmental IGOs. The ordering across these issue areas supports the logic that states use the institutional venue for building a security coalition, whether directly coordinating security policies or drawing on economic benefits. Environmental organizations that regulate

---

25. See the supplemental materials in Davis and Pratt (2021) for the full set of coefficients and standard errors when replicating Table 1, Models 1–5, using *S-scores* and *UN Ideal Point similarity*. The alliance measures of geopolitical alignment are significant and positive across samples for entry and enlargement.

26. IGOs are coded as "broadly" part of an issue area if there is any mention of topics related to the issue in the IGO charter document or the description in the Yearbook of International Organizations, and as "narrowly" part of an issue area if there is no mention of another issue. Thus the eight security IGOs are those that only focus on security and the nine environment IGOs are those that only focus on the environment. The broad category "all economic" includes IGOs that address economic issues and also security and/or environmental issues.

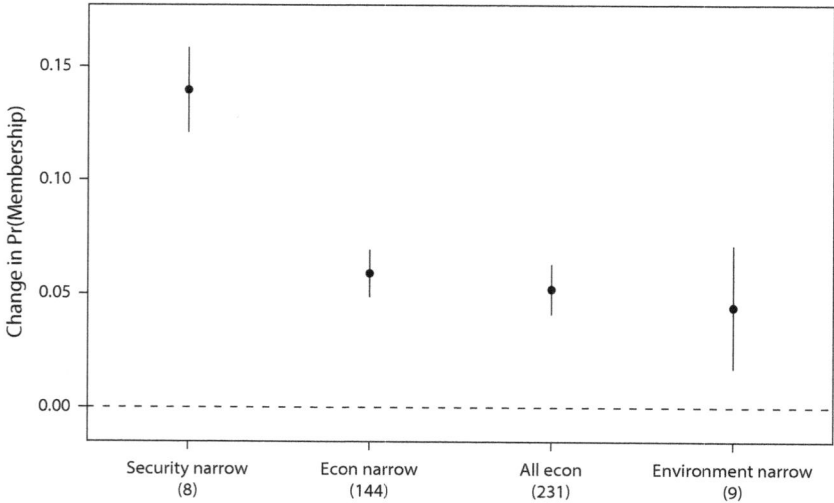

FIGURE 3.2. *Effect of alliances on IGOs in different issue areas:* The figure displays the change in the predicted probability of membership when shifting the Average Alliances variable from each sample mean to one standard deviation above the mean. Predicted probabilities and confidence intervals are generated via 1,000 quasi-Bayesian Monte Carlo simulations of the full model.

by restricting harmful policies for the sake of public goods provision offer fewer opportunities for side payments to allies.

In additional robustness checks, we ensure that our results are not driven by a specific type of economic IGO by separately removing trade, banking, and commodity organizations from the sample. Geopolitical alignment has a positive effect in each case, mitigating concerns that the results rely on one subset of organizations.

We assess how rules limit or augment the impact of geopolitics by including an interaction between the *Stringent Approval* variable and the *Average Alliances* variable. The negative interaction effect implies that geopolitics plays less of a role in IGOs that set a high threshold for member approval. Similarly, estimating the model on the subsample of 75 organizations with stringent approval procedures shows a smaller effect of geopolitical alignment.

We estimate a model with separate coefficients for geopolitical alignment in the Cold War and post–Cold War eras to confirm that the relationship is not specific to one era. Indeed, there is no significant difference in the effect of alliances during and after the Cold War.

Results are also robust to the use of defense pacts instead of all alliances; the exclusion of NATO members; the exclusion of eight economic IGOs that serve as alliances (e.g., Commonwealth of Independent States); a lagged dependent variable; and additional controls for foreign direct investment, total alliance memberships of the state, and geographic distance between the state and IGO members. We fit a Cox proportional hazards model to test whether geopolitical alignment influences states' time to entry for each IGO.[27] We expand the sample to all state-IGO-year observations, including those that had been dropped, to construct the "potential but not automatic" sample. In all cases, shared security interests continue to exert a strong influence on IGO membership. Finally, we investigate the interactive effect of *Average Alliances* and *Trade with Members*. While alliances and trade represent independent forces of attraction, the negative interaction effect suggests the two dimensions more likely function as substitutes rather than as complements. States with greater geopolitical alignment with existing IGO members receive a smaller boost in membership from trade ties than those with lower levels of geopolitical alignment.

3.2.3 *Finite Mixture Model of Weighted Decision-Making*

We have seen that across a large sample of economic institutions, geopolitical alignment is a significant predictor of IGO membership. This is important evidence for the effect of geopolitical alignment, but leaves two additional questions unanswered. First, how powerful is our hypothesized geopolitical model compared to the functional economic explanation? Second, under what conditions do states privilege geopolitical considerations over economic interests? To answer these questions, we estimate a finite mixture model. The mixture model allows for multiple distinct theoretical processes to drive outcomes. As Imai and Tingley (2012, p. 218) explain, "each observation is assumed to be generated either from a statistical model implied by one of the rival theories or more generally from a weighted combination of multiple statistical models under consideration." In a single framework, researchers can judge the relative explanatory power of competing theories.

27. Our key explanatory variable for average alliances meets the proportional hazard assumption. However, diagnostic tests reveal a potential violation of the trade ties variable, which has an effect that changes over time. We add a time interaction that captures the conditional effect of a variable that violates the PHA with years of eligibility, as recommended by Licht (2011).

In our case, we hypothesize that some membership decisions are consistent with the geopolitical alignment logic and others are consistent with a functional explanation. The analysis assumes that each observation comes from a probability distribution over the two competing models. For example, the observation corresponding to Turkey's potential membership in the European Union in 2010 may have a 25% likelihood of arising from the geopolitical model, and a 75% likelihood for the functional economic model. These probabilities can be interpreted as the relative weight placed on geopolitics and economics when determining membership in a given state-IGO-year. The estimation of weights is guided by a set of *model-predicting* variables that help determine which model is most appropriate. For state i and IGO j in year t, the probability of assignment to the geopolitical model (π_G) is:

$$\pi_{G,ijt} = logit^{-1}(\delta + \delta_1 \text{Cold War}_t + \delta_2 \text{Polity}_{ijt-1} + \delta_3 \text{Stringent Approval}_j).$$

The *model-predicting* variables are akin to scope conditions, informing the relative applicability of each competing model. These variables are measured at different levels of analysis, matching the multilevel nature of our state-IGO-year sample. The first is an indicator for the Cold War period, reflecting the realist expectation that geopolitical considerations will be strongest when the distribution of power is characterized by bipolarity. The second is a measure of domestic regime type (Polity scores), capturing the liberal notion that the structure of state-society relations shapes foreign policy decisions. Third, we include the indicator for whether an IGO's charter contains stringent accession procedures to limit membership.

For each observation, the outcome (IGO Membership) is generated via a weighted combination of the geopolitical and functional economic models:

Geopolitical: $\Pr(\text{Membership}_{ijt}) = logit^{-1}(\alpha + \beta_1 \text{Alliances}_{ijt-1} + \beta_3 D_{ijt-1}).$

Economic: $\Pr(\text{Membership}_{ijt}) = logit^{-1}(\alpha_2 + \delta_1 \text{Trade}_{ijt-1} + \delta_3 D_{ijt-1}).$

We specify the geopolitical model using the *Average Alliances* variable and the control variables included in the full model from Table 3.1 (column 2), while excluding the measure of trade ties. The functional economic model excludes the alliances variable and instead includes *Trade with Members*.[28] These specifications make it possible to identify a "geopolitical" and "economic" model a priori.

---

28. Though both models include the same control variables, the coefficients are allowed to vary across the two theories.

	Dependent variable: IGO Membership		
	Geopolitical model	Economic model	Pooled model
Average Alliances	4.964***		1.949***
	(0.166)		(0.171)
Trade with Members		0.826***	0.296***
		(0.033)	(0.033)
Polity	−0.018***	0.010	0.011*
	(0.007)	(0.007)	(0.006)
GDP	0.242***	−0.181***	0.053
	(0.047)	(0.054)	(0.062)
GDP per capita	−0.215***	−0.467***	−0.245***
	(0.040)	(0.045)	(0.043)
Trade Openness	0.020***	−0.172***	−0.014***
	(0.002)	(0.009)	(0.005)
Stringent Approval	0.389***	−0.326***	0.069
	(0.053)	(0.063)	(0.049)
Regional IGO	0.529***	0.128	0.325***
	(0.118)	(0.115)	(0.102)
Existing Members from Region	0.094***	0.304***	0.139***
	(0.007)	(0.011)	(0.010)
Fatal MIDs with Members	−0.044	0.896***	0.243*
	(0.097)	(0.164)	(0.129)
Cold War	−0.130**	−0.029	−0.038
	(0.053)	(0.042)	(0.039)
Observations	251,500	319,195	570,695

TABLE 3.2. *IGO membership: Geopolitical vs. economic models*: Models 1 and 2 display results of a finite mixture model that assumes IGO Membership is driven either by a geopolitical process (Model 1) or an economic process (Model 2). Model 3 is a pooled specification in which all observations are assumed to arise from the same data-generating process. All are estimated by a logistic regression with cubic polynomial terms to correct for time dependence (not shown). Statistical significance is denoted by: *p<0.1; **p<0.05; ***p<0.01.

We first provide results for the two competing models—geopolitics versus functional economic preferences—that drive patterns of state membership in economic IGOs. Table 3.2 displays coefficient estimates from the geopolitical (column 1) and economic (column 2) components of the mixture model, as well as a pooled model of IGO membership formation for comparison (column 3).[29]

29. We use the main sample of state-IGO-year observations from Table 3.1, Model 2. These results are also consistent in the entry-only sample. The model is estimated using the *flexmix*

In the geopolitical model, the estimated effect of *Average Alliances* is more than twice as large as the original pooled estimate (shown in column 3). A one standard deviation (0.27) increase in the *Average Alliances* variable is associated with a 15.04% increase in the probability of IGO membership, and the shift from no alliance with a lead state to holding such an alliance is associated with a 19.43% increase in the probability of IGO membership. The larger effect suggests that among the observations identified by the model as consistent with a geopolitical logic, security relationships have a very powerful influence on IGO membership decisions. The key independent variable in the economic model, *Trade with Members*, is similarly larger in magnitude than in the pooled model.[30] Some control variables have different effects across the two models. For example, IGOs with stringent accession procedures tend to attract more members among observations driven by geopolitics, while stringent accession depresses membership among observations driven by economic considerations.

The mixture model compares the explanatory power of each theory. In our case, the model estimates that the geopolitical explanation is nearly as powerful as the functional one: 44.1% of observations in the sample are consistent with the geopolitical model, while the remaining 55.9% are more accurately explained by the functional economic model.[31] Very few observations are entirely explained by one model. This is notable, given that the sample includes only economic institutions. When we measure trade and alliances with the lead state in an IGO, the mixture model assigns an even greater proportion of observations to the geopolitical model, with 56.0% of membership decisions driven by geopolitics.[32]

Because each observation is assigned to a weighted combination of the competing geopolitical and economic models, we can assess the conditions under which the geopolitical logic dominates functional economic considerations. Figure 3.3 demonstrates that as the Cold War progressed, states put

---

package in R (Grun and Leisch, 2008). Coefficients and standard errors are obtained by estimating a weighted logistic regression, with weights corresponding to each observation's assignment to the two competing models.

30. Increasing *Trade with Members* by one standard deviation (4.20) is associated with a 31.24% increase in the probability of IGO membership.

31. We calculate this measure by summing over all observations' probability of assignment to Model 1 and Model 2. We get similar results on the entry-only sample and for estimates of the geopolitical and trade models' prevalence among IGO formation and IGO enlargement observations.

32. See the online appendix of the full article for these additional results.

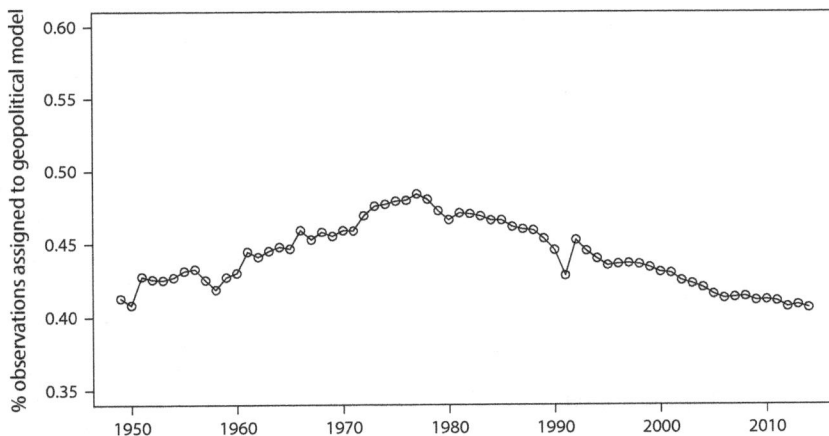

FIGURE 3.3. *Geopolitical model estimates by year*: The figure displays the proportion of state-IGO-year observations estimated to be consistent with the geopolitical model by the finite mixture model for each year in the sample.

a greater emphasis on geopolitics in their IGO membership decisions. This trend declined slightly in the waning years of the Cold War, before increasing sharply as the fall of the Iron Curtain shifted states' geopolitical orientations. Although the tendency to prioritize geopolitics has declined in the post-Cold War era, our results suggest that the post-Cold War observations in our sample are driven by geopolitical considerations approximately 41.8% of the time. This evidence counters the view that Cold War bipolarity is necessary for security to shape membership decisions.

We can compare the geopolitical and functional economic models across a range of other dimensions (See Figure 3.4). For example, democratic states appear to be significantly less geopolitical in their approach to IGO membership. Approximately 30% of democratic country observations are consistent with the geopolitical model; the remaining 70% are driven by economic concerns. Among non-democracies, 51% of observations are driven by geopolitics and 49% by economics. This is also evident in country patterns, as Russia and China both hold higher levels of geopolitical variables influence over their membership outcomes.

3.3   Conclusion

Multilateral economic organizations represent an important segment of international cooperation. From preventing financial crises to harnessing global trade, the stakes for coordinating policies are large. This could lead to all

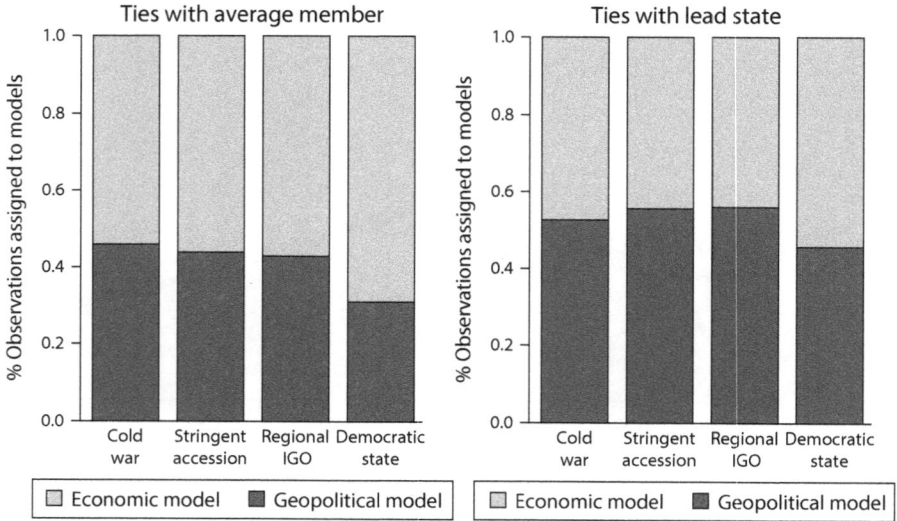

FIGURE 3.4. *Mixture model results for different samples*: The figure displays the proportion of state-IGO-year observations consistent with the geopolitical model. Each barplot represents a different sample for the specified subset of observations. The left graph uses the average state alliance measure, and the right graph shows estimates from the lead state alliance measure.

states joining together in universal organizations that would maximize coordination. Or fears of free riding could force small groups to pursue deeper cooperation. Economic issues are a strong candidate for meritocratic IGOs because benchmarks of economic potential are observable, and substantial economic benefits could incentivize policy reforms to meet rigorous compliance reviews. Nevertheless, multilateral economic organizations often form discriminatory clubs.

This chapter has shown that geopolitical alignment increases the probability that states will join the same multilateral economic institutions. This relationship holds both when institutions form and when they expand. We find that geopolitics more fully accounts for nearly half of state membership in economic IGOs, roughly equivalent to the explanatory power of economic interdependence. Far from being the exception, security ties are a prominent factor that shapes who joins and remains in multilateral economic organizations. These results suggest that existing studies about political favoritism within multilateral institutions may understate the role of geopolitics (e.g., Thacker, 1999; Stone, 2008; Dreher et al., 2013). Even before the odds can be stacked in the favor of certain states, geopolitical concerns influence who gets to play the game.

States weigh security and economic interests when making decisions about multilateral economic cooperation, and our evidence indicates that in many cases the former loom larger than the latter. Security externality and security linkage strategies motivate this pattern; while such logic is well known to shape bilateral trade and aid flows, we demonstrate that states act on these incentives to use multilateral economic organizations as tools of economic statecraft via geopolitical discrimination over membership.

Geopolitical discrimination over membership opens the possibility for more impact by the institution on state behavior because entry is not simply derivative of preferences within the issue area. Subordinating membership choices to security interests, however, could undercut effectiveness. Just as political allocation undermines the efficacy of foreign aid (Dreher et al., 2013), the geopolitics of IGO membership may distort the credibility of institutional commitments. As security ties take precedence over policy reform, compliance levels may worsen and result in lower cooperation. This in turn creates pressures for institutional proliferation to address the shortcomings of existing IGOs. The widening number of preferential trade agreements and regional development banks helps states continue to seek economic gains and add new layers of security linkages among overlapping groups of states.

The foreign policy role of IGOs should shape how scholars assess institutional effectiveness. Evaluating outcomes based on economic reform neglects the foreign policy benefits of membership. Identifying a causal relationship between institutions and peace becomes even more difficult, however, in light of the geopolitical bias in membership. To the extent that states join IGOs because they already have common security interests, a spurious relationship could generate the observed correlation between IGO membership and peace.

The question of why and how states cooperate is fundamentally connected to the question of *who* states choose as partners for cooperation. Joining an institution is not the same as signing a contract with an anonymous actor. In the small community of states, political relations provide a rich context as both sources of information and mutual interests. Against this backdrop, states form club-style IGOs that favor entry by friends and exclude rivals.

4

Accession to the GATT/WTO

Christina L. Davis and Meredith Wilf

LOOKING MORE closely at one institution, this chapter continues the empirical investigation into the conditions that lead states to become members.[1] The trade regime represents an organization with open eligibility terms and a focused issue area scope for its jurisdiction. This offers an opportunity to evaluate the role of geopolitical alignment in shaping cooperation, because any state could be considered for entry and there is no direct coordination of policies on security within the organization. The discretionary rules for accession allow leeway for selection. Using detailed information on when states apply and their accession negotiations, the chapter will demonstrate that the timing and terms of accession in the trade regime support both the geopolitical discrimination and favoring friends hypotheses.

Membership patterns in the multilateral trade regime—who joins and when—are difficult to explain from a narrow focus on trade policies. The GATT and Trade (GATT) has grown from a small club of 23 founding countries in 1948 into the near-universal WTO, with 164 members that represent 98 percent of world trade.[2] Figure 4.1 shows that, more than a decade after regime establishment, in 1960, fewer than 50 percent of all countries were GATT

1. This chapter is based on the article Christina L. Davis and Meredith Wilf (2017), "Joining the Club? Accession to the GATT/WTO," *The Journal of Politics*, Vol 79, no. 3: p. 964–978.

2. "The WTO in Brief," available at https://www.wto.org/english/thewto_e/whatis_e /inbrief_e/inbr_e.htm.

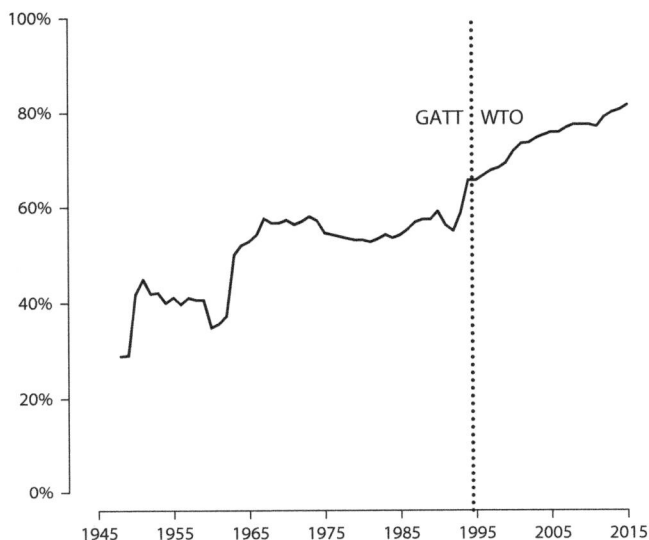

FIGURE 4.1. *Membership in trade regime*: This graph plots the number of GATT/WTO members in a given year as a percent of total countries.

members. There were relatively large increases in membership in the early 1960s as many former colonies became independent and joined, and in the early 1990s just before WTO's establishment. The transition from GATT to the WTO in 1995 brought more members through gradual expansion. To the extent that literature documents substantial trade gains from membership, it is puzzling why many countries wait to apply and join.[3] To the extent that the regime promotes free trade, it is surprising to observe countries such as India and Brazil who joined the GATT in 1948, remaining staunchly protectionist. Socialist Yugoslavia joined in 1966, showing that states could enter the trade regime without even becoming full market economies.

The economic rationale to join early is strong. For example, had China been allowed to join the GATT in 1989 (three years after its application), trade by 2001 (the year it actually joined) might have been more than twice as large as observed. Instead, the Tiananmen Square massacre led GATT members to halt accession talks in 1989, and China underwent one of the longest

---

3. On the positive effect of membership on trade, see Gowa and Kim (2005); Subramanian and Wei (2007); Goldstein, Rivers, and Tomz (2007); Mansfield and Reinhardt (2008); Liu (2009); Chang and Lee (2011); Allee and Scalera (2012); Dutt, Mihov, and Van-Zandt (2013). Others find little effect on trade (Rose, 2004; Eicher and Henn, 2011).

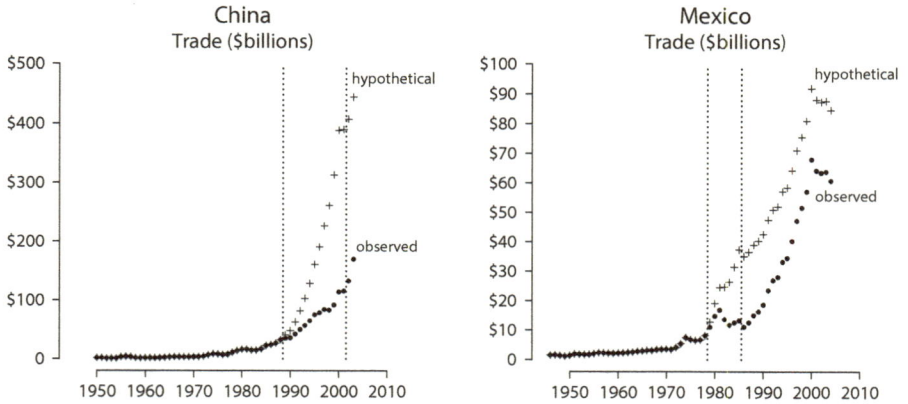

FIGURE 4.2. *Cost of delayed entry: China and Mexico*: This illustrative example, based on calculations using the estimated coefficients of annual membership trade gains from the analysis of Goldstein, Rivers, and Tomz (2007), extrapolates the value of accumulated trade for China and Mexico in a hypothetical early entry into GATT in 1989 for China and 1979 for Mexico.

accession negotiations of any state in the regime, while losing the trade gains of membership during the intervening years. In another case, Mexican president José López Portillo broke off the nearly completed GATT accession talks of Mexico in 1979 to show independence from the United States (Story, 1982). Within Mexico, widely publicized domestic deliberation and a high-profile cabinet vote about whether to join GATT illustrated how seriously governments take the question of whether or not to enter the regime (Ortiz Mena, 2005, p. 221–222). Mexico joined seven years later, forfeiting potential trade gains of membership during the intervening period. Figure 4.2 details annual estimates for China and Mexico for comparing the observed trade levels with a hypothetical entry at the earlier date.[4]

We explain such puzzling trade regime membership variation by considering how geopolitics shapes both the supply and demand of membership. We argue that members encourage the application of like-minded states with

4. Using Goldstein, Rivers, and Tomz (2007, p. 55, Table 3) estimates, and replication trade and membership coding data, we estimate the hypothetical trade for the earlier entry option; had China joined in 1989, trade in 2001 might have been $389.6 billion (hypothetical), a 258% increase over the $115.2 billion observed trade. Mexico nearly completed accession negotiations in 1979, before postponing entry for domestic reasons, later joining in 1986; had Mexico joined in 1979, by 1986, hypothetical trade might have been $35.0 billion rather than the $11.1 billion observed trade, a 216% increase over 1986 trade levels.

similar foreign policy interests, while raising the entry bar or blocking the entry of states with different policies. Even before members screen applicant states, we argue that nonmember decisions about whether to apply are conditional on shared geopolitical alignment with members. Under each scenario, foreign policy interests offset potential trade gains. This challenges a functional view of the international trade institution as a forum for cooperation to achieve issue-specific benefits, which would suggest that liberal trade policies should form the core precondition for membership. Indeed, existing research on GATT/WTO explains accession variation through the lens of distinct trade interests (Pelc, 2011; Copelovitch and Ohls, 2012; Neumayer, 2013). Instead, we expect that nonmembers with higher geopolitical alignment with members join faster. We analyze accession as the gatekeeping moment that precedes membership commitments of trade reciprocity and nondiscrimination. Because formal GATT/WTO accession rules are vague and flexible, members are able to promise easy accession negotiation to certain nonmembers while imposing obstacles for others. The result is that nonmembers with a variety of economic policies can join the regime. Qualitative case studies illustrate geopolitical dynamics at play.

In statistical analysis of GATT/WTO applications and negotiation timing, we examine the geopolitical conditions that increase the likelihood of countries joining the GATT/WTO. Whereas many organizations only record membership dates, the GATT archives include detailed records on when each state requests to join. This enables us to create a new dataset that measures both when states apply and the length of accession negotiations. We find that higher geopolitical alignment with members, measured by alliances and United Nations voting, has a positive and statistically significant relationship with early application and short negotiations. This contrasts with the ambiguous relationship of greater trade openness and the insignificant effect of applicants' trade dependence with existing members. We also consider the role of democracy as another condition that shapes the demand for trade and has a strong correlation with geopolitical alignment. While from its origin the GATT emerged within the context of American hegemony and was shaped by the U.S. Cold War foreign policy to support economic integration and alliances as twin pillars (Stein, 1984; Lake, 2009), we demonstrate that foreign policy goals have continued to shape membership decisions in the post-Cold War period, and we explore geopolitical alignment measures that incorporate interests beyond the United States.

Geopolitical alignment does not directly determine trade interests— economic theories for the gains of trade make no assumptions about political ties among the trading states. The evidence that trade flows nevertheless reflect political relations at the bilateral level highlights the need to look beyond economic interests (Gowa, 1994; Mansfield and Bronson, 1997). We demonstrate that even the multilateral institution that is most rigorously focused upon substantive policy coordination and nondiscrimination is more fundamentally based upon the political ties among its members. Most importantly, we identify accession as the critical window at which discrimination takes place. The importance of non-trade issues for entry into the trade regime makes it a discriminatory club.

4.1   Supply and Demand of Membership

We argue that the multilateral trade regime membership is driven by the similarity of foreign policy preferences. The role of geopolitical alignment in shaping accession decisions is distinct from the institution's substantive focus to promote economic gains through solving trade coordination and enforcement problems. From the perspective of economic interest, membership brings trade benefits such that the presence of laggards, who wait to join, is surprising. Functional theories of international institutions would predict rapid membership expansion upon the establishment of a regime. Once created, reciprocity and self-enforcing institutions are expected to sustain cooperation by a broad membership to provide free trade as a public good (Keohane, 1984; Bagwell and Staiger, 2002). Rational design theories, on the other hand, would predict more limited expansion, as enforcement problems motivate states to design rules that restrict membership to a small group with a strong commitment to liberalize trade (Downs, Rocke, and Barsoom, 1998; Koremenos, Lipson, and Snidal, 2001; Jupille, Mattli, and Snidal, 2013). Koremenos, Lipson, and Snidal (2001, p. 784) cite the WTO accession process and arduous negotiations by China to join as evidence consistent with the conjecture that enforcement fears and uncertainty over preferences lead members to impose strong conditionality over membership in trade institutions. From this perspective it is surprising to observe protectionist Brazil among the founding members of GATT in 1948 and the accession of East European communist countries, such as Poland and Hungary, in the 1960s, before they had embraced free market economic policies. Characterizing GATT/WTO accession as having tight supply side restrictions on membership neglects those cases when membership has been granted with very few strings attached.

Existing empirical literature gives little attention to the question of who joins the trade regime, a gap that is problematic because membership status plays a central role in the debate about whether the regime is effective.[5] The coding of "membership" is the key difference between the finding of Rose (2004) that formal trade regime membership has little effect on trade and the finding of Goldstein, Rivers, and Tomz (2007) that states participation in the regime, as opposed to formal membership, has positive effects upon trade flows. Several studies highlight how accession processes and country characteristics condition the effects of regime membership upon trade (Gowa and Kim, 2005; Allee and Scalera, 2012; Carnegie, 2014). Others show that expanding membership has shifted the power structure of the regime and forms one of the greatest challenges to its governance (Barton et al., 2006). But all of these studies take the decision to join as given.

The trade regime represents a hard test of the importance of geopolitical alignment because the GATT/WTO is an institution that coordinates economic policies. Extant research on GATT/WTO accession focuses on the economic determinants of entry to the regime. Certainly one expects economic size and the structure of trade to influence membership in the trade regime. Large states established the regime's rules that sustain open markets, leading to these large states' gains from trade and economic stability (Krasner, 1976; Bagwell and Staiger, 2002). The export interests of members shape the bargaining dynamic for accession negotiations; any existing member can participate in and veto accession agreements, such that applicants with the most valuable markets are forced to offer the most concessions (Jones, 2009; Kim, 2010; Pelc, 2011; Neumayer, 2013). Smaller states that face higher demand for international market access, and former colonies with high levels of trade dependence on members, are thought to be among the most eager to join (Copelovitch and Ohls, 2012). For nonmembers considering application, resistance from industries demanding protection can prevent accession (Kucik and Reinhardt, 2008).

The GATT has been portrayed as a "like-minded group on trade issues" that succeeded as an institution by starting from a small group of Western industrial states with relatively homogeneous preferences in support of free trade that could govern the institution (Jupille, Mattli, and Snidal, 2013, p. 68). This conforms to the *sequential liberalization* argument of Downs, Rocke, and

---

5. Pelc (2011); Neumayer (2013) examine the terms of entry, but do not address which states join.

Barsoom (1998), whereby members hold more liberal preferences for trade than nonmembers, and expansion is conditional on nonmembers becoming more liberal in their trade preferences. We argue that, beyond the trade dimension, the regime has been like-minded on foreign policy preferences.

4.1.1   Discretionary Rules for GATT/WTO Accession

The discretionary nature of the formal GATT/WTO accession process *enables geopolitical factors to pull states into the trade regime.* In principle, any government with autonomous control over its trade policy is eligible to accede on terms agreed upon between the applicant and members (formally referred to as contracting parties) (GATT, 1947, Article XXXIII). No specific conditions, whether economic or political, are formally required. GATT accession has been likened to a "big tent" approach that welcomes governments with different policies in order to maximize exposure to its rules (Jones, 2009, p. 289).[6]

Accession processes were guided by GATT Article 33 and GATT Article 26 until 1994, and by WTO Article 12 beginning in 1995. Under GATT Article 33 and WTO Article 12, membership formally occurs on terms accepted by the applicant and approved by a two-thirds majority of members. In practice, a subset of member states forms a working party to investigate the applicant's trade policies and negotiate accession terms, which include trade policy and tariff commitments. Any member may opt in, such that the working party size ranges from a small handful of members to as many as 50 for Russia's case (Neumayer, 2013). When negotiations are complete, the working party's report and negotiated schedule of applicant commitments is voted on by the full membership, typically by consensus. GATT Article 26 was available to former colonies of members and did not require negotiations or a vote by members.[7] The establishment of the WTO in 1995 eliminated the Article 26 exception, and WTO applicants face more rigorous demands from members to bring their policies into conformity with a broader set of rules (Jones, 2009).

---

6. Use of the term "government" rather than "state" in the charter has helped the regime to skirt sovereignty issues with regard to membership.

7. Specifically, Article XXVI:5(c), GATT 1947. We identified 78 countries eligible to apply under this process and 64 countries that applied/acceded under this process. After data limitations, 48 Article 26 eligible countries enter into time to apply analysis, 43 of which join under Article 26 and five of which apply after 1994 under WTO Article 12.

Negotiations—between application and accession—for GATT Article 33 and WTO Article 12 applicants exhibit wide variations in length and final level of policy commitments (Evenett and Braga, 2006; Pelc, 2011).[8] New members' trade policy commitments may be deeper than current members' commitments in some areas, and not as deep in others. Stone (2011, p. 101) argues that while the trade regime upholds a primary norm against seeking concessions on non-germane issues, informal procedures allow powerful states to strategically disregard this norm, such as the U.S.' insistence to link human rights to China's accession and to hold up Russia's accession over a series of security conflicts. Overall, obstacles on both applicant and member sides may produce delays, and negotiations continue until both sides reach agreement. This flexibility in the terms of accession makes it credible for existing members to promise an easy negotiation process for some, and block or delay the negotiations for others. Nonmembers may defer their application if they anticipate tough negotiations.

4.1.2   The Geopolitical Basis of the Multilateral Trade Regime

Although the trade regime regulates trade policies, on both the demand and supply sides of membership decisions, states incorporate foreign policy goals. Member states maximize utility *across* both trade and foreign policy dimensions. On the supply side, members may use flexible accession terms to favor an ally's entry into the regime. Granting allies easy entry provides income gains to states that share security interests and, through increasing interdependence, reinforces cooperative relations.[9] To grant new membership on the basis of geopolitical alignment, however, existing members may incur opportunity costs associated with foregoing potential trade gains. Member states' exporters and consumers stand to gain more from using accession conditionality to pursue high levels of applicant trade liberalization, while import-competing industries would benefit from blocking applicants to exclude new exporters. Applicants could *become* competitors or large export market destinations in the future. We argue that members accept these costs when they anticipate significant foreign policy benefits.

In parallel with the recruitment of allies, members exclude their rivals. Keeping hostile states out of the trade regime denies trade gains to

---

8. GATT Article 26 applicants did not undergo negotiations.

9. On the theory about the security externalities of trade, see Gowa (1994); Mansfield and Bronson (1997); Gowa and Mansfield (2004); Gowa (2010).

adversaries.[10] But it also generates an opportunity cost for members through lost trade. Furthermore, through exclusion, states forsake the opportunity to use interdependence and socialization within the organization to build cooperation with adversarial states. We contend that states make this choice because delaying a rival's entry maximizes leverage over that state if it applies and while it negotiates accession. Excluding hostile states allows members to retain full use of trade to "hold up" the outsider with demands for other foreign policy concessions. Carnegie (2014) demonstrates that states with more divergent foreign policies and regime type gain the most from joining the trade regime because of nondiscrimination rules that protect them from such threats. Knowing that entry into the organization could offer asymmetric trade gains for the rival, members discriminate against them at accession. Letting in more states based on broad geopolitical alignment increases the punishment strategy for rivals because the cost of remaining outside the club grows when more states have joined. We expect that these states with divergent foreign policies are the last to seek entry and face high demands from members that delay their negotiations.

On the demand side, nonmembers weigh the benefits of greater market access and closer ties with members against the costs associated with any undesired policy changes that may be asked of them during accession negotiations. The ability for members to promise aligned states that they will enjoy relatively easy accession negotiations helps to lower these anticipated adjustment costs. Furthermore, the increase of trade dependence that may accompany membership will be viewed differently across states—potential applicants who share similar foreign policy positions with members will view this as a benefit while those with foreign policies less aligned may be wary of such trade dependence.

Overall, nonmembers more closely tied to the major powers of the multilateral trade institution—those with greater geopolitical alignment—are the most likely to receive favorable terms during negotiation, as allies offer a free ride on trade by suspending reciprocity demands. We conceive of geopolitical alignment broadly as common foreign policy objectives.[11] From the

---

10. This conforms to the need to internalize security externality of trade gains. In addition, it is consistent with Donno, Metzger, and Russett (2015), who show that across a large range of organizations states prevent entry of conflict-prone states as a strategy to avoid entanglement.

11. In statistical analysis we examine several proxies, including democratic regime type, UN voting patterns, and alliance ties with existing trade regime members.

perspective of members, supporting economic opportunities for states that share similar geopolitical alignment offers both a reward for cooperation and encouragement to remain aligned in future foreign policy issues. The accession process may proceed more quickly, as current members refrain from excessive demands and stalling actions that contribute to long accession negotiations. From the perspective of an applicant, economic interdependence will appear less risky when states share common interests. Nonmember states that share geopolitical alignment with members will apply more quickly because encouragement from current members leads them to expect to be granted admission to the club. On top of economic gains, these countries receive foreign policy benefits from membership. This leads us to our central hypothesis: *Geopolitical alignment with GATT/WTO members increases the speed of application and accession.* The main alternative explanation is that economic alignment with the trade regime—that is, greater trade and trade with regime members—drives states to apply.

4.1.3   Examples of Accession Negotiations

Illustrative cases establish the plausibility of the above dynamics—that existing members may actively encourage the accession of some states while discouraging that of others on the basis of non-trade concerns. We examine variation in the accession experience for countries that range from close U.S. allies to hostile states. U.S. allies Japan and Korea have lower distance from the United States in their UN voting; Iran and China are more distant on average, and divergence sharply rises during crises (see Figure 4.3). Differences in the accession timing and negotiation outcomes are clearly evident across the cases.

Japan's accession in the 1950s is an example of the United States actively supporting an ally's application and accession into the GATT. Japan was a competitive manufacturing powerhouse with the capacity to flood international markets with its exports, while being reluctant to open its own markets to foreign goods. Early debates within a foreign ministry committee meeting about the decision to enter GATT raised concerns that joining GATT could restrict industrial policy tools, but eventually the multilateral section of the ministry, with support from Prime Minister Shigeru Yoshida, won in the push to apply for GATT membership in 1952 as a core foreign policy goal (Akaneya, 1992, p. 89, p. 302). The United States actively advocated for Japan's GATT accession, including conducting negotiations with other GATT

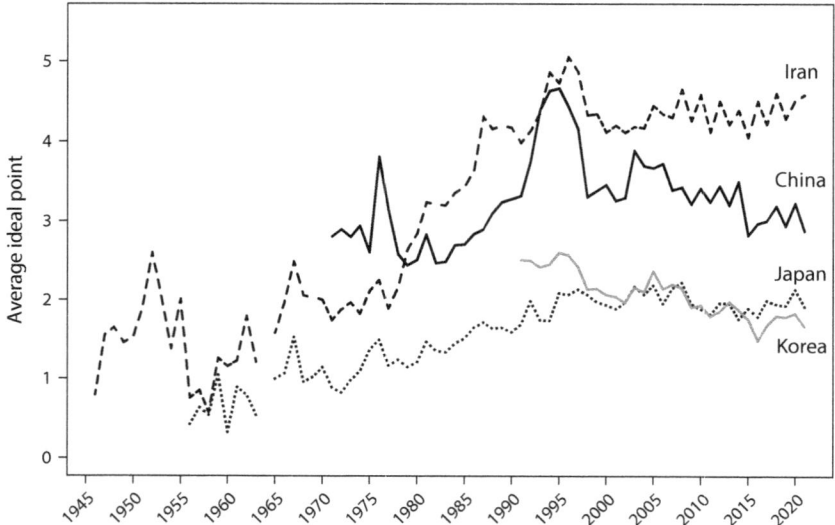

FIGURE 4.3. *Comparison of UN ideal point distance from United States*: The graph shows the ideal point distance, which represents the dyadic difference between the ideal points of two individual countries calculated from their voting record in the UN General Assembly. Higher values indicate more distance from the United States in their voting patterns. Data is from Bailey, Strezhnev, and Voeten (2017). The line for each country begins when it becomes a UN member (China begins from 1971 UN recognition of the People's Republic of China. Korea begins from 1991.)

members (Forsberg, 2000, p. 112). The United States went so far as to offer tariff concessions for improved access to U.S. markets to GATT members that gave tariff concessions to Japan (Komatsu, 1963, p. 161). Japan gained entry into the GATT in 1955 without having made many trade policy concessions.[12] More recently, the United States actively encouraged Afghanistan and Iraq to apply for membership, reflecting foreign policy interests more than demands from U.S. businesses for market access. In a similar logic, former colonies of members were offered the accelerated Article 26 accession process as much because they had an existing member sponsor in the club as because of any distinct trade policy features.

12. Japan's accession was unusual insofar as a subset of existing members approved membership but denied Japan most-favored-nation (MFN) treatment for several years after its accession. See chapter 6 for more on this case.

The Republic of Korea's accession in 1967 provides another example of a U.S. ally that was actively encouraged to join the GATT despite trade policies that ran counter to the regime's free trade objectives. In November 1965, Korean president Park Chung-hee urged his government to apply for GATT membership and established a research team to assess membership effects.[13] The committee's report emphasized market access benefits but also highlighted the downside if accession terms forced the Korean government to reduce its high tariffs and export subsidies that supported domestic industry competitiveness.[14] After assurances that significant liberalization was not necessary to become a member, Korea applied in 1966.[15] Korea joined in 1967, after only three meetings of the working party. Over the course of negotiations, the United States withdrew its original demands for automobile industry concessions, and other members did not make additional demands (Kim, 2005, p. 186). Members expressed concerns about active state intervention in the economy, and Korea promised that its export promotion measures would conform with GATT rules and that it would lift trade restrictions as soon as its balance of payments situation improved.[16] While government policy was turning toward export orientation, it was far from embracing liberal trade policies. Only with the encouragement of the U.S. officials and benefit of lenient terms did the government come out in support of membership.

The experience of communist applicants illustrates how foreign policy interests shaped entry and exclusion even among those who were not allies. During the Cold War, the U.S. policy of differentiation sought to create distinct foreign policies toward Soviet Bloc states, based upon a state's degree

13. 16 November 1965, *The Chosun Ilbo*. Previously, Korea began negotiations to join as a participant in the Torquay round GATT negotiations in 1950 (GATT Documents C/M/36 (1966 June 17), GATT/CP.5/46/Add.1 (1950 December 18), BUDGET/6 (1950 March 20)), but participation was interrupted by the outbreak of the Korean War. With little trade at this time, Korean application would have been largely a symbolic statement about joining the international community (Kim, 2005, p. 185).

14. 12 December 1965, *The Chosun Ilbo*.

15. The special and differential treatment for developing countries (GATT chapter IV) would allow Korea to join without significant constraints on its own trade policy (Kim, 2005, p. 186). In a telegram to the Korean government in November 1963, GATT Secretary General Eric Wyndham White encouraged Korea's government to seek membership, telling the Korean government that members only expected it to reduce or bind customs duties on a few measures as a gesture of liberalization (Korean National Archives, AW/101/KOR).

16. GATT Archive Documents L/2720 (14 December 1966) and L/2704 (14 November 1966).

of alignment with the USSR. Under this policy, the United States identified Poland in the late 1950s as a Soviet Bloc country with which to expand relations (Haus, 1992, p. 15). Seeing the possibility that Poland could break from USSR alignment, the United States extended foreign aid to Poland beginning in 1957 and MFN status in 1960 (Kaplan, 1975, p. 153, p. 160). Poland applied in 1959 and joined in 1967 under innovative accession terms that allowed it to retain its non-market economic system.[17] Bulgaria—with consistently closer ties to the Soviet Union—did not apply until 1986, and saw no action on its request until 1990, when the working party began to hold its first meetings.[18] In contrast, the GATT denied the Soviet Union's 1986 request for observer status in the Uruguay Trade Round talks, citing non-market status (Kennedy, 1987, p. 23). Foreign policy strategies on both sides favored entry by some communist states over others, irrespective of each one's progress toward becoming a market economy.

In the case of China's 1986 application, GATT members agreed to establish a working party, and talks calling for moderate economic reforms within the state-controlled economy quickly advanced—until members suspended working party action in response to the 1989 Tiananmen massacre (Cross, 2004). When talks with China reopened in 1992, they called for significant trade and regulatory policy changes—China would not receive fast track treatment. In the ultimate penalty paid by the People's Republic of China (PRC) for not joining earlier, its membership path now occurred in parallel to accession for Taiwan as an independent WTO member, under the name "the Separate Customs Territory of Taiwan, Penghu, Kinmen, and Matsu."[19]

---

17. Rather than make typical commitments to bind tariff rates, Poland committed to annual increases in GATT member imports and to undergoing an annual review process. GATT Documents L/2736 (13 January 1967) and L/2851 (19 September 1967).

18. GATT Archive Documents L/6667 (10 April 1990).

19. China was among the founding members of GATT in 1947. Correspondence among U.S. officials indicates that during the civil war they considered ways to suspend trade with communist controlled China, which had abrogated GATT commitments (FRUS 1949, Volume IX, 960–961). Instead, after the Nationalist government retreated to Taiwan, the ROC announced unilaterally in 1950 its withdrawal from GATT. It may have felt this was the most effective way to deny trade to the Mainland, given that Czechoslovakia had objected to the seating of the nationalist government (Report of the 122nd Meeting of the Executive Yuan, 3 March to 22 March 1950). Since China's GATT tariff schedule covered products traded by the Mainland, and Taiwan had not yet developed substantial trade, the exit may not have seemed costly to the KMT (Cho, 2002, p. 172). The PRC did not seek GATT membership in 1971, when it was recognized

The accession talks were again interrupted by security tensions with the United States during the 1996 Taiwan Straits crisis and the accidental U.S. bombing of the Chinese Embassy in Belgrade in 1999. These incidents further delayed negotiations fraught with domestic politics on both sides while trying to navigate the breadth of the WTO agreements and the nature of the Chinese economy. Skillful diplomacy and leaders determined to improve relations saw past these crises, and by the end of the 1990s relations had stabilized (see Figure 4.3 and leveling of UN voting distance). The U.S.-China trade agreement would be essential for the multilateral approval of WTO entry for China, and neither side wanted to rush into a bad deal. Among the G7 countries, Japan had been the strongest advocate for China to enter, and concluded its bilateral agreement with China first. Other WTO members also negotiated terms in bilateral negotiations as well as in the formal WTO working party.

Few thought that the WTO could turn China into a liberal market democracy, but it was hoped that engagement with rules-based trade might support political and economic changes in China that would improve human rights. Since China's economy was on a growth trajectory even outside the regime, WTO accession negotiations were a window to impose rules and extract concessions from China. Prior to joining the WTO, China had full access to other markets, as countries, including the United States, granted it MFN tariff treatment. China sought entry into the WTO to avoid the annual debate over human rights that had become the condition for U.S. approval of MFN and presented the high-stakes risk of facing non-GATT tariffs of over 50 percent of the value of imports. The threat from the United States was part of a wider potential that countries would impose quotas against low-cost labor production as Chinese exports increased (Chow, 2013). Of course, recent U.S. sanctions restricting trade with China in the name of national security and human rights allegations, such as the 2018 tariffs imposed by the Trump administration and the the Uyghur Forced Labor Prevention Act signed by President Biden in December 2021, demonstrate that WTO membership does not end linkage politics. On both sides there may have been more optimism about the constraining power of rules.

---

as the representative of China in the UN, which left both governments outside the trading system. Taiwan submitted its application to join GATT in 1990 and was admitted in January 2002, one month after China, pursuant to an understanding that China would not block its membership. I thank James Lee for research on this interesting stage in the membership question for China.

China's accession package exemplifies the flexibility possible in a process that relies on reaching terms acceptable to members. In comparison to other accession countries, China agreed to WTO-plus terms that required deep tariff cuts and transitional reviews, while also accepting WTO-minus terms that allowed other members to impose safeguards and other limits against Chinese exports (Tan, 2021a, p. 25). As part of WTO accession, China undertook major transformation of domestic rule of law, including regulatory reform and the establishment of patent and trademark offices and courts to enforce intellectual property rights. Implementing these changes required development of legal capacity within the government, corporations, and the legal profession (Shaffer and Gao, 2020). Tan (2021a) explains that WTO entry altered politics within the state to simultaneously strengthen developmental industrial policies as well as market-enhancing regulatory approaches. In contrast to allied states that joined the trade regime as part of "favoring friends," with easy entry, China had to prove itself committed to the rules and accept extra obligations to overcome distrust of members.

To the extent these reforms released a surge of economic growth, they benefit China and its economic partners. Amidst growing geopolitical rivalry, however, these gains appear dangerous. The Chinese government retains policies of state socialism that challenge the WTO system (Wu, 2016; Mavroidis and Sapir, 2021). So while, from China's perspective, it paid a high price of entry, others contend that letting China into the club was a mistake. Objective evaluation shows that much of the original optimism that WTO entry would make China into a liberal market democracy and the current pessimism that China fails to follow the rules are both overblown (Tan, 2021b). One point is clear – China had to wait longer and do more to enter than U.S. allies, and it gained admission only in 2001, through the combination of extensive promises and leaders who wanted better relations and thought it might be possible.

Finally, Iran's ongoing membership negotiations illustrate how foreign policy may hold up accession negotiations. After several years of economic reforms, Iran announced in 1996 that it would apply to the WTO: "The Islamic Republic of Iran has, for the last several years, embarked on an extensive programme of reconstruction and development leading to expansion of economic relations and trade with its regional and global partners. The Government is, therefore, prepared at this stage to engage in the procedures that follow this application."[20] Through 2004, however, the United States refused

20. WTO Document WT/ACC/IRN/1 (18 October 1996).

to approve the establishment of a working party, in effect blocking negotiations.[21] The two governments lack diplomatic relations and frequently clash in the United Nations (Figure 4.3). After years of not even making it onto the agenda of WTO meetings, the General Council meeting in May 2001 briefly touched on the issue. The discussion began with Egypt drawing attention to Iran's 1996 application, followed by a statement by the United States that it was reviewing the matter and not in a position to discuss Iran's application. Malaysia urged attention to the matter following normal procedures, and the EU delegate said the application should be considered on the "merits," but recognized the need for consensus. Then members moved on to the next item on the agenda, taking no action on Iran's application.[22]

Only in 2005—nine years after Iran's application—did the United States and Europe agree to the establishment of a working party as an economic incentive to encourage Iran in nuclear talks.[23] European nations were explicit about the linkage between the nuclear program talks in Paris and their support for the start of WTO accession negotiations, as they warned Iran that "this sort of progress will be jeopardized if Iran now moves away from the Paris agreement."[24] Iran also appeared reluctant to push forward accession negotiations. After the establishment of a working party in 2005, it took Iran four years to submit the required memo reviewing its trade policies.[25] Between 2011 and 2015, the working group took little action, as members would not agree to appoint a chairperson for the accession working party.

The breakthrough nuclear agreement endorsed by the UNSC in July 2015, the Joint Comprehensive Plan of Action, created another opening. Speaking at the WTO Ministerial Council meeting as an observer in December 2015, the Iranian representative renewed his country's call for membership: "Finalizing our WTO membership is therefore a priority for the Iranian Government. As the largest nonmember economy in the world, our full membership will be a win-win for all and a significant step toward creating a truly universal

21. Officially, each year when the matter was raised at the WTO General Council Meeting, the United States repeatedly said that it was still reviewing Iran's trade policies. *Inside U.S. Trade* (27 May 2005) Vol. 23, No. 21.

22. Minutes of Meeting, 18 June 2001. Document number 01-3041. WT/GC/M/65.

23. *Inside U.S. Trade* (16 June 2006) Vol. 24, No. 24.

24. Direct quote reported in Elaine Sciolino, 2005. "Trade Group to Start Talks to Admit Iran," *The New York Times*, 27 May.

25. WTO Document WT/ACC/IRN/3 (24 November 2009).

organization."[26] The unilateral withdrawal of the Trump administration from the Iran nuclear deal in 2018, followed by Iran announcing it would not honor the agreement, however, set back any expectation for improving relations between the United States and Iran. Iranian officials still express interest in joining the WTO. In 2019, the Iranian government sent a delegation to Geneva for meetings at the WTO, and attended the Eighth China Round Table on WTO Accession held in Moscow (a meeting organized by the WTO secretariat and including 11 acceding country delegates).[27] But without an accession working party chair, no substantive negotiations have taken place. One Iranian scholar described Iran's accession "non-process" as caught between U.S. hostility and lukewarm efforts from Iran, and noted, "In the particular context of WTO accession, most of Iran's geopolitical rivals have leveraged, and are expected to continue to leverage, their veto power as members to extract political and economic concessions."(Bigdeli, 2018, p. 178). On balance, the trade policy reforms it would take to join the WTO could support economic growth in Iran and market opportunities for WTO members. Iran would want to phase in policies and receive assurance that sanctions would end for it to begin a serious engagement in trade reform, and currently there is no prospect of that happening.

The unilateral nature of negotiations can lead to what are called "WTO-plus" and "WTO-minus" obligations. Some states are allowed to join without fully meeting commitments in the treaty texts as a condition of accession. Others must offer extra commitments in their accession protocol. And in the cases of China and Iran, there has been linkage to issues entirely outside of the trade regime.

The accession process is flexible, such that some nonmembers are encouraged to apply and other accession processes are drawn out to prioritize geopolitical objectives over maximizing economic opportunities. The next section presents statistical analysis of the full population of potential trade regime members, and controls for economic alternative arguments to test the key hypothesis that geopolitical alignment drives faster application and shorter accession negotiation.

---

26. WTO 10th Ministerial Conference Plenary Statement by H. E. Mr. Mohammad Reza Nematzadeh, Minister of Industry, Mine and Trade of the Islamic Republic of Iran, 17 December 2015. https://www.wto.org/english/thewto_e/minist_e/mc10_e/statements_e/irn_e.pdf.

27. WTO, *WTO Accessions Newsletter* no. 97, December 2019. Available at https://www.wto.org/english/thewto_e/acc_e/nl_e/2019_07_acc_newsletter_e.pdf.

4.2 Empirical Analysis of Entry into GATT/WTO

Statistical analysis of the relationship between geopolitical alignment and trade regime membership tests our hypothesis. We use a survival model to analyze time to apply and length of accession negotiations for the years 1948 through 2014. The unit of observation is the country-year. Time to apply tests the demand side of membership—potential members' revealed interest to become members—for 144 potential applicants.[28] As a test of the supply side of membership—existing members' willingness to extend membership to a nonmember—we analyze negotiation length for 80 countries that require accession negotiations.[29]

4.2.1 Data on GATT/WTO Application and Accession

Our main analysis focuses on the number of years between country eligibility and formal application to the GATT/WTO. As a public action initiated by a nonmember country's government, application represents the best measure of a government's interest in joining. It isolates the demand side by measuring the decision of a country like Iran to apply in 1996 even when member resistance would block its accession. Analyzing time to *apply* also limits endogeneity associated with reforms undertaken during a country's negotiation process, which makes it a better identification strategy than time to *accession*. For example, in the extreme case of China, trade openness grew from 25 percent of GDP when it applied in 1986 to 43 percent upon accession in 2001. The former colonies of members are also included in this analysis because they represent a unique test of the variation in demand for membership, given that they were guaranteed entry without negotiation through the Article 26 accession process, but they nevertheless exhibit wide variation in their time to apply.

For the full history of the regime, we identify the year that each country is eligible to join and the year that each country applies for membership. Under formal GATT rules, a country becomes eligible to apply once it holds

28. Of 205 independent countries, 185 apply to join. Due to missing data on measures for democracy and trade openness, our time to apply analysis includes 144 countries, of which 137 apply to join.

29. This includes countries that apply under GATT Article 33 and the WTO Article 12 process that requires active negotiation. Our data identifies 101 applicants under these processes; due to missing data, 80 countries enter into negotiation length analysis.

Distribution of time to apply

Distribution of negotiation time

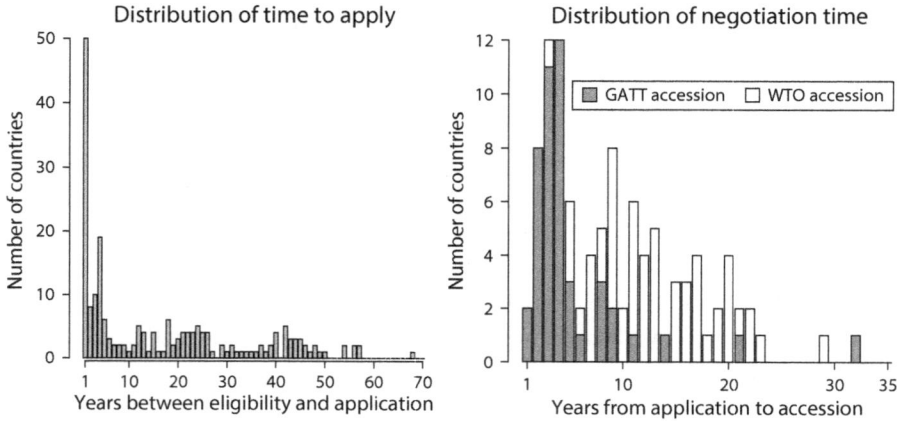

FIGURE 4.4. *Variation in timing of accession to GATT/WTO:* The left graph shows the distribution of countries by the number of years between 1948 (or year of independence) and application to join GATT/WTO. Founders are coded as joining in year 1. The right graph shows the distribution of country-years between application and accession for countries that negotiate entry through either GATT Article 33 or the WTO Article 12 accession process.

"full autonomy in the conduct of its external commercial relations" (GATT, 1947, Article 33). We consider a state to hold trade policy autonomy when it becomes an independent state as identified by the State System Membership List in the Correlates of War Project (2011) dataset. We code the year that each country applies for membership using the Stanford GATT Digital Library and the WTO website. The left graph in Figure 4.4 plots the distribution of countries by time to apply to the GATT/WTO. The figure reveals wide variation in when states apply to join the regime. While almost 25 percent of all countries apply the first year they are eligible and 45 percent apply within the first five years of eligibility, others substantially delay their applications.[30]

A secondary analysis focuses on negotiation length, the time between country application and formal accession. The favoring friends hypothesis suggests that the flexible accession process allows existing members to make it easier for certain states to become members. One implication is that geopolitically aligned states will enjoy faster negotiations. The right graph in

---

30. For countries that never apply, time to apply counts the years between country year of eligibility and the end of the dataset in 2014 (or the year of country dissolution).

Figure 4.4 displays wide variation for the length of accession negotiations. While applicants who seek entry after WTO establishment in 1995 face longer negotiations on average, some GATT outliers experienced negotiations that lasted multiple decades.

We examine several measures of a country's geopolitical alignment with GATT/WTO member states. To assess foreign policy orientation more broadly, we use similarity of UN General Assembly voting, which we interpret as a measure of revealed state policy preference (Bearce and Bondanella, 2007). As the United States was the leading major power throughout the regime, our base specification measures UN voting similarity to the United States (*UN Voting Similarity*).[31] Results are consistent when using an ideal point measure of UN voting and when measuring similarity of each nonmember with the five largest regime members beyond the United States alone. To measure how alliances encourage states to join the trade regime, we include a count of all alliance partners with the applicant that are members of the trade regime (*Ally Member Count*).[32] We also test for dynamic effects by using two-year change in level of geopolitical alignment.

Although the book focuses on UN voting and alliances as measures of geopolitical alignment, in this analysis we also consider democracy because of its strong association with trade and alliances. Democracy was a defining feature of Cold War rivalries, and continues to form the basis of foreign policy alignment, whether as condition for EU enlargement or foreign aid allocation. Based on lower probability for conflict and shared norms, democratic governance is a pillar of foreign policy cooperation among states (e.g., Russett and Oneal, 2001; Dafoe, 2011). Democratic regime type (*Polity Score*) represents one source of shared interests.[33]

We control for the structure of trade. First, we include trade openness (*Ln(Openness)*), which is a general measure of the importance of trade in

---

31. We use the *s3un* variable, multiplied by 100, from Voeten (2013). Values range between −100 (country voting is least similar to that of U.S. UNGA) and 100 (country voting is most similar to that of U.S. UNGA).

32. From the ATOP dataset, we code as allies pairs of countries with active offense or defense commitments. We code years 2004 through 2012 using the ATOP data update from Mansfield and Milner (2015), and we extend 2012 values through 2014. Results are not sensitive to ending the sample in 2012.

33. We use Polity IV's *polity2* index measures, which ranges from −10 (most autocratic) to 10 (most democratic).

the economy.[34] A second measure of economic alignment with the regime is the trade by a nonmember with GATT/WTO members as a percent of total trade (*GATT/WTO Trade %*). Copelovitch and Ohls (2012) argue that higher trade dependence increases the benefits of membership, and they find support in the case of former colonies. One could also posit that low levels would motivate entry as a tool to increase trade shares. Including the control variable accounts for both possible effects on demand for membership.

Additional country and year characteristics could affect a nonmember's decision to apply. In all specifications we control for market size (*Ln(GDP)*) and wealth (*Ln(GDPpc)*).[35] An indicator for the Cold War period (*Cold War Period Indicator*) controls for systemic changes. To incorporate changes across the trade regime itself, we include an indicator variable for whether a GATT/WTO trade round is occurring in a given year (*Trade Round Indicator*), since these rounds were historically used as a time to expand membership with accession negotiations occurring alongside each trade round. A measure of percent of all countries in the world that are members of the GATT/WTO (*Percent World Members*) controls for diffusion of membership that increases market gains for entrants and the cost of remaining outside.

We also measure the percent of total trade with preferential trade agreement (PTA) partners (*PTA Trade %*), which captures the degree to which a nonmember country receives preferential trade terms outside of the multilateral trade regime.[36] We expect that higher levels of PTA trade indicate more private benefits for the country outside of the regime, and thus reduce incentives to apply to join the multilateral trade regime. We control for whether the country is a historic colony of a trade regime member (*Former Colony Indicator*), which could be associated with ties to the trade regime and shorter time to apply (Gowa, 2010). Finally, Mansfield and Pevehouse (2006, p. 147) argue that democratizing states are more likely to join international organizations. We include their measure of democratization to control for the possibility that their general finding applies to the trade regime (*Democratizing Country Indicator*).

---

34. Openness is the log of imports plus exports as a percent of gross domestic product (GDP), with trade data from the IMF Direction of Trade database.

35. We use the natural log of these data; GDP in constant 1967 USD and population data are from World Bank and Goldstein, Rivers, and Tomz (2007).

36. PTA data from Mansfield and Milner (2015) are combined with trade figures from the IMF Direction of Trade database.

4.2.2   Geopolitical Alignment and Trade Regime Membership

Survival analysis examines the relationship between the length of time to an event of interest (application or accession) and the explanatory variable (geopolitical alignment with the trade regime members). The likelihood that an observation experiences the event at any given point in time is modeled as a function of a time-varying baseline hazard and covariates.[37] We use the Cox proportional hazards model with country-year observations and the Efron method of ties.[38]

For our primary, demand-side analysis of time to apply, each country becomes eligible to join in 1948 (the year the GATT came into force) or, if it becomes an independent state after 1948, then the country's year of independence. For example, Australia was independent upon the establishment of the regime, and its first year of eligibility is 1948, while Vietnam became independent—and thereby is first eligible to apply—in 1956. We code each country-year between eligibility and application as "survival," and treat the country-year of application as the failure event, after which the country leaves the sample.[39] Countries eligible to apply under GATT Article 26 (former colonies of members) are modeled as a distinct strata, which accounts for the possibility they may have a different baseline propensity to join, because they did not face any requirement to negotiate over commitments.[40]

37. The formal equation estimated is $h(t, \mathbf{X}) = h_0(t) \, exp \left[\sum_{i=1}^{p} \beta_i X_i \right]$, where the hazard ratio h at a given time t for a set of p observed covariates $\mathbf{X} = (X_1, X_2, \ldots, X_p)$ is a function of time-specific baseline hazard $h_0(t)$ and the exponential of the least squared estimates based upon time-independent covariates $exp \left[\sum_{i=1}^{p} \beta_i X_i \right]$.

38. The Cox model makes no assumption about the shape of the baseline hazard and allows it to vary each time period. We confirm that covariates in each model meet the proportional hazard assumption at 0.05 percent (Box-Steffensmeier and Zorn, 2001).

39. For example, when analyzing time to apply, the model considers all countries that are eligible to apply in a given time period (e.g., eligibility year 1), and observes those that apply ("fail") and those that do not ("survive"). Country-year observations that do not fail are coded as censored; countries that never apply are censored in each country-year of eligibility. The original contracting members to join GATT in 1948 are included in the regression analysis as having applied to GATT in their first year of eligibility.

40. We code the variable based on lists from the GATT archive that designate in each period which nonmember countries were eligible to join under Article 26. This represents an institutional rule for application status and differs from the historic colony variable that is included as a control. We confirm that stratification is appropriate through log-rank tests comparing time

A secondary, supply side analysis of negotiation length analyzes 80 countries (with full data) that apply to join under accession processes that require active negotiations (i.e., GATT Article 33 or WTO Article 12). Here we use a Cox proportional hazards model to estimate the relationship between covariates and completing negotiations for accession. Each applicant begins negotiations in its application year (negotiation year 1), and remains in the dataset until the country formally joins. Each year that a country has applied but not joined is coded as censored.

Table 4.1 presents our results, showing support that geopolitical alignment is associated with faster application and accession. Point estimates are hazard ratios (the exponential of the coefficient), such that less than 1 indicates a negative effect on the speed of application (i.e., slower application) relative to expected time to apply in the baseline group. Hazard ratios greater than 1 indicate positive coefficients correlated with faster application.

Model 1 maximizes sample size (144 potential member states) and year coverage (1948 through 2014). Higher levels of democracy are associated with faster time to apply. Model 2 adds additional geopolitical variables and controls for trade with GATT/WTO members, reducing the sample size to 134 countries. In support of the geopolitical discrimination hypothesis, states with a greater number of allies that are GATT/WTO members and those with similarity in UN voting with the United States are more likely to apply to join the trade regime. Model 3 introduces additional control variables.

States with closer geopolitical alignment consistently joined more quickly than others, even when controlling for the main alternative explanations of economic alignment. Furthermore, higher economic alignment is not robustly associated with faster application. While higher levels of openness are associated with greater likelihood of applying in the base specification for Model 1, the association is statistically insignificant when adding additional variables in Model 2 and Model 3.[41] Further, trade dependence upon GATT/WTO members is not systematically associated with time to apply in

---

to apply of Article 26 and non-Article 26 countries. With stratification, the Cox proportional hazards model estimates a baseline hazard ($h_0(t)$) for each of the two strata, and assumes that covariates affect both in the same proportion.

41. Further tests show that openness moving from statistically significant in Table 4.1, Model 1 to statistically insignificant in Table 4.1, Model 2 is due to the addition of geopolitical variables rather than the sample size change.

Dependent Variable	Model 1 Time to apply	Model 2 Time to apply	Model 3 Time to apply	Model 4 Time to apply	Model 5 Negotiation length
Geopolitical Alignment					
Polity Score	1.080*** [1.05, 1.11]	1.055*** [1.02, 1.09]	1.057*** [1.02, 1.09]		1.037* [1.00, 1.08]
Polity Score, 2-Yr Change				0.977 [0.90, 1.06]	
UN Voting Similarity		1.012*** [1.00, 1.02]	1.013*** [1.00, 1.02]		1.011*** [1.00, 1.02]
UN Voting Similarity, 2-Yr Change				1.012* [1.00, 1.02]	
Ally Member Count		1.068*** [1.02, 1.12]	1.062*** [1.02, 1.11]		1.030 [0.99, 1.07]
Ally Member Count, 2-Yr Change				1.224*** [1.09, 1.37]	
Control Variables					
Ln(Openness)	1.254***	1.153	1.219		1.328
Openness, 2-Yr Change				1.894	
GATT/WTO Trade %		0.474	0.929		0.698
GATT/WTO Trade %, 2-Yr Change				2.547	
Ln(GDP)	1.413***	1.435***	1.440***	1.252***	0.907
Ln(GDPpc)	0.858*	0.837	0.809*	0.931	1.120
Cold War Period Indicator	0.258***	0.192***	0.207***	0.220***	28.083***
Cold War Period X Ln(Negot Yrs)					0.252***
Trade Round Indicator			0.240***	0.088**	
Trade Round X Ln(Yrs Eligible)			1.813***	2.263*	
Percent World Members			2.506	3.204	
PTA Trade %			5.729**	2.698	
Former Colony Indicator			1.231	0.742	
Democratizing Country Indicator			0.688		
number of observations	2,167	1,751	1,750	1,450	680
countries	144	134	133	91	80
events	137	121	120	78	62
year coverage	1948–2014	1948–2014	1948–2014	1950–2014	1948–2014

Significant at: *** <1%; ** <5%; * <10%.

TABLE 4.1. *Estimates of time to GATT/WTO accession*: Results of time-varying Cox proportional hazards models. Each point estimate is the hazard ratio with 95 percent confidence interval in brackets. Model 1 through Model 4 estimates are based upon time from eligibility to application for all countries; these models include stratification by Article 26 eligibility status and standard errors are clustered by country. Model 5 estimates are based upon time between application and accession for countries that apply to join under GATT Article 33 or WTO Article 12. Due to space constraints, we report control variables' point estimates and significance indicators only. All models attain robust logrank p-values of <0.05.

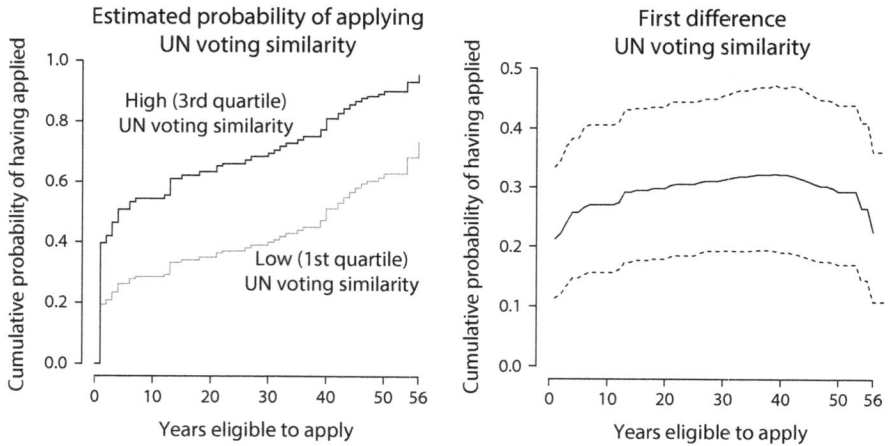

FIGURE 4.5. *Substantive effect of UN voting similarity*: The left graph shows the estimated application probability when moving from low (1st quartile values, light line) to high (3rd quartile values, dark line) values of UN voting similarity with the United States. The figure to the right shows the estimated first difference of this shift to become more aligned with the United States in UN voting similarity. The 95 percent confidence interval is shown with dashed lines.

Model 2 or Model 3. PTA trade dependence in Model 3 has a positive impact on application.

Market size is important, as shown by the positive correlation of GDP with membership. While our theory focuses on variation across country-specific measures of geopolitical alignment, the Cold War period indicator is also relevant. The highly significant point estimate below 1 indicates that the geopolitical context of the Cold War period suppressed the average tendency of states to apply to the free trade regime. In Model 3, an indicator for countries undergoing democratization has no statistically significant relationship with time to apply, leading us to conclude that level of democracy, rather than the period of transition to democracy, is associated with earlier application. Both the variable indicating whether a state is a former colony of a member and the measure for the percent of countries in the world that are members of GATT/WTO in a given year are insignificant. The impact of trade rounds is contingent on how long a country has been eligible.

The substantive effect of UN voting similarity is illustrated in Figure 4.5, based upon estimates from Table 4.1, Model 3. Holding other variables at their means, the left graph plots probability of having applied when moving from lower (1st) quartile to higher (3rd) quartile values of UN voting similarity to the United States.[42] The graph shows that a country with greater UN voting similarity is associated with higher probability of having applied for membership. The right graph shows the first difference, or difference in probability of application, between the two groups of low and high UN voting similarity. Moving from the 1st quartile value of −44.1 (the approximate annual average of Bulgaria between 1981 and 1986) to the 3rd quartile value of 25.9 (the approximate annual average of Bolivia between 1948 and 1987) increases the likelihood of having applied by 23.4% in the first year of eligibility.[43] This difference in application probability reaches a maximum of 32.3% in year 39 of eligibility (1986 for countries eligible to apply since the beginning of the regime in 1948).

Model 4 tests two-year changes in geopolitical alignment and levels of trade dependence. We find that increases in the number of allies that are members is associated with faster time to apply at a 1% level of significance, and that more similar voting to the United States within the UN is associated at a 10% level. Consistent with Model 3, we do not find a democratization effect; two-year changes in level of democracy are not systematically associated with applying to join.[44] Neither change in openness nor change in trade dependence with members has statistically significant effects on time to apply in Model 4.

In Model 5 the dependent variable changes to negotiation length and the sample is limited to applicants that engage in accession negotiation processes. We find evidence that UN voting similarity to the United States and higher levels of democracy at the time of application are associated with faster negotiation times. The third measure of geopolitical alignment, alliance ties, does

---

42. Because in this research design "survival" implies that a country has not yet applied, it is the complement of the survival curve—the probability of having applied—that provides the most intuitive interpretation of the effect magnitude. Formally, the left graph of Figure 4.5 plots $1 − S(t)$, where $S(t)$ is the estimated probability of having not applied at a given time t.

43. Using the Model 3 sample, we create bootstrap simulations in R to replicate application probability estimates at 1st and 3rd quartile values of each quantity of interest, holding all other variables at their means. Point estimates are the average of the simulation at each year from eligibility, given 1,000 sample replications.

44. *Democratizing Country* is dropped as a control variable because it is collinear with changes in Polity Score level. The null finding for democratization is also consistent with Poast and Urpelainen (2013), who find that democratization leads states to form their own *new* organizations, but not join existing organizations. In the area of trade, Kono (2008) shows democratization introduces conflicting trade interests that could induce discrimination rather than liberalization.

not reach statistical significance. A large proportion of allies joined as founders or former colonies without negotiations, and so they are not included in this analysis even though they experienced the quickest entry possible. Higher levels of openness and GATT/WTO trade dependence have no statistically significant associations with negotiation time.

Our findings are robust to different specifications.[45] We find similar results when using accession as the dependent variable. While the main models use eligibility years as a theoretically appropriate measure to compare states during equivalent intervals, geopolitical variables retain significance when using an alternative specification that evaluates each country during the same calendar year. Our findings hold if we constrain the model to the GATT years only, and if we exclude founders and early joiners. Statistical significance of geopolitical alignment is robust to adding an indicator for WTO period observations.

Key associations are consistent when using alternative proxies for geopolitical alignment. Results hold when we analyze democracy as the difference between the applicant level of democracy and the average level of democracy for members of the GATT/WTO. We replace the affinity measure of UN Voting Similarity with the United States with an ideal point measure of UN voting that creates a one-dimensional measure of how a country's UN voting reflects its preferences toward the U.S.-led liberal order (Bailey, Strezhnev, and Voeten, 2017). This analysis produces similar conclusions. Since 1983, the U.S. State Department has deemed certain UNGA votes to be important to U.S. national interest; UNGA voting similarity with the United States on this subset of important votes is statistically associated with faster application. Further, a measure of a country's average UN Voting Similarity with the five regime members with the largest economies remains correlated with faster application.[46] This provides evidence that our findings may not be driven solely by the United States. We also consider the possibility that certain member allies might be more important than others, and create two weighted measures of member allies: Member Allies' Trade as a Percent of Total GATT/WTO Member Trade, and Member Allies' GDP as a Percent

45. Robustness checks are based upon changes to Table 4.1, Model 3, and are presented within tables and figures in the supplementary figures of the original article (Davis and Wilf, 2017). Appendix Section A.

46. For each year, we identify the largest five GATT/WTO member economies by GDP size and take the average of each nonmember's UN Voting Similarity with these five countries.

of Total GATT/WTO Member GDP. Although not statistically significant in the full model, the measures are positive and statistically associated with shorter joining in a reduced model. We find substantial evidence that geopolitical alignment is associated with faster time to apply in both the Cold War *and* post-Cold War periods. There is no statistically significant interaction between the Cold War Period and any of the three geopolitical alignment variables, and patterns are consistent when we subset the data to separately examine each period of time.

Analysis of the sample of Article 26 countries offers an additional test of the demand side argument. Since these countries were eligible to join without negotiations, given their status as former colonies of members, they did not need to consider supply side restrictions that might limit others from joining. Within this smaller group of countries, higher levels of geopolitical alignment remain associated with faster application.

To further test the supply side of our argument and the favoring friends hypothesis, we examine how geopolitical alignment shapes the terms of accession. Here we use data from Allee and Scalera (2012) that measures the applied tariff decrease (from pre-application to the year after joining) and compiles the number of working party members and the count of commitment paragraphs. We consider the linear relationship of UN Voting Similarity at application year on these three measures of negotiation rigor. The negative correlations shown in Figure 4.6 offer additional evidence that more geopolitically aligned applicants experience an easier negotiation process. States with geopolitical alignment can join sooner because they face less rigorous accession negotiations, and may not have to make the extensive tariff cuts and regulatory commitments of other states.

4.3   Conclusion

Although the GATT/WTO is best known as an economic organization, geopolitical factors attract some toward the trade regime while making others hesitant to join. The variation in applications to the trade regime more closely resembles formation of a political club than a free trading club. Members refrained from imposing strong conditionality to screen for liberal trade policies in order to use the organization as a foreign policy tool. Discretionary accession provisions allowed members to adjust the cost of entry on a case by case basis. States applied as a way to affirm their position within the liberal international order with all of the benefits that came with it, including market

Applied tariff decrease
(n = 45)

UN Voting Similarity

(−) **10%**

Working party (WP) member count
(n = 45)

UN Voting Similarity

(−) **5%**

Commitment paragraph count
(n = 45)

UN Voting Similarity

(−) **10%**

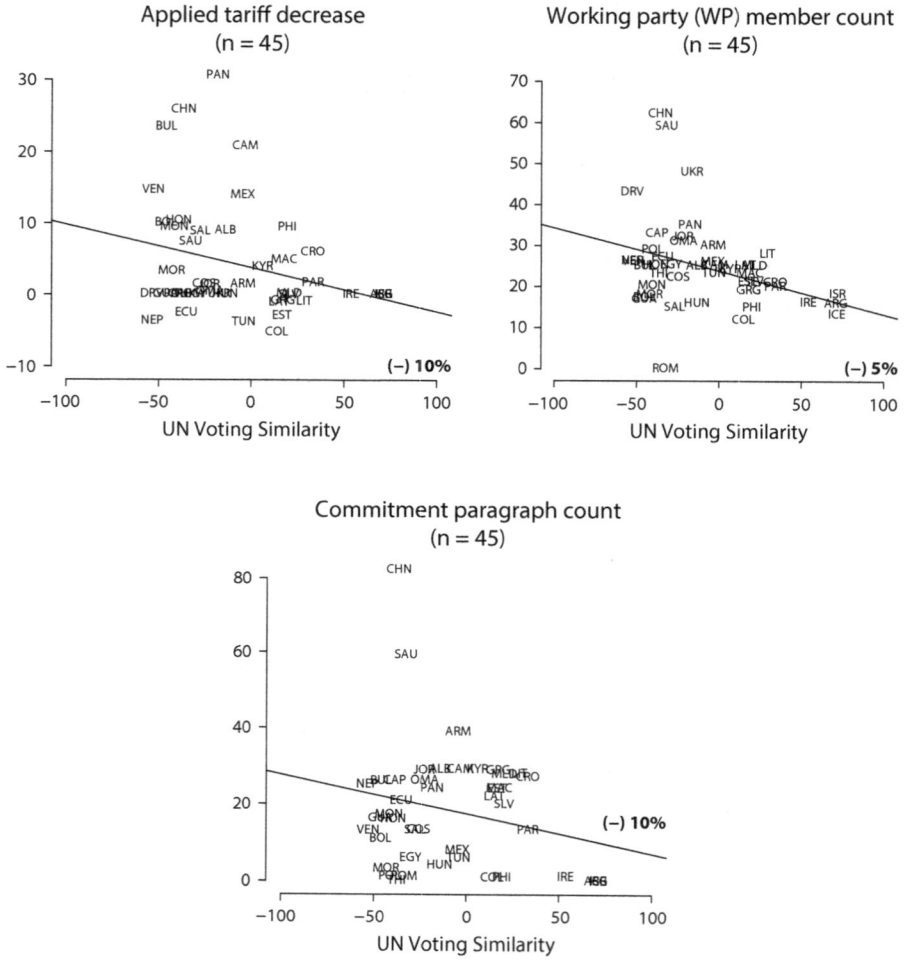

FIGURE 4.6. *Geopolitical alignment and accession rigor*: Using data from Allee and Scalera (2012), we plot UN Voting Similarity at year of application and three measures of negotiation rigor. The line in each graph is the simple linear regression between the two measures, and statistical significance is noted in the bottom right corner of each graph. All measures of negotiation rigor are negatively correlated with UN Voting Similarity and the above measures are statistically significant at the 10% level or greater.

access. Common foreign policy orientation formed conditions favorable for applying to join and for completing timely accession negotiations.

Members of the leading economic organization enticed new members with lenient conditions when engaged in Cold War rivalry, and only began to impose more economic conditions after the end of Cold War. Nevertheless, it would be wrong to conclude that foreign policy linkage strategies ended. Security and human rights concerns, along with high conditions for economic reform, held China outside the system for 15 years of negotiations after its request to join in 1986. The applications of Iraq and Afghanistan in 2004 to join the WTO under the urging of the United States represent two examples of sponsorship, although their accession negotiations have proceeded slowly, as Afghanistan completed the accession process in 2016 and Iraq continues its negotiations. The application of Iran remains blocked by concerns about its nuclear program rather than by trade policies. Our statistical analysis shows that UN voting and alliances have a significant impact that is not conditional on the Cold War period—foreign policy and democracy continue to shape the trade regime today.

Chapter 3 shows that governments make decisions about joining multi-lateral economic organizations through a weighted decision process that considers economic and geopolitical calculations. Therefore it is surprising to see that variables measuring trade have little impact on decisions to join the trade regime. Our statistical analysis of time to apply and negotiation length fails to show consistent effects on membership from either trade openness or trade dependence on members. Since our focus has been to examine geopolitical alignment, we would caution against concluding that trade interests do not matter. Some states with lower trade openness and trade flows may join as a commitment device to advance market reforms and build trade relationships, and others may join after reaching higher levels of trade interdependence. The structure of trade and its political influence within a country may also filter how economic interests impact engagement with the regime.

Open eligibility for accession rules and the economic interest in widening participation meant that others could also join. The trade regime now includes both China and Russia. But the evidence here shows a strong pattern that those with closer geopolitical alignment were more likely to apply sooner and their applications were approved more quickly. These favored members could pursue liberalization that would eventually raise the level of commitments from within the institution. The delayed or incomplete liberalization by some new entrants was acceptable to members who welcomed them into the club for reasons that went beyond the calculation of trade gains. Meanwhile, discrimination denied trade gains to rivals and established strong rules before they would eventually be allowed to join. Through geopolitical discrimination and favoring friends, the trade regime consolidated around an early core of like-minded states that shared alliance ties, democratic governance, and held similar positions on major world issues.

5

The OECD: More Than a Rich Country Club

THIS CHAPTER contributes to understanding entry into organizations through investigation of one organization, the Organisation for Economic Co-operation and Development (OECD). I examine how membership evolves through an informal process of self-selection and screening, and I demonstrate how this process of conditional membership brings policy reform. I challenge the conventional view that states join organizations because of a functional demand for cooperation on the specific policies regulated by the organization. Rather, they join due to common interests beyond the purview of the organization and adopt policies that may not fit their specific economic circumstances. The case illustrates that states seek status by associating with a group of like-minded and powerful states. Joining the OECD represents a choice of social category within the international system that brings with it both norms of behavior and benefits for reputation. Similarly to the evidence from the GATT/WTO presented in the previous chapter, alliance ties and UN voting affinity correspond highly with membership in the OECD.

The OECD grew out of the Organisation for European Economic Co-operation (OEEC), which had been the organization established in 1948 to oversee implementation of the Marshall Plan aid. European governments were divided over the form of European integration. States disagreed over proposals for an intergovernmental free trade agreement (EFTA) and a more centralized approach to delegate supranational authority within the European Coal and Steel Community. The OEEC membership was split with seven in the former group and six in the latter. At the same time, the tensions of the Cold War had placed necessity behind efforts to strengthen NATO, and there were even proposals to form an economic council within NATO to take over the OEEC role (Carroll and Kellow, 2011, p. 48). Against this background, 20 countries agreed to transform the OEEC into a new organization that would include the United States and Canada, shifting focus from European development to a broader mandate of economic cooperation. The organization incorporated the codes of liberalization and peer review monitoring practices that had been central to the OEEC and adopted the goal of achieving a 50 percent increase of GNP for the aggregate membership over the first decade, from 1961 to 1971 (Carroll and Kellow, 2011, p. 51).

The OECD pursues a broad mandate to promote development. As such its policy scope extends across a range of different economic policy dimensions, including aid, trade, finance, and investment, where its mission overlaps with other multilateral and bilateral agreements. The organization has weaker enforcement than the WTO but actually appears to have a larger effect on trade liberalization among members. In one study, Rose (2005) finds that OECD membership increases the average value of bilateral trade by over 50 percent, which is more than the increase attributed to belonging to either the GATT/WTO or the IMF. The OECD plays a central coordinating role for development aid and provides oversight for policies on bribery and taxation. More broadly, its reports include environmental, labor, and education policies. Through monitoring reports and production of consolidated data on policies, the organization functions as a think tank and center of information sharing among members and the broader international community.

The challenge to understanding the effectiveness of the OECD, however, is that selection into the organization is highly correlated with decisions to undertake economic reforms and to improve relations with existing members. On the one hand, trade liberalization prior to joining would cause a downward bias that could mean the results above underestimate the effect on trade.[1] On the other hand, if these reforms are undertaken for reasons unrelated to joining the organization itself, the positive effect attributed to membership represents a spurious correlation. Membership may screen for those states that already have positive economic reform preferences (e.g., Downs, Rocke and Barsoom, 1996; von Stein, 2005; Gray, 2009). Furthermore, membership selection is a function of not only economic reform trajectory but also political relations. Turkey was a founding member of the OECD because it had been among the recipients of Marshall Plan aid as a NATO member. In contrast,

---

1. Rose (2005, p. 688) makes this point directly.

East European membership in the OECD came after the end of the Cold War opened political relations with the West. Other values considered important by members enter into consideration for the selection of new members over time. Democracy has become a criterion for membership. Most recently, some argue that policies for environmental protection should be part of evaluating candidates. To the extent that economic reform trajectory, positive political relations with the West, and democracy are all likely to correspond with benchmark measures of economic outcomes such as trade, it is very difficult to identify the causal effect of membership.

The evolution of the OECD from 20 founding members in 1961 to 38 members today reveals several puzzles. How did an organization with no formal conditions required for accession maintain core features as a group of like-minded countries while expanding beyond its origins as the economic counterpart to NATO? Contrary to the conventional portrayal of the OECD as the "rich country club," the organization includes developing states. Turkey was a founding member, Mexico joined in 1994, and Costa Rica is the most recent addition to join on 25 May 2021. Nevertheless, the OECD remains a small club with high entry barriers. This presents a second puzzle. Why would countries make reforms on entry to an organization that offers benefits to members and nonmembers alike? The liberalizing reforms completed by members are nondiscriminatory in their effect, and economic information is widely shared as policy advice. Joining an organization such as the WTO or EU provides differential market access, but OECD services as a think tank are equally available to all states.

The answer to these puzzles lies in the role of the OECD to allocate status. It is the clubby nature of the organization that both attracts countries to join and mandates restrictive entry barriers. In addition to income, similarity along the dimensions of democracy and foreign policy underlie the appeal of the OECD brand. For states that value association with democracies in the United States-led alliance system, membership offers more than just coordination of policies and provision of information. Joining the OECD represents recognition as belonging to the most exclusive club of "the West."

The chapter gives attention to the supply and demand side of the membership decision within the context of enlargement from a small club. I further develop the argument of the book about IGOs as discriminatory clubs by using this case to explore strategic status-seeking. I use the case of the OECD to show that states choose whom to emulate when deciding to join international institutions. The appeal of closer affinity with the rich democracies of the Western alliance attracts applicants who want closer association. This dynamic allows for more agency by applicant states than is commonly seen in the literature on diffusion, where states respond to competitive pressures or common culture and region as basis for policy convergence. At the same time, the supply side restraint, which may be dictated by noneconomic considerations at the whim of current members, creates space for agency on the side of the IGO as a collective group of members. Existing members act as gatekeepers to exclude those who do not appear likely to fit in the club. Screening on the basis of shared democracy and geopolitical alignment ensures that peer pressure will be a sufficient enforcement mechanism. Those that join must meet both criteria: preference to become like the advanced industrial democracies and sponsorship by existing members.

Using case studies of "outsiders" who join the club, Mexico, South Korea, and the Czech Republic, I illustrate how leaders valued the status of entry (the case of Japan's entry to the OECD is in chapter 6 as part of the country study). The goal of OECD entry provided a rationale for making policy concessions. The Mexican and South Korean cases both serve as warnings that the rush to membership can be destabilizing—banking reforms and capital inflows that accompanied membership also laid the conditions for their subsequent financial crises. These accession case studies are contrasted with Brazil's. Among nonmember states, Brazil stands out for its broad and sustained engagement with OECD activities. Despite OECD encouragement to consider membership, Brazilian leaders have been reluctant to join the organization. Only recently has the government indicated it will seek to become an accession candidate, even as Colombia and Costa Rica completed their accession process. The change of attitude by the Brazilian government toward the OECD closely followed an improved relationship with the United States and ushered in a surge of structural reform proposals as part of trying to earn an invitation to join the club.

The next section builds on the argument about institutional accession and membership as applied to the OECD. Membership decisions are based on geopolitical alignment as states deepen cooperation with allies. Their goals encompass regulatory harmonization as well as the status they gain from association with a like-minded club. Descriptive statistics show the profile of OECD members in section 5.3, and in section 5.4 I analyze selection into the organization with a duration model of time to OECD entry that highlights the importance of political variables. Democracy and geopolitical alignment bring more rapid membership even when controlling for key economic measures and regional location. Trade and financial openness are surprisingly not predictive of which states join the OECD. Using case studies, section 5.5 explores more closely the decisions to join in terms of the motives of the applicants and the specific policy reforms they agree to undertake as the price of membership.

5.1 Vague Rules and Selective Enlargement

What is the right size for an organization? The depth-breadth problem is especially sharp in the case of an organization such as the OECD that began as a small club but seeks to govern global issues. As a feature of institutional design, membership varies across the dimension of selectivity and precision of entry conditions (see chapter 2). These help define whether a subset of countries forms an exclusive "club" or whether a large group of countries aspires to achieve universal membership. Different kinds of cooperation problems give rise to restrictive membership. In the provision of public goods, as in the OECD's function to support open markets and regulatory coordination, the non-excludable and non-rivalrous nature of the project gives rise to free riding because states can benefit equally regardless of their input. A small group can more easily achieve cooperation through joint effort and monitoring. Exclusivity is necessary when states face congestion problems for the provision of a club good (Buchanan, 1965; Cornes and Sandler, 1996). Both the services of the OECD secretariat and status gain from membership could diminish with the number of members.

The small-club configuration may also be endogenous to the power distribution. When the interests of the great powers diverge more vis-à-vis other states than amongst themselves, Drezner (2007, p. 67) argues that they will adhere to club standards; "Club IGOs, such as the Group of Seven countries (G7) or the OECD, use membership criteria to exclude states with different preference orderings and bestow benefits for in-group members as a way to ensure collective action." He points to the 1997 OECD Anti-Bribery Convention which was quickly concluded among OECD members after a failed attempt to negotiate on this issue at the United Nations (ibid., p. 77). Once negotiated within the smaller group, the United States and Europe effectively exported these standards to a wider range of countries. More recently, global tax reform proposals also take place within the OECD forum even as their effectiveness will require a broader implementation beyond the OECD.

But the OECD has grown. Expanding membership beyond the small club offers several advantages. Larger membership can promote cooperation by supporting diffuse reciprocity, issue linkage, and broader total gains (Keohane, 1984; Koremenos, Lipson, and Snidal, 2001). To serve the interests of powerful states, the OECD must still elicit the cooperation of other states—the more the better.[2] Regulatory coordination has more impact when everyone agrees on the standards. Likewise, theories that emphasize the role of socialization of members as a key function of an international institution suggest broader membership will support cooperation (Johnston, 2001). The peer review mechanism of enforcement in the OECD could draw on a larger peer group.

One solution to this depth-breadth trade-off is to form institutions that involve *similar states* and add other states after convergence of preferences. A small club can maximize cooperation by expanding to the point at which the returns from a new member joining equal the costs (Downs, Rocke, and Barsoom, 1998; Gray, Lindstädt, and Slapin, 2017). In a second approach, states construct differential membership through varying the entry conditions and commitments across the membership (Gilligan, 2004). For example, Schneider (2009) shows that during eastern enlargement negotiations of the EU, differences across the concessions and transition periods introduced what in effect was discriminatory membership. Viola (2020) examines the United Nations with its Security Council privileges for major powers as the premier example of hierarchy within a multilateral organization. These strategies adjust the timing and structure of membership.

Some aspects of sequential and differential membership play out in the OECD enlargement process, but they are insufficient. Geopolitical discrimination is the missing piece to explain the form of conditional and selective enlargement that has taken place in the OECD. A more comprehensive definition of interests is necessary to explain which preferences were aligned to select new members. Conditions were imposed with variation across members, but without adopting a formal hierarchy.

Enlargement forces decisions about what constitutes similarity of interests. The preferences and capabilities of states within the issue area of the regime rules form baseline performance criteria for selecting partners for enlargement under the conventional theories of institutions. Geopolitical discrimination occurs when states instead look outside of the issues governed by the OECD to choose partners on other criteria.

---

2. Stone (2011) connects *voluntary* participation as the foundation of legitimacy for an international organization, but does not focus on the breadth of participation.

5.2   Selecting for Similar Type in the OECD

These arguments about the depth-breadth trade-off are at the forefront of decisions about enlargement for the OECD. From a functional perspective, the organization can better serve its own mission to coordinate economic policies for growth and prosperity if it includes more countries. At the end of his term as OECD Secretary General, Donald Johnston made the pointed remark that "how are you going to shape the global economy if you're basically working with a minority of it?"(Woodward, 2009, p. 105). At the same time, inevitably the addition of more countries introduces greater heterogeneity of preferences which can block decisions. Sociological perspectives are also not free of this trade-off. Broadening membership adds further legitimacy and greater weight of peer pressure, but also reduces the sense of community and shared norms. Committee meetings that are overcrowded with participants are less likely to build small-world networks through discourse. Finally, the status premium of OECD membership could be lost if the group expands too broadly.

The OECD has undertaken gradual expansion based on similarity across multiple dimensions. Table 5.1 lists members by year of accession with data on their income, democracy, and alliances. The accession process involves exclusion through screening mechanisms and attraction through the provision of club goods. The requirement for commitments to liberal economic policies keeps out states that would diminish quality within the group. The appeal of association with the rich club attracts states to meet the entry requirements. But this only applies to those countries that share liberal orientation in their foreign policy and political values. Through an informal process, geopolitical alignment with the United States and democratic regimes has become a condition of membership.

5.2.1   The OECD Accession Process

The OECD does not establish precise conditions for eligibility or compliance review in its formal accession process. The OECD Convention sets out the following rules in Article 16:

> The Council may decide to invite any Government prepared to assume the obligations of membership to accede to this Convention. Such decisions shall be unanimous, provided that for any particular case the Council may

Country	Accession Year
Japan	1964
Finland	1969
Australia	1971
New Zealand	1973
Mexico	1994
Czech Republic	1995
Poland	1996
Hungary	1996
South Korea	1996
Slovakia	2000
Chile	2010
Slovenia	2010
Estonia	2010
Israel	2010
Latvia	2016
Lithuania	2018
Colombia	2020
Costa Rica	2021

TABLE 5.1. *OECD member enlargement*: The table lists enlargement to 38 members for countries who joined by accession. The following twenty states were founding members in 1961: Austria, Belgium, Canada, Denmark, France, Greece, Iceland, Ireland, Italy (ratification in 1962), Luxembourg, the Netherlands, Norway, Portugal, Spain, Sweden, Switzerland, Turkey, United Kingdom, United States, and Western Germany

unanimously decide to permit abstention, in which case, notwithstanding the provisions of Article 6, the decision shall be applicable to all the Members. Accession shall take effect upon the deposit of an instrument of accession with the depositary Government.

These general terms allow considerable discretion for the current members to admit or exclude applicants. But the charter does not have any provisions for the suspension or expulsion of members. The OECD typically requires new members to have both market economy and democratic political institutions. This context has allowed deviations from the norm that OECD members uphold democratic principles. Founding members included states under authoritarian rule (Spain and Portugal) at the time, and democratic reversals in Greece and Turkey were not grounds for exclusion. Likewise, even as Cyprus has met the demanding conditions for economic and political reforms necessary to join the EU, it remains excluded from the OECD due partly to objections by Turkey on the basis of tense political relations.

A 2004 agreement in the Ministerial Council Meeting accepted a working group proposal that was intended to provide more specific guidelines for selecting candidates for accession, and yet the OECD instead reflects the ongoing discretionary nature of admitting countries to the club. Carroll and Kellow (2011, p. 123) concluded that the criteria for suitability boiled down to four points: "there had to be 'like-mindedness'; the state had to be a 'significant player'; there needed to be 'mutual benefit' from membership; and there had to be regard given to 'global considerations,' particularly keeping some sort of agreed 'balance' between European and non-European members." The report states that like-mindedness should be judged by fundamental yardsticks for a country having a market economy and democratic principles, while additional factors should include: economic performance, good governance, human rights, participation in other IGOs, provision of development assistance, and observance of the OECD *acquis*.[3] The chairman of the working group, Ambassador Seiichirō Noboru, expressed dismay at the failure of subsequent council meetings to consolidate the principles into more concrete admission criteria.[4] But the OECD member states have chosen to retain their flexibility with informal principles for screening applicants. Ambassador Noboru noted that the European states that seek admission for more EU members favored more explicit requirements for democracy and market economy, while Japan, Canada, and Australia were insistent that states needed to be significant players, by which they hoped to encourage entry by some of the BRICS (Brazil, Russia, India, China, and South Africa), which held a larger share of world GDP than many EU states seeking entry. The United States wanted to keep the organization small to avoid budget increases, but sought entry for Israel. The report notes explicitly that the "significant player" criterion does not take precedence over "like-mindedness." Flexibility allows states to navigate such differences among members.

At first it would seem that income represents a critical threshold to define a subset of countries eligible to join. Yet this belies the early membership of Turkey as a founding member and the entry of Mexico in 1994. Both fall within the World Bank classification category for "upper middle income" developing countries. Furthermore, recent entrants are far down the list of countries

3. OECD (2004), "A Strategy for Enlargement and Outreach," report by Chair of the Heads of Delegation Working Group on the Enlargement Strategy and Outreach, Ambassador Seiichirō Noboru.

4. Telephone interview by author, 28 October 2014.

in terms of economic size measured by total GDP. Woodward (2009, p. 105) refers to "minnows" like Estonia that ranked between Uganda and Jordan in terms of World Bank rankings of GDP in 2007 when they were invited to initiate accession talks for joining the OECD. Of course, their per capita GDP is much higher. The latest countries accepted for membership included Colombia and Costa Rica. These countries are both poorer on a per capita income basis and smaller in total GDP than Brazil, Malaysia, Russia, and Singapore which remain outside of the organization. The other recent entrants include Lithuania and Latvia, which along with Estonia stand out as small but relatively wealthy members.

The European origins of the OECD continue to privilege those from the region even as the organization embraced Japan and Australia early on. Today members span all continents, with the exception of Africa, South Africa being among the countries involved in the "enhanced engagement" with the OECD that is intended to prepare countries for membership. Thus we can see that even while there is a set of common characteristics shaping the organization, it does not represent rigid criteria for democracy, wealth, or location.

5.2.2   The Price of Admission

The three dimensions for screening out applicants are dues, transparency, and policy reform. The first is the easiest, because the OECD has progressive budgeting. Member dues are assessed based on paying a share of the OECD budget according to proportion of national income, such that larger states pay more, up to a cap of 25 percent, of total budget (Carroll and Kellow, 2011, p. 15). The G7 group of large states provide three fourths of the core budget and also fund "pet projects" through voluntary contributions (Woodward, 2009, p. 46). In 2019, the United States paid 20.5 percent of the budget while Iceland paid the smallest share at 0.6 percent.[5]

The requirement for transparency represents a hurdle for some governments. States agree to provide information to the OECD, and thus to expose their performance to public assessment. Although membership in the IMF and WTO may have already elicited considerable economic reporting from countries, the OECD economic surveys and other studies are far more wide-ranging in scope. The peer review process builds on this information to

5. OECD (2019), "Member Countries' Budget Contributions for 2019." Available at http://www.oecd.org/about/budget/member-countries-budget-contributions.htm. Accessed 12 March 2021.

provide the primary enforcement mechanism of the organization, as states' policies are examined in detail within a given area with the purpose of evaluating whether the state is meeting the best practice standards that have been established through OECD decisions (Woodward, 2009, p. 57). The widely used economic surveys represent an extensive review of economic data through a process that incorporates the members' self-assessment as well as analysis by the secretariat and questioning by other members before the completion of a final public report. OECD rankings of government performance according to common benchmarks provide ammunition to domestic groups critical of their own government. For states that have a record of political interference and "cook the books" of accounts, compliance with objective data categories and reporting standards represents unwanted transparency.

The most important objective requirement of membership is for the applicant to conform with OECD policies. The Codes of Liberalization (formally two agreements, Code of Liberalisation of Current Invisible Operations and the Code of Liberalisation of Capital Movements) form the core OECD agreements. They embody the commitment of the organization to pursue open trade and capital markets. Lowering trade barriers and establishing convertibility of currencies and free capital movement were primary conditions. The codes call for more comprehensive liberalization of finance and investment policies than membership in other multilateral economic organizations, although reservations allow for states to carve out exceptions. Subsequent agreements such as the 1994 decision on National Treatment for Foreign-Controlled Enterprises and the Anti-Bribery Convention have since expanded commitments to FDI and other areas. In all cases, states are allowed to make reservations that carve out individual exceptions. Governments notify members of their policies related to the codes, and are subject to peer review. The organization lacks formal procedures for sanctions, and instead relies on a state's concern for reputation and the role of persuasion in shaping policy choices.

5.2.3   Why Bother? Understanding Demand for Membership

Many of the public goods provided by the OECD in its role as policy think tank are available to all states. Each year the organization publishes more than 200 reports (Woodward, 2009, p. 57). The organization actively disseminates its reports. Even the peer review assessment OECD Economic Survey has been undertaken by countries that are not members, such as China and Brazil. Furthermore, when member governments change their policies to conform with OECD recommendations, they do not discriminate among members and nonmembers in their application of these policies (i.e., adoption of anti-bribery rules does not favor OECD members over other states). When governments seek to liberalize trade and capital according to the Codes of Liberalization, they do so on a most-favored-nation basis rather than as preferential access limited to fellow OECD members.

Therefore one must look further to understand why applicants would be willing to jump these hurdles for membership. On the demand side, states seek the status benefits of closer association with other members. While to some the stereotype of the OECD as a "rich country club" is derogatory, joining the ranks of this group offers an imprimatur of acceptance in the top ranks of international society. In particular, OECD membership means self-identification as an advanced country aligned with the United States and Europe. States may experience rivalry over the status of association, given that more members in the organization will only dilute the signal attained by those who join. As a discriminatory club, the OECD offers both provision of shared goods in the form of policy expertise and regulation, and also the benefits of association that are a function of the status of other members.

From a market perspective, the value of association with the rich club can pay off in real terms through the channel of investor confidence. One benefit from membership that was especially important for the countries that joined in the 1990s came in the form of lower interest rates on capital. Due to the Basel Committee on Banking Supervision's decision to apply zero risk weighting for bank loans to all OECD governments, accession to the OECD would substantially lower the cost of capital for Mexico and Korea (Claessens, Underhill and Zhang, 2008, p. 317). In part due to recognition that this led to excessive capital inflows into Korea that contributed to its financial crisis shortly after joining the OECD in 1996, the 2004 revision to Basel rules on banking introduced a more complex risk assessment procedure that would end the zero risk weighting for emerging market OECD members that had been enjoyed by the Czech Republic, Hungary, Mexico, Poland, Slovakia, South Korea, and Turkey (ibid., p. 327). Nevertheless, nothing will stop market actors from taking into account OECD membership as a sign of quality when they evaluate country risk levels.

Countries that are considering accession refer to expected improvement in credit as one motivation for joining. For example, on its website the Russian Ministry of Foreign Affairs mentions in the description of reasons for Russia to seek OECD membership, "One of the most important functions of the OECD for Russia is the OECD's determining of states' credit ratings, on which the borrowing conditions in global financial markets depend."[6] The importance of such signals are widely acknowledged—when talks about potential Russian accession arose again, Sergei Guriev, former chief economist at the European Bank for Reconstruction and Development, said that the move would represent a "substantial positive signal for investors and entrepreneurs" because of the expected reforms to corporate governance and tax policies that would accompany joining the OECD.[7] Similarly Lithuania's president issued the following statement after a meeting at the OECD about its application to begin negotiations for accession: "Joining the OECD would make Lithuania more attractive to foreign investors, improve our debt ratings and reduce borrowing costs."[8] Argentina is a prospective member that issued its request to join in 2016 with a strong push from the top level of the government under the administration of Mauricio Macri. Marcelo Scaglione, Deputy Secretary of State, who led the talks with the OECD from 2016 to 2019, emphasized that completing accession would attract investment that could fund specific projects in Argentina, lamenting the fact that the new government was slowing talks to join the OECD and that "Today, that financing is not available in the country because we are not able to give investors confidence. It can only be available if Argentina is aligned with the good practices of the OECD."[9] The OECD does not issue credit ratings or have any direct role aside from the signal of membership.

Market actors responding to uncertainty may rely on the OECD as a brand. The status premium of OECD membership holds value in financial markets and in competition for investment. More generally, the literature has shown that organizational membership can impact country risk ratings and

6. The Ministry of Foreign Affairs of the Russian Federation, "Rossiia na puti integrasii v mirovuiu ekonomiku: Rossiia I OESR (Russia on the Road to Integration into the Global Economy: Russia and the OECD)" (19 July 2005). Retrieved February 2 2014 from http://www.mid.ru/ns-vnpop.nsf/osn_copy/6ED794F5B1C4B629C325704300315446.

7. Ilya Arkhipov and Evgenia Pismennaya, "Putin's New Premier Reaches Out to West with Bid for OECD Ties," *Bloomberg*, 3 March 2020.

8. Bryan Bradley, "Lithuania Seeks OECD Invitation to Start Accession Talks in May," Bloomberg (9 April 2013). Accessed at http://www.bloomberg.com/news/2013-04-09/lithuania-seeks-oecd-invitation-to-start-accession-talks-in-may.html.

9. Guadalupe, Alan Soria, "The Impact the Delay on Entry to the OECD Has on Argentina," *La Nacion* 17 January 2020. https://www.lanacion.com.ar/politica/el-impacto-para-la-argentina-del-retraso-en-el-ingreso-a-la-ocde-nid2324797.

bond yields. Dreher and Voigt (2011) find that independently of the quality of domestic institutions, membership in international organizations improves the risk rating. Gray (2013) argues that investors face uncertainty and rely on cues about countries' reliability based on their peer group, and provides evidence that membership in international organizations can increase bond ratings. Her theory contends that independently of actual policies, the reputation of a country as measured by bond ratings will rise or fall in accordance with whether they associate with good or poor quality countries in regional economic associations. Yet such branding has its limits. Dreher and Voigt (2011, p. 340) find that the subset of OECD members *do not* receive any boost from their membership in other international organizations. Presumably their status as OECD members and the accompanying features that characterize this unique group obviates any role for additional information from IGO membership.

To preserve its brand value, the OECD must remain exclusive. More so than other membership benefits from the OECD, the brand value in markets will form a club good that is subject to crowding effects. Should too many countries be allowed to join, there would no longer be new information from membership status. Expansion to include countries of lower quality on core economic policies would risk damage to the OECD's reputation as the gold standard for a business environment. To the extent that states value association with high status members, they will refuse entry to others who do not uphold the level of the group.

5.2.4   Seeking Status through Association

Beyond their motivation to improve their credit ratings, states are drawn to applying when they want to become more like the members. Membership offers a direct pathway to following members' policies. The greater access to policy learning is cited by many participants as a key benefit of engaging in the OECD. In extensive interviews with OECD member governments and the organization secretariat, Carroll and Kellow (2011, p. 38) remark that all without exception emphasize policy learning. Being "in the room" for committee meetings and technical discussions matters, for both the influence to shape the output of decisions and the opportunities to receive information. Staffing of the organization is largely from members, who send their officials to attend committee meetings or to serve within the organization. These national representatives play a critical role in the information exchange that is central to the OECD mission. Emile van Lennep, former OECD Secretary General, said "ninety-nine percent of our work concerns the exchange of experience and the elaboration of lines of action" (Woodward, 2009, p. 24). Through directly participating in this process, member states can tap into the wealth of knowledge from the experience of their peers and the technical materials prepared by the secretariat.

Rather than passively responding to economic competition or following role models defined by social relationships, governments select into a group as a deliberate choice to expose themselves to peer pressure within a particular group. States seek status through association with the elite club. This process combines aspects of learning and emulation as well as competition. The accession decision goes beyond learning described in the policy diffusion literature because it involves accepting a broad set of principles and participation in an ongoing dialogue over future policy direction.[10] Applicants do not assess the efficacy of specific policies. Rather, emulation occurs in the sense that OECD members are the "advanced nations" with valuable information on a wide range of policy issues. Joining their circle confers status by virtue of membership and offers opportunities to learn how to be successful like them. Where the sociological tradition rightly gives attention to how countries can be shaped by following a lead country or prevailing policy trend, this overlooks the goal-oriented nature of deciding to join a group of countries. The applicants seek to have their position in international society defined by their attributes as liberal states by means of deepening their association with the rich, liberal democracies of the Western alliance. For some, this simply consolidates their current position, but others are trying to change perceptions, whether shedding a regional stereotype or distancing from a former communist legacy.

The association with the OECD appeals to states holding similar political values and foreign policy positions. The key features of the OECD are democracy and U.S.-centered foreign policy. For democratic countries and U.S. allies, the domestic public responds with more favor to steps by their government to deepen interactions with countries that they see as positive examples. In contrast, leaders of an authoritarian government may worry about unfavorable comparisons to OECD countries rallying opposition, and avoid the closer association with OECD countries that would accompany membership. Survey analysis suggests that the public may care more about the reputation of

10. On diffusion literature, see Simmons, Dobbin, and Garrett (2006).

the countries that states form an agreement with than the depth of design in the agreement itself (Gray and Hicks, 2014).[11] In approaching prospective trade partners, public opinion favors agreements with allies (Carnegie and Gaikwad, 2022).

This explanation is distinct from commitment theories whereby states endeavor to buy credibility through increasing the costs of defection. Mansfield and Pevehouse (2009) contend that democratizing states signal their commitment to consolidate political reforms and responsible economic policies by joining organizations that set standards and regulate economic policies. Such logic fits well to explain a part of the demand for joining the OECD, but not the wide variation among democratizing states. Moreover, with its weak mechanisms of enforcement, the OECD is a poor tool for tying hands. At entry countries can make reservations to exclude sensitive policies, and after entry the worst cost of violating OECD principles lies in critical commentary. Real policy commitments are made as part of accession and the peer review mechanism raises costs of defection, but stronger commitment tools lie in other multilateral organizations – the WTO, regional agreements, or bilateral trade and investment agreements include enforcement provisions that incorporate third-party arbitration and retaliation/compensation.

Status goals upend the sequential liberalization theory. Rather than selecting on convergence of preferences over the regulated policy areas, applicants seek to join before they have all of the OECD policies in place. To achieve membership, they initiate substantial reforms as part of the accession process and aspire to change future policies through the interaction with members. As an institution, the OECD juxtaposes forward-looking goals for change and an organization that will do little to lock-in such policy reforms. This does not fit either the story of states binding their hands nor one of rubber-stamping.

The status-seeking emulation motive for accession does not relegate the action to symbolic politics. Applicants must undertake some policy reforms to earn entry to the club. Current members recognize the cost of admitting new members when there are only weak enforcement mechanisms. They carefully screen for countries with strong commitment to OECD principles and responsiveness to OECD peer review. Here the members look for friends,

---

11. The survey included responses by 471 U.S. respondents to a Mechanical Turk poll that included embedded experimental treatment to vary information on type of agreement and whether the counter party had "good" reputation (e.g., Canada) or "bad reputation" (i.e., Iran).

Average income

Income distribution

Per capita GDP (million constant U.S. dollars)

OECD members

Non-OECD

1960   1970   1980   1990   2000   2010

Per capita GDP (in 2005 U.S. dollar prices)

OECD   Non-OECD

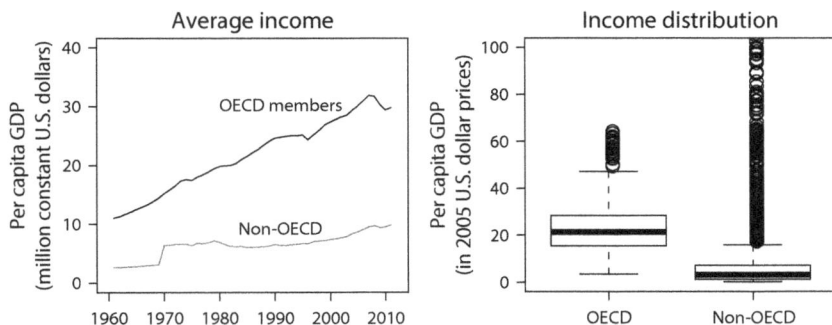

FIGURE 5.1. *Income comparison of OECD members and nonmembers*: The left figure displays the mean per capita GDP of OECD members and nonmembers over time. The right figure displays the distribution of per capita GDP for OECD members and nonmembers over the period 1961 to 2012.

who are expected to remain cooperative within the broader context of the diplomatic relationship.

Both the demand and supply side of membership suggest that noneconomic conditions of similarity will attract members to an organization. Specifically, political regime type and geopolitical alignment form important criteria to shape membership decisions. On the basis of common interests, states seek status by association and are welcomed into a club that relies on weak tools of enforcement and offers benefits that include both public goods and club goods.

5.3   Common Features of the Like-Minded Club

A brief overview of the characteristics of members confirms the expectation that the OECD, which is often referred to as a "rich country club," has a membership with high income. Figure 5.1 shows the average per capita GDP for OECD members relative to nonmembers over time. Nevertheless, it is also important to examine the distribution of income. The box plot of OECD members is centered at the mean income of 22.55 thousand U.S. dollars (over the full period 1961 to 2012, taking the average income for all members in each given year), with a large cluster of high income outliers above the fourth quartile. The nonmember distribution is more skewed, with a lower mean income of 6.65 thousand U.S. dollars and a cluster of high income states. This clearly demonstrates that while the OECD members are rich on average,

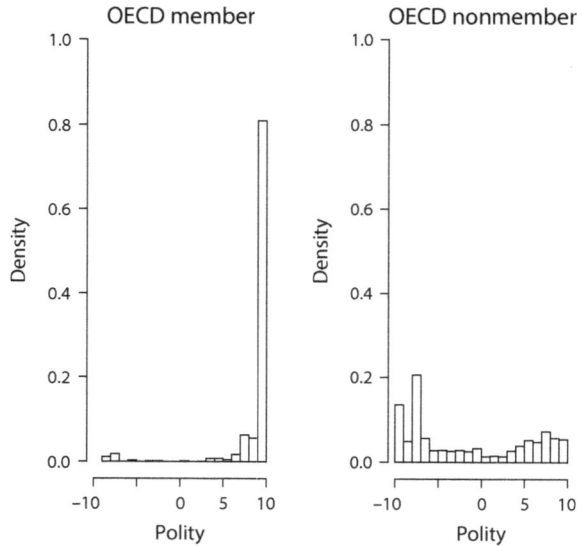

FIGURE 5.2. *Democracy and OECD membership*: The figure compares the frequency of government institutions across the range of Polity score index in which −10 is authoritarian and 10 is fully democratic.

there are also many wealthy nonmembers, including those with oil wealth, tax havens, and some industrial economies such as Russia. Furthermore, the most recent admitted countries, Colombia and Costa Rica, are both upper middle income.

Figure 5.2 shows the dominance of democratic regime types among OECD members, where the modal polity score is the highest level of 10 for consolidated democracies. Nevertheless, authoritarian governments have been members of the OECD. Nonmembers over this period from 1961 to 2012 have authoritarian regime as the modal polity score, but many states achieve high democracy scores without entry to the liberal club.

Within the nonmember grouping are important actors that have embraced many of the liberal economic and political policies advocated by the OECD. India and Brazil stand out as two democracies that are major emerging markets of importance to the global economy but remain outside the OECD. As the target of outreach by the OECD, they participate in "enhanced engagement" and undertake peer monitoring by requesting an economic survey report on their economic policies, and yet India has explicitly stated it does not seek to formally join the OECD and Brazil only recently started negotiations

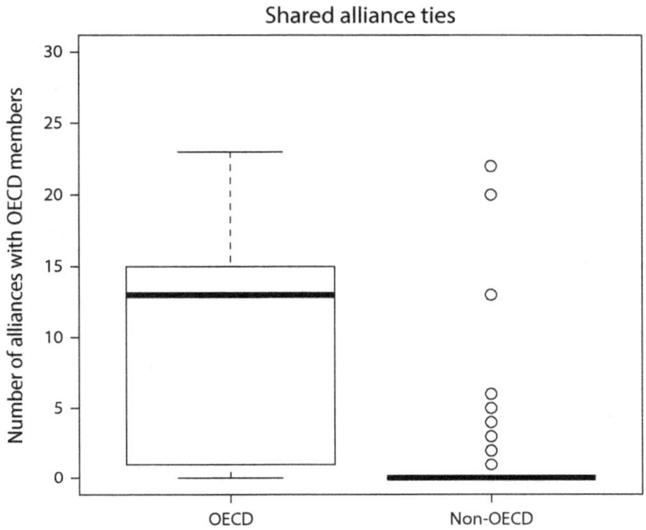

FIGURE 5.3. *Alliance ties of OECD members*: The box plot graphs display the distribution within the OECD membership in comparison to the nonmember countries in terms of the number of shared formal alliances with OECD members.

toward accession. Their international status derives from leadership of the developing world, rather than seeking entry to the advanced industrial world. Singapore long ago achieved income levels that surpass that of many OECD members and would easily meet most of the policies for liberal market economy. Its non-democratic status may be one obstacle, but Carroll and Kellow (2011, p. 122) emphasize that Singapore has not applied because regional identity makes Singapore seek to avoid any step that could upset its neighbors or detract from the image as a "Chinese island in a Malay sea."

This leads to the third dimension of similarity that shapes the OECD members: geopolitical alignment. Figure 5.3 clearly displays the pattern of shared alliances among OECD members, who on average have alliances with ten fellow OECD members.[12] The organization had its origins within the effort to use economic cooperation to build cohesion in the Western Alliance and all NATO members joined the OECD. This accounts for why Turkey as a politically unstable democracy and poor country joined the ranks of the OECD's

12. The alliance data is from the Correlates of War Formal Alliances Version 4.1 dataset, with correction to add the second post-Cold War NATO enlargement.

founding members in 1961.[13] Nevertheless, the founding group of the OECD also included nonaligned Switzerland, Austria, and Sweden, and many non-NATO countries joined the OECD in subsequent enlargement decisions. The sequence of joining NATO and the OECD has varied; the Czech Republic, Poland, Hungary, and Slovakia joined the OECD before they were invited to join NATO accession talks, whereas Estonia, Latvia, Lithuania, and Slovenia became NATO members before joining the OECD. Four members of NATO have not yet become OECD members (Albania, Bulgaria, Croatia, and Romania). Other countries such as Japan and Korea are not in NATO but stand as firm U.S. allies. Indeed, most OECD members share an alliance with the United States, with the exceptions of Ireland, Switzerland, Austria, Finland, Sweden, Israel, and New Zealand. And while a country like Israel does not hold a formal alliance with the United States, it is the recipient of extensive military aid and holds close foreign policy affinity with the United States, as seen in its UN voting record. Two thirds of the OECD members are U.S. allies, and 20 percent of nonmembers are U.S. allies.

Geopolitical differences account for some outliers who otherwise appear to fit the member profile—Indonesia, Malaysia, and South Africa have income that surpasses that of several current OECD members, and have completed the transition to democratic institutions. Yet as leaders in the nonaligned movement, they have greater geopolitical distance from the OECD. Similarly, India, another prominent leader of the nonaligned movement, has explicitly said it will not seek OECD membership.

A more general measure of geopolitical alignment is voting similarity in UN General Assembly roll call votes.[14] Voting within the United Nations has been used to identify states with similar interests (Voeten, 2000; Bearce and Bondanella, 2007). The trend of UN voting patterns for the OECD and non-OECD subset of countries in Figure 5.4 shows the consistency across different periods in the higher similarity of OECD member voting affinity with the United States (left graph) and three major European states (right graph).

The importance of foreign policy orientation can be seen in the example of Russia. The government surprised many when it submitted its application

13. Although Turkey held democratic elections since the 1950s, a military coup in 1960 highlighted that it had not completed a transition to become a consolidated democracy.

14. The data here are from the s3un variable in Anton Strezhnev; Erik Voeten, 2013-02, "United Nations General Assembly Voting Data." https://dataverse.harvard.edu/dataset.xhtml ?persistentId=doi:10.7910/DVN/LEJUQZ.

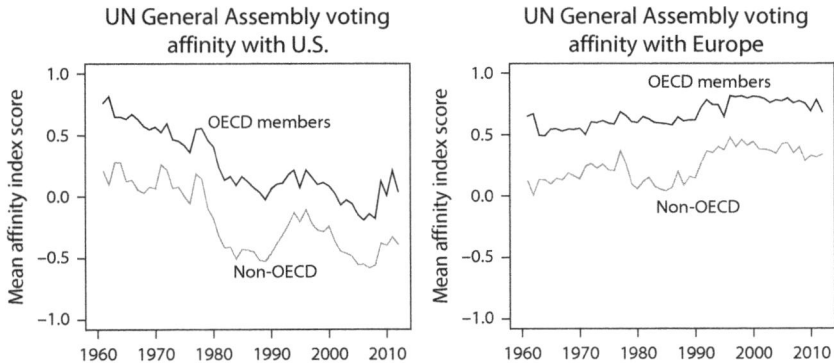

FIGURE 5.4. *UN voting and OECD membership*: The graphs display the mean affinity scores for UN voting across the OECD membership in comparison to the nonmember countries. The affinity index ranges from −1 to 1 and is calculated based on voting across the three categories of affirmative, abstain, and negative votes, with higher values reflecting greater similarity in voting. The figure to the left represents similarity with the United States and the figure to the right represents similarity with the United Kingdom, France, and Germany (taking the average of similarity with each of the three European states).

to join the OECD in May 1996, following up on a declaration by Russian President Boris Yeltsin in a speech during the Halifax meeting of the G7 countries in June 1995 that Russia would join the OECD. In a close election with resurgence by the Communist Party, Yeltsin may have seen the call to join the OECD as an easy way to appeal to those in Russia seeking further reforms, and skeptics reported the development as an election stunt.[15] Joining the OECD would have shown that Russia was becoming a full partner with the West and confirmed its new direction. The declaration that Russia wanted to join the OECD was more aspirational than realistic. As Russian foreign policy shifted, the economic hurdles remained, and accession negotiations did not formally begin until 2007. Studies within Russia acknowledge the challenges for Russia to complete the economic reforms necessary, and an OECD report in 2011 highlighted problems with state involvement in the economy, weak rule of law, and restrictive trade and investment policies.[16] While it ratified

15. "OECD Backs Britain on Jobs." *The Independent* 22 May 1996. Retrieved 2 February 2014 from NewsBank on-line database (Access World News).

16. OECD. 2011. *OECD Economic Surveys: Russian Federation 2011*, OECD Publishing, Paris, https://doi.org/10.1787/eco_surveys-rus-2011-en.

the Anti-Bribery Convention, weak enforcement has drawn criticism and an OECD working group was formed to monitor the situation.[17] The Russian government has actively participated in OECD committees across a range of issues. Russia completed several chapters of the negotiations toward accession before foreign policy crises arose as an insurmountable obstacle.

Security conflict has derailed any progress toward membership for Russia. First, the 2008 Russian-Georgian war led to claims on both sides about unnecessary delays in accession through politicization.[18] The Russian intervention in Ukraine in 2014 led the OECD's governing Council to announce it would postpone activities related to Russia's accession. Yet neither side wanted to cut off communication. The government continued to engage with the OECD as a participant in its committees and signatory to its conventions. After a major government turnover in January 2020, the incoming prime minister Mikhail Mishustin was an individual reported to have been active in these OECD policy discussions when in his prior role overseeing Russian tax policies.[19] Only three months after taking office, he was reported to be working to renew efforts for Russia to join the OECD. According to a Bloomberg story that was widely cited in other media outlets, Russian officials explained that "the push to restore ties—even if it doesn't immediately lead to restarting accession efforts—signals the new government's desire to reach out to the West and to improve the business climate," and that "the move comes as the new government has recognized that Russia's pivot away from the West since the imposition of sanctions has taken it too far toward China."[20] The story about Russian interest in restarting talks to join the OECD was carried on a government news portal.[21] The timing also corresponded to a shift in relations

17. OECD, "Russia Must Urgently Step Up Fight against Foreign Bribery," 26 April 2019. Available at https://www.oecd.org/russia/russia-must-urgently-step-up-fight-against-foreign -bribery.htm.

18. "Politics Should Not Affect Russia's Accession to OECD," BBC Monitoring International Reports, retrieved 28 January 2014 from NewsBank on-line database (Access World News); 19 September 2008 "Commentary of Russian Foreign Ministry on Rice's Speech at German Marshall Fund," BBC Monitoring International Reports, retrieved 28 January 2014 from NewsBank on-line database (Access World News).

19. Max Seddon and Henry Foy, "Putin's New Prime Minister Steps from Tax Office into Limelight," The Financial Times, 16 January 2020.

20. Ilya Arkhipov and Evgenia Pismennaya, "Putin's New Premier Reaches Out to West with Bid for OECD Ties," Bloomberg, 3 March 2020.

21. Ministry of Economic Development of the Russian Federation, "Russian government to analyze potential revival of relations with OECD," 5 March 2020. Available at http://www.ved .gov.ru/eng/general/news/19/26395.html. Accessed 16 April 2021.

with the United States. Russia enjoyed improving ties with the United States, and the Trump administration even called for its readmission to the G7.[22] The window of opportunity was closing, however, as the Biden administration shifted to a less supportive position toward Russia, which was excluded from the virtual Summit for Democracy in December 2021. Russian government steps toward more transparent tax policies and enforcement of anti-bribery rules helped Russia to show its compliance with more OECD rules but could not overcome the worsening geopolitical climate. As Russia undertook a full invasion of Ukraine, the OECD Council condemned its actions and voted to formally terminate the accession process that had been suspended since 2014, close the OECD Moscow office, and end invitations for Russia to participate in OECD committees.

In summary, the descriptive statistics support the general view of OECD membership representing wealthy democracies of the Western alliance system. On the margins, however, the criteria for advanced income, democracy, and geopolitical alignment were substitutes, such that meeting one dimension would compensate for falling short on another dimension. This chapter examines how states on both sides of the membership question weighed their readiness to join.

5.4 Statistical Analysis of OECD Accession

To more fully examine the correlates of membership in the OECD I use a duration model to estimate the time for a country to join the OECD from the date of its establishment in 1961. The question of interest here is why Turkey would be among the original members to join in year 1 while Mexico would join 33 years later, and others such as Singapore remain outside of the organization.

I first look at how different groups have distinct baseline survival trends when describing the rate of failure. Figure 5.5 shows the estimated survival curves using Kaplan-Meier estimates. The first graph on the left shows the significant difference for European countries relative to non-European countries, as the former are less likely to remain outside the OECD for each year following the establishment of organization. For the display of descriptive comparison of the variation in survival probability, U.S. allies offer easy comparison as a dichotomous measure for geopolitical orientation. The right

22. Maggie Haberman, "Trump Postpones G7 Summit and Calls for Russia to Attend," *The New York Times*, 31 May 2020.

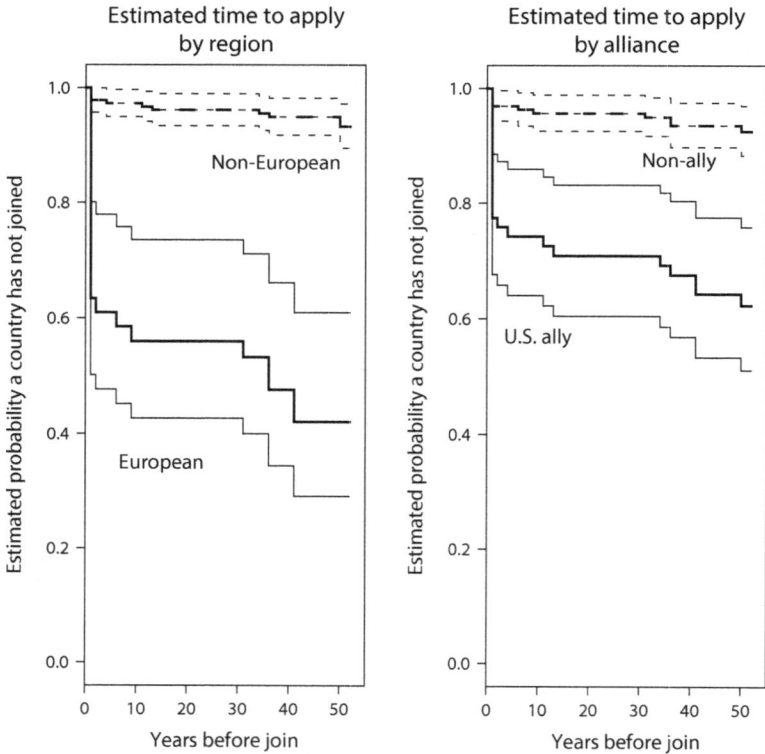

FIGURE 5.5. *Estimated negotiation survival curves*: Using Kaplan-Meier estimates of survival, the figure shows the estimated probability for a country to remain a nonmember.

graph reveals the smaller but nonetheless statistically significant difference between the survival probability of U.S. allies and non-allies, with the former more likely to have joined at any specific period in time. The figure highlights the clear pattern for European countries and U.S. allies to be among the first OECD members.

Given the expectation that there is not a constant rate of failure, the Cox proportional hazards model is the appropriate specification that allows me to include time-varying covariates. The sample includes 161 countries for the period from 1961 to 2014. Standard errors are clustered on country to take into account possible correlation of error terms across years within the same country. Because the organization has its roots in European development and location in Europe continues to form strong bias toward membership, I stratify based on European and non-European countries to allow for a distinct baseline hazard (this model specification is similar to adding a fixed effect for the region).[23]

The key relationships highlighted above in descriptive statistics are tested in the regression analysis with focus on how not only income but also alliances and democracy exert positive pressure on countries to join the organization. My main variable to measure geopolitical interests is an alliance with the United States, and I also examine the effect of UN voting affinity with the United States. I use the polity 2 index to measure democracy. Membership in the European Union is included as a control variable. Three variables control for economic determinants of membership. Income is measured as per capita GDP (million 2005 US$ from Penn World Table), and is expected to have a positive effect, conforming to the notion that the OECD represents a rich country club. Liberal trade and financial policies form key benchmarks for economic policies conducive to participation in the organization; I include measures of trade openness (imports and exports share of GDP) and an indicator of whether a country has ratified IMF Article 8, which indicates a commitment to maintain an open current account.[24]

A test for whether covariates meet the proportional hazard assumption shows that this assumption is not met by the polity measure of democracy, which indicates that the residuals are not constant over time. Therefore it is necessary to model the effect of democracy as conditional on time through adding an interaction term between polity and the log of time since 1961 (Box-Steffensmeier and Zorn, 2001). All other covariates in the model meet the proportional hazard assumption without interaction.[25]

Table 5.2 presents the coefficient estimates indicating the direction and significance of effects (coefficients in the Cox proportional hazards model are not otherwise informative about substantive effect size). The results in model 1

23. I apply the Efron method of ties. Countries enter the dataset in 1961 with the founding members experiencing failure in year 1. All countries exit the dataset after year of failure to join OECD or in 2014 for those that do not join and are right-censored. The definition of Europe as a region follows the UN Statistics Division geographic regions.

24. IMF Article 8 signature has been described as an important signal to investors of open environment for trade and investment (Simmons, 2000; Nelson, 2010).

25. Including GDP in some additional specifications, however, is problematic because it does not meet the proportional hazard assumption. The model does not converge when including multiple covariates interacted with time. I focus on the polity variable where conditional effects on time are most plausible in theory. Results are consistent when ending the sample in 2011, or in the full sample shown here that extends the 2011 alliance data and merges World Development Indicator per capita GDP data for the final three years.

	Model 1	Model 2
U.S. ally	0.946***	
	(0.345)	
UN voting affinity with U.S.		1.479**
		(0.738)
Polity	−0.070*	−0.063*
	(0.041)	(0.038)
Polity × log(time)	0.124***	0.109***
	(0.042)	(0.041)
EU	−0.871*	−0.421
	(0.460)	(0.416)
Per capita GDP (logged)	1.985***	1.654***
	(0.335)	(0.302)
Trade openness	−0.006	−0.005
	(0.005)	(0.005)
IMF Article 8	0.699*	0.552
	(0.402)	(0.400)
Observations	5,031	4,917
# Countries	161	160
# Accession events	33	32

TABLE 5.2. *Effect of geopolitical alignment on OECD membership.* Models examine whether a U.S. alliance (Model 1) or UN voting similarity with the United States (Model 2) affects the probability of membership in the OECD. The Model 2 sample does not include Switzerland, which was not a UN member at time of entry. West Germany is not included in both models due to missing data at time of entry. The table shows estimates from Cox proportional hazards regression with stratification for Europe as a region and standard errors clustered by country. Statistical significance is denoted by: *p < 0.1; **p < 0.05; ***p < 0.01.

confirm that U.S. allies have higher probability of joining at any given time than those not having common security interests. Model 2 measures geopolitical alignment with UN voting affinity to the United States. Table 5.2 shifts to replace the alliance variable with UN voting affinity to the United States as a measure of geopolitical similarity. In both specifications, there is a significant and positive effect on the predicted time to join the organization.

Democratic institutions have a more complicated relationship that is conditional on time. Only later in the time period does the polity score measure become significant to increase the hazard rate. The OECD members shifted to embrace democracy as an informal condition for membership after starting as a group that included the non-democratic founding members Greece, Portugal, and Spain. During the evolution of the OECD, democratic institutions became an important factor for increasing the speed with which countries join. This may reflect both the role of democracy as a principle for geopolitical alignment and the fact that political institutions can shape preferences for economic policies.[26] Unfortunately it is difficult within the research scope of this chapter to differentiate among these dual pathways in which democracy could shape OECD membership.

As expected, income accelerates membership. Trade openness, if anything, slows entry into the OECD, although the effect is not statistically significant and the variable could also reflect the smaller share of trade in GDP for many advanced industrial democracies. Article 8 signatories are more likely to have joined, although these results are only significant in the analysis of countries that joined after 1961. These variables represent rough proxies for a country's capacity to accept the OECD Codes of Liberalization. The negative coefficient for the EU suggests that geographic location in Europe matters more for OECD membership than membership in the EU; for several countries, joining the OECD was the precursor to EU entry.

In summary, the regression analysis has revealed the multiple dimensions upon which countries consider membership. Those that are the most likely to have joined early are not only wealthy, but also aligned to the United States in security and UN voting. Over time, democracy has emerged as a factor that also speeds some countries to higher rates of joining.

5.5   Case Studies of OECD Accession

Three case studies shed light on the features that shape the demand and supply of membership for OECD accession. Japan's entry in 1964, discussed in chapter 6, was the first example for the organization to step outside of the transatlantic scope of its origins. Here, in this chapter, I highlight the Mexican and Korean cases that stretched the organization both in regional scope and in economic conditions, as the OECD welcomed developing country members. A final case examines the Czech Republic as the first of the former communist countries to join the OECD.

5.5.1   Mexico

The case of Mexico's accession to the OECD must be viewed within the context of its negotiations to join the North American Free Trade Agreement

---

26. See, for example, Milner and Kubota (2005); Mansfield, Milner, and Pevehouse (2008); Steinberg and Malhotra (2014).

(NAFTA). Having already agreed in 1990 to pursue a free trade agreement with the United States and Canada, the decision by the government the next year to announce its intent to join the OECD was a complementary step to further broaden the scope of its economic reforms beyond the United States and Canada. Indeed, during the anxious period when U.S. ratification of NAFTA was uncertain, some reported that OECD membership would provide an alternative way to lock in reforms of Mexico even if NAFTA were rejected by the U.S. Congress.[27] Ultimately, the negotiations to join the OECD from 1993 to 1994 followed the signing of NAFTA in 1992, and formal acceptance of invitation to join the OECD on 18 May 1994 occurred during the first year that NAFTA entered into force. While NAFTA attracts more attention, joining the OECD also provided a framework to guide the transformation of Mexican economic policies.

The Salinas government that launched the series of economic reforms within Mexico also took the first step to deepen its relationship with the OECD. The OECD Observer report at the time of Mexico's joining the OECD notes that in 1990 the Mexican government "took the initiative of broadening the scope of its dialogue with the OECD . . . by sending an exploratory mission to learn about the Organisation and the possibilities for strengthening ties with it."[28] Whereas the government had declined an earlier OECD invitation to participate in the OECD Steel Committee, it chose to join the committee in a September 1990 agreement with the OECD and quickly moved forward on privatization of the industry the following year. Speaking to the OECD Council in 1992, Salinas confirmed that Mexico would like to join the organization and take a larger role in the world economy.[29] To the extent that the government was undergoing deep trade liberalization through NAFTA, following its accession to GATT in 1986, the challenging aspects of OECD reforms were focused in other areas, outside of trade. In particular, Mexico expressed early reservations about whether it could undertake liberalization of capital account and in areas of oil privatization and telecommunications.[30] Despite the clear reluctance of Mexico to allow free

27. *The Financial Times*, "Survey of North American Free Trade—Impact on Mexico," 12 May 1993; *Wall Street Journal*, "Nafta or Not, Salinas Pursues Free Market," 15 June 1993.

28. *The OECD Observer*, "Mexico, 25th Member of the OECD," Jun/July 1994.

29. Reuters News, "Mexico Seeks OECD Membership and Active World Role," 22 July 1992.

30. Agence France-Presse, "Mexico to Hold Talks on Entering OECD in 1993," 2 December 1992.

capital movement, finance stood as an area for gains—the likely improvement of Mexico's status on credit markets was noted within Mexico by leading financial groups.[31]

After negotiating with members, Mexico made several reservations but also agreed to reforms in critical areas. In particular, the reservations allowed Mexico to continue to restrict some cross-border capital operations such as foreigners conducting transactions in pesos and in areas of financial services and transport services.[32] At the same time, FDI liberalization went beyond NAFTA commitments, with new legislation passed to open Mexico to investment from all countries, without restriction to either NAFTA or OECD members, and a new stock market law passed to offer access to the domestic market for foreign issuers. Daniel Dutzin Dubin, a Mexican official leading the accession process, said that OECD countries were concerned about the lack of a mechanism for the settlement of disputes, which led to the Mexican government including a multilateral mechanism for the protection of investments in the new Foreign Investment Law.[33] Mexico also agreed to the request from OECD members to liberalize maritime services.

While surging forward on liberal economic reforms, Salinas took a slower pace toward democratization. After Mexico joined the OECD in May 1994, Mexico held elections at the end of the year that allowed international observers and were recognized as step toward partial democracy. Yet it would be several more years before Mexico would represent a consolidated democracy. While some consider OECD membership pushing along this process, it is largely in a backup role. Peer review in the OECD does not extend to political institutions, and socialization is the main channel through which it could exercise positive influence on political reforms. Clearly at the time of accession negotiations, members were willing to accept Mexico more on the promise of liberal political reform than through actual completion of the process.

From the OECD perspective, the question of Mexico's joining brought conflicted views. Carroll and Kellow (2011, p. 97) cite statements by a Belgian minister calling for postponement of formal dialogue with Mexico (and

---

31. *El Siglo de Torreón*, "Disminuirá el riesgo de invertir en México al entrar a la OCDE," 1 September 1992. See also commentary in *International Herald Tribune*, "Cut in Mexico's Debt Cost Is Likely if It Joins OECD Capital Markets," 7 June 1993.

32. Pierre Poret *The OECD Observer* no. 189, "Mexico and the OECD Codes of Liberalisation," August/September 1994.

33. *El Siglo de Torreón*, "Cambiar La Ley de Inversion Extranjera, Compromiso de Mexico con la OCDE," 6 April 1993.

Brazil and Indonesia) by warning against "watering down and disorganizing the group at the expense of the close co-operation among the 24 of us." At the same time, expansion offered an opportunity to increase influence both through the reforms demanded of applicant countries and through the greater reach that the organization would have based on larger membership.

When it came to selection of whom to favor for admission, it was clear that political ties and not only the assessment of policies mattered. European members emphasized the importance of including East European countries in transition while the United States, Canada, Australia, and Japan led the side calling for enlargement to broaden the geographic scope of the OECD. Colonial legacies also shaped positions as Spain and Portugal took more favorable positions toward including Latin American countries in OECD work and were advocates for Mexico. Ultimately Mexico would join one year earlier than the first of the Eastern European applicants (Czech Republic in 1995). The United States and Canada strongly pushed for Mexico while opposing a German request for rapid acceptance of the East European countries.[34] Pushed by political interest, the OECD Council took an unusual step to establish the Centre for Co-operation with European Economies in Transition to promote their ability to fulfill conditions necessary for accession to the OECD through assistance and advice.[35]

Upon entry to the OECD, Mexico left the Group of 77 coalition of developing countries that coordinate policies in the United Nations. Its having been a founding member and leader among the coalition, this represented a clear shift of Mexico's identity. Nevertheless, in many multilateral fora Mexico remains an advocate for the developing country perspective. The inauguration in 2006 of Angel Gurria as the first OECD Secretary General from a developing country put a spotlight on Mexico's ascendance to the pinnacle of international society and the place of the OECD as a global institution.

5.5.2   Korea

Korea's accession to the OECD has been blamed by some in Korea for rushing its liberalization of capital flows and setting the stage for its descent into financial crisis and IMF bailout one year after joining the organization.[36]

---

34. *The Financial Times*, "OECD to Open Its Doors to Mexico," 4 Jun 1993.

35. Statement of Chair of working group of Council cited in (Carroll and Kellow, 2011, p. 159).

36. This is widely noted in media commentary in Korea, and also a point in scholarly research (e.g., Lee, 2000; Kalinowski and Cho, 2009).

Fierce criticism in parliament called for government officials to testify on why financial liberalization was so mismanaged. The causes of Korea's crisis are too complex to attribute to one source, and such an explanation lies beyond the scope of this paper. In many ways the problem is that Korea tried to partially implement capital liberalization, while not implementing the appropriate supervisory structures to regulate against risk. Unlike for Mexico, which negotiated to join the OECD largely as a backup to NAFTA, for Korea this would be the first major liberalizing commitment.

Korea first expressed interest in OECD membership under the military rule of President Chun Doo-hwan in 1983, when it was at the start of its remarkable economic growth miracle. The leading conservative daily reported the president saying that in order for South Korea to be treated as a developed country, one possible way would be to join the OECD, a group of countries already labeled as such.[37] The repeated theme was that "challenging" itself through OECD membership would be a way to speed up Korea's economic progress. At the same time, critical commentary warned against expensive dues and costly liberalization.[38] After a year of preliminary investigation into what membership would entail, Shin Myoung-ho, who was then serving as the counselor to the Korean Embassy in Paris, met with OECD Secretary General Jean-Claude Paye. He was told that Korea was unlikely to be accepted, with an explanation that "the OECD was an exclusive club not one that accepted all who want to join and that the members did not want new members since they already felt there were too many and it was not efficient for dialogue. So he told me no."[39] Korea shelved the idea, without launching a formal application process. As with a social club, the informal process dictates that countries are invited to apply, and so this exchange set aside Korea's potential membership for the next decade.

Changes at the OECD signaled that Korea would now be treated as a serious candidate for membership. From 1990, as the collapse of communist regimes foreshadowed the end of the Cold War, the OECD began outreach to both the East European economies in transition and other "dynamic nonmembers," including Korea. This outreach encouraged their participation in OECD committees and initiated a dialogue toward their eventual membership. The eagerness of European members to welcome the transition economies of Eastern Europe and the pushback from other members

37. *Chosun Ilbo*, January 21, 1983.
38. *Chosun Ilbo*, January 23, 1983.
39. Interview by author, Seoul Korea, 10 July 2013.

wanting broader geographic scope pushed forward both Mexico and Korea as prime candidates for the OECD (Carroll and Kellow, 2011, p. 96). Korea had already started on the path to becoming a liberal market democracy, with its first democratic elections in 1987 and its decision to accept IMF Article 8 in 1989. In its 1991 five-year plan, the Korean government outlined a schedule to join the OECD by 1996.[40]

Presidential leadership advanced Korea's bid for membership in the OECD in 1992. As a former activist for democracy under authoritarian rule and the first civilian to be elected, Kim Young-sam consolidated the democratization process that had begun in 1987. He advocated a *"segyehwa"* policy for the globalization of Korea, in terms of both society and economy. Joining the liberal democratic club of advanced countries to guide international economic cooperation formed one concrete target within this overall program, calling on Korea to undertake liberal economic and political reforms in an outward-looking process. Kim Young-sam included a pledge to seek OECD membership as part of his election platform in his successful bid for the presidency in 1992. Lee (2000, p. 125) writes that "Kim expected that accession to the OECD could elevate the nation's status in the international community while also increasing his own political popularity." Choi Byung-il, the president of the Korea Economic Research Institute, also stated that it was a political decision to apply: "President Kim Young-sam had strong motivation to globalize Korea, using the phrase 'segyehwa' as the Korean language word for globalization. Presidential power at that time was very strong. He may have believed that if during his tenure Korea could join OECD it would make for better society. Some thought that if Korea joined, the code of conduct and information sharing would help lift up the management skills for Korean business."[41]

Within Korea the question of membership was fiercely debated and challenged by the opposition party.[42] The government undertook a proactive effort through creating pamphlets about OECD membership to distribute widely, not only to politicians and scholars but also, through broader outlets, to the public. Shin Myoung-ho, who would play a key role in negotiations for Korea to join the OECD in his role as Deputy Minister of International Finance, stated:

40. *Asian Wall Street Journal*, "South Korea: OECD Application," 17 October 1991.
41. Interview by author, Seoul, Korea, 4 July 2013.
42. *Kyunghang Shinmun*, 16 March 1995.

We had to educate on why [we] need to join [the] OECD. We said that now is the time for us to have rules and regulations so as to be a really developed country, and so we must learn and get information. We argued that the easy way to learn would be to join the OECD where information exchange and discussion would help us. We say now is the right time and that we are not taking on excessive liberalization and are doing what is within our competence. We also held seminars and summoned groups to come for meetings so we could explain banking policies.[43]

The government sales pitch for joining the OECD included, in addition to the above-mentioned opportunity to learn from advanced countries, the concrete benefits for businesses from improved international credibility and lower interest rates on loans (Lee, 2000, p. 126). The influential chaebol sought to benefit from greater access to capital from abroad and favored the introduction of competition to strengthen the domestic financial industry.

This case represents a clear example of demands for substantial reforms as condition of membership. Between June 1993, when the OECD agreed to negotiate toward Korean membership, and the formal application in 1995 and approval in 1996, the government engaged in multiple rounds of talks at the OECD. Although Korea had opened the capital account, the governments of the OECD member states were clear that further financial reforms would be necessary to meet OECD standards prior to accession (Carroll and Kellow, 2011, p. 152). Typical are the comment by U.S. ambassador to the OECD, David Aaron, in October 1994: "OECD membership is not the beginning point of the liberalization process, it really has to be seen as something near the climax of that process."[44]

Demands made on Korea included raising the foreign investment ceiling and ending foreign bank restrictions, allowing full currency convertibility, lifting capital controls on large Korean companies, relaxing rules on mergers and acquisitions, trade liberalization, and labor law revisions. In each of these areas, particular OECD members pushed hard for Korean reforms, using the OECD accession process as a form of leverage. The strong political backing in Korea to gain OECD membership created a window of opportunity for outside pressure. Making reforms in the context of OECD accession was more palatable in Korea than doing so under U.S. demands, and certainly Japan

---

43. Interview by author, Seoul Korea, 10 July 2013.

44. David Brunnstrom, "Seoul Must Speed Liberalization for OECD Place." Reuters News, 21 October 1991.

could not have requested reforms outside of a multilateral venue, given the tense bilateral political relationship.

For joining the OECD, the biggest challenge for Korea would be liberalization of the financial sector—the won was not fully convertible and restrictive market regulations prohibited foreign takeover and limited equity holdings. Choi described the changes: "the government completely controlled the financial sector such that in truth there were no 'private' banks. The OECD membership would bring a sea change."[45] Although the changes of policies were large relative to the closed financial markets in place in Korea, the government limited the scope and pace of liberalization. When the Korean government brought its financial liberalization plan to the OECD for negotiations, days of negotiations ultimately led members to accept its plan for sequencing the reforms according to its own gradual plan.[46] The government favored liberalizing short-term capital inflows first while maintaining controls on long-term investment (e.g., strict limits on foreign ownership of Korean companies), and refused to open bond market participation to foreigners. The rationale was that the government could more readily restrain chaebol through restrictions on long-term investment and needed to play "traffic cop," allocating funding among the small group of large firms to avoid market distortions. Supervision of the banking industry was supposed to help manage influx of short-term capital, and allowing liberalization here for financing trade and bank transactions promised immediate gains to boost the economy. Korea's large conglomerates stood to benefit from increased access to capital, while restricting long-term capital flows reflected the old, developmental state bias against foreign direct investment (Kalinowski and Cho, 2009, p. 225). Later, critics would cite this as the mistake that weakened the Korean financial system, given that the supervision of banking remained inadequate. Failures of the newly established merchant banks would form the onset of the financial crisis in 1997, and large short-term debt made the country vulnerable when foreign creditors lost confidence and decided to withdraw funds. Yet at the time, commentary in the Western media focused on how Korea had not gone far enough. According to the *Financial Times*, "Korea accepted only 65% of the OECD codes on financial liberalisation against an 89% acceptance rate by the average OECD member."[47] Critics emphasized the importance of the

45. Choi Byung-il, Interview by author, Seoul Korea, 4 July 2013.
46. Shin Myoung-ho, Interview by author, Seoul Korea, 10 July 2013.
47. *Financial Times*, 14 October 1996, "South Korea Braces for Restructuring."

pledge by Korea that it would continue its liberalization reforms in the coming years.

In an example of the shifting benchmark for membership, Korea faced demands on labor law policies. European members were critical of the restrictions limiting the number of unions in a firm, barring third-party arbitration of labor disputes, and the ongoing arrests of labor activists. In response to the demand for assurance that it complied with labor laws deemed essential by OECD members (although none were listed as criteria in OECD agreements), the Korean government formed a labor law committee to draft the outline of changes. When the Korean government was late in its proposal for labor policy reforms, the OECD's governing Council delayed its final decision meeting on Korean membership, thus holding the issue as a breaking point for the conclusion of the accession deal.[48] Ultimately, members decided to accept a letter of assurance from the Korean government that it would reform its laws so as to follow the core labor standards of the International Labour Organization (ILO).[49]

Although much of the draw of membership is aspirational—to follow the successful example of members and learn from their policies—Korea also faced a counterexample from the Mexican experience. At the height of Korean efforts to liberalize its financial policies for OECD membership, the most recent member, Mexico, was undergoing a financial crisis that would require massive bailout by the United States, to underwrite the value of the peso as currency flight threatened to erode the last of the country's foreign reserves. Cautious voices within Korea pointed to the Mexican example as they urged that Korea should wait to undertake reforms. Yet President Kim was undeterred in his push for joining the OECD, although the application was delayed by a few months as Korea negotiated over the need to follow its gradual plan for liberalization.

Once the OECD accepted the Korean terms, the membership question had to go before the Korean Parliament, where it faced considerable debate. Opposition ranged from those who favored accession, but sought further delay to lengthen the transition for slower liberalization process, to those who strictly opposed accession. Financial firms whose interests were directly threatened had formed a lobbying coalition. Many leading scholars in Korea also voiced opposition. Several ruling party member legislators joined the opposition

48. *Financial Times*, "Labour Law Threat to Korean OECD Bid," 10 October 1996.
49. *Financial Times*, "South Korea Braces for Restructuring," 14 October 1996.

parties with criticism that hurrying into the OECD could bring in excessive financial inflows that would make Korea vulnerable to a crisis similar to the peso crisis experienced by Mexico. For example, one member of the ruling party, Park Myung-hwan, said, "The price we will have to pay by entering the OECD is too great in consideration of our lack of preparation."[50] Ultimately, the government proposal was ratified in November 1996 with a vote of 159 in favor and 101 against.[51] Korea would become the twenty-ninth member of the OECD the next month.

In light of the subsequent financial crisis, many came to regret the price paid to join the OECD. Both the media and scholars blamed the Kim government for having rushed into the organization and undertaken reforms against the economic interests of Korea (Lee, 2000). Nevertheless, even for critics who see the reforms undertaken in the early 1990s as faulty, withdrawal from the OECD is not raised as a serious proposal. Choi noted that when the 2008 financial crisis led him to advocate for imposition of short-term capital controls, "the government officials would say no, giving as the reason the OECD commitments. Bureaucrats think of the OECD as setting a global standard that we must abide by. As if we need to be good students! Korea is obsessed with country ranking and the comparison of countries in the OECD is taken very seriously. In the 2008 crisis, I argued that there was reasonable necessity to impose restrictions on short-term flows, but their final defense was always the commitment to the OECD."[52] For better or worse, Korean leaders are too proud of OECD membership to consider withdrawal or rejection of its principles.

5.5.3   Eastern Europe

The expansion beyond Europe occurred against the backdrop of strong pressure to include new European members. From 1989, Germany and other European members of the OECD called for early entry of East European members; non-European members of the OECD pushed forward their own candidates outside of Europe. This regional balancing was also constrained by the conditions of alignment, democracy, and economic reforms rather than

---

50. Agence France-Presse, "South Korea's Ruling Party Faces Mounting Opposition to OECD Membership," 1 October 1996.

51. Agence France-Presse, "South Korean Parliament Ratifies Controversial OECD Entry," 26 November 1996.

52. Choi Byung-il, interview by author, Seoul, Korea, 4 July 2013.

geography alone. Clearly it was only the end of the Cold War and the move toward market economic policies and democratic reforms that set the stage for East European countries to join the OECD. This geopolitical shift shaped both the demand to join by East European governments and the willingness to accept them by the OECD members.

The first successful East European country to join the OECD was the Czech Republic. In January 1990, with the Cold War drawing to a close, the government of Czechoslovakia expressed interest in joining the OECD.[53] As the Soviet Union itself sought closer dialogue with the OECD, it opened the door for Czechoslovakia to directly seek membership in an early courtship with Europe. The 1993 split that formed the Czech Republic and Slovakia was successfully managed, and stable macroeconomic performance raised expectations for the Czech Republic's joining early. The government oversaw major reforms for privatization and reduction of state subsidies and price controls as part of the transition to a market economy, and moved forward on trade and investment liberalization. With the establishment of a convertible currency in October 1995, the government had met the demands from the OECD and became an OECD member in December that year. Yet many areas of reform remained unfinished, with concerns voiced about the expected capital inflows causing instability when financial reforms, price liberalization, and privatization remained incomplete.[54] As with the Czech Republic, the entry of Poland and Hungary in 1996 followed substantial reforms that represented a down payment on their transition to a market economy.

The U.S. Minister-Counselor for Economic Affairs to the OECD from 1992 to 1996, William Weingarten, said—regarding enlargement to include the Czech Republic, Poland, and Hungary—that the countries wanted "some form of link with the West," and the OECD played this role; "They basically asked to be tutored, and we were happy to do it."[55] He also acknowledged that this process required willingness to bend the rules to let countries in so that they could be guided through an ongoing transition process, with reviews to assess shortfalls.

53. David Marsh and Strasbourg Bonn, "Czechoslovakia Asks to Join OECD," *Financial Times* 18 January 1990.

54. Kevin Done, "Czech Economic Achievements Rewarded," *Financial Times*, 22 November 1995.

55. Association for Diplomatic Studies and Training, Oral History Project interview of William Weingarten. Available at https://adst.org/OH%20TOCs/Weingarten,%20William %20A.toc.pdf. Accessed May 12 2014.

Notably, EU enlargement and OECD enlargement have not followed a fixed pattern. The statistical analysis showed significant negative association between EU membership and OECD membership. For countries like the Czech Republic, Poland, and Hungary, entry to the OECD preceded entry to the EU. Other countries, such as Slovenia and Estonia, joined the EU before they joined the OECD. Finally, five of the 28 EU members are not members of the OECD.[56] Poast and Urpelainen (2013) find that new democracies often form new organizations rather than join existing ones as they cannot yet meet entry requirements for the best clubs, and so must seek other ways to lock in reforms and signal quality. This argument applies to circumstances of the new democratic regimes of Eastern Europe, but we also observe eagerness on the part of OECD members to support the democratization of Eastern Europe through encouraging their entry into the OECD and accepting incomplete reforms as good enough.

The Eastern European enlargement followed the shift of geopolitical alignment that was paired with economic and democratic reform. This further highlights the challenge to disentangle which aspect was most important for the entry to the OECD. Rather than making causal arguments about any variable as an explanation of membership, the cases highlight how these variables were jointly assessed as part of a wide set of criteria for what constituted like-minded states.

5.6   Brazil as a Nonmember Partner

What goes into the decision process of states that represent plausible candidates for membership but have not joined? This section will examine the case of Brazil, which stands out as a nonmember with strong potential to join. It is one of the states that has been highly engaged with the OECD, as can be seen by its involvement in OECD committees (Figure 5.6). This section will consider why Brazil has been late to show interest in membership, only to rapidly jump-start talks for accession since 2017.

The OECD Council of Ministers in 2007 named Brazil, along with China, India, Indonesia, and South Africa, as a partner for enhanced engagement, with a view toward membership. The enhanced engagement process was launched as part of the OECD strategy to become a more global institution through expanding membership and outreach to nonmembers. The key partners relationship represents an invitation to engage with possibility of

56. These are Bulgaria, Croatia, Cyprus, Malta, and Romania.

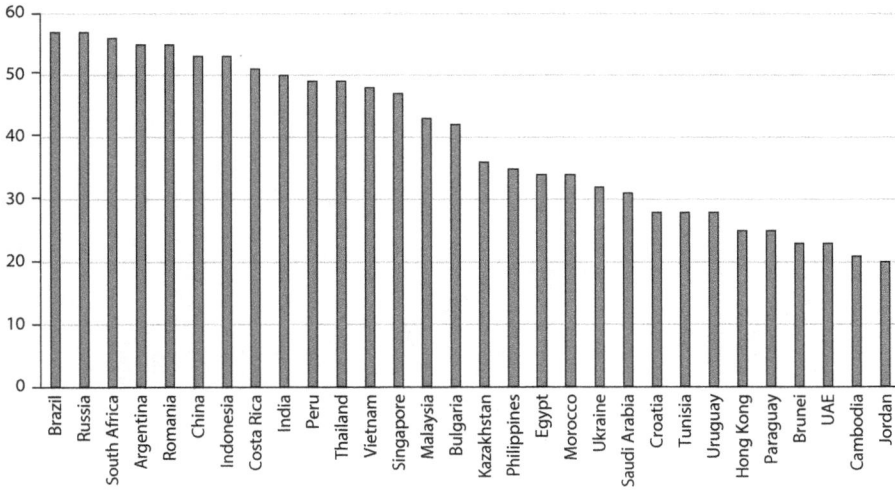

FIGURE 5.6. *Participation in OECD committees by nonmembers*: Numbers reflect partnership in OECD bodies, including committees, subcommittees, and working groups as of September 2020, as reported in data given to author from the OECD Secretariat. This figure is inclusive of all forms of engagement in the body, whether in associate, participant, or invitee status.

accession—at the time, the common view was that the OECD membership would take a positive position toward their application for membership. As the share of the global economy held by OECD members declined with the rise of emerging markets, the organization felt the threat of becoming marginalized. This prompted strategic planning to expand its outreach to nonmembers. The five partners for "enhanced engagement" have been encouraged to participate in OECD activities. The OECD Convention calls for members to contribute to economic expansion in member and nonmember countries and provides for inviting nonmember governments to participate in the organization.

Although nonmembers lack decision-making power and are not obligated to pay dues, they have several ways to access policy information and influence debate over standards. Many OECD activities are open to nonmembers, including full participation in OECD committees on the basis of invitation and approval of the members and attendance in OECD Ministerial Council meetings. Some voluntarily adhere to OECD instruments and participate in regular economic surveys.[57] In the year 2014, prior to its government's

57. See "OECD Global Relations: Engaging with Nonmember Economies" at www.oecd .org/globalrelations.

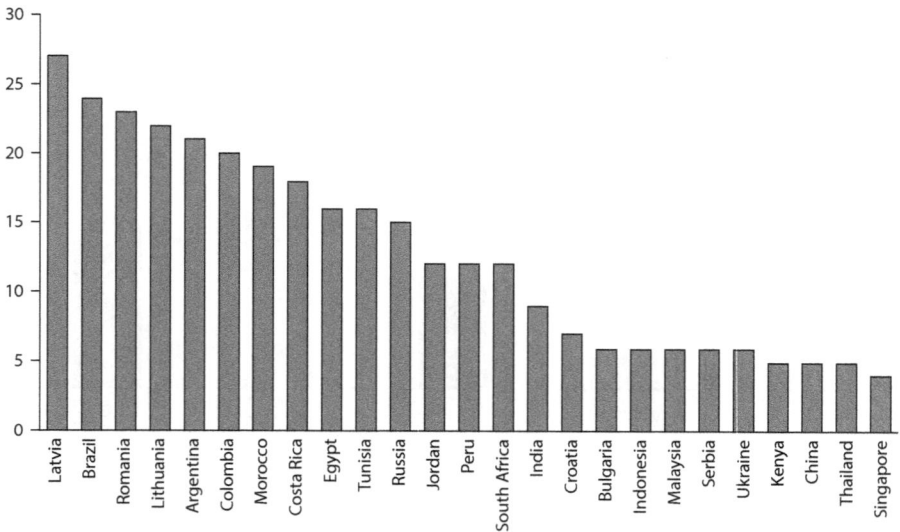

FIGURE 5.7. *Signature of OECD instruments by nonmembers*: The graph shows the instruments accepted as of 2014 as reported in data given to author from the OECD Secretariat.

request to join the OECD, Brazil was among the top nonmember countries to have ratified OECD instruments, with a level that was comparable to that of Latvia, Lithuania, Colombia, and Costa Rica—all governments in the accession process that would go on to become members before Brazil (Figure 5.7).

Brazil began active engagement with OECD committees as a nonmember in 1996 when it joined the steel committee, and it quickly expanded involvement the next year to participate in leading committees, including those for trade and investment, and the competition policy committee. It has accepted key OECD instruments, including the OECD Anti-Bribery Convention. Since 2001, the OECD has routinely completed economic surveys of Brazil involving extensive information exchange between the government and the organization. Through a 2015 cooperation agreement, the government began an ongoing working party level coordination with the OECD for regular meetings between the OECD and Brazilian officials to address mutual priorities. Brazil now serves as an associate in the Governing Board of the OECD's initiative for education reform, the Programme for International Student Assessment (PISA). Its ministers frequently attend OECD Council of Minister summits.

Early Reluctance to Join

Yet despite engaging with the organization, Brazil showed little interest in seeking full membership. It would not be easy for Brazil to meet OECD standards for entry, but for many years the slow progress on this front was attributed to lack of desire to undertake the reforms for the sake of entering the organization (Woodward, 2012, p. 213). At a time when the OECD was expressing eagerness to expand and include BRICS for broader legitimacy, there could have been flexibility on accession standards to make it possible for Brazil to enter; the government already accepted many OECD instruments and shared its economic and social data for public reporting. Other governments had joined the OECD without full liberalization of capital and trade flows.

Following Mexico's accession to the OECD in 1994 could have triggered an application from Brazil. Yet the market-oriented centrist governance led by Fernando Cardoso from 1995 to 2002 never showed interest in membership in the OECD. Even as Brazil began to engage with OECD committees, the government of Cardoso eschewed seeking to join. The Cardoso government undertook many neoliberal reforms to bring Brazil into closer engagement with the world economy and consolidated democracy (Hammond and Filho, 2007). But Brazil was seeking its own direction, especially in foreign policy. The pursuit of autonomy without alignments remained the guiding priority of foreign policy for Cardoso, with leadership in the region anchored around Brazil's role in Mercosur (Vigevani, de Oliveira and Thompson, 2007). Association with its region was more important to Brazilian foreign policy in the 1990s than the possibility of association with the OECD.

More than inability to join, lack of interest in joining delayed Brazil's entering the OECD. The former Brazilian finance minister Rubens Ricupero said in comment for a Brazilian politics and economic site, "OECD membership would be the equivalent of political suicide. Most of the time, on all those issues, the positions assumed by Brazil are not only different from but often opposed to those of OECD member countries. Mexico opted to join the OECD in the euphoria following the celebration of the Free Trade Agreement with the US and Canada (NAFTA); today, the country is quite isolated and unremarkable in multilateral diplomacy forums."[58]

58. See John Fitzpatrick, "Brazil Would Commit Political Suicide by Joining the OECD, Says Ex-Finance Minister Rubens Ricupero," *PRlog*. http://www.prlog.org/10256031-brazil-would-commit-political-suicide-by-joining-the-oecd-says-exfinance-minister-rubens-ricupero.html. Quoted in Woodward (2012, p. 213)

States have many options for joining groups. A point of resistance to join-ing the OECD lies in the conflict between leadership of developing nations and OECD membership. One OECD official, asked about why the BRICS have not joined the OECD, said, "The emerging markets like China and Brazil want to engage with OECD but for the moment are not looking for member-ship. China joins discussion on SOE reform, but signing [an] instrument is too much for them. Brazil does sign many instruments and is already very closely engaged with the OECD. But until now they have considered membership impossible. For these countries as a leader [sic] of developing countries, they see the OECD as anathema. This is more about the image that is attached to the OECD than anything else."[59] Seiichirō Noboru, the former Japanese ambassador to the OECD who chaired the OECD working group that pro-duced the 2004 A Strategy for Enlargement and Outreach, commented in an interview that "there is an outdated notion among some countries that in order to maintain unity of the G77 they should not join the OECD, since it is regarded as [a] rich man's club and its activities could not be helpful. But that view is totally wrong and the OECD needs to counter it through out-reach efforts."[60] He continued, to note, "The G20 work is of more interest for Brazil and other emerging markets, and it does not cost as much. Joining the OECD has financial cost in terms of budget contribution and also requires that a country make its system open and transparent. Some countries are not quite ready for this. BRICS could gain a lot from joining the OECD." Others who work with the OECD concurred that Brazilians will often say it is about the G77 and they see a political cost to joining the OECD because it would be perceived as turning their back on the G77 in the same way that Mexico did when it joined the OECD.

Nothing in OECD procedures or norms would require members' leav-ing other organizations. Mexico and Korea both exited the G77 upon entry to the OECD, but Chile remained a G77 member after OECD accession. Many OECD members, including Mexico and the Republic of Korea (but not Chile), are also members of the G20. Thus there is not a *necessary* con-flict of membership for Brazil when considering its membership in the G77, G20, and OECD. Rather it is a relative choice about which grouping it values, based on both status of association and the cost benefit analysis of belonging to the organizations.

59. Interview by author, OECD Secretariat, 20 October 2014.
60. Telephone interview by author, 28 October 2014

For some countries, closer association with the United States and Europe attracts them into joining the OECD, but this same association repels others. The influence of countries like Brazil in multilateral diplomacy relies on their identification as leaders of developing market economies. In some cases, this has been deemed more important than trying to shape the determination of "best practices" and standards in the OECD or any positive benefit from association with wealthy democracies.

Brazil Applies for Membership

From May 2017, the attitude of Brazil toward the OECD began to shift, and the government requested to be considered for membership. Amidst the scandals engulfing the Rousseff presidency, leading figures in economic ministries and the private sector hoped to borrow some credibility in the eyes of investors through entry into the OECD, with its reputation for high standards.[61] Others also saw it as a political shift, whereby the government could distance itself from the predecessor regime's leftist policies that strongly identified Brazil as a leader of developing countries in world affairs.[62] After the brief caretaker regime of Michel Temer, the election of Jair Bolsonaro to serve as president from January 2019 further entrenched the shift to conservative economic and social policies. Successful pension reform and proposals to change fiscal policies and competition rules marked a fresh engagement with structural reform. Where many previous tax reform efforts failed, Brazil is moving toward a value-added tax system in accordance with OECD recommended practice. While leaders embraced the goals of market-based economic policies and anti-corruption efforts at home, OECD policy assessments continued to warn that the Brazilian policies to safeguard domestic markets with tariffs and other barriers hindered effective integration in the world economy.[63]

Since expressing interest in membership, Brazil has pushed forward rapidly to expand the number of instruments it will ratify, including the Codes of

61. "Brazil Seeks OECD Membership to Impress Investors," plus55 30 May 2017; Esmerk Latin American News, "Brazil: Country Wants to Join OECD's Free Movement of Capitals Code," 23 May 2017.

62. Economist Intelligence Unit, "Brazil Economy: Quick View—Brazil applies for OECD membership," 5 June 2017.

63. See OECD, 28 February 2018 "Further Reforms to Spur Trade and Investment Key for Brazil's Inclusive Growth." Available at http://www.oecd.org/brazil/further-reforms-to-spur-trade-and-investment-key-for-brazil-s-inclusive-growth.htm.

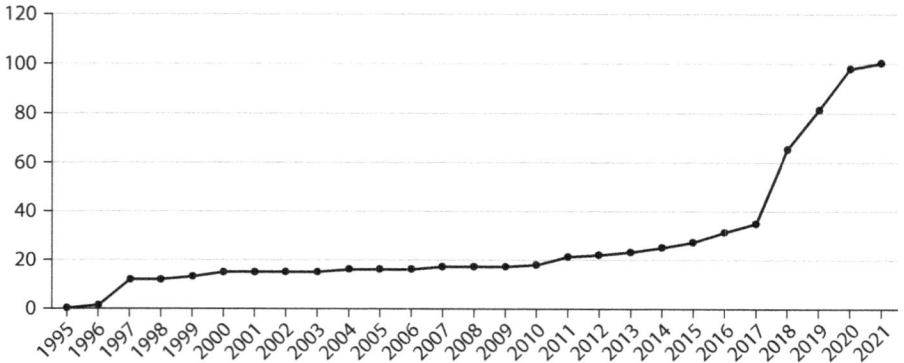

FIGURE 5.8. *Signature of OECD instruments by Brazil*: The figure shows the cumulative number of OECD instruments adhered to by Brazil, with the noticeable uptick from 2017 when the government requested membership.

Liberalisation of Capital Movements and Current Invisible Operations (see Figure 5.8). The government has established high-level coordination for a whole government approach, led by an interministerial council and a parliamentary "friends of the OECD" group working to harmonize laws and guidelines. The ambassador to the OECD from Portugal, Bernardo Lucena, remarked that "as a prospective candidate to full membership, Brazil has shown that the political will is real and ambitious."[64]

The changed approach toward the OECD accompanied a broader reorientation of foreign policy. For decades, Brazil had distanced itself from the United States to preserve its own autonomy as a regional leader of and advocate for developing country economic policies. Bolsonaro brought a sharp reversal with his open admiration for Donald Trump. His foreign minister for his first years in office, Ernesto Araujo, was known for controversial positions both referring to Trump as "the saviour of the west" and condemning Chinese leaders.[65] Drawing closer to Trump with a quickly convened summit meeting in which he highlighted the effort to join the OECD, Bolsonaro broadcast the departure from the past emphasis of Brazilian leaders on the

64. OECD, "Active with Brazil," 17 January 2021. Available at https://issuu.com/oecd .publishing/docs/active_with_brazil_2020__en_web-1a_ .

65. "Brazil's Foreign Minister, Who Bashed China and Praised Trump, Resigns," *The Guardian*, 29 March 2021.

Group of 77 and BRICS.[66] In addition to embracing the United States, Brazil's application to join the OECD has taken away from its role as leader of the developing nations. At their summit meeting, the joint leaders' press release linked the two points: "President Trump noted his support for Brazil initiating the accession procedure to become a full member of the OECD. Commensurate with its status as a global leader, President Bolsonaro agreed that Brazil will begin to forgo special and differential treatment in WTO negotiations, in line with the U.S. proposal."[67] This concession by Brazil would end flexibilities allowed to developing nations when they implement trade agreements, which represented a lightning rod issue in the Trump administration trade agenda that has featured prominently in the U.S.-China trade war, as China defends its developing country status (as do India, South Africa, and many others). Bolsonaro signaled clearly that he was taking the U.S. side on the matter, against the opposition from other developing countries. A leading Brazilian newspaper reported the Trump endorsement of Brazil's OECD candidacy as a "win" for Bolsonaro, noting that "it was the primary goal of Bolsonaro's first visit to the United States as president. The Brazilian government sees OECD membership as a sort of 'seal of approval' of its macroeconomic policies."[68] After years of strained ties, overcoming U.S. resistance was seen as critical to Brazil's chance of joining.[69] News that the United States had indicated to senior OECD officials that it supported priority to Brazil over Argentina was heralded as if it were a soccer victory: "Washington defends that Brazil occupy the spot that belonged to Argentina in the queue of candidates for a place in the so-called club of rich countries."[70] Bolsonaro proclaimed that not only had he won American support, but also "we are overcoming resistance and showing that Brazil is a viable country. . . . And the advantages for

66. Rathbone, John Paul, and Andres Schipani. "Brazil's 'Tropical Trump' Seeks to Reset Ties with White House Visit," *The Financial Times,* 18 March 2019.

67. "Joint Statement by President Trump and President Jair Messias Bolsonaro of Brazil," 19 March 2019. https://www.govinfo.gov/content/pkg/DCPD-201900159/pdf/DCPD -201900159.pdf. Accessed 24 February 2023.

68. Dias, Marina. 2019. "After Bolsonaro's Flattery and Concessions, Trump Announces Support to Brazil Joining OECD," translated by Natasha Madov. *Folha de Sao Paulo.* https:// www1.folha.uol.com.br/internacional/en/world/2019/03/after-bolsonaros-flattery-and-conce ssions-trump-announces-support-to-brazil-joining-oecd.shtml. Accessed 17 April 2020.

69. Schipani, Andres, and James Politi. 2019. "Brazil and US Hit Restart Button on Trade Relations," *The Financial Times,* 14 May 2019.

70. "Brazil: Bolsonaro Celebrates US Support of Bid to Join OECD." *Folha de Sao Paulo,* 15 Jan 2020 'translation by BBC Monitoring Americas.'

Brazil are many, it is the equivalent of our country entering the first division" (ibid.).

The Trump administration increased U.S. cooperation with Brazil more broadly. In a significant step, in July 2019, the Trump administration designated Brazil a Major Non-NATO Ally, which made it only the second country after Argentina from Latin American nations to receive this status, alongside other major allies like Australia, Japan, Korea, and Israel.[71] The designation allows U.S. funding for joint research and development and production of U.S. defense equipment, exemption from some arms export control provisions, along with other forms of security cooperation. Trump even referred to the prospect of Brazil's joining NATO, which others later qualified as a possibility for it to become a NATO partner country, as distinct from alliance member. Many recognize the outreach to Brazil as part of a strategy to improve ties during a period of growing rivalry with China for influence. As China has risen to be the top trade partner of Brazil and many other countries in Latin America, it has also expanded political influence. Against this backdrop, Daniel Runde, a former official of the U.S. Agency for International Development, notes that "OECD membership would strengthen the Brazilian-U.S. bilateral relationship, countering China's increasing presence in the Western Hemisphere."[72]

In an odd juxtaposition, the populist and bombastic leadership of Bolsonaro and Araujo also amplified the rhetoric about Brazil's joining the OECD, a technocratic organization dedicated to regulation of the global economy. In a speech about OECD cooperation on 26 October 2020, Araujo extolled the value of joining for Brazil—"We are convinced that full membership will be relevant to the dynamics of reforms by intensifying Brazil's integration in the international economy, as well as the adoption of higher regulatory standards to the benefit of our economic ties with the member countries"—and went on to urge the OECD—"We are convinced that the OECD shall also have much to gain from Brazil's full membership, which would allow for the reinforcement and broadening of the OECD range of standards and practices and for the strengthening of its presence in other

71. "Designation of the Federative Republic of Brazil as a Major Non-NATO Ally," 31 July 2019. https://www.federalregister.gov/documents/2019/08/19/2019-17998/designation-of-the-federative-republic-of-brazil-as-a-major-non-nato-ally. Accessed 24 February 2023.

72. Daniel F. Runde, "Brazil's OECD candidacy is best chance for reform," *The Hill*, October 21, 2020.

regions, especially in our region. Also, for the maintenance of the fundamental values of the OECD, around freedom and democracy."[73] The government rapidly increased its participation in OECD bodies and accepted additional OECD instruments to prepare its candidacy. Brazilian outlets reported on the potential creditor rewards from association with the OECD, with one quoting Brazil's Central Bank president Ilan Goldfajn having said that "OECD membership would improve Brazil's international image—and could even lead to the reduction of interest rates for loans contracted by the federal administration."[74] Speaking in October 2020, the Brazilian Finance Minister Paulo Guedes declared, "We are about to join the OECD. We are fulfilling two thirds of what the requirements are, and probably in one year we should be joining," and listed the advances in transparency, regulatory, anti-corruption, and procurement protocols as evidence of meeting expectations for membership.[75] Progress in 2021 to complete domestic reforms consolidating autonomy for the central bank represented another important benchmark in harmonizing policies consistent with OECD country practices.

The embrace of the OECD by a populist leader can also be seen as part of a legitimation strategy. After years in which parties on the left sought legitimacy as leaders of the South, Bolsonaro could rebel by pushing Brazil into the camp of the North.[76] According to Wajner (2022), populist leaders that rally against domestic elites can find that the international stage offers sources of legitimation back home. This was certainly a goal for Bolsonaro in his relationship with Trump, and may have been a part of the application to join the OECD. Trying to join a group of democracies could serve as a response to critics of his authoritarian tendencies.

73. Speech text available at https://www.gov.br/mre/en/content-centers/speeches-articles-and-interviews/minister-of-foreign-affairs/speeches/interventions-by-minister-ernesto-araujo-at-the-releasing-ceremony-of-oecd-studies-201cgoing-digital-in-brazil201d-and-201coecd-telecommunication-and-broadcasting-review-of-brazil-2020201d. Accessed 17 March 2021.

74. The Brazilian Report, 2018, "What Would Joining the OECD Mean to Brazil?" https://brazilian.report/business/2018/03/01/joining-oecd-mean-brazil/. Accessed 17 April 2020.

75. Jamie McGeever, "Brazil to Join OECD in a Year, Plans 'Digital Bank' IPO: Economy Minister," Reuters, 20 October 2020. Available at https://www.reuters.com/article/us-brazil-economy-guedes/brazil-to-join-oecd-in-a-year-plans-digital-bank-ipo-economy-minister-idUSKBN2751W3. Accessed 15 March 2021.

76. The OECD has a global reach that defies geographic location. It now cuts across the cleavages of north versus south in its membership, but retains the core identity associated with its origin as an IGO of the northern countries in the Western alliance.

The economic groups in Brazil that stand to benefit from membership also recognize the need for a wide campaign to win entry into the club. In the lead-up to the 2018 presidential election, Brazil's National Confederation of Industry urged election candidates, "it is important that presidential nominees express their interest in Brazil's accession to the OECD," and informed them of the broader sets of expectations. The report noted, "To be accepted as a member of the organization, Brazil will have to negotiate the terms of its entry with its current members, which may impose conditionalities/requirements to accept it as a member of the club. These requirements may also include reforms in areas not regulated by the normative instruments of the OECD. . . . During the accession period, a country applying for membership of the OECD must show that it shares the world view of its peers. It is therefore during this period that a prospective member must promote the most relevant reforms to conform to the normative framework of the organization."[77] Far from single-issue lobbying, domestic actors must treat accession as a package of reforms they will support.

Nevertheless, not everyone is positive toward Brazil's accession, and opposition from any member could hold up entry, given the requirement for unanimous approval. This uncertainty offers leverage to demand reforms from Brazil. Although the terms for membership are vague, the process has grown increasingly strict, as each major OECD committee conducts a review of policy adherence to OECD instruments. This reaches well beyond the core codes of liberalization.

Concerns about whether Brazil is like-minded arise when considering new policy dimensions. Stewardship of the environment is an increasingly high priority to OECD members. When major burning of the Amazon forests sparked outrage at Brazil's government, many connected it to the OECD bid. Gabriel Petrus, executive director of the International Chamber of Commerce in Brazil, raised the alarm that criticism of deforestation could block OECD membership, and he urged the Brazilian minister of environment to take action to protect forests and show accommodation when meeting with the OECD Environment Policy Committee.[78] The committee postponed Brazil's

77. National Confederation of Industry, "Brazil on the OECD: A Natural Path to Follow," Proposals from Industry for the 2018 election (Brasilia, 2018), p. 15.

78. Boadle, Anthony. "Amazon Fires Could Burn Brazil's Bid to Join OECD Rich Nations Club." Reuters, 23 Aug 2019. Available at https://www.reuters.com/article/us-brazil

participatory status instead. Critical letters from NGO groups continue to weigh against Brazil, with direct lobbying of the OECD Environment Policy Committee not to relent.[79] A group of U.S. senators wrote in a letter to President Biden that failure by the Brazilian government to counter deforestation would affect their willingness to support Brazil's accession to the OECD.[80] Likewise, concerns about human rights violations and intervention in the federal police to prevent a bribery investigation led to remarks implying that the news could harm Brazil's standing as an OECD candidate. Drago Kos, chairman of the OECD working group on bribery, expressed alarm over accusations made by a Justice Minister who resigned to protest Bolsonaro's firing of the federal police chief. Earlier in 2019, an OECD press release from the working group had publicly admonished the Brazilian government that as a founding party of the 1997 Anti-Bribery Convention it should strengthen, not weaken, its framework to combat foreign bribery and corruption. Kos issued a warning: "Our member states are very, very rigorous when discussing accession to the OECD, so I'm hopeful that Brazil will use this as an opportunity. But if this goes otherwise, our member states will know how to deal with it. . . . We have to be absolutely sure that Brazil is not going backward."[81] This brought the unusual step of establishing a special anti-corruption monitoring group from the OECD within Brazil. On the economic front, transfer pricing rules for tax policies stand out as an area that has received high-profile attention by OECD officials in comments about changes Brazil must undertake to complete accession.[82]

-environment-wildfires-oecd/vamazon-fires-could-burn-brazils-bid-to-join-oecd-rich-nations-club-idUSKCN1VD2A9. Accessed 7 July 2020.

79. Luciana Téllez Chavéz, "Attempt to Greenwash Bolsonaro's Environmental Record Backfires at OECD," Human Rights Watch, 11 February 2021. Available at https://www.hrw.org/news/2021/02/11/attempt-greenwash-bolsonaros-environmental-record-backfires-oecd. Accessed 15 March 2021.

80. David Biller and Joshua Goodman, "Senate Democrats Urge Biden to Condition Aid to Brazil," AP News, 16 April 2021. Available at https://apnews.com/article/joe-biden-donald-trump-brazil-deforestation-climate-b25195150ea4c20343e4c61581341624.

81. Adghirni, Samy. "Brazil's OECD Bid under Scrutiny after Bolsonaro Allegations," Bloomberg, 6 May 2020. https://www.bloomberg.com/news/articles/2020-05-06/brazil-s-oecd-bid-under-scrutiny-after-bolsonaro-allegations. Accessed 23 June 2020.

82. OECD, "Launch of the Transfer Pricing Work Programme." Available at http://www.oecd.org/fr/fiscalite/prix-de-transfert/launch-of-transfer-pricing-work-programme-brazil-2018.htm. Accessed 27 May 2020.

Another obstacle to Brazil lies in the complex bargaining among members over multiple candidates for enlargement. The current list of countries that have expressed interest in joining includes Argentina, Bulgaria, Croatia, Peru, and Romania. Where trade issues or legislative policies often benefit from logrolling to create package deals, IGO enlargement in the EU or OECD has often occurred through joint entry by countries that together can appeal to enough countries for consensus support to emerge. As members hold different priorities for economic and geopolitical interests and regional balance when considering applicants, approval of one at a time is less likely to achieve the winning coalition. This is evident in the tendency to have waves of enlargement. Hence members must agree not only on Brazil but also on the combination of other countries that could enter together. In Latin America, Argentina requested to join in 2016, a year prior to Brazil. The EU would like more of its members to join the OECD with Romania, considered next in line. Japan hopes to see representation from Southeast Asia. Rather than wait for these other cases to get worked out, however, Brazil's government has been intent on continuing to deepen its involvement in OECD activities and reform of policies at home. As one of the five key partners selected by OECD members in 2007 for enhanced engagement, Brazil has the presumption of approval on its side now that it has decided it wants to join.

The shift from a leftist government to a conservative administration helped the Brazilian government embrace the economic reform policies consistent with joining the OECD as it began its pursuit of membership in 2017. But this change of orientation was not sufficient. Earlier governments, such as the long administration of Cardoso, had engaged in economic reforms and liberalization without pairing it with the goal of OECD membership. The change that emerged since 2017 has been the combination of conservative leadership open to economic reforms *and* willing to take sides within emerging geopolitical rivalries to join hands with the United States. In 2017, Brazil was ready to look toward the OECD for a new pathway to influence and leadership. Instead of trying to lead the developing world, Brazil would demonstrate that it was ready to enter the rich country club. The personal admiration of Donald Trump by Bolsonaro helped to cement closer ties between the countries. Nevertheless, the request from Brazil had preceded the election of Bolsonaro and the pursuit of membership by Brazil remains strong after the departure of Trump. One cannot ignore the importance of economic interests and personal politics, but they are also shaped by the underlying shift of attitudes toward foreign policy relations.

The case of Brazil illustrates that the effect of membership begins long before a state completes its formal entry into an organization. As part of trying to enhance its candidacy, Brazil has pushed forward a broad range of reforms to increase consistency of policies with the OECD instruments and the expectations of the members with whom it hopes to join as a peer. To the extent that such reforms at times occur through close engagement with OECD working groups and ongoing participation in its committees, the effect of the OECD on Brazil began even before it requested to join. The final benefit that awaits acceptance as a member lies in the status of being a member of this exclusive club.

5.7   Conclusion

The OECD serves as a clear example of selective membership, as one observes strong patterns of correlation in income, alliance, and democracy. This is an important caveat in light of the large number of political science studies that use OECD membership as the criterion for analyzing a subset of countries, without explicit attention to the determinants of OECD membership and potential biases or outliers that could arise in the research as a result of sample selection. Selection occurs through the attraction of like-minded states and screening for countries that favor economic cooperation. But the impact of the organization is not simply because states that have already made economic policy reforms choose to join. The chapter provides empirical evidence of how conditional membership brings policy change. Entrants make substantively important commitments to liberalize trade, finance, and investment policies during accession in order to achieve membership approval.

The OECD represents an unusual organization in its broad scope of policy mandate, accompanied by low levels of legalization with peer review as the primary form of enforcement after entry. Failed negotiations at the OECD for a multilateral investment regime in 1998 demonstrated that its powers are no greater than what members decide they support as best practice. Yet it has emerged as an effective organization—whether by increasing trade among members or by establishing common regulatory frameworks. The influence of the organization in the complex milieu of instititutions with a hand in guiding global governance, lies in its size and credibility—small enough to offer serious deliberations among members who often share similar preferences and can be trusted to move in the recommended policy direction. This has made the question of enlargement especially important.

From the perspective of institutional design, there are important implications and lessons from the OECD about discretionary accession. The rational design volume of *International Organization* (Koremenos, Lipson, and Snidal, 2001) raises the expectation for organizations to be inclusive or exclusive in membership based on the type of cooperation problem that countries face. Given the wide scope of issues addressed in the OECD, it defies such categories. It addresses multiple issues with very different types of cooperation problems. The vague formal rules and ad hoc practice applied in the accession process suggest that OECD members favor discretion about how inclusive or exclusive to be for any given period or applicant.

On the one hand, the membership remains a small set of 38 states with a club identity. On the other hand, the OECD has admitted developing countries and widened its geographic scope beyond the transatlantic partnership and allowed more heterogeneity of interests. As with any social club, it suits members to retain their own autonomy to define whom to admit. Thus even when the OECD attempted to clarify terms of membership, its guidelines were vague and the list of new applicants defied any template of membership criteria. The vague but selective accession process of the OECD conforms to the "discretionary rules" hypothesis. This club-style form of multilateral cooperation opens space for geopolitical discrimination.

The value of association with the West helps to explain why some countries seek membership and willingly undertake reforms during accession while others do not. OECD accession offered leverage for policy change in applicants who were motivated by a strong desire to join the organization for the sake of joining, above and beyond their expected gains from specific reforms. Although the countries examined in the case studies had all embarked on a turn toward liberalization of their economic policies and sought OECD membership as one tool to deepen those reforms, they made difficult concessions as part of accession. Japan gave up key instruments of industrial policy, while Korea undertook significant reform of its state-centered banking system. Even Mexico, which had largely completed its substantial economic liberalization as part of concluding NAFTA, found that OECD membership required additional steps. In a process similar to that described for EU enlargement by Schneider (2009), complex bargaining over interests led to different terms of accession. For Korea, those members engaged most closely in security cooperation (the United States and Japan) were strong advocates and accepted some reduction of liberalization even as more reluctant members in Europe added on new conditions such as labor law revisions. Through the changing demands of the members as well as the applicant use of reservations that excluded policy areas from liberalization, each case took on a different set of commitments. And yet the premise was that aspiring members would continue their reform process to reduce the reservations and bring themselves up to the OECD standards. In ways that parallel the experience of the GATT/WTO, the OECD has had geostrategic ties as the glue to motivate economic cooperation.

The odd case of Russia's application to join the OECD highlights some important points. The use of alliance ties to measure geopolitical alignment captures the most obvious and certain cases of inducing discrimination and favoring friends. But a broad scope of activity often necessitates looking beyond allies. In some cases this meant including non-allied but clearly aligned states like Switzerland and Israel. But for other cases, the selection of friendly states relies on more transitory indications of changing geopolitical orientation. Russia was never on track to become a NATO ally, but it has improved relations and different Russian leaders have tried to increase the association with Europe through applying to the OECD. In some periods, the OECD members flirted with the possibility that Russia would join during these moments of improved foreign policy relations. The flexibility of OECD accession rules meant that any country could potentially join if the members agreed. Any hopes that Russia might shift toward geopolitical alignment with the West, however, ended with the Russian invasion of Ukraine.

As a like-minded club, the OECD consists of countries that share values, whether those are achieved by liberal political institutions, economic policies, or commitment to the Western alliance. Rather than a rigid package, these criteria form a multidimensional space in which the members have discretion to prioritize one criterion over the other for a particular country or era. From the applicant side, the countries applied at a time when they wanted closer ties to the other members. They saw the benefits of membership in terms of both policy coordination and status. Similarity with current OECD members on the dimensions of political, economic, and geostrategic policies made these states seek membership where others would not. Ambitious political leaders latched onto OECD accession as a symbolic gesture to build support for their economic reform programs because they knew it held resonance within their domestic public. Even as opponents warned of the risks and disparaged the need to make concessions for vain efforts to gain status, leaders pushed through the necessary reforms and ratification to join.

At the same time, the case of Brazil illustrates how different alignment could dissuade a state from seeking membership even when it is proffered. The turnaround by Brazil to now seek entry offers a window into what conditions on the demand side within countries shape their motivation to join. The choice to join organizations reflects a broad association with a group of countries, and states choose carefully based on political relations. Functional demand for gains from cooperation are certainly important to members and applicants, but membership decisions go far beyond the issues at stake in the regulations of the regime.

6

Japan's Multilateral Diplomacy

THIS CHAPTER explores the experience of Japan from 1853, when it first opened to the West, through today, when it is a member of more than 80 international governmental organizations (IGOs). Tracing Japanese foreign policy through its approach to IGO membership choices highlights different ways in which geopolitical alignment shaped its decisions. Whether trying to win free of the unequal treaties during the Meiji period, or reentering international society after defeat in war, IGOs have played an important role in the interaction of Japan with the world. Foreign policy goals motivated Japan's membership decisions, and entry into organizations provided leverage to bring about domestic reforms.

In this chapter, I examine the hypothesis that geopolitics influences the choice by Japan to join international organizations. Through close focus on one country, I offer a broad view of like-minded foreign policy orientation to consider why Japan sought to pursue closer affinity with states. Japan offers a useful test case because it had so little connection with the outside world in 1848 when IGOs began to form, so one can evaluate the evolution of its foreign policy parallel to the growth of IGOs as a diplomatic tool. When first entering organizations in the late nineteenth century, Japan lacked alliances. It sought to build ties and establish sovereignty. In the early twentieth century, Japan formed an alliance with Britain, achieved great power status, and then chose alignment with Germany in a reversal of geopolitical alignment that impacted its participation in IGOs. Subsequently, the war reset Japan's position as an outsider, and we can observe how its new alliance with the United States shaped its desire and ability to enter organizations. Across these different periods, the chapter evaluates Japanese goals and the reforms it made in order to join IGOs. Examples of geopolitical discrimination and of favoring friends are evident as Japan joins organizations together with allies and without rigorous review of compliance.

Japan offers insights that can help us to understand a broader set of countries. Achieving independence and prosperity allowed Japan to consider joining many organizations. But it has also faced difficult times when leaders feared outside threats and economic decline. Japan is neither a hegemonic power nor is it tied to a strong regional organization. We can learn more from Japan about how typical states approach membership decisions than is possible from studying the United States or European states. Swings between periods of extreme national chauvinism and those with liberal internationalism arise over Japan's history as evidence of malleability, not cultural determinism. While this chapter provides a close-up view of Japan's experience, my goal is to test the general hypotheses about the geopolitical logic of membership in international organizations.

Unpacking the domestic decision-making process, I consider where the initiative to join organizations arises. The conventional view that institutions serve as a functional tool to promote cooperation within an issue area points to demand arising from interest groups connected to the issues that will be regulated by the organization. From this perspective, those who seek gains from free trade should advocate for membership in the trade regime. In contrast, when foreign policy and relations with other countries determine entry, the foreign ministry and political leadership may take on a more prominent role than would be otherwise expected. This chapter will examine case studies to assess whether domestic lobbying by interest groups and their supervising bureaucratic agency in the issue area or elite level leadership and foreign policy officials took the initiative to bring about Japan's entry into organizations. Where geopolitical goals favor entry, membership may also serve economic goals. But in some cases the geopolitical logic must offset resistance from interest groups. Here I examine the process by which discretionary rules soften the terms of entry and national interest tips the balance within domestic decision-making.

For the contemporary period of Japanese democracy, the chapter uses testimony in the Japanese legislature (called the Diet) as evidence to evaluate priorities of politicians as they consider whether to join. A functional approach to institutions suggests that Diet testimony would revolve largely around the nature of policy commitments and benefits from cooperation in the issue area of the institution. The relational approach of my theory expects significant attention to foreign policy and the membership composition of an organization. The split in foreign policy orientation across Japan's political parties appears in the debates, as the Liberal Democratic Party (LDP) favors closer ties with the United States to shore up the alliance, and opposition parties include some hostile to the alliance who warn against dependence on the United States. My theory would expect commentary to reflect these different views on the value of closer association with the United States within international organizations.

Research into Japanese foreign policy has long emphasized the role of foreign pressure. Membership in international organizations, however, highlights the earlier question of whether Japan chooses to generate this foreign pressure. By entering IGOs, the government triggers external monitoring and enforcement of policy changes. It can also negotiate the level of pressure when entry consists of partial reforms. As a great power that had joined the allied victors of WWI, Japan could join the ILO before offering recognition to unions. The GATT case offers evidence of the United States favoring friends as it sponsored Japan's membership without substantial liberalization of trade policies. Such examples are consistent with the argument that IGOs allow states to enter without prior enforcement of compliance.

The chapter also provides insight into outcomes that are not predicted by the theory. Geopolitical alignment is only one of many factors that shape entry decisions, and economic interests sometimes outweigh security considerations. The GATT example highlights how not all allies in the Western alliance were willing to give Japan favorable access. And while rivalry with China was a major reason for Japan to remain outside of the Asian Infrastructure Investment Bank (AIIB), it did not stop Japan from joining the Regional Comprehensive Economic Partnership, a major trade agreement including China. Choices over which development banks to join fit expectations of the theory, but the trade agreement decisions offer mixed support.

Often the complex decisions over membership seen up close in a case study allow a more nuanced approach to geopolitical alignment. Japan joined early organizations in the nineteenth century to assert sovereignty and it pushed forward the Trans-Pacific Partnership (TPP) agreement to build regional leadership. Analysis of the decision process highlights how membership expands relational ties as part of geopolitical balancing even when these cases do not represent a simple test about allies joining organizations together. In this way, the chapter expands on the insights from the main argument about geopolitical discrimination and favoring friends.

The IWC case probes what can happen when any state can join an organization. The evolution of the IWC mandate from resource management to conservation put Japan in the position of belonging to an organization

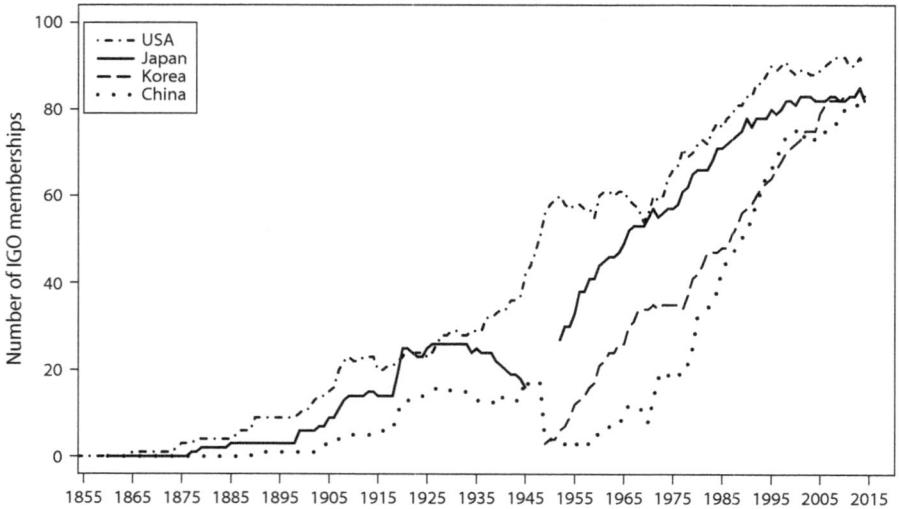

FIGURE 6.1. *Japan's IGO membership in comparison*: The figure displays the number of all existing IGOs in which Japan was a member in each year, along with the totals for the United States, Korea, and China.

opposed to its interests. This shifts the question about membership to asking why Japan chose to remain in the organization so long and what prompted its eventual exit. The case serves to emphasize that interests affected by the regulatory rules will always play an important role in membership, but one that can be moderated by relational ties.

6.1   Japan's Membership in International Organizations

The engagement of Japan with the world can be traced through its membership in international organizations. Figure 6.1 shows the number of IGOs that Japan has joined in comparison to the United States, China, and Korea. Since only autonomous countries are included in the data on membership, Japan experiences a gap from 1946 to 1951, with zero memberships, when it is not included in the state system while under the Occupation.[1] Similarly, Korea was outside of the state system while under Japanese colonial rule, and enters

---

1. In 1945, Japan was listed as a member of 16 organizations. It may have remained a nominal member in some cases, but for my analysis of state membership it is excluded from the data during these years.

IGO	Full Name	Start Date	Japan Entry Year
UPU	Universal Postal Union	1874	1877
ITU	International Telecommunication Union	1865	1879
BIPM	International Bureau of Weights and Measures	1875	1885
IUPCT	International Union for the Publication of Customs Tariffs	1890	1891
IUPIP	International Union for the Protection of Industrial Property	1883	1899
PCA	Permanent Court of Arbitration	1899	1899
IAS	International Association of Seismology	1903	1903
IIA	International Institute of Agriculture	1905	1905
RadioU	Radiotelegraph Union	1906	1906
CBI	Central Bureau for the International 1:1,000,000 Map of the World	1909	1909
IBIER	International Bureau for Information and Enquiries regarding Relief to Foreigner	1907	1907
ICTM	International Commission on the Teaching of Mathematics	1908	1910
IPrizeC	International Prize Court	1907	1910
PIARC	Permanent International Association of Road Congresses/World Road Association	1908	1910
IBCS	International Bureau of Commercial Statistics	1913	1913
ILO	International Labour Organization	1919	1919
ICAO	International Civil Aviation Organization /International Commission for Aviation	1919	1919
ICDR	International Commission for the Decennial Revision of the Nomenclature of Causes of Death	1900	1920
IES	International Exchange Service	1886	1920
IICom	International Institute of Commerce	1919	1919
IOPH	International Office of Public Hygiene	1907	1920
IPentC	International Penitentiary Commission	1875	1920
LoN	League of Nations	1920	1920
RepCom	Reparation Commission	1919	1920
IHO	International Hydrographic Bureau/International Hydrographic Organization	1919	1921
IIF	International Institute of Refrigeration	1920	1924
ITTC	International Telegraph Consultative Committee	1925	1925
ITCLE	International Technical Committee of Legal Experts on Air Questions	1926	1929
BIS	Bank for International Settlements	1930	1930
IOEz	International Office of Epizootics	1924	1930
PICS	Permanent International Commission of Studies on Sanitary Equipment	1925	1936

TABLE 6.1. *Japan's Membership in IGOs*: The abbreviation, name, and start date for IGOs are from the Correlates of War IGO dataset. Japan's membership dates have been confirmed with some corrections based on primary sources.

IGO	Full Name	Start Date	Japan Entry Year
ICAI	International Commission of Agricultural Industries/International Commission for Agriculture and Food Industries	1934	1938
FAO	Food and Agriculture Organization	1945	1951
ICAC	International Cotton Advisory Committee	1939	1951
IGC	International Wheat Advisory Committee/Int'l Grains Council	1949	1951
IWC	International Whaling Commission	1946	1951
UNESCO	United Nations Educational Scientific and Cultural Organization	1945	1951
WHO	World Health Organization	1946	1951
APFIC	Indo-Pacific Fisheries Council/Asia Pacific Fishery Commission	1948	1952
IBRD	International Bank for Reconstruction and Development/World Bank	1945	1952
IMF	International Monetary Fund	1944	1952
INTERPOL	International Criminal Police Commission/ International Criminal Police Organization	1923	1952
IRC	International Rice Commission	1948	1952
IRSG	International Rubber Study Group	1944	1952
IWSG	International Wool Study Group	1947	1952
NPAFC	International North Pacific Fisheries Commission/North Pacific Anadromous Fish Commission	1952	1952
ISuC	International Sugar Council	1937	1953
WMO	World Meteorological Organization	1947	1953
COLOMBO	Council for Technical Cooperation in South and Southeast Asia	1950	1954
UNDROIT	International Institute for the Unification of Private Law/UNIDROIT	1926	1954
GATT	General Agreement on Tariffs and Trade	1948	1955
IBE	International Bureau of Education	1929	1955
AALCO	Asian-African Legal Consultative Committee	1956	1956
ICMMP	International Committee of Military Medicine and Pharmacy	1921	1956
IFC	International Finance Corporation	1956	1956
IGCC	Intergovernmental Copyright Committee	1952	1956
ITC	International Tin Council	1956	1956
UN	United Nations	1945	1956
HCPIL	Hague Conference on Private International Law	1955	1957
IAEA	International Atomic Energy Agency	1957	1957
IMO	International Maritime Organization	1948	1958

TABLE 6.1. *(continued)*

IGO	Full Name	Start Date	Japan Entry Year
NPFSC	North Pacific Fur Seal Commission	1958	1958
ILZSG	International Lead and Zinc Study Group	1959	1960
IOcC	Intergovernmental Oceanographic Commission	1960	1960
APO	Asian Productivity Organization	1961	1961
IOLM	International Organization for Legal Metrology	1955	1961
ICfO	International Coffee Organization	1963	1964
OECD	Organization for Economic Cooperation and Development	1961	1964
WCO	World Customs Organization	1950	1964
IEXB	International Exhibitions Bureau	1928	1965
AIDC	Asian Industrial Development Council	1966	1966
ADB	Asian Development Bank	1966	1966
ASPAC	Asian and Pacific Council	1966	1966
UNIDO	United Nations Industrial Development Organization	1966	1966
ICCROM	International Center for the Study of the Preservation and the Restoration of Cultural Property	1958	1967
AOPU	Asian-Oceanic Postal Union/Asian-Pacific Postal Union	1962	1968
CMAEC	Council of Ministers for Asian Economic Cooperation	1968	1968
IATTC	Inter-American Tropical Tuna Commission	1949	1970
ICSEAF	International Commission for the Southeast Atlantic Fisheries	1969	1970
IUPLAW	International Union for the Protection of Literary and Artistic Works	1886	1970
AVRDC	Asian Vegetable Research and Development Center	1971	1971
ICCO	International Cocoa Organization	1973	1973
INTELSAT	International Telecommunications Satellite Organization	1964	1973
IEA	International Energy Agency	1974	1974
WIPO	World Intellectual Property Organization	1967	1975
WIPO	World Intellectual Property Organization	1967	1975
IOPCF	International Oil Pollution Compensation Funds	1975	1976
IFAD	International Fund for Agricultural Development	1974	1977
WTOURO	World Tourism Organization	1975	1978
APT	Asia-Pacific Telecommunity	1976	1979
IMSO	International Mobile Satellite Organization	1979	1979
INRO	International Natural Rubber Organization	1980	1980
NAFO	Northwest Atlantic Fisheries Organization	1979	1980

TABLE 6.1. (*continued*)

IGO	Full Name	Start Date	Japan Entry Year
IUPNVP	Union for the Protection of New Varieties of Plants	1961	1982
AfDB	African Development Bank	1963	1983
IJO	International Jute Organization	1984	1984
IAIC	Inter-American Investment Corporation	1985	1985
ITTO	International Tropical Timber Organization	1986	1986
MIGA	Multilateral Investment Guarantee Agency	1988	1988
APEC	Asia-Pacific Economic Cooperation	1989	1989
CFC	Common Fund for Commodities	1989	1989
INSG	International Nickel Study Group	1990	1990
EBRD	European Bank for Reconstruction and Development	1990	1991
GEF	Global Environment Facility	1991	1991
ICSG	International Copper Study Group	1992	1992
PICES	North Pacific Marine Science Organization	1992	1992
IOMig	Intergovernmental Committee for European Migration/International Organization for Migration	1951	1993
Montreal	Multilateral Fund for the Implementation of the Montreal Protocol	1990	1993
ICRI	International Coral Reef Initiative	1994	1994
WTO	World Trade Organization	1995	1995
ISA	International Seabed Authority	1994	1996
Wassen	Wassenaar Arrangement on Export Controls for Conventional Arms and Dual-Use Goods and Technologies	1996	1996
ASEF	Asia-Europe Foundation	1997	1997
GHSI	Global Health Security Initiative	2001	2001
AFEXIMB	African Export Import Bank	1993	2002
IASAJ	International Association of Supreme Administrative Jurisdictions	1983	2002
CBFP	Congo Basin Forest Partnership	2002	2011
CSLF	Carbon Sequestration Leadership Forum	2003	2003
ICWMD	International Commission on Weapons of Mass Destruction	2003	2003
PSI	Proliferation Security Initiative	2003	2003
GEO	Group on Earth Observations	2005	2005
GICNT	Global Initiative to Combat Nuclear Terrorism	2006	2006
ICC	International Criminal Court	2002	2007
MOPAN	Multilateral Organizations Performance Assessment Network	2002	2014

TABLE 6.1. (continued)

the data recording its IGO participation in 1949. See Table 6.1 for the list of IGOs that Japan has joined by the year of its entry.[2]

The IGO membership trend shows Japan's entry into international society during the late nineteenth century as it joined the early handful of international organizations. Declining membership also corresponds to Japan's retreat from international society in the late 1930s as the military-led government went on a path toward autarky with the exit from the League of Nations and other organizations. During the postwar burst of creating new international organizations, both Japan and Korea as newly independent states rapidly expanded their memberships. China exhibits a later entry into international society and a retreat at the time of the communist revolution in 1949.[3] The United States has outpaced both Japan and China, but the gap has closed. States have choices about which organizations to join, and these choices shape their position in international society.

6.2   Entry into International Society

After 200 years of self-imposed isolation during the Tokugawa period, Japan faced rapid adjustment to integrate with the world. Following the arrival of Commodore Matthew Perry in 1853, the weakening shogunate was forced to sign a succession of unequal treaties with foreign powers. These agreements imposed low tariffs and established separate legal status for consular jurisdiction that allowed foreign residents immunity from Japanese laws. After a brief civil war brought new leadership to power in the Meiji Restoration of 1868, Japan's government set out on a remarkable path to modernize the nation. Learning from foreign models played a prominent role, as epitomized by the departure on December 23, 1871 of several top leaders in a large delegation called the Iwakura Mission that toured the United States and Europe for almost two years of observation. The opening up to the world occurred against the backdrop of a society that had very little exposure to the ideas and goods of, and personal encounters with the non-Japanese. The government had no alliances with foreign governments.

2. The aggregate data for Figure 6.1 draws on the COW IGO dataset that includes data at five-year intervals prior to 1960.

3. Following the COW IGO dataset, China represents Mainland China, and Taiwan is a separate member after 1949.

The expanding contact with foreign governments brought new demands for coordination. Beyond these functional needs, the government also sought to rid itself of the unequal treaties. To do so, it had to provide evidence that it could manage its own tariff and legal system. Joining international organizations served both to facilitate integration with the world and to demonstrate the authority of the government. Membership represented a visible seal of approval by other states of their recognition of Japanese sovereignty, and participating in these fora allowed the government to protect its rights. This can be seen across a range of venues from the technical to political—indeed the distinction between technical and political organizations lost meaning, as even a narrowly defined economic organization could affirm sovereignty or turn into a forum for criticism.

6.2.1   Communicating with the World: UPU and ITU

Effective management of postal services was the first step to upholding Japan's sovereignty and became a route to international recognition. Postal services in Japan were unified in 1870 as an early step by the Meiji government to centralize the feudal society of Japan. As mail services extended throughout the country, private services were replaced by a government monopoly and regulated rates. From the outset, the issue was entangled with international relations. During the early years of centralizing postal services, private sector interests opposed the state's role, which would undercut courier businesses, while the role of postal services in international relations was one of the reasons given by the government to justify the state monopoly (Maclachlan, 2011, p. 41).

Alongside the unequal treaties, postal relations were another dimension where Japan lacked full sovereignty. Initially, foreign mail was managed by separate postal offices operated by Britain, France, Germany, and the United States to serve their own residents in Japan. Japan's need to exchange mail abroad grew as it established its own embassies in the United States and Europe and expanded communication. Lack of postal control meant Japanese living abroad had to route mail back to Japan through a foreign treaty port post office. The United States was the first to negotiate a treaty with Japan for direct exchange of postal services shortly after the 1872 consolidation of the Japanese domestic service to include provisions allowing for foreign postal service, and at that time closed its postal office. Germany soon followed, but France and

Britain refused. These negotiations played a key role to prepare Japan for entry into the UPU (Howland, 2014, p. 28).

The proposal to join the union came from the Japanese minister based in Germany, Shūzō Aoki.[4] He was actively assisted by the German government officials, who favored Japan's joining the UPU (Howland, 2014, p. 28). Germany had played a leading role in the establishment of the international organization, although its headquarters were in Switzerland. Writing to Tokyo in February 1876, Aoki reported that Turkey had joined the UPU, and followed up in April with an inquiry about whether Japan would join.[5] Foreign Minister Munenori Terashima requested the opinion of the head of the Postal Office, Hisoka Maejima, who argued that the postal system was a necessary function of the state and could form the basis for international recognition.[6] Maejima emphasized the bargaining advantages of negotiating for control over postal relations at the UPU instead of separately with each foreign government, and alluded to the goal of heightening national sovereignty. Noting that Egypt had successfully closed foreign postal offices after joining the UPU, he stated that through joining the UPU, "the government shall press in the negotiation for the closure of the French and British post offices."[7] News stories in Japan reported that entry would allow Japan to simplify handling of foreign mail with standard and low-priced fees.[8]

In 1877, Japan notified the Swiss government that it would adhere to the Berne Postal Treaty of 1874, and this led to the recognition of their membership in the General Postal Union and participation in the Paris Postal Congress of 1878 (Codding, 1964, p. 37). Within the UPU, the approval process offered other members a period to object to new members. The United States played

4. *The Japan Times*, 21 June 1902, p. 3.

5. Ministry of Foreign Affairs. "Bankoku Yūbin Rengō Jyōyaku Teikoku Seifu Kamei Ikken [One Issue Concerning the Adhesion of the Imperial Government to the Universal Postal Union]." 1875–1877. Japan Center for Asian Historical Records. https://www.jacar.go.jp/. Accessed 11 April 2021.

6. Maclachlan (2011, p. 38), citing William Beasley.

7. Letter between Munenori Terashima, Foreign Minister, and Hisoka Maejima, Head of Postal Office. 1875. Ministry of Foreign Affairs. "Bankoku Yūbin Rengō Jyōyaku Teikoku Seifu Kamei Ikken [One Issue Concerning the Adhesion of the Imperial Government to the Universal Postal Union]." 1875–1877, pp. 113, 115.

8. "Nihon, bankoku yūbin rengō ni 1877 nen kamei, yūbinjigyō no kōsō wo kakuritsu [Japanese accession to International Postal Union in 1877 establishes framework for postal services]," *Yomiuri Shimbun* 10 May, 1902 morning edition, p. 2.

the lead role as sponsor, given it already held postal relations with Japan and ongoing cooperation with shipping lines and mail transfer. Despite hostility to opening Japanese postal services that could compete with its own routes, the UK did not object (Howland, 2014, p. 30). Joining the General Postal Union led the UK and France to also close their postal offices in Japan, although they did not do so until 1879 and 1880, respectively (Den, 1970, p. 410). The organization changed its name to Universal Postal Union the next year, reflecting the broader scope as it expanded beyond Europe, with independent Latin American and African states joining along with Japan (Codding, 1964, p. 37–38). Yet Japan would remain the sole Asian member country until 1885, when Thailand joined as the Kingdom of Siam; China did not enter until 1914.

Closure of the foreign operated offices represented an important step toward Japan's establishment of administrative sovereignty (Howland, 2014). Henceforth the government would be responsible for following common practices for postal exchange, including the guarantees on fixed rates for different weights and the treatment of lost mail. The presence of European colonies including India and Hong Kong as members of the UPU shows that organizational membership alone would not bring full sovereignty—Japan did not complete revisions of the unequal treaties until 1894. Nevertheless, UPU membership offered a forum to enhance relationships from a position of mutual recognition. At the twenty-fifth anniversary of joining the UPU, Communications Minister Akimasa Yoshikawa made the following remarks about joining the UPU:

This event not only afforded much convenience to the general public and became one of the causes that contributed to the progress of society, but also secured our autonomy in postal matters because by the time that the General Postal Union Treaty came into force in our country, the postal agencies of Great Britain and France, established in our country, had been closed one after another. Our entry into the Postal Union, then, should be regarded as one of the greatest landmarks in the history.... Not only does it promote the welfare of the nations by providing them with expeditious means of transporting letters and goods throughout its territory, but as the promoter of universal peace, it also binds together with a strong chain the different states of the world and helps to foster happy relations between them.[9]

9. *The Japan Times*, 21 June 1902, p. 3.

Foreign governments also acknowledged the role of the UPU in bringing Japan into international society. Speaking at the twenty-fifth anniversary event as the representative of members of the UPU, a diplomat of the United States, Colonol A. Buck, reflected that the organization "tends to foster more friendly relations among the powers of the world" and highlighted the significance of Japan's early participation:

> The Government and people of the Empire are to be congratulated on this country having been the first of all the countries of the Orient to become, in cooperation with Western powers, a member of the Postal Union. It might well and truthfully be said, in addition, that it is also the first of all Asiatic countries to inaugurate within itself, in the various departments of the Government, improved systems of administration which have necessarily and happily resulted in bringing this country into full and complete fellowship with other great Powers.[10]

Where other countries of Asia relied on foreign consular posts, Japan asserted its autonomy to handle its own postal service. Broadening communication with the world would support its rush of modernization, but equally important was the development that the government would control this critical service both internally and externally.

Although the International Telegraph Union, established in 1865, was one of the first international organizations, Japan's late introduction of telegraph communications delayed its entry to 1879. While a telegraph machine was among the gifts brought to Japan by Commodore Perry during his historic visit to the shogun in 1854, the first official telegraph line was not laid until 1869, with the first message transmitted on 7 January 1870 between Yokohama and Tokyo, on a machine equipped to carry messages in both English and Japanese (Brunton, 1991, p. 28). The British Consul-General, Sir Harry Parkes, provided the Japanese government with a copy of the recently revised Paris Agreement of the International Telegraph Union in March 1871, and the governments of Australia, Hungary, and Denmark that year encouraged Japan to attend the ITU meeting to be held later in the year (Association, 1996, p. 16). As the Danish Company, Great Northern Telegraphic Company, had entered into contracts with the Japanese government to lay telegraph lines in Japan, the Danish government was a strong advocate for Japan's participation. Two notable points stand out in the international communications to Japan: it was

10. *The Japan Times*, 21 June 1902, p. 3.

emphasized that the ITU membership was limited to sovereign nations that had established a telegraphic service and that it would be "in the interest of Japan and desirable to the European Powers" for Japan to attend the meeting.[11]

An observer sent to the Rome International Telegraph Conference (December 1871–January 1872) represented Japan's first contact with the organization, preceding its international telegraph communication. Atsunobu Shioda, who was then serving as the Japanese representative in London, attended the conference.[12] The agreement reached at the conference notably included a reference to fixing the transit rates to be charged for messages interchanged with China and Japan by some but not all countries (British India, Persia, Russia, Turkey set rates for Japan and China, while other countries set single rate to apply to all countries).[13] The first international connections were built by the Great Northern Telegraph Company between Nagasaki and Vladivostock and between Nagasaki and Shanghai; international telegraph services became fully operational in 1878 (Den, 1970, p. 420). The government again sent representatives as observers to the 1875 International Telegraph Convention in Saint Petersburg. Once the country had established a network of telegraph lines within the country and established a foreign telegraph office, it joined the ITU on 1 January 1879 as the thirty-third member of the organization and participated in the Plenipotentiary Conference held in London that June as a full member. Such membership provided access to necessary information and coordination for participation in the international telegraph networks while also affirming Japanese sovereignty in its dealing with other powers.

The ITU and UPU represented opportunities for the Japanese government to take a place as an equal at the international fora discussing regulations for global communication. It was the first Asian country to join the organizations. Given the absence of cables connecting Japan with Europe and America

---

11. Letter from H. Calice, Austro-Hungarian chargé d'affaires to Nobuyoshi Sawa and Munenori Terashima, Ministers of Foreign Affairs. 5 July 1871. In Intelligence Division, Ministry of Foreign Affairs. "*Dainippon gaikō bunsho Dai yon kan.* [Documents Related to Japanese Diplomacy, Vol. 4]." Nihon Kokusai Kyōkai, 1938–1940, pp. 943–945. National Diet Library Digital Collections. DOI: 10.11501/1450084.

12. Intelligence Division, Ministry of Foreign Affairs. "*Dainippon gaikō bunsho Dai yon kan.* [Documents related to Japanese Diplomacy, Vol. 4]." Nihon Kokusai Kyōkai, 1938–1940, pp. 949–952. National Diet Library Digital Collections. DOI: 10.11501/1450084.

13. "The International Telegraph Convention Revised at Rome, 1872." Available at: https://search.itu.int/history/HistoryDigitalCollectionDocLibrary/5.3.61.en.100.pdf.

at the time, one may question what functional value the government gained from the discussions about rates of exchange among these densely interconnected regions, technological development pushed forward the organization, but in the case of Japan its participation at the diplomatic level went ahead of its actual communications. Seeking information about the latest technologies and approach to communications provided incentives to join even when Japan did not confront an immediate need to coordinate policies. In the case of the postal union, functional needs for coordination over postal exchange joined with the reality that any shortcoming would be filled by other states' incursions on Japan's sovereignty. The forward-looking search for information and the constant pressure to prove itself competent as a sovereign government supported the need for Japan to join the UPU and ITU.

6.2.2   International Bureau of Weights and Measures

In the same period, France led a move by a number of European states together with Russia, the United States, and a handful of Latin American states (Brazil, Peru, and Venezuela) to establish the International Bureau of Weights and Measures (known by the abbreviation of the French name as BIPM) on May 20, 1875. By the late nineteenth century, the need for common measurement standards had become widely recognized (Quinn, 2011, p. 4). Harmonization of measurements was important to scholars and business, as it would help scientific comparison of research findings and aid commercial exchange. The standardization of weights and measures was a classic coordination game where there were multiple ways to measure but mutual gains from having a unified approach. And yet the need to transfer measurement systems involved distributional costs of adjustment. A scientific consensus emerged around the efficiencies of the metric system through several meetings conducted alongside international exhibitions in the mid-nineteenth century. At the time of developing the Bureau, governments expected that the organization would facilitate comparison of the standards in use by all states without a requirement for conversion, although the goal of a single standard was implicit in the work being undertaken (Quinn, 2011, p. 48).

Japan was not included in the original set of invitations that were issued by the French government to diplomatic missions in 1869 to attend a meeting for the establishment of an International Meter Commission (Quinn, 2011, p. 29). But after the negotiations in Europe had progressed to the stage of drafting a convention, the French decided to engage in outreach, and in November 1873 its diplomats in Tokyo invited the Japanese government to participate in the drafting exercise (Quinn, 2011, p. 62). The Japanese government took note of the institution, but deferred entry for another decade.

As the world was beginning to harmonize measurements, Japan was trying to establish common measurement within its own jurisdiction. The Ministry of Finance conducted studies to compare the various measurements used across regions within Japan to those used in France and Britain, which was reported by Finance Minister Shigenobu Okuma to the Army Minister Aritomo Yamagata in February 1874.[14] The Ministry of Finance's Division of Weights and Measures drafted regulations for domestic measurement. In August 1875, the Meiji government's Council of State issued the first edict calling for a standardization of existing Japanese measurement units.[15] That same year, other governments signed the Metre Convention.

The Ministry of Foreign Affairs joined the Ministry of Finance to advocate for Japan to join the Metre Convention and become a member of the International Bureau of Weights and Measures.[16] The arguments expressed in favor referred to both advancing academic research and helping Japan build ties with other countries. There was no mention of commerce. The records from the time of joining indicate that the foreign ministry had voiced its support as early as 1875, when the organization was founded, but do not explain why the government waited until 1885.

Entry brought a self-imposed expectation of adoption of the metric system. Accession did not require that Japan change its traditional measurements. Indeed, it was not until 1891 that the government passed the law on weights and measures to assign equivalency values between the traditional measurement units and the metric system; the law referred to adoption of the metric system as a future necessity.[17] At the time when the first proposal to adopt

14. "Nigatsu mikka Ōkura-kyō kou-futsu doryōkō hikaku no gi otoiawase no ken oyobi gokaitō [February 3, Minister of Finance: Matters Concerning the Comparison of Japanese and French Weights and Measures (Reply)]," 1874 and "Doryōkō kaisei gakari [Division of Weights and Measures]," 1875. Japan Center for Asian Historical Records. https://www.digital.archives .go.jp. Accessed 21 April 2021.

15. "Doryōkōhō torishimari jyōrei to kensakisoku shuruihyō wo seitei."*Mainichi Shimbun* 6 August 1875.

16. Tsugumichi Saigō. Letter to Sanetomi Sanjo. 17 January 1885. In "Furansu pari ni oite doitsu hoka jyurokkoku no aida ni teiketsu seru metoru jyōyaku ni kanyū su. [Accession to the Metre Convention, signed by Germany and 16 other countries in Paris, France]." Japan Archive for Asian Historical Records. https://www.digital.archives.go.jp. Accessed 21 April 2021.

17. "Shindoryōkōhō wo kōfu," *Mainichi Shimbun* 13 April 1921.

the metric system was introduced in 1890, government officials pointed to the membership of Japan and twenty-two countries in the Metre Convention as the reason for taking this step. A business representative noted that the convention did not require adopting the metric standard, which was not not even the dominant system in use at the time, as many countries followed the British measurement standard.[18] Nevertheless, the government position was that by joining the BIPM, Japan had expressed its intent to move toward the metric system. The final conversion to the metric system in Japan was completed in 1966.

Why was Japan quicker to join the ITU and UPU and delayed for the BIPM? One notable difference is the role of Britain. It sent delegates to the early convention of meetings for the BIPM, but chose not to sign until 1884.[19] Japan joined one year after the British entry. There is no evidence of any external pressure by the UK on Japan to join or remain outside of the organization. Rather, the delay by Britain may have had an indirect effect. The contestation over choice of standard between the British and French systems weakened the focal power of the institution. The decision by Britain not to join until 1884 may have contributed to the lower priority given to this particular institution. From a commercial perspective, the dominant trading role of Britain would have favored adoption of the British measurement standard.[20] While the actual choice of measurement did not pose a barrier to entry in the BIPM, this question may have inhibited earlier entry. One can infer that the focus on domestic consolidation of measurements took priority. At the same time, the foreign policy interest in coordination through the international organization added incentives to joining the organization, as expressed by the Ministry of Foreign Affairs. By 1885, there were no more barriers to entry as Japan had completed its domestic reform process and the UK's membership increased the appeal of the organization as a forum for deepening international ties.

Across the three organizations, joining represented a step toward *strengthening* Japanese sovereignty. Indeed, Japan joined the UPU first as the organization that supported a strategy to replace foreign offices. In each of the cases, domestic debate over the organization included an expectation that

18. "*Doryōkō-hōan ika ni ketsugi saru bekiya* [How Should the Diet Vote on the Law on Weights and Measures?]," *Yomiuri Shimbun*, 6 December 1890.

19. The founding members were Germany, Austria-Hungary, Belgium, Brazil, Argentina, Denmark, Spain, the United States, France, Italy, Peru, Portugal, Russia, Sweden and Norway, Switzerland, Turkey, and Venezuela (Quinn, 2011, p. 87).

20. In 1885, over a third of Japanese trade was conducted with the British Empire, which was double the size of trade with France (Davis, 2008/9, p. 159).

membership would help establish recognition for Japan as a state through strengthening its ties to other countries. Contemporary debates from the perspective of dominant states refer to the sovereignty costs arising from membership in organizations that constrain autonomy of states. Yet in the context of Meiji period Japan, international organizations were sought as a route to establish sovereignty.

6.3   Acting like a Great Power: Japan in the League of Nations

As Japan's national power grew, no one questioned its sovereignty. The formation of the Anglo-Japanese Alliance in 1902 brought Japan into its first alliance. Victory over both China and Russia and participation as an ally in WWI had clearly established the ability of the state to defend its territory. Rapid modernization had consolidated a strong state and growing industrial economy. Entering international organizations meant Japan would accept constraints on its own behavior—sovereignty costs. But entry offered benefits, including status and the ability to participate in decisions over rules. A close examination of the engagement between Japan and the League of Nations illustrates the role of political relations in shaping the willingness of governments to accept constraints and peer pressure within an institution rather than to exit the institution to avoid such constraints.

6.3.1   Joining the League

By joining the League of Nations in 1920, Japan gained recognition of its standing as one among the five great powers (France, Italy, Japan, the United Kingdom, and the United States). The institution designated that the five powers would hold a permanent seat on the League Council, and the requirement of unanimity for decisions in the council conveyed veto authority to each of the members. The League formed around the signatories to the Versailles Peace Treaty, so the organization began as the victors' ambitious plan to restructure the world order. At the level of forming the organization and debating its design, there was less interest on the Japanese side at both government and public levels, such that it was often a "silent partner" at the Paris Peace Conference of 1919 (Shinohara, 1959, p. 56–62). Japan would go forward to accept this role even as the United States decided not to join.

Before this decision was made, however, a fierce debate ensued within the foreign ministry and among elites of the government. The primary concern was whether Japan would be marginalized within the organization and find its military strength curtailed by the constraints of armament controls. Miyoji Itō of the Privy Council criticized the vague principles of Wilson's Fourteen Points, and declared that "the League of Nations is a political strategy of first-rank Euro-American powers to maintain the status quo . . ." (Burkman, 2008, p. 51). Fumimaro Konoe, who would later be prime minister when Japan, exited the League and wrote a scathing article against it in a newspaper to condemn the "economic imperialism" and domination by the Anglo-American alliance that was upheld by the organization (ibid., p. 57). In his statement in 1918 calling for Japan to support the negotiations to establish the League, Foreign Minister Kōsai Uchida rebutted such concerns by emphasizing the requirement of unanimity. He made the analogy that, similarly to its approach to the Anglo-Japanese alliance formed in 1902, joining the League of Nations would allow Japan to merge Western chivalry with Eastern bushido.[21] Others emphasized the dangers of isolation if Japan did not join. Japan's ambassador to the Paris Peace Conference, Nobuaki Makino, argued that nonparticiation would bring ostracism while joining would allow Japan to shape the League and increase its own international standing (Burkman, 2008, p. 53). The notorious Twenty-One Demands issued in 1915 to extend Japan's influence over China had backfired to instead spark Chinese domestic resistance and international suspicions toward Japan, while anti-Japanese sentiment had also begun to sour the Anglo-Japanese alliance. Joining the League of Nations with the UK offered a new forum for cooperation to offset those tensions.

The Paris Peace Conference was an opportunity for Japan to show common cause with China in demanding racial equality and to display Japan's role as regional leader (Burkman, 2008, pp. 20-23). Writing in 1927 to reflect on Japan's membership, Inazō Nitobe, who was a scholar and diplomat and would later go on to serve as an official in the newly established League of Nations, wrote that joining was part of the need to follow world trends rather than specific interests:

> When, therefore, the League of Nations arose from the ashes of the battlefields, with a banner on which was writ large the motto of world cooperation, Japan showed no hesitation in joining it. There was murmured some legal quibble about sovereignty and super-state; but this fell into oblivion before the grand ideal of universal peace and harmony. . . . Her foreign

21. *Yomiuri Shimbun* 8 September 1918.

interests are most vitally interrelated with America, Russia and China. As long as neither America nor Russia is in the League, Japan reaps scant advantage from her connection therewith. As to China, would she not be far freer to deal with that country outside the League, unencumbered with the opinions of more than two score nations that know nothing of the Far East? All these points of view have not escaped the attention of our people. But what goes under the name of "interests" should not be confined to material advantages; for there are immaterial interests as well. . . . Among the mental luxuries which Japan enjoys as a member of the League is the feeling that she has won this position by her own exertions. . . . Then there is another advantage we reap from our membership in that body. The league has for us a publicity value of the first order.[22]

Notably, few made the positive argument for gains that would accrue to Japan from the rules. Makino's defense of the League did not turn to the reasons that disarmament could benefit Japan's interests (Burkman, 2008, p. 53). While the ruling *Seiyūkai* party was close to business interests that sought to end discriminatory barriers against Japanese exports, the agreement would not bring such liberalization. Commentary on the agreements condemned the absence of specific provisions to achieve tariff and immigration liberalization.[23] The call for racial equality, which constituted Japan's major demand at the Paris conference and attracted considerable domestic public interest, was firmly rebuffed by Woodrow Wilson—even when a majority at the Paris conference supported its passage, Wilson ruled that the matter required unanimity and blocked inclusion of a racial equality clause in the League's covenant (Burkman, 2008, p. 85). Furthermore, it was clear that the sanctions rules stood as a source of future pressure on Japan more than representing a necessary tool for its own use vis-a-vis others. Advocates of membership emphasized, far more than the direct benefits from membership, the importance for Japan to participate in world governance and join the great powers in the new organization. Media coverage took this tone, with articles such as a *Tōyō keizai shinpō* editorial that urged readers to support the promise of "mutual international life" without considering their interests in the specific agenda items (Burkman, 2008, p. 67). In his report to the prime minister at

22. Nitobe, Inazō. "Why Is Japan in the League of Nations?" *The Japan Times and Mail*, 9 November 1927, p. 4.

23. "League of Nations and International Economy," *The Japan Weekly Chronicle*, 22 May 1919.

the conclusion of the Paris Peace Conference, the head of the Japanese delegation, Kinmochi Saionji, listed recognition as a great power to be the greatest accomplishment of the Japanese delegation at the conference (ibid., p. 95). The committee report to the Privy Council seeking ratification of the treaty acknowledged that the creation of the League was not itself in Japan's interests, but supported joining as part of world trends (ibid, p. 100). The Council approved the decision without objection.

6.3.2 The International Labour Organization

Among the affiliated organizations created alongside the League of Nations, the International Labour Organization (ILO) presented the biggest challenge to Japan. The primary appeal lay in standing alongside great powers in the international governance framework—Japan was invited to hold a permanent seat on the governing board. Membership in the League was seen to automatically confer membership in the ILO even while the ILO retained autonomous status as an organization (Howard-Ellis, 1929, p. 233). The government sent representatives to join the organizing committee for the first session of the International Labour Conference in 1919 and continued to regularly send large delegations for meetings and was the first country to appoint a permanent delegation to the ILO (Thomann, 2018, p. 332). Through this participation the government gathered information on labor and industrial conditions in Europe while also defending Japanese labor practices. At the Paris Peace Conference, other delegates had pilloried Japan for holding outdated employment practices that fell below European standards (Garon, 1987, p. 64). Taking its seat at the ILO allowed Japan to engage as an equal.

Participation came at a cost. For a government that refused to recognize labor unions and was intent on repressing the communist movement, it was anathema to send representatives of labor unions alongside government officials to represent Japan at an international conference that would set new labor standards opposed by the government. The ILO required changes in Japan through both its conventions on labor rights and the process of bringing together representatives of government, employers, and workers.

Business interests in Japan were hostile to the imposition of the higher wage standards called for in the ILO. The conference debated regulations to restrict child labor, impose a forty hour work week, set a minimum wage, and guarantee the right to organize labor unions. All of these measures would require changes of policy in Japan. The Japan Industrial Club opposed recognition of labor unions and resisted governmental labor reforms of any kind (Garon, 1987, p. 44–45). Businesses protested that while the ILO proposals could be readily adopted by European states, they would be impractical for Japan. A newspaper reported on rising unease among businesses in the face of little government information about whether Japan would join the organization or opt out of the rules.[24]

From the outset, the representation of labor formed a crisis point for Japan's relationship with the ILO, which had a tripartite structure that called for representation from labor, management, and government. Not having any publicly recognized trade unions, the Japanese government instead sent a labor representative who was widely viewed as "handpicked" by the government (Howard-Ellis, 1929, p. 241). This was criticized in Japan and abroad as a perversion of the principles of the organization (Garon, 1987, p. 44). At first the government found the ILO tolerant of its special circumstances—the first International Labor Conference in October 1919 accepted the labor delegate from Japan and exempted Japan from some of the rules (ibid., p. 70). With Japan's partial compliance to the basic provisions and adoption of only one major ILO convention in its first three years of membership, one could conclude that it was member in name only. This is a clear example of discretionary accession, where Japan could join without compliance at time of entry.

The government continued to participate in the ILO meetings, and through this engagement officials and the designated labor representatives formed ties that would shape subsequent development of labor policies in Japan. Progressives within society and some in the government began to call for recognition of labor organizations and guarantees for worker rights. The demands of workers who formed unions and led strikes across several industries gave urgency to the issue. Garon (1987) highlights how, on top of these forces, ILO membership led to public recognition of unions by their framing the labor issues as a threat to Japan's prestige abroad as well as its stability at home. By 1922, the government had established a Social Bureau within the Home Ministry to better manage policies and to create a unified front for engaging with the ILO (ibid., p. 95). Several modest reforms were directed to improve worker conditions. Nevertheless, the representation issue continued as a problem. The ILO credentials committee issued strong criticism of Japan for not consulting with the labor movement to select its delegate, while labor officials called on the government to support the ILO. Finally, in 1924 a

24. "International Labour," *The Japan Weekly Chronicle* April, 24 1919.

conservative and nonparty cabinet agreed to recognize that the membership of Japan's large unions would be allowed to elect Japan's delegate to the ILO (ibid., p. 108).

The government gradually embraced more ILO regulations. In particular, the minimum age rules set in the Employment Exchange Act in 1921 and limits on working hours set in a 1923 revision to the Factory Act represented two important changes that responded to ILO conventions (Thomann, 2018, p. 333). The ILO representative visiting Tokyo in 1928 grudgingly admitted that with ratification of 9 of 12 ILO conventions and accompanying changes to domestic laws, "Japan is all things considered not in a dishonorable state" relative to the other ILO members, many of whom also had chosen to selectively ratify a subset of all conventions (Thomann, 2018, p. 333). Having started from a lower level in terms of its labor policies, Japan's changes wrought from participation represented significant cooperation. Some in the government recognized that upgrading labor relations was necessary to achieving higher productivity in new industries, but the government sought to keep the reforms to a minimum as a concession to moderate unions and the ILO while continuing to suppress left wing unions (Thomann, 2018, p. 337). For the Privy Council that issued the decisions on ratification of ILO conventions, enhancing the standing of Japan in the international order was the primary objective.

6.3.3   Exiting the League and ILO

Just as the effort to improve relations with foreign powers led Japan into international organizations, the deterioration of its relations with those states prompted its exit. The dramatic departure from the League of Nations represented a turning point in Japan's path to war. Since its establishment, Japan had seen the organization as a forum for cooperation among the great powers. According to Thomas Burkman in his history of Japan's role in the League, "So long as Japan maintained reasonably good ties to the powers, League membership would present no insurmountable obstacle to Imperial Destiny" (Burkman, 2008, p. 165). When its relations to other powers worsened, the League lost its value. Japan's dramatic exit in 1933 was the culmination of its estrangement from international society.

Disagreements between the major powers and Japan were tied to differences over arms control and China policy. The London Naval Treaty of 1930 was bitterly resented in government circles and the public for constraining

Japan's military capacity. At the same time, radical military actors challenged the government's control through assassination plots and the 1931 Manchurian incident that began the steady expansion of Japan's war in China. Acting in response to the worsening situation in China with the onset of Japanese planes bombing Shanghai, the League of Nations sent the Lytton Commission to investigate and report back to Geneva. The report concluded that the Japanese military actions in Manchuria had not been self-defense and that the newly declared independent state of Manchukuo was only supported by Japanese troops; the report endorsed Chinese sovereignty and called for the withdrawal of Japanese troops. The only hope for Japan would have been a mediated compromise in the council, but failing here, Japan faced a vote in the General Assembly in February 1933, which it lost decisively (Burkman, 2008, p. 172). Japan's delegate to the League, Yōsuke Matsuoka was accompanied by one of the military colonels who had been a mastermind of the entire Manchuria incident. Matsuoka himself believed strongly in the importance of Manchukuo to Japan's national interest. He refused to accept any criticism, choosing instead to give an inflammatory speech and walk out of the room. Jansen (2000, p. 585) writes that "in a matter of weeks the goals that Japanese diplomacy had pursued since 1868—gaining equality through cooperation with the largest of the great powers—were thrown to the wind." Yet it was not a personal decision—the cabinet had voted unanimously before the assembly meeting to order withdrawal from the League in the case of a vote against Japan's policy (Burkman, 2008, p. 174).

Japan remained in the ILO for five years after it had walked out of the League. This differentiation did not arise from any inherent greater interest in the work of the ILO, but rather an attempt to limit the effect of the departure from the League on Japan's relations with other governments. Indeed, the decision to remain in the ILO occured as part of high-level consultations during the decision-making prior to exit from the League.[25] The imperial rescript issued in March expressed hope that good relations would continue so that by its League withdrawal Japan would not "isolate itself thereby from the fraternity of nations" (Burkman, 2008, p. 175). This spirit explains why the

---

25. "*Kokusai rōdō kikan kyōryoku keizoku ni kansuru kakugi kettei, shōsho, kokuyu tō no shiryō* [Material such as Cabinet Decision, Emperor's Order, and Declaration Concerning Decision to Continue Cooperation with the International Labour Organization]," National Archives of Japan Digital Archive. https://www.digital.archives.go.jp/das/meta/M0000000000 00001239665. Accessed 20 February 2021.

government continued to participate in the subsidiary organizations, including the ILO, after ending membership in the League. In his explanation to the cabinet, Foreign Minister Kōsai Uchida justified that the government would stop participation in the parts of the League that had "political nature" but continue to join the conferences held by the League on topics such as disarmament, health, and labor, which he said held distinct purposes for peace and culture.[26]

It was not an easy time for Japan to remain in the ILO. The early 1930s had witnessed progressive proposals for a union bill that would legally recognize all unions and protect them against discrimination, but strong opposition from employers' groups who joined forces with conservatives in the *Seiyūkai* party defeated these efforts (Garon, 1987, p. 184). Japan came under criticism at the ILO conferences such as the 1934 conference, where Western delegates accused Japan of "social dumping" through its export of products made cheaply under terrible working conditions (ibid., p. 203). By 1937 the government was oppressing labor-based opposition to the government and rolling out patriotic associations to subsume any alternative social organization. With the dissolution of unions at hand, none inside the country could protest the end of Japan's membership in the ILO, which was part of the 1938 decision by the government to withdraw from all of the League's humanitarian organizations that went into effect in 1940, two years after providing notice.

Foreign relations helped tip Japan toward leaving the ILO. One reason cited for staying in the ILO after exiting the League was the value of retaining connections with other countries.[27] But as criticism of Japan within the ILO grew, this turned into a negative point. Further, the desire for close ties with the UK and United States when Japan entered the ILO had since been replaced by increasing coordination with Italy and Germany, as represented by the signing of the Anti-Comintern Pact in 1936. Germany had exited the ILO in 1933 and Italy a few years later. According to Kamiyama (2014, p. 71–72), the government perceived that the ILO was increasingly aligning itself with democratic and populist movements and showing politicization. Officials within

---

26. "*Renmei dattai tetsuzuki* [Process of Withdrawal from the League]," *Yomiuri Shimbun*, 26 February 1933.

27. Minstry of Labor, Minister's Secretariat. "*Kokusai renmei no dattai to kokusai rōdō kikan to no kankei* [The Relationship between Withdrawal from the League of Nations and the International Labour Organization]," 1937. National Archives of Japan Digital Archive. Accessed 20 February 2021.

the Division of Labor of the Health and Welfare Ministry favored sending representatives to defend Japan's position within the ILO, but others disagreed. Several Diet members argued that Japan should withdraw from the ILO in line with the principles set out in the Anti-Comintern Pact and should create a new international labor front with Germany and Italy, which had already withdrawn from the ILO.[28] Some reported that Germany and Italy were putting pressure on Japan to withdraw from the ILO.[29] At the ILO conference in 1938, the representative of China used the forum to condemn Japan's military assault in China. This prompted the government to withdraw on the basis that the ILO had become too politicized (Kamiyama, 2014, p. 77–81).

Desire for prestige and cooperative relations had drawn Japan into the League and ILO. It is remarkable that Japan joined after having failed to win concessions on the issues of concern—racial equality and free trade—and despite misgivings about constraints on its ability to exercise power in Asia and fear of interference in its domestic issues. A relatively smaller level of possible sovereignty costs kept the United States out of the organization that it had helped to create. Japan's primary and perhaps sole reason to join was the effort to establish stronger relations with other major powers. Likewise, the decision to leave reflected the end of internationalism as the goal of Japanese foreign policy and its shift of alignment toward the Axis countries.

6.4   The Return to International Society

Following defeat in the war, Japan under the U.S. Occupation lacked sovereignty and did not participate in international organizations. With the conclusion of the San Francisco Peace Treaty in 1951, Japan regained its autonomy. Immediately the government began to seek memberships in international organizations. As seen in Table 6.1, 1951–55 brought a surge of organizational membership for Japan as it entered the large multilateral organizations like the WHO, IMF, and World Bank, as well as many smaller commodity organizations such as the International Whaling Commission or the International Rubber Study Group. Membership was proclaimed to offer specific gains and a diplomatic link between Japan and the world. Typical of such commentary

---

28. "Rōdō daihyō haken wo maeni jeniiba dattai no sakebi [Calls for Withdrawal 'from Geneva' before Sending Representatives of Labor]," *Asahi Shimbun*, 16 January 1938.

29. "Japan's Withdrawal from ILO is Denied: Delegate at Geneva Says That He Will Represent Tokyo at Next Labor Conference." *New York Times* 25 January 1938, p. 9.

was the report on Japan's entry into the WHO, which noted the importance of cooperation for health and also that "Japanese membership in this
international organization is another step toward Japan's goal of joining the
peace-loving nations of the world."[30] Through working with other countries
on technical matters, the government could hope to restore trust with them.
Domestic groups also rallied behind the cause; both the Japan Chamber of
Commerce and many labor unions supported the government outreach to
reenter the ILO in 1948 while Japan remained under the Occupation.[31] Joining international organizations played an important role in Japanese foreign
policy in the post-WWII era as it tried to end its pariah status as a defeated
nation and engage fully in the international community.

Not all organizations readily accepted Japanese membership. Inclusive organizations with a universal mandate still could exclude Japan, which remained
an enemy state in the eyes of many. Indeed, Japan's request to join the United
Nations was caught up in Cold War politics that led to several years of delay, as
the USSR objected to its membership. Even when Japan did join, some institutions used weighted voting to differentiate among members in hierarchical
organization. In these cases, the voting power allocation favored the founding Allied powers (Lipscy, 2008, p. 135). Switching from enemy to ally with
the United States alone did not change Japan's position in international society. It would take years to restore trust. But the alliance with the United States
opened the door.

One feature that was common in its campaign to rejoin international society, was the role of the United States as sponsor. While Japan remained
under the Occupation, the United States urged that Japan should accede to
international treaties in order to promote its return to the international society. Amidst the deepening Cold War, U.S. security interests favored a strong
Japanese government closely tied within the alliance. Records of discussion
within the Japanese Diet indicate that there was active coordination between
Japan and the Occupation authorities on selecting international organizations
to which Japan would apply even before conclusion of the San Francisco Peace
Treaty in September 1951.[32] Not only did the United States encourage Japan's
outreach, but it also pressured other countries to accept Japan. For example,
when UK officials expressed concerns about Japan's impact on world wheat

30. "Japan Joins WHO," *Japan Times* 19 May 1951.

31. *Yomiuri Shimbun*, 26 May 1948.

32. Diet records, 8 March 1950. 7th Session of the Diet, Lower House Committee on Foreign
Affairs no 7.

markets, U.S. officials offered concessions in their own purchasing patterns and assurances about limits on Japanese trade so that the UK came to support Japanese entry into the International Wheat Council.[33] The next section provides a close-up examination of how the United States supported Japanese accession to the multilateral trade regime.

6.4.1   GATT Entry

The accession of Japan to the GATT in the early 1950s severely tested the principle of open membership. As a state with industrial capacity that had been expanding market share in the 1930s, Japan was viewed with fear in business circles in the United States and Europe following World War II. Low-cost wages combined with high skill levels made Japan a competitive threat, while fears of cheating loomed large on a range of issues from brand-copying to dumping below price. Japan sought export markets but was unwilling to open its own markets. In short, theories that assume convergence of preferences prior to entry into a regime would suggest that Japan in the 1950s would neither have sought entry nor been allowed by current members to join the regime (Downs, Rocke, and Barsoom, 1998). Its critical role as a U.S. ally on the front lines of Cold War containment strategies in East Asia, however, added an argument in favor of its membership.

Events in East Asia and poor performance of Japan's economy convinced the United States that integration of Japan into the Western trading bloc was a foreign policy priority. First with the victory of communists in the Chinese Civil War and then with the outbreak of war in Korea, East Asia took on new importance in the battle against communism at the start of the 1950s. The United States had a strong interest in Japan as the base for U.S. troops in a strategic perimeter and as a democratic protege emerging from occupation. Yet the Occupation reforms had opened the way for liberal sentiment and organized labor that could turn radical in the face of continued poverty. Socialist victory in the 1948 elections made real the possibility that Japan would turn to embrace neutrality in the Cold War, and the problem of political and economic stability in Japan took on renewed importance. George Kennan's visit to Tokyo in March 1948 convinced him that economic failure posed a greater risk of communist subversion from within than any risk of Russian

---

33. "*Kokusai komugi kyōtei ni sanka: Nihon e 50 man ton wariate.* [Japan Admitted to the International Wheat Agreement: 500,000 Tons Allocated to Japan]," *Asahi Shimbun,* 16 June 1951; P. J. Philip, "U.S. and Canada Agree on Wheat Exports: Prepare Plan to Meet Needs if Tokyo and Bonn Join International Accord," *The New York Times* 5 March 1950.

invasion or future Japanese return to aggression (Forsberg, 2000, p. 62). He led in urging the new approach to Japan that would soon be codified in NSC 13/2, which called for the United States to focus on economic recovery in Japan and make "a vigorous and concerted effort . . . to cut away existing obstacles to the revival of Japanese foreign trade."[34] Continued U.S. aid was expensive, and exports offered one route to economic recovery in the devastated nation. The need to gain Japan's cooperation with trade sanctions against China also made it essential for the United States to provide Japan with alternative markets as the United States compelled a reluctant Japanese government to restrict trade with its most natural regional trade partner (Forsberg, 2000, p. 112).

Within a year of the conclusion of the San Francisco Peace Treaty in September 1951, on 18 July 1952, Japan applied for GATT membership. The decision had strong backing within the Japanese government, as the GATT held promise for both foreign policy and economic needs. "Japan's viability required access to export markets, which the United States did not wish to provide alone. Japan itself had every reason, political as well as economic, to seek admission to the newly established trading club, the General Agreement on Tariffs and Trade (GATT)" (Trezise, 1978, p. 2). And yet, as commentators noted at the time, the government seemed to expect entry as an act of "charity" for its hard economic circumstances while at the same time it was increasing protection for uncompetitive industries and launching new controls on prices and production contrary to the market logic of GATT.[35] In a foreign ministry discussion council debating the decision to enter GATT, the primary concern raised was the possibility that joining GATT could restrict industrial policy tools (Akaneya, 1992, p. 89). Despite its reluctance to open its own markets, however, the government recognized the vital need to negotiate lower tariffs abroad for its exports. Some within the foreign ministry advocated reliance on bilateral treaties to gain the best terms for tariff reduction, but the multilateral faction with the support of Prime Minister Shigeru Yoshida won in the push to apply for GATT membership in 1952, and this became the focus of Japan's foreign trade policy over three years of tough negotiations (Akaneya, 1992, p. 302).

---

34. NSC 13/2 "Report by the National Security Council on Recommendations with Respect to United States Policy toward Japan" (7 October 1948), in *Foreign Relations of the United States*, 1948, Volume VI, The Far East and Australasia, Document 588. https://history.state.gov /historicaldocuments/frus1948v06/d588. Accessed 1 August 2022.

35. Sheldon Wesson, "How Japan Seeks to Win Economic Independence," *Nippon Times* 17 February 1955, p. 6.

Japan's accession was discussed by members as problematic even before Japan's GATT application in 1952. An original suggestion in 1949 by the United States, speaking on behalf of Occupied Japan, that it should be allowed to join GATT was rebuffed, as the GATT Contracting Parties declined to invite Japanese participation in tariff negotiations. The U.S. representative said, "The inclusion of Japan in the framework of the General Agreement on Tariffs and Trade would contribute to the political stability of the Pacific area and of the world. . . . The contrary course with all its implications may breed serious resentment and political dissatisfactions."[36] Opposition, led by the UK, was motivated by fears that Japan would flood markets with its exports and not comply with trade rules.

Returning to membership in the ILO was one step to addressing concerns about social dumping that stood as an obstacle to joining the trade regime. A report by an ILO committee in 1949 warned that other countries would not tolerate trading with Japan unless it upheld labor rights protecting unions.[37] The Japanese Constitution included the right to collective bargaining, but the Occupation's General Headquarters had suppressed strikes in 1947 and some feared the Japanese government would undermine labor rights in practice. In 1948 the Japanese cabinet voted to seek ILO entry and began sending delegates as observers while passing laws to conform with ILO labor rights. Both industry groups and labor unions spoke in favor of entry.[38] After conclusion of the San Francisco Peace Treaty in 1951, a majority of ILO members voted to approve Japan's reentry. Eastern bloc countries objected that Japan and West Germany were puppet regimes, unqualified as sovereign states, but they could not block the decision.[39] Despite this success, even more lobbying would be necessary to win support for Japan's entry into GATT.

36. GATT/CP3/WP10/2/3; GATT/CP3/WP10/2/9.REV.1.

37. *The New York Times* 12 September 1949.

38. "Kokusai rōdō kikan e no fukki ni tsuite. [Regarding re-entry into the ILO]," National Archives of Japan Digital Archive. Accessed 7 April 2021.

39. "Report of the International Labour Organisation (E/2050)," UN Economic and Social Council Official Records, thirteenth session 512th meeting, 21 August 1951. The Japanese records indicate the vote passed 177 in favor with 11 opposed and seven abstentions, with the negative votes recorded by Poland, Czechoslovakia, Philippines, and Guatemala (countries had multiple delegates). Ministry of Foreign Affaris and Ministry of Labor. "Kokusai rōdō kikan kenshō no setsumeisho [Explanations Regarding the ILO Charter]," pp. 17–19. In "Kokusai rōdō kikan kensho no judaku ni tsuite shōnin wo motomeru no ken (Gaimushō). [Seeking Approval for the Acceptance of the ILO Charter (Ministry of Foreign Affairs)]," 1951, National Archives of Japan Digital Archive. Accessed 7 April 2021.

Within the U.S. government, the State Department took the lead to advocate for Japan's rapid accession to GATT and negotiate the bilateral agreement that would lay the foundation for accepting its entry as a new member of GATT. Opposition from nationalist Republican senators in Congress complicated efforts to negotiate lower bilateral tariffs with Japan. U.S. officials entered negotiations with modest offers to lower tariffs on Japanese goods (and no concessions on textiles, where Japan had major export interests) and demanded concessions from Japan on politically important products such as automobiles. The Japanese resisted making any major tariff reductions and maintained import quotas that protected domestic industry. The United States increased its concessions on textiles, such that the final agreement concluded in May 1955 was heavily criticized in the United States. The bilateral agreement benefited the United States only when viewed from the larger perspective that Japanese economic growth was in the U.S. national interest (Forsberg, 2000, p. 156). Based on this calculation, the administration expended considerable capital, first at home to accept the agreement, and then abroad in negotiations with other GATT members to encourage approval of Japan's GATT accession. In an extreme gesture of support for Japan, the United States was reported to have offered tariff concessions for improved access to U.S. markets to those GATT members that gave tariff concessions to Japan (Komatsu, 1963, p. 161).

Faced with the same trade-off between foreign policy goals and domestic industry opposition, Britain made a different choice. Britain's foreign office recognized the foreign policy reasons to favor accession for Japan but faced strong resistance from Lancashire textile interests represented by the Board of Trade (Forsberg, 2000, p. 126). Opponents frequently complained that Japan engaged in unfair trade by dumping its products, stealing designs, and not opening its own markets, and therefore they supported the need for Britain to be able to discriminate against imports from Japan. The foreign office counterargued that Britain would be blamed if GATT members rejected Japan and this led Japan to ally with the Soviet Union (Yokoi, 2003, p. 114). A British government report carefully laid out the risk that rejecting Japan's GATT membership would destabilize Japan and anger the United States just as the new Prime Minister Ichirō Hatoyama was wavering in support for the Western alliance. The report noted that some British industries could gain from exports to Japan but others faced the potential of serious injury (Yokoi, 2003, p. 111). In an odd compromise, Britain chose to approve membership as a way to affirm Japan's position in the Western club of nations while continuing to exclude its trade. The government voted in favor of Japan's GATT accession while exercising the escape clause in GATT Article 35, by which existing members could deny MFN privileges to new members on a selective basis. The UK was not alone, as 14 of the 34 GATT members invoked Article 35.[40]

Japan had not convinced states that it was embracing liberal market reforms, but nonetheless gained full de jure membership on 10 September 1955. The United States and 19 other members agreed to open their markets to Japan as they conferred MFN treatment to Japan at the time of membership in exchange for the limited reciprocity of market access in Japan. Japanese exports grew rapidly in markets like the United States and Canada, which conferred full GATT status, but remained stagnant in those refusing to provide MFN tariff treatment to Japan (Uchida, 1959, p. 170). The security interests of the United States and Japan's interest in rejoining the international community through membership in organizations explains the willingness of both countries to go forward under these conditions (Akaneya, 1992, p. 305). It took a decade of negotiations before all members agreed to extend regular GATT terms to Japan in the mid-1960s.

Theories of international relations suggest that leaders use international institutions such as trade regimes as leverage to overcome domestic resistance (e.g., Maggi and Rodriquez-Clare, 1998; Rosendorff and Milner, 2001). This argument finds a parallel within studies of Japanese foreign policy that emphasize the role of *gaiatsu* (foreign pressure) (e.g., Campbell, 1993; Calder, 1988). But Japan's entry into GATT reveals a different logic—negotiators insisted on the lowest number of concessions as terms for entry and succeeded in avoiding substantial liberalization. There is little evidence suggesting that the government wanted to commit itself to liberalization through taking on binding commitments or that it was agreeing to liberalize in reaction to foreign pressure. In an editorial article on the day after accession was concluded, Shigeo Horie, the executive director of the Bank of Tokyo, portrayed the gains in terms of the "voice Japan acquires in the arena of international commerce," and the costs as commitments to follow rules, given that Japan could only afford to liberalize trade slowly.[41] In 1955, mercantilist attitudes remained entrenched within the government, and the Ministry of International Trade and Industry (MITI) was at the height of its active intervention to promote

40. British and French colonies would also invoke Article 35 against Japan to increase by an additional 18 the total number of members that refused to provide full GATT status to Japan.

41. Shigeo Horie, "New Benefits and Obligations," *Nippon Times* 10 September 1955, p. 5.

exports while restricting imports. Instead of strategic lock-in, Japan's leaders hoped to gain market access without undertaking significant liberalization. It would take decades for Japan to offer concessions as part of the reciprocal bargaining process within the regime over the long term and under pressure outside the regime, in bilateral negotiations. Japan gained entry into the institution through issue linkage with geopolitical strategy, and later the force of the institution brought liberalization reforms. Importantly, this counters the view that states only agree to enter institutions that confirm the policies they already plan to implement. Further, it highlights the double-edged leverage from alliance ties. Japan extracted favorable market terms from the United States during critical periods even as tables were turned later when the United States used GATT to apply pressure on Japan to open its markets.

The GATT case offers support of the hypothesis about favoring friends from the perspective of the U.S. actions on behalf of Japan. The economic interests threatened by Japan as a potential economic competitor were a strong counterpoint. In the case of the UK and other European countries in the Western alliance, security was not enough to justify an open ticket to Japan for these states. Japan faced ongoing discrimination against it on trade terms, being treated as a former enemy alongside its nominal equality as a member.

6.4.2   OECD Entry

Admitting Japan in 1964 was the first expansion of the OECD beyond the founding group of 20. For the OECD it was a major step to show that the new organization would not remain tied to its roots as an organization for post-war recovery in Europe. To Japan, the entry marked its position as a peer among the leading industrial countries and the Western alliance. Prime Minister Ikeda had trumpeted an income-doubling plan that would be the hallmark of his four years in office from 1960 to 1964. To achieve this goal he launched a series of economic reforms that achieved remarkably high growth. His foreign policy also placed new emphasis on the need for Japan to build ties with Europe alongside the United States to form "three pillars" in support of the free world (Iwanaga, 2000, p. 214). As part of this strategy, Ikeda went on a 1962 tour of European capitals and expressed interest in Japan's membership in the OECD.[42]

42. A Ministry of Finance official attributed the initiative for OECD membership as arising during the prime minister's trip. "*OECD kamei to shihon torihiki no jiyūka* [OECD Membership and Capital Account Liberalization]," Kin'yūkai (August 1963), p. 24.

In 1960, Japan had joined the Development Assistance Group, which later became the Development Assistance Committee in the OECD. For Japan, a country limited by its constitution from substantial military contribution to international security, foreign aid has evolved from its role as a quasi-reparation policy after the war to an area for Japanese leadership and burden-sharing with the United States. For the trade-dependent state, promoting development and investment opportunities in other countries was central to its own prosperity. This sometimes raised tensions. Trade interests encouraged giving aid tied to projects that would benefit Japanese firms, while the OECD monitoring of aid policies pushed all countries including Japan to reduce the amount of tied aid. The government made the decision that greater prominence through participation in OECD aid coordination was worth the cost of inviting scrutiny over its aid policies.

When discussing the prospect of OECD membership in the Diet, Prime Minister Ikeda engaged in a long speech about the praise from other nations for Japan's economic revival and democracy, expressed the priority of his new cabinet to raise the level of the economy, education, culture, health, and social welfare of the Japanese, and declared that the scheduled accession to the OECD and IMF Article 8 demonstrated a growing international role for Japan.[43] According to a detailed report on the input from key government and business leaders on the prospective accession to the OECD, which was published in 1964 by the leading Japanese think tank Japan Economic Research Institute (JERI, *Nihon Keizai Chōsa Kyōgikai*), "Our country has now come to hold economic power as a first class industrial nation comparable to that of the European and American nations. In light of this economic reality, Japan's participation in the OECD is not only extremely 'obvious' but also 'necessary' for both our country and the OECD"(Shimomura, 1964).[44] To mark Japan's position as the first Asian country to have achieved high levels of economic development, many Japanese elites embraced the role of adding an Asian perspective within a European-centered organization.

Joining the OECD also promised contribution to economic growth through access to information. In the debate in the Japanese Diet prior to ratification of the agreement to join the OECD, Seiichi Inoue stated that there were two reasons for Japan to seek OECD accession: first, OECD membership would increase Japan's voice in international society, and second, learning

---

43. Lower House Diet Testimony, 18 October 1963, parliamentary record [008/010] 44 no. 3.
44. I thank Shirō Kuriwaki for extensive help translating this book.

from the experiences of other countries would help Japan to weather the currents of the liberal economic order.[45] As one example, the JERI report noted Japan's ongoing struggle to counter high inflation. The report recommended that "Japan should seriously learn from these OECD countries," which at the time enjoyed lower inflation rates than Japan (Shimomura, 1964, p. 127). Speaking at a forum shortly after conclusion of the negotiations for Japan to join the OECD, a finance ministry official extolled the main benefit of membership would be through the interaction with officials from other countries in committee meetings, where Japan could learn from the practice of other countries—"reflecting on experience of other countries, Japan should adopt those policies that are good"—and also share where it may have excelled with a unique approach to economic policy.[46]

Entering the OECD presented an opportunity for Japan to move toward more active engagement as "peer" (*nakama*) taking its part to shape the international order (Shimomura, 1964, p. 128). Beyond opening its own market, Japan saw OECD membership as adding new leverage in its effort to eliminate the discriminatory trade policies held against Japanese exports by many OECD members.[47] Here the symbolic and material benefits overlap, as the JERI report suggests that by becoming a member of the economic club Japan would gain a new forum and a voice to protest these policies, which it described as a problem given that Japan was an "equal peer" (Shimomura, 1964, p. 135).[48] An official with the Ministry of Finance warned that the discriminatory trade policies would not be dropped immediately upon Japan's entering the OECD, but through a gradual process as other countries came to see Japan as one of them, and not so different.[49]

45. Upper House, Diet Testimony of the Foreign Affairs Committee, 24 April 1964. Diet Record [001/001] 46 no. 18.

46. "*OECD kamei to shihon torihiki no jiyūka* [OECD Membership and Capital Account Liberalization]," *Kin'yūkai* (August 1963), p. 43.

47. When Japan acceded to GATT in 1955, 14 GATT members invoked Article 35 of GATT as a means to deny MFN treatment to its trade, and this number increased further as the European colonies also invoked Article 35. By fall of 1961, with support of the United States, Japan had seen the GATT commission report on the problem, and the Japanese government was involved in intense negotiations with each of the governments to win their removal of Article 35 exclusion (Komatsu, 1963, p. 165). Although by 1964 several countries had revoked Article 35 treatment, the weak negotiation position of Japan to win MFN status left many discriminatory barriers in place against key Japanese exports.

48. I thank Shirō Kuriwaki for highlighting this important point.

49. "*OECD kamei to shihon torihiki no jiyūka* [OECD Membership and Capital Liberalization]," *Kin'yūkai* (August 1963).

Japan undertook significant policy reforms as part of joining the OECD. Some concessions included limits on key industrial policy tools such as government support of the shipping industry and restrictions on the use of Foreign Capital Law and Foreign Currency Law to screen approval of new technology, which had often been used by governments to favor targeted industries and reduce so-called "excess competition" through centralized control of access to new technology from abroad (Shimomura, 1964, p. 92). At a time when the government saw its shipping industry in crisis, there was considerable reluctance to make these reforms. But when it became apparent that refusal on this point would delay accession, the government agreed to phase out the policies that were limiting use of foreign shipping (Shimomura, 1964, p. 68).[50]

Financial liberalization would be a struggle for Japan, and it only went partway toward fulfilling the OECD codes. Leading up to OECD accession, Japan negotiated with the IMF to become an Article 8 signatory, which involved ending many import quotas that had been justified for balance of payments reasons. Some within Japan argued that these steps were being taken too quickly as a result of the government's eagerness to join the OECD. An official with the Bank of Japan commented in an August 1963 roundtable discussion that there was a sense that Japan was rushing capital liberalization, but the official also recognized that further delays would only make things more difficult because European states were liberalizing and the gap between them would further widen.[51] The government was especially reluctant to liberalize foreign investment. At the time of accession, Japan included reservations that would allow it to maintain its restrictions on direct investment in the manufacturing sector, uphold the government's role in auto insurance, and continue to limit participation in securities markets by non-residents. Nevertheless, there was recognition that the reservations could exclude particular policies from liberalization for a limited period but would face ongoing pressure through debate in the OECD (Shimomura, 1964, p. 92).

The attention to the OECD in the Japanese Diet was limited largely to the ratification period. The United States and France were the prominent partners

50. At the same time, as a global leader in shipbuilding, the Japanese government was frustrated by subsidies of OECD member governments to their shipbuilding industries that would remain unchanged. Accession bargains are a one-way street with the applicant holding no capacity to issue its own demands.

51. "OECD kamei to shihon torihiki no jiyūka [OECD Membership and Capital Liberalization]," Kin'yūkai (August 1963).

relevant to the Diet discussion of OECD membership for Japan, which is consistent with the perception that it would deepen ties with both the United States and Europe.[52] Indeed, this sparked opposition from left wing politicians. The Socialist Party objected to accession on grounds that the organization was anti-communist and represented an "economic version" of NATO (the Socialist Party had just lost out in the fierce 1960 revision of the U.S.-Japan Alliance Treaty) (Iwanaga, 2000, p. 216). One Socialist Party member, Sōji Okada, said in testimony before the Foreign Affairs committee that Japan seemed to only be trying to pretend to be a member of advanced countries, while its preparation was weak and it was too soon for it to join.[53] Opposition party members criticized pressures on the shipping industry and wages with specific criticism of French policies. Foreign Minister Masayoshi Ōhira defended the importance of becoming a member in order to urge France and others to change policies that Japan saw as a problem. Finance Minister Kakuei Tanaka remarked that the OECD was a club where countries discuss policies to make consensus recommendations without adopting strict policies; he insisted Japan would never yield to pressure from the OECD.[54] With the LDP holding a majority in the Diet, ratification went forward smoothly.

OECD members approved Japan's entry in a consensus decision. While this chapter focuses on the demand side perspective of Japan as the applicant, the successful outcome reflects the agreement of members that including Japan would add to the organization. As a member Japan would join the peer review process and rule-making of the organization with equal authority to that of the other members. Allowing Japan to make reservations to the financial codes and retain high levels of trade protection, they eased its entry. Growing economic importance, along with its role as a U.S. alliance partner, made Japan an attractive new partner for the OECD to expand beyond the North Atlantic region and the NATO origins of its membership.

52. In a text search of Diet testimony from the Upper and Lower House during 1964, colocation analysis for pairing a country and OECD reference within 20 words shows 123 such references to the United States and 27 to France, followed by the UK (9) and Germany (6).

53. Testimony of the Japanese Diet Upper House Foreign Affairs Committee, [005/134] 46 no. 18, 24 April 1964.

54. Summary of selected speeches during Diet testimony in the 46th Session of the Diet. See Lower House Committee on Foreign Affairs, no. 7, 28 February 1964; Lower House Joint Session between the Committee on Foreign Affairs, Finance Committee, and Committee on Transportation, no. 2, 25 March 1964; Upper House Committee on Foreign Affairs, no. 18, 24 April 1964; Upper House Finance Committee, no. 11, 4 March 1964.

Beyond supporting the expected pattern of allies joining earlier and with a lower entry fee, the OECD case supports the importance of foreign policy within the domestic process. Japanese elites emphasized the value of association with other states in the OECD. The accession process brought to the forefront discussion of economic reforms as well as geopolitical strategy.

6.5   Leadership in East Asia

Japan has turned to international institutions to become a leader within its own region. Japan's leading the Asian Development Bank but remaining outside the Asian Infrastructure Investment Bank highlights the continued role of the United States as the anchor of Japan's diplomacy. Yet in the TPP negotiations for a trade agreement, Japan stepped forward to fill a vacuum left by U.S. withdrawal.

6.5.1   The Tale of Two Banks: ADB and AIIB

Following recovery from wartime devastation, Japanese leaders began to consider how to support growth of its neighbors with a regional development bank. An earlier proposal by Japan for a Southeast Asia Development Fund in 1957 had failed on account of suspicions by other countries about domination of Japan (Nishihara, 1976, p. 7). This time, Japanese officials first discussed a plan for an ADB on their own in early 1963, and then proposed the idea to the UN Economic Commission for Asia and the Far East (ECAFE) (Watanabe, 1973). After two years of deliberation focused around an expert group appointed by ECAFE, the ADB was established in 1966. Equally important, it was a framework expected to gather U.S. support.[55]

Japan pledged $200 million capital for its starting base, which was 20 percent of the total expected funds for the bank.[56] The government emphasized that building prosperity in its region would support the economic and security interests of Japan.[57] Prime Minister Eisaku Satō supported the bank under the rationale of regional leadership:

---

55. *Japan Times*, 13 January 1965, p. 1, "Tanaka Sees Backing for Asian Bank."

56. Nozaki, Shinroku, "Development Bank for Asia," *Japan Times* 10 July 1965.

57. Ministry of Foreign Affairs, Japan. "*Showa 40 nen ban waga gaikō no kinkyō* [Showa Year 40 Present State of Diplomacy]." Diplomatic Bluebook (1965). https://www.mofa.go.jp/mofaj/gaiko/bluebook/1965/s40-contents.htm. Accessed 14 April 2021.

As a nation in Asia, Japan is in a position to take the initiative among the developed countries of the world to show a warm understanding toward these countries close to her and at the same time to positively promote cooperation and assistance which will contribute to the improvement of their prevailing situations. It is in this spirit that our country actively participated in the establishment of the Asian Development Bank at the end of last year.[58]

The growing trade deficits of Southeast Asian countries with Japan also provided a context for development assistance: a way to positively show Japanese economic contributions.

Working through the ADB helped Japan balance sensitive political relations with neighbors and the United States. Unilateral actions as a rising power would have triggered fears of domination given Japan's past aggression against neighbors and its position as the largest indutrial power of the region. Animosity toward Japan lingered in the region and working through a broader group could dispel worries about its economic imperialism. But Japan also faced expectations to do more for the U.S.-Japan alliance during a tense period in which the United States was ramping up its activities to combat expanding communism in East Asia. At one level, Japan's aid policy during these years was evolving from post-war reparations to burden-sharing with the United States through economic means (Arase, 2005). At the same time, it was critical to avoid the appearance of serving the United States. The British ambassador at the time noted that Japan's search for influence in the region through leadership in the ADB and bilateral aid followed its commercial interests, "coupled with the avoidance of any political responsibility or identification with any of the power blocs to an extent [to] which [it] might lose friends and damage exports."[59]

Attention to the membership balance in the design of the ADB supported the goal to reassure regional countries while still engaging the United States. During the deliberation among ECAFE meetings, some governments favored restricting membership to countries within the region. Many felt the purpose of the new bank was to serve specific needs of the region and that it should be a bank run by Asian people for Asia. Yet Japanese officials recognized that the ability to raise capital would benefit from including developed countries

---

58. *Japan Times*, 29 January 1966, p. 2: "Text of Sato's Administrative Policy Speech."

59. Sir Francis Rundall's Valedictory Dispatch (British Ambassador to Japan, received 13 July 1967, FJ 3/4), cited in Cortazzi (2015, p. 6)

like the UK that were not part of ECAFE (Okura, 1964, p. 7). Top political leadership in Japan insisted on American participation, and the Japanese delegate to ECAFE, Takeshi Watanabe, strongly pushed to include all developed countries with interests in the region (Watanabe, 1973, pp. 15–17). He succeeded, and the founding charter established an inclusive mandate allowing both regional and non-regional members. The United States indicated it would join, and Watanabe personally campaigned in European capitals to seek their participation. Most agreed to join, but not the French; Watanabe explained of the French refusal that "France was under the impression that the Asia Development Bank was part of America's Asia policy" (Watanabe, 1973, p. 21).[60] Four years later, France would eventually join the bank too. Within East Asia, the "Western" camp orientation of the bank was clear and the PRC would not join until 1986.[61] Neither the USSR leadership nor the successor Russian government showed interest in the ADB.

As the Japanese parliament discussed ratification, the role of the United States loomed large. Indeed, Figure 6.2 reveals that attention to the United States was greater than to any other country or region.[62] Involvement by the legislature focused on the period around institutional formation (membership for Taiwan and China also emerged as a topic in 1972). Given the structure of Diet exchange, a large share of comments about the ADB in 1966 arose from the opposition Socialist Party members. They favored a regional institution without the United States. Responses by the cabinet and ministry officials were evenly divided between the finance ministry and Ministry of

60. At founding, the ADB was composed of 14 members: Australia, Ceylon, India, Iran, Japan, Korea, Malaysia, Nepal, Pakistan, Philippines, Republic of Vietnam, Thailand, the Federal Republic of Germany, and the United States of America. Its charter specifically notes membership is open to all UN members.

61. A critical point regarding PRC membership was the status of Taiwan. Starting in 1983, PRC contacts indicated an interest in its joining the ADB, but also objected to the fact that Taiwan was a member. Eventually, an agreement was reached to allow Taiwan to remain a member while changing its name to Chinese Taipei (Fujioka, 1986, p. 153). The U.S. Congress passed a resolution that threatened to cut ADB funding if Taiwan were removed, as a condition of membership for the PRC (Cho, 2002, p. 163).

62. The text analysis presented in Figure 6.2 uses the package quanteda in R to break up sentences into "words." The Japanese language text corpus is based on Diet testimonies in all committees and plenary sessions in both the Upper House and the Lower House. The frequencies in the graph represent a count of the names of countries or regions that appear within 20 "words" before and after the word "ADB" (search terms included the full Japanese name and abbreviation for ADB and a country name dictionary).

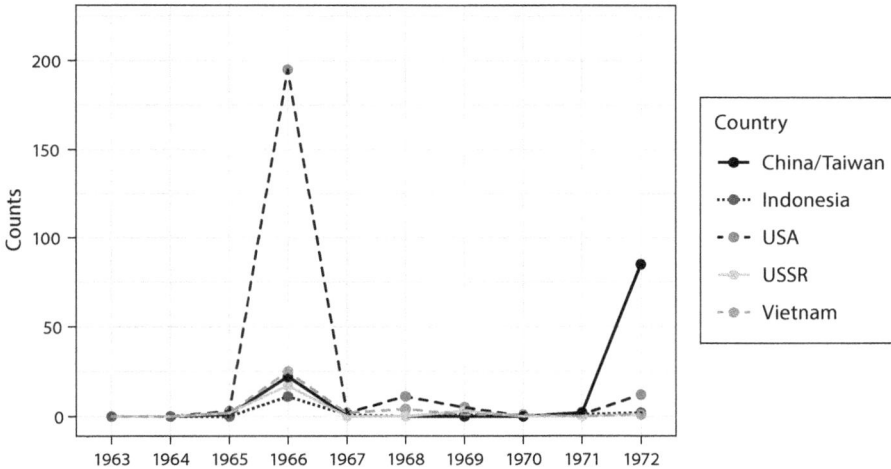

FIGURE 6.2. *Attention to ADB in Diet testimony:* The graph displays total count of references to the top five countries mentioned together with discussion of the ADB in a search of Diet testimony for all committees and plenary sessions in the Upper and Lower Houses.

Foreign Affairs. Deliberation focused on the location of headquarters and questions about the choice to include non-regional members, with fears raised about control, with the United States as a provider of a large share of funds. While opposition politicians saw U.S. involvement as undermining neutrality, Foreign Minister Etsusaburō Shiina insisted that the ADB represented the concept advanced by ECAFE's, not the United States' goals, and emphasized that the organization would serve developmental goals without a military agenda.[63] Overall, more time was devoted to the discussion of how to organize the bank and calibrate U.S. influence, and relatively less attention was given to economic issues such as budgetary outlays or gains for Japanese firms (see Figure 6.3).[64]

Japan has shown restraint in its leadership of the bank. Speaking during the Diet ratification debates in 1966, Finance Minister Takeo Fukuda emphasized

63. Testimony of the Japanese Diet Lower House Foreign Affairs Committee, Session 51, 25 May 1966.

64. This description of Diet testimony is based on hand-coding the topics of 572 full text speeches that mention the ADB during 1966. Speeches are divided among the four substantive topic categories displayed in Figure 6.3. A speech is placed in one category based on its most dominant theme.

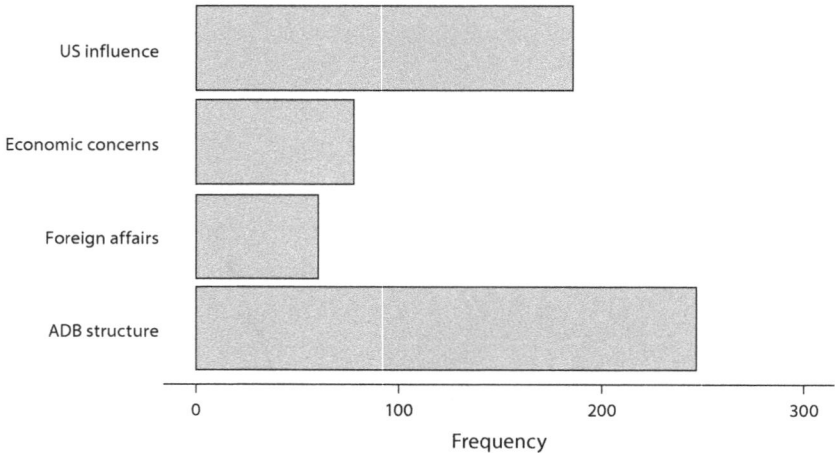

FIGURE 6.3. *ADB Diet deliberation topics:* The graph summarizes topics of speeches that make reference to ADB for the year 1966 from a search of Diet testimony for all committees and plenary sessions in the Upper and Lower Houses.

that governance provisions clearly mandated that the bank should not serve the interests of any country—Japan would not use appointment of a Japanese official as president of the bank to influence its policies.[65] Allowing the head-quarters location to be Manila drew criticism in some circles within Japan, but also proved useful to deflect the perception that the bank would become a political tool used by Japan on behalf of a U.S. Cold War mission. Subsequent analysis generally supports the position that Japan upheld high governance standards in its role as leading donor. Through influence over personnel placements within the bank, Japan had the capacity to significantly shape operations (Yasutomo, 1983). Some find evidence of strategic manipulation to gain leverage over countries critical to Japanese foreign policy goals (Lim and Vreeland, 2013). But even as the Japanese share of ADB funding rose over the 1970s and 1980s, it did not seek expanded voting rights in the institution, and a declining number of procurement awards went to Japanese firms or favored its trading partners (Wan, 1995, p. 526). The Ministry of Finance officials posted to serve at the bank held an internationalist view and used Japanese spending

---

65. Testimony of the Japanese Diet Lower House Finance Committee, Session 51, 8 June 1966.

to win broad goodwill from the region and the United States rather than to advance a specific agenda.

Within Japan, the ADB served foreign economic diplomacy and domestic politics. The split between nationalists, who wanted to assert independent Japanese policies, and socialists, who wanted to reject reliance on the United States, had escalated with the signing of the U.S.-Japan Security Treaty in 1960, which also led to the resignation of Prime Minister Nobusuke Kishi. The income-doubling goal of Prime Minister Ikeda and his successor Satō fit well with a turn to focusing on economic development of the region. Leadership on the economic front focused within the region could substitute for security topics that were better left untouched while the polity recovered from the massive protests surrounding alliance renewal. Partnering with the United States showed the relationship held broader significance than the controversial aspects of defense guarantees and hosting bases for U.S. troops in Japan. From this perspective, the membership politics of the ADB highlight two sides of security linkage in economic policies, as Japan tried to offer support to the alliance with economic cooperation and the alliance became more palatable within Japan as a broad partnership.

Yet Japan's leadership in the region has not meant joining every organization. Notably, it has refrained from joining the AIIB. With a rationale similar to that underlying the founding of the ADB, in 2013 China proposed establishing a regional bank that would pool resources to provide a more flexible response to the unique needs of Asia for infrastructure investment. At the United States' insistence in the mid-1990s, the ADB had shifted to focus more on social issues such as education, health, and environment despite demands from India and China to focus on infrastructure lending (Wan, 1995, p. 524). As with Japan in the early 1960s, China sought to contribute to regional development and enhance its influence through a multilateral institution that would appear less threatening than unilateral policies, as a form of 'soft balancing' against U.S. power in the region (Chan, 2017). Japan's reluctance to partner with China for the initiative reflects the overlap between the two development banks and fear that the AIIB would undercut Japan's signature international endeavor, the ADB. But Japan also found support in the United States, which spoke out against the formation of the AIIB and refused to join. Even as the UK and other European states decided to become AIIB members and its signatories reached 57 founding members by the end of 2016, Japan and the United States remained outside the institution.

The Japanese government has adopted a consistent position against membership in the AIIB. Officials emphasize that for Japan to join, the bank must address two concerns: first, the board must implement a transparent process to evaluate and approve projects, and second, loan conditions should assure sustainability for debt repayment and consider environmental/societal impacts.[66] Speaking in July 2014, Minister of Finance Tarō Asō focused on the risk of poor lending decisions leading to non-repayment, and noted that this would be the same perspective held by the IMF or World Bank.[67] In the Japanese Diet testimony, Liberal Democratic Party members made similar comments about poor governance as the reason for Japan not joining. Communist Party Member Mikishi Daimon countered that such concerns would be more effectively addressed by Japan joining the institution—he urged Japan to join with a strong comment that its refusal was only because the United States had refused to participate.[68] Some members indicated clearly the matter of China's role in the bank as the underlying problem. For example, a senior-ranking LDP politician Kōzō Yamamoto expressed his strong opposition to joining the AIIB, pointing out the lack of transparency in governance and that its purpose was to serve China's national interests.[69] Even as Prime Minister Abe in 2017 spoke in favor of targeted cooperation with China on development assistance to the region, his administration still objected to joining the AIIB.

Government officials were defensive about whether the decision would harm Japanese economic interests. A Ministry of Economy Trade and Industry official explained that since few Japanese companies receive orders to build ADB projects, they would not expect to receive many projects from the AIIB, and he noted that Japanese companies had not requested that the government

66. Statement by Vice-Minister of Finance Sugawara, press interview, Ministry of Finance, Japan 17 July 2017. https://www.mof.go.jp/public_relations/conference/my20150319.htm accessed 2 August 2017.

67. https://www.fsa.go.jp/common/conference/minister/2014b/20140718-1.html. Accessed 2 August 2017.

68. Statement by Mikishi Daimon, Upper House Finance Committee, Diet session 189, 23 April 2015.

69. "*Yamamoto Naikakufu Tokumei Tantō Daijin Kishya Kaiken Yōshi* [Summary of Press Conference by State Minister Yamamoto, May 23, 2017]," Cabinet Office. Available at https://www.cao.go.jp/minister/1608_k3_yamamoto/kaiken/2017/0523kaiken.html. Accessed 2 February 2021.

should join the organization.[70] Indeed, the corporate procurement reports of AIIB and ADB for the years 2017–2019 reveal that neither bank included Japanese firms among the top five suppliers.[71]

Overall, business sentiment favorably viewed engagement with the institution, but there was not enough interest to generate a large lobbying campaign. In public statements, the Japanese business federation Keidanren would make a reference to the AIIB that avoided taking a position on the question of membership even as it encouraged the government to engage in international leadership. Speaking in 2017, Keidanren chairman Sadayuki Sakakibara said the U.S.-Japan relationship should be the top priority while also indicating that he would join LDP Secretary General Toshihiro Nikai in Beijing for the summit on China's foreign One Belt One Road initiative; he encouraged cooperation in infrastructure projects between the AIIB and ADB.[72] The leader of another prominent business group, Yasuchika Hasegawa, cautiously noted that he hoped that the infrastructure businesses in Japan would not be disadvantaged by staying outside of the AIIB.[73] The Osaka region business organization stood out for directly issuing a public recommendation that Japan should join the AIIB.[74]

The pros and cons of membership were largely discussed in terms of relations with other states. The government draft paper about the bank released in 2015 listed the positive value of joining as a step to improve Japan-China

70. Statement by Minister of Economy, Trade and Industry Miyazawa, press release after cabinet meeting, Ministry of Economy, Trade and Industry, 17 July 2017. http://www.meti.go.jp/speeches/kaiken/2014/20150331001.html. Accessed 2 August 2017.

71. "2019 Annual Corporate Procurement Report," Asian Infrastructure Investment Bank, March 2020, https://www.aiib.org/en/opportunities/business/.content/index/_download /2019-Annual-Corporate-Procurement-Report-final.pdf (accessed 15 February 2021); "Projects and Tenders," Asian Development Bank, https://www.adb.org/projects/tenders/type /contracts-awarded-1541 (accessed 15 February 2021).

72. "Chairman Sakakibara's Statements and Comments at His Press Conference," Keidanren, 8 May 2017, https://www.keidanren.or.jp/en/speech/kaiken/2017/0508.html. Accessed 8 February 2021.

73. Keizai Dōyūkai Director Yasuchika Hasegawa's comments in Press Interview, 31 March 2015. https://www.doyukai.or.jp/chairmansmsg/pressconf/2014/140331a.html. Accessed 2 August 2017.

74. Johnston, Eric. "Kansai Business Lobby Calls for New Diplomatic Initiatives to Strengthen Ties with Other Asian Nations." The Japan Times, 25 January 2018. https://www.japantimes.co.jp/news/2018/01/25/national/politics-diplomacy/kansai-business-lobby-calls -new-diplomatic-initiatives-strengthen-ties-asian-nations/. Accessed 2 February 2021.

relations, but concluded it would be better to use Japan's role as outsider arguing for governance reforms as "the biggest card against China."[75] An editorial in the *Asahi Shimbun* noted that while Japan valued joining together with the United States, it could be left behind and "miss the bus" as other countries joined.[76] Such concerns only grew with the surprise decision of the UK to join, which was shortly followed by those of other G7 members (even Canada announced in 2017 that it would join). In an interview, Kenya Akiba (head of LDP Foreign Relations Council) defended the strategic calculus for Japan to remain outside AIIB while acknowledging that the one demerit of remaining outside the organization was a concern about what other Asian countries would think, as they were likely to want Japan to join for its larger provision of capital.[77] And of course the central point was relations with the United States, as "There are reports of an active effort—quiet lobbying—by Washington and like-minded governments to keep other nations from joining the AIIB."[78]

In the Diet, discussion arose largely in 2015 (see Figure 6.4). Following the decisions of the LDP policy leaders and the cabinet not to sign the AIIB agreement, the Diet discussion was explanatory. The level of attention was less than had been given to the ADB during the peak year of its discussion in 1966.[79] During Diet meetings in 2015 that did touch upon the question of AIIB, governance standards were the most prominent topic, along with the view that Japan should seek to hedge against China's influence from outside the AIIB (see Figures 6.5 and 6.6).[80] Among those testifying in 2015, more than half

75. "Japan still on fence about AIIB but envisages $1.5 billion contribution if it joins," *Japan Times* 8 April 2015.

76. *AIIB dou ikasuka ga kanyo da* (AIIB: Trying to Make the Most Out of It), *Asahi Shimbun* May 11, 2015.

77. Reuters, "*AIIB, Chūgoku ni kyohiken ga arunara sanka wa konnan da* [AIIB, Difficult to Join as Long as China Has Veto Power]," *Tōyō Keizai Online* June 5 2015. https://toyokeizai.net /articles/-/72349. Accessed 17 July 2017.

78. "China Banking on Infrastructure," *The Japan Times* 29 October 2014.

79. In a text search of testimony in the Upper and Lower House counting speeches with at least one reference to the institution name, there were 572 speeches for ADB in 1966 and 113 speeches for AIIB in 2015.

80. This description of Diet testimony is based on hand-coding the topics of 113 full text speeches that mention the AIIB during 2015. First, speeches are divided among three substantive topic categories displayed in Figure 6.6. Second, speeches are analyzed with attention to the tone toward China, and divided among the four topic categories displayed in Figure 6.5. For the classification shown in each of the two graphs, a speech is placed in one category based on its most dominant theme.

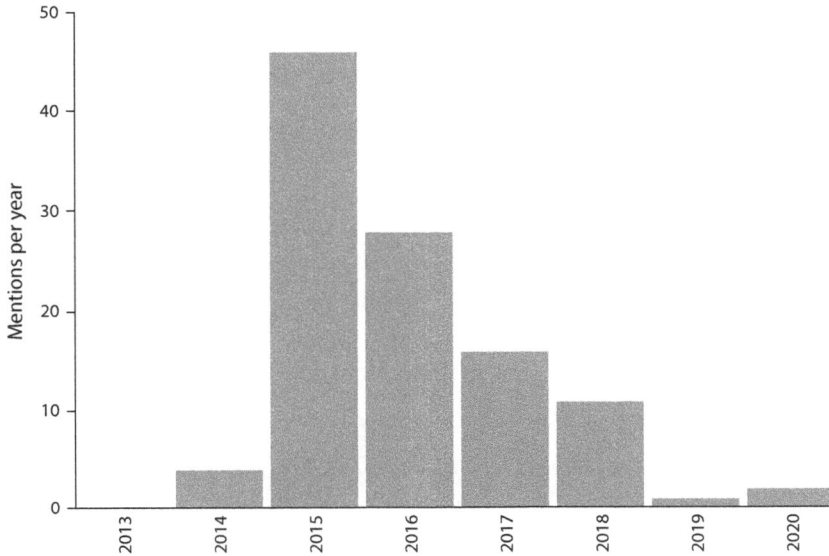

FIGURE 6.4. *Attention to AIIB in Diet testimony:* The graph displays total meetings that make a reference to AIIB in a search of Diet testimony for all committees and plenary sessions in the Upper and Lower Houses.

held affiliation with the Ministry of Foreign Affairs. Many questions came from the opposition, and several scholars and NGO representatives also spoke at hearings. Most supported the decision to remain outside of the AIIB, and comments were made that Japan could work with the United States in existing multilateral institutions and the ADB. Nearly half of the speeches raised concerns about AIIB governance, and many urged that Japan should not join until the AIIB demonstrated high standards of lending and governance. Only 20 percent of the speeches focused on economic interests such as Japanese exports and infrastructure investment opportunities.

Public opinion supported the decision of the government not to join AIIB. In a 2015 poll, 59 percent responded that they agreed with the decision by the Abe administration not to join the AIIB (eleven percent were opposed to the decision). Thirty percent of respondents were recorded as don't know/no response.[81]

81. TV Asahi, telephone survey with 1,000 respondents from national sample with two-staged stratified random sampling. "April 2015 Public Opinion Poll." https://www.tv-asahi.co.jp/hst_archive/poll/201504/index.html. Accessed 11 February 2021.

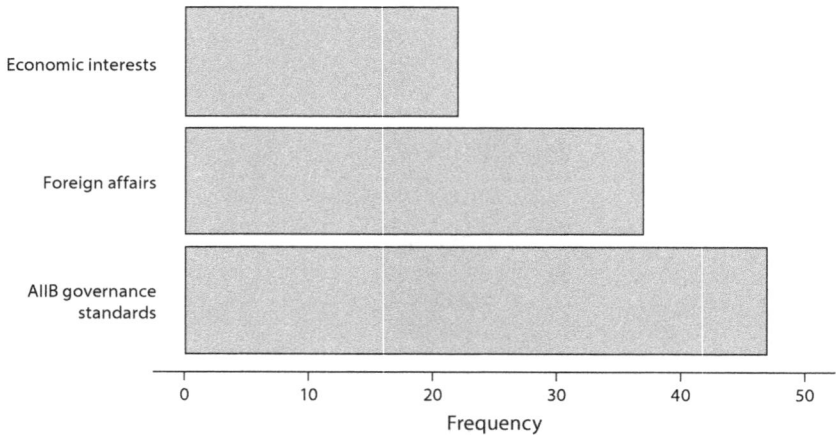

FIGURE 6.5. *Topics raised in AIIB Diet testimony*: The graph summarizes major themes in Diet speeches that referenced the AIIB in 2015 (Upper and Lower Houses).

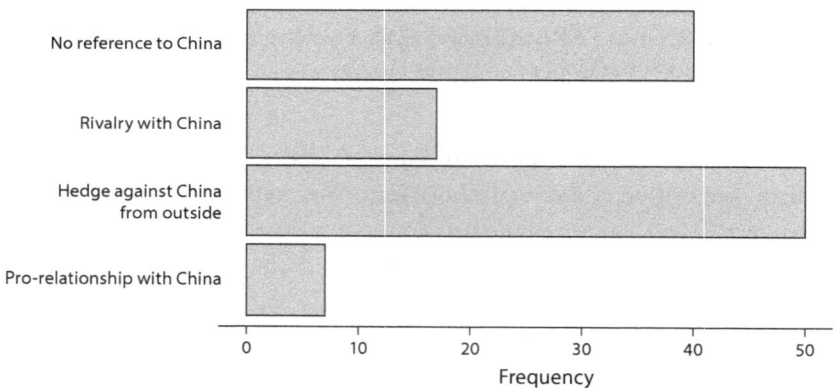

FIGURE 6.6. *Views of China in AIIB Diet testimony*: The graph summarizes perspectives on China in Diet speeches that referenced the AIIB in 2015 (Upper and Lower Houses).

To date, the AIIB has demonstrated strong performance as an international lending organization. Former ADB president Takehiko Nakao confirms that "the AIIB is run according to international standards." Having European countries, Australia, and ROK as members is one constraining factor, but he argues that "the PRC's vision for the establishment of the AIIB was to show its international leadership and prestige. It did not make sense to create it if it was going to do something it would be criticized for" (Nakao, 2022, p. 141). Nakao also dismisses fears about rivalry between the ADB and AIIB. The amount of lending by the ADB was five times that of the AIIB in 2019 and cooperation between the two banks has proceeded smoothly. Despite the evidence of good performance by the AIIB, however, few expect to see the Japanese government change its position regarding the membership question.

At the same time Japan refused to join the AIIB, it increased its own aid provision to the region. In May 2015, at an international aid conference held in Tokyo, the government released a "Partnership for Quality Infrastructure" plan that called for a 30 percent increase in quality infrastructure investment in the Asian region from 2016 to 2020 through collaboration between Japan and the ADB.[82] The levels of development assistance by Japan show a marked increase from 2015. The government sought to emphasize the focus on "quality," to differentiate Japanese aid in rivalry with China.[83] The scope of these projects has included transportation and telecommunications as well as investment in extractive industries for oil and mineral development. The government has carefully avoided a confrontational approach with China. Public statements have expressed willingness by Japan to cooperate with China's OBOR initiative. Moreover, the ADB and AIIB have jointly financed a growing number of development projects.

The controversy over AIIB highlights the point that membership decisions are about more than the qualifications of states to contribute to a public good. Any evaluation of which countries have an interest and capacity to play a role in supporting development policies for Asia would put Japan and the United States at the top of the list. Moreover, China welcomed their participation.[84] It was on the demand side where Japan and the United States both decided they did not want to join the organization. Their public rationale has focused on concerns of governance. But other governments such as the UK share the same concerns, and the AIIB rules are largely similar to those of other multilateral governance banks. Taking sides with China on the other hand helps

---

82. Ministry of Foreign Affairs. https://www.mofa.go.jp/files/000081298.pdf. Accessed 30 April 2021.

83. The annual report on Japanese foreign policy expands on Japan's focus on quality infrastructure. "Diplomatic Bluebook 2017: Japanese Diplomacy and International Situation in 2016." Ministry of Foreign Affairs, Japan. https://www.mofa.go.jp/files/000290287.pdf. Accessed 18 April 2021.

84. Kaya and Woo (2021) show that countries with more distant UN voting records from China actually received a small benefit in their influence within the organization through a larger voting share, although China retained veto privilege as the largest shareholder. The first four years of lending by the AIIB do not appear to have favored members politically close to China (Kaya, Kilby, and Kay, 2021).

explain unlikely joiners such as Russia, which did not have a strong financial interest (or surplus capital!) and had not been a participant in the ADB. Resisting China emerges as a central reason to explain why Japan has to date preferred to lobby about AIIB governance concerns from outside the organization. Rivalry with China has stimulated greater effort by Japan to demonstrate its own leadership for quality development assistance to the region.

6.5.2   From Follower to Leader: Japan in TPP

The experience of the TPP offers another perspective on how Japan's evolving relationship with China shapes its foreign economic policy through the prism of forming new organizations. After years of reluctantly opening its markets in the face of pressure from abroad, Japan led the campaign to save the TPP. How did this happen? The TPP confronted Japan with the unusual scenario where the United States pushed forward a high-level agreement and then unexpectedly withdrew. Instead of backing out, the Japanese government led negotiations for the new TPP11 agreement that preserves the core provisions of the original text and holds open the door for the United States to reenter the agreement in the future.[85] In a marriage of diplomatic necessity and domestic reform agenda, Prime Minister Shinzō Abe played a critical leadership role. The commitment to TPP despite the exit of the United States reflects a new role for Japan as the broker between East Asia and the United States.

Japan had been late to start negotiating free trade agreements, and even the 13 agreements that it had concluded since the year 2000 were with smaller partners and covered only 19 percent of Japan's exports (Solís and Katada, 2015, p. 156). TPP represents by far the most ambitious free trade agreement undertaken by Japan. It has been subject to tremendous resistance from farm groups and other interests and moderate advocacy from industry. Against this backdrop, the value of the agreement as part of a geopolitical strategy was essential to overcoming domestic obstacles to liberalization. But geopolitics in Japanese trade policy has moved beyond reactions to U.S. pressure for liberalization. In the proactive use of economic statecraft, Japan seeks to deepen

85. The official name of the agreement is Comprehensive and Progressive Agreement for Trans-Pacific Partnership. For more information on how Japan came to play a leading role in the CPTPP, see Davis, Christina L. 2019. "Japan: Interest Group Politics, Foreign Policy Linkages, and the TPP." In Megaregulation Contested: Global Economic Ordering After TPP, edited by Benedict Kingsbury, David M. Malone, Paul Mertenskötter, Richard B. Stewart, Thomas Streinz, and Atsushi Sunami, p. 573–591. Oxford: Oxford University Press.

regional integration in East Asia and offset China. The decision to position the international trade agreement within the framework of policies for domestic economic restructuring further strengthened the resilience of Japanese commitment to the agreement.

The twelve countries that would eventually sign the TPP in February 2016—Australia, Brunei, Canada, Chile, Japan, Malaysia, Mexico, New Zealand, Peru, Singapore, the United States, and Vietnam—span a wide geographic region as well as diversity in their political and economic characteristics. From a starting point based around talks among Chile, New Zealand, and Singapore, the cooperative enterprise came to include many more than anticipated at the outset. In particular, even after the United States announced in December 2009 that it would join the negotiations, there was no expectation for Japan to be a part of the project. Longstanding resistance by Japan to the liberalization of agricultural trade, along with the persistent trade deficit between the United States and Japan in auto trade, contributed to deep skepticism on the United States' side that Japan would engage in a deep free trade agreement.

The question of whether Japan would join TPP first arose in 2010, when the Democratic Party of Japan (DPJ) led the government. Prime Minister Naoto Kan declared in an October speech that he would consider the possibility. TPP participants were planning a meeting on the sidelines of the upcoming APEC Summit meeting to be hosted in Japan in November, which would serve as a catalyst for Japan's interest in joining. The government was already negotiating an economic partnership agreement with Australia that challenged Japan's protectionist agricultural policies. Prime Minister Kan said the Australia agreement could break Japan's "*sakoku*" (closure) policy for a second reopening.[86] His successor to represent the DPJ, Prime Minister Yoshihiko Noda, declared that TPP was one of the three priorities of his administration. Ultimately Noda would be unable to formally join TPP negotiations as he faced fierce resistance from agricultural interest groups and his own agriculture minister threatened to resign if he entered the negotiations (Sakuyama, 2015, p. 166). Nevertheless, his administration took a critical step that helped to convince the United States that Japan might be able to join TPP when it initiated a review in 2011 of the health-related restrictions on beef imports from the United States that had been a major source of tensions between the countries.[87] The DPJ campaigned on a pro-TPP platform during the December

86. *Asahi Shimbun* 11 February 2011.
87. Former USTR official, telephone interview by author, 16 May 2017.

2012 election, which it lost in a landslide defeat that brought the Liberal Democratic Party back to power.

Surprisingly, the change in ruling party did not influence Japan's position on TPP. The incoming LDP government formally accepted the deal with the United States to revise beef market regulations in January 2013, which signaled the continued commitment on this front. The government undertook intense consultations at home about the question of joining TPP, and it received briefings by other participants that outlined the broad contents of the agreement and ongoing issues. When Prime Minister Abe announced the government would join the TPP negotiations in March 2013, his speech emphasized three main points: the importance of the agreement to revitalize Japan's economy, reassurance that the government would support the interests of the agricultural sector in the face of liberalization, and the need for Japan to join with the United States as its ally and other countries with shared values to create new rules for the economic order.[88] He called for Japan and the United States as economic powers to participate in establishing a new economic order. The Liberal Democratic Party statement went even further to emphasize explicitly that the agreement was not only a commercial agreement, but also contributed to national security.[89] In discussions before the Diet, Prime Minister Abe and others would repeatedly return to the need for the agreement as a matter of national interest on both economic and security dimensions.

ECONOMIC MERITS OF THE AGREEMENT

As a high standard trade agreement, the TPP would open foreign markets with comprehensive tariff liberalization and deepen discipline on trade and investment with WTO-plus rules. The United States has been at the forefront of pushing ambitious liberalization through preferential trade agreements, while Japan presents a mixed picture, with many agreements having less tariff coverage even as the government supports deeper rule commitments (Solis, 2017, p. 21). Upgrading the standards for the trade architecture can bring gains through improving market access and business efficiency for investment.

88. Official statement of Prime Minister Shinzō Abe issued 15 March 2013. http://www .kantei.go.jp/jp/headline/tpp2013.html.

89. Liberal Democratic Party official party statement on the decision to join TPP, 15 March 2013. Available at https://www.jimin.jp/news/discourse/128489.html.

The economic studies of the original TPP12 agreement forecast positive effects on Japan's economic growth. The Japanese government Cabinet Office study estimated 2.6 percent increase of GDP from the 2014 level of the annual GDP.[90] The new provisions of TPP on e-commerce, labor, and state-owned enterprises were supported by the Japanese government. Japan shared the U.S. priority to resist practices such as requiring domestic location of servers, forceable transfer of source code, and discriminatory tariffs on digital trade. World Bank researchers' investigation about projected TPP income gains also highlighted that larger gains accrue from liberalizing non-tariff measures and services than from traditional market access.[91]

Japanese manufacturing industries supported Japan's decision to join TPP negotiations in 2013. Industry organizations such as Keidanren and the Japan Automobile Manufacturers Association urged the government to quickly conclude negotiations. The Japan Electronics and Information Technology Industries Associate chairman Ryōji Chūbachi emphasized that for his industry to succeed amidst fierce international competition, it needed the government to push forward more free trade agreements with high-level standards going beyond tariff reductions to include intellectual property rights and investment rules.[92] More regulatory coherence would facilitate investments for multinational firms and lower the costs of complying with rules of origin across multiple overlapping agreements. Yet this was not a primary factor driving TPP, in part because the agreement does not include all countries in the region. Moreover, the weak utilization of earlier preferential trade agreements (PTAs) by firms operating in the Asia Pacific region has meant that businesses did not consider it a priority to lobby for their consolidation (Capling and Ravenhill, 2012). To the extent that regional production chains are deeply embedded in China as well as some of the smaller countries outside

90. Cabinet Office, TPP headquarters, 24 December 2015. Available at https://www.cas.go .jp/jp/tpp/tppinfo/2015/pdf/151224_tpp_keizaikoukabunnsekio2.pdf.

91. The World Bank estimated that the original TPP would generate an overall lift of 1.1 percent in annual GDP by the year 2030. These studies rely on simulations utilizing the Global Trade Analysis Project (GTAP) model, which is a widely used macroeconomic model that incorporates trade into forecasts of economic growth. Assumptions about key relationships between prices and inputs underlie such modeling exercises (*Global Economic Prospects: Spillovers and Weak Growth*, 2016, p. 227).

92. 15 March 2013 Statement available at http://www.jeita.or.jp/japanese/topics/2013/0315 /1303XX_TPP.pdf.

of TPP such as Thailand, TPP would be an inadequate tool to achieve full harmonization of rules.

The new provisions of TPP on e-commerce, labor, and state-owned enterprises were supported by the Japanese government. In particular, a Japanese government official gave as an example that there are rules initiated by Japan and incorporated into the electronic commerce chapter.[93] Japan shared the U.S. priority to resist practices such as requiring domestic location of servers, forceable transfer of source code, and discriminatory tariffs on digital trade. It is a major provider of digital service exports in the region. Japan was largely on the defensive in market access talks where it resisted full liberalization of agricultural markets and in turn had to be satisfied with small concessions for its key industries. Notably, auto concessions by the United States had such a long phase-in time that benefits would not have been achieved for decades even if the United States joined the agreement.

Smaller but still significant economic gains remained for TPP11. Writing in 2017, Petri et al. (2017) estimated that the TPP would have increased global income by $492 billion, while TPP11 would generate a much reduced annual income gain of $147 billion. The loss of U.S. participation reduced the expected gains to Japan by almost one third. Notwithstanding such changes following U.S. withdrawal, the business community reaffirmed its support for Japan to pursue the TPP11. The chairman of Keidanren praised the government efforts to push forward: "Japan is taking leadership in Trans-Pacific Partnership (TPP) talks aimed at creating a TPP11 agreement following the withdrawal of the United States. Prime Minister Abe's diplomatic initiatives have succeeded in bolstering the presence of Japan in the global economy and international politics, and these achievements should be rated highly."[94] In a January 2018 survey of 121 firms, 75 percent reported expectations that TPP11 would have a positive effect on the Japanese economy and 18 percent said they would seek out new business opportunities as a result of the agreement.[95]

Although the TPP promises economic gains to Japan, they are modest in scope. Alone, they failed to motivate entry over strong domestic opposition by entrenched agricultural interests. Even the business community frames the

93. Interview by author, Tokyo, 5 July 2017.

94. Chairman Sakakibara's statements and comments at press conference, September 25, 2017. Available at http://www.keidanren.or.jp/en/speech/kaiken/2017/0925.html#p5. Accessed 30 October 2017.

95. *Sankei Shimbun* 4 January 2018. Available at http://www.sankei.com/economy/news/180104/ecn1801040003-n1.html. Accessed 30 March 2018.

agreement within its diplomatic context. It is necessary to consider a broader array of interests to get the full picture of Japan's decision.

CHINA BALANCING

Proponents of TPP were explicit in emphasizing its role as an instrument of foreign policy. This "securitization" of the agreement can be seen in the United States, which has long used PTAs to reinforce its alliances, and indeed lies behind many of the earlier PTAs in the Asia Pacific region (Mansfield and Bronson, 1997; Capling and Ravenhill, 2012). TPP represents an economic partnership that reinforces ties among allies.[96] Speaking at the ASEAN business and investment summit on 21 November 2015, President Obama declared, "TPP is more than just a trade pact; it also has important strategic and geopolitical benefits. TPP is a long-term investment in our shared security and in universal human rights." He went on to emphasize the role of the agreement to build trust among members and deepen U.S. ties to its allies in the region, concluding that the "TPP sends a powerful message across this region—across the Asia Pacific. It says that America's foreign policy rebalance to the Asia Pacific will continue on every front. It says that the United States will keep its commitments to allies and partners, and that we are here to stay and that you can count on us."[97]

The connection to security interests was equally present in Japan. For Prime Minister Noda, TPP helped foreign policy on two dimensions by strengthening ties with the United States and by responding to Chinese challenges in the region (Sakuyama, 2015, p. 192). The DPJ had poor relations with the United States due to difficulties over the question of the Okinawa military bases. The DPJ had issued an election pledge in 2009 to close the Futenma base and then confronted increasing local hostility when the United States insisted upon the existing relocation plans that are deeply unpopular

---

96. The United States has formal alliances with Canada, Australia, and Japan. Capling and Ravenhill (2012) note that Malaysia and Brunei Darussalam have defense arrangements with the United States, and the U.S. military engages in cooperative exercises with New Zealand, Vietnam, and Singapore. Canada, Peru, and Chile engage in U.S. regional cooperation and collective security as part of the Organization of American States. Other allies such as Korea, Taiwan, and the Philippines were not included—geopolitical ties helped some move forward but were not alone enough to bring entry for all allies.

97. Statement available at https://www.whitehouse.gov/the-press-office/2015/11/20/re marks-president-obama-asean-business-and-investment-summit.

in Okinawa. Unable to turn the base issue around, the government hoped that supporting TPP talks would appease the U.S. administration. It was especially important to restore good relations with the United States in the face of growing hostility with China. In 2010, Japan confronted a dramatic increase in tensions over the Senkaku/Diaoyu islands off the coast of Okinawa that are claimed as Japanese territory and disputed by China. The arrest of a Chinese fishing boat captain in the area sparked widespread protests in China. Protesters vandalized Japanese companies, and the government restricted exports of rare earth minerals, which are a vital input for some industries in Japan. Nationalization of the islands by the Japanese government in 2012 was interpreted by China as escalation of the dispute, and led to challenges from China through repeated incursions into Japanese territorial waters by both fishing boats and government surveillance ships. Additional confrontations took place in the South China Seas over disputed islands, with China taking an aggressive approach that heightened alarm in the region.

These security concerns loomed even larger for the new LDP administration upon election in December 2012. Having lambasted the DPJ for harming diplomatic relations with the United States and neighbors through weak foreign policy, the newly elected Prime Minister Abe needed something to demonstrate an immediate foreign policy success. The U.S. rhetoric about TPP as a strategic agreement to shore up its own commitment to regional partners facing a hostile China reinforced the impression in Japan that security cooperation should naturally lead to economic cooperation, and that Japan's joining the TPP was a corollary to supporting the U.S.-Japan alliance.[98] Given his strong orientation to security as a policy priority, Abe was naturally inclined to support the linkage between the TPP and national security interests (Akiyama, 2015, p. 49). Economic trends reinforce Japanese interest in balancing against China. As China has grown in economic size and world market shares, so have Japanese fears of Chinese economic competition. Furthermore, easing customs procedures and providing higher levels of support to data and intellectual property rights in Southeast Asia would counter the allure of the Chinese market. Terada (2015, p. 383) suggests that the high-level rules of TPP were viewed by the government as a way to make markets outside of China attractive to Japanese investors and thereby reduce dependence on China.

---

98. "TPP wa anpo [TPP Is the alliance]," *Nihon Keizai Shimbun* 23 December 2012.

But the agreement does not preclude membership for China. Rather, it sets high standards that would be difficult for China to meet. In particular, the mandate for collective bargaining rights for labor goes beyond anything contained in the WTO to impinge on domestic policies. Provisions on transparency and competition policies with regard to state-owned enterprises would also force changes in sensitive policies in China. The digital trade provisions further strike at issues that have been sources of tension in other negotiating fora, as the Chinese censorship regime emphasizes a domestic server requirement while TPP promotes free flow of data and restricts such data localization requirements.

Japan's government has engaged in TPP negotiations as part of a foreign policy strategy to contain, shape, and entice China toward cooperation. By joining as a founding member in TPP, the government hoped to ensure its own role in writing the rules that would set the standard for China to later join. Speaking at a press conference in Tokyo, Japan's lead TPP negotiator and Minister of Economic Revitalization, Akira Amari, emphasized the importance of setting rules for investment transparency and other critical topics, and holding them out as the entry requirements for the agreement—he commented that many other countries were lining up to enter but would be told they must accept the rules as a condition to join.[99] The large role of state capitalism and state-owned enterprises competing directly with Japanese firms worries METI officials. Coercing China to moderate its industrial policy would be difficult for any country, let alone Japan, given that tense bilateral relations cast a shadow over Sino-Japanese negotiations. Far better for Japan to hold up the TPP rules, leaving the choice to China about whether it will make the necessary reforms to join.

Certainly from the Chinese perspective, the agreement was first perceived as hostile to its interests. An editorial in the *China Daily* at the time of Japan's entry into TPP stated that "TPP has been heavily criticized for its spirit of confrontation and containment, as China, the world's second-largest economy and a traditional powerhouse in the eastern Pacific, is excluded from the Pacific trade pact. By participating in the talks Japan will further alienate its geographic neighbor and closest economic partner."[100] Alongside the

99. Akira Amari press conference, 7 October 2015. Available at http://www.cao.go.jp /minister/1412_a_amari/kaiken/2015/1007kaiken-1.html. Accessed 15 November 2016.

100. Hong Cai, "Japan Looks to Board US' 'Black Ship,'" *China Daily*, 28 March 2013, http://usa.chinadaily.com.cn/opinion/2013-03/28/content_16351746.htm.

warnings of "encirclement," however, others noted China could someday join and benefit from the high standards set in the agreement [101]

In 2021, the PRC submitted its application to join, closely followed by Taiwan. This move has put the current members into a dilemma. Some are favorably inclined toward accepting China, while others including Japan are caught between the open structure of the agreement and their anxiety about China joining. Japan's approach has been to delay issuing any decision and renew calls for U.S. entry in the agreement.[102] Ultimately, members are likely to engage in a similar approach to that taken for WTO entry for China. Strongly insisting on compliance with TPP standards to promote reform and delay negotiations will raise the cost of entry for China. When open agreements confront rival states, entry conditions are held to their most rigorous test.

BUILDING SUPPORT FOR TPP IN DOMESTIC POLITICS

During the domestic approval process in Japan, foreign policy played an important role in offsetting resistance to the agreement. Long before the TPP had become a rallying point for political attention in the United States, it was widely discussed in Japan. Indeed, it has been called the "debate dividing the nation into two" with a close split in public opinion and fierce opposition from farm groups (Naoi and Urata, 2013, p. 326). Yet despite the controversy over the agreement, Japan emerged as one of the most committed advocates of the agreement and among the first to push forward the domestic ratification process. How did Prime Minister Abe overcome the fierce domestic resistance?

First, Abe had the benefit that the prior administration under the Democratic Party of Japan had supported the prospect of joining TPP. In the early rounds of discussion about TPP in the Diet, which were quite extensive in 2011, the DPJ had been on the side promoting the agreement. Tables were reversed for the debate in 2013 around the decision by Prime Minister Abe to join talks. From the opposition party position, the DPJ criticized the LDP for being inconsistent. But the LDP did not face a battle over the merits of free trade or deepening integration with the United States. Moreover, the 2012

101. Qifang Tang, "TPP's High Standards Conflict with Goal of Expanding Membership," *Global Times,* 22 April 2013. http://www.globaltimes.cn/content/776655.shtml.

102. "TPP hukki yōsei e shushō, Biden daitōryō ni [Prime Minister Requests to Biden a Return to TPP]," *Mainichi Shimbun* 21 January 2022.

election victory ensured that the LDP in coalition with the Kōmeitō party held two thirds of the seats in the Lower House of the Diet.

Abe was able to make this policy shift appear consistent by his emphasis on the national gains. TPP fit easily into the overall economic growth strategy termed "Abenomics" that was central to the administration. In the common description, the "three arrows" of the policy consist of monetary easing, fiscal stimulus, and economic restructuring. The third arrow has been highlighted as the most important foundation for a growth strategy and the most difficult to deliver. Abe seized on TPP as the concrete policy that would force competition and globalization on Japanese industries from abroad. This pattern follows a long tradition of Japanese liberalization under foreign pressure, *gaiatsu*, and is consistent with theories of free trade agreements as a domestic commitment device (e.g. Schoppa, 1993; Davis and Oh, 2007; Milner and Mansfield, 2012).

Absent the geopolitical logic of the agreement, however, it is less apparent that this would have emerged as the core policy for economic restructuring. TPP offered only limited economic gains for Japan, with the largest income benefits attributed to Japan's own liberalization of its markets (Kawasaki, 2014). The long transition for U.S. auto concessions delays the gains it can expect from market access, while Japanese agricultural concessions are equally gradual in their implementation. The fact that China and Thailand, both critical cogs within Japan's regional production networks, are outside of the agreement, substantially weakens the benefits of harmonization.

TPP confronted entrenched opposition from Japanese agriculture interest groups. The sector has been steadily contracting through a combination of structural factors related to small-scale production and demographic shifts, along with liberalization. But it nevertheless continues to win high levels of protection.[103] The Japanese agricultural cooperative organization Nōkyō criticized the decision to join the negotiations as a threat to agriculture and incursion on sovereignty.[104] Specific sectoral organizations such as the dairy farmers' association and pork farmers' association linked their political campaign contributions with TPP policy positions.[105] In massive mobilization

---

103. The Japanese agricultural sector continues to receive generous government assistance, with 48 percent of farm income over the years 2013–15 coming from government policies, three times higher than the OECD average (OECD, 2016, p. 96).

104. http://www.zenchu-ja.or.jp/pdf/press/130315_tpp_release.pdf.

105. *Asahi Shimbun*, 29 November 2014.

against the agreement, "agricultural cooperatives collected more than 11 million petitions against Japan's participation in the TPP within a 10-month period since 2011, which constituted more than 10 percent of Japan's total eligible voters" (Naoi and Urata, 2013, p. 334). The primary goal of agricultural groups was resistance to liberalization of the five sensitive commodity groups: rice, wheat/barley, beef, dairy products, and sugar. The protection of these "sanctuaries" was the rallying cry to hold the line against threats to the sectors that had low competitiveness and retained substantial shares of farm employment.[106] Signalling the continued political influence of agricultural goups, the Diet passed resolutions opposing liberalization of these five important commodity groups.

Reflecting this pressure, the government insisted that it could not promise zero tariffs, and Japan preserved 19 percent of its agricultural commodities from any tariff elimination (Solis, 2017, p. 186). Nonetheless, the government accepted major new cuts for agricultural protection in the agreement for the most ambitious liberalization to date. The TPP represents the first of Japan's preferential trade agreements to reach the WTO standard for liberalization of 90 percent of tariff lines, and this included the immediate elimination of tariffs on 51 percent of agricultural commodities (Solis, 2017, p. 186). This came at a political cost, with agricultural groups portraying the tariff cuts on sensitive products as a violation of the Diet resolutions, and surveys showing a loss of support for the administration among farm voters (Solis, 2017, p. 208).

Several factors undermined the ability of the agricultural groups to achieve their full demands. The demographic shift of an aging sector on top of the 1994 electoral law change prioritized larger size districts and national policymaking interests. Internal dynamics of the agricultural iron triangle also changed with the retirement of leading politicians in the hard-core *nōrin zoku* faction of the LDP representatives tied to agricultural interests and with the erosion of the agricultural cooperatives' monopoly through several deregulation measures. Starting with the Koizumi administration, one began to see the government focus more on consumer interests. Yet after noting these trends in the long-term decline of influence for agricultural interests, Akiyama (2015) points to the importance of the security linkage to place agricultural groups on the defensive. He writes that "the growing importance of the U.S.-Japan alliance associated with the rising anxiety about the security environment in Asia became linked to the TPP and, combined with the conservative beliefs of

106. http://www.zenchu-ja.or.jp/pdf/press/130315_tpp_release.pdf.

Prime Minister Abe, created a situation in which opponents had no choice but to recognize that Japan would accept the agreement even if forced to undertake some liberalization of the five critical products."[107] As in the case of the Uruguay Round negotiations that ended the ban on rice imports, farm groups came to recognize that compromise was necessary to avoid blame for a major international setback for Japanese national interests.[108]

Those conservative LDP politicians most likely to support agricultural interests are also susceptible to the appeals for security gains. With the DPJ weakened and on the record as having supported TPP in the past, LDP politicians were safe in the knowledge that angry farm groups had no alternative party to choose. The coalition partner in the LDP administration was a small religion-based party, Kōmeitō, which had a lower-income urban base and historically was the most favorable to agricultural liberalization. Indeed, to the extent that the Kōmeitō party was more supportive of TPP than it was of some of the more ambitious security policy reforms planned by Abe, the trade agreement strengthened the policy mix for the coalition.

The Abe administration changed the tone of agricultural liberalization with emphasis on the positive imaging that a strengthened Japanese farm sector could increase agricultural exports and take advantage of the Japanese food culture boom. Some argued that the liberalization of agricultural markets would promote consolidation of land as smaller farmers retire, and a stronger agricultural sector would emerge with lower prices to consumers and direct income compensation by the government to support farmers' living standards (Ishikawa, 2014). At the same time, the government has continued the long tradition of using subsidies to ease the transition even when they undercut reform goals. Budget allocations for TPP adjustment have targeted the rural sector with public works and subsidies. This strategy successfully diffused the opposition to the agreement. In the October 2017 Lower House election, the TPP was largely absent as an issue.[109]

107. Author's translation from Japanese Akiyama (2015, p. 50)

108. See Davis (2003) for analysis of the domestic politics in Japan related to agricultural liberalization in the Uruguay Round.

109. A comparison of the campaign policy platform of eight major parties reveals a brief mention from LDP about helping rethink agricultural policies to adapt to impact of TPP while the Communist Party urges withdrawal from the agreement, and the six other main opposition parties fail to even mention the deal. See summary of campaign platforms. https://mainichi.jp/senkyo/48shu_koyaku/.

The final consideration that facilitated Japan's participation in the TPP negotiations was the greater centralization of policy authority within the Cabinet Office. Japan has long been notorious for turf wars between rival ministries. It is not uncommon for the government to send ministers from two or even three ministries as part of the negotiation team. While the Ministry of Foreign Affairs holds the formal role of lead negotiator, Finance, Agriculture, and of course the Ministry of Economy, Trade and Industry (METI) all take strong interest in trade agreements. Even the assessment of the economic impact of the TPP had competing studies issued from different ministries.[110] This ended with the decision by Abe to locate TPP negotiations within the Economic Revitalization headquarters, which was the cabinet-level organization established to formulate economic growth strategy. The appointment of Akira Amari in December 2012 assigned him the role of lead negotiator for the TPP as part of his duties as minister of economic revitalization. He helped to ensure that there would be one voice for the Japanese negotiating team and one authoritative cabinet source to assess the impact of the agreement.[111] According to a former USTR official, "The TPP negotiations were completely different than prior negotiations with Japan. In TPP, all of the Ministries were on board and Japan played a leadership role. They were committed to finding creative solutions, and worked hard to bring other countries on board. Moreover, it was important that Minister Amari was reporting straight to Prime Minister Abe and he could see the totality of negotiations, not just through the lens of individual issues affecting one Ministry."[112] A lasting legacy of the TPP for Japan could be a more centralized approach to trade negotiations. Dealing with the complexity of megaregional agreements spanning such a range of issue areas and partners forces domestic institutional adaptation in ways that may persist.

The TPP instigated a process within Japan that has entrenched support for the agreement in the government. Linking the agreement to Prime Minister Abe's centerpiece economic reforms and geopolitical strategy made this an

110. The Ministry of Agriculture study concluded that the agreement would cause 3.4 million job losses in the agriculture sector, while a METI study instead concluded that the net impact on the economy was positive, such that *not joining* would cause 0.8 million lost jobs. Analysis indicates that the choice by a regional government to publish one study over the other correlated highly with opinion toward the agreement by firms in that region (Naoi and Kuno, 2012, p. 6).

111. Amari's resignation in January 2016 over a corruption scandal left a temporary leadership vacuum, but came after the agreement had been signed.

112. Interview by author, 16 May 2017.

irreversible commitment. Attributing economic gains from the deal to domestic structural reforms of the Japanese economy created an economic rationale that was not contingent on market access gains per se. Furthermore, the two-pronged geopolitical role to deepen ties with the region and exercise rule-making authority over economic governance represented a nuanced strategy toward balancing Chinese influence that went beyond the U.S.-Japan alliance. Compensation to losers helped to soften the distributional impact on weak sectors. These factors made Japan's support for TPP resilient in the face of the U.S. withdrawal.

While the Japanese government was pushing the agreement through the Diet ratification process, the U.S. Presidential campaign openly condemned TPP as a bad agreement. After the victory of Donald Trump in the November 8, 2016 election, Congressional Republicans said they would not bring the agreement to the floor. At the time, the U.S. House Ways and Means Committee member Rep. Lloyd Doggett (D-TX) said, "TPP in its current form is dead . . . and the only question is will it come back in some zombie trade agreement to stalk us next year?"[113] Nevertheless, the Diet voted to approve the agreement in December 2016, and the Japanese government issued its formal notification of ratification on 20 January 2017—the inauguration day for President Donald Trump.[114] Fulfilling his campaign promise, President Donald Trump declared the exit of the United States from the agreement as one of his first acts in office.

The decision to bring TPP forward for ratification in the Diet during the fall of 2016 even as the U.S. government turned against the agreement raises important questions. If the primary motive of the agreement was to support U.S.-Japan relations, why did Prime Minister Abe advance the agreement with uncertainty over its ultimate future? Of course, the decisive win in the 2016 July elections gave him a surplus of political capital, so that the party was assured of the votes to win passage. Nevertheless, in a consensus-driven society, ramming through legislation over objections risks negative public reaction and could potentially freeze out cooperation on other issues coming before the legislature. Nonetheless, Prime Minister Abe went ahead with the ratification process in the hopes to encourage other TPP signatories to follow suit. His stated goal was to "send a message about the TPP's strategic and economic

113. *Inside U.S. Trade*, 15 November 2016

114. "Japan Taking Final Step for TPP Ratification Friday," *Nikkei Asian Review* 20 January 2017.

significance of creating a fair economic grouping."[115] In many ways, the geo-political framing created a momentum of its own. Having once portrayed the agreement as the lynchpin of U.S.-Japan cooperation against a hostile China, the Japanese government feared that failure to conclude the TPP agreement would represent weakness.

Filling the vacuum left by the United States to bring the agreement to fruition put the spotlight on Japan's regional leadership role. A series of bilat-eral meetings followed, with the December 2017 meeting, when negotiators from the 11 parties gathered in Tokyo before the upcoming APEC meeting. Japanese negotiators sought to hold open the door for the United States to later join. For this reason, they resisted efforts from other governments to change the terms of the agreement, which could complicate U.S. entry. An official with Japan's Cabinet Secretariat noted, "The only option is to con-vince them not to renegotiate," in response to suggestions that New Zealand would introduce a new restriction on foreign real estate investment and to a series of requests from Vietnam on textile tariffs and other matters.[116] Japan was largely successful in this goal—the parties removed 22 clauses in the orig-inal text but retained the core principles and all tariff schedules. The rules on digital trade, state-owned enterprises, environment, and labor have not been changed. Most of the suspended clauses relate to items that had been reluctantly accepted, at the United States' insistence, such as some aspects of the investor-state dispute mechanism and specific items related to intellec-tual property right protection.[117] In a clever legal maneuver, these provisions have been "suspended" in the TPP11 agreement but could be reinstated if the United States later joined the agreement. On 8 March 2018, in Santiago Chile, the 11 remaining countries signed the TPP11, renamed as the Comprehensive and Progressive Trans-Pacific Partnership.

In part, Japan went forward with the belief the United States would even-tually join, and hoped that implementation of TPP11 would encourage this movement. Petri et al. (2017, p. 8) estimate that U.S. gains from joining TPP would have stood at as much as $131 billion in the year 2030, relative to the baseline of no agreement, while the United States risked an annual loss of $2 billion when the agreement among the 11 remaining countries went into

115. "Japan's Ratification of the TPP," *The Japan Times* 14 December 2016.
116. 29 October 2017, "TPP11 Faces New Challenges as Clock Ticks Down," *Nikkei Asian Review*.
117. See Asian Trade Centre Policy Brief, "CPTPP: Unpacking the Suspended Provisions." Available at http://www.asiantradecentre.org/. Accessed 30 March 2018.

effect. Others gained preferential market access and first-mover advantage for investment and setting product standards. U.S. agricultural exporters faced a significant disadvantage. For example, U.S. beef exports faced a beef tariff rate of 38.5%, while Canada and Australia stood to benefit from the lower 9% rate negotiated under TPP. In a role reversal to practice the art of two-level game diplomacy on the United States, Japanese trade officials were reported to comment, "Tokyo hopes that U.S. meat industry leaders will speak up in favor of rejoining the trade deal."[118] Japan's lead negotiator Kazuyoshi Umemoto affirmed that "putting the TPP 11 into effect will not only give us an open and free Trans-Pacific trade system, but it will also act as a strong message to the U.S. to return to the trade pact."[119] Keidanren chairman Sakakibara stated, "The Japanese business community is anticipating the United States will rejoin in the future."[120]

The centrality of the United States to Japanese interest in the TPP is evident from the content of Japanese Diet members' speeches about the agreement (see Figure 6.7).[121] From the outset to the conclusion, the United States has clearly been the most frequently referenced country in the Diet discussion of the agreement. Indeed, its departure from the agreement only heightened the need to discuss TPP in terms of how it related to the U.S.-Japan relationhip.

TPP AS STEPPING STONE TO FTAAP

TPP is one of several trade agreements in the Asia Pacific region. Beyond the existing agreements with ASEAN and a web of bilateral agreements, APEC leaders called for a Free Trade Area of the Asia-Pacific (FTAAP) at an APEC meeting in 2010, and ASEAN leaders joined China to initiate the RCEP. Japan stands in the middle as the pivotal country that belongs to all three of these groupings, whereas the United States is outside of RCEP and China is outside of TPP.

118. "Revived TPP May Exclude Trade Concessions Sought by US," *Nikkei Asian Review*, 24 August 2017.

119. "TPP 11 negotiators make headway before crucial summit next week," *Nikkei Asian Review*, November 1, 2017.

120. Adam Behsudi, Morning Trade, *Politico*, 3 November 2017.

121. As in the earlier analysis of the ADB and AIIB, the text analysis uses the package quanteda in R to break up sentences into "words." The Japanese language text corpus is based on Diet testimonies in all committees and plenary sessions in both the Upper House and the Lower House. The frequencies in the graph represent a count of the names of countries or regions that appear within 20 "words" before and after the word "TPP" (search terms included the full Japanese name and abbreviation and a country name dictionary).

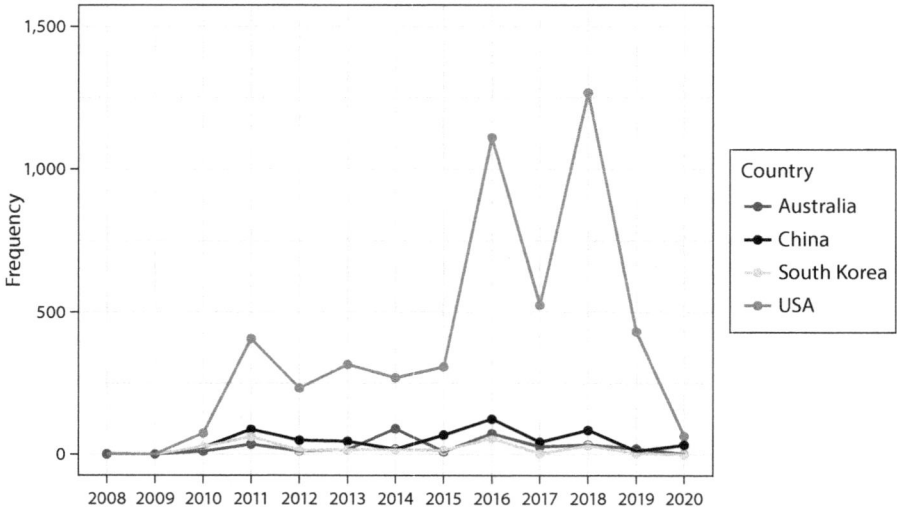

FIGURE 6.7. *TPP partners in Diet testimony*: The graph displays total count of references to each country and TPP (within 20 words surrounding the text including the English acronym or the Japanese name) in a search of Diet testimony for all committees and plenary sessions in the Upper and Lower Houses.

The long-term economic interests of Japan encourage further integration with China, which remains the natural trading partner for Japanese business.[122] Whereas many of the income gains to Japan from TPP come from its own liberalization measures, the RCEP agreement brings market access gains achieved through the participation of China and Korea (other partners in TPP and RCEP already held agreements with Japan). From the beginning, the Japanese government offered assurances that it would pursue multiple strategies with continued interest in RCEP even as it joined TPP. In his March 2013 speech about joining TPP negotiations, Prime Minister Abe explicitly mentioned the hope to see RCEP concluded and eventually a broader Free Trade of the Asia and Pacific Region.[123] This comprehensive approach found broad-based support. When business associations endorsed the decision to join TPP, they also made reference to RCEP as another goal. Similarly, even

122. Early research conducted for the Economic Planning Agency examined gains from different forms of free trade agreements in terms of selection of partners. It predicted highest gains from pursuit of both TPP12 and RCEP agreements (Kawasaki, 2014).

123. Official statement of Prime Minister Shinzō Abe issued 15 March 2013. http://www.kantei.go.jp/jp/headline/tpp2013.html.

while urging the government to protect agricultural interests in the negotiations, the criticism of the government from the DPJ Leader Banri Kaieda on 15 March 2013 noted that the Democratic Party of Japan had planned to simultaneously negotiate the TPP, the trilateral agreement between Japan, South Korea, and China, as well as RCEP, with the long-term objective of creating an Asia-Pacific free trade zone.[124]

TPP also advanced other FTA negotiations. When Prime Minister Noda engaged in preliminary talks about the possibility of joining TPP in November 2011, it sparked the interest of China in the trilateral talks and also triggered engagement by the EU to push forward talks with Japan for an EU-Japan FTA (Ishikawa, 2014, p. 231). First, Japan's decision to enter TPP negotiations surprised many who had seen the government as only weakly committed to liberalization of trade and investment (Solís and Katada, 2015). Second, each new agreement generates fears of trade diversion (Chase, 2003; Manger, 2009; Mansfield and Milner, 2015). Here it was the actual threat of deepening integration among TPP members that pushed others to action for their own negotiations to gain access. In an ironic turn of events, Japan and the EU announced the conclusion of their agreement on the eve of the July 2017 summit of G20 leaders in Hamburg, as a clear message from Japan and Europe to President Trump that they would continue forward on trade liberalization.

The trilateral talks for China, Korea, and Japan stalled over politics; RCEP became the back door to circumvent these problems and allow Japan to join a free trade agreement with Korea and China. Political tensions among these countries loom large on both sides when they are negotiating on their own. In the context of the larger regional agreements, however, both sides can portray concessions as part of regional cooperation rather than as zero-sum exchanges.

Ultimately, Japan concluded a bilateral FTA with the United States in 2019 while simultaneously implementing CPTPP and negotiating RCEP. As Japan navigated options for multiple overlapping agreements, political relations and rivalries loomed large. Some within the Abe administration voiced concerns that going forward with RCEP could abandon chances of bringing the United States around to join the TPP. A METI official was quoted during a round of meetings on RCEP expressing the belief that the government should prioritize

124. https://www.dpj.or.jp/article/102149/

the talks with the United States over the RCEP negotiations.[125] In the final bilateral agreement, the "phase one" deal offered the United States largely equivalent terms to those of the TPP for access to Japanese markets. For political expediency, Japan agreed to defer talks over auto market liberalization in the United States to a phase two agreement, even as it offered the sought-after liberalization for U.S. beef exports; the United States agreed not to impose tariffs on Japanese autos and did not demand rice market liberalization by Japan. With the bilateral agreement in place with the United States, Japan was free to pursue RCEP.

Geopolitical interests helped push the TPP and U.S.-Japan agreements in line at first, but the attraction of preferential access to the Chinese market and consolidation of rules of origin within the region was too great for Japan to resist. Not all cooperation is driven by a security logic. After years of negotiations to uphold high standards and broaden participation, Japan accepted the RCEP agreement, to join the largest free trade agreement in its region. During negotiations, Japan supported the core principles that it had developed in partnership with the United States in the TPP negotiations. One Japanese government official explained that "the terms of the TPP agreement could serve as standards for RCEP. We hope that TPP can raise the level of the RCEP agreement."[126] Pushing high standards risked delaying the talks, and many Japanese firms would benefit from a simpler focus on market access in key sectors and basic investment protection. Nevertheless, the government urged a high-level agreement with continued pressure for further rounds of talks. Some of the provisions pushed by the Japanese government included digital trade terms for free cross-border transfer of information as well as for open locations of servers, and intellectual property rights to protect against technology transfers or other violations. The trade minister Hiroshige Sekō reported to the Diet in 2017 that although some RCEP member states called for an early agreement that only covered market access, Japan would seek a treaty that sets the rules of the game, and he felt that solidarity in the TPP11 talks built momentum for this effort.[127] During the most intense discussion of the agreement in 2018, politicians repeatedly emphasized Japan's role as the standard-bearer of free trade.

125. *Asahi Shimbun* 25 February 2017.

126. Interview by author, Tokyo, 5 July 2017.

127. Diet Record, 26 May 2017. 193rd Session of the Diet, Lower House Committee on Economy and Industry, no. 16.

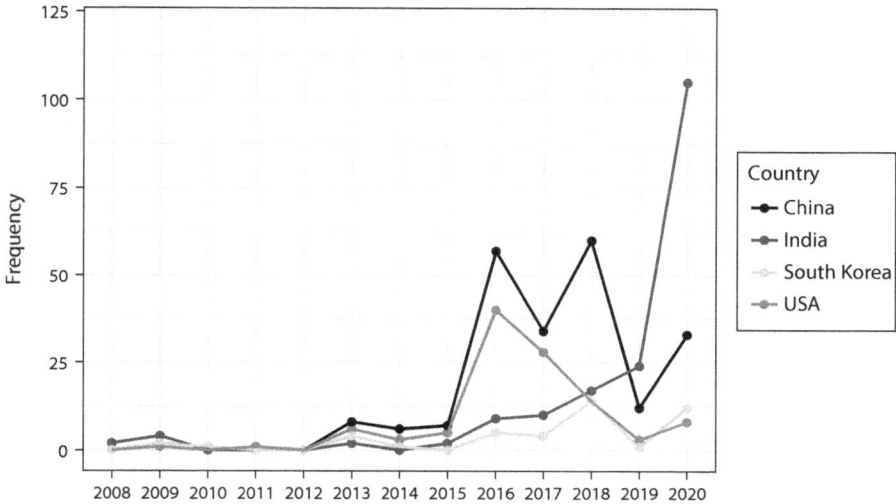

FIGURE 6.8. *RCEP partners in Diet testimony:* The graph displays total count of references to each country and RCEP (within 20 words surrounding the text including the English acronym or the Japanese name) in a search of Diet testimony for all committees and plenary sessions in the Upper and Lower Houses.

Originally China and ASEAN had envisioned a smaller grouping, without India, but Japan encouraged inclusion of India. On November 14, 2018, in a RCEP summit held in Singapore, Prime Minister Abe argued that "RCEP is becoming more and more strategically important as protectionist policies are on the rise, and we must create a free market based on fair rules in this region and thus realize a free and open Indo-Pacific region."[128] Yet the Japanese goals for a high standard agreement that included India proved too ambitious. India backed out of participation in the final year, despite strong encouragement from Tokyo to remain. The question of India's participation attracted significant attention in the Japanese Diet discussion of the agreement, with concerns about its decision to withdraw and how best to go forward (Figure 6.8). Noting India's absence when signing RCEP on 15 November 2020, Prime Minister Suga emphasized that "India remains an essential player in the regional

128. Sugime, Shingo, "RCEP 2019 daketsu itchi. [RCEP Agrees to Conclude Negotiations in 2019]," *Yomiuri Shimbun*, 15 November 2018.

economic framework. Japan is determined to continue playing a leading role in India's return in the future to this Agreement."[129]

There was no significant public debate related to RCEP. Sentiment in support of free trade has been generally high, with the exception of the sensitive issues of agricultural trade. Flexibility in the agreement meant Japan would not have to offer significant new liberalization of its agricultural sector, which helped it to avoid backlash from farmers that had opposed earlier talks about the TPP. At the same time, the Japanese public was cynical about the prospect of economic cooperation with China. When asked whether the future of economic relations between Japan and China would be complementary or competitive, 45 percent said it was competitive, relative to 25 percent indicating they expected a win-win relationship.[130] The lack of specific polling on RCEP—itself an indicator of low public interest—prevents direct assessment of public sentiment.

The agreement completed the full set of economic partners critical to Japanese trade. This clearly served economic interests dependent on global supply chains and market access. Through the balance of partners in different agreements, Japan could achieve the highest level of rules possible while still maximizing breadth. On the trade dimension, far from excluding rivals, Japan sought to both hedge against and engage China. Through careful sequencing, leaders kept Japan's foreign economic policy close to the United States while they advanced ties with other states.

6.6   Japan and the International Whaling Commission

Even as Japan advocated for multilateral institutions, one action sent a discordant note. In December 2018, the government announced it would withdraw from the IWC. Amidst a wave of negative rhetoric toward multilateralism from President Donald Trump and the Brexit referendum of 2016, did Japan choose to mimic others and turn away from organizations? Not really. Japan left the organization when long-held discontent with the organization reached a tipping point. In this case, geopolitical ties were a factor to explain why Japan did

129. Ministry of Foreign Affairs of Japan, "The 4th Regional Comprehensive Economic Partnership (RCEP) Summit and RCEP Agreement Signing Ceremony," 15 November 2020. https://www.mofa.go.jp/policy/economy/fta/page1e_000291.html. Accessed 28 January 2021.

130. The Japan-China Joint Opinion Survey, 2019. https://www.genron-npo.net/. Accessed 7 February 2021.

not exit sooner from an organization that had long since stopped functioning in the way Japan expected. The rise of exit by other countries from multilateral organizations helped to release the brakes.

Along with many other organizations, Japan immediately signed up to join the IWC in 1951 at the end of the Occupation. The organization has an inclusive charter that only requires applicants to notify that they will adhere to the agreement, without any review by the organization or vote of members. As a whaling nation, Japan had interest in supporting an organization dedicated to the management of whale stocks as a natural resource. Japanese interests aligned with the goals stated in the preamble: "Recognizing that the whale stocks are susceptible of natural increases if whaling is properly regulated, and that increases in the size of whale stocks will permit increases in the numbers of whales which may be captured."[131] The organization was also actively supported by the United States, with the charter signed in Washington, DC in 1946. Its secretariat was based in the UK.

At the time of joining the IWC, there was no tension between the United States and Japan on the question of whaling. Indeed, Japan's whaling industry's revival and development was fostered by the U.S. Occupation. After the war, the Supreme Allied Commander General Douglas MacArthur approved Japanese whaling vessels fishing in the region around the Antarctic Ocean, while sending SCAP officials on ships to supervise them, and the US represented Japan at the IWC (Japan could not itself join because it lacked sovereignty).[132] Since Japan had already brought its policies into conformity with the IWC regulations under the guidelines of the U.S. Occupation, it would not have to make changes now in order to join. Furthermore, the standards were viewed as loose enough not to limit Japan's whaling activity. In Diet deliberation regarding the decision to join, the head of the Fisheries Agency assured politicians that membership would be "neither plus nor minus" in its impact on Japanese whaling.[133] He went on to argue that the value of accession lay in the opportunity for the government to show other countries that Japan was trustworthy.

131. "International Convention for the Regulation of Whaling" United Nations Treaty Series Vol. 161, no. 2124 (1953), p. 72.

132. Nakashima, Leslie. "30 Nippon Ships to Hunt Whales," 29 July 1950, *The Japan Times* p. 3.

133. Diet records, 28 February 1951. 10th Session of the Diet, Upper House Committee on Fisheries, no. 15.

Over time, the IWC evolved from a resource management organization to one dedicated to the preservation of whales, and Japan found itself in the minority of members that still conducted commercial whaling. The end of the commercial whaling industry in the United States and global advocacy against whaling by activist groups led the U.S. government to support the call for a moratorium on commercial whaling. Following the 1972 passage by Congress of the Marine Mammal Protection Act that prohibited whaling in the United States, U.S. officials sought to internationalize the ban. They did so by threatening sanctions against states deemed to "diminish the effectiveness" of IWC regulations (DeSombre, 2000, p. 208). Other states had not yet converged on this view, and a 1972 proposal for a moratorium on commercial whaling was voted down by the IWC. But without any restrictions on membership, more non-whaling countries became members who joined the United States, Europe, Australia, and New Zealand in a coalition that opposed whaling. In the case of Chile, Peru, and South Korea, the United States certified them for harming the IWC when they exceeded IWC quotas on whaling, which led them to join the organization and agree to respect IWC whaling quotas (DeSombre, 2000, p. 209). A decade later, another proposal for a moratorium passed in the IWC. This began the era of Japan's tense relationship with the organization. Several outcomes could have resulted: Japan could have been socialized within the organization to oppose whaling, its government could defy the IWC with unrestrained whaling, it could lobby for changes in the rules, or it could exit from the organization.

For decades, Japan chose the third course, to formally comply with IWC rules while trying to minimize the restrictions on whaling imposed by the organization. The long cultural tradition and political support for local whaling communities, combined with a fear of restrictions on other fishery stocks, provided a strong bulwark against the shift of norms toward whaling that took place in other countries (Catalinac and Chan, 2005). At the outset of IWC pressures, Japan objected to the 1973 quota on commercial whaling of Minke whales. The Japanese catch exceeded IWC limits until U.S. threats of sanctions led it to agree to comply (DeSombre, 2000, p. 209). Later, Japanese delegates reported pressure from a "certain nation" not to object to the IWC vote in 1982 adopting a moratorium on commercial whaling (ibid.). Given the pressure from its ally, the issue had come to be seen as a matter where Japan needed to conform to trends in what constituted responsible international behavior (Catalinac and Chan, 2005). The Japanese government agreed in 1988 to halt commercial whaling. Its catch was immediately cut from 2,769 whales in

1986 to 241 in 1988, with low levels upheld in subsequent years (Strausz, 2014, p. 457). Public opinion and government support for whaling remained strong, but the government relented to the IWC pressures for change in the scope and form of whaling by Japanese fishermen.

Whaling continued in the form of a scientific whaling program. Following the rules issued by the IWC scientific committee and fishing from the abundant population of Minke Whale in the Southern Ocean allowed the government to maintain IWC compliance and also sustain a limited amount of whaling. Even as other whaling nations withdrew (Canada announced its withdrawal in 1981 and Iceland in 1992), Japan stayed in the organization. Japan later advocated for Iceland's having the right to rejoin the organization while making a reservation to the moratorium.[134] Within the IWC, the Japanese representative voted against proposals, such as those to create a Southern Ocean Whale Sanctuary in 1994, and it introduced plans to allow for community-based whaling to support traditional practices of coastal towns.

Working within the IWC constraints with the establishment of the scientific whaling program was seen as the choice to support the international order. Yet it neither formed the basis for a robust industry nor avoided international criticism. The rules of the IWC allowed nongovernmental organizations to present papers at plenary sessions, which resulted in the IWC serving as a platform for them to advance arguments against whaling (Catalinac and Chan, 2005, p. 139). A new challenge arose when Australia brought a complaint against Japan's whaling practices to the International Court of Justice. The ICJ ruling in 2014 against Japan's scientific whaling program in the Antarctic forced a new approach and the government announced it would comply with the

134. Norway objected to the moratorium and has remained a member while conducting commercial whaling. After leaving the IWC, Iceland sought to join with a reservation excluding its actions from the moratorium. It rejoined as a nonvoting observer after a series of contested votes, and eventually gained full membership over objections of United States. The U.S. government position was that "the United States encourages Iceland to rejoin the IWC, but cannot accept that its adherence is conditioned on a reservation to the commercial whaling moratorium." National Oceanic and Atmospheric Administration, Department of Commerce Washington, DC, 15 May 2002, "Iceland Rejoining International Whaling Commission: Fact Sheet." Available at https://2001-2009.state.gov/p/eur/rls/fs/10228.htm. Accessed 24 July 2019; IWC, "Iceland and her re-adherence to the Convention after leaving in 1992." Available at https://iwc.int/index.php?cID=119. Accessed 24 July 2019. Japan's government protested US efforts to exclude Iceland as going against international law (*Asahi Shimbun* 24 July 2001.

ruling. Indirectly, the ICJ ruling reduced incentives for Japan to remain in the IWC; ending scientific whaling in the Southern Ocean freed it of the need for IWC supervision of fishing in international waters.[135] In a final effort at persuasion, the government advanced a proposal to renew commercial whaling at the IWC meeting in 2018. After losing the vote on its proposal at the IWC, the question turned to exiting the organization.

During debate in the Japanese legislature, some politicians urged the government to reconsider its adherence to IWC regulations. Foreign ministry officials insisted that for a state committed to rule of law and international order, Japan must strive to follow IWC rules and accept the ICJ ruling.[136] Prime Minister Abe declared plans to continue whaling; along with a group of politicians from whaling districts and at the insistence of the Fisheries Agency, he pushed back against the pro-compliance voices in the foreign ministry (Ida, 2019, p. 33).

Both sides of the debate were concerned with the broader impact on international affairs. On the one hand, advocates for leaving the organization argued that exiting the IWC was an important way to signal to other governments the resistance of Japan to any spread of regulations to other marine resources, such as tuna. The director for fisheries' negotiations at the Fisheries Agency, Hideki Moronuki, described Japan's position on whaling as a "sea wall" to prevent other bans on fishing.[137] Others worried that exiting the IWC would weaken Japan's stature when it urged other countries to follow international rules to reduce over-fishing by its neighbors, or even on issues beyond marine resources. Foreign ministry officials worried that exiting would harm diplomacy. The opposition parties expressed fears about negative reaction in other countries. Constitutional Democratic Party leader Yukio Edano said, "Japan could be isolated from the international community if it withdraws."[138]

This question arose at a time when the United States was changing its position toward multilateralism under the leadership of Donald Trump. Since the 1970s, the United States had consistently led the international pressure on Japan against whaling. Facing a stand-off between strong anti-whaling

135. The International Convention on the Regulation of Whaling requires that IWC members issue permits when killing whales for research, which was the basis for Japan's research program in the Antarctic (JARPA).

136. Diet Lower House Foreign Affairs Committee, 1 no. 4, 28 November 2018.

137. Okutsu, Akane "Why Japan Risked Condemnation to Restart Commercial Whaling," *Nikkei Asian Review* 19 February 2019.

138. *NHK World News*, "Why Japan Withdrew from the IWC," 2 February 2019. Available at https://www3.nhk.or.jp/nhkworld/en/news/backstories/367/. Accessed 24 July 2019.

consensus in the U.S. Congress and pro-whaling consensus in the Japanese Diet, top leadership on both sides had to intervene to avoid spillover that could harm the alliance (Strausz, 2014, p. 467). While environmental policy issues were not a top priority for Reagan, it is remarkable nevertheless that these rose to his attention—he notes in a diary entry that "Japan fudged in Internat [sic]. Whale Protection Agreement. If continues we can deny them fishing rights in our waters."[139] Prime Minister Nakasone worked with the Reagan administration officials to resolve the sanctions episode in the 1980s. The overriding importance of maintaining strong alliance relations helped Japan and the United States work out compromises within the framework of the IWC oversight of Japan's scientific whaling program. Yet tensions continued. The Clinton administration raised the possibility of trade sanctions in the year 2000. Even when Japan modified its whaling program and prevented sanctions, bipartisan resolutions from Congress and statements from the Clinton and subsequently the Bush administrations continued to criticize Japan's scientific whaling program (Ackerman, 2002). After 2016, this pressure lightened. With Donald Trump exiting international organizations and openly skeptical of environmental movement activists, there was less reason to fear criticism from the United States.

The decision to exit was announced with fanfare in December 2018. The prominent pro-whaling Liberal Democratic Party Secretary General Toshihiro Nikai stated:

> The IWC has changed as an organization and its anti-whaling members don't have the slightest consideration toward the livelihoods of the fishermen who depend on whaling. . . . We have no choice but to pull out. This decision is a dream come true for the many Japanese people who have long awaited the resumption of commercial whaling. . . . We repeatedly warned that we may withdraw but they never listened to us.[140]

The sense that the organization had been inflexible to Japan's position was echoed by a former IWC Chair from Australia, Peter Bridgewater, who was reported to have said he was not surprised by Japan's withdrawal and agreed that the debates at IWC had often been a "dialogue of the deaf."[141]

139. Reagan and Brinkley (2009), cited in Strausz (2014, p. 464).

140. *NHK World News*, "Why Japan Withdrew from the IWC," 10 February 2019. Available at https://www3.nhk.or.jp/nhkworld/en/news/backstories/367/. Accessed 22 July 2019.

141. *The Independent*, "Japan Ushers in New Era of Commercial Whaling" 7 April 2019. Available at https://www.independent.co.uk/news/world/asia/japan-whaling-commercial-research-shimonoseki-iwc-a8858511.html. Accessed 22 July 2019.

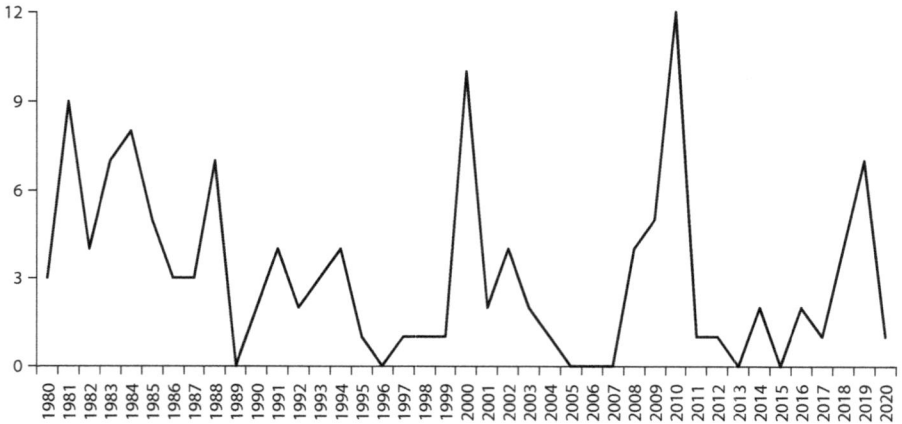

FIGURE 6.9. *Media attention to Japan and the IWC:* The graph displays total count of references to "Japan and International Whaling Commission" in a search of *Washington Post* articles in the Proquest database from 1980 to 2020.

After the requisite transition period, Japan formally exited in June 2019, with commercial whaling resuming the next day. Its decision was condemned in statements by the environment ministers of governments from the UK, Australia, and France.[142] Yet there was no statement issued by the U.S. government. A moderate level of media attention in the United States was focused on the exit announcement, but less than earlier events, such as the backlash that had occurred in 2000 when Japan expanded its scientific whaling or the news surrounding the filing of a complaint to ICJ in 2010 (see Figure 6.9).

It first seems puzzling why Japan risked international opprobrium by exiting. Although whaling was once an important food source, whale consumption has declined to be inconsequential in the daily diet of most Japanese.[143] Only a few hundred fishermen are actively engaged in whaling, and the size of their communities is too small to constitute a voting bloc. The fact that both Prime Minister Abe and the LDP Secretary General Nikai came from districts including whaling added political heavyweights behind the pro-whaling voices, but their political strength did not make them beholden to such

142. *NHK World News,* "Why Japan Withdrew from the IWC," 2 February 2019. Available at https://www3.nhk.or.jp/nhkworld/en/news/backstories/367/. Accessed 24 July 2019.

143. Consumption has been under 5,000 tons in recent years compared to 200,000 tons in the 1960s. Okutsu, Akane, "Why Japan Risked Condemnation to Restart Commercial Whaling," *Nikkei Asian Review* 19 February 2019.

groups. Much stronger was the reverberance of nationalism and cultural tradition against external pressure, which resonated among the public at large. An NHK survey in January 2019 found that a majority approved the decision to withdraw from the IWC.[144] The coalition of local communities, fishery agency officials, and politicians could appeal to nationalism in Japan while the silence of the United States mitigated the risk that exiting would raise tensions in U.S.-Japan relations.

From a Japanese perspective, the puzzle is why it stayed in the organization so long after the views of the membership had diverged from Japan's position on whaling. Strong commitment to international society and rule of law contributed to Japan's adherence to the IWC moratorium on commercial whaling. The government also accepted the ICJ ruling against its scientific whaling program. The government only left in 2018, when U.S. pressure on the issue was lower than in previous years and a nationalist and pro-whaling leader held strong political control. Japan had joined the organization in 1951 to gain the trust of other governments, and some worried that departure would harm its international reputation. But such logic was less compelling when the United States was departing many organizations and even Britain was leaving Europe. At this time, Japan could leave the IWC without condemnation from the United States or damage to its reputation.

6.7   Conclusion

Many comment that the Japanese government and public appear to be especially sensitive to the perception abroad of Japan's role in international society. Some contend that social relations of hierarchy at home are extended to international relations, so that Japan seeks to establish its place in a community (Satō, 1977, p. 376–378). Others see the reactive policy response to foreign demands as a function of domestic political structures that require external pressures to break vested interests and ministry rivalries (Calder, 1988). But the conventional wisdom overlooks a key mechanism by which the government shapes its position in international society. By entering organizations, Japan chooses which countries to engage with more deeply. Security interests were often the metric to favor cooperation with specific groups of states.

144. Sekiguchi, Yuya, "Why Japan Withdrew from the IWC," *NHK World News* 2 February 2019. Available at https://www3.nhk.or.jp/nhkworld/en/news/backstories/367/. Accessed 24 July 2019.

The value of association with European states drew Meiji Japan into the earliest organizations. Long after its power had grown, the government joined the League of Nations as a strategy to sustain relations with the UK and other major powers. The U.S.-Japan alliance fostered a wide range of cooperation within IGOs, while the OECD tied Japan to the Atlantic alliance of Western states. In each case, geopolitical interests guided decisions by Japan, to create diplomatic opportunities. Building on relationships with other states, the government sought entry into international organizations.

Discretionary rules, alliance sponsors, and variable entry conditions all played in favor of Japan's being able to join. Japan won support from allies which eased its entry by allowing it to join the ILO as a country with poor labor rights and join the trade regime as a country that retained an active industrial policy. These choices to join organizations then brought to bear foreign pressure through the commitments and deep network of interdependence with other states. As a peer acting within international organizations, Japan could then rise in status within international society.

From the perspective of theories on international institutions, the Japanese approach to joining international organizations suggests that it saw more value in the political dimension of the organizations. Japan would join organizations well before its economic interests suggested accession would serve material needs of the country. The League of Nations and ILO stand out as IGOs Japan entered to advance diplomatic relations. The benefit of membership brought status more than material gains. But even in discussion over entry into the GATT and OECD, which promised direct benefits for the economy, decision-makers highlight the significance of entering the IGO as part of consolidating ties as a staunch member of the Western camp. Within East Asia, focusing on the ADB while staying outside of the AIIB reflected geopolitical strategy to closely cooperate with the United States as Japan expanded its regional role through development assistance. Functional theories are too narrowly focused on the gains within an issue area. States are equally interested in whom they will cooperate with and how the engagement in the organization will strengthen political relationships.

Broadening cooperation with allies through international organizations can offset domestic resistance. In the first decade of the U.S.-Japan alliance, cooperation over development assistance and economic strategies allowed Japanese leaders to deflect criticism of the military dimension. Later, when the alliance had broad acceptance within the public, cooperation for strategic goals with the United States could justify difficult economic concessions.

In these cases, foreign ministry officials and political leaders guide the decision process. Their comments about joining organizations reveal the close attention paid to other countries, and especially the United States. Diet testimony over two development banks showed divergent perspectives between the LDP and opposition party members. The LDP politicians defended U.S. involvement in the ADB and warned about China's influence over the AIIB. Representatives of the socialist and communist parties warned against U.S. influence over the ADB and emphasized the benefits from working with China in the AIIB. These examples demonstrate that decision-makers evaluate who belongs to an organization as well as what the rules require of members.

Not all of the cases line up according to alliance politics. Despite the U.S. rejection of TPP under the Trump administration, Japan went forward to join the agreement. And while staying distant from China on the AIIB, Japan entered the RCEP agreement in partnership with China. Nor could one ascribe exit from the IWC to a breakdown in relations with the United States, which remains a member. These cases still offer some supportive evidence for the argument. In its maneuvering over trade agreements, the Japanese leadership sought first to partner with the United States. Faced with the Trump administration rejecting TPP, Japanese negotiators kept an open door for its reentry and negotiated similar terms with the United States later in a bilateral agreement. Only after taking these steps did the government join RCEP, where economic interests to deepen regional market integration were compelling for membership. By sequencing agreements with allies first, Japan shaped RCEP terms and maximized its autonomy as the pivotal state in a network of agreements. Alliance politics cannot account for Japan's exit from the IWC but likely had an impact on the timing. For decades after the organization moved away from Japanese whaling interests, the government remained a member as part of a strategy to avoid tensions with the United States. The lack of interest in multilateralism and environmental activism by Donald Trump was a permissive condition to allow Japanese leaders to finally leave the organization. Although the cases diverge in terms of joint membership, geopolitics shaped the approach taken to the membership decisions.

Decisions on membership in international organizations have not been left to technocrats. From the top leadership in the Meiji period to an Imperial order regarding the League institutions, Japan's engagement with international society has held high-level priority. As a democracy after independence in 1951, Japanese politicians deliberated in the Diet over the decision to join or not join organizations. Their attention focused on the implications of the decision for international relations at a political level—even the development banks ADB and AIIB were discussed in terms as much of their foreign relations significance as of their economic costs and benefits to the nation.

For an outsider trying to join the circle of great powers, international organizations have played an important role in Japanese foreign policy. It has seen both sides of discrimination—as a "former enemy" after WWII, Japan struggled to join the UN, and its pathway forward depended on its ally the United States. For regional trade strategies, the government joined multiple groupings to bridge the growing rivalries in the region and balance security and economic interests.

7

Club Politics in Regional Organizations

THE UNITED STATES, Japan, and Australia have declared a commitment to co-operation in the "Indo-Pacific Region"—and a new grouping of countries has emerged. But until there is a regional organization, it is unlikely to gain traction as a region. Indeed, with the addition of India the grouping took on the name "Quad," perhaps to acknowledge that it did not constitute a region. The difference between summitry and regionalism lies in the institutional layering that occurs to entrench patterns of association. To form an Indo-Pacific region, the states would need to establish institutional arrangements for ongoing regional cooperation with membership requirements. The impetus for whether states form an "Indo-Pacific Association" in the coming years will lie in balancing against the rise of China. As regionalism shifts in response to changing security coalitions, it creates a dynamic in which politics, more than geography, determines when and where the lines between regions are drawn.

Common practice in policy circles and scholarship assigns states across regions based on geographic categories. The assignment determines bureaucratic jurisdiction for meetings, benchmarks for policy evaluation, or control variables and sampling strategies for cross-national studies. At the same time, theories of regional integration explain how social and political forces account for variation across regions in the institutions for joint decision-making and cooperative behavior that create a meaningful collective identity.[1] The intersection of these two perspectives lies in the selection of states for membership in regional organizations.

1. For some examples, see Milner and Mansfield, 1997; Solingen, 1998; Buzan and Waever, 2003; Mansfield and Solingen, 2010; Hooghe et al., 2016; Thomas, 2017.

Do regional organizations form around a prior regional identity or do they constitute this identity by formally bringing together a particular set of states? Could one know who belongs to Europe or Southeast Asia separately from the organizations among states? On the one hand, nobody would doubt that Switzerland is European, irrespective of its choice to remain outside of the EU. On the other hand, Estonia joining the EU and rejecting participation in the Commonwealth of Independent States brought to the forefront its identity in Europe over Eurasia and deepened its association with the European states and distance from Russia. When Bangladesh found its application to the Association of Southeast Asian Nations (ASEAN) rejected, it led in the formation of a South Asian Association for Regional Cooperation. Sri Lanka had once been invited to join the ASEAN and declined. These examples highlight the fuzzy boundaries of regional identity that become more clear as the result of membership decisions for regional organizations.

Regional organizations represent a hard test of the theory about IGOs as a discriminatory club because these organizations have a primary membership criterion based on geography.[2] More so than in other organizations, there is a premise that membership politics would follow an objective criterion to welcome those from the region and exclude those outside of the region. Nevertheless, borders of regions are not objectively defined. This creates the opening for other factors to define a region through their role as conditions promoting regional organizations. I apply to the regional context the broader argument in the book that international organizations form discriminatory clubs built around a core of shared security interests. As an additional test of hypotheses 2, I expect states will be more likely to belong to regional organizations with other states sharing their geopolitical alignment.

Through statistical analysis of regional organizations, the chapter evaluates the correlates of membership to compare the role of geopolitical alignment with those of other conditions. The regional organizations analyzed in this chapter encompass comprehensive mandates to bring prosperity and peace to the region as well as more narrow projects to protect a shared resource. Almost all of the regional organizations conform to the club model, with restrictions on participation that are not based on objective performance criteria.

In two case studies, I more closely assess the decision process that led to enlargement. I select the EU and ASEAN as two important regional

---

2. In the analysis of IGO charters in chapter 2, limiting eligibility to countries within a region stood out as one of the most frequent ways to restrict participation.

organizations that vary in their security context. While the NATO alliance unifies the core members of the EU, ASEAN is led by states committed to the nonaligned movement. At the same time, the geographic regions have both confronted deep rivalries and experienced shifts that transformed the strategic balance in the neighborhood. Looking at the decisions to join or abstain from the regional project over time highlights where differences in orientation toward critical foreign policy issues shaped the contours of expanding regional borders. Importantly, the case studies look at smaller differences in geopolitical alignment. The EU also stands out as a more meritocratic organization relative to the club-style informality of ASEAN, although the two organizations have evolved over time in their approach to the accession process. Despite these differences, both exhibit wide discretion by states over whom to let in and variation in what to expect of their policies.

7.1   Defining Regions

While regionalism is widely studied, "observers do not agree on what constitutes a region" (Mansfield and Solingen, 2010, p. 146). I will discuss the role of geographic, economic, and political conditions before expanding on the importance of security interests. While my argument focuses on geopolitical alignment and joint membership, this represents only one dimension of a complex process shaping regional integration. The goal is to establish underlying conditions that make some states potential members of a regional category. A standard definition of "region" is "an administrative area, division, or district; an indefinite area of the world or universe; a broad geographic area distinguished by similar features."[3] This sets up the task of considering the organizational structures based on area and evaluating which dimensions of similarity matter when it comes to delimiting regions from the perspective of the world state system.

Geography

The defining attribute of a region arises from geography, which could also constitute an eligibility criterion for membership in a regional organization. Drezner (2007, p. 68) describes neighborhood IGOs that "use geography to

---

3. Merriam-Webster online dictionary definition of "region." Available at https://www .merriam-webster.com/dictionary/region.

place a natural and fixed limitation on membership." The functional theory of regimes, with its focus on density of interactions and coordination for provision of public goods, complements this premise for regionalism based on location (Keohane, 1984). The resource constraints of a specific context shape the response of the population and the evolution of institutions (Abbott, Green, and Keohane, 2016). Early international institutions in the nineteenth century formed around issues like river management and infectious disease, where externalities were greatest among neighbors. Models of trade also include distance as a variable to predict trade flows between countries. The potential for gains from cooperation are highest among states that are closer together. Yet how close is close enough to belong in a region?

A good starting point is to consider states located in a geographic area defined by distance, continent, and population centers. Yet it is not straightforward to draw lines on this basis alone. The division of the world into geographic regions imposes more than location onto the choice of category. This matter was highlighted by the UN Statistics Division:

> A large number of official reports are produced every year by specialized agencies and other UN entities, which present country data according to a regional/geographical classification and often regional and sub-regional aggregates (based on average or other aggregation methods). Regional aggregates are a convenient way to show trends and assess progress over time and differences across the various areas of the world. However, practices vary among the various international agencies and regional groupings and classification of countries are based on different criteria.[4]

The problem arises because we cannot neatly split all of the Eurasian continent or the Americas into distinct regions based on geography. Arbitrary lines become taken for granted, such as the common association of Middle East and North Africa as a region distinct from Sub-Saharan Africa, or the separation of North America and South America into distinct regions, with some including Central America with the North and others with the South. The indicators generated for the Millennium Development Goals by an inter-agency expert group based on UN geographical groupings have been widely used, with one tier of regions for developed countries comprising Europe and other states (Canada, United States, Australia, New Zealand and Japan); and

---

4. Committee for the Coordination of Statistical Activities SA/2006/15, Eighth Session Montreal, 4–5 September 2006, Item 6 of the provisional agenda.

another tier of regions for developing countries, comprising: Northern Africa, Sub-Saharan Africa, Latin America and the Caribbean, Caucasus and Central Asia, Eastern Asia, Southern Asia, South-Eastern Asia, Western Asia, and Oceania. Previous versions had different groupings and included an "other" category for the transitional economies of Europe and the Commonwealth of Independent States, but the latest effort avoids such obviously political designations. However, the UN follows a separate classification of regions for UN elections, where all members are divided among five regions, Latin America and the Caribbean (GRULAC), Western Europe and Others (WEOG), Eastern Europe, the Asian Group, and the African Group. A country like Turkey, at the crossroads of regions, has run for seats at the UN Security Council in different years as Eastern Europe, Asia, and Western Europe.[5] The UN Technical classification attempts to follow continents to define macro regions that are further subdivided into categories of sub-regions to create homogeneity in sizes of population.[6]

From the perspective that geographic allocation of states across regions is based on a notion of proximity, distance represents the underlying latent force generating a propensity for regional formation. Any other category inserts economic and political characteristics into the definition of region. Yet as a continuous measure, distance fails to set limits on regional categories, so we must look further to understand regional borders.

Economic Integration

Regional trade agreements have long been a part of the international trade system. From the interwar trade blocs to the proliferation of free trade agreements since the late 1990s, much of trade occurred among regional partners. In part, this arose from the logic of the classic gravity model of trade, whereby distance enters as a key determinant of the expected volume of trade between a pair of countries (Anderson and van Wincoop, 2003). But a more complex range of factors related to strategic linkage and effort to augment bargaining power in multilateral economic fora also drives regional trade agreements (Whalley, 1998).

Trade gains motivate efforts to lower trade barriers and harmonize regulatory standards among regional partners, and this process can also generate demands

---

5. I thank Christoph Mikulaschek for bringing to my attention this distinction and the information on Turkey's example.

6. See https://unstats.un.org/unsd/methodology/m49/.

to share decision-making authority that lead to more comprehensive integration. Mattli (1999) argues that market structure and growth prospects among complementary economies explain variation in formation and expansion of regional organizations. Economic competition also serves as a mechanism to spur the diffusion of policies, including the establishment of regional organizations (Jetschke and Lenz, 2013, p. 628). Bargaining over enlargement is driven forward by those states that expect welfare gains from bringing new entrants into the regional organization (Moravcsik, 1998; Schneider, 2009). This provides a core economic logic to anchor development of regional organizations.

At the same time, it is not clear where the economic logic should stop to define a region with fixed borders. As each customs union or preferential trading agreement sets up borders that favor trade among members over outsiders, the discrimination generates economic incentives for others to join.[7] Economic regionalism in one location tends to spur regionalism in other regions (Milner and Mansfield, 1997). Moreover, in a world of global value chains, interregional trade has grown apace, so that any description of trade as narrowly restricted within regions would be misleading.

Identity and Political Community

Religious, linguistic, and historical conditions also bind together neighboring countries as part of a common region. Here one can refer to region in the sense used by Katzenstein (2005) as reflecting the power and purpose of states along both material and symbolic dimensions. Whether as the result of a colonial legacy or interactions from the movement of people and trade, many cultural and economic dimensions cluster among neighboring states. These cultural dimensions form the basis of a regional identity. They are intertwined with power relationships that may lead one central state to shape the character of its surrounding region. Yet local actors and the social interactions among leaders can emerge as critical determinants for the direction of regional identity (Acharya and Johnston, 2007). Where policies diffuse through mimicry, states may follow the example of neighbors (Simmons, Dobbin, and Garrett, 2006). Shared values that build trust will also facilitate cooperation.

At the political level, regime type offers another source of regional identity. Diffusion may produce strong regional patterns in democratic consolidation

---

7. This discriminatory source of expansion was evident among nineteenth century agreements (Pahre, 2008), and can arise today through investment channels and multinational production (Manger, 2009).

or authoritarian rule. This in turn shapes the ability to cooperate for regional integration. Democracies have found it easier to engage in deep regional integration (Mansfield, Milner, and Pevehouse, 2008). At the same time, these organizations also promote democracy (Pevehouse, 2002; Mansfield and Pevehouse, 2006). Regional organizations, most notably in Europe, have explicitly adopted human rights and democracy as conditions for membership (Duxbury, 2011). We also see affinity among like-minded authoritarian regimes, where political similarity can reinforce their interest in similar sets of regional organizations. The counterpoint to democracy as informal membership criterion for the EU arises in the authoritarian orientation among the states in the Eurasian Union (Obydenkova and Libman, 2019). Other organizations, such as the Bolivarian Alternative for the Americas, bring together populist governments united by left-leaning ideological beliefs (Gray, 2013, p. 126). This highlights that political similarity may represent an important dimension across the full spectrum of regimes.

Bounded Security

Security interests are embedded within a geographic space. *Bounded security* operates as a regional level of geopolitical alignment. Neighbors both fight more with each other and ally against common threats they share because of their location (Walt, 1985; Morrow, 2000). The vulnerability of states to conquest, their strategies to balance as maritime or landlocked powers, and the network dependencies of alliance ties are among the many strategic variables that may cluster by region (Fazal, 2007; Levy and Thompson, 2010; Warren, 2010). Solingen (2015) explains regional orders in terms of convergent trends within states that support their cooperation as a region: when an internationalizing coalition emerges in the domestic politics of the more powerful states in a region that see openness as key to their own political survival, they are more likely to form a zone of peace. These studies of security regionalism share a common focus on how political ties among states provide the impetus for regional integration (Mansfield and Solingen, 2010). Decisions over membership in regional organizations set the borders for this process.

Expansionary security goals undermine regional cooperation. Territorial ambition generates spatial rivalries that produce local conflict (Mearsheimer, 2001; Dreyer, 2012).[8] Only major powers can project power at a global level,

8. Katzenstein (2005, p. 7) offers a useful review of how scholars have presented territoriality as basis for the geopolitics of regions.

and most other states can only compete as "players" in their own neighbor-hood (Thompson, 2001, p. 560). Such localization can concentrate conflict within regions. In its most coercive form, regional integration takes place through imperialism. Even short of occupation, coercion may give rise to forms of regional order shaped by power and domination. Repeated conflict incidents may inhibit collective institutions. High vulnerability to potential aggression by a neighbor can exacerbate the security dilemma for states in close proximity.

In contrast, common security interests support forming and joining re-gional organizations. An external threat can serve as a catalyst for regional cooperation. Alliances offer a direct response. To the extent that alliance cohe-sion benefits from economic exchanges, states will seek to link issues (Long and Leeds, 2006; Poast, 2013). This helps to generate alliances that include terms for economic cooperation. More comprehensive forms of cooperation can emerge, whereby security interests lead states to work together on a range of regional problems. Bringing states together in a forum facilitates side pay-ments that support long-term contractual relationships as well as short-term needs of security actions (Lake, 2009; Henke, 2017). Indeed, Haftel and Hof-mann (2019) show that regional economic organizations use their shared security interests to expand into the arena of security cooperation, especially when the regional security organization includes strategic rivals. In some cases the security mandate is explicit, but in other cases states that share security interests may not be able to commit to security objectives, let alone joint military action in an alliance. Fear of provoking a negative reaction from neigh-boring powers or domestic audiences can inhibit direct alliances. Hence it may actually be easier to cooperate through a regional organization among a sub-set of states than it would be for the same group to use a security organization. The facade of regional cooperation offers cover for security cooperation by another name.

Understanding the membership of regional organizations sets the basis for revisiting why these organizations could increase security. Haftel (2007, 2012) shows that regional economic institutions have a significant effect on reducing conflict. Yet some share of the cooperation also results from the fact that states select into the organization based on common security interests. Where real-ist theory has emphasized how competition over relative gains between rivals would limit willingness to cooperate, liberal theory leaves open the poten-tial for a virtuous circle in which states form institutions in order to prevent conflict (e.g., Grieco, 1993; Russett and Oneal, 2001). At the level of mid-range theorizing, the question is one of timing and mechanism—to what extent do allies join international organizations together such that their security affinity precedes joint institutional cooperation? An affirmative answer to this first question does not deny the role of the institution to support peace through helping states to consolidate their positive relationship (Haftel, 2012, p. 57). Rather, the security basis of membership indicates that the mechanism for regional institutions supporting cooperation is more likely to arise through reinforcing ties among like-minded states rather than as a forum for building trust among rivals. Conferring benefits to fellow member states locks in their cooperative path by raising opportunity costs to conflict.

7.2   Evolving Membership Patterns

This section examines regional organizations to evaluate how distance, trade ties, democratic regime, and geopolitical alignment contribute to explaining the membership patterns. As selective organizations with a participation restriction for regional focus, they could operate strictly based on geographic criterion. But the discretion of accession rules allows states to take into consideration other factors. Within some group of potential regional members, states could impose meritocratic screening for those more qualified to contribute to the joint project. Trade dependence and democracy offer economic and political metrics for states that could be expected to form high-value cooperation partners. As a club, regional organizations may use other criteria to determine who offers high value as a member. Geopolitical alignment introduces an extra quotient for high-value partners to be enticed into cooperating not only on security matters but also on broader regional projects.

Data: Regional IGOs

Building on the analysis of chapter 3, I subset the data on IGOs to 197 IGOs with a regional scope in their mandate, based on their including a reference to a geographic region in the organization name or in its founding charter document. The policy scope is not limited by issues since for many regional organizations they are quite broad.[9] The sample includes organizations that

9. As in the full sample of IGOs, the most frequently referenced issue is economic policy. Eighty percent of the regional IGOs include economic issues, relative to 35 percent including social issues, 20 percent including environment, and ten percent including security.

are primarily military in focus, such as NATO; those with narrow economic domain, like the Nordic Patent Institute; and many that span a wide range of issues such as ASEAN. The membership may or may not be restricted to states within the region. Many organizations with a regional scope referenced in their purpose are open to non-region members, e.g., the United Kingdom is a member of the Asian Infrastructure and Investment Bank. In other cases, organizations simply change their regional scope and even the name of the organization to accommodate an enlargement of the membership.[10] Therefore the population consists of the 156 states included by COW in the state system for which there is data available on basic covariates. The period for analysis is 1949–2014.

As in the aggregate pattern of the IGOs presented in chapter 2, membership procedures of regional IGOs are at once selective and discretionary. The Organization for Security and Co-operation in Europe is an exception, explicitly being open to all.[11] Figure 7.1 shows the different means of restriction. Most include an eligibility restriction with some geographic reference. Yet even among regional organizations, a handful refrain from such limitation. For example, the Southern African Development Community (SADC) has 16 members, all located in the southern part of the African continent, but its charter membership provisions explicitly note that it will consider any application for membership—allowing an expansive view of region as a possibility. Yet SADC also has a stringent level of member approval that requires consensus.[12] As in the larger set of organizations, the formal charters rarely call for compliance review as a condition of entry or expulsion. When present, such references are quite vague. Twenty-five organizations have hierarchical membership, evidenced by weighted voting rules that differentiate among states, which is most common among the regional development banks.

---

10. For example, the South Pacific Forum changed its name in 1999 to become the Pacific Islands Forum after allowing states north of the equator to join. See Hooghe et al. (2017) for detailed accounts of variation in the accession provisions and the experiences of regional organizations.

11. Only three percent of the regional IGOs are fully open like the OSCE, with the others being smaller technical organizations. The OSCE membership includes the United States, Canada, and Russia, in addition to many European states.

12. Among the 69 regional IGOs that require member approval, 57 hold the high threshold of supermajority or consensus.

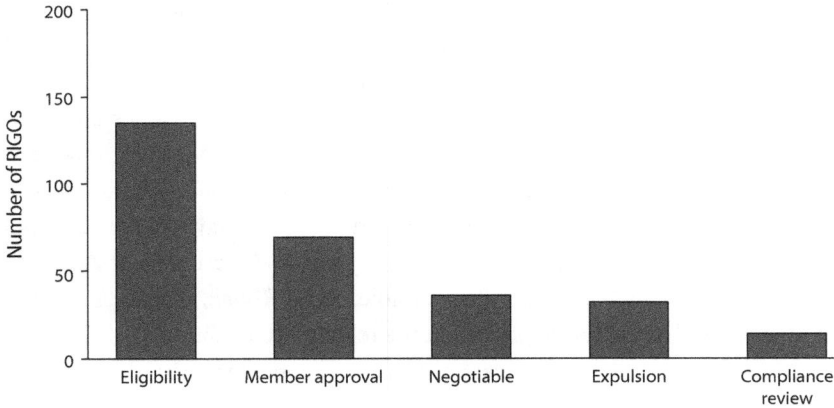

FIGURE 7.1. *Regional IGO charter restrictions on participation mandate*: The figure shows the number of regional IGOs by the type of membership restriction present in the charter. Note that any single IGO may include multiple types of restrictions.

The analysis examines membership in the broadest sense, including states' entry into an IGO and each year of continued membership.[13] For comparison, I use the same specification as that of chapter 3 to estimate membership for the sample of regional IGOs.[14]

One challenge is the measurement of region. Having just explained it is a problematic distinction, how should I incorporate the concept into analysis? First, I use geographic proximity as a "raw" indicator of location. The distance variable measures the average geographic distance between the state and other members of the organization.[15] Without my imposing any external region

13. This is consistent with Stone (2011), who theorizes participation in IGOs as an ongoing process of decisions to enter and continue cooperation. Earlier chapters explore differences across each distinct phase of IGO membership: entry at formation, entry through enlargement, and exit. But as an overview, this chapter aggregates across these to simply measure participation as whether the state belongs to the organization.

14. The statistical analysis uses logistic regression to estimate the dichotomous outcome variable, IGO membership with state-IGO-year units of observation. All independent variables are lagged by one year, and standard errors are clustered at the country level.

15. Data on geographic distance are from the dyadic measures of distance in kilometers between states in the CEPII dataset (Mayer and Zignago, 2011). The simple distances are calculated following the great circle formula, which uses latitudes and longitudes of the most important city (in terms of population) or of the official capital. The log transformation of this average is used as the distance variable.

categories, distance taps into the underlying importance of proximity as a source of demand for localized cooperation. Second, I measure neighborhood diffusion with reference to conventional region indicators. I include a measure for *Region Members* indicating the number of states residing in a state's geographic region that are members of the IGO. This measure uses eight regions based on commonly referenced geographic divisions: Sub-Saharan Africa; Middle East and North Africa; Europe and Central Asia; Western Europe; Latin America and Caribbean; North and Central America; East Asia and Pacific; South Asia.[16] An indicator variable, *Same Region*, measures when a state is located in the region named in the regional IGO charter.

As in chapter 3, the role of geopolitical alignment is measured in terms of alliances and foreign policy positions taken on votes in the United Nations. The first model uses the *Average Alliances* variable, which is the proportion of IGO member states with which a state shares a formal alliance in a given year.[17] In the sample of regional IGOs, it ranges from 0 to 1 with a mean value of 0.10. The second model examines a dichotomous indicator for whether the state has an alliance with the lead state of the IGO, which is defined in terms of the largest power, measured annually by gross domestic product (GDP). The mean value in the sample is 0.14. The third model also focuses on shared issue positions between a potential member and the lead state, using *UN Ideal Point Similarity* to measure geopolitical alignment. This variable increases as the UN voting records of two states converge (Bailey, Strezhnev, and Voeten, 2017).[18]

Other important factors include positive pressure for membership from joint trade and negative pressure from joint conflict. The *Trade with Members* variable measures average (logged) volume of imports and exports between a state and each other member of an IGO.[19] Conflict-prone states may lack the interest in joining organizations, and also face exclusion from members

16. This draws on the region definitions used in Milner and Mansfield (Milner and Mansfield, 1997; Mansfield and Milner, 2012), modified from World Bank categories to include "Western Europe" and "North Central America" as regions. For World Bank categories, see http://data.worldbank.org/about/country-and-lending-groups.

17. Data on alliances comes from version 4.1 of the COW Formal Alliances dataset (Gibler, 2009).

18. For other studies using this as metric of foreign policy interests, see (e.g., Bearce and Bondanella, 2007; Vreeland and Dreher, 2014).

19. Bilateral trade data is from the IMF Direction of Trade dataset. I add 1 before taking the log to ensure values of zero trade are not excluded due to the mathematical transformation.

who have a stake in the conflict or simply fear contagion (Donno, Metzger, and Russett, 2015). I include a control variable measuring the average number of fatal militarized disputes (MIDs) between the state and other members of the IGO.[20] An indicator for the Cold War period (1947–1991) allows for more macro-level systemic changes that were important for the evolution of regional organizations. Separate control variables measure shared colonial history.[21] Variables for income (GDP per capita, logged), market size (GDP, logged), and trade openness (total trade / GDP) control for economic interests at a monadic level.

The organizations with a higher threshold for supermajority or consensus support of members as an entry requirement are measured with an indicator for *Stringent Approval*. To address general diffusion effects, the variable *Total IGO Membership* is a count of members in each IGO, which could exert positive attraction for other states to enter.

Analysis of Membership Patterns

Table 7.1 presents the main results. The correlation between security ties and membership in regional IGOs is quite robust across specifications. Whether measuring alliances in terms of average of all members or an alliance with the lead state, these ties correspond to an increased likelihood of joining. In the second model, the broader measure of UN voting similarity is also positive. Importantly, these findings take into account distance, former colonial experience, and regime type. Table 7.2 shows robustness to a difference-in-differences specification for changes of geopolitical alignment.

The substantive size of the effect of alliances is larger than either distance or democracy when considering comparable alternative scenarios (see Figure 7.2). Shifting the average alliances with members from its mean value to one standard deviation above the mean increases the probability of membership in the organization by 1.6 percentage points. A more dramatic change from zero alliance partners in the organization to a scenario of a state holding shared alliance ties with all members of the organization leads to an eight percentage point increase in probability of membership.[22] UN voting similarity with

---

20. MIDs data are from the dyadic version of the COW Militarized Interstate Disputes Dataset (Ghosn and Bennett, 2003).

21. Data on colonial linkages are from CEPII (Mayer and Zignago, 2011).

22. The first difference estimate is 0.016 with standard error of 0.003. The estimate when shifting from 0 to 1 on alliance measure is 0.078 with standard error of 0.014.

	Dependent variable: IGO Membership		
	Model 1	Model 2	Model 3
Avg. Alliances	2.124***		
	(0.175)		
Lead State alliance		1.303***	
		(0.125)	
UN Voting similarity with Lead state			0.205***
			(0.047)
Trade with Members	0.372***	0.374***	0.492***
	(0.037)	(0.035)	(0.041)
Distance to Members	−0.556***	−0.700***	−0.680***
	(0.098)	(0.095)	(0.107)
Same Region	1.124***	1.372***	1.469***
	(0.169)	(0.184)	(0.189)
Region Members	0.201***	0.206***	0.211***
	(0.014)	(0.014)	(0.015)
Polity	0.013	0.005	0.008
	(0.008)	(0.009)	(0.009)
GDP	0.007	−0.091	−0.227***
	(0.057)	(0.070)	(0.071)
GDP per capita	−0.333***	−0.318***	−0.326***
	(0.058)	(0.065)	(0.069)
Trade Openness	−0.009	−0.011	−0.025
	(0.007)	(0.007)	(0.024)
Stringent Approval	0.022	−0.034	−0.180*
	(0.085)	(0.091)	(0.098)
Cold War	−0.032	−0.014	−0.038
	(0.049)	(0.049)	(0.051)
Constant	−4.231***	−1.148	0.456
	(1.009)	(1.320)	(1.289)
Observations	895,116	888,690	829,762
# IGOs	197	197	197
# States	156	156	156

TABLE 7.1. *Effect of foreign policy on regional IGO membership*: These models examine how geopolitical alignment measured by alliance ties (Models 1 and 2) and UN voting record (Model 3) influence the probability of membership in regional organizations. Coefficient estimates are displayed with robust standard errors in parentheses. Models include the following controls (not shown): *Fatal MIDs with Members, IGO Membership Size, Total State Memberships, Former Colony, Common Colonial History,* and a time polynomial. Statistical significance is denoted by: *p<0.1; **p<0.05; ***p<0.01.

	Dependent variable: IGO Membership		
	(1)	(2)	(3)
Avg. Alliances	0.300***		
	(0.027)		
Lead State alliance		0.155***	
		(0.013)	
UN Voting similarity with Lead state			0.012***
			(0.002)
Trade with Members	0.004***	0.004***	0.006***
	(0.0004)	(0.0004)	(0.001)
Same Region	0.008	0.019	0.048***
	(0.013)	(0.013)	(0.014)
Distance to Members	−0.037***	−0.054***	−0.061***
	(0.006)	(0.006)	(0.006)
Polity	0.001**	0.001	0.001***
	(0.0003)	(0.0004)	(0.0005)
GDP	0.007***	0.004	0.002
	(0.002)	(0.003)	(0.003)
GDP per capita	−0.004*	−0.003	−0.0003
	(0.002)	(0.002)	(0.003)
Trade Openness	−0.0002**	−0.0002*	−0.0003**
	(0.0001)	(0.0001)	(0.0002)
Stringent Approval	0.005	0.002	−0.0001
	(0.004)	(0.004)	(0.005)
Regional Members	0.024***	0.025***	0.025***
	(0.001)	(0.001)	(0.001)
Constant	0.206***	0.434***	0.569***
	(0.065)	(0.076)	(0.084)
Observations	919,929	913,814	848,001
# IGOs	197	197	197
# States	164	164	164

TABLE 7.2. *First differences of foreign policy on regional IGO membership*: The table shows estimates from a difference-in-differences specification based on a linear probability model including year fixed effects to examine how changes in geopolitical alignment influence shifts in membership among state-IGO pairs. On estimation approach, see Lechner (2011). Statistical significance is denoted by: $^*p<0.1$; $^{**}p<0.05$; $^{***}p<0.01$.

the lead state in the organization also holds a positive and significant effect, although with smaller magnitude relative to alliance change. A standard deviation shift to increase the distance results in a one percentage point reduction in the probability of membership. As one would expect, those states within

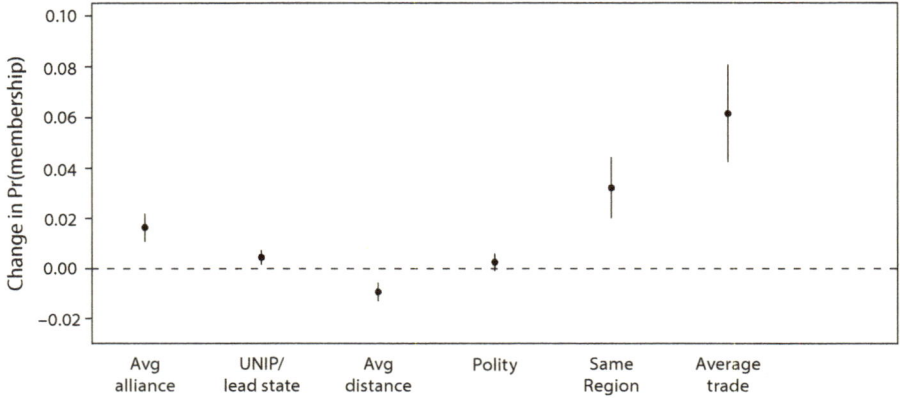

FIGURE 7.2. *Estimates of membership probability in regional IGOs*: The figure displays the change in the predicted probability of membership when shifting the Alliances with Members variable from the sample mean to one standard deviation above the mean (far left). Other variables similarly display the predicted probability for membership when shifting the specified variable from the sample mean to one standard deviation above the mean, with the exception of the indicator for *Same Region*, which is shifted from 0 to 1. Predicted probabilities and confidence intervals are generated via 1,000 quasi-Bayesian Monte Carlo simulations of the full model (Table 7.1, Model 1). The estimate of UN ideal point similarity with lead state is based on Table 7.1, Model 3.

the same region as the geographic region specified as part of the IGO mandate are more likely to be members.[23] The *Same Region* variable reflects the strong tendency for states within a region to join the regional IGO, and the *Region Members* variable controls for how many other states in the same region are also members of the organization. Results are also robust when dropping the two region measures.[24] Trade with members also holds a strong pull for states in regional organizations.

The effect of democracy is small. Based on the estimates of Table 7.1, Model 1, a one standard deviation shift of the polity measure corresponds to a 0.25

23. The shift of the indicator from 0 to 1 results in a corresponding estimate of 3.2 percentage point increase in the probability of membership (point estimate 0.032 with standard error 0.006).

24. There is a small increase in magnitude for the coefficient measuring the effect of geopolitical alignment and a substantial increase in the effect of distance when omitting the region variable, which is to be expected in light of collinearity.

percentage point increase in probability of membership and does not reach standard levels of statistical significance.[25] Even a large shift from −10 to 10 for the polity indicator equivalent to the complete transformation of an absolute dictatorship into a full democracy would only increase the probability of membership by 0.7 percentage point. It is only in the difference-in-differences specification of Table 7.2 that the control for democracy has a significant positive effect.

Of course, considering these shifts of variables as if they could occur in isolation is unrealistic; they aid in the interpretation of the regression output for comparing the relative effects predicted by the sample averages. Figure 7.2 shows the estimates with confidence intervals to account for uncertainty, with a comparison of the average first difference estimates for alliance measure relative to the distance measure. But the analysis remains largely a descriptive exercise subject to all of the challenges in observational data of social processes. All covariates are lagged by one period, but one cannot avoid the endogeneity that may emerge in long-term connections across the variables with unobserved factors related to security ties and probability of cooperation.

The next set of analyses (Tables 7.3 and 7.4) allows for unique contextual effects within regions. I divide the sample into regional IGOs according to the regional scope of the IGO and rerun models on the subsamples.[26] This does not change the importance of geopolitical alignment, and I also find consistent results when replacing the alliance measure with UN ideal point distance. The regional sub-samples shed light on the sensitivity of the estimates for democracy. The results of Table 7.1 show a weakly positive relationship between democracy and membership in regional organizations, but it is both small in magnitude and not statistically significant at standard convention.[27] When disaggregating to examine regional organizations with a separate analysis for

25. Changing the specification to instead include an indicator for democracies, based on coding those with a polity score above 5 as democracies, does not change this finding that democracy has an insignificant effect on membership in regional organizations. The positive coefficient for the polity variable is significant at 90 percent level in the specification that drops the region control.

26. The choice of eight regions is defined above. Note that some IGOs are included in more than one regional category.

27. These results are sensitive to the specification of standard errors. In the preferred specification shown in the results of this book, I treat heterogeneity by country through clustering standard errors at the country level. This step contributes to polity losing significance, relative to a specification that does not cluster standard errors.

	Dependent variable: IGO Membership			
	Western Europe	E. Europe Central Asia	East Asia Pacific	South Asia
Avg. Alliances	1.685***	0.969***	2.167***	3.595***
	(0.316)	(0.355)	(0.560)	(0.672)
Trade with Members	0.186	0.235**	0.430***	0.513***
	(0.114)	(0.107)	(0.092)	(0.153)
Distance to Members	−0.854***	−1.158***	−1.869***	−2.028***
	(0.234)	(0.216)	(0.273)	(0.285)
Same Region	0.196	0.055	0.760***	1.637***
	(0.391)	(0.354)	(0.241)	(0.388)
Polity	0.018	0.029*	0.070***	0.078***
	(0.015)	(0.016)	(0.016)	(0.018)
GDP	0.069	0.061	0.144	0.101
	(0.105)	(0.108)	(0.122)	(0.170)
GDP per capita	0.057	−0.026	−0.436***	−0.383***
	(0.108)	(0.111)	(0.100)	(0.134)
Trade Openness	−0.026	−0.026	−0.009	−0.004
	(0.051)	(0.050)	(0.014)	(0.010)
Stringent approval	−0.272**	−0.0002	0.038	−0.570***
	(0.118)	(0.127)	(0.171)	(0.208)
Region Members	0.246***	0.239***	0.243***	0.203***
	(0.021)	(0.019)	(0.026)	(0.038)
MIDs	11.685***	14.602***	8.299***	8.534**
	(3.809)	(3.737)	(3.035)	(3.556)
Common colony	0.301	2.816***	1.887***	1.666***
	(3.540)	(0.837)	(0.626)	(0.624)
Former colony	−3.651	−3.311	2.548*	3.920**
	(4.185)	(4.147)	(1.404)	(1.655)
Cold war	0.108	0.101	0.202**	0.030
	(0.102)	(0.115)	(0.099)	(0.115)
Constant	−1.527	0.809	4.657	5.632
	(2.267)	(1.907)	(3.263)	(3.562)
Observations	259,233	245,274	134,386	73,939
# IGOs	53	53	28	15
# States	156	156	156	156

TABLE 7.3. *Analysis of regional IGOs by separate region samples (1)*: These models examine the effect on membership of geopolitical alignment measured by alliance ties for the sub-sample of regional IGOs for each region. Coefficient estimates are displayed with robust standard errors in parentheses. Models include the following controls (not shown): *IGO Membership Size, Total State Memberships,* and a time polynomial. Statistical significance is denoted by: *p<0.1; **p<0.05; ***p<0.01.

	Dependent variable: IGO Membership			
	Sub-Saharan Africa	Latin America & Caribbean	North/Central America	Middle East N. Africa
Avg. Alliances	1.463***	2.293***	2.804***	2.778***
	(0.190)	(0.441)	(0.342)	(0.313)
Trade with Members	0.329***	0.716***	0.673***	0.271***
	(0.044)	(0.082)	(0.073)	(0.054)
Distance to Members	−1.263***	−1.059***	−1.174***	−0.909***
	(0.143)	(0.312)	(0.189)	(0.168)
Same Region	1.802***	1.390***	1.215***	1.522***
	(0.311)	(0.287)	(0.316)	(0.270)
Polity	0.025*	−0.009	−0.018	0.005
	(0.014)	(0.013)	(0.014)	(0.014)
GDP	0.068	−0.589***	−0.421***	0.029
	(0.083)	(0.151)	(0.142)	(0.073)
GDP per capita	−0.260***	−0.365***	−0.181	−0.291***
	(0.084)	(0.138)	(0.127)	(0.074)
Trade Openness	0.0002	−0.096	−0.304***	−0.005*
	(0.002)	(0.061)	(0.062)	(0.003)
Stringent Approval	0.248*	−0.692***	−0.709***	0.210
	(0.142)	(0.236)	(0.159)	(0.159)
Region Members	0.127***	0.161***	0.139***	0.118***
	(0.011)	(0.027)	(0.036)	(0.012)
MIDS	11.629***	5.571	6.367**	9.575***
	(2.911)	(3.403)	(2.589)	(2.299)
Common colony	1.808***	1.484**	1.821***	2.402***
	(0.276)	(0.577)	(0.500)	(0.351)
Former colony	−0.520	3.517***	3.607***	−0.004
	(0.770)	(0.614)	(1.260)	(0.732)
Cold war	−0.178**	−0.055	−0.061	−0.264***
	(0.083)	(0.119)	(0.095)	(0.073)
Constant	0.612	4.501	2.430	−0.845
	(1.646)	(3.483)	(2.402)	(1.797)
Observations	246,107	202,965	254,536	191,097
# IGOs	60	43	54	43
# States	156	156	156	156

TABLE 7.4. *Analysis of regional IGOs by separate region samples (2)* These models examine the effect on membership of geopolitical alignment measured by alliance ties for the sub-sample of regional IGOs for each region. Coefficient estimates are displayed with robust standard errors in parentheses. Models include the following controls (not shown): *IGO Membership Size, Total State Memberships,* and a time polynomial. Statistical significance is denoted by: *p<0.1; **p<0.05; ***p<0.01.

each region, democracy has a significant effect within the regions that have more variability in democracy: East Asia and Pacific, South Asia, and Sub-Saharan Africa. Where there are stronger democratic norms in Europe, North and Central America, and Latin America and Caribbean, the polity measure does not have significant impact. Neither is an effect evident for the low democracy region of Middle East and North Africa.[28]

The relationship between security and entry holds across larger samples of IGOs. In Table 7.5, one can see a consistently positive and significant coefficient for the alliance variable across the regional organizations in the larger set of 321 regional organizations, including those that did not have a formal charter (column 1). The second column shows the full sample of all 491 IGOs from the COW dataset, with basic covariate data for the estimation of membership patterns. On average, states have a lower probability of joining regional IGOs (RIGOs), but those in the same region are more likely to join the regional IGO. There is little evidence here that regional organizations have a neighborhood effect with a unique integration dynamic; regional organizations can be understood as one kind of international organization that exhibits many similar trends with others.

The rules can moderate the impact of geopolitics. In the high-stakes security of a regional context, veto players can block entrants. I interact the *Stringent Approval* indicator with the *Average Alliances* variable (see Model 1, Table 7.6). Fifty-seven regional organizations meet this high threshold for supermajority or consensus approval requirement for enlargement. The base effect of the stringent voting rules indicator is positive, which suggests that despite the high approval threshold, a state is on average more likely to join. A more restrictive organization may hold appeal for its signaling value or correspond to greater distributive benefits upon joining (Poast and Urpelainen, 2013). Of particular interest for my argument, the interaction term indicates that there is a significant relationship between stringent approval and geopolitics. The negative interaction effect implies that geopolitics plays *less* of a role in IGOs with a stringent accession process than in those with lower approval threshold.[29] Achieving consensus within a geographic area requires a different kind of appeal. Alliances can be a positive force of attraction for one group

---

28. In their analysis of democratic transition and IGO membership, Poast and Urpelainen (2018) also find that East Asia has a strong effect, in contrast to weak or even negative results for the Americas.

29. The basic specification in Table 7.1 controls for stringent approval process, which was insignificant. Interacting geopolitical alignment with the stringent approval variable does not

	Dependent variable: IGO Membership	
	(1)	(2)
Average alliance	2.090***	1.993***
	(0.177)	(0.185)
Trade with members	0.371***	0.302***
	(0.037)	(0.033)
Distance to Members	−0.596***	−0.294***
	(0.100)	(0.090)
Same Region	1.043***	1.569***
	(0.167)	(0.160)
Polity	0.007	0.009
	(0.007)	(0.006)
GDP	−0.044	0.071
	(0.052)	(0.057)
GDP per capita	−0.257***	−0.194***
	(0.057)	(0.044)
Trade openness	−0.011	−0.016**
	(0.007)	(0.007)
IGO membership size	0.043***	0.026***
	(0.003)	(0.001)
Total State Memberships	0.008*	0.018***
	(0.005)	(0.004)
Fatal MIDS with member	11.652***	9.241***
	(2.568)	(2.005)
Common Colonial History	2.283***	2.530***
	(0.216)	(0.195)
Former colony	1.098	−0.514
	(0.717)	(1.057)
Cold War	−0.013	−0.041
	(0.047)	(0.036)
Region members	0.194***	0.154***
	(0.012)	(0.010)
RIGO		−1.501***
		(0.113)
Observations	1,219,768	1,989,094
# IGOs	321	491
# States	156	156

TABLE 7.5. *Regional IGO Sample Comparison*: The RIGO sample in the first column expands to all 321 regional organizations from COW without limiting to those with data on the IGO charter terms. The second column removes the restriction to regional organizations for full sample of 491 IGOs while adding a control indicator for the regional IGOs. Statistical significance is denoted by: *p<0.1; **p<0.05; ***p<0.01.

	Dependent variable: IGO Membership		
	(1)	(2)	(3)
Average alliance	2.345***	2.185***	2.440***
	(0.195)	(0.180)	(0.185)
Trade with members	0.372***	0.312***	0.332***
	(0.038)	(0.036)	(0.037)
Distance to Members	−0.567***	−0.595***	−0.781***
	(0.098)	(0.109)	(0.111)
Same Region	1.099***	1.240***	1.575***
	(0.168)	(0.180)	(0.209)
Region members	0.200***	0.202***	0.186***
	(0.014)	(0.014)	(0.015)
Polity	0.013	0.019**	0.029***
	(0.008)	(0.008)	(0.010)
GDP	0.009	0.086	0.139**
	(0.056)	(0.057)	(0.058)
GDP per capita	−0.327***	−0.363***	−0.409***
	(0.057)	(0.062)	(0.068)
Trade openness	−0.009	−0.005	−0.006
	(0.007)	(0.004)	(0.004)
Stringent approval	0.269***	0.057	0.204**
	(0.104)	(0.095)	(0.097)
Fatal MIDS with member	11.696***	10.336***	10.479***
	(2.629)	(2.541)	(2.905)
Common Colonial History	2.283***	2.317***	2.223***
	(0.223)	(0.229)	(0.259)
Former colony	0.720	0.925	−3.897**
	(0.999)	(0.926)	(1.728)
Cold War	−0.035	−0.067*	−0.044
	(0.049)	(0.035)	(0.042)
Alliance*Stringent	−0.805***		
	(0.213)		
Rivalry		−0.255	−0.035
		(0.388)	(0.299)
alliance*Rivalry		1.027	
		(0.631)	
Observations	895,116	604,983	479,592
# IGOs	197	184	174
# States	156	156	129

Note: *p<0.1; **p<0.05; ***p<0.01.

TABLE 7.6. *Voting and rivalry regression results:* Model 1 interacts the alliance measure with supermajority approval requirements. Model 2 interacts the alliance measure with the indicator for rivalry with the IGO lead state. Model 3 omits all NATO states and the IGOs that also represent alliances. Models include the following controls (not shown): *IGO Membership Size, Total State Memberships,* and a time polynomial.

and a veto point for another. IGOs with a less formalized way of restricting membership, such as requiring accession by invitation or negotiation, rely on political ties, without the risk of veto players.

In order to consider another perspective on vetoplayers, I also look at the presence of rivalries. In the context of regional organizations that often bring together bordering states with a long history of war, rivalries may become embedded for deep animosity. Adding a control variable for the presence of rivalry between a state and the largest "lead state" of the organization tests for this concern.[30] Table 7.6 shows in Model 2 that the base effect of rivalry is insignificant, and there is no apparent interaction with the alliance ties to members.

A final test examines sensitivity of the findings to the IGOs with high-security orientation. Model 3 omits all NATO countries as well as 11 IGOs, including NATO, that have their primary focus as a security IGO. The alliance ties with members remains important, and rivalry is unchanged as an insignificant control variable. The weak finding for strategic rivalry matters as an assurance that the attraction through alliances is not simply the inverse of historic rivalry. But there may also be challenges to understanding the impact of rivalry that would merit separate analysis. Within a region, proximity and conflict behavior generate competing pressures for cooperation. Depending on the case, regional organizations bring such states together for governance projects or deepen the separation through drawing another line of insider and outsider politics. Rivalries may also influence membership through different channels, such as by suppressing the creation of an organization rather than stopping entry.

Aggregating across the experience of many countries and regional organizations has demonstrated a robust correlation between security ties and joint membership in regional organizations. I next turn to review critical case studies of two prominent regional organizations in Europe and the Asia Pacific. From its formation in 1957 among six countries at the core of Europe to twenty-eight members, the EU merits study as the largest economy and a regional organization that exercises considerable authority over governance.

---

change the direction and significance for the baseline positive effect of geopolitical alignment in the larger set of regional organizations that do not have stringent voting approval.

30. The strategic rivalry variable is from Thompson (2001). It measures the intensity of conflict between a pair of states through the reported perception of rivalry by decision makers. The data ends in 2002, which limits the sample time period for the model.

Membership remains one of its most conflictual questions, as seen by the controversial exit of the UK and the eager requests to join by Ukraine and Moldova, among others. In contrast, ASEAN has been slow to expand to its current membership of ten states, and has been more reluctant to delegate authority to a central institution. Yet it also brings to the forefront controversies over membership and unexpected turns in the expansion to include more states. From a security perspective, the EU and ASEAN offer interesting variation with the NATO alliance anchoring the EU, while non-intervention is the key unifying principle of ASEAN. At turning points in the institutional development, perceptions of threat levels vary in ways that allow comparison across potential members of each institution in their choice about accession. Close examination of these enlargement decisions within each case study allows me to identify which actors initiate the process seeking membership and review the government rationale.

7.3   EU: The Security Prerequisite for Entry

The EU has struggled with the place of foreign policy within its mandate. Outside of trade and commercial affairs, there has not been a common foreign policy. There are no references to security commitments as a condition of membership, nor do states engage in systematic coordination of their defense policies as members. The Treaty of Rome elaborates on the common policies in all areas of commerce, ranging from free movement of goods and people to agriculture and transportation, while making no stipulation for a common foreign policy or defense policy. This stands in contrast to other regional organizations such as the Organization of American States.[31] Weiler (2003, p. 11) notes that until the 1990s, any "overt foreign policy" role would have been contested, and comments that leaders would even hold separate meetings, under different umbrellas, when ministers were to discuss foreign policy. The attempt to include a foreign policy was among several points that doomed the proposal for an EU Constitution in 2004, only to lead to more modest foreign policy mandate in the Lisbon Treaty. Nevertheless, geopolitical alignment has played a central role in European integration. It does so through the path of membership.

The EU imposes more rigid conditionality for membership than most organizations. The nature of conditions, however, has gone beyond compliance

31. For example, the Organization of American States chapter VI stipulates collective security commitments.

with economic and social regulations. The East European experience stands out, as applicants undertook extensive reforms to implement the body of EU laws in order to gain entry into the European club. On some dimensions the applicants had to adopt higher standards than current members. Most notably, political criteria for human rights and democracy were upheld alongside economic policy demands (Duxbury, 2011). In addition, I argue that common security orientation formed an informal prerequisite for entry. A large literature lays a strong foundation for understanding the European enlargement process, and it is beyond the scope of this chapter to offer a comprehensive review (e.g. Schimmelfennig, 2001; Jacoby, 2004; Vachudova, 2005; Kelley, 2004; Schneider, 2009). Rather, this section will explore how security interests shaped membership choices.

While all would acknowledge that basic goals for peace and prosperity underlie the pursuit of European integration, differences arise over the relative importance of foreign policy goals and economic interests in determining the process (Moravcsik, 1998). Some place more emphasis on entrepreneurial leaders like Jean Monnet and their ideals for a larger European project. This perspective places a premium on geopolitical concerns and grand strategy alongside evolving norms about what it means to be European. Neofunctional theory points to goals for cooperation on specific problems and the spillover that occurs as technocrats entrench federalism in the process of implementing policy (e.g. Haas, 1958; Mitrany, 1965). Others look at the distributional stakes for economic interests. The wealthy markets of the core members draw in states that seek preferential access, and nonmembers face costs from exclusion, including trade and investment diversion (Baldwin, 1995; Mattli, 1999). Beyond free trade agreements, joining the EU allowed states to consult on economic regulations as participants in the decision process and embed their policies in a broader context. The normative commitment to the idea of Europe, which is conceived as liberal democracy forms another factor shaping enlargement patterns (Schimmelfennig, 2001). Across these debates about grand strategy for a greater Europe and narrow economic interests at the national level, states faced the question of who should be the right partner for pursuit of peace and prosperity.

Founders

The origins of the European Union extend back to the Concert of Europe and other forms of international cooperation centered in Europe. But a more specific proposal dates to the interwar years. In his massive study of international organization, Eagleton (1957, p. 564) attributes the first significant step toward a European organization to French Premier Aristide Briand's proposal to a gathering of 27 European states in 1929 that they create "some kind of a federal bond." Governments offered support and joined follow-up commissions and diplomatic meetings, but they failed to produce any concrete organization, given mixed views about how to sequence economic and political cooperation and rivalries between states. Leaders revisited the idea after WWII, which led to the establishment of the Council of Europe in 1949.[32] The Treaty of Rome in 1957 initiated deeper cooperation envisioned for economic and social unity among European states.[33] Why did a potential grouping of nearly 30 European states ultimately become six founding members: Belgium, France, Germany, Italy, Luxembourg, and the Netherlands?

In the aftermath of war, states sought to bind Germany to prevent it from ever threatening the security of Europe. At the same time, the emerging conflict with the USSR set high stakes on building European unity to defend against the threat from the East. These twin forces supported a general commitment to use economic integration to strengthen their economies and uphold peaceful cooperation in Europe. But beyond this general acknowledgement, the foreign policy dimension often became subsumed within a narrative that placed central focus on whether integration served the functional demand for economic cooperation from national governments or served federalist aspirations for political consolidation (e.g. Haas, 1958; Moravcsik, 1998; Dedman, 2010). Alongside these sources of integration, specific security interests pushed some states ahead and held others back.[34]

32. This organization began with ten members: Belgium, Denmark, France, Ireland, Italy, Luxembourg, the Netherlands, Norway, Sweden, and the United Kingdom. It has since expanded to the current 47 members, including Russia, Turkey, and Ukraine. The charter clearly envisioned broader expansion to achieve the goals of supporting rule of law and human rights in the region, and held open that any European Country invited by its Committee of Ministers—based on supermajority vote of approval—could deposit a ratification instrument.

33. Following COW, the European Coal and Steel Community (1952–1992) and European Economic Community (1958–1992) are treated as distinct IGOs because they are independent legal entities recorded in the International Organization Yearbook. Both end with establishment of the EU, which is treated as a new IGO. A historical perspective highlights the overlapping nature and evolution of a single effort to unite the region.

34. Some of those states opting to remain outside of the EEC formed the European Free Trade Association, which counts as a regional international organization but represents much more shallow integration based on establishing a free trade area. Austria, Denmark, Norway,

The UK government offered early support for the idea of a customs union in Europe in 1948. Foreign Minister Ernest Bevin and the foreign office initiated the proposal as part of his political strategy, and he acted over the resistance of the economic ministries that were more worried about disadvantages for British industry (Dedman, 2010, p. 33). But ultimately the strategic priority led the UK to focus on a collective self-defense commitment among European States (the Western European Union) and favor ties to the United States over deepening commitments to European economic cooperation (ibid., p. 36). Indeed, Dedman (2010, p. 38) argues that once the UK had gained its security commitment from the United States through NATO, the foreign office in 1949 switched its view to see European integration as unnecessary and potentially even harmful to British foreign policy. Given resistance by major economic stakeholders, none in government remained in favor of the enterprise. In an odd turn of events, the U.S. security guarantee reduced the interest of the UK government in building ties with the continent, despite the fact that U.S. officials strongly urged the UK to lead the movement for European integration. Ultimately, France led the effort to build a customs union in Europe, and the UK chose to stay out.

France favored a smaller union for both economic and foreign policy reasons. The foreign policy benefits arose from standing out as a regional leader. Through negotiations in the smaller group dominated by France, it could control the level of liberalization to shelter its interventionist economic policies and weak sectors (Dedman, 2010, p. 46). Moravcsik (1998, p. 104) counters the common narrative that geopolitical goals and European ideology alone motivated the French leadership for creation of an integrated Europe. He argues that, if anything, geopolitics was secondary to its commercial goals, and the decisive role of French agriculture played in favor of integration. Nevertheless, economic interests in France were mixed, as economic ministries lined up against the union, along with several sensitive economic sectors, including the powerful small business groups (Moravcsik, 1998, p. 115).

German leaders were eager for any opportunity to restore positive relations with its neighbors. Having only achieved limited sovereignty with the end of the Occupation, joining the French initiative for a European customs union offered recognition of its equality as diplomatic partner and a deal to reclaim control of the industries in the Ruhr industrial region (Dedman, 2010,

---

Sweden, Switzerland, and the UK founded EFTA, while Iceland, Liechtenstein, and Portugal later joined. As countries joined the EEC, they left EFTA.

p. 56). Chancellor Konrad Adenauer pursued Western alignment as the way to achieve security and combat the alternatives of nationalism or Social Democratic Party proposals for talks with the USSR, and for him, integration with European economies was paired with rearmament in NATO, a part of committing Germany to the Western camp (Moravcsik, 1998, p. 94). Business interests favored a free trade agreement over a customs union with the "small Europe" grouping, and the German economics minister advocated global free trade; so it was Adenauer and the foreign ministry officials who led the German enthusiasm for joining the EEC (ibid., p. 100).

The governments of Austria, Finland, Norway, and Switzerland gave their status as neutral states as reason to stay outside of the EEC at its formation. When Sweden considered possibly joining the EC in 1971, it deferred with the rationale that it could not reconcile membership with neutrality (Subedi, 1993, p. 255).[35] Speaking in 1987, Kalevi Sorsa, Prime Minister of Finland, stated that "membership of the EC is barred to any country that wishes to preserve its neutrality" (Subedi, 1993, p. 239). Even with over half its trade flowing to the members of the European Community over most years from 1955 to 1988, and the united front of business, labor, and agriculture in favor of integration with Europe, critics of integration within Austria pointed to treaty terms of neutrality as preventing its membership in the EC (Schultz, 1992, p. 176). The Soviet Union insisted that the EC was the economic arm of NATO and Austria could not join as a neutral state, and its objections resurfaced at each stage of Austrian discussion of association with the EC (ibid., pp. 179, 182). Soviet objections loomed even larger for Finland, which did not become a full member of the European Free Trade Association until 1986 (Beyer and Hofmann, 2011, p. 296). Mattli (1999, p. 82) acknowledges that the neutrals form an outlier for his theory that demand for economic growth opportunities will drive regional integration.

Many, but not all, of the neutral states would eventually join the EU. The signing of the 1986 Single European Act had set the course for deepening integration of Europe from 1992, raising the economic stakes of remaining outside the Union. At the same time, the end of the Cold War shifted the security conditions in the neighborhood to allow for loosening the interpretation of neutrality. In the case of Austria, its accession negotiations explicitly note its ongoing commitment to neutrality (Subedi, 1993, p. 240). Yet this step toward

---

35. Sweden claims its neutral foreign policy is "not allied between power blocs in peace in order to be able to remain neutral in a war" (Subedi, 1993, p. 246).

a more flexible interpretation would not have been possible without the collapse of the Soviet Union that both ended external objections and the use of its threats by domestic critics of integration (Schultz, 1992, p. 196). The meaning of neutrality has evolved and varies by country, based on how domestic audiences have shaped the norm adoption and how the end of Cold War shifted security interests (Beyer and Hofmann, 2011). While Switzerland long stayed outside of the UN, other neutral states including Austria and Sweden joined the UN in the 1950s and later became EC members without revoking neutrality. Ireland ascribes itself as holding a neutral foreign policy, but has never seen this as presenting a conflict with joining the EC. The Irish government insists that the treaty obligations do not prejudice defense policies of its members (Subedi, 1993, p. 258). Indeed, given the absence of a military component in the organization, the puzzle is why any state would consider entry a problem from the perspective of neutrality. Yet informal linkages between geopolitical alignment and economic cooperation form an obstacle for the most strict adherents to neutrality like Switzerland, and has delayed the entry of others.[36]

Accession rules

Since its founding, the EU has expanded to 28 members. How has enlargement gone forward? The EU treaty terms of membership explicated in the 1992 Treaty on European Union (the Maastricht Treaty) in Article O are quite precise about the accession process.

> Any European State may apply to become a Member of the Union. It shall address its application to the Council, which shall act unanimously after consulting the Commission and after receiving the assent of the European Parliament, which shall act by an absolute majority of its component members. The conditions of admission and the adjustments to the Treaties on which the Union is founded which such admission entails shall be the subject of an agreement between the Member States and the applicant State. This agreement shall be submitted for ratification by all the contracting States in accordance with their respective constitutional requirements.

36. Ultimately the accession decision reflects both economic and security interests, and one cannot say neutrality alone keeps Switzerland outside of the EU. High resistance to CAP from its agricultural sector, concerns from banking industry about finance regulations, and public rejection as revealed in 1992 referendum on whether to join the European Economic Area all contribute to Switzerland's decision to remain outside of the EU.

The provisions set clear expectations that conditions of admission in the form of "adjustments to the Treaties" will be negotiated and reviewed as part of the evaluation of membership. The requirement for unanimous approval of the council puts the EU squarely in the stringent approval category. The decision is ultimately determined by voting at both transnational and national levels of members. Potential veto players may limit the consideration of candidates through rigorous review or voting. The basic terms governing membership to the EU remain largely unchanged from those set forth in the original 1957 Treaty of Rome.[37] Working procedures establish greater transparency over accession, but the legal parameters remain consistent. On the one hand, the EU rules call for more rigorous review than do those other regional organizations. It is closer to the ideal type of meritocratic selection. On the other hand, the terms still leave room for discretion that allows the EU to form a club with discriminatory evaluation of criteria for entry.

The British experience highlights this point, as France vetoed its first applications to join the European Economic Community. By 1961, the British Prime Minister Harold Macmillon's government had come around to seeking membership. Economic growth on the continent outpaced that in the UK, and freeing barriers for trade with its major trading partners promised new stimulus. Nevertheless, it was not simply an economic pull that led the UK to seek membership.[38] Membership promised to improve UK foreign policy ties not only with Europe but also with the United States, which favored European integration as a political project over the free trade association that the UK had been pursuing (O'Rourke, 2019, p. 68). The prospect of UK influence within Europe, however, prompted concern in France. French President Charles De Gaulle vetoed British entry twice, first in January 1963 and again in 1967. This occurred at the same time that France was reducing its security

---

37. The 1957 treaty states: "Any European State may apply to become a member of the Community. It shall address its application to the Council which, after obtaining the opinion of the Commission, shall act by means of a unanimous vote. The conditions of admission and the amendments to this Treaty necessitated thereby shall be the subject of an agreement between the Member States and the applicant State. Such agreement shall be submitted to all the contracting States for ratification in accordance with their respective constitutional rules." (1957 Treaty of Rome Article 237, UN Treaty Series 1958, p. 92)

38. In fact, in the first UK referendum on membership in the EU that took place in 1975, it would be the Secretary of Industry and Secretary of State for Employment who voted against entry to the UK (O'Rourke, 2019, p. 76).

cooperation with NATO.[39] In 1963, de Gaulle criticized UK Atlanticism as a threat that would lead to American dependence overwhelming the European Community and cited a recent missile deal between the United States and United Kingdom as a reason for vetoing its membership (Freedman, 2020). There is debate over whether de Gaulle was motivated by his aspirations for a French foreign policy role in Europe and suspicions of the UK as being too close to the United States, or simply sought protection of French agricultural interests.[40] Nevertheless, the case highlights that even the most qualified democracy with deep economic engagement with members was not assured entry. Only after the passing of de Gaulle and several years of negotiations could the UK join in 1973, alongside Denmark and Ireland, in the first round of European enlargement.

In considering the norms underlying the legal provisions, it is useful to contrast the EU with the Council of Europe. The latter includes democracy and respect for human rights as formal membership criteria, but when establishing the Coal and Steel Community, states omitted any reference to democracy or human rights. Thomas (2017, 224) notes that from the first draft to final text, such conditions were never present in negotiations as leaders such as Jean Monnet favored an inclusive project to achieve production gains and did not want to be constrained by fixed entry criteria. Critically, this flexibility would leave open the door to possible entry by noncommunist states in alignment against the Soviet Union, such as Portugal, Spain, and Greece. Ultimately the enlargement to include these countries would hinge on democracy, human rights, and foreign policy items as well as on economic reforms, which they accepted as an informal condition of participation (Duxbury, 2011).

Eastern Enlargement

The rise and fall of Cold War tensions triggered discussion of expanding membership to Eastern Europe in 1989. Reductions in the threat level and signs of internal shifts earlier during the Cold War had led Western governments to welcome several communist states into the GATT and extend foreign aid. But it was the end of the Cold War that rapidly led to demands for broadening the European project. Under the leadership of Mikhail Gorbachev, the USSR

39. After years of De Gaulle threatening to quit NATO, in 1966, France ended the Status of Forces Agreement, which meant it halted participation in the integrated NATO command.
40. See Moravcsik (1998) for the argument that economic interests played the larger role in the expansion of Europe.

in 1988 assented to members of the Warsaw Pact and the Council for Mutual Economic Assistance (COMECON), establishing their own relations with Europe, and he praised engagement with Europe and the vision of a "common European house" (Mastny, 2009, p. 205). Freed of Soviet control, newly independent governments sought to anchor their geopolitical alignment with Western Europe. Thereafter, loss of aid and trade following Soviet collapse placed a new imperative on access to European markets for growth.

Foreign policy and economic motives are closely intertwined for applicants. To the extent loss of Soviet aid and economic need drove demand for access, one would expect economic ministries to have advocated early entry and the countries that had been most dependent on the USSR to have headed to the front of the line in seeking a new patron. But this was generally not the pattern. Among Eastern governments, the executive and foreign ministries led the call for entry into the EU. Governments that had been more independent on the USSR—Poland, Hungary, and Czechoslovakia—were first to issue the request. Their demands emphasized being part of Europe, with economic gains often coming as a secondary justification (Grabbe and Hughes, 1998, p. 7). Of course, the idea of "Europe" aggregates both a sense of history and geography as well as alignment with the foreign policy and ideology of the member governments, such that one cannot simply extract one motive. But for the countries between the Western and Soviet camps, declaring themselves to be part of Europe was a deliberate choice to shift outside of the Russian sphere into Europe. In their analysis of the original demand side of Eastern enlargement in the early 1990s, Grabbe and Hughes (1998, p. 8) emphasize the importance of the "implicit security guarantee that is effectively part of EU membership."

On the member side, foreign policy loomed large to push for accommodation of new entrants. Germany stood up as the institutional leader and "paymaster" supporting Eastern enlargement, and its motives reflect the economic benefits of regional production networks and a hope for rehabilitation of relations with the East (Mattli, 1999, p. 104–105). The UK had long favored widening over deepening of the EU, and Tony Blair emerged as a strong advocate (O'Rourke, 2019, p. 168). France at first had expected to use the Organization for Security and Cooperation in Europe (OSCE) as a kind of halfway house for coordinating aid and foreign policy with Eastern Europe when they were far from ready to join the EC (Mastny, 2009, p. 209). When it was clear such options would not accommodate the aspirations of the Eastern countries, France assented to EU enlargement.

Following the Copenhagen criterion established in 1993, the EU accession process approached the meritocratic model to conduct rigorous review of policy changes that are required as a condition for entry. Vachudova (2005) makes the distinction between the passive and active leverage applied by the accession process on the East European countries. The former arose from the appeal of joining the EU for economic benefits and consolidation of democratic reforms, which encouraged political elites to engage in the accession process. The latter, however, was more direct negotiation over specific reforms through review of policy changes. This active leverage differentiates the meritocratic model of accession and was relatively new with the Eastern enlargement. Where other organizations would often accept a promise of committing to the policies of the organization without inspection, reviews of the legislative changes brought intense scrutiny on applicants. Indeed, the eastern enlargement of the EU was more severe in its insistence on the completion of reforms prior to accession than NATO's. In 1999, Poland, Czechia, and Hungary became the first former Warsaw Pact countries to join NATO, well before achieving requested levels of military readiness (Jacoby, 2004, p. 32).[41] One scholar refers to the experience of conditionality for Eastern enlargement: "For the house Delors was building was much like a New York co-op—with a board setting up strict conditions for admission and screening all the applicants"(Mastny, 2009, p. 207). The rigorous compliance review fits with the expectation that non-allied states must work harder to prove their qualifications. The end of the Cold War opened a door, but the Eastern enlargement negotiations were long and demanding.

Yet one should not exaggerate the rigor of conditionality. By no means did the EU impose a single template on all applicants. Jacoby (2004, p. 6) notes that the EU favored "rough and approximate" standards over checklists because it neither wanted to promise approval if a country met the rules nor demand all should be fulfilled. In his analogy of a *menu*, governments made a range of choices over the conditions demanded for entry. Schneider (2009) reveals the political bargains that took place between powerful members sponsoring entry for favored applicants and the leverage seized by smaller members who could insist on concessions to offer assent. Variation in the level of subsidies and transition periods to implement reforms characterize differences across the accession packages that were negotiated. The

41. On 31 December 1992, Czechoslovakia split into two new states: the Czech Republic (Czechia) and Slovakia.

constrained choice for the applicants arose insofar as they could not pull apart these complex agreements, largely shaped by the terms agreed upon by members. Indeed, in some cases the legislatures of applicant countries did not even debate many of the legislative changes as they were taken as part of negotiating to implement the *acquis*, rather than as deliberation over individual policies (Jacoby, 2004, p. 4).

The case of Poland as the largest of the entrants during the Eastern enlargement reveals the complex nature of the process. From an early start, it would take fifteen years to enter the EU. In September 1989, Poland signed a trade agreement with European states, and in February 1990 its foreign minister, Tadeusz Mazowiecki, publicly expressed the wish to join the European Community. The urge to join has been described as "Poles' longing to be part of the West" and avoiding ever again falling into dependence on Russia (Taras, 2003, p. 3, 14). Lech Walesa proposed a NATO II and EU-2 that would allow Poland to lead a wave of Eastern members to reform under European tutelage (Mastny, 2009, p. 216). The left party of SLD and its many former Communist Party members were at the forefront of the push for European integration, but there was a broad consensus across the political elite in 1989, and it was only later that right wing parties would pick up on Euroskepticism to offer an alternative rallying point (ibid., p. 4).

In a sequence of steps toward membership, Poland first established rapprochement with Germany and France in 1992, and according to Mastny (2009, 214), its close relations with both countries "gave Poland a head start for admission to the EU." It soon assumed associate membership in the EU in 1993 and began negotiations for full membership five years later. The review was not a free pass—well after shock therapy had converted Poland into a market economy and elections established its democratic credentials, reports from accession negotiations in 1999 highlighted remaining gaps, where policies across agriculture, industry, and transportation and labor were all faulted as falling short of EU harmonization with the *acquis* (ibid. p. 11). Writing of their experience as lead negotiators for Poland, Kulakowski and Jesień (2007) argue sectoral interests were taken up within a larger sense of history that the project would end the Cold War division of Europe. Ultimately the hard decisions fell to the top leadership. Only at the Copenhagen European Council Summit meeting in December 2002 did Poland agree on a compromise for phasing in direct payments to farmers and allocating additional funds to rural areas (Kulakowski and Jesień, 2007, p. 301). The labor regulations on working conditions also required direct intervention by the Prime Minister to reconcile different positions. Finally, in 2003, countries signed the accession treaty and in 2004 Poland became a member after all EU members voted for ratification of the accession protocol.

The negotiations to join the EU occurred alongside efforts to also join NATO. Early requests to join in 1991 were rebuffed. Strong Russian opposition led to worries among European states. Such resistance from Russia only deepened the urge in Poland to go forward. In 1997, the Polish Defense Minister spoke of "Association with, and then membership in, the European Union will also further our participation in [NATO]" (Terry, 2000, p. 11). With heightened U.S. pressure in support of East European countries joining NATO, however, the alliance talks proceeded ahead of regional integration and Poland joined NATO in 1999, along with Czechia and Hungary (Mastny, 2009, p. 216).

The literature on the Eastern enlargement of the EU points to both economic and foreign policy forces to account for expansion. The treaty terms for rigorous review left room for negotiation over sectoral interests while security interests helped bridge the gap when economic differences might have otherwise loomed too large. On the one hand, geopolitical realignment at the end of the Cold War opened the prospect of former Warsaw Pact countries entering the EU. On the other hand, even after joining NATO, tough negotiations remained before Poland could be accepted into the EU. The Cold War danger motivated European integration, and its end also sparked further integration with a new set of countries. The change of alliance affiliations reconfigured which states wanted to join and the timing of their requests.

The Excluded Neighbor Turkey

European enlargement has not expanded so far as to include Turkey. In its first bid for membership, Turkey requested to join the European Economic Community in 1959. This led to deepening economic exchange through commitments for association that could lead to consideration for accession. In 1986, Turkey formally applied for full membership, but the European Commission deferred the case (Ilgaz and Toygu, 2011, p. 4). It was over a decade before European states would engage in serious negotiations on the matter. During this period Turkey consolidated its political institutions as a democracy.[42] By 1995 Turkey had concluded an agreement to join a Custom's Union

42. The polity measure of democracy for Turkey is 9 out of 10 for the years 1989–1992, with some losses of rights leading to declines to 7 or 8 in the following years, with return

with the EU, which further highlighted the question of its political integration. Following the decision of the Helsinki European Council Summit in 1999, Turkey became an official candidate for accession. Within a few years, it had put forward a plan for adoption of the European *acquis* and in 2004 the European Council determined that Turkey had met the Copenhagen political criteria so that accession negotiations could begin. But after many rounds, these talks have been deadlocked, with few on either side holding expectations of a revival.[43]

Many focus on how cultural and political differences stand as obstacles. The presumption that Europe as a "Christian club" opposes giving membership to Turkey as a country with a large Muslim population, has been widely discussed in the media if not in official statements. Writing in 2001 prior to becoming the foreign minister, Ahmet Davutoglu wrote that Europe "regards Turkey culturally as part of the Islam-centred East, economically and politically as an extension of the South. Because of this, Europeans regard Turkey as a hard-to-absorb element, and avoid saying 'yes' to full membership, while keeping relations in limbo by calculating the potential costs of saying 'no.'" (Ilgaz and Toygu, 2011, p. 13). The gulf between Turkey and Europe has grown as the result of political shifts within Turkey. Political repression by President Recep Erdogan has been given as the reason by those in the European Parliament that call for suspending accession talks.[44] First coming into office in 2003 as prime minister with wide popular support for his pro-democracy and pro-European views, Erdogan emerged as a forceful advocate for Turkey to join the EU. Later he increasingly turned toward restricting political rights, and his politicization of economic policies has worsened the perception that his government falls short of what Europe expects of accession candidates. The Europa website states, "Turkey is a key strategic partner of the EU on issues such as migration, security, counter-terrorism, and the economy, but has been backsliding in the areas of democracy, rule of law and fundamental rights. In response, the General Affairs Council decided in June 2018 that

---

to a higher score of 9 in 2011–13. The polity level 9 is equivalent to Bulgaria's and Romania's at the time of their accession to the EU. The 2014 repression of rights pushed Turkey's polity score to 3.

43. Notwithstanding this reality, rumors about imminent membership in the EU for Turkey were used as a red herring in the Brexit debates, as will be discussed below.

44. European Parliament, European Parliament resolution of 6 July 2017 on the 2016 Commission Report on Turkey, 6 July 2017, P8TA(2017)0306.

accession negotiations with Turkey are effectively frozen."[45] One cannot know whether accepting Turkey within the European fold earlier could have set the country on a different path of economic and political reforms. Yet prior to democratic backsliding, that door was closed as accession talks deadlocked over other issues.

The role of foreign policy looms large over why Turkey is even mentioned as a potential member of the EU. As a NATO ally, Turkey stood alongside Europe in the Cold War confrontation with the USSR. This status was a factor bringing it into the OECD and GATT much sooner than might have been expected by its economic position alone. Its importance as a strategic partner on security and regional conflicts account for why Turkey could become a formal accession candidate even when cultural or geographic lines could have been drawn to exclude it. Marti Ahtisaari, former president of Finland and Chair of the Independent Commission on Turkey, stated that "the unique geopolitical position of Turkey at the crossroads of the Balkans, the wider Middle East, South Caucus, Central Asia and beyond, its importance for the security of Europe's energy supplies and her political, economic, and military weight would be great assets" (Burak, 2007, p. 44). Moreover, the United States has often been seen as a critical broker necessary to push the Europeans to accommodate the request from Turkey to join.[46]

On the other hand, Turkey is directly involved in a territorial dispute with EU members over Cyprus. Since 1964, a UN Peacekeeping force has remained on the island to prevent fighting between the Greek Cypriot and Turkish Cypriot communities. Turkey does not recognize that the government of the Republic of Cyprus has the right to rule the entire island; Turkey is the only government to support the legitimacy of the government in north Cyprus. Ever since Greece joined the European Community in 1981, it has held a veto over Turkish membership, given the European rule for consensus on member enlargement. With enlargement in 2004 to include Cyprus—despite the Greek Cypriots' rejection that same year of Kofi Annan's peace plan for unification of the island—the territorial dispute became even larger a problem for Turkey's entry into the EU. Accession talks in 2005 and 2006 were held

45. https://ec.europa.eu/neighbourhood-enlargement/enlargement-policy/negotiations -status/turkey_en. Accessed 10 September 2021.

46. For example, in 2006 *The Economist* (9 December 2006) reported that Turkey's hopes were "pinned on the Americans" and the upcoming 'telephone diplomacy' by President George Bush with European leaders, at a stage when talks were deadlocked.

up over difficulties related to the Cyprus conflict, as the EU insisted it could not open negotiations until Turkey agreed to accept goods from the port of Cyprus, while Turkey insisted that European states end their trade embargo on northern Cyprus (Ilgaz and Toygu, 2011).

The unspoken role of cultural differences and the heavily negotiated topic of Cyprus lie outside of European policies in the formal chapters that constitute the accession review of compliance. But given a process where membership relies on an open-ended negotiation over what terms states must accept in order to join and the need for unanimous support of current members, anything could emerge as a barrier to membership. Indeed, it is because of complicated cases like Turkey that states prefer discretionary rules over membership. Security ties cannot form a box for checking eligibility when a country like Turkey can simultaneously represent an alliance partner and be a conflict participant. In this sense, the exclusion of Turkey from the EU is the exception that proves the rule. Even within a meritocratic club such as the EU, sufficient discretion remains to allow states to determine what constitutes a suitable partner.

Brexit

The British decision to exit the EU was determined through a referendum on 23 June 2016 after years of tension over the role of the EU. With a close vote of 52 to 48 percent, British voters chose to leave. Some argue that structural trends of economic decline in regions hurt by integration with larger European markets for trade and labor fueled nationalism and disaffection with the EU, while others point to more contextual dynamics that arose at a particular historical moment in a closely fought campaign. Here I will briefly consider whether we gain new insights into Brexit when viewing the process from the logic of geopolitical alignment and membership politics that are central to this book.

At first, the exit from an international organization that had partnered the UK with its NATO allies serves as a counterpoint to the earlier accession cases in which geopolitical alignment supports membership in the EU. Was this a decision at the popular level without consideration for geopolitical alignment? Did Conservative Party leaders sacrifice foreign policy to settle internal political rivalries? Certainly both public sentiment and political maneuvers loom large in the outcome. Nevertheless, at both the popular and elite level, views about Britain's place in world affairs were one factor that fostered the decision to go it alone. A broader view of foreign policy identity helps to reconcile this breakup among allies.

The push for Brexit drew upon a populist messaging that gained favor among enough of the public to tilt the UK from Euroskepticism into full exit. Prime Minister David Cameron called for the referendum in a strategy to remain in the EU, and the Labor party joined him to support the remain side. Brexit was not the choice of the establishment. Extensive work by scholars and news analysts addresses the campaign and voter opinion, and I will not revisit this question here. It is difficult to dissect public opinion on an issue that was presented as a take-it-or-leave-it over membership, without details on the terms of exit. In what *The Economist* would describe as "fifty-fifty nation," a panel of voters was asked about coordination with Europe on specific issues of migration, trade, welfare policies, and the results show that the public "likes to have its cake and eat it."[47] After the referendum, the prolonged negotiations over when and how to leave brought forth clearly this uncertainty. Sovereignty and fears of losing control over policies loomed large in the referendum to leave. But during the post-referendum period, opinion polls showed trade as the largest concern of the public for negotiations of a new relationship with the EU (Vasilopoulou and Talving, 2019). The Brexit vote rejected membership but did not deliver a clear mandate for ending all cooperation with Europe or a roadmap for the future relationship.

On the dimension of economic integration, the UK benefited greatly from ties with the EU. Growing shares of trade went to Europe following member-ship and London thrived as the financial gateway servicing investment in the region, and benefited greatly from the ability to operate across the continent. At the same time, opt-outs on several dimensions of European integration, including the common currency, allowed the UK some autonomy; it weath-ered the 2008 financial crisis with more rapid recovery than other European states. As noted by O'Rourke (2019), this disparity may have made the EU look less attractive as a partner, but also means the UK should not have blamed EU constraints for its economic problems.

The foreign policy side of economic relations, however, pushed toward separation, as Leavers campaigned that the UK should negotiate free trade agreements on its own. One must ask why the UK would want its *own* free trade agreements when the larger market size of the EU promised stronger

---

47. "Fifty-Fifty Nation: Brexit and Public Opinion," *The Economist* 19 November 2016.

leverage in any negotiation over market access. Less sensitivity over agriculture might allow the UK to contemplate some partnerships that would be difficult for the EU. In addition, freed of the EU collective decision-making, the UK could focus on those partners attractive to UK foreign policy. As a former imperial power, the UK has long been intertwined with its trade ties to former colonies, and the Commonwealth nations' trade preferences were the primary delay for the original decision to join the EEC. Brexit promised to free the UK to pursue an active trade agenda that could advance both economic and foreign policy goals through new trade agreements.

Immigration served as the lightning rod in the Leave campaign. This policy issue intersects economic, social, and foreign policy interests. Workers held concerns about growing inequality and employment competition with immigration from Eastern Europe. Nativist fears were provoked by flagrant campaign ads. In particular, the Leave campaign included posters about imminent EU membership for Turkey (O'Rourke, 2019, p. 176). These not-so-subtle ads portrayed the EU as bringing hordes of immigrants to threaten British jobs and social fabric.

Many foreign policy interests favored Britain's remaining in the EU. When the government conducted a thorough review of the "balance of competencies" to evaluate the UK relationship with the EU across policy issues, the report on foreign policy issued in 2013 reached an affirmative conclusion that it was "generally strongly in the UK's interests to work through the EU in foreign policy."[48] British security depends on the NATO alliance, which includes many EU members. The United States has long supported UK membership in the EU. The internationalists of the Foreign and Commonwealth Office favored the UK's ongoing engagement as a member of the EU, more aware than any about the difficult negotiations ahead for exit and the tense relations that could follow. The threat of an increasingly hostile Russia called for unity with Europe to present a strong front. Despite these common security interests, "Few argued—as was argued in the 1970s—that the EU represented a grand geopolitical project that could enhance British influence" (Freedman, 2020).

An alternative narrative declared that UK foreign policy required its independence from Europe. In a speech on 17 January 2017 that laid out the vision for negotiating the exit from the EU in terms of embracing a "global Britain," Prime Minister Theresa May declared, "I want us to be a truly Global

---

48. Report cited in (Whitman, 2016).

Britain—the best friend and neighbour to our European partners, but a country that reaches beyond the borders of Europe too. A country that gets out into the world to build relationships with old friends and new allies alike. . . . Many in Britain have always felt that the United Kingdom's place in the European Union came at the expense of our global ties, and of a bolder embrace of free trade with the wider world."[49] As with many issues related to the choice of remain or leave, not only the current EU but the anticipation of *future* deepening led some to favor exit. The rejection of the Constitution had ended formal establishment of an EU foreign policy, but movement toward ever deeper union promised further coordination on this dimension. As the Common Foreign and Security Policy of the EU grew more cohesive, it posed a potential constraint on UK's autonomy.[50] Talk of a European foreign ministry had not died out in Brussels with the defeat of the Constitution proposal, and some called for majority voting to ease decision-making on common foreign policy decisions. The Leave campaign even warned of a future European army that would entangle the UK in foreign adventures not of its choosing. Whether seeking different trade agreements or a stricter approach toward Russia and Chinese cybersecurity threats, some felt the UK should formulate an independent foreign policy and feared an imminent deeper union on this dimension. An unspoken possibility for the UK also lay in favor of a smaller foreign policy, in which the UK would neither strive to regain its historic dominance as an imperial power nor merge with European leadership (Freedman, 2018).

Fears of losing foreign policy autonomy mattered because the UK was not always in harmony with EU foreign policy. The gap is evident in their voting record at the UN. Mapping its foreign policy based on the average ideal point in UN voting, Figure 7.3 shows that the UK consistently lies closer to the United States than the average for EU members. The divergence on specific policy issues loomed large in 2003 during the second Gulf War, when Tony Blair joined George Bush to support the invasion to overthrow Saddam Hussein against opposition from most other EU members. Britain stood by the "special relationship" with the United States when France cautioned against following the American "hyperpower." During the Libyan crisis in 2011, different approaches to competing international obligations within NATO and

49. BBC, "In Full: Theresa May's Speech on Future UK-EU Relations." Available at https://www.bbc.com/news/uk-politics-43256183.

50. On the Europeanization of national foreign policies, see Gross (2009); Hill and Wong (2011); Hill, Smith, and Vanhoonacker (2017).

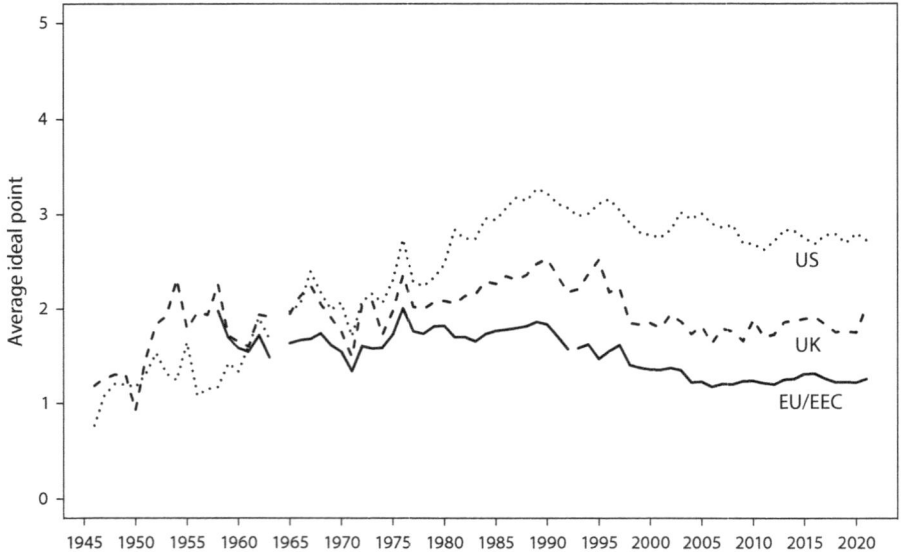

FIGURE 7.3. *UN voting comparison of the UK and Europe*: The figure plots the UN voting ideal point distance between the US, UK, and EU/EEC from all other countries. Europe data is based on the average for the ideal points of the EEC (1958–1992) and EU (1993–2021) membership in each year. The ideal points are calculated from UN General Assembly voting as a dyadic variable indicating the differences in voting patterns in a given session of the UN General Assembly (Bailey, Strezhnev, and Voeten, 2017).

the EU, alongside domestic opinion, helps to explain why EU members were unable to reach a common European response and the UK favored a NATO-led operation with minimal European involvement (Michalski and Norman, 2016). These episodes were part of a broader move in British foreign policy to take an active approach to intervention and make its foreign policy less EU-centric (Whitman, 2016).

The role of the United States is also complex. Speaking in 2016 against the Leave campaign, President Obama stated, "It leverages U.K. power to be part of the EU. I don't think the EU moderates British influence in the world, it magnifies it," and he warned that the United States would not be quick to negotiate a free trade agreement post-Brexit.[51] Many U.S. foreign policy experts worried that Brexit would make it harder for the United States to coordinate with Europe on key issues such as sanctions against Iran and

51. Calamur, Krishnadev. "Obama's 'Brexit' Plea," *The Atlantic* 22 April 2016.

Russia.[52] Yet Brexit was not a break with the United States, and the day after the referendum, President Obama issued a statement accepting the decision of the British people, and affirmed the enduring special relationship with the UK and its importance as a NATO member.

The election of Donald Trump six months after the Brexit referendum shifted the U.S. position to be more favorable of Brexit.[53] The tone of rhetoric from the U.S. leadership abruptly changed with President Trump applauding Brexit as the British voting to "take back their country." Such words encouraged the British leaders seeking to fulfill the referendum mandate with a full exit from the EU. Lawrence Freedman, a leading British scholar of global strategy, wrote that in ordinary times the United States would have helped to broker a solution after the referendum. Moreover, he attributes the association between Trump and Brexit as hardening the position of European leaders to resist any accommodation to Britain (Freedman, 2018). The Trump administration position in favor of Brexit acted as gas on the pedal where an alternative U.S. administration may have urged caution for a soft exit that left Britain in a position to continue as a bridge between Europe and the United States.

None of these factors suggests that geopolitical alignment caused Brexit. There is no indication that a rift over foreign policy goals between the UK and EU members had become a significant problem in 2016. Far from the UK breaking with NATO, the UK is a strong supporter. At this level, Brexit seems to contradict the expectations of my argument that geopolitical alignment brings states together in organizations. Yet at another level, there is evidence consistent with the importance of geopolitics in shaping how states view the benefits of membership. Some in the UK saw exit as compatible with building stronger foreign policy relations with other states beyond the EU. Both the legacy of empire and importance of the relationship with the United States allowed Britain to pull away from the EU and hold its own independent foreign policy identity. In contrast, other EU members have foreign policy positions that align more closely with the logic of integration and see exercising leadership within Europe as enhancing their global position.

52. "Obama Says 'Special Relationship' with Britain Will Endure," *The New York Times* 24 June 2016.

53. Some see parallels with the Brexit movement as populist backlash against internationalist elites. This misses differences such as the point that Brexit advocates argued Britain could form more trade agreements rather than less.

Given the close vote for Brexit, any one factor may be attributed as consequential. The different views on whether the EU was an asset or liability to British security interests should be weighed among the many contested issues. The case is also rare as a public referendum on membership, which allows for a different set of explanations than account for most decisions over membership.

A final reflection on Brexit lies in its implications for enlargement. At a triumphal moment following the end of the Cold War, Europe embraced the project of expanding the security community and upholding democratization by supporting membership in the EU for Eastern European governments. The UK was at the forefront of advocating for this inclusive approach. Nevertheless, economic competition from low-cost labor and production in the new members raised problems for the UK, and its government also lost influence over policies within the unwieldy decision-making of the large group of heterogenous countries. Indeed, the challenge of collective decisions among such an expanded group lay at the center of the push to increase the policies subject to majority voting, with more pooling of sovereignty. The resulting backlash led to disintegration. Would the UK have stayed part of a smaller and more homogenous European Community in the absence of broadening and deepening? We cannot answer this question, but the case highlights how foreign policy influence over membership decisions changes the course of cooperation in ways not anticipated by more narrow interests over the coordination of economic policy.

7.4   ASEAN: Noninterference Elevated to Security Principle

Where alliances and democratization drove forward the European integration process, they were not a factor in Southeast Asia. The absence of alliance pairs within ASEAN makes it an outlier among regional organizations. Nevertheless, security ties and the Cold War emerge alongside economic interests to determine the path to regional integration. Only after states reconciled security conflicts could they join the regional organization. Alliances may proxy for one form of security tie, but geopolitical alignment can take other forms which are evident in this case study.

The Association of Southeast Asian Nations emerged in a region referred to as the "Balkans of the Orient." Weak state formation, the colonial legacy of artificially imposed borders, and heterogeneity along fault lines of religion, ethnicity, and political systems laid the basis for deep pessimism about the prospects for cooperation in the region after the end of the colonial era (Acharya, 2012, p. 87). Previous attempts at regional integration had failed to consolidate into any lasting enterprise. A series of conferences in the region took place in 1947 and 1949, and a 1954 "Conference of the South-East Asian Prime Ministers" showed unity in the anti-colonial sentiments of leaders but not much beyond this. Participants in this final meeting included the ten current members of ASEAN, along with India, Pakistan, and Sri Lanka, which Acharya (2012, p. 116) notes as evidence that the regional boundaries were uncertain at this time. Even larger groupings took place in efforts to unite the anti-colonial sentiments of Southeast Asian and African nations. Indonesia hosted the Bandung Conference in April 1955 that included Asian and African nations. The declaration would condemn colonialism and call for peace but not establish an institutional framework for cooperation. A smaller regional organization—the Association of Southeast Asia (ASA) formed by Thailand, Malaysia, and the Philippines in 1961—accomplished little in the face of conflicts between the countries.

Formal security arrangements for regional cooperation failed to unite the region. First, an Anglo-American initiative during WWII established a Southeast Asia Command in 1943 to coordinate battle operations and to aid planning for the future transition from Japanese rule. Initially based in Ceylon (Sri Lanka), the jurisdiction encompassed Ceylon, Myanmar, Malaya, Singapore, and Thailand (Acharya, 2012, p. 83). Thereafter, external threats supported ideological convergence within the opposing camps in the Cold War divisions (Roberts, 2012, p. 26). But any possibility of the region forming a consolidated pro-Western camp ended as Vietnam, Cambodia, Laos, and Sri Lanka leaned communist while Indonesia took leadership of the nonaligned movement. The next major step for regional security coordination came with the formation of the Southeast Asia Treaty Organization (SEATO) in 1955. As a Cold War proposal from the United States and United Kingdom, however, the alliance aroused fears of external intervention and neocolonialism that led to opposition from Malaysia, Singapore, and Indonesia (Roberts, 2012, p. 36). Only Thailand and the Philippines joined from the region, along with Australia, New Zealand, France, and Pakistan. SEATO activities remained limited to joint military training exercises and consultation, without spurring broader integration. The alliance was dissolved in 1977 in the wake of U.S. withdrawal from Vietnam and the Nixon Doctrine. The United States retained bilateral defense pacts with Thailand and the Philippines, while the British led several security agreements with its former colonies.[54] China formed alliances with Myanmar and Cambodia during the 1960s, but these too had elapsed by the end of the decade.

The states of Southeast Asia did not form alliances with each other. Indeed, avoiding war over territorial conflicts was their first challenge. In the early 1960s, Malaysia and Indonesia engaged in what was referred to as the *konfrontasi* period of sustained tensions around the independence of Malaysia, which sparked fears in Indonesia that foreign bases in Malaysia would become a source of external intervention. Resolving these issues in a series of declarations to deny foreign bases use against others and mutual recognition of independence set the stage for moving forward on reconciliation by the forming of a regional organization (Frost, 2016, p. 17–19).

Founders

The founding countries of ASEAN shared an anti-communist orientation and commitment to the principle of noninterference in domestic affairs. As former colonies (with the exception of Thailand), they emerged newly independent and fiercely protective of sovereignty (Dent, 2008, p. 86). Their security concerns included external threats, internal communist insurgencies, and regional tensions. With China, Russia, and Japan looming as powerful neighbors and the U.S. and European governments maintaining strong interests, there was a high sense of vulnerability amongst the new nation states.

Given that alliances were largely in place as bilateral arrangements with states outside of the region, and others rejected alliances altogether, regional cooperation did not have a military focus. Instead, states sought to advance cohesive diplomatic policies and economic development. Geopolitics mattered because it shaped which countries wanted to coordinate their foreign policy and support mutual economic gains. Membership politics in a regional organization would facilitate the goal of subsetting *whom* to cooperate with in regional activities.

Thailand hosted the summit of leaders that issued the Bangkok Declaration, establishing ASEAN on 8 August 1967. ASEAN brought in Indonesia and Singapore for a larger group than the three that had formed ASA (Thailand,

---

54. Of these bilateral alliances, only the U.S.-Philippines alliance meets the threshold to count as defense pact alliance in COW, based on the definition that "highest level of military commitment, requiring alliance members to come to each other's aid militarily." See http://www.correlatesofwar.org/data-sets/formal-alliances. Accessed 14 September 2018.

Malaysia, and Philippines). The decision to form a new organization rather than build on the earlier ASA reflected the preference of Indonesia to begin fresh without the strong Western orientation of ASA (Frost, 2016, p. 20). Acharya writes that Indonesia saw ASA as a "front" for SEATO even though it did not have any security activities in its mandate (Acharya, 2012, p. 153). The support of Indonesia was critical, and it sought to brand the new organization as its regional initiative. Having resolved their own territorial conflicts and clearly laid out principles of independence from outside intervention, the five states of Thailand, Malaysia, Philippines, Indonesia, and Singapore could form a political consensus on their mutual interest to pursue development and resist communism. Indonesia's foreign minister, Adam Malik, ascribed the main motivation for the five states to join ASEAN as arising from the "convergence in the political outlook of the five prospective member-nations" with regard to both national objectives and views about the ideal "strategic configuration of East Asia" (Acharya, 2012, p. 156).

The importance of geopolitical alignment surfaced as reluctance to join rather than to exclude. The first moves, for a regional organization, were remarkably inclusive. The five members who founded ASEAN embraced the policy that it should open the doors to North and South Vietnam in addition to Myanmar, Cambodia, Laos, and Ceylon (Sri Lanka) (Acharya, 2012, p. 155). But they were unable to persuade them. "ASEAN had informally approached Myanmar and Cambodia about membership at the time of the Association's formation. However, the two countries declined due to their membership in NAM and the associated bipolar cleavages generated by the Cold War" (Roberts, 2012, p. 60). In Myanmar, General Shu Maung Ne Win had seized power in a 1962 military coup and led his country into a path of isolation and his own version of socialism. Even with nonaligned movement leader Indonesia at the head of ASEAN's formation, Ne Win refused to join an organization including U.S.-allied Thailand and Philippines. Similarly, Cambodia's effort to remain outside of the communist and anti-communist spheres included dropping U.S. aid in 1963 and refusing the invitation to join ASEAN. There is no indication that Vietnam ever seriously considered joining at this juncture, but it is nonetheless significant that the choice lay with Vietnam.

In parallel with the regional organization, the five founding members of ASEAN signed a nonintervention pact in 1976. The Treaty of Amity and Cooperation in Southeast Asia (TAC) committed the states to pacific settlement of disputes. Originally limited to accession by other states in Southeast Asia, an amendment in 1987 allowed for states outside of the region to accede based on consent of the Southeast Asian signatories. This treaty expanded to encompass Australia, China, Japan, and the United States and serves as a regional code of conduct. It remains a separate treaty, but ASEAN members hold control over membership in TAC, and it is implicit that states would ratify TAC prior to joining ASEAN. From 1994, ASEAN has also sponsored the ASEAN Regional Forum as a diplomatic venue for discussing security issues with a broader range of partners. Far from selecting those with similar security interests, ARF includes potential adversaries—United States, Russia, China, India, and Japan—in an attempt by ASEAN members to reduce uncertainty about behavior toward critical issues in the region (Khong and Nesdaurai, 2007, p. 80). These engagement strategies complement the decision that ASEAN itself would remain centered around a core group of states that shared strategic goals to protect their autonomy.

Accession Rules

The membership rules of ASEAN are as important for what they do not say as for what is included. The Bangkok Declaration Article 4 provides that "the Association is open for participation to all states in the South-East Asian Region subscribing to the aforementioned aims, principles and purposes." It does not outline either decision-making procedures for approval of enlargement nor a criterion to define the geographic scope of the region. Not until adoption of the ASEAN Charter in 2008 did the organization embrace a rule-governed member enlargement process based on recommendation of new members by the ASEAN Coordinating Council and unanimous approval of members in the ASEAN Summit (Hooghe et al., 2017, p. 436). This reform lays out criteria for admission to include location in Southeast Asia, recognition by ASEAN members, and the willingness to accept the ASEAN agreements and member obligations. The possibility of suspension was absent in the Bangkok Declaration, and first appears with the vague reference in the ASEAN Charter about matters of noncompliance being referred to the ASEAN Summit.

The informality and emphasis on consensus found in accession rules more broadly represent the organization. In what became known as the "ASEAN way," states eschewed a legalistic and bureaucratic approach to regional integration.[55] The organization centers around ministerial meetings, with each member having a national secretariat to support the work for the

---

55. While this informality stands in contrast to the EU's procedures, there are many regional organizations in Europe and other regions that are informal. Variation in the institutional form of cooperation does not have an inherent regional preference (Snidal and Vabulas, 2022).

organization. A small ASEAN General Secretariat was established in 1976 and expanded its capacity over time based on a series of amendments to the ASEAN Charter by the members to delegate broader authority for it to lead organization activities. After adoption of the ASEAN Charter, the organization established a centralized executive in the form of the ASEAN Coordination Council meeting of foreign ministers that is supported by specialized councils with staff and working groups (Hooghe et al., 2017, p. 434). In the wake of the Asian financial crisis, ASEAN leaders followed parts of the EU regional model that appeared effective, even while not adopting an EU-style court (Jetschke and Murray, 2012).

Enlargement Experience

Despite inclusive membership provisions, over a decade passed before the prospect of enlargement arose. As Brunei began steps toward independence from British colonial rule, its foreign minister, Prince Mohammad Bolkiah, requested membership in ASEAN when attending the annual foreign ministers' meeting in June 1981 as an observer (Weatherbee, 1983, p. 723). Its candidacy was attractive on several dimensions, including a strategic location central in the region and oil resources, along with historic and cultural links as one of the former Malay states. The conservative monarchy was not an obstacle given the prominence of non-democratic regimes among ASEAN members. Malaysia had led the campaign to end British colonial rule of Brunei, while Indonesia sought to prevent Brunei's gaining independence through assimilation in a Malaysian federation. To the extent that welcoming it within the regional organization would facilitate the transition to an independent state, both Malaysia and Indonesia supported prospective membership for Brunei and were reported to have encouraged its application from as early as 1978 (Weatherbee, 1983, p. 730). At the same time, Brunei shared close economic and security ties with Singapore, including military exercises in Brunei by Singaporean forces (Weatherbee, 1983, p. 732). Brunei was approved as ASEAN member one week after its formal independence in January 1984, which was prior even to its entry into the United Nations later in September of that same year.

One decade later, the entry of Vietnam further broadened the organization. The end of the Cold War loosened divisions in the region and weakened ideological orientation among states on both sides of the historic division over communism. The loss of Soviet aid and a broader security umbrella were tied to the political changes in Vietnam to reform its diplomatic and economic policies starting in 1986. Yet Vietnam remained firmly committed to upholding communist rule. Its entry required ASEAN to set aside its anti-communist consensus. Vietnam made its first request to join ASEAN in November 1988 (Acharya, 2012, p. 210). These overtures met a generally positive response. That December, Malaysian prime minister Mahathir declared that "if Vietnam subscribes to the ideas of ASEAN, the system of government it practices should not be something that stands in the way of becoming a member of ASEAN" (Acharya, 2012, p. 199).

Since 1967, the position of ASEAN toward Vietnam had adjusted to the threat level rather than regime change or ideological affinity. At its origin a regional project, the growing war in Vietnam strengthened ASEAN unity. The vacuum left by U.S. withdrawal after the war raised fears that a newly powerful communist Vietnam would dominate the region. Nevertheless, the end of the Vietnam war brought outreach from ASEAN for joint regional projects with Vietnam. Indeed, Indonesia and Malaysia were open to the prospect of working with Vietnam to join ASEAN at this early stage (Acharya, 2012, p. 187). Then Vietnam's invasion of Cambodia in 1978 renewed hostility, which again unified ASEAN as it pushed for the UN General Assembly to condemn Vietnam's invasion (Acharya, 2012, p. 190). Resolution of the conflict in Cambodia helped to open the way for including Vietnam. In April 1989, Vietnam announced it would unconditionally withdraw the rest of its troops from Cambodia, where they had long propped up the puppet government. Another key security issue was the 1995 decision to agree on a nuclear-free zone in Southeast Asia. This period also witnessed the opening and growth of China, with both the promise and peril it presented to smaller neighbors. Vietnam could help ASEAN members to counterbalance the growing influence of China in their resistance to outside interference and nuclearization.

The accession process for Vietnam was much longer and more involved than what Brunei had experienced. Although ASEAN has an informal process, this can also be dragged out. Since its first request in 1988, the Vietnamese negotiators engaged in multiple rounds of talks and finally joined in 1995. By 1995, ASEAN had expanded its scope to include agreements on economic cooperation, with the 1992 addition of a framework on enhancing economic cooperation. To join ASEAN, Vietnam also committed to these related agreements. After joining ASEAN in July 1995, it completed negotiations in December of the same year to ratify a protocol of accession to the ASEAN Framework Agreements on Enhancing ASEAN Economic Cooperation and accepted the

Common Effective Preferential Tariff Scheme for the ASEAN Free Trade Area. While not formally required as conditions for membership, these steps demonstrated that Vietnam did indeed subscribe to the ideas of ASEAN.

The resulting organization remains quite heterogenous across economic, social, and political dimensions. Members include democracies and repressive regimes and a wide range of ethnic groupings. After Vietnam's entry, Laos and Myanmar joined in 1997 and Cambodia became a member in 1999. Dramatic reversals contribute to political uncertainty in the region as democratization proceeds for some (Indonesia and Malaysia) while reversing for others (Thailand) and facing contestation in many (Philippines, Myanmar, and Cambodia). The GDP of members ranges from $861.9 billion for Indonesia to a mere $12.3 billion for tiny Laos.[56] But internal changes are not a problem within an organization where the consensus around noninterference forms a unifying security principle.

Outsiders

In addition to the first case of Sri Lanka, other states could be considered potential members. East Timor applied to join ASEAN in 2011 and continues to seek approval. East Timor had been a Portuguese colony, and was annexed by Indonesia after Portuguese withdrawal in 1975. After years of conflict and a UN mediated settlement, it became independent in 2002, thereafter joining the UN, IMF, and World Bank. Its membership in ASEAN remains an open question, with member disagreement as the primary obstacle. Some express concerns about it as an economic laggard while others fear adding a liberal democracy (Ortuoste, 2019). The government decision to abstain on the April 2021 UNGA vote condemning the military coup in Myanmar was seen by outsiders as a crude attempt to avoid angering a potential veto player over its ASEAN membership (despite several other ASEAN members voting in favor of the resolution) (Cardoso, 2021). Even as a small actor, East Timor could shift the balance of geopolitical alignment. The government has conducted joint military exercises with the U.S. army and Australia maintains a substantial defense cooperation program in the country. While some ASEAN

---

56. GDP figures from World Bank, World Development Indicators, 2015, reported in Council of Foreign Relations, "ASEAN: The Association of Southeast Asian Nations." Available at https://www.cfr.org/backgrounder/asean-association-southeast-asian-nations. Accessed 2 January 2019.

members also conduct military exercises with the United States and Australia, others are closer to China. Getting all to agree is a high barrier.

In the end, it is up to the members to decide whether a state can join. Even as ASEAN has added more rigor to the accession procedures with the addition of provisions on qualifications, they leave considerable room for interpretation. In particular, the need to demonstrate "ability and willingness to carry out the obligations of membership" is such a loose phrase that can be used to indefinitely hold up a country like East Timor from joining, when it otherwise meets the geographic requirement and has seen its independence recognized by ASEAN members.

Australia opted to remain outside the regional cooperation movement while engaging strongly to build bilateral relations. One could conceive of an alternative formation in which Australia and New Zealand would have joined, and a larger conception of Southeast Asia and Oceania would have formed the basis of regional identity. The Australian government backed the independence movement of Indonesia and joined the early conferences on regional problems, but its anti-communist orientation led it to refuse participation in the Bandung conference (Frost, 2016, p. 12). While Australia joined SEATO, it did not join ASEAN.

When ASEAN was initiated, the question of Australian (and New Zealand) membership was raised. The Malaysian government was in support, but Indonesia worried about Western bias if Australia joined. Since the Australian government did not express interest in joining, the matter never went further (Frost, 2016, p. 21). The Australian government immediately endorsed ASEAN after the Bangkok Declaration. Its membership was never revisited; at a 1971 meeting a Malaysian official was quoted saying Australian membership was out of the question, and a few years later an Australian diplomat said that due to "differences in character" Australia did not stand as potential member of ASEAN (ibid, pp. 21 and 27). Yet cooperation at the diplomatic level was high, and Prime Minister Gough Whitlam in 1974 proposed that Australia should send an ambassador to ASEAN (Frost, 2016, p. 26).

Lessons from Regional Case Studies

ASEAN represents an important case where security interests bring together states that could not otherwise form an alliance. This is the form of "laundering" influence where security interests support IGO membership. "Like-minded" in the Southeast Asian context centers around regional autonomy from great power interference and strong defense of sovereignty embodied in the "ASEAN Way" for informal cooperation. States rejected the notion that one must have a common political regime type as basis for cooperation. The evolution of the consensus on nonintervention helped ASEAN to embrace communist Vietnam. The principle of regional autonomy took precedence over anti-communist views such that binding together with Vietnam represented freedom from outside interference. In contrast, anti-communist principles were inextricably linked to the democratic values and Western alignment that formed prerequisites for who could join the European regional project.

Both Europe and Southeast Asia highlight the challenge of defining a geographic region. In ASEAN, clearly the region was not predetermined in its borders, as a country like Sri Lanka or Australia could begin as a potential member but later be excluded as outside of the region. Political affinity and geographic proximity form two dimensions that mutually constitute the identity of a region, with neither being sufficient on its own. Security ties that appear either as an alliance or as an informal alignment can still represent an important component of political affinity that binds together some neighbors more than others. The formal organization becomes the de facto source of authority to define the concept of region through the process of selecting members.

7.5   The Missing Northeast Asian Regional Organization

The absence of a regional project for Northeast Asia (NEA) serves as a reminder that geographic proximity and economic complementarities alone do not compel states toward integration. Rozman (2004, p. 10) commented, "If economic conditions suffice to produce regionalism, NEA would already be noted as the world's third great regionalism." Over a decade later, the levels of economic integration are even greater, with little political coordination in the form of regional architecture.

It is not for lack of past attempts. Alongside ASEAN formation, the Republic of Korea took the initiative to put forward a proposal for an Asian and Pacific Council. The group held its first meeting in Seoul in June 1966 with Australia, the Republic of China, Japan, Malaysia, the Philippines, New Zealand, Thailand, and the Republic of Vietnam (South Vietnam) joining the South Korean government to become nine founding members. The organization's members "declared their common determination to preserve their integrity and sovereignty in the face of external threats and invited other free countries in the region to join the newly formed Asian and Pacific Council (ASPAC)" (*Asian And Pacific Council*, 1966). The organization suffered from differences over its role, as the United States backed the hardline position of the governments of South Korea and South Vietnam that ASPAC should support regional military coordination, but Japan and Australia resisted the securitization of the organization, which was largely focused on economic and cultural topics (Frost, 2016, p. 14). In the end, recognition of the PRC diminished the anti-communist impetus behind the grouping, so that meetings were suspended in 1973 and the organization stopped operations. It had modest scope and influence.[57]

There were also false starts, such as the Australian Prime Minister Whitlam's 1974 proposal for an Asia-Pacific Forum that would include ASEAN members plus Australia, New Zealand, Japan, China, and India (Frost, 2016, p. 29). This proposal for a broader regional grouping failed to gather support and did not materialize as an organization.

Despite growing levels of economic integration, Northeast Asia remains an arena for security tensions. Japan, China, and Korea cannot resolve their ongoing territorial disputes and recurringly spar over historical legacy from WWII atrocities by Japan. In the most recent iteration of tensions that have included a range of economic measures and public protests, Korea announced it would terminate its security information sharing agreement with Japan. Without a rapprochement for closer diplomatic relations, any prospect for political coordination remains impossible.

7.6   Conclusion

The analysis of regional organizations offers several insights into how international organizations form clubs of states. In regional organizations, an objective criterion based on geographic location establishes a benchmark criterion for entry. Nonetheless, geography is far from determinative. Consistent with the discretionary rules hypothesis, regional organizations often do not specify

---

57. The organization is included in the full dataset of IGOs in COW because it is listed in the International Yearbook. It is omitted from the data analyzed here because we could not locate any indication of a written charter document, which is a selection criterion for inclusion in my IGO data. For discussion of ASPAC, see (Braddick, 2006).

the borders of the region and have charter provisions that require member approval for enlargement. The analysis shows a strong correlation between security interests and membership in regional organizations, in support of the geopolitical discrimination hypothesis. Indeed, the proximity of states to the geopolitical interests of other members matters as much as their proximity by distance. The debates over whether Turkey belongs in Europe or Vietnam in Southeast Asia spotlight that maps could allow for multiple definitions of regional borders.

Yet bounded security is also more nuanced. Within the context of a region, geopolitical alignment is focused on positions taken on the crises facing the region. The case studies of the EU and ASEAN show variation, where membership decisions have turned on foreign policy but not always along the dimensions of allies versus non-allies. The Eastern enlargement of the EU clearly fit the pattern of geopolitical restructuring as the necessary condition to trigger a new group of applicants to join the EU as they left the Soviet orbit. Yet the exclusion of Turkey and complicated saga over British membership occurred as tense decisions about regional organization membership taken among NATO allies. France twice vetoed British membership in the EU for fear it would bring the EU under U.S. domination, and later the UK exited over concerns that it risked losing sovereignty within the European project. Turkey's repeated rejection puts in a spotlight the tensions among allies as Greece and Cyprus held up integration because of their disagreement over northern Cyprus. Within ASEAN, non-allied states have coalesced for political cohesion to balance against threats in the region.

In contrast to the consistent effect of security ties, the findings for democracy are mixed, and highlight the different trajectories of democratic conditionality in the formation of regional organizations. Democracy has been central to the regional integration process in the European Union. Yet the findings here show that taking into account geopolitical alignment is necessary—in the statistical analysis of regional organizations as a whole, democracy has a small and often insignificant role in the pattern of membership in organizations. Many democratizing states form new organizations to show their capacity to participate in governance projects (Poast and Urpelainen, 2013). In the Americas and Europe, however, democracies that choose not to join, and organizations that accept all states irrespective of regime, counteract any democratic propensity to participate in these activities. In another trend, authoritarian regimes form their own coalitions of like-minded groups (Libman and Obydenkova, 2013; Obydenkova and Libman, 2019).

The flexibility of accession rules that are common in international organizations also characterizes regional organizations. Even while charters specify that the organization is open to accession by all "European states" or any state in "Southeast Asia," they do not define these regions. This allows for exceptions. The vague provisions also enhance bargaining leverage as applicants are never sure if they can gain entry (Schneider and Urpelainen, 2012). In some cases, meritocratic criteria may screen for democratic regimes or high compliance (Kaoutzanis, Poast, and Urpelainen, 2016). But more often, security ties slip in as a source of favoritism encouraging shared club membership.

Regions evolve as a concept that is shaped by a wide set of forces. Katzenstein (2005) refers to *porous regions* that are bound in material and symbolic ways within an area but also reflect international pressures that shape their identity. In trying to assess the determinants of membership in regional organizations, this chapter contributes to ongoing debate about the evolution of regions. Security, trade, and politics influence membership in regional organizations, which then solidify the identity of the region through further deepening these connections. The lines we draw that divide the world map into regions are based on politics as well as geography.

8

Exclusion from Universal Organizations

WHY DISCRIMINATE over membership in organizations that support global health, clean environment pursuit of knowledge, and international peace? Such universal goals imply universal membership. But when membership confers sovereignty as a collective recognition of statehood, it is a high-stakes outcome that cannot be given out easily. This chapter examines the conditions that allow politics to influence who joins organizations that claim to welcome all states.

Wide participation strengthens the legitimacy of inclusive international organizations. Most countries agree at an aspirational level to the desirability of peace, prosperity, and protection of the environment. But making a formal commitment as a member of an organization goes one step further. Affirmation of a goal by most countries reinforces its normative force as a universal principle. In contrast, outsiders and defection threaten to undermine this perception of the norm and the legitimacy of the organization.

The challenge of collective action is most severe for the provision of public goods, which are non-rival and non-excludable. States may support the normative goal but not contribute to the effort of IGO activity as they free ride on the actions of others. In some cases, broad membership takes on heightened importance, not because each state's contribution is necessary but because their participation reassures members that everyone will do their fair share. This is the dynamic for climate change policies, where smaller states have a trivial impact on the problem but their nonparticipation could weaken the willingness of larger players to take costly adjustment measures. In other cases, partial contribution by a subset of states is insufficient to achieve the goal and broad membership is essential. For example, the smallpox immunization campaign led by the WHO could not have eliminated the disease without access to every country.

Therefore many multilateral organizations uphold the goal of universal membership. Indeed, the broad trend of global governance includes further opening of international organizations to participation by non-state actors and wider coordination (Tallberg et al., 2013; Abbott and Zangl, 2015). But when it comes to membership decisions, universal organizations still impose conditions. Accepting actors who do not affirm the goals of the organization or openly flout its rules would hardly build the power of the norm. Including every entity would worsen the collective action problem by straining the organizational capacity to monitor behavior. This brings us back to the core question—what criteria determine the limits of universal organizations?

Based on the typology from chapter 2 (see Figure 2.1), universal organizations allow entry for any state that ratifies the terms of the treaty. The inclusive participation mandate and vague conditionality terms support wide membership. Since they do not review policy implementation, ratification is not a high barrier. But eligibility for any *state* highlights the core challenge of defining sovereignty. There is not an authoritative list of states. Rather, multiple criteria in terms of diplomatic recognition and demonstrated autonomy leave open to interpretation the question of statehood. This shows up in the politics of membership in international organizations.

Some states could readily qualify by most definitions of statehood. Others stretch the concept on one or more dimensions. A small set of outliers face contested sovereignty. Several cases illustrate the wide range of entities that may or may not be deemed to be states, depending on who makes the decision. For example, the tiny South Pacific Island of Niue joined the WHO in 1994 despite the fact that its foreign affairs are conducted by New Zealand and it has not been recognized as a member of the United Nations or other organizations. Taiwan has been unable to join the WHO or United Nations even as it stands as a full member of the WTO and ADB.[1] Palestine has joined UNESCO and the International Criminal Police Organization but not the WTO or UN. Consider the gap between participation in the Olympics

1. This chapter will refer to Taiwan as general reference to the Republic of China. In each international organization, the designated official name varies. For example, Taiwan entered the WTO under the name "Separate Customs Territory of Taiwan, Penghu, Kinmen and Matsu (Chinese Taipei)," while in the ADB it is listed as "Taipei, China."

and the UN: there are 193 members of the United Nations, while 206 countries competed in the 2021 Olympics, from tiny Nauru (a member of the UN since 1999), with a population of 11,500, to Kosovo, which joined the International Olympic Committee in 2016 but has not yet joined the United Nations. Both Taiwan and Palestine compete with independent delegations to the Olympics.[2]

The flip side of entry lies in expulsion, whereby members vote to deny membership. Suspending a government from the activities of the organization may impinge on participation without challenging sovereignty. But expelling the state from membership begins a process that could reverse the recognition of sovereignty. The rarity of this action emphasizes its role as an extreme sanction.

Membership selection matters for organizational effectiveness and legitimacy. The potential to include unqualified entities or to exclude those able to contribute to the public good leaves IGOs open to a range of abuse that could reduce functionality. At the level of *process*, the role of power and influence to politicize membership selection could undermine legitimacy. Outcomes may also be affected by insufficient participation. What if the United Nations had continued to exclude the PRC and denied representation to all of its people? Rules hold less effectiveness if they do not include key actors. Overriding the preferences of the United States to include Palestine in UNESCO has led to U.S. withdrawal from the organization, which presents a challenge of another kind.

This chapter evaluates the argument of geopolitical discrimination in the context of universal organizations. In section 8.1, I examine why gatekeeping arises over membership in the club of sovereign nations. Legal standing and performance capacity could justify differentiating among potential candidates for the purpose of upholding the legitimacy and effectiveness of the organization. But drawing on the broader theoretical framework of this book, I argue political requirements can take priority over these principles. Section 8.2 looks at data on IGO membership to analyze how states exclude. Alongside open eligibility provisions, selection by membership approval forms a screening process. The discretionary design of membership rules also encompasses many universal organizations. Analysis of entry into IGOs with open eligibility confirms the importance of political ties while controlling for measures

---

2. The Olympics are not an intergovernmental organization and as such are outside the scope of this book. The Taiwanese delegation to the Olympics uses the name Chinese Taipei.

that proxy for legal standing and performance capacity. This aggregate analysis includes a wide range of 88 IGOs that are in principle open to all states but vary significantly in the scope of activities and realized levels of participation.

The following sections examine three cases of controversial membership applications to the United Nations and its affiliated agencies. The cases each involve a major power campaign against the membership of a candidate. At a lower level of shifting geopolitical power balances across coalitions of states with rivalry for spheres of influence, we see variation in the ability of great powers to dictate outcomes. Geopolitical rivalry in the Cold War excluded North and South Korea from the United Nations. Shifting alignment toward China was clearly mapped onto dramatic changes in IGO membership for Taiwan. The back and forth over temporary participation in the WHO for Taiwan illustrates another level of conditioning IGO membership on political orientation. Palestine advanced its sovereignty claim through gaining membership in UNESCO over strong U.S. opposition, but has made limited advances in other organizations. A fourth case turns to the example of exclusion from universal organizations as a sanction against Apartheid in South Africa. Letting Palestine into UNESCO and pushing South Africa out of the UPU highlight how accession rules allow considerable flexibility. The chapter concludes with a discussion of how international organizations bias the definition of statehood by means of politicized accession into international organizations.

8.1   The Political Logic of Exclusion

The puzzle of exclusion from universal organizations lies in the contradiction between a mandate for including all states and actions to the contrary. Three sets of reasons could account for screening: performance capacity, legitimate standing, or political relations. The first reflects the fact that universal organizations address public goods. As such, even if they exclude participation, they are unable to prevent the outsider from reaping the benefits provided by others. Nevertheless, there could remain the functional demand to limit participation to those with sufficient capacity. This supports a baseline performance threshold for entry. Alternatively, a second line of reasoning invokes the need for normative coherence. The principle of universality upholds inclusion on the basis of legitimate standing rather than capacity. Here one expects a legal criterion for establishing who has standing. The final dimension for screening relies on political relations, which requires a subjective evaluation of who belongs. The geopolitical discrimination hypothesis suggests this political screening will be biased by security interests. Consent determines who gains entry, and the political interests of other states determine whether they will offer consent.

Screening based on performance capacity encompasses both the functional and the power perspectives in international relations scholarship. Theories of institutions emphasize the potential for mutual gains based on some overlap in shared preferences for cooperation in an issue area where coordination would yield long-term gains (Keohane, 1984). Self-interested states can commit to coordinated behavior conditional on reciprocal actions of others. The problem of free riding may be overcome by institutions that select those willing and able to engage in joint cooperation. Powerful states may play a significant role in providing for public goods; even as debates in the literature have largely rejected the view that a dominant hegemon is necessary for cooperation, the distribution of capabilities remains an important condition in enforcing rules. In their discussion of the breadth and depth trade-off faced by international institutions, Stone, Slantchev, and London (2008) contend that the capacity to contribute for the marginal member and credibility of punishment by the largest member determines the overall depth of cooperation. Including dysfunctional actors lowers cooperation by worsening the free rider dilemma and creating a race to the bottom for ambition of cooperation. Large states will prefer to discriminate against small states below a threshold of capacity. This logic supports a minimal capacity criterion for entry.

To achieve legitimacy, however, universal institutions may look beyond capacity. The organizations uphold the multilateral norm of nondiscrimination and their founding charters call out for the participation of all states. Rules of accession that are consistent with these norms will contribute to the legitimacy of an organization. Scholars attribute legitimacy as a significant factor to enhance compliance that forms an alternative mechanism to coercive enforcement and self-interest (Hurd, 1999). The sources of authority of international organizations arise from both shared functional interest and a sense of community (Hooghe, Lenz, and Marks, 2019). The procedures to select members determine the scope of the norm's applicability; only members are subject to the obligation of compliance. The universal organizations aspire to embrace one global community and draw greater authority from this universalism. Open eligibility rules reinforce their broad mandate.[3] Following customary international law rules on statehood as the criteria for membership

---

3. Hooghe, Lenz, and Marks (2019) distinguish between task-specific and general-purpose organizations, with the latter embracing transnational community and openness to membership growth.

eligibility offers a baseline decision procedure that conforms to the multilat-eral norms of the organizations. This could lower the bar of entry, to allow entry to states that may be too weak or unwilling to contribute to cooperative outcomes but which nonetheless belong to the global community insofar as they should be subject to the normative obligation of the institution.

The interests of states and community norms could also give rise to dis-crimination based on political relations. Favoring one group over another with selective membership access enhances their share of gains and increases the cohesion of the group. Political ties between states may also support cooperation if the expectation of in-group favoritism in the allocation of ben-efits increases levels of trust and reciprocity (Cook, Levi and Hardin, 2009). Yet this exclusionary dynamic runs counter to the norms of multilateralism. Theories of collective action emphasize the need for diffuse reciprocity and community to support a wider view about the distribution of gains when cooperation goes beyond two-person exchanges (e.g., Ostrom, 2000).

Political exclusion fits within the larger theme of this book. I argue states use IGOs as a discriminatory club. States reduce the efficiency and legiti-macy of a universal organization when they restrict the membership of states that otherwise would meet a requirement based on performance or legal standing. Legitimation processes call for IGOs to maximize procedural and performance standards (Tallberg, 2019). Alongside efforts to establish such processes for decision-making among members, however, other standards apply to the question of who is a member. Through *geopolitical discrimination*, states let security ties play a large role in their choice of partners for coop-eration in multilateral organizations. By doing so, they pursue political goals outside of the mandate of the organization for policy coordination within a given issue area.

These efforts take on special significance in the context of universal organiza-tions. Membership confers access to benefits. This alone makes it worth holding up as a tool for geopolitical discrimination. Membership in universal organiza-tions also represents status within international society, as those excluded are marked as either pariah or periphery countries. Hurrell (2004, p. 40) writes that "control over the membership norms of international society and the capac-ity to delegitimize certain sorts of players through the deployment of these norms represents a very important category of power." Finally, membership can implicate core security interests. In many cases of exclusion from universal organizations, states disagree about the authority to control territory in the potential applicant. This raises new stakes, as accepting membership implies recognition, which connects to sovereignty. In cases of secession and independence, recognition of the contested applicant challenges the sovereignty of an existing state. For those caught in the middle of a great power rivalry, recognition could shift the boundary of great power spheres of influence.

The importance of sovereignty makes it worth fighting over. In one conception, sovereignty forms a property right both in the sense of control and participation (Barkin, 2021). The way states exercise these rights evolves in a changing international context, but the significance of sovereignty has not diminished. Territorial disputes lead to wars, and the hint of disputed borders can scare away investors (Simmons, 2005; Carter, Wellhausen, and Huth, 2018). Even before or after the outbreak of conflict, disagreements over sovereignty appear as a factor in the membership politics of international organizations. Actors in the international system care deeply about the recognition of their sovereignty, and this manifests itself in their demand to control both land and seats in organizations.

When establishing order within the system, great powers utilize organizations as a tool to withhold benefits from rivals and build cohesion among allies (Gilpin, 1981; Lake, 2009). Lascurettes (2020) argues that at critical moments of change after wars or shifting power balance, great powers have countered comprehensive threats of military and ideological power by creating "orders of exclusion." A key feature of his theory lies in the role of membership rules about which kinds of units are considered participants of the order. The dominant state reinforces its favored status quo by keeping out threatening states.

As great powers determine the broad contours of membership in the international order, accession politics forge the link between systemic interests and cooperation outcomes. Even the most powerful state does not impose membership on others. Through negotiation and persuasion based on organizational rules, states decide to include or exclude applicants. The process requires balancing the trade-off between universal norms for inclusion and systemic interests in exclusion. States will lean toward providing recognition through membership approval for those that would expand their coalition of allies in the organization. Sharing benefits to strengthen allies and increasing a like-minded group for voting on favorable policies form two reasons to support entry by allies. Exclusion of others will diminish rivals.

International organizations offer the means to differentiate between who is in or out of the order. Yet the precision of IGO membership as a dichotomous decision comes up against the ambiguity of sovereignty. If statehood were an objective condition, there would not be any room for geopolitical considerations to arise in the context of universal organizations that claim to consider entry by all states. A neutral bureaucrat acting on behalf of members could simply confirm receipt of application by eligible states and register new members. Instead, the contestable nature of sovereignty opens the door for states to define it according to their geopolitical interests. The institutional rules for approval of members by other states allow their views to shape the outcome. Through their decisions over membership in international organizations, states determine what constitutes a state.

8.1.1 Gatekeeping over Sovereignty

Sovereignty represents the baseline from which states engage in international cooperation. Hurd (1999, p. 393) calls it the "foundational principle" by which states interact such that the "organization of territorial space into recognized states remains a fundamental fact of politics." The principle of sovereign equality has long been accepted alongside the clear inequality of resource distribution. Yet sovereignty is complex and not allocated with a citizenship card to define which states meet its standard. It represents an institution rather than an attribute inherent in states. Coggins (2011, p. 435) writes that "most theories take the fundamental units of political life to be exogenous" even as governments can disagree over which actors are legitimate members of the international community. Some critical mass of governments must offer recognition for a new state to emerge, and in this process it helps to have "friends in high places" (Coggins, 2011). According to Barkin (2021), sovereignty is a "recognition cartel" of a small group of actors over rights to global governance. Domestic efficacy *and* international validation must occur for an entity to achieve statehood with all of the privileges that come with sovereignty. One form of international validation comes through IGO membership.

There is a circular relationship between sovereignty as one of several conditions to gain membership in international institutions at the same time that membership in international organizations offers a building block to establish sovereignty. On the path to independence or secession, the acceptance as a member of the United Nations is the culminating step for success in establishing statehood. In the case of South Sudan, the 2011 vote admitting it to the United Nations came prior to most states having established formal diplomatic relations and represented collective recognition (Dugard, 2013, p. 64). Through membership, states gain a seat at the table. This is the first step by which international institutions distribute authority so that similar functional units achieve legal and political equality (Viola and Zürn, 2015).

Membership in international organizations relates to all four categories of sovereignty examined by Krasner (1999)—domestic, Westphalian, interdependence, and legal sovereignty. Domestic sovereignty is based on competent domestic authorities that establish governance within the borders. Westphalian sovereignty requires only that states have autonomy to exclude external actors from authority structures within their borders. Interdependence may compromise state control as market forces shape critical outcomes. Control over domestic affairs within a territory is a prerequisite to joining organizations, including the United Nations. Yet what constitutes *control* is subjective. Some weak governments are unable to conduct the most basic state functions in large sections of territory, but they are still treated as a state (Lee, 2020). There are failed states devastated by civil war, such as Yemen or those like Somalia and the Congo, that are unable to overcome the legacy of internal conflict and low development to provide basic human services. Some small states outsource their foreign policy to another, such as in the example of the Pacific Island of Niue. Others have achieved recognition in international organizations while remaining under foreign control: the Ukrainian Soviet Socialist Republic became a founding member of the United Nations, as did India while still under British colonial rule. For the case of Taiwan, the PRC asserts One China and sovereignty over Taiwan, but all functions of governance are conducted by the Taiwanese government, which possesses an independent military that would resist any direct incursion on its territory. When conceiving of sovereignty as *organized hypocrisy*, Krasner explains that few states achieve all four types of sovereignty in practice. Neither do international organizations require all four types of sovereignty.

The recognition of a state for membership represents the public judgment of other states about control and legitimacy. The formal role of organizations offers efficiency to negotiate agreements and establish a stable forum (Abbott and Snidal, 1998). The technocratic nature of an organization, with membership rules, budget dues, and meetings, facilitates the act of recognition. At this level, IGO membership confers sovereignty. Organizational membership means both participation in a contract and status in international society. Once given, membership is rarely revoked. Hence states that assert independence may gain membership in international organizations at a moment of emerging strength and retain it long after descent into civil war or subordination by another state has eroded the very notion of control over territory. The recognition of a state through its IGO membership preserves contacts that will be distinct from the recognition of a particular government—states may cut ties with another government while they continue to interact with it in a multilateral organization.[4] Recognition of governments in a civil war context also changes through discretionary decisions taken in multilateral organizations. Landau-Wells (2018, p. 103) notes that in most cases UN recognition of a rebel group through transfer of the UN seat precedes military victory. IGO membership becomes a form of "congealed ties" to bind a state within a larger network of relationships (Hafner-Burton, Kahler and Montgomery, 2009, p. 579).

There are other forms of interaction open to quasi-states. These range from an invitation to attend a meeting or formal approval of observer status. As seen in the case of the OECD, non-member participation by states can also be extensive. This participation may provide some of the benefits of cooperation, but as a step short of membership it denies recognition as a peer. The intermediary forms of participation do not convey sovereignty.

Upon entry, IGO membership can protect sovereignty. First and foremost, membership in the United Nations offers at least the principle of collective security to defend the borders of its members against aggression. Scholars have also found membership can help prevent civil wars (Tir and Karreth, 2018). Committing to abide by international rules constitutes one way in which states voluntarily reduce their sovereignty according to Krasner (1999). Yet when conceived as a participation right, the external constraints that come with multilateralism enhance sovereignty (Barkin, 2021). Membership in international organizations provides governments access to the regulations that moderate the interface between the global economy and domestic markets. Populist discourse and scholarship on globalization often pose that international law conflicts with nationalist claims, but in many cases governments navigate transnational issues with their claims about national rights asserted within a framework of international law (Greenhouse and Davis, 2020). Holding a voice in setting those regulations as a rule-making member changes the terms of exchange. Even for smaller powers that cannot shift the content of the rules, taking part in decision-making can facilitate more proactive engagement and understanding of the rules. Coalitions of small states have acted to change rules in some important cases, such as for intellectual property rights and access to medicine (Sell and Odell, 2006). Officials of member states may take defensive actions, seek aid, or utilize institutional mechanisms for flexibility while outsiders must simply react.

---

4. See Peterson (1983) for discussion on distinction between recognition of governments and recognition of states.

Legal sovereignty is based on recognition of other states and is therefore most directly tied to membership in international organizations. In effect, the United Nations issues the imprimatur of legal sovereignty (Dugard, 2013, p. 74). In this role, UN membership differentiates between Kosovo (not a member) and North Macedonia. Both have a population of around two million, represented in a parliamentary republican government that exercises effective control over the territory after their having emerged from the disintegration of the Former Yugoslavia and a civil war that followed, and they stand as candidates for accession to the European Union. It would be difficult to ascertain the nature of qualifications that would produce this contrasting outcome. Both have similar capacity to represent themselves at a world forum as an independent legal entity. Under an alternative legal order, factual conditions could define statehood for any entity that declares itself ready to represent a group of people. This is the perspective in the 1933 Montevideo Convention on the Rights and Duties of States, which outlines that statehood requires that a government represent a permanent population on a defined territory and have capacity to enter into relations with other states.

When states rushed to recognize newly independent states during the era of decolonization, they did so with little regard for the traditional criterion of statehood set out in the Montevideo Convention (Dugard, 2013, p. 40). So long as the metropole state granted independence, states approved UN membership irrespective of the fact that some entities lacked a stable government or sizable population. This shift to prioritizing self-determination over capacity to exercise sovereignty was possible because UN admission was by member approval, without any limiting criterion for eligibility or review.

Over time, sovereignty has evolved from a dynastic basis in Europe to an institution rooted in territoriality and nationalism that has achieved universal scope, whereby sovereignty equates to membership in international society (Buzan, 2017). The boundaries of this expansion have been set through the practice of flexible criterion for joining international organizations. Where Bull and Watson (1984) observe a rational incorporation of new states to expand international society, they do not focus on the mechanism by which this happens. A society of mutual recognition based on shared values emerged. Reus-Smit and Dunne (2017, p. 25) make the important point that law shaped this process as the European powers replaced older standards of civilization with new legal guidelines to admit new members. Yet even in a codified process, the system lacks rules for who qualifies. Instead, organization by organization, the incremental judgments over membership form the basis of international society.

While replacing the rhetoric of civilization with that of universal values, organizations have not embraced openness and equality. Viola (2020) explains the exclusionary multilateralism that shapes many institutions. In her theory, powerful states restrict entry to retain their privileged access to distributional benefits in the international system. Even as institutions expand their geographical scope they entrench inequality within their procedures, as with the United Nations' authority for the permanent members of the Security Council, and new groupings such as the G20 allow subgroups to determine policies outside of larger institutions. Stone (2011) explicates how even universal membership may accompany differential authority within an organization through exceptions to rules. Such deviations from universalism accommodate the tensions between widening participation and the interests of powerful states.

Scholars of international law acknowledge the political process on the path to recognition (Crawford, 2006; Vidmar, 2013). The act of recognition is "constitutive, as between the recognizing State and the new community, of international rights and duties associated with full statehood," but at the same time,"recognition is a matter of absolute political discretion as distinguished from a legal duty" (Lauterpacht, 1944, p. 386). Because of this discretion, the practice of states forms the de facto criterion used within international law. For example, the Vienna Convention on the Law of Treaties (Article 81) stipulates that for the purposes of resolving interstate disputes over treaties, states are defined as parties to the International Court of Justice, as members of the UN or its specialized agencies, or as those invited by the UN General Assembly. This preserves a gatekeeping role over the definition of state. From this interpretation, membership in UNESCO conferred statehood to Palestine even as the legal status of its territorial claim remains contested; Soviet Republics like Ukraine when under complete control of USSR were also states by virtue of holding separate UN seats.[5] Rather than meeting a legal definition, states must pass the political threshold of recognition—which often means membership in international organizations.

An alternative mark of recognition comes from diplomatic ties. This represents the formal establishment of relations between states with a diplomatic mission. States seek this level of contact for the functional purpose of facilitating business and travel of citizens as well as of supporting cooperation on

5. See Vidmar Jure, "Palestine v United States: Why the ICJ does not need to decide whether Palestine is a state," 22 November 2018 post on blog of the *European Journal of International Law*. https://www.ejiltalk.org/palestine-v-united-states-why-the-icj-does-not-need-to-decide-whether-palestine-is-a-state/. Accessed 31 January 2020.

international affairs. Kinne (2014) argues that both prestige and signaling are important motives for states to establish diplomatic ties and reflect strategic choices given limited information and resource constraints. Establishment of ties reflects expected patterns of proximity and power that can measure position in the international system (Small and Singer, 1973; Neumayer, 2008). Nevertheless, as a dyadic relationship, these ties are less informative of status within a community than are memberships in multilateral organizations.

States may also seek to form communities of democracy to support higher levels of cooperation. Research demonstrates the value of international organizations for democracies to advance their goals for peace and prosperity (Pevehouse and Russett, 2006). At the same time, bringing states into the fold of an IGO can promote democracy (Pevehouse, 2002). Democracy is not necessary for sovereignty, but may well form an important condition for membership in international organizations that can enhance the chance for democratic regimes to achieve recognition.

Because states desire recognition, "nonrecognition" itself becomes a policy tool (Krasner, 1999, p. 8). The time from independence to recognition can vary considerably, with some left in limbo as de facto states. The puppet regime of Manchukuo established by Japan in northern Manchuria faced the public policy declaration by the United States and League of Nations Assembly of nonrecognition. The intention to use the measure as a sanction was discussed in the assembly, along with steps to ensure that other state parties would refuse Manchukuo's accession to selective international organizations and object to its joining open international organizations, including the ITU, and even the most technocratic ones, such as the an International Union for the Publication of Customs Tariffs (Middlebush, 1934, p. 679). States were urged to also object to participation in activities of representatives of Manchukuo. The length to which states went to shun Manchukuo from any form of international recognition is quite remarkable. Today the Chinese government adamantly opposes any form of recognition of Taiwan as a state. Recently it blocked even the reference to Taiwan on Twitter accounts of the International Civil Aviation Organization (ICAO) during the period of air travel restrictions related to the coronavirus health crisis.[6] Taiwan holds more claim to legitimacy as a state than Manchukuo on any dimension of sovereignty, but it suffers a similar fate of nonrecognition.

---

6. See U.S. criticism of this policy. https://2017-2021.state.gov/icaos-outrageous-practice-of
-blocking-twitter-users-who-reference-taiwan/index.html. Accessed 3 February 2020.

At a social level, recognition means acknowledging another actor as a peer. Renshon (2017, p. 4) refers to status community as a group in which states perceive themselves in competition with each other for ranking in a hierarchy. The complicated role of status for states lies in its combined value of the psychological benefit for their leaders and of the instrumental benefit for the influence of their state (Renshon, 2017, p. 2). The importance of status represents one source of demand but also a reason to restrict access. Because of its inherent nature as a positional concept, status is a club good subject to crowding (Renshon, 2017, p. 21). This reinforces the fact that recognition does not itself mark equality beyond the notion that an actor is worth ranking because it belongs in a common reference group. The tribute system of East Asia embedded hierarchy within its exchange of tribute, whereby a neighboring state was recognized by the Chinese emperor. Even within contemporary international organizations members may not be equal, as weighted voting in the international lending institutions or veto status for the permanent five members of the United Nations Security Council differentiates among the members. Nevertheless, recognition confers entry into the small club of sovereign states subject to the rights and obligations of customary international law and to the symbolic trappings that accompany statehood in diplomatic protocol. In this way, entry into a universal organization confers membership in a status community.

Institutions structure relations between states to form a society that is between anarchy and hierarchy. In his classic work, Bull (1977, p. 44) presents a theory about a society of states where common values and interests unite actors, and emphasizes that these states must "regard each other as subject to the same set of rules and as co-operating in the working of common institutions." This differentiates between states that interact through commerce, diplomacy, or war in an international system. For Bull, institutions did not have to take the form of an organization with a legal charter documenting the rules and listing members. So long as the group of states understood the principles of differentiation that guided their conduct toward members of society from those outside, it was sufficient to provide order. For Bull, membership forms a social category rather than simply a matter of legal standing. Yet he also refers to the example of Turkey signing the Treaty of Paris of 1856 as the first case of a non-European state gaining recognition as a member of international society through admission to the Concert of Europe (Bull, 1977, p. 34). The surge of treaty-making in the nineteenth century would solidify connections between states in a network of legal agreements, although still sharply differentiating those accepted as civilized nations (Keene, 2007, 2012). After the end of World War II and establishment of the United Nations, the growth of international organizations would continue, with some as small clubs and others embracing a universal scope. Their membership rolls created, and reflect, the lines of international society.

8.1.2   Evaluating Conditions for Exclusion

Given the overlap between sovereignty and membership, what is the way forward to evaluate the conditions for membership in universal international organizations? One can revisit the three benchmarks for evaluating membership in universal organizations: performance, legal standing, and political ties. To contribute to provision of public goods, the state must at a minimum control its territory and domestic policies. Distinct from this functional criterion, however, lies the universal mandate of some international organizations, whereby participation itself strengthens the legitimacy of the organization. Here a state must have achieved recognition of its legal sovereignty to qualify as an actor that would expand the organization's scope of universal participation. Thirdly, political relations favor membership by states who seek benefits from association with each other independent of collective goods. All three criteria could be applied, but the third may substitute for the first two in extreme cases. This would occur if positive political ties allowed states with less control or legal status to join because they hold value of association for allies; in other cases political ties could exclude states that meet functional performance but represent a threat to political cohesion due to other sources of dissent.

Capacity. In order to function as an efficient collective for the provision of global public goods, international organizations will need to attract states with competent governments. Including more powerful states will enhance the prospect for the organization to contribute to global governance with effective policies supported by the key actors whose cooperation is necessary. At a basic level, economic indicators of market size and national income correspond with the performance of the government and proxy for national power.[7]

---

7. Population size also measures resources vital to determining whether a state could play a meaningful role. The Correlates of War state membership definition uses a threshold of 500,000 population as one of its minimal criteria for inclusion in the state system. Correlates of War Project, 2017, "State System Membership List, v2016." Available at http://correlatesofwar.org. Accessed 15 September 2020.

Legal standing. For an organization to uphold its appeal as a universal body, the entry threshold should be objective and inclusive. Relying on legal sovereignty will enhance the legitimacy of an international organization. Recognition by other states through diplomatic contacts and membership in international organizations form the path to legal sovereignty. Each additional dyadic tie and membership success adds a precedent. Not all organizations are equal; the United Nations and its specialized agencies play a leading role in international society such that membership in any of these organizations offers a prima facie case for legal standing as a sovereign state. Once a state gains entry to one of the UN family organizations, it has enhanced its standing for entry into other organizations.[8]

Political ties. One can assess the expectation that political relations shape membership through the role of alliances. Security commitments form the most significant indicator of a positive political relationship between countries. Those with more allies within an organization stand to benefit with sponsors for their request for admission. Diplomatic relations with embassy representation of senior officials indicates a basic level of political relations; yet states typically hold embassy relations with friend and foe alike, so this measure is distinct from shared interests.

All three conditions would be expected to increase the prospect for a country to join an international organization. The next two sections present empirical analysis of data for a large sample of potential candidates and specific case studies of difficult membership decisions.

8.2   Exclusion Mechanisms

In presenting the argument that IGOs are a discriminatory club, I contrast the selection of favored states based on geopolitical discrimination with universal, meritocratic, and hierarchical models. This chapter examines whether IGOs with universal principles can act as a discriminatory club. How do states screen out applicants while calling for all to join?

A small number of international organizations accept all countries that apply. These would fit the universal IGO model of accession process. But

---

8. The Correlates of War state membership definition uses diplomatic recognition by major powers or membership in the League of Nations or United Nations as criteria for inclusion in the state system. Correlates of War Project, 2017, "State System Membership List, v2016." Available at http://correlatesofwar.org. Accessed 15 September 2020.

most international organizations are selective. Requiring an invitation or a vote of approval or establishing specific criteria of eligibility are different ways of limiting who joins (see chapter 2 Figure 2.4).

This section will analyze the IGOs that are open in terms of eligibility based on coding the IGO charter provisions. They aspire in principle to a universal scope of membership. Eighty-eight IGOs in the sample of 322 are open in terms of eligibility. Their charter does not restrict ex ante which states are eligible to join, whether by reference to a regional scope of activity or other criteria.[9]

As expected by the discretionary design hypothesis, however, states still control entry. The primary means of selection is through member approval. There are different thresholds for approval, from a simple majority to unanimity. Requiring consensus holds advantages to extract concessions from entrants and to preserve rights of members, while different vote thresholds could accommodate variation over preferences (Downs, Rocke, and Barsoom, 1998; Kaoutzanis, Poast, and Urpelainen, 2016; Schneider and Urpelainen, 2012). The analysis differentiates between open eligibility IGOs that are inclusive, allowing any state to join that deposits the application with a commitment to organization principles, and those that have a higher threshold for stringent approval. A frequent formulation for an inclusive organization is to allow any UN member to simply ratify the treaty without member approval, while holding the proviso that non-UN members will require member approval. Others may require a majority of members to approve an applicant. The set of open eligibility IGOs that impose stringent approval require a super-majority vote by members, or a consensus, or grant a veto to a subset of members.

The subject matter and scope of cooperation in the sample of open eligibility IGOs vary widely. Some IGOs in the sample have a narrow mandate that would only hold interest to a small number of states, while other IGOs are expansive to address issues of importance to all states. Even among the 88 open IGOs, states do not join them all. In Figure 8.1 we observe an overall increase in the number of IGOs that states could choose to join, and a fairly

9. Organizations that require membership in the United Nations or have higher bar for accession by non-UN members are considered open eligibility. But this sample leaves out commodity organizations such as OPEC or the International Copper Study Group that limit by producer profile; regional organizations like the EU, with a geographical restriction; and IGOs that limit membership by ethnic or religious categories, such as the Arab League and Organization of Islamic Conference.

Average membership in IGOs, 1865–2014

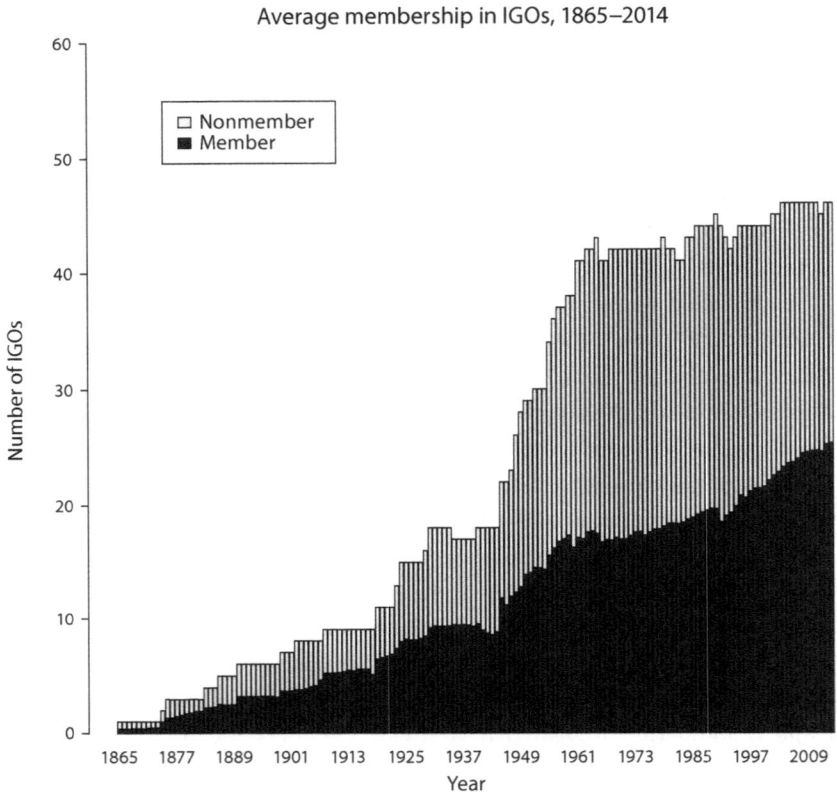

FIGURE 8.1. *Average membership rate in open eligibility IGOs*: The figure displays the average membership rate for states over time with reference to the IGOs that have open eligibility rules.

steady rate of countries belonging.[10] Some of this variation may arise from the difference in interest and resource constraints on the demand side, while other variation may arise from exclusion.

8.2.1   Statistical Analysis of Accession to Universal Organizations

I examine political relations as geopolitical alignment based on formal alliances.[11] Following Davis and Pratt (2021), I use a relational measure that

10. Each year presents the average of membership and nonmembership given the available IGOs in that year.

11. Data on alliances, which include defense pacts and neutrality or nonaggression pacts, come from version 4.1 of the COW Formal Alliances dataset (Gibler, 2009).

takes the average number of alliances of a potential member with all other states that belong to the organization. The variable *Average Alliances$_{ijt}$* measures the proportion of IGO j's member states with which state i shares a formal alliance in a given year. In a secondary test, I measure geopolitical alignment with an indicator for whether the state has an alliance with the lead state of the IGO.[12] Models will control for trade ties as well as for the other conditions for entry into universal organizations based on capacity and legal standing.

The analysis estimates the probability of joining an IGO as a function of geopolitical alignment. This requires a state-IGO-year unit of analysis to reflect that states are choosing to join a set of countries in the foundation of an organization or are applying to join an existing organization. The dependent variable is entry into an organization as a full member.

The model estimates the probability of IGO membership for state i in IGO j and year t:

$$\Pr(\text{IGO membership}_{ijt} = 1) = logit^{-1}(\alpha + \beta_1 \text{Alliances}_{ijt-1} + \beta_2 X_{ijt-1}).$$

Control variables X_{ijt} are measured at the level of the state-IGO-year (e.g., Trade and fatal MIDs with IGO Members); state-year (Trade Openness, GDP, GDP per capita, Polity); and IGO (member count as indicator of IGO size, UN). To mitigate simultaneity, all independent variables are lagged by one year. Standard errors are clustered at the country level in the baseline specification to address cross-national heterogeneity in patterns of joining, and another specification will add country and IGO fixed effects.

In addition to political ties, performance and legal standing form benchmarks for recognition of sovereignty. I include country-level indicators that should correspond with these underlying conditions of sovereignty. GDP and per capita GDP provide a basic measure of performance. Economic prosperity is one indicator that a government effectively manages its territory. Legal standing raises the problem of circularity because states are expected to have recognition in order to hold legal standing. Measuring membership by a state in other international organizations serves as a proxy for legal standing with the logic that with each successful entry into an international organization the state gains legal status that could help it join additional organizations. The variable *State IGO count* serves to control for legal standing. Membership in the UN or any of its specialized agencies, which constitute independent international organizations with close affiliation to the UN, offers a strong signal of legal stature of statehood within international

---

12. Lead state is measured by the state with the largest GDP among the IGO members.

law.[13] *UN Family Member* is an indicator for states with membership in the UN or a UN specialized agency. The United Nations holds a unique place among all international organizations, and so an indicator at the IGO level controls for a potentially different dynamic arising in the context of joining the UN.

The main specification controls for the potential that economic interdependence forms the basis for strengthening relations with other states in an IGO to build support for membership. Trade with IGO members and trade with the IGO lead state measure the impact of shared economic ties.[14] In addition, the *polity* measure controls for the higher rate of membership among democracies and the potential for their different appeal as prospective entrants (Russett and Oneal, 2001; Pevehouse and Russett, 2006; Poast and Urpelainen, 2015). Including a variable for the number of fatal militarized disputes (MIDs) between state *i* and members of IGO *j* controls for the likelihood that conflict-prone states could be screened out as threats to peace (Donno, Metzger, and Russett, 2015).[15] The variable *Total IGO Membership* is a count of members in each IGO, given that states may have a stronger interest in joining large organizations. Separate control variables measure shared colonial history as well as a state's average geographic distance from IGO *j*'s

13. The 15 specialized agencies include: Food and Agriculture Organization, International Civil Aviation Organization, International Fund for Agricultural Development, International Labour Organization, International Maritime Organization, International Monetary Fund, International Telecommunication Union, United National Educational Scientific and Cultural Organization, United Nations Industrial Development Organization, Universal Postal Union, World Bank Group, World Health Organization, World Intellectual Property Organization, World Meteorological Organization, and the World Tourism Organization. While there is significant overlap in their membership, differences are possible with states that belong to one or more specialized agencies but not the UN. Their funding is independent of the UN, and each has its own charter document and secretariat.

14. Bilateral trade data is from the IMF Direction of Trade dataset. The "trade with members" variable measures average (logged) volume of merchandise imports and exports between state *i* and each member of IGO *j*. The "trade with lead state" variable measures (logged) trade volume with the lead state, adding 1 before taking the log to ensure values of zero trade are not excluded due to the mathematical transformation.

15. MIDs data are from the dyadic version of the COW Militarized Interstate Disputes Dataset. One could alternatively hypothesize conflicts would lead states to have a stronger interest in entry to organizations, given evidence that IGO membership can contribute to conflict resolution (Tir and Karreth, 2018).

member states.[16] A Cold War indicator (1947–1991) adjusts for baseline differences in membership rates during the bipolar era. The specification models time dependence with the inclusion of a cubic polynomial for time (Carter and Signorino, 2010).

Table 8.1 displays results across different samples. First, Model 1 maximizes the sample availability over the full period of 1865–2014 and 177 countries, without any missing data arising from economic control variables. Then, important control measures for economic ties with members and national-level income and GDP, along with conflict propensity, are added in as control variables in Model 2. This restricts the time period to 1949–2014 and 164 countries.[17] Model 3 subsets to the sample of observations when states form the founding group to establish the organization.[18] Then in Model 4, the specification focuses on the subject of much research on IGO membership that examines the enlargement phase. Here the analysis is subset to examine the decision on whether to join an existing IGO during enlargement. Finally, concerns about specific features of states and IGOs that may systematically shape membership decisions are controlled for by state fixed effects and IGO fixed effects in Model 5.

The results offer support that political ties with members promote successful entry for a state. Table 8.1 shows a positive correlation between alliances and membership in IGOs, even in this set of inclusive organizations. In the full specification of Model 2, a one standard deviation increase in the *Average Alliances* measure increases the probability of membership, on average, by one percentage point. This is a small substantive effect, but remains robust across the five model specifications as a statistically significant finding. In the fixed effects specification Model 5, the effect is slightly larger.

There is also support for the importance of legal standing, as shown by the consistently positive and significant effect of state memberships in other IGOs, on the probability of joining another organization. Membership in the UN and its affiliated special agencies holds a strong legitimating force

16. Data on colonial linkages are from CEPII (Mayer and Zignago, 2011). *Colonial ties* is an indicator variable for an IGO-state-year in which the potential entrant and a current member have a history of colonial ties.

17. The sample is currently limited to those defined as states by Correlates of War, which omits Palestine but includes Taiwan. One challenge is that much of our data comes from international sources that rely on reporting by international organizations and may not include the unrecognized states.

18. This leads to a smaller subset of IGOs because those founded prior to 1949 are dropped.

	Dependent variable: IGO Entry				
	Baseline (1)	Entry (2)	Formation (3)	Enlargement (4)	State-IGO FE (5)
Average Alliances	2.373*** (0.229)	2.190*** (0.320)	2.932*** (0.374)	1.945*** (0.357)	5.249*** (0.350)
Trade with Members		0.026** (0.011)	0.119*** (0.018)	0.026* (0.014)	0.009 (0.015)
Polity	0.031*** (0.005)	0.024*** (0.004)	0.015*** (0.005)	0.028*** (0.005)	0.036*** (0.007)
UN		0.422 (0.317)		−0.098 (0.356)	
UN family IGO member		2.668*** (0.473)	1.506** (0.688)	3.267*** (0.573)	3.512*** (0.572)
GDP		0.111*** (0.034)	0.003 (0.040)	0.104*** (0.038)	0.285** (0.143)
GDP per capita		−0.021 (0.026)	−0.025 (0.037)	−0.050 (0.035)	−0.263** (0.129)
Trade Openness		−0.012*** (0.004)	−0.052*** (0.017)	−0.010** (0.004)	−0.011*** (0.004)
IGO member count	0.012*** (0.001)	0.012*** (0.001)		0.026*** (0.001)	−0.018*** (0.001)
State IGO count	0.005* (0.003)	−0.006*** (0.002)	0.010*** (0.003)	−0.009*** (0.003)	−0.034*** (0.005)
MIDS		−0.171 (0.146)		−0.204 (0.161)	−0.203 (0.176)
Colonial ties		0.260*** (0.072)	0.481*** (0.086)	0.221** (0.093)	0.068 (0.083)
Cold War	−0.451*** (0.071)	−0.865*** (0.080)	−1.030*** (0.114)	−0.859*** (0.107)	−0.733*** (0.089)
Number IGOs	88	86	51	86	86
Number States	177	164	164	164	164
Observations	281,985	239,861	5,821	234,040	239,861

Note: *p<0.1; **p<0.05; ***p<0.01.

TABLE 8.1. *Effect of alliances on membership in open IGOs*: The logit regression models estimate the effect of geopolitical alignment (average alliances with IGO membership) across different stages with an opportunity for IGO entry. Statistical significance denoted by: *p<0.1; **p<0.05; ***p<0.01.

correlated with entry into other organizations. However, despite including a range of controls for conditions that may support higher membership levels, it remains difficult to distinguish between underlying factors that make a state more likely to join all organizations and the recognition effect gained from these other affiliations. The State IGO count variable is not significant in Model 5, which incorporates fixed effects. The expectation that organizations would screen based on state capacity to perform as a significant player in the organization receives mixed support, as per capita GDP is insignificant or negative in its effect, although GDP has a positive relationship in some models.

Geopolitical discrimination is easier when states have stringent approval procedures that allow voting to exclude states. In Table 8.2, we see the interaction effect between geopolitical alignment and accession procedures. As a baseline effect, stringent approval blocks entry for some, as one would expect—there is a negative relationship between stringent approval and entry. But when accession procedures are interacted with geopolitical alignment, one observes a positive relationship, suggesting that among organizations with stringent approval, there is a positive effect of geopolitical alignment on a state's prospects for entry. Based on the comparison of analyses run separately on each subsample of stringent approval, non-stringent approval, and UN family IGOs, Figure 8.2 presents the substantive effects as the change in the probability of membership that results when the model estimates a standard deviation movement in the alignment measure. The figure also compares estimates using geopolitical alignment with the lead state as an alternate measure, in case it is the alliance with the largest member of the IGO that is determinative of results. Effect sizes are small, as one might expect in organizations that aspire to be open to all states. But nonetheless, when voting on membership, discrimination to favor allies serves as a significant tip toward entry.

Diplomatic recognition is one mark of sovereignty. Holding formal diplomatic relations as measured by hosting or sending an embassy proxies for legal standing of the country. This could serve as a criterion of legal standing for entry into universal organizations. In one pattern, states establish bilateral ties that will pave the way for acceptance by a larger group of members in an international organization. This would suggest a positive relationship between diplomatic contacts and IGO membership. Figure 8.3 shows the bivariate correlation between embassies and IGO membership for the final year of the dataset, 2014. The positive correlation is readily apparent, but many factors could be affecting the incidence of both variables. In one study, Kinne (2014) finds evidence from a network model that IGO memberships correspond to lower probability of diplomatic ties through recognition. He concludes that IGOs may substitute for diplomatic ties. This would suggest a negative correlation, whereby states with extensive diplomatic contacts would feel less demand to join IGOs and those with few contacts would strive to join as a shortcut to building their political connections.

	Dependent variable: IGO Entry			
	Interaction model (1)	Stringent Approval (2)	Inclusive (3)	UN Family (4)
Average Alliances	1.916***	3.088***	1.678***	1.329***
	(0.328)	(0.367)	(0.326)	(0.448)
Trade with Members	0.024**	0.038***	0.020*	−0.002
	(0.010)	(0.012)	(0.012)	(0.022)
Polity	0.024***	0.025***	0.023***	0.029***
	(0.004)	(0.005)	(0.004)	(0.009)
UN	0.651**	0.488*		
	(0.312)	(0.287)		
UN family member	2.662***	3.436***	2.388***	
	(0.466)	(0.616)	(0.433)	
GDP	0.113***	0.105***	0.118***	−0.019
	(0.034)	(0.035)	(0.034)	(0.045)
GDP per capita	−0.020	0.009	−0.027	−0.047
	(0.026)	(0.035)	(0.028)	(0.072)
Trade Openness	−0.012***	−0.022**	−0.010***	−0.018
	(0.004)	(0.011)	(0.003)	(0.025)
IGO member count	0.012***	0.016***	0.010***	−0.008***
	(0.001)	(0.001)	(0.001)	(0.001)
State IGO count	−0.006**	−0.019***	−0.001	−0.004
	(0.002)	(0.003)	(0.002)	(0.007)
MIDS	−0.171	−0.183	−0.165	−0.060
	(0.146)	(0.288)	(0.161)	(0.175)
Colonial ties	0.253***	0.421***	0.179**	0.599***
	(0.071)	(0.086)	(0.072)	(0.116)
Cold War	−0.861***	−2.203***	−0.536***	−1.544***
	(0.080)	(0.191)	(0.089)	(0.217)
Stringent approval	−0.361***			0.258***
	(0.041)			(0.098)
Approval:alliance interaction	0.622***			
	(0.188)			
Number IGOs	86	28	58	16
Number States	164	164	164	164
Observations	239,861	87,618	152,243	12,460

Note: *p<0.1; **p<0.05; ***p<0.01.

TABLE 8.2. *Effect of alliances on membership with comparison of selection process*: The logit regression models estimate the effect of geopolitical alignment (average alliances with IGO membership) conditional on a stringent approval process for accession. Model 1 presents interaction effect, while Models 2 and 3 estimate on separate subsamples of IGO populations. Model 4 restricts the sample to the UN and 15 specialized UN agencies. Statistical significance denoted by: *p<0.1; **p<0.05; ***p<0.01.

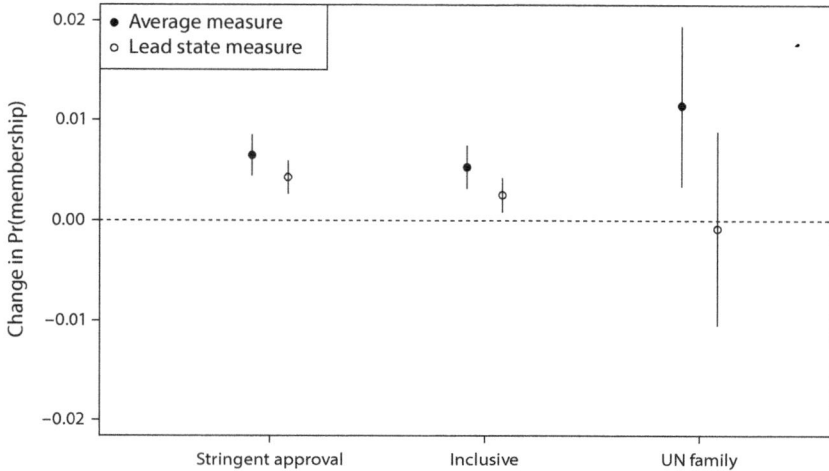

FIGURE 8.2. *Substantive effect of geopolitical alignment on open IGO membership*: The figure displays the change in the predicted probability of membership when shifting the alliance variable. Solid circles indicate estimates from the shift of proportion of allies with all members and open circles estimate the shift in holding an alliance with the lead state of the IGO. Predicted probabilities and confidence intervals are generated via 1,000 quasi-Bayesian Monte Carlo simulations of models from Table 8.2.

Therefore, as a separate test, I revisit the models with the addition of data from the Diplomatic Contacts Database on embassy representation (Rhamey et al., 2013) and the Correlates of War Diplomatic Exchange dataset (Bayer, 2006). The data records the sending and hosting of embassies and the presence of an ambassador or other high-ranking representative official.[19] The

19. The data for 1948–1969 are from the COW diplomatic exchange dataset. Since COW does not differentiate between levels of diplomatic representation from 1950 to 1965, these variables count all levels of representation for those years as sufficient to being equivalent to holding an embassy. The diplomatic contacts database, which is available for the years 1970–2010, codes a country as having an embassy when there is a diplomatic structure with an ambassador or high commissioner in residence. Merging the two series allows for continuity of sample period with the earlier analysis and inclusion of the early IGOs. Robustness checks confirm similar results with the subsample using only DIPCON data. Both data series have been coded in five-year increments, and the intervening years are extrapolated from the last observation with data, given the expectation that embassy representation is generally stable. Indicator variables for the COW data period, cubic splines, and Cold War are included but not shown.

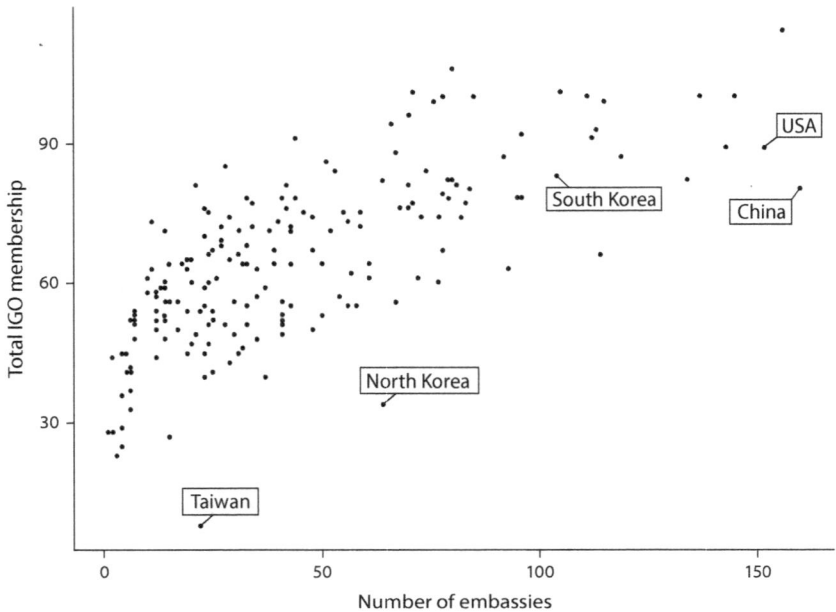

FIGURE 8.3. *Embassies and IGO membership*: The figure displays the bivariate correlation between the number of embassies sent outward by a country in 2010 and IGO memberships for the year 2014.

relational measure of diplomatic ties incorporates the share of states in the IGO with which the given state has diplomatic ties. Then Models 2 and 3 examine the country-level total diplomatic contacts. Model 2 uses the count of all embassies that a country sends to other countries in a given year as outward ties, and Model 3 uses the count of embassies hosted in the country as inward ties (both variables include a log transformation to smooth the skewed data distribution). As with other covariates, the measure is lagged by one year. Hosting an embassy of the United States represents a final measure to consider its outsized role in influencing recognition by other states (this model drops the United States). The results are shown in Table 8.3.

The first model examines the proportion of member states in an IGO with which a state has diplomatic relations as measured by sending an embassy. States are less likely to join IGOs when they have a higher share of diplomatic relations with the current members. The increase of one standard deviation in the relational measure corresponds to a 0.8 percentage point decrease in the probability of joining the IGO. The measure becomes insignificant, however, when estimated in a specification that includes state and IGO fixed

	Dependent variable: IGO Entry			
	Relational IGO ties	Outward ties	Inward ties	U.S. ties
	(1)	(2)	(3)	(4)
Average Alliances	2.606***	2.094***	2.094***	2.530***
	(0.385)	(0.355)	(0.353)	(0.277)
Embassies (IGO avg)	−1.547***			
	(0.292)			
Embassies (sent)		−0.102		
		(0.078)		
Embassies (received)			−0.125	
			(0.086)	
U.S. Embassy				−0.075
				(0.109)
Trade with Members	0.055***	0.026**	0.027**	0.018*
	(0.016)	(0.011)	(0.012)	(0.009)
Polity	0.023***	0.021***	0.021***	0.027***
	(0.005)	(0.004)	(0.005)	(0.004)
UN	0.445	0.433	0.392	0.356
	(0.303)	(0.305)	(0.304)	(0.310)
UN family member	2.850***	2.437***	2.496***	2.833***
	(0.407)	(0.423)	(0.426)	(0.497)
GDP	0.192***	0.140***	0.141***	0.149***
	(0.042)	(0.048)	(0.045)	(0.024)
GDP per capita	−0.072**	−0.050*	−0.043	−0.033
	(0.030)	(0.028)	(0.027)	(0.026)
Trade Openness	−0.013**	−0.009***	−0.008***	−0.011**
	(0.005)	(0.002)	(0.002)	(0.004)
IGO member count	0.011***	0.011***	0.011***	0.013***
	(0.001)	(0.001)	(0.001)	(0.001)
State IGO count	0.0001	−0.002	−0.002	−0.007***
	(0.003)	(0.003)	(0.003)	(0.002)
MIDS	−0.131	−0.124	−0.121	−0.087
	(0.134)	(0.132)	(0.132)	(0.129)
Colonial ties	0.219***	0.241***	0.250***	0.327***
	(0.084)	(0.078)	(0.079)	(0.061)
Cold War	−0.907***	−0.895***	−0.892***	−0.967***
	(0.087)	(0.084)	(0.084)	(0.088)
Number IGOs	86	86	86	86
Number States	164	164	164	163
Observations	239,810	236,550	236,550	238,535

Note: $^*p<0.1$; $^{**}p<0.05$; $^{***}p<0.01$.

TABLE 8.3. *Embassy representation and IGO membership*: The table presents logit regression on membership outcomes for the sample of open eligibility IGOs during the period 1949–2014 with data on embassy representation. Statistical significance denoted by: $^*p<0.1$; $^{**}p<0.05$; $^{***}p<0.01$.

effects (not shown). There is also an insignificant relationship when looking at the country-level measures of the absolute number of embassies sent to and received from all other countries in the world in Models 2 and 3. The negative direction of embassies on membership would be consistent with the logic of a substitution effect.[20] States that achieve strong representation through bilateral ties may have less need for IGO membership. But there is also a possibility of a reverse relationship, where it is the inability to join the IGO that fuels the need for more bilateral ties. Countries like North and South Korea sent diplomatic missions to other countries even in cases when the other side did not reciprocate, as they competed for influence through recognition, and rising powers such as China, Brazil, and India also send more embassies than they receive (Neumayer, 2008, p. 232). Furthermore, U.S. embassy hosts are no more or less likely to join IGOs. The small number of states excluded from the extensive U.S. network of embassies are still able to join some IGOs. Even when subsetting to the sample of open IGOs where the United States is the largest member (measured by GDP), the presence of a U.S. embassy is not a significant predictor of membership. Although Figure 8.3 shows a positive correlation, once controlling for other features in the regression analysis, there appears to be a negative or insignificant relationship. The mixed findings for these estimates on diplomatic contacts may reflect the dual logic whereby recognition through embassies could both facilitate IGO membership and reduce demand. In all specifications, the role of alliances remains robust.

Membership patterns at the aggregate level for a broad sample of open eligibility IGOs show evidence of political bias. While controlling for relevant features associated with performance capacity and legal standing, the role of security ties remains a positive factor for joining organizations. The next section will examine the United Nations system to provide a different perspective into the politics of exclusion for the most prominent universal organization and its affiliated agencies. The cases will consider how candidates experience the path to membership with attention to functional and legal competence relative to political shifts in relationships with major powers. Whereas the statistical analysis focused on alliance ties as the key indicator of geopolitical alignment, at the level of case study we can explore more nuanced shifts in the political ties among states.

20. Kinne (2014) shows the negative relationship between IGO ties and diplomatic ties. In my analysis here, there is less concern about reverse causality since I drop observations after the country joins an IGO.

8.3 Korea

The division of Korea into North and South remains one of the most tragic legacies of Cold War rivalry. Neither war nor decades of negotiations between the two sides and their great power backers have resolved the problem. Both North and South Korea have functioning governments that demonstrate their capacity as sovereign states by regulating the population of their territory. Each has diplomatic recognition from a critical number of other states as formal evidence of legal standing. IGO membership, however, has a mixed pattern.

Divergent political relations reinforce the conflicted goals of each side with regard to its position in international society. Geopolitical disputes have spilled over into international organizations in debates over which government should represent Korea. These have sometimes been resolved through applications and votes to allow both governments in, but often have left both outside. As a result, by 1975, North and South Korea were both members of universal organizations such as the WHO, UNESCO, the UPU, and the World Intellectual Property Organization (WIPO). Yet they struggled to join the organizations with stringent approval rules. The two could not gain UN membership until 1991, and North Korea remains outside the WTO and IMF, while South Korea is a member.

The challenge of membership for divided countries lies in the fear that simultaneous entry as two governments with separate membership will entrench the division while entry of one without the other will tip the balance in the quest for legitimacy as the sole representative government. With the Soviet Union backing the North and the U.S. backing the South, the stakes were amplified as struggles of influence and credibility. This case study examines how debates played out to shape the long battle over entry into the United Nations. The change of geopolitical alignment at the end of the Cold War tipped political relations to favor entry into the UN for North and South Korea.

8.3.1   United Nations

In a detailed account of the Korean effort to join the United Nations, Jonsson (2017) describes how South Korea began its pursuit to be the sole representative of Korea at the UN, while the North sought simultaneous entry; but over the years their positions shifted, so that the South took the side of requesting simultaneous entry, at which point the North sought a confederation sharing one seat. When it eventually came to the final approval of membership for South Korea and North Korea as two fully sovereign members of the United Nations in 1991, the Security Council voted after less than ten minutes of discussion, and the General Assembly issued its approval without a roll call vote to resolve what had long stood as one of the most divisive UN membership questions. According to Jonsson (2017, p. 62), "Thanks to the end of the Cold War, South Korea had eventually accomplished the most important target of its foreign policy."

The UN Charter embraces universal principles in the membership provisions of chapter II, which declares that membership is open to all "peace-loving states" that accept the obligations of the charter. At the same time, the rules call for the "judgment of the Organization" about whether a state is "able and willing" to carry out the charter obligations. This member approval process opens the door for screening applicants. The procedures require a recommendation from the UN Security Council, where each of the five permanent members holds a veto, and a two thirds majority vote of approval by the General Assembly. In a catch-22, UN membership has become a critical threshold in the path to recognition as a state, yet UN membership rules presume statehood as if there exists some prior definition of what constitutes a state. Politics can intervene where objective criteria are absent, and the Security Council gatekeeping role provides major powers with a veto authority. In practice, they rarely exercise this veto.[21] Cold War politics were underlying the exceptions, including the long struggle over the membership of North and South Korea that is the focus of this section.

When 51 countries founded the UN in 1945, Korea had just emerged from Japanese colonial rule under the supervision of the U.S. and Soviet occupation. Thus it did not join the group of founding governments, nor immediately seek entry. The UN temporary Commission on Korea was to oversee elections for an independent Korea, but failed in this task; elections in the South established the Republic of Korea (ROK), which immediately requested recognition by the UN as the representative of Korea. But a Soviet-backed Democratic People's Republic of Korea (DPRK) formed in the north, rejecting UN authority (Jonsson, 2017, p. 25). A majority in the General

---

21. The United States voted against the Security Council recommendation for Angola to join the UN as it disputed the role of Cuban troops in the newly independent state. But the United States decided not to veto membership, and entry was approved in the General Assembly with both United States and China abstaining on the vote (*New York Times* 2 December 1976).

Assembly supported the ROK, but USSR opposition effectively blocked its first formal application for membership in 1949. That same year, the ROK attained membership in organizations including the WHO and UPU; where the USSR lacked a veto, the ROK could receive support for entry.[22] The involvement of the UN Command in the Korean War from 1950 to 1953 further complicated the standoff over membership. The war had left the country divided, with the UN Command joining the United States to offer security in the South and the USSR backing the North. UN debates that included the South and not the North supported calls for elections and UN membership for a single Korea, while rejecting the request from the North for parallel entry. In subsequent years Taiwan, Australia, and others would issue new resolutions in support of membership for the ROK, only to face a Soviet veto.

Universality was secondary to rivalry. In 1957, the Cold War politics laid out the two sides on the question of Korean membership. In January, the Soviet Union requested simultaneous membership for both North and South Korea as full members, which was blocked by the United States, as it rejected the two-state solution and considered the North to have been an aggressor in the war (Jonsson, 2017, pp. 35–36). The U.S. coalition of supporters (Australia, Taiwan, Colombia, Cuba, France, the Philippines, and the UK) voted later in the year in favor of a Security Council resolution to admit South Korea as the sole representative, which was blocked by the Soviet Union. In contrast, the North objected to the presence of foreign troops in the South and insisted that any proposal for elections and unification should be conducted between two equal Korean delegations. Each year the UN General Assembly took up what was referred to as the "Korean Question" for regular debate. But its handling of the matter changed over time. When South Korea indicated it would consider entry for two Koreas in 1961, the Security Council refused to take up the issue.

The shifting geopolitical balance in the UN worsened the position of the ROK. Many newly independent states entered the UN with closer alignment to the USSR and DPRK position, and the 1971 recognition of the PRC as the representative of China added another Security Council veto player of the ROK petition for membership.[23] Abandoning the possibility for the ROK to

---

22. As a non-UN member, Korea would need to receive support from a two-third vote of members to join organizations such as WHO and UPU that would otherwise have allowed UN members to join without member vote.

23. Choi (1975, p. 401) shows the pro-DPRK support in UN growing from 17 percent of membership in 1966 to 35 percent in 1974, with new support largely coming from entrants to the UN in Africa.

become the sole representative of Korea, the South started a new campaign for simultaneous entry. Now, the North adopted the former position of the South, which objected that simultaneous entry would render the division to be permanent. Nevertheless, the North successfully pursued membership in the WHO in 1973. This brought observer status and rights to speak in the UNGA. Deadlock was apparent in 1975, when the General Assembly adopted resolutions on proposals to reduce tensions on the peninsula, with conflicting claims about settlement terms and UN representation. At this time, the full membership was divided over the issue. The impasse continued at the UN even as both North and South Korea were approved to join other UN affiliated agencies and international organizations, where the major powers lacked veto authority.[24]

The final status of UN membership proved elusive until the end of the Cold War. The geopolitical realignment reduced the distance between South Korea and its rivals, such that they lifted their veto over its accession. South Korea benefited from the shift in views within the USSR led by Mikhail Gorbachev, who favored universal diplomacy without restricting relations based on ideology and hoped to open ties with the booming Asia Pacific region as a way to support the failing Soviet economy (Joo, 1993). Jonsson (2017) argues that expanding political ties by the ROK and the examples from other divided countries pushed forward the momentum toward membership. As Germany and Yemen negotiated their membership in the UN after reunification, they demonstrated that two-state solutions could also form a path toward eventual unification. Indeed, political leaders in South Korea who were averse to abandoning the unification goal made references to these examples.[25] South Korea established diplomatic relations with the USSR and East European countries and displayed its growing economic prosperity while hosting the Olympic Games in 1988. Growing trade and promises of loans to the USSR

24. In one exception, the Koreas did not join the ILO until 1991, when it used the UN membership path to join without a vote simultaneously with the DPRK. Commentary suggests that while the ROK had been an observer at the ILO since 1982, earlier efforts to join were set aside over concern it could not win a two-third vote from members and its reluctance to accept commitments on labor provisions. "South Korea hesitated about joining ILO in late 1980s over labor unrest concerns: Declassified dossier," *Yonhap News* 31 March 2020. Available at http://yna.kr/AEN20200331004500325.

25. "Kim Dae Jung Asks UN Leader to Help Seoul, P'yang Get Simultaneous Entry," *The Korea Times*, 4 May 1991.

further cemented South Korea's quest for normalization with the Eastern bloc (Joo, 1993). At the 1990 summit with South Korean president Roh Tae-woo, Gorbachev agreed to support the South Korean entry into the UN *either* as simultaneous entry with the North *or* as unilateral membership by the ROK (Joo, 1993, p. 442). In the 1990 General Assembly both President George Bush and President Mikhail Gorbachev spoke in favor of South Korean membership. Nonetheless, negotiations between the North and South remained deadlocked over whether to join with a shared seat or separate membership. Finally, the South decided to apply on its own for full membership.

At this stage, China provided the final push. According to some, President Bush helped mediate this outcome, whereby China informed the North it would not veto the South Korean membership proposal (Jonsson, 2017, p. 57). With 71 member states, including the Soviet Union, having spoken in favor of South Korea, and China itself trying to restore its international standing by removing the sanctions imposed after Tiananmen Square, China had little reason to stand beside the North on the UN question. One month after a visit by the Chinese Premier Li Peng, in which he was reported to have told President Kim Il-sung that China would not veto the ROK request for UN membership, the North made the surprise announcement that it would seek membership.[26] Completely isolated, North Korea had to accept that it could not stop the South from gaining a seat, and so would seek its own seat. Thus ended the long path to UN membership for two governments of a divided nation that aspires to unification.

Alongside the multilateral recognition through joining international organizations, both countries had been expanding their bilateral ties through diplomatic recognition. Figure 8.4 shows the closely matched competition between South and North Korea in their sending representatives to other countries in the years leading up to UN membership. Then their trajectories diverge. South Korea continues to accelerate its ties, but the shifting allegiances of East European countries leads North Korea to reduce the embassies it sent after the end of the Cold War. The loss of aid from the USSR may also have contributed to reduction, as a step for cost cutting. Both South and North Korea send more than they receive, but the disparity is greater for the North. In this particular case, UN membership may substitute for bilateral ties with North Korea. Many countries do not seek additional representation in

26. Sanger, David, "North Korea Reluctantly Seeks U.N. Seat," *New York Times* 29 May 1991.

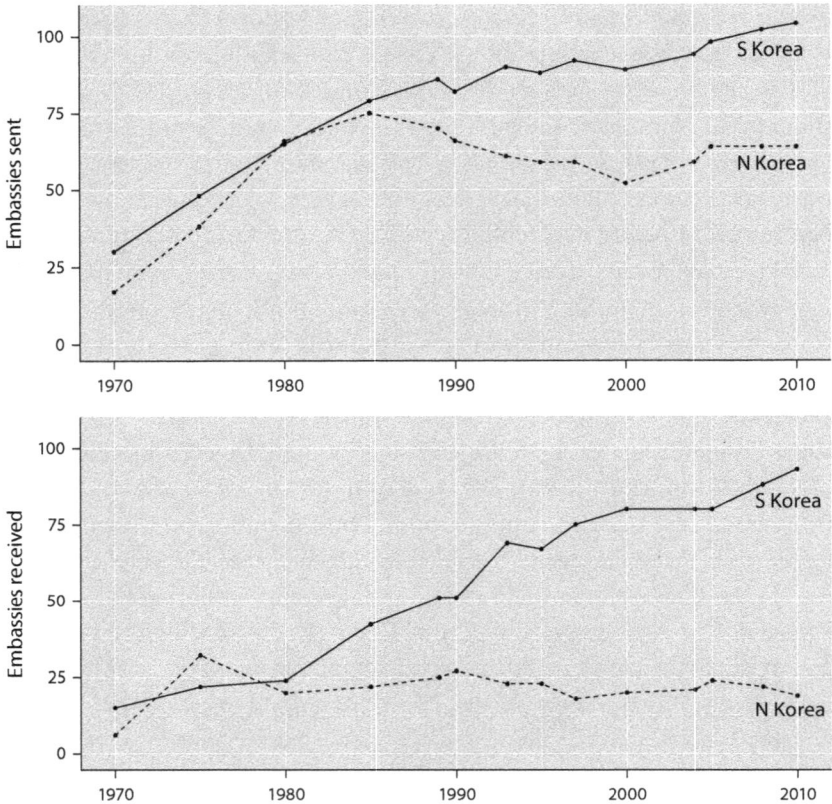

FIGURE 8.4. *Diplomatic representation of North and South Korea*: The graphs show the growing number of diplomatic contacts through sending embassies (top) and hosting embassies (bottom).

North Korea, and the DPRK leadership holds onto its isolated status within the international system.

There is evidence that the dual entry of North and South Korea into the United Nations also reduced the conflict over sovereignty status at the level of bilateral ties. Prior to UN entry, a dozen countries had diplomatic ties with both the North and the South, relative to 35 states that recognized only the North and 44 that recognized only the South.[27] Amidst contested sovereignty, ties to other states fell along clear ideological lines. Following UN entry, there

27. Descriptive numbers are based on the DIPCON database.

are now 35 states that recognize both. The largest grouping, however, constitutes the 70 states that have recorded high-level representation only with South Korea. By virtue of its UN membership, North Korea can claim equal sovereignty and opportunity for communication that expands its audience through UN venues. South Korea benefits from seeing UN membership open both multilateral fora and doors for wider bilateral ties than had been possible when its sovereignty was at the center of Cold War geopolitical rivalry.

UN recognition for the Koreas was long overdue from the perspective of governance capacity and legitimacy. The inability to agree on a way forward to allow participation by North and South Korea had been a symbol of how Cold War rivalries undermined the core ideals of the United Nations. Their absence limited the reach of collective security. The timing of the change closely conforms to the expectations of geopolitical pressures, and arose through top-level coordination among leaders of key allies with the United States and Japan advocating for the South, and the Soviet Union and China pushing the North to accept the broader association in the UN alongside the South.

8.4   Taiwan

Taiwan represents an extreme case, in which a high-performance government with domestic sovereignty has been excluded from even the universal international organizations. Following the conclusion of the civil war that resulted in the Chinese Communist Party establishing the People's Republic of China (PRC), Kuomintang (KMT) representatives who fled to Taiwan from the mainland asserted their right to control the full country.[28] They insisted that the Republic of China (ROC), established on the mainland in 1912, remained the true representative of the Chinese nation. Both governments only agreed on the principle that there was "one China," while contesting who was the legitimate representative. This differs from secession, where a region declares independence and demands recognition as a new state. Two claimants to single representation of China creates one of the most difficult cases for defining sovereignty. The act of diplomatic recognition leads to high-stakes decisions

---

28. The Qing Empire had asserted its control of Taiwan (Formosa) in 1885, only to cede it to Japan in 1895 under the Treaty of Shimonoseki following defeat in the Sino-Japanese war. The end of Japan's colonial occupation of Taiwan in 1945 returned the island to Chinese control. The KMT suppressed those in the local population who sought self-determination for Taiwan as an independent state.

that signify a move to "break" with one side to recognize the other. While the decisions over diplomatic ties occur at the national level, international organizations have been faced with the need to reach a collective decision over recognition when determining membership. Standard criteria are insufficient. Both governments enjoy de facto statehood from the perspective of autonomous control over a well-defined territorial unit in the sense of Westphalian sovereignty. But legal sovereignty changed as a function of other states' decisions about IGO membership representation for China.

From the outset, states confronted a choice with membership in the United Nations. China holds a permanent seat on the UN Security Council, so the question of which government represents China is of central importance to the organization. As the incumbent government when the UN was founded, the ROC could insist that it remained the true representative, despite having lost control over the main territorial entity of China. The Soviet Union presented a resolution to deny the ROC credentials at the UN Security Council, but failed to gain majority support, which left the ROC to hold the UN seat representing China.[29] This standoff continued for more than two decades, as the US-led opposition excluded the PRC. Eastern bloc countries submitted resolutions calling for PRC representation that were rejected in the Security Council, and the General Assembly voted to postpone consideration of the matter.

The dramatic change in geopolitical alignment was initiated by the United States opening up to China. Amidst rising Sino-Soviet tensions, the United States shifted policy to engage the PRC. Writing in 1967 in a prominent *Foreign Affairs* article, President Richard Nixon signaled the new policy direction. After warning against a rush "to grant recognition to Peking, to admit it to the United Nations and to ply it with offers of trade—all of which would serve to confirm its rulers in their present course," he insisted that "we simply cannot afford to leave China forever outside the family of nations" (Nixon, 1967, p. 9). This was followed by Nixon's surprise announcement on 15 July 1971 that he planned to visit China. The shift in the U.S. position from hostility to cautious engagement renewed the membership question in the UN. While the United States would not formally change its own policy of recognition to establish diplomatic ties with the PRC until 1979, officials let it be known that

29. The UN Charter provision on membership in Article 4 requires that states uphold the values of the organization and also requires that "the admission of any such state to membership in the UN will be effected by a decision of the General Assembly upon the recommendation of the Security Council."

the United States would no longer block those in the UN who pushed for the PRC to represent China. The agreement established during Nixon's visit in 1972 that "there is but one China and Taiwan is part of China" left the issue framed as a decision about *which* government to recognize rather than pushing a two-state solution.[30]

Most attention to the question of Taiwan's status in international cooperation focuses on the critical turning point brought by the UN Resolution 2758 of 25 October 1971, which conferred on the PRC the status as sole lawful representative of China to the United Nations. This stripped the ROC of legal sovereignty. Having allowed the recommendation of the Security Council to proceed without veto, the United States voted against the resolution in the General Assembly even as it passed with majority approval. This itself did not end the Taiwan question. Diplomatic recognition diverged among UN members, and membership decisions also varied across affiliate organizations over time. While many organizations followed the UN decision to strip Taiwan of membership, others allowed it to retain membership (i.e., ADB), and some would later offer membership to China while also providing full membership to Taiwan (i.e., WTO). Having been a member of 39 organizations in the 1960s, the membership portfolio of Taiwan had shrunk to six in the 1980s after Taiwan was forced to leave both prominent organizations such as the IMF and seemingly innocuous technical organizations like the International Hydrographic Bureau and the International Sugar Council (Li, 2006, p. 598).

The Taiwanese government under President Lee Teng-hui in 1993 began a campaign to achieve participation in international organizations. Serving as Premier at the time, Lien Chan wrote an appeal for Taiwan to be allowed membership in the United Nations that was published in *Orbis* (Lien, 1993). He lays out how Taiwan meets "all the prerequisites of a sovereign state," and offers the examples of East and West Germany holding seats prior to unification and North and South Korea holding membership in the UN to insist that Taiwan's own bid to join the UN does not presume to displace the PRC within the organization. Lien writes, "We feel strongly that the United Nations should take up its moral responsibility by accepting all nations that are willing to join." In 2007, the Taiwanese government launched a campaign for full membership in the UN. Its bid was declined by UN Secretary-General Ban Ki-moon, with the United States also discouraging Taiwan from such a provocative initiative.

---

30. See review of the Nixon visit to China in February 1972 available at https://www.nixonfoundation.org/exhibit/the-opening-of-china/. Accessed 1 July 2020.

The matter was not brought to a vote. The stalemate at the UN continues even as Taiwan has broached different forms of participation across a range of organizations. By 2001, Taiwan held membership in 31 organizations in an IGO-rich international society, where the least active participants, such as the micro-state Andorra, had over 60 IGO memberships (Li, 2006, p. 599). Where Taiwan does hold membership, name changes are a nontrivial part of each negotiation on membership, as it appears under different names. Figure 8.5 shows that among the full set of 322 IGOs analyzed in this book, Taiwan has a low and declining number of memberships.[31] See table 8.5 (p. 381) for a list of the IGOs where Taiwan has held membership.

This case study will examine the experience of Taiwan from the perspective of understanding how political ties shape outcomes for participation in international organizations. Given the controversy over its status, this section examines a broader range of participation as the outcome of interest—when does Taiwan gain access as an observer, if not full membership? There are two dimensions to the role of political ties in conditioning the access for Taiwan: relations between members of the organization with the PRC and ROC and relations between the PRC and the ROC. As ties of other states with the PRC improve, there is less support for the ROC gaining access. At the same time, the PRC's position has ranged from adamant opposition to a more accommodating one, allowing some participation. When the government of Taiwan has emphasized closer ties to China, it has achieved some gains for access to international organizations as a response. Election of governments that emphasize distance from China in turn has been met with reductions of access to international organizations.

The shift of the geopolitical alignment at stake revolves around the United States' position toward the PRC. On the one hand, the United States stands firm in its support as the key guarantor of Taiwan's security autonomy.[32] Formal warnings to China against military action, and military sales to Taiwan that bolster its self-defense capacity, serve as signals of resolve in a tense standoff. On the other hand, the United States has sought to improve relations with China as part of wider strategic goals. For example, Nixon made his

31. This represents the sample of multilateral organizations in the COW IGO dataset where I could identify a charter document. Note that Taiwan may have membership in other international associations that are not intergovernmental, or those without a formal charter and secretariat.

32. See Kan and Morrison (2014) for background.

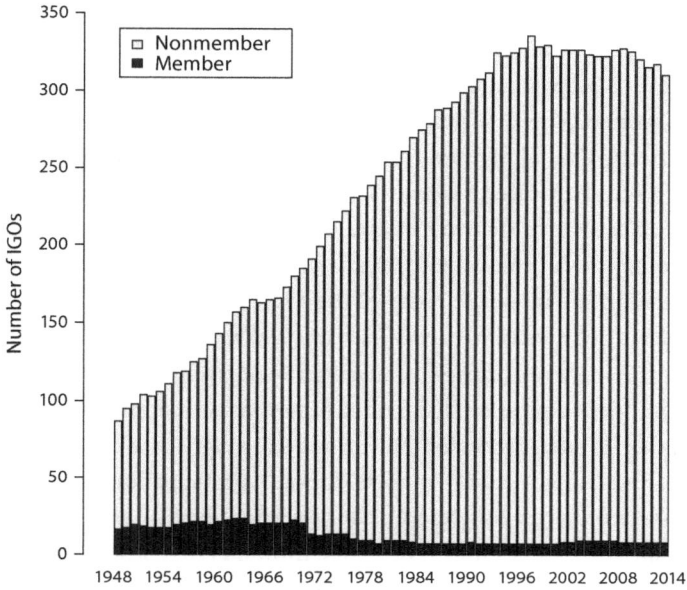

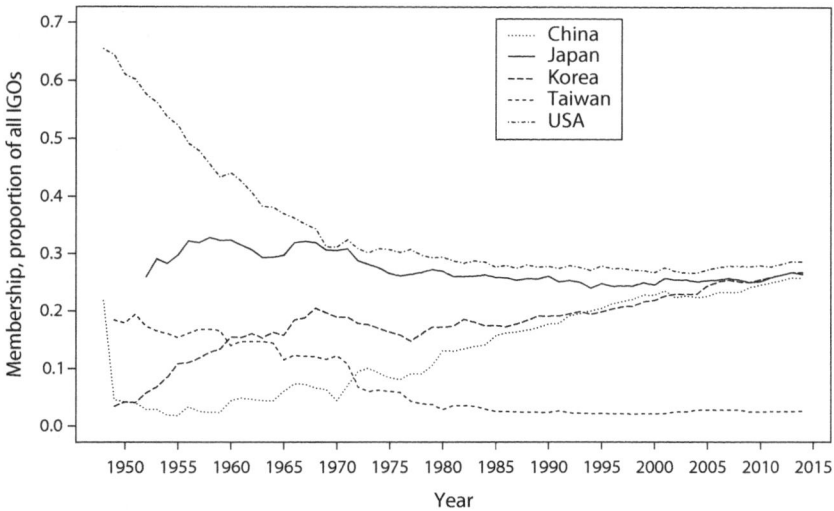

FIGURE 8.5. *Taiwan's membership in IGOs*: The declining share of IGOs in which Taiwan is a member can be seen here as a count of Taiwan's IGO membership relative to the total number of IGOs (top) and as a membership proportion in comparison to other countries (bottom) for the period 1948–2014.

historic step to normalize ties with China as a way to counter the USSR and retreat from the Vietnam war, and the Clinton administration engaged closely with China as a growing economy to allow its entry into the WTO. These steps did not end the U.S. support for Taiwan, which held a mutual defense treaty with the United States until 1979, and remains a frequent purchaser of weapons from the United States.[33] The Taiwan Relations Act (TRA) specifically emphasizes that the shift of U.S. diplomatic recognition did not imply expulsion of Taiwan from international organizations.[34] And as the Clinton administration brokered the entry of the PRC into the WTO, it insisted on the parallel negotiation for entry of Taiwan (Nakatsuji, 2001). Nevertheless, in the face of Chinese resistance to Taiwan achieving status in IGOs, closer relations with China require that the United States remain committed to the status quo that denies recognition for Taiwan as a sovereign state.[35] In keeping with the TRA, the United States supports Taiwan's participation in international organizations in which statehood is not a requirement.

Party shifts within Taiwan reverberate through cross-straits relations. The issue of membership in international organizations emerges as a political matter of highest importance in the politics of Taiwan (Chen, 2002). Leaders of the KMT are committed to the One China policy but have taken different approaches to foreign policy. The step by President Lee Teng-hui to raise Taiwan's status in the UN began the foray toward a more nuanced policy. As democratization progressed, the KMT had to engage in contestation with opposition parties that chose different stances on relations with China and the world. The rise of the Democratic Progressive Party (DPP) in 2000 renewed emphasis on UN representation as a goal of the government. The DPP government led by President Chen Shui-bian issued the formal UN membership request in 2007, followed by his calling a referendum on UN membership among the public in 2008, at the same time as the national election. Marking

33. The 1979 Taiwan Relations Act commits the United States to providing defensive weapons in support of self-defense for Taiwan, and provides that the United States retains its "capacity to resist any resort to force or other forms of coercion" harmful to Taiwan. During the Taiwan Straits crisis, the United States deployed two aircraft carriers as a strong sign of defense for the autonomy of Taiwan in the face of missile tests from China (Kan and Morrison, 2014).

34. See Section 4d, "Nothing in this Act may be construed as a basis for supporting the exclusion or expulsion of Taiwan from continued membership in any international financial institution or any other international organization."

35. Officially, the U.S. government adopts a neutral stance that neither supports nor opposes the independence of Taiwan.

the high stakes of the moment, President Bush ordered two U.S. aircraft carriers to position in the Taiwan Straits at the time of voting (Kan and Morrison, 2014, p. 5). In the end, the competing proposals from DPP and KMT about the name under which Taiwan might pursue participation in international organizations (Taiwan or Republic of China) both failed to gather sufficient votes; knowing the PRC could veto any application for membership to the UN, while approval would provoke a crisis with the PRC, even those who might have supported the goal were not willing to vote for the measure. The KMT won the election with a solid margin. The return of the KMT to power under the leadership of President Ma Ying-jeou shifted the policy toward the softer approach to pursue participation and not membership in organizations. Ma would accept the name Chinese Taipei and the policy of "three noes"—no unification, no independence, and no use of force. This period saw new flexibility from the PRC about Taiwan engaging in international affairs, although not any relaxation of the core rejection for membership in the UN.

The election of a DPP government led by President Tsai Ing-wen in 2016 again raised tensions between Taiwan and the PRC over independence. When she refused to endorse the One China policy, Beijing protested and ended the diplomatic contacts that had grown under the Ma administration.[36] Her January 2020 reelection victory has set a continued course for a tense standoff with Beijing, which was rumored to have tried to intervene in the election on behalf of the losing KMT candidate. Having retreated from its original campaign for UN membership as a distinctly separate Taiwanese delegation, and modified strategy to focus on "meaningful participation", the DPP continues to seek the goal of expanding Taiwan's status in international organizations, and is viewed by Beijing as doing this to step toward independence. The KMT has also shifted priorities over time, from wanting the return of its old seat at the UN as sole representative of China, to slowly pursuing IGO connections through informal party networks to build ties with diplomatic allies, as well as deepening economic and diplomatic connections to Beijing. By continuing its endorsement of the One China policy and flexibility on names, the KMT reassures the PRC.

In sum, the election of pro-independence parties in Taiwan and foreign policy cooperation between the United States and the PRC both reduce the

---

36. Javier C. Hernández, "China Suspends Diplomatic Contact With Taiwan," *The New York Times*, 25 June 2016.

chance for Taiwan to gain participation. In contrast, the combination of a pro-China KMT government in Taiwan and rivalry between the United States and the PRC would be more conducive to Taiwan's expanding its role, albeit as a non-state observer.

One sees these trends when looking closer at the case of the WHO. The Taiwanese government has in the past requested full membership. Currently, the ROC government says that it seeks *meaningful participation* as a way to dodge the larger question of membership while focusing on a request for observer status. Dual representation for Taiwan and the PRC in organizations such as APEC and the WTO has been facilitated by simultaneous negotiations toward entry and careful references to member economies rather than member states. De facto sovereignty may arise through such paths to membership that skirt the political challenges of defining statehood.

8.4.1   World Health Organization

The Covid-19 pandemic highlights the dilemma of membership for Taiwan as an urgent issue for the world. The Taiwanese representative to London, David Lin, wrote in a letter to *The Economist*, "Taiwan sent an early warning to the international health body about the risk of transmission of the coronavirus between humans at the end of December. However, the warning was not shared with other countries by the WHO because of its relationship with China. That error ultimately delayed the global response to the pandemic."[37] In its own editorial, *The Economist* advocated for admission of Taiwan to the WHO. Wide praise acknowledged the effective measures taken by the government in Taiwan to limit the spread of the disease.

The WHO embraces a universal goal with a preamble in the Charter that affirms that the organization principles are "basic to the happiness, harmonious relations and security of all peoples" and "Membership in the Organization shall be open to all States." The organization has open selection for UN members, who can accept the charter provisions to join without any policy screening or vote by members. For those not gaining access by virtue of UN membership, membership requires approval by a simple majority vote of the Health Assembly. Once approved, all members have equal vote within the organization.

37. 26 March 2020, *The Economist*.

The Taiwanese government campaign to join the WHO began in 1997 with efforts to gain recognition as a "health entity." After several years of failed attempts, the requests escalated with the DPP victory in 2000. After the severe acute respiratory syndrome (SARS) outbreak in 2003, which led to a hospital overcome with infection and several deaths, there was a deep sense that lack of membership creates problems. SARS was a new disease that came from China, and there was little information about it. When Taiwanese officials asked for information from the WHO, they were told to go through Beijing. Unwilling to take that step, the government instead relied on the U.S. Center for Disease Control and friendly governments. The Chinese government insisted it was taking care of Taiwan, with offers of medical advice and essential materials. In the midst of the crisis, Taiwanese medical researchers complained about their inability to obtain samples for research, with one epidemiologist traveling to Beijing for direct access after having his request denied by the WHO, even as it led a global study on the disease (Cyranoski, 2003). Taiwanese doctors were refused access to antibody tests. "We can't get any information from the WHO," said Chen Yuan-Tsong, director of the Institute of Biomedical Sciences at the Academia Sinica in Taipei (ibid.). This situation increased the levels of urgency within Taiwan and sympathy from other countries for its appeal to gain access to the WHO. The government request to join the WHA as an observer in 2004 was rejected, with only 25 votes in favor and 133 opposed, but this result was still evaluated as a positive step for Taiwan. Jich Wen-chich, deputy director-general of the foreign ministry's department of international organization, emphasized the symbolic meaning of Taiwan's application to have Japan and the United States vote in favor, while noting that the PRC had tried to stop the vote from taking place.[38] President Chen Shui-bian next sought full membership in the WHO in 2007 and 2008, but could not win approval (Winkler, 2012).

The United States' support for Taiwan has focused on the WHA, where statehood is not a condition for participation. The U.S. Congress passed legislation with a unanimous vote in support of Taiwan's efforts to gain observer status in the WHO that was signed by President Bush in June 2004. In March 2020, the Trump administration endorsed the call for greater effort to support Taiwan's international presence with the Taiwan Allies International Protection and Enhancement Initiative (TAIPEI) Act. With a strong

38. Melody Chen, "Taiwan: Twenty-five countries voted for Taiwan's WHO bid," *Taipei Times* 19 May 2004.

bipartisan consensus in Congress and the signature of President Trump, the move demonstrates the unified front backing U.S. support of a role for Taiwan in international organizations "as appropriate," while not going so far as to deviate from the official U.S. policy recognizing the PRC as the representative of China.[39]

The leadership in Taiwan has placed a priority on the WHO across administrations. Differences arise over the form of cooperation. The return to power of the KMT in 2009 brought a shift in sentiment to emphasize technical cooperation and observer status. The PRC showed new flexibility in a statement from President Hu Jintao: "Taiwan compatriots' participation in international activities would be discussed with priority given to participation of the World Health Organization's (WHO) activities after the cross-strait consultations were resumed" (Winkler, 2012). In response, President Ma Ying-jeou focused the government effort on expanding participation—not membership. His government emphasized the WHO as a priority and willingness to participate under the name Chinese Taipei. In exchange for his more accommodating position, the PRC aided in the decision to allow Taiwan's participation in the WHA in 2009 and every year since through 2016 (Sullivan and Sapir, 2012, p. 36). These concessions were seen as valuable for Ma to rally public opinion in Taiwan. In an analysis of the full record of transcripts, Sullivan and Sapir (2012, p. 54) show Ma giving attention to sovereignty topics, including issues such as participation in WHO, with the trend increasing over time during his presidency, and focused on prominent domestic audiences in his National Day and New Year speeches. In an appeal to voters, the KMT argues that its focus on strong economic ties with the Mainland will contribute to both economic growth and opportunities to expand participation in international organizations.

Although the decisions on new membership and participation lie in the hands of the full membership, the PRC has worked with the WHO secretariat officials to reach an accommodation that maximizes its range of control. Following the SARS outbreak, in 2005 PRC health officials made statements supportive of technical exchanges that led to more access to WHO by experts in Taiwan.[40] After the 2009 election, the government relented toward the

39. Mercy Kuo, "Trump and theTAIPEI Act Insights from Russell Hsiao," *The Diplomat* 21 April 2020.

40. "Beijing Okays Technical Cooperation between WHO and Taiwan," *China Daily*, 17 May 2005. https://www.chinadaily.com.cn/english/doc/2005-05/17/content_443095.htm.

participation by the Health Minister of Taiwan. Since the WHO Director General issues the invitations to attend the WHA, it is a discretionary decision made each year rather than a formal status with rights of participation. The 2009 decision rested upon an informal understanding that was reached between the PRC and the WHO that they would both have to agree in order to issue any subsequent invitations (Kan and Morrison, 2014, p. 24). Moreover, the invitation did not include complete access to WHO technical meetings, where much of the information exchange takes place. Relaxing the restrictions on participation for Taiwan while retaining the right to remove this benefit left China fully in control, while simultaneously presenting a softer diplomatic stance to the public in Taiwan and to others in the international community (Tubilewicz, 2012).

With the election of the DPP again in 2016, the PRC increased its effort to isolate Taiwan. Its observer status at the WHA was revoked as the Director-General declined since to again invite a representative of Taiwan to attend the annual meeting. The first invitation to the WHA, in 2016, added a provision conditioning Taiwan's participation on acceptance of the One China principle, and thereafter Taiwan has not been sent an invitation. Li Bin, head of China's WHA delegation, stated Taiwan's removal was due to the DPP's decisions, and that by refusing to recognize the One China policy, the DPP had "undermined the political basis of cross-Straits relations and brought the cross-Straits contact and communication mechanism to a standstill."[41] By noting that DPP policies made it impossible to continue the "special arrangements" that had allowed Taiwan's government officials to attend the WHA, the Chinese government announced that any access for Taiwan was conditional on the permission of the PRC—*for a particular governing party*—not on Taiwan's aspirations as an actor in international society. President Tsai criticized the exclusion, "The WHO's secretariat has again, under pressure, refused to invite Taiwan to attend the WHA, and I would like to use this opportunity to express my solemn protest. Refusing Taiwan's participation because of political factors does not conform to the common interests of the international community."[42]

41. "Official: Taiwan Can Blame Itself," *China Daily* 23 May 2017. http://www.chinadaily .com.cn/china/2017-05/23/content_29454155.htm.

42. Yen, William. "President Tsai Protests Taiwan's Exclusion from WHA," *Focus Taiwan* 19 May 2020, https://focustaiwan.tw/politics/202005190014. Accessed 13 August 2020.

The issue of international space is a highly charged political matter in Taiwan. Both parties share in the goal to achieve greater participation for Taiwan in international organizations even as they differ in their strategies. The KMT showcases its ability to deliver better outcomes on this front. Lien Chan, who had argued that China should be able to join the United Nations, promised as a candidate for the presidency in 2000 that he would address the need for Taiwan to participate in functional international organizations.[43] Eric Chu, former Taipei mayor and the 2016 KMT candidate for the presidency, declared that if the KMT returned to power in 2020, Taiwan would be able to participate in the WHA and other international organizations.[44] Yet these appeals have been insufficient to deliver electoral success, and the KMT may start to move closer to the DPP and rethink its position on the One China policy. The public gave a resounding margin of victory to Tsai for her reelection in January 2020.

The United States has protested the exclusion of Taiwan. At meetings of the WHA representatives of the United States, along with those from other supportive countries such as Japan and Germany, have spoken in favor of allowing Taiwan to participate.[45] They make a distinction between supporting participation in the WHA, which does not require statehood as a condition of membership, and the larger question of full membership in the WHO. Support for Taiwan in the U.S. Congress is bipartisan, and has grown stronger in proportion to rising hostility toward Beijing. A year prior to the coronavirus outbreak, in January 2019 Democratic Senator Bob Menendez and Republican Senator Jim Inhofe introduced legislation urging the U.S. government to develop a strategy for Taiwan to rejoin the WHO as observer. Speaking in favor of the bill, which detailed the many contributions of Taiwan to global health and condemned the effort by the PRC to resist such engagement by Taiwan, Sherrod Brown said, "For years, Taiwan participated at the World Health Assembly in observer status helping to promote the fundamental human right of access to medical care. Excluding Taiwan limits meaningful exchanges

43. China TV News, last modified 18 October 2003. https://news.cts.com.tw/cts/general/200310/200310180121994.html. Accessed 30 August 2020. Translated from Chinese.

44. "If the Kuomintang Returns to Power, Taiwan Will Participate in the International Organizations that the People Care About." China Taiwan Net, last modified March 22, 2019. http://www.taiwan.cn/taiwan/jsxw/201903/t20190322_12150546.htm. Accessed 30 August 2020. Translated from Chinese.

45. Aspinwall, Nick, "Taiwan Picks Up International Support after Being Barred from World Health Assembly," *The Diplomat*, 10 May 2019.

on infectious diseases that disregard international borders and have a global impact."[46]

U.S. advocacy for Taiwan has increased further during the Covid-19 outbreak. Speaking in May 2020, Secretary of State Mike Pompeo declared, "I want to call upon all nations, including those in Europe, to support Taiwan's participation as an observer at the World Health Assembly and in other relevant United Nations venues."[47] After months of criticizing the WHO with calls for organizational reform and accusations over excess influence by China, in July 2020 the Trump administration began the formal process of withdrawal. In a high-profile step, U.S. Secretary of Health and Human Services Alex Azar traveled to Taiwan in August 2020 to meet with President Tsai. In his speech to the National Taiwan University on 11 August Azar said, "Taiwan was not invited as an observer to the 2017 WHA, and it has not been invited since—even in the midst of a global pandemic, with so many lives at stake. Representing the United States, I have spoken out against this decision at each WHA I have attended. This spring, we issued our first joint statement with Taiwan on the issue, highlighting how much more illogical and counterproductive this decision has become during a global pandemic."[48] While the Biden administration reversed the decision about exiting the WHO, it remained firmly supportive of Taiwan both as a security and economic partner and in its right to international space.

Taiwan's role in offering early reporting of the outbreak in Wuhan with human transmission, and its strong national response to Covid-19, with remarkably low levels of cases, became ammunition to support its right to contribute directly as a participant in WHO discussions of the pandemic response. Eventually the WHO allowed experts from Taiwan to join online fora about the pandemic, but the government remains shut out of the WHA. This leads some to conclude that the organization "puts politics before public health" (Chen and Cohen, 2020). Whereas the PRC and ROC can share equal status within the WTO and ADB in discussions over economic policies,

46. "Menendez, Inhofe, Senators Urge Taiwan Participation in WHO," United States Senate Committee on Foreign Relations. https://www.foreign.senate.gov/press/ranking/release/menendez-inhofe-senators-urge-taiwan-participation-in-who. Accessed 27 August 2020.

47. Drew Hinshaw and Lukas I. Alpert, "U.S. Makes Diplomatic Push for Taiwan to Attend WHO Summit," *Wall Street Journal* 7 May 2020.

48. "Remarks by HHS Secretary Alex Azar at National Taiwan University," American Institute in Taiwan, 11 August 2020. http://www.ait.org.tw/remarks-by-hhs-secretary-alex-azar-at-national-taiwan-university/.

they are unable to do so within the WHO. Rivalry over economic gains is less severe than rivalry over representation. Since the WHO is a UN agency, the sovereignty stakes for participation in it are higher than those for other organizations. Governments among the WHO membership and in China and Taiwan have decided that the significance of sovereignty overrides the incentives to compromise for more efficient coordination within a multilateral setting.

The worsening relations between the ruling parties in Taipei and Beijing ensure that China will mobilize states to vote against any future entry into the WHO by Taiwan. While U.S. tensions with China increase its support for Taiwan's appeal to join the organization, they have also led China to issue vocal comments that it would use force to stop any steps by Taiwan toward independence. Consequently, there is little prospect for Taiwan to gain participation status, let alone membership. One could not find a more clear case for functional demand to achieve universal membership than the need for information sharing about a global pandemic in the WHO. Taiwan meets the criterion for performance as a strong state capable of contributing to global public health coordination, but its entry continues to be stymied. Because membership confers sovereignty, even universality has its limits.

8.5   Palestine

From the outset, membership in international organizations was central to the recognition of statehood for Israel and it increasingly plays a prominent role in the Palestinian search for equality as a sovereign state. Some would contend that the multilateral fora simply ratify decisions set in place by power politics. Yet major powers could not dictate the outcomes. Where superpower agreement ushered in recognition of Israel, steps toward recognition for Palestine show the limits of the U.S. ability to exclude actors from recognition as a state. The case of Palestine touches on complex politics that bring the Arab-Israeli conflict into debates over membership in international organizations.

As with the Koreas, the UN tried to broker the birth of states with the end of colonial rule. With the prospect following the end of WWII that Britain would end its mandate for Palestine, the UN established a commission in 1947 to examine the "Palestinian question." The commission recommendation to partition the land between two states formed the basis for the UN General Assembly to adopt Resolution 181 in November 1947, calling for the establishment of a Jewish state of Israel and an Arab state.[49] In the plan, the two states would form an economic union with a shared currency, and Jerusalem would be an autonomous international regime. The Palestinian groups and Arab states rejected the Partition Plan, however, and instead launched a failed attempt to seize the full territory through military force. This doomed the UN proposal of partition as a path to an independent state for Palestine. Israel rushed forward to declare independence even as war broke out. Ultimately, Israel won control over the land allocated by the Partition Plan for a Jewish state as well as part of the land that had originally been allocated to the Arab state. The remainder of the territory designated for the Arab state came under control of Egypt and Jordan through armistice agreements negotiated with Israel through UN mediation efforts.[50]

The establishment of Israel as an independent state in 1948 was quickly recognized by both the United States and the USSR in May 1948. Its government immediately applied for UN membership. A year later, the Security Council recommended UN membership for Israel. On 11 May 1949, the General Assembly voted in favor of membership over opposition by Arab states that walked out of the room to protest the outcome. The resolution noted that "in the judgment of the Security Council, Israel is a peace-loving State and is able and willing to carry out the obligations contained in the Charter," and was approved by 37 in favor, 12 opposed, with nine abstentions.[51] The ambassador of Lebanon, Charles Malik, objected to allowing Israel to claim territory beyond its share in the Partition Plan, and the representative of Denmark said it was premature to approve membership without resolving Israel's treatment of refugees, the status of Jerusalem, and justice against the radical Jewish group attributed with assassinating a UN mediator (Stauer, 2016, p. 87). But others insisted that the Security Council recommendation made further debate unnecessary. In a period when Cold War rivalries held up other membership cases, Israel benefited from the remarkable agreement between the United

49. The U.S. government backed Resolution 181. See https://history.state.gov/milestones /1945-1952/creation-israel.

50. See Stauer (2016) for detailed discussion of Partition Plan and its aftermath.

51. "Admission of Israel to membership in the United Nations: Resolution/adopted by the General Assembly," United Nations, 11 May 1949. https://digitallibrary.un.org/record/671023 ?ln=en. Accessed 1 August 2020. An initial Security Council vote taken in December 1948 failed due to abstentions from governments concerned about the ongoing conflict (Belgium, Canada the UK, France, and China). After fighting had ended, several of these governments agreed to support the recommendation, although the UK abstained from the 1949 vote.

States and the USSR. The USSR may have expected that Israel would lean toward it given the socialist orientation of some leaders (Stauer, 2016, p. 81). At the critical moment, Israel found both sides considering it a potential ally. In his first speech to the UN after the approval vote, the Israeli foreign minister, Moshe Sharett, emphasized Israel's policy of "loyalty to the fundamental principles of the United Nations Charter and friendship with all peace-loving states, especially with the United States of America and the Union of Soviet Socialist Republics."[52]

Israeli membership in the affiliated UN agencies soon followed. Israel faced some obstacles to entry into other international organizations due to opposition by Arab states, and at times suffered unequal treatment as a member, such as when Arab states refused to allow Israeli delegates to participate in activities in the regional offices of WHO. Nonetheless, Israel's gaining IGO entry allowed it, from the insider position as an established member, to confront later efforts by Palestine to join.

The future for Palestine as an entity in international society, however, remains undecided.[53] The Palestinian Authority (PA) continues its unsuccessful effort to gain UN membership. Even as many report the end of a viable two-state solution, Palestine has received recognition as a state by over two thirds of the UN member states.[54] Since 1974, Palestine has enjoyed observer rights at the United Nations, which was elevated to official status as a non-member observer state in 2012.[55] As one indicator of basic capacity, the per capita income of Palestine exceeds that of the bottom quartile of UN members (see Figure 8.6). But its requests for full membership in the UN in 2011 and again in 2019 were blocked by opposition led by Israel and the United States. While both North and South Korea were able to join the WHO and UPU in the 1970s long before the end of the Cold War and entry into the UN, Palestine has been rejected in its application to both.

---

52. Thomas Hamilton, "Israel Wins a Seat in U.N. by 37-12 Vote," *New York Times* 12 May 1949.

53. It is not included as a state in the COW IGO dataset, in contrast to Taiwan.

54. As of 31 July 2019, 138 of the 193 UN member states recognize the State of Palestine. Paul Scruton, Paddy Allen, and James Ball, "Which Countries Recognize Palestine Already?" *The Guardian*, 20 September 2011. Updated figures available at http://www.theguardian .com/world/interactive/2011/sep/20/palestinain-state-israel-un-interactive, Accessed 1 August 2020.

55. "3237 (XXIX) Observer Status for the Palestine Liberation Organization," United Nations General Assembly, 22 November 1974.

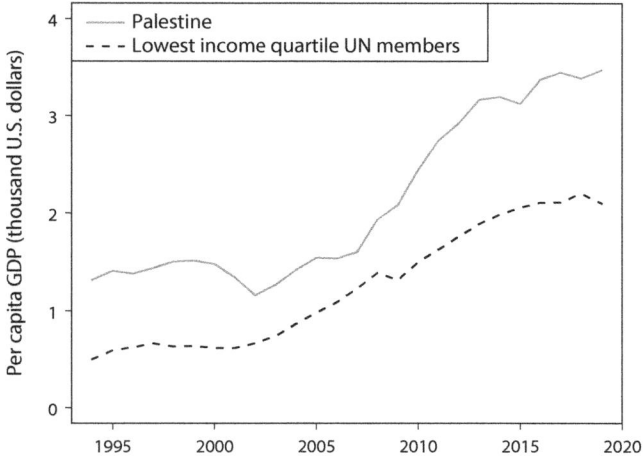

FIGURE 8.6. *Palestine income comparison*: The graph shows the per capita income in U.S. dollars for the Palestinian territories measured as the average for Palestine, West Bank, and Gaza. The second line indicates the average per capita income of the bottom quartile of UN members. Data are from World Bank 2020 World Development Indicators.

The Palestinian quest for international status has gone forward on two fronts, with direct negotiations with Israel and with indirect pressure through a campaign for entry into international organizations. As talks with Israel stalled, Palestinian diplomacy over membership gained increasing priority. PA president Mahmoud Abbas has insisted that the PA only seeks recognition of the natural borders of Palestine based on the 1967 settlement, and does not seek to delegitimize Israel (McMahon and Masters, 2012). While the U.S. government endorses the peace process goal for the creation of an independent Palestinian state, it has insisted that the conclusion of the peace process with Israel must precede entry into international organizations. At the time of the 2012 request for UN membership for Palestine, a State Department spokesperson articulated this viewpoint ahead of the vote: "We do not think that this step is going to bring the Palestinian people any closer to a state."[56] The opposition from the United States raises the stakes for its membership applications. When considering whether to apply for full membership in the WHO in 2018—Palestine has held observer status in the WHA since

56. "Palestinian Statehood at the UN," Council on Foreign Relations. https://www.cfr.org /backgrounder/palestinian-statehood-un. Accessed 18 June 2020.

1974—officials were persuaded against causing a controversy that could jeopardize their funding from WHO projects (Zarocostas, 2018). In this section, I focus on Palestine's 2011 membership entry into UNESCO, which itself sparked the eventual withdrawal from UNESCO by the United States and Israel.

8.5.1   UNESCO

The United Nations Educational, Scientific, and Cultural Organization is a UN-affiliated agency with a broad mandate. Central activities include education and preservation of culture. They relate to efforts focused on science and education, such as funding of schools and coordination for scientific societies. The scope of the mission allows UNESCO to actively engage in work promoting sustainable development and human rights. Its work for cultural preservation is most prominent in its role to determine World Heritage sites. The agency seems like a technical organization that might be apolitical, but it also intervenes in issues where there are controversial differences among members.

The inclusive mandate for membership is apparent in the accession terms, which allow automatic entry for UN members and a second track open to membership for non-UN members.[57] States that are not UN members must receive a recommendation from the elected Executive Board and approval by a two-thirds majority of members voting in the General Conference. In a critical point for Palestine, the United States does not hold a veto over membership in UNESCO.

The first request for Palestine's admission as a member state to UNESCO was submitted by Algeria, Indonesia, Mauritania, Niger, Senegal, and Yemen in May 1989, following the declaration of Independence of the State of Palestine on 15 November 1988 by the Palestine National Council. The document notes that "under public international law, a State is made up of three constituents: a population, a territory and a government."[58] This proposal failed to win approval. Twenty-two years later, however, Palestine succeeded in its

57. Automatic entry for UN members makes UNESCO more inclusive than the Food and Agriculture Organization or other such organizations that have open eligibility but still impose a stringent approval process of a two-third majority vote for all applicants.

58. Explanatory Note Concerning the Request for the Admission of the State of Palestine to UNESCO, UNESCO Executive Board Hundred and thirty-first session meeting (131 EX/43), Paris, 12 May 1989.

bid to join. Its engagement in the peace process with Israel expanded the legitimacy of the Palestinian state to represent territory. While not overcoming opposition from the United States, Palestine won the necessary support among members. Where China could sway opposition to Taiwan in the WHO, U.S. opposition was insufficient to exclude Palestine from UNESCO.

The vote on membership for Palestine followed the lines of geopolitical alignment, as the United States stood beside Israel and also swayed many of its allies to oppose or at least abstain from the vote. Palestine was approved by the required two-thirds majority, with 107 in favor, 14 voting no, 52 abstentions, and a few absences.[59] Australia, Canada, and Germany joined the United States to vote no, while Mexico, the UK, Japan, and South Korea were among the allies abstaining. Some allies, however, were among those that voted in favor of Palestine. NATO allies France and Turkey both joined the group voting yes. Many states in Latin America supported Palestine, with the two states most closely tied to the United States, Mexico and Colombia, joining the group to abstain. The leading push in favor of Palestine came from its Arab allies, along with support from Russia and China. Among the first countries to recognize Palestine as a state, China supports it with aid and diplomatic engagement at the highest levels, including at summit meetings.[60] Figure 8.7 shows the difference in geopolitical alignment across the groups for the vote on Palestine's membership in UNESCO, based on their overall pattern of voting in the United Nations General Assembly in 2011.[61] The group voting in favor of Palestine is notably more distant from the United States in overall foreign policy positions in the UN than the group that voted against Palestine. This reveals divisions along geopolitical lines even when the outcome itself went against U.S. demands.

Gaining membership had significant consequences for Palestine. Entry into a UN agency as a state immediately bolstered its standing within international law. On this basis, Palestine brought its first case to the International

59. "UNESCO Votes to Admit Palestine as Full Member," *UN News* 31 October 2011. Available at https://news.un.org/en/story/2011/10/393562-unesco-votes-admit-palestine-full-member. Accessed 9 April 2019.

60. "Xi Backs Palestinian Efforts," *People's China Daily* 19 July 2017.

61. The graph displays distance from the United States based on the UN ideal point. The measure aggregates UN voting records to estimate the dyadic difference between two countries' ideal points. Distance increases as the UN voting records of two states diverge (Bailey, Strezhnev, and Voeten, 2017).

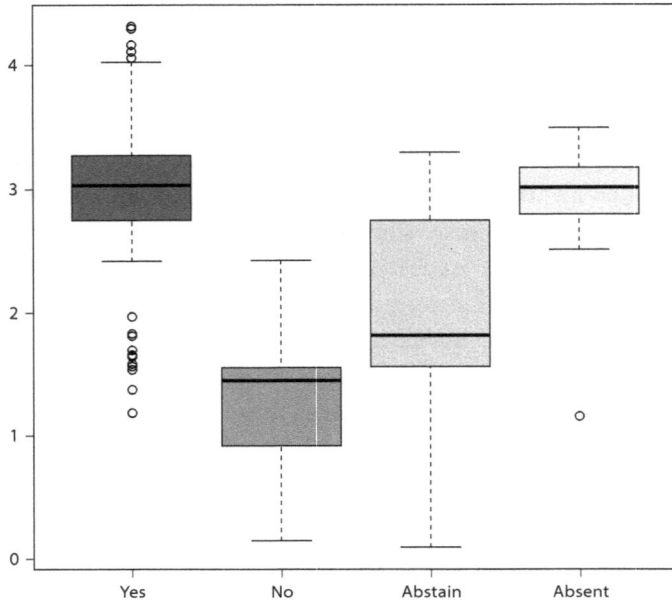

FIGURE 8.7. *Geopolitical alignment and UNESCO vote for Palestine*: The figure displays the UN ideal point distance from the United States for countries grouped by their vote in the 2011 vote on Palestine's membership in UNESCO. Data on UN ideal points are from Bailey, Strezhnev, and Voeten (2017).

Court of Justice, which has jurisdiction limited to states.[62] In a September 2018 claim against the United States, Palestine challenged that the U.S. decision to move its embassy to Israel from Tel Aviv to Jerusalem violated the Vienna Convention on Diplomatic Relations. The PA has also pursued membership in other UN agencies, with a few successes. More directly, Palestine enjoys benefits as a member of UNESCO, to influence important policies. When seeking membership in UNESCO in 2011, Palestine requested recognition of Bethlehem as a World Heritage site. The 2012 approval of the site served as a prominent acknowledgement of Palestine's new status as a UNESCO member, and would be followed by recognition of several more sites.

62. See the discussion, Vidmar, Jure, "Palestine v United States: Why the ICJ Does Not Need to Decide whether Palestine Is a State." Blog of the European Journal of International Law, 22 November 2018. Available at https://www.ejiltalk.org/palestine-v-united-states-why-the-icj-does-not-need-to-decide-whether-palestine-is-a-state/. Accessed April 2019.

UNESCO Director-General Irina Bokova described the vote as "a chance for all to commit once again to the values we share and not to be divided," but also noted,"I am worried we may confront a situation that could erode UNESCO as a universal platform for dialogue. I am worried for the stability of its budget."[63] On the other side, the decision was condemned by Israel, whose ambassador to the UN, Nimrod Barkan, stated that UNESCO members "have adopted a science fiction version of reality by admitting a non-existent state to the science organisation. . . . UNESCO should deal in science not science fiction."[64] Remarking on the juxtaposition of Palestine winning membership in UNESCO with the fact that its request, at the same time, for full membership in the United Nations had been denied, U.S. Secretary of State Hillary Clinton was reported to say, "I found quite confusing and somehow inexplicable that you would have organs of the United Nations making decisions about statehood or statehood status while the issue has been presented to the United Nations."[65]

The membership of Palestine triggered the United States to stop funding UNESCO in 2012. Legislation dictates ending payments to any UN organization that admits the PLO as a member.[66] Withdrawal of funds was a significant blow to the organization, given that U.S. funding had constituted a 22 percent share of the annual budget.[67] As provided for in the UNESCO charter, after a year of not paying dues, the United States lost voting privileges from 2013. UNESCO votes critical of Israel, such as one in 2016 that condemned Israeli policies to limit access to the Al-Aqsa Mosque, worsened the view of the organization in Israel and the United States. For several years this status quo continued, until in October 2017 both the United States and Israel announced their intention to withdraw from the organization.

63. See "UNESCO Votes to Admit Palestine as Full Member," 31 October 2011. Available at https://news.un.org/en/story/2011/10/393562-unesco-votes-admit-palestine-full-member.

64. "Palestinians Admitted to UNESCO as Full Member," Agence France Presse—English, 31 October 2011.

65. "Palestinian State Quest Wins First Victory in UNESCO Vote," *The Telegraph* 6 October 2011. Available at https://www.telegraph.co.uk/news/worldnews/middleeast/palestinian authority/8810255/Palestinian-state-quest-wins-first-victory-in-UNESCO-vote.html.

66. Section 414 of P. L. 101-246.

67. "Palestinians Admitted to UNESCO as Full Member," *Agence France Presse* 31 October 2011.

This divisive case highlights the role of membership approval as the key to sovereignty. Palestine has opted for a strategy to build its status through international organizations. After UNESCO membership, approval by the UN General Assembly of a resolution supporting nonmember observer state status was hailed by Palestinians as international acceptance of statehood. At the same time, without a breakthrough in its relationship with Israel and the United States, Palestine cannot become a UN member. Despite that reality, in January 2019, the PA renewed its formal application for UN membership. In terms of legal standing based on recognition by states, Palestine now has a strong case for membership. While unable to uphold full conditions of domestic sovereignty within its territory, Palestine is no weaker than other UN members such as South Sudan. But these are not the criteria on which states are selected to enter the UN.

8.6   Ostracism of South Africa under Apartheid

As discussed in chapter 2, expulsion of states from membership is extremely rare. Yet there are circumstances where joint association with another state becomes untenable. In order to become members in a discriminatory club, actors value joint association as well as the collective effort for provision of public goods. Factors that diminish the value of association can strain perceptions about continued cooperation independently of the capacity of the state to contribute. For an individual, a club's change in social norms toward in-group identification may lower its attractiveness to a fellow member. For governments, the perception of security interests and the collective perception of the like-minded status of another member country can also change. Other states may come to view such a state as a pariah unfit for peer association.

The experience of South Africa represents a unique prism for viewing membership politics in universal organizations. The state entered many multilateral organizations despite the pervasive racism in its domestic institutions and society. Two factors gave rise to the pressure for exclusion and expulsion of South Africa. First, as more African countries gained independence to become members themselves, they formed a core coalition opposed in principle to any interaction with the regime. The racist system of Apartheid represented an existential threat to newly independent governments fighting to establish their sovereignty as equals within international society. Second, as awareness of the injustices committed by the regime grew and values to

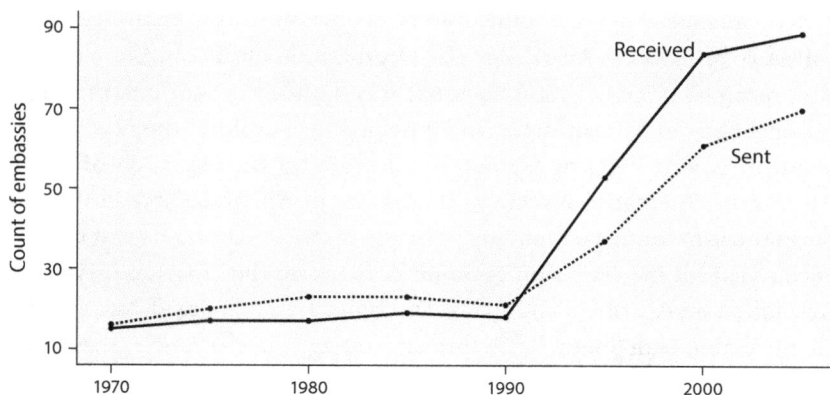

FIGURE 8.8. *Diplomatic ties of South Africa:* The figure shows embassies sent to foreign governments and received by South Africa.

protect human rights rose in the international arena among all countries, more and more governments sought to demonstrate their opposition to Apartheid. Both factors changed the willingness of other countries to engage in joint association with South Africa in international organizations. While unrelated to the ability of the South African government to comply with rules and contribute to cooperation on the issues regulated by IGOs, the change in association value directly impacted membership politics.

Much attention has been given to the economic sanctions imposed on the regime by national governments. They were more comprehensive than witnessed for almost any other human rights abuse, with a wide range of countries participating and a broad scope of trade and investment affected. Beginning in 1962, when the UNGA passed a resolution urging all UN members to cease trading with South Africa, the sanctions movement grew in momentum over the years. With the Comprehensive Anti-Apartheid Act passed in 1985, the United States deepened its effort with sanctions of not only trade but also airline travel and all investment. The sanctions are attributed to have played a significant role in the decision of the South African government to end the Apartheid system. The reliance on access to oil markets and foreign capital flows, and dependence on exports of materials, all made the regime vulnerable to the economic pressure (Manby, 1992). Refusing to exchange diplomatic representation was one way governments shunned the regime. Figure 8.8 shows the unusually low number of governments that maintained an embassy in South Africa under the Apartheid regime, and the rapid increase following the end of the system. Even sporting events excluded the country.

IGO membership was another means for governments to coordinate their collective rejection of Apartheid. The Organisation of African Unity (OAU, later renamed African Union, in 2002) was founded in 1963 constituting a regional body of African states, and it helped to coordinate the newly independent African states as a group to advocate for the expulsion of South Africa from international society. Elimination of Apartheid and all vestiges of colonialism formed a founding principle of the OAU, and its first conference called for the expulsion of South Africa from the UN, and it issued a Resolution on Apartheid and Racial Discrimination that urged states to end all interaction with South Africa through cutting consular relations and economic exchange.[68] In many of the most universal international organizations, repeated proposals demanded the expulsion of South Africa. Critical resolutions forced South Africa to exit the ILO, the WHO, UNESCO, the Food and Agriculture Organization (FAO), and others. The government was expelled from the UN General Assembly meetings, but did not lose its UN membership. These steps established South Africa as a pariah within international society. Manby (1992, p. 211) describes this pressure: "White South Africans see themselves as part of the Western democratic tradition: The isolation—sporting and cultural as well as economic—brought about by sanctions gave them an acute sense of vulnerability and a desire to be accepted back into the international community. This sense became that of the government also."

The end of the Apartheid system led states to withdraw sanctions and welcome South Africa as a full member of international society. After the election of Nelson Mandela to lead a new South Africa, the government entered many organizations where it was welcomed with open arms. Figure 8.9 shows that during the critical period of the 1980s, when opposition was at a peak, South African membership was held at a plateau, as it could not join new organizations and had been forced out of some. Other peers such as Egypt, Ethiopia, and Nigeria all saw a steady increase of memberships at this time, given the expansion of international organizations. With the 1990 release of Nelson

68. Alongside its exclusion of South Africa from its ranks, the OAU embraced universality for all states on the African continent to join; debates about whether to expel states for actions that undermined OAU principles, such as holding relations with South Africa or violations of human rights within their own borders, did not lead to expulsion (Tandon, 1972). The organization members defended sovereignty and resisted any interference in domestic affairs as part of the anti-colonial mission even as they opposed South Africa for its domestic system as part of the opposition to racism and colonial legacies.

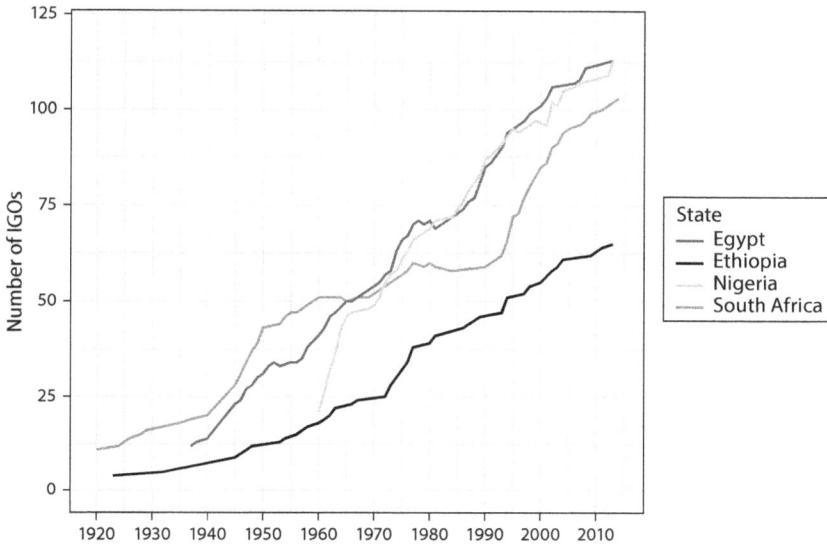

FIGURE 8.9. *South Africa's membership in IGOs*: The figure shows the number of IGOs to which South Africa belongs as a member in comparison with some other states in Africa.

Mandela and the start of negotiations to dismantle Apartheid, South Africa began to catch up with a rapid pace of IGO entry.

This case has many unique dimensions and revolves largely around a human rights debate, which is distinct from the argument of this book about geopolitical alignment. Nevertheless, it is important to ask whether even in the most sensitive issues geopolitical interests could intervene. In the debates over membership, states took sides along Cold War lines. Western governments condemned Apartheid but defended the right to membership for South Africa. Even as they accepted independence for their former colonies and took steps toward more racial equality at home, security dictated support for the South African regime that upheld Western interests in Africa. At the same time, the USSR and China rallied alongside the newly independent nations of Africa and the Middle East to pillory South Africa and call for its removal. Their statements on these matters both won points with other countries and contributed to removal of a state long seen as hostile.

The efforts to expel South Africa arose across many international organizations and reached different levels in limiting interaction. For some IGOs, this led to multiple instances of exit and reentry by South Africa (see Table 8.4). In an early exit, South Africa left UNESCO in 1955 to protest critical documents

IGO	IGO entry	IGO exit	Reentry	Exit	Reentry
ITU	1881				
UPU	1893	1979	1982	1984	1994
ILO	1919	1967	1994		
ICAO	1935				
FAO	1945	1964	1993		
World Bank	1945				
IMF	1945				
UN	1945				
UNESCO	1945	1955	1994		
WHO	1947				
WIPO	1975				
IMO	1995				
WTOURO	1997				
UNIDO	2000				

TABLE 8.4. *South Africa's membership in UN family IGOs.*

that it claimed were an interference in its domestic affairs; research studies that rejected doctrines of race superiority and called for the end of prejudice were seen as attacks (Phillips, 1968). The exits under criticism would continue. The ILO approved resolutions that invited South Africa to withdraw from participation, refused to approve credentials for South African workers to join in deliberations, and called for reports on Apartheid in labor matters—upon which the government chose to end membership in 1964 (ibid). Similarly, the WHO voted in the 1964 WHA to suspend South Africa from voting and the government gave notice it would stop participation. That same year the FAO voted to exclude South Africa from all activities in Africa, after which the government announced it would leave the organization (Bissell, 1974). The ITU voted to exclude South Africa from participating in plenary sessions in 1965, but allowed it to retain membership, and the government accepted this situation. ICAO passed resolutions of condemnation but did not exclude South Africa from activities. There was no attention to the case by the IMF or the World Bank, where South Africa has been a member from their founding, although not drawing on IMF loans during the Apartheid period. South Africa also could join WIPO in 1975 without any objections through automatic entry for UN members. UNIDO was established in 1966, and South Africa could have also joined as a UN member but chose not to join until well after the end of Apartheid. The UPU example of expulsion will be the focus of this case study.

8.6.1   Expulsion from the UPU

The UPU is both one of the oldest and one of the most open international organizations. Established in 1874 and integrated into the UN family as a specialized agency in 1948, the UPU seeks wide participation to facilitate its core function of coordinating the exchange of mail to achieve a *universal* postal service. Indeed, the charter refers to "country" rather than "state," as part of the original intent to include more than sovereign governments, and also territories under colonial administration. In 2021 the membership included 192 states. The original Treaty of Berne lacked any provisions on accession—it was an open treaty any entity could join by unilateral declaration, and membership status was simply indicated by the list of members. The 1947 Paris Congress added an accession process to require application, consultation, and approval by two thirds of members. But when formalized in the 1964 treaty revision Article 11, accession was simplified for UN members, who only need to provide notification of accession without any vote of approval, while non-UN members must receive approval by vote of two thirds of the members.[69] The treaty contains no provision on suspension or expulsion of members, although Article 12 outlines provisions for voluntary withdrawal. It also does not refer to human rights or democracy as a principle in the preamble to the organization.

In the midst of contending colonial forces and state formation, South Africa had joined the UPU in 1893.[70] Over 80 years later, it faced expulsion. It seems contradictory to discuss discrimination against South Africa over racial discrimination. The South African example represents international society ostracizing a state that was abhorrent to other members. Placing its expulsion from the UPU within a framework of discrimination against states does not imply a normative judgement. Rather, the intention is to focus on how global governance addresses the tension between inclusion and exclusion when dealing with states that reject accepted values of the community. The tool of discrimination that the South African regime applied to harshly

69. International Bureau of the Universal Postal Union (2018), "Constitution and General Regulations: Rules of Procedure Legal Status of the UPU with Commentary by the UPU International Bureau." Available at https://www.upu.int/UPU/media/upu/files/UPU/aboutUpu /acts/manualsInThreeVolumes/actInThreeVolumesConstitutionAndGeneralRegulationsEn .pdf.

70. This is the date that is listed as its entry date in UPU records. The data analysis for this book considers only independent states, so South Africa begins its membership in 1920.

oppress the Black population was invoked at the level of diplomacy against the state of South Africa with the goal of improving human rights.

South Africa's racist policies of separation drew broad condemnation from international society. From the outset, the UN General Assembly served as a forum for this criticism. The Indian delegation spoke of unjustified racial discrimination in remarks at the 1946 meeting of the newly formed international organization. While South Africa defended its position that the UN Charter excluded domestic policies from its jurisdiction, its challengers insisted that the human rights violations constituted a threat to international peace, and was subject to chapter 7 of the UN Charter (Ferguson, 1981, p. 205). In a 1974 debate in the UN Security Council over a proposal to expel South Africa from the UN, the delegate of Egypt said membership required adherence to the principles of the UN Charter, and "Once those principles have been violated purposely and repeatedly, it goes without saying that such membership would be nonexistent, null and void" (ibid, p. 208).

In these early years, the South African position in support of noninterference received backing from the U.S. and UK. In the first sally of membership disputes, when South Africa withdrew from UNESCO, the United States and UK passed a resolution calling for it to rejoin as a member (ibid, p. 206). In 1974, France, the United States, and the UK vetoed the draft resolution at the UN Security Council calling for the expulsion of South Africa from UN membership. The support for South African membership by the United States and UK lay partly in legal interpretation of sovereignty and the UN Charter, and fear of setting a precedent that would erode the institution's framework. The U.S. delegate John Alfred Scali explained that "we believe that a just solution of South Africa's racial dilemma indeed lies within South Africa itself. . . . Expulsion would set a shattering precedent. . . . It would bring into question . . . the concept of a forum in which ideas and ideals are voiced and revoiced along with conflicting views until elements of injustice and oppression are forced to give way to reason." UK representative Lord Ivar Richard said expelling South Africa would not change the government policy, and "The principle of universality is not one which my delegation will lightly sacrifice. We will certainly not sacrifice it for no sure return."[71] But at a more basic level, the defense of South Africa's UN membership also protected the status of a country that served their economic and security interests.

71. Security Council Official Records, 29th Year, 1808th Meeting, 30 October 1974, New York. http://digitallibrary.un.org/record/54817.

The geopolitical alignment of South Africa lay firmly in the Western camp during the Cold War. Troops from South Africa fought in the Korean War and the government coordinated with NATO on defense plans, which signaled clearly its geopolitical alignment with the United States (Bissell, 1974, p. 180). Alongside its policies of racial suppression, the Afrikaner Nationalist Party led the government from its election in 1948 and pursued brutal suppression of communism. The 1950 Suppression of Communism Act banned the Communist Party and defined communism broadly, so that any opposition could be portrayed as subject to its harsh rules for detention and torture, without access to legal defense. In regional proxy wars, South Africa found itself in opposition to the USSR and Cuba, who aided the Southwest African People's Organization in the border conflict during the Namibian war of independence in the 1960s and then aided the Popular Movement for the Liberation of Angola during the Angolan Civil War that raged for nearly thirty years from 1975. Even as the U.S. position grew more critical of South Africa on human rights, it did not reject dealing with the government that stood as a strategic outpost in a critical region with a staunchly anti-communist government (Thomson, 2008). Later evidence revealed that the U.S. support for South Africa in the Angolan conflict was quite extensive with military cooperation.[72] In the push between public sentiment and national security, divisions appeared within the U.S. government. When the United States shifted its foreign policy strategy toward South Africa from covert support and diplomatic pressure to one of comprehensive sanctions in 1986, the policy change came at the initiative of Congress over a veto by President Reagan, who continued to praise reform efforts of the government and criticize the African National Congress as "Soviet-armed guerillas"(Thomson, 2008, p. 146).

The UPU was a hard case for exclusion. First, under its rules, the United States and UK could not veto proposals to exclude South Africa, but neither could the members prevent South Africa from simply rejoining the next year. A UN member such as South Africa enjoyed automatic entry to the UN agency. This set up the spectacle of repeated exit and reentry. The commitment to universality made it challenging to exclude a country (Duxbury, 2011, p. 236). Second, the UPU charter did not provide a clear basis to judge South Africa's human rights as noncompliance. Its focus is postal service coordination as a technical agency—the core purposes of the organization as laid out

72. French, Howard W., "From Old Files, a New Story of U.S. Role in Angolan War." *The New York Times* 31 March 2002.

in the UPU Constitution Article 1 on Scope and Objectives include free transit of postal services and technical assistance to members for improvement of postal services. Third, there were no rules in the charter for suspension or expulsion.[73] This stands in sharp contrast to the UN rules, where expulsion of countries not following the principles of the organization was enshrined in Article 6 of the UN Charter, and Article 1 included explicit endorsement of human rights as part of the mission of the United Nations "To achieve international co-operation in solving international problems of an economic, social, cultural, or humanitarian character, and in promoting and encouraging respect for human rights and for fundamental freedoms for all without distinction as to race, sex, language, or religion."[74] From the standpoint of IGO purpose and design, we would expect that South Africa could have been expelled from the UN. This would also have ended its relationship with other organizations. But instead, South Africa retained its UN membership while losing in the UPU.

A series of proposals at the annual meetings of the Congress of the UPU demanded the expulsion of South Africa. The supporters used the violation of the Universal Declaration of Human Rights and UN Charter to call for expulsion but could not directly frame Apartheid as a violation of the UPU charter. The first initiative to expel South Africa came in June 1964, when the Congress of UPU adopted a resolution expelling South Africa. The vote passed with 58 in favor, 30 opposed, and 26 abstentions. Yet because the UPU did not have any rules for expelling a member state, the Secretary General interpreted the action as only suspending South Africa from the meeting of the Congress that year and it remained a member in good standing (Magliveras, 1999, p. 69). Countries that had voted negatively, including the United States, said it was wrong to vote on such a measure when the UPU charter did not provide for expulsion. A separate vote on the procedural question of whether Congress was competent to expel a member failed to achieve a quorum, as 59 countries refused to vote (six voted in favor, 55 against, and two abstained) (ibid, p. 71). The second initiative came in 1974 as a proposal from African members to amend the Constitution to include terms for expulsion of members

73. An attempt in 1947 to expel Spain through refusing to invite its attendance at the UPU conferences was rejected by members who supported continued UPU membership for Spain even as it was kept out of the United Nations. An attempt to expel Israel in 1984 was also rejected by members. See Magliveras (1999, pp. 68–69, 75).

74. UN Charter. Available at https://www.un.org/en/about-us/un-charter/full-text.

who have a policy of Apartheid or racial discrimination. Failing to achieve a two-third majority support, the amendment failed. But a motion did carry to prevent South Africa from participating in the Congress, which was a de facto suspension of its rights as a member.

Then in the third attempt, African and Arab states at the 1979 conference put forward the motion to take away membership status by a majority vote. In a secret ballot, this was passed by a majority (77 in favor, 44 against, 13 abstentions), over the objection by some that it was null and void, without legal effect (Magliveras, 1999, p. 74). The members of the European community opposed the measure as they said it had no legal basis in the UPU charter.[75] Japan objected to the amendment as "unconstitutional and inadmissible" (Duxbury, 2011, p. 236). Over objections, the resolution temporarily ended South Africa's status as a UPU member. Nevertheless, Given the open process for accession to the UPU by UN members, South Africa simply rejoined the organization in 1981. This replayed. Finally, in 1984, members voted to approve a resolution that South Africa could not use its UN member status to reenter the organization, and South Africa did not try again to challenge the point and let its membership status end.

The proposal to expel South Africa coincided with a period of reorientation in U.S. foreign policy to be more critical of the regime. The Carter administration brought in new attention to human rights, and specifically a high degree of pressure on South Africa to reform, as seen by U.S. support of a UN Security Council Resolution condemning Apartheid and the 1977 UN-imposed arms embargo on South Africa. The administration led a rethinking about Cold War diplomacy to recognize that support for harsh authoritarian regimes contributed to Soviet influence over countries and movements opposed to those regimes. Zbigniew Brzezinski told the South African ambassador that under no circumstances would the United States intervene to support the White-led government in Pretoria, "even if the communists were involved" (Thomson, 2008, p. 98–99). At the time of the 1979 conference, other foreign leaders could sense that the shift against South Africa included high-level pressure from the United States. While the Reagan administration favored working with the South African government over ostracism, support for sanctions within Congress signaled to other governments that their vote

75. Written Question No. 948/79, *Official Journal of the European Communities* 23, no. C41 (February 18, 1980). https://eur-lex.europa.eu/legal-content/EN/TXT/PDF/?uri=OJ:C:1980:041:FULL&from=RO.

to support isolation policies toward South Africa was unlikely to draw criticism from the United States. Geopolitical alignment with the West had helped South Africa withstand the campaign waged against its racist policies, but would no longer be sufficient.

The consequences of exclusion were largely symbolic. The government lost input into decision-making, as debates in the UPU over terminal dues for postal charges and the monetary units accepted for exchange led to decisions without input from South Africa. But mail continued to be delivered. In a South African newspaper, readers were assured that postal services would continue uninterrupted; Postmaster-General Mr. Louis Rive condemned the vote as "nonsense and mere political chicanery," and added that "it would appear that the Western bloc voted against our expulsion which is an encouraging sign."[76] Other stories noted that Taiwan as a nonmember of the UPU also receives mail without problems. Even the normative pressure of exclusion was lowered by the extra-constitutional nature of the action. Duxbury (2011) notes that an ad hoc application of membership sanctions such as those witnessed in the case of South Africa and the UPU will have lower perceived legitimacy than in cases where the sanctions have a basis in the violation of clear commitments within the organization.

Nevertheless, the status by association that comes from joint membership can signal the stability of a country as a partner. Whether in the eyes of investors or of internal resistance forces, a government shunned by the world looks weaker than a government with leaders posing for pictures at summits and deliberating the rules of global governance. Indeed, to be excluded from even the most technocratic and universal organization—the UPU—was a dramatic signal of rejection from international society.

None would attribute the loss of UPU membership as a decisive factor in persuading the government of South Africa to accept racial equality and end Apartheid. Even the role of economic sanctions is hard to identify given the concurrence of many pressures on the government for change. The end of the Cold War also played a role by reducing the value of the South African regime as a strategic ally and removing the excuse of countering a Soviet threat as justification for political suppression. Within months of the Berlin Wall coming down, the government released Nelson Mandela from prison in February 1990.

76. "SA postal expulsion "not serious," *The Argus*, 21 September 1979.

With the election of Nelson Mandela as president in 1994, South Africa entered a new period of hope for integration among people and in the world. The end of Apartheid opened the door for South Africa to return to membership in many organizations, including the UPU. In 1994 the UPU Congress meeting in Seoul passed the Resolution on the Removal of the Ban on Readmission of South Africa (Magliveras, 1999, p. 75). The end of discrimination within South Africa brought an end to discrimination against its association with international society.

8.7 Conclusion

Despite the soaring rhetoric about universal principles in the preambles of international organizations, most are selective. This chapter has shown the significance of alliance ties for entry into open eligibility international organizations, where one would least expect to find political favoritism. While open to all states, voting approval lets members exclude those they wish to keep out of the state system. The universality of the organizations magnifies the cost of remaining outside as both a loss of benefits and denial of association status.

When considering the screening of membership based on political ties, legal standing, and performance capacity, there is consistent if small support for the importance of geopolitical alignment. The relationship for diplomatic ties through embassies is less clear, contrary to the expectation that recognition by other states would enhance legal standing as a state and thereby increase the probability of acceptance in IGOs. Future work should examine the sequence by which IGOs and diplomatic embassies offer first recognition as a path to establishing sovereignty. The open eligibility organizations examined in this chapter show little preference for high income countries, although those with a large economy are more likely to become members. At a more disaggregated level, one would want to consider performative capacity tailored to the specific mandate of each international organization. Analysis of individual organizations would also offer more leverage into the demand side conditions that shape which countries seek entry; chapter 4 reveals a similar dynamic for security interests in shaping applications to the multilateral trade regime, but this chapter was not able to bring to bear detailed application data across organizations.

The case studies probe more closely the multiple levels at which political relations emerge in the context of membership debates. The Korean experience shows superpower rivalry as an obstacle for membership, and improved political ties as the solution. Taiwan confronts a sovereignty dispute with the PRC, which stands as a major power that is determined to both veto and mobilize opposition votes. This reality precludes Taiwan's membership in the UN family organizations in the forseeable future. Where opportunities have arisen to expand its participation, they have relied on the orientation of Beijing toward the party in power in Taiwan. The mixed record for Palestine falls along the lines of accession rules as it gains entry to inclusive organizations but remains outside organizations that provide a veto role to the United States. This was also the pattern for South Africa in reverse—majority voting allowed states to expel the Apartheid government from universal organizations even as the United States and its allies protected its UN seat. The rules are enabling of the geopolitical logic for inclusion and exclusion.

The process of gatekeeping over sovereignty involves veto rights and mobilization of coalitions for votes on membership. Great powers have shown their willingness to insist on their preferred roster of members in universal organizations, with other states often going along. The membership outcomes differ from those one would expect from a perspective of legitimacy or effectiveness.

IGO	IGO Formation	China (mainland) member years	Taiwan member years	Taiwan name
AARO	1962	Nonmember	1968–2021	ROC
ACWL	2001	Nonmember	2004–2021	Chinese Taipei
ADB	1966	1986–2021	1966–2021	Taipei, China
AIDC	1966	1972–1974	1966–1972	China
AOPU	1962	1975–2021	1962–1975	China
APEC	1989	1991–2021	1991–2021	Chinese Taipei
APFIC	1948	1993–2021	1949–1954	China
APO	1961	Nonmember	1961–2021	ROC
FAO	1945	1945–1948, 1973–2021	1949–1952	China
IAEA	1957	1984–2021	1957–1971	China
IBE	1929	1934–1949, 1971–2021	1949–1971	China (Formosa)
IBRD	1945	1945–1949, 1980–2021	1949–1980	China
ICAC	1939	Nonmember	1963–2021	Taiwan
ICAI	1934	1936–1951, 1960–1968	1951–1959	China
ICAO	1919	1947–1948, 1971–2021	1949–1971	China
ICMMP	1921	1931–1949, 1990–2021	1949–1989	China
IHO	1919	1921–1949, 1977–2021	1949–1977	ROC
ILO	1919	1919–1949, 1971–2021	1949–1971	China
IMF	1944	1945–1949, 1980–2021	1949–1980	China
IMO	1950	1973–2021	1958–1971	China
INTELSAT	1964	1977–2001	1972–1976	ROC
INTERPOL	1923	1984–2021	1961–1984	China
IOEz	1924	1992–2021	1954–2021	Chinese Taipei
ITU	1865	1920–1949, 1972–2021	1949–1972	China
IUPCT	1890	1890–1949, 1977–2021	1949–1976	China
PCA	1899	1910–1949, 1973–2021	1949–1973	China
UN	1945	1945–1949, 1971–2021	1949–1971	China
UNESCO	1945	1946–1949, 1971–2021	1949–1971	China
UPU	1874	1914–1949, 1972–2021	1949–1972	China
WHO	1946	1946–1949, 1972–2021	1949–1972	China
WMO	1947	1972–2021	1951–1972	China
WTO	1995	2001–2021	2002–2021	Chinese Taipei

TABLE 8.5. *Taiwan's membership in IGOs*: The table lists the shift of membership between the government located in mainland China and the government located in Taiwan, along with the name used by Taiwan. The list of IGOs are from the Correlates of War International Organizations data, and Taiwan member years have been corrected for accuracy when information is available. The year span of this table ends in 2021. Note that in some cases the organization has ceased to exist or the end year of membership has not been confirmed. In the WTO and ACWL, the formal name of Taiwan is Separate Customs Territory of Taiwan, Penghu, Kinmen and Matsu. Where no information differentiates a specific name for Taiwan, the table entry is "China."

9

Revisiting Anarchical Society

THE MEMBERSHIP politics of IGOs hold broader implications for our understanding of international institutions. This chapter reviews the findings of the book and examines how the process of joining IGOs transforms cooperation. The geopolitical logic of IGO membership channels the interaction of states in ways that strengthen security coalitions and broaden economic exchange. This can lead to challenges for understanding the overall impact on cooperation. First, to what extent do institutional ties reinforce or even aggravate geopolitical divisions? When institutions form discriminatory clubs, cooperation expands along familiar cleavages of security interests. Geopolitical rivalries also generate balancing in the sphere of multilateral governance. The biases that arise from membership selection must be taken into account when researchers evaluate the impact of IGOs on security cooperation. Second, does the practice of discriminatory membership help or hinder the effectiveness of IGOs to promote cooperation? On the one hand, building on prior ties promotes the cohesion of a community, but on the other hand, selecting on characteristics outside the rules may reduce performance. Politicized selection also connects to the legitimacy of IGOs. This highlights the difficulty of accurately assessing the net gains for policy outcomes.

Finally, the chapter examines how IGOs evolve to provide structure for international society. Given an underlying demand to discriminate, expanding membership in IGOs will in turn generate new pressures for the proliferation of international organizations. States create new institutions as a tactic to continue the practice of discrimination and adapt to the problem of overexpansion. Forming institutions also follows major changes within states in their regime or foreign policy, which can lead them to change their circle of association. In their membership choices, states adjust their position within international society. Through setting standards for recognition and expulsion, they guide the behavior of other states.

9.1   What We Have Learned

This book encourages a view of organizations as a community based on relationships. States come together to accomplish specific tasks for mutual gain, but these acts occur within a larger process of social engagement. Any task represents an opportunity to build association with others. The theory of IGOs as discriminatory clubs builds on the assumption that the utility of membership consists of both the provision of goods and the association with other states. For states, these conditions lead to favoring allies. To the extent this introduces selection on criteria unrelated to performance, it is discriminatory and can bias the cooperation that results.

Design Choices

When designing rules over membership, states must decide what will serve as the exclusion mechanism. From comparison of more than 300 IGOs, this book reveals high barriers to entry are common, but the conditions of entry are not very specific. Through limiting eligibility, states narrow the range of potential applicants. Regional boundaries are the most common, and yet even in this category of IGO selection, states can leave room for interpretation and choice. The additional requirement for member approval plays the largest role in selecting members, and is entirely discretionary. Given the absence of precise conditions in the charter, members can make their decisions on approval based on the qualifications they deem to be important for selecting members. The book finds broad support for the hypothesis that states choose to design IGO membership to provide discretion over selection.

It is the combination of selective eligibility with vague conditions that helps IGOs to form a discriminatory club. The accession rules form an exclusion mechanism that gives discretion to states, which facilitates the subjective evaluation of applicants based on capacity and the value of association. The prevalence of this design affirms that states seek to maximize their control and flexibility in the domain of choosing partners. They neither view potential applicants as anonymous actors nor seek to bind their choices with fixed rules.

Alternative design choices address the depth-breadth trade-off. Organizations can be more rigorous in evaluation or more inclusive of eligibility. The strongest option for deep cooperation within an issue area occurs when states conduct meritocratic screening with an assessment of policy consistency. This ideal type assures maximal coherence within a group, and it envisions gradual enlargement when preferences among states converge or the benefits induce reforms for the sake of entry. In contrast, universal organizations that allow open eligibility promote broader cooperation. Full equality in an inclusive organization is consistent with the mandate to allow participation by all states. But given distributional conflict and inefficiency of collective decisions in a heterogenous group, these organizations often exhibit lower ambition of commitments. Within inclusive organizations, differentiation among members can establish a hierarchical organization for allocation of benefits that may support deeper cooperation.

The large majority of IGOs are designed as clubs, but meritocratic or universal IGOs also engage in geopolitical discrimination. Rather than a new way of categorizing IGOs, we need a new perspective on the logic of cooperation. Because IGOs produce both cooperation and community, states select partners with attention to the performance capacity and association value. This dynamic is present to some degree across all IGOs.

State behavior can deviate from the formal rules for membership. In practice, organizations may impose meritocratic screening for compliance even when the charter terms are general. Indeed, we see organizations like the WTO and OECD conduct extensive working party and committee meetings to evaluate candidates despite the vague terms in the charter over accession. Over time the accession process for the WTO and OECD increased demands for reforms on recent applicants relative to applicants in earlier years. Nevertheless, there is wide latitude for exceptions within this practice of rigorous review. The working parties can demand more than existing rules and allow reservations that exempt some areas from compliance. Looking at the pattern of entry we see strong evidence for geopolitical favoritism that continues in the OECD and WTO. The informal practice of rigorous review does not constrain states acting within a club IGO, and in some cases will become a mere charade. The most meritocratic organizations are also susceptible to manipulation of membership, as seen in the case of European enlargement.

Nevertheless, members send a stronger signal to applicants when the charter mandate includes rigid entry criteria or specific terms for expulsion based on noncompliance. The review processes conducted by IGO officials and national-level representatives takes place within a principal agent context, and guidance to participants on both sides of the review process about the criteria would limit their autonomy. Hooghe et al. (2017, p. 20) write that "the formal rule casts a long shadow even in the presence of an informal rule." A charter that specifies that compliance with all terms of the agreement will be reviewed as a condition for membership sets the benchmark for higher review than one without any such clause. Formal provisions to expel states that fall out of compliance with rules reinforces the expectation of member adherence to commitments. In the design of IGOs, what is *not included* matters as much as the rules that are specified. Even when practice includes a performance review, the absence of precise accession terms in the charter lowers the level of attention to compliance.

One can contrast the flexibility over exclusion with the enforcement of compliance through dispute settlement and suspension. Many IGOs, especially those in the area of economic policy, include specific and detailed provisions on how to resolve disputes. Legalization and the use of dispute settlement represent important trends for international cooperation (Abbott et al., 2000; Alter, 2014). The embrace of a punitive approach to noncompliance has been much slower in the domain of membership rights. Some regional IGOs with a formal commitment to democracy have begun to add to their toolkit explicit terms for suspension of member rights in democratic backsliding by members (Emmons, 2022). But across the larger sample of IGOs examined in this book, suspension for noncompliance (as opposed to nonpayment of dues) is rare. Expulsion is largely absent. The terms for dispute settlement set moderate punitive steps within a specific claim, without reference to potential suspension of membership for noncompliance. The equivalent is a renter agreement that includes details for a tenant to be fined for failure to pay rent or being a public nuisance, without any reference to actions that would justify eviction.

A common feature of membership provisions for IGOs is the lack of definitions. Regional organizations mention a region without setting geographic boundaries. This has been a permissive factor to allow geopolitical alignment to play as large a role as distance to shape who joins a regional organization. Universal organizations refer to eligibility of all states without resolving the challenge of defining what constitutes statehood. This sets up the role of international organizations as gatekeepers—as a form of recognition, IGO membership validates the sovereignty of a state.

The evidence of this book shows that international organizations often follow the discriminatory club model. This appears in both the evaluation of the formal charters, and in observation of practices across different sets of organizations. Multilateralism upholds the principle of nondiscrimination among members for their policy coordination, but does not restrict the range of criteria that could discriminate in the choice of members.

Favoring Friends

Having given themselves wide range for discretion, states frequently use geopolitical alignment to guide membership decisions. This arises on the demand side, when states choose whether to seek entry or form an organization, and also shapes evaluation by other states on whether to approve membership. In the case of the multilateral trade regime, where detailed information tracks when states apply for membership, it was possible to isolate the demand side to show that security ties were a significant factor in explaining who applied more rapidly for membership. In the invitation-only OECD, the leadership of the organization and member governments encouraged Brazil to apply, but met with little interest from Brazilian leaders, who preferred to distance Brazil from the West. Only after a foreign policy shift did Brazil ask to be considered for membership. These cases highlight geopolitics as a force of attraction for entry into international organizations, irrespective of the issues regulated by the rules.

Security ties also smooth the pathway into the organization, with shorter and easier negotiations for allies than adversaries. While the trade regime now appears like a nearly universal organization, countries like Japan and Korea joined sooner than expected, with fewer concessions at entry, while those like China and Russia were delayed in their entry. Later entry meant there were more agreements to implement as part of accession, and bargaining also extracted deep concessions. The U.S. holdup of Iran's entry into the WTO and Russian entry into the OECD continues today. Comparatively, Japan and Korea were allowed into GATT and OECD while retaining substantial dimensions of industrial policy and capital controls.

Even within regional organizations and universal organizations that offer less scope for discretion, there is a positive effect of security ties with members. In case studies, a more nuanced look at foreign policy interests shows evidence of geopolitical interests outside of what could be captured by alliance ties or UN voting patterns. The exclusion of Turkey from Europe and departure of Britain both reveal the limits of the NATO alliance to push integration, but also highlight local conflicts in the region over foreign policy goals. The evolution of ASEAN closely followed shifting security interests, although none of the states held alliances with each other. From its origin as a regional organization built around an anti-communist security orientation to its more general commitment to nonintervention and balancing against outside powers, ASEAN's borders of Southeast Asia expanded. UN membership for the two Koreas was impossible until the end of the Cold War, and the breakthrough came from improved relations for South Korea with the Soviet Union and China, rather than from a shift of alliances. No single variable can explain a complex decision over membership. Foreign policy issues shape the political relations between states in ways that can provoke a veto player or thaw tensions.

Alongside geopolitical alignment, the gains of expected cooperation on other dimensions also come into play. The evidence from chapter 3 on membership in multilateral economic organizations highlights that security ties sort states into organizations as part of a weighted decision balancing trade and security ties between states. Security ties contribute to sorting more than 40 percent of membership outcomes in the dataset, which is substantial considering that these are *economic* organizations. The importance of security interests as a condition for joint military action is not itself surprising, but the significance of security interests as a factor for multilateral economic cooperation is notable. The example of Japan revealed how far the United States would go to support an ally's entry into the GATT, as the United States offered concessions without requiring substantial reforms by Japan. Letting Turkey join the OECD or Bulgaria join the EU may not have raised the standards of the organization for corporate governance or for trade in goods and capital. Such entry cases placed a heavier weight on the security component, while other entrants earned their entry more on the promise of their contribution to uphold trade and capital flows.

Alternative criteria are possible—individual cases will give rise to their own logic, whether it be religion, race, or another source of affinity. In their classic study about the expansion of international society, Bull and Watson (1984) ascribe standards of civilization that dictated who belonged. They explain how a new order of sovereign states emerged out of the European state system. First through imperialism and then through the adoption of European norms in a postcolonial order, the new order included those who accepted a European structure of states as sovereign entities. Other research has highlighted the importance of ideology and regime type as unifying frames for understanding shared features of states within international institutions (Mansfield and Pevehouse, 2006; Poast and Urpelainen, 2013; Obydenkova and Libman,

2019; Voeten 2021). These concepts overlap with geopolitical alignment in theory and measurement, making it difficult to identify distinct causal arguments comparing European civilization, liberal ideology, and democracy.

This book presents evidence for the importance of geopolitical alignment as one prominent criterion, but it is not at the exclusion of the other factors. The core claim about discriminatory clubs is that selection arises from features connected to association value, not just performance capacity. When civilization, ideology, democracy, or other factors contribute to the value of association to bias selection, these alternative criteria still follow the discriminatory logic. Evidence that alternative criteria dominate to the exclusion of security ties would falsify my claim about the importance of geopolitical alignment. Evidence that membership selection is a function of expected performance without attention to relational attributes of states would falsify my claims about the importance of IGOs as a discriminatory club. The consistent pattern in which security ties influence membership in economic organizations, where security lies outside the performance of the IGO, provides strong support for both the discriminatory logic and the geopolitical criterion that produce geopolitical discrimination.

It would go beyond the scope of this book to explain the origins of alliances, but it is also important to acknowledge that alliances are not exogenous to the wider system of relationships. The argument of this book could equally apply to the choice of alliance partners—states select allies based on both performance needs (classic realist theories of threat and capability) and non-security attributes of the partner that create value from association. Concepts such as civilization, ideology, and regime also contribute to alliance ties and the broader geopolitical alignment that is central to this book. Some alliances rise and fall directly with security threats, such that one might entertain a notion of independence from shared values, but in most cases alliances represent complex institutions based on a multifaceted set of interests. Threat perceptions underlie whether states decide to balance or bandwagon, and interoperability of war plans as well as exit options shape bargaining over alliance agreements (Walt, 1985; Wallander and Keohane, 1999; Poast, 2019). Yet constructivist critics highlight the subjective nature of threats, and the Copenhagen School portrays security as a set of interests that are embedded within a regional security complex arising from interdependence as well as geography and power (Buzan and Waever, 2003). Any measure of security ties will inevitably capture these other conditions that contribute to alliance formation. Voeten (2021, p. 102) comments that his measure of ideology in terms of UN voting shows high similarity to that of alliance portfolios. The endogeneity of security ties to other characteristics of states limits our ability to make strong causal inference about how security ties shape cooperation. At best, we can observe that the correlation is very robust across specifications that control for confounders related to development levels, location, colonial history, and regime.

At the same time, the neglect of the relationship between security ties and membership in IGOs leaves out a key component of cooperation. Several studies find that states with more membership in IGOs are less likely to engage in conflict (Russett, Oneal, and Davis, 1998; Boehmer, Gartzke, and Nordstrom, 2004). Others compare how the member composition of IGOs influences their success at conflict mediation (Hansen, Mitchell, and Nemeth, 2008). The selection effect demonstrated in the analysis of this book points to complementarity of security interests prior to joining the IGO. Any study examining the effect of cooperation in the IGO on security cooperation is open to the possibility of a spurious correlation generated by the selection bias at entry—some component of the IGO effect on security arises from this selection bias. As a result, research into the pacifying effect of IGOs may overestimate the security gains. More attention to the overlap of membership and interests across issues can yield important new insights. For example, the security interests of members in regional economic organizations has led some to engage directly in security cooperation (Haftel and Hofmann, 2019). The research agenda on how IGOs impact peace should take into account the selection effect of alliances on IGO membership.

9.2 Geopolitical Discrimination and Cooperation

This book focused on the politics of membership from the perspective of decisions to join or exit organizations. These choices naturally anticipate the effect of membership. From functional theories to relational theories, states are viewed as strategic actors who pursue goals based on their preferences for outcomes. A large body of scholarship examines the effects of institutions. How do the biases in IGO membership highlighted in this book shape the effectiveness and legitimacy of institutions? This section will discuss some of the implications and ideas for a future research agenda.

Deepening Relationships and Rivalries?

By sorting states into like-minded groups for joint activities, IGOs deepen their relationships. After entry, states engage in collective action for mutual gain, as expected from the functional theories of international institutions (Keohane, 1984). Repeated interactions offer opportunities for socialization for states to bring their behavior closer to expected norms (Johnston, 2001; Greenhill, 2010). Where disagreements arise, dispute settlement mechanisms offer an outlet for managing the problems (Davis, 2012). All of those mechanisms by which institutions are expected to promote cooperation help the members achieve better outcomes.

States that have agreed to cooperate within the institution gain opportunities to further expand their security cooperation. First, they are less likely to engage in conflict as a direct function of their membership. Kinne (2013a, p. 660) argues that the difficulty of joining IGOs makes them useful signals that "convey strategically valuable information to prospective partners" that a state is trustworthy. In his theory, sharing a portfolio of IGO memberships creates a *friends of friends* dynamic that corresponds to lower conflict. Second, joint membership helps promote new cooperation achievements. Security coalitions that led states into the IGO continue to require consolidation with additional side payments and favors. Many missions will require skillful negotiation to persuade others to join—an alliance formed against one threat does not automatically transfer to joint action on all security issues, and states may also seek support from more states that are not joined in formal alliances. Henke (2019) shows that states use their diplomatic embeddedness as a resource to strengthen security cooperation. In Henke's theory, IGOs support allied partners as a forum for exchange of information and venue with opportunities for issue linkage, and she presents evidence of how multilateral institutions outside of security organizations help states to negotiate specific actions, such as participation in a peacekeeping mission. This brings a social-institutional perspective to understanding cooperation—Henke's theory presents network ties in multilateral institutions as a cooperation multiplier. The starting point of network ties in discriminatory IGO clubs lays a foundation for this process, which will further expand cooperation among member states.

While the in-group selection dynamic deepens cooperation within IGOs, it is possible that out-group hostility could worsen as a result of exclusion from IGOs. The opportunity to offset conflict on the security dimension with cooperation in other spheres is lost by the tendency to screen adversaries out of IGOs. Indeed, Carnegie (2015) argues that adversaries benefit the most when allowed to join institutions, because they would otherwise be constantly subject to the threat of holdup, which can suppress cooperation. The neo-functional theorists who saw European integration as the way to end wars in

Europe aspired to using cooperation over mundane technocratic issues as an opportunity for spillover to build better relations between the former enemies Germany and France (Haas, 1958). In the formation of discriminatory clubs based on geopolitical alignment, states are closing off this route to cooperation among rivals. Furthermore, the act of exclusion as a negative sanction raises hostility. The refusal to cooperate also conveys reluctance to share information. In short, the possibility of joint membership itself raises the stakes by presenting states with a choice that will signify a parting in the road toward more or less cooperation. When considering the counterfactual to joining an IGO, nonmembership represents a step back from the pre-IGO level of relations.

Impact for IGO Effectiveness

Discrimination over selection may lower the quality of cooperation on the single dimension of cooperation on the issue. The attention to extraneous factors to select members lowers their quality relative to those that would be selected strictly on a meritocratic review of performance capabilities. Of course, the characteristics that bring high status of association may positively correlate with characteristics that bring high performance, which would reduce any impact on cooperation outcomes. In some cases, allied states may be the most capable cooperators on the issue. But when states with strong security ties may otherwise be less qualified, the tip in their favor will lower the average capabilities.

Favoritism to friends also represents a form of patronage that lowers the effort when applicants are not expected to earn entry by showing their willingness to reform. The case study evidence highlighted allies that gained entry while making few reforms. Absent alliance ties, a government would have had to offer more concessions to persuade other states it is a suitable member.

The evaluation of institutions on the single dimension of performance is misleading, however, given the wider goals states hold for organizations. States discriminate over entry because their utility function includes both performance contribution for the collective good and the attributes of those they associate with in the organization. Letting security impact selection lowers the group production of the collective good but offers value on the association dimension of IGO membership.

Candidates that gain entry through discrimination will raise cooperation levels when they comply. The prestige of a golf club membership may bring into the club some who have no aptitude for golf but aspire to belonging to elite circles, and eventually they too will learn the game of golf! Indeed, as states that would not otherwise have had convergent preferences and high performance, the unlikely cooperators make a significant contribution. For example, when Poland joined the GATT before adopting a market economy, it still agreed to expand the volume of imports. Japan's membership in the ILO in 1919 led it gradually to offer more rights to labor unions. Even if these states are joining to signal their foreign policy orientation, their entry begins the process of commitment and socialization with real reforms implemented over years. The lack of rigid accession based on compliance reviews means such countries could join, and then they are subject to all of the pressures imposed by the IGO to adjust their policies.

Furthermore, the similarity of security interests may compensate for lower performance capacity and bring greater compliance. Like-minded states with higher levels of trust can sustain cooperation through community norms. The OECD upholds some of the most rigorous standards for conduct of business and other regulatory policies, despite the absence of any legalized dispute resolution mechanism. Its peer review process applies compliance pressure, which is more effective among a group of states that are held in high esteem and share overlapping interests. Therefore, in equilibrium the discriminatory club may yield high benefits through alternative channels that yield broader and deeper cooperation.

The rarity of exclusion preserves its strength as leverage against pariah states. Decades of exclusion and the extreme actions of expulsion from universal IGOs raised the pressure on South Africa until it ended the Apartheid system. Iran came to the table for nuclear talks in the hopes it would gain a release on the hold for entry into the WTO, and normalize trade to free its economy from the burden of sanctions. But the sovereignty role of IGO membership may increase the stakes of membership in a way that limits cooperation, such as seen in the cases of Palestine and Taiwan. Few would disagree on the value of their participation in the WHO for the sake of global public health cooperation, but their path to entry is fraught with political controversy, because it means so much more than sharing information about health. In the case of South Africa, exclusion brought dramatic internal reforms, while in the case of Taiwan, exclusion denies the IGOs the input from a prosperous and successful government.

It is challenging to analyze the net effect of membership on cooperation because the intentional screening at entry makes it impossible to consider IGO members as a random sample of countries. The effect of the sorting process on cooperation is equally hard to identify. Future research must consider what are the appropriate benchmarks for cooperation outcomes. Should states' compliance be judged on a single performance dimension of IGO rules when they were not selected on that basis? If not, how would one assess the wider range of relational output gained from joint interaction in the IGO?

Impact for IGO Legitimacy

Although discrimination carries the connotation of unfair and negative bias, what does it mean at the level of states? In the domestic context, selection procedures are deeply connected to the legitimacy of government. IGOs need legitimate authority to exercise power over state behavior. Scholars examine the characteristics that endow international institutions with legitimacy and the limits on their authority (Franck, 1990; Hurd, 1999; Hooghe, Lenz, and Marks, 2019). Therefore, it is important to consider how the politics of membership could impact legitimacy.

The discretionary rules of IGO accession leave decision-making authority about membership in the hands of states. This increases actor-based legitimacy from a perspective of deference to the authorities that represent governments. Rather than international bureaucrats reviewing applications, a state-centered approach respects sovereignty and the decentralized nature of international cooperation in anarchy. When governments decide whether to join IGOs with states that are high performers or like-minded states, their choice will attain legitimacy through the authority of the states.

Excluding states with an interest in global governance, however, undermines equality, and adding informal criteria outside the IGO mandate reduces transparency and rule of law. This may lower procedural-based legitimacy. On the one hand, perception of universal principles and fair procedures uphold legitimacy for IGOs (Lenz and Viola, 2017; Tallberg, 2019). Some argue that impartiality and heterogenous membership endow IGO approval with force over public opinion when it comes to authorization of military intervention (Thompson, 2006; Chapman, 2011; Recchia and Chu, 2021). On the other hand, the public of a member state may be more likely to support cooperation conducted by allied states (Carnegie and Gaikwad, 2022).

Most importantly, selection bias over who joins could support maintenance of other norms of multilateralism that call for collective decision-making and nondiscrimination among members. International affairs has long been unequal, with compromised sovereignty and exclusionary practices in international organizations and balance of power politics (Krasner, 1999; Las-curettes, 2020; Viola, 2020). The discriminatory club nature of IGOs is one more piece of evidence that international norms are subject to compromise. It may be necessary to allow discrimination over entry in order to achieve nondiscrimination among members.

9.3   The Evolution of Cooperation

Proliferation of IGOs

The twentieth century witnessed an explosion in the number of IGOs. From a small number of universal organizations, the population has expanded to include narrow technical organizations, regional groupings, and many that govern wide swathes of policy-making from trade to environmental policy. Often this gives rise to overlapping institutions (Aggarwal, 1998; Alter and Meunier, 2009). Whether in trade, environment, or development assistance, we observe multiple institutions dedicated to supporting cooperation on the same issues, with some including overlapping memberships and mission goals, while others separate states into different clusters (Davis, 2009; Keo-hane and Victor, 2011; Pratt, 2021). Resources available within the context of competing organizations offer an ecological perspective on the evolving population of IGOs (Abbott, Green, and Keohane, 2016). Failures of exist-ing institutions to adjust to shifting power balances or issue agenda can lead disgruntled states to support the formation of a new IGO (Morse and Keo-hane, 2014; Pratt, 2021). The nature of the issue area for externalities will constrain the ease with which states exit and the pressure on IGOs to adapt (Lipscy, 2017). Alongside these structural explanations, how do relationships among states within international society contribute to the pattern of IGO proliferation? There are several reasons to expect that the nature of IGOs as discriminatory clubs encourages the creation of new IGOs.

First, the status benefit achieved from membership in IGOs carries a higher premium in a small club than in an organization that has accepted nearly all states. This need for differentiation supports a larger number of IGOs. From the perspective of institutional choice, Jupille, Mattli, and Snidal (2013) argue that the transaction costs of building new institutions turns existing arrange-ments into the default option; states only create new institutions when the current ones are inadequate. The relational value of being a member in an IGO adds a new dimension in this calculation. To the extent a new IGO lets states signal their quality through advertising their close association with a particular group of states, the creation of a new IGO may be justified. The case studies of Eastern Europe in this book showed early efforts to join GATT as the first movement toward more independence from the USSR, which was cemented with membership in the OECD and EU after the end of the Cold War. Postwar Japan raced to join any organization that would accept it as part of the road to normalization after its defeat in WWII. Alongside joining existing institutions, states trying to establish their new identity can also form new IGOs. Poast and Urpelainen (2013) argue that the formation of new IGOs serves a special role for democratizing states that must demonstrate a capacity to provide public goods before they are able to join the higher demand institutions. Given crowding for status, existing IGOs may be reluctant to allow newcomers to join, making IGO formation the necessary first step to entering international society with those who will agree to common association.

Second, balance of power politics can also lead states to form rival IGOs. This book highlighted how the OECD plays a role as the economic complement to NATO, forming a broader quasi-alliance to unify the "West." Its counterpart in the East was the COMECON, formed in 1949, and subsequently the Commonwealth of Independent States, formed in 1991. There are some indications that the Shanghai Cooperation Organisation fills this role for China and Russia today. We cannot think about the emergence of these organizations independently of the population of IGOs, and how states that cluster in their IGO memberships could lead to the separation of states into competing diplomatic blocs. The interdependence of ties among states that form a network has been shown in the context of bilateral agreements as well as diplomatic recognition (Kinne, 2013b, 2014). There is also evidence that IGOs form clusters among regions (Greenhill and Lupu, 2017). Regional organizations show interdependence in their evolution in terms of design elements and membership (Jetschke and Lenz, 2013). This highlights the importance of future research into dynamic trends in the IGO network from a perspective of membership and geopolitical alignment. Do nodes that connect rival states decrease over time as the logic of separation pulls states into distinct clusters, with fewer and fewer shared ties?

Third, this book highlighted the near absence of expulsion from IGOs. The logic of community formation supports entry by friends but sets a high bar for terminating their membership. Simple failure to comply with some rules is insufficient. In their role to confer sovereignty as a form of recognition, IGOs have established a significance around belonging that goes well beyond compliance. Collective decision-making also reinforces the status quo. Diminishing security alignment does not produce actions to expel, although it may prompt exit and exclusion from new IGOs. In short, states find it easier to add members than to terminate them. Vague rules allow entry by some states that are not high compliers, and the lack of membership conditionality to expel for noncompliance means they can stay. Together this dynamic generates momentum toward overexpansion. The consequence dilutes status benefits and worsens performance, which further increases the incentive to form new institutions.

All three processes are readily apparent in the trade regime. Having nearly reached universal membership, new entrants are not able to differentiate themselves through accession. With the shift to rivalry with China, moving trade activity into other arenas offers more potential to build on a security coalition. Notably, states do not seriously discuss expelling China even as they share frustrations about the consequences of state-led capitalism of an export powerhouse on their economies and of the rule-based trade system. Strengthening and building alternative trade fora has emerged as part of the balancing act. This also reflects dissatisfaction with the regime, which has begun to suffer from the problems of overexpansion. Two decades of deadlock in the Doha round negotiations contribute to states' turning to other fora. A country like Japan shifted to favor regional groupings like the TPP to strengthen its diplomatic leverage and to expand trade opportunities. U.S. leaders rejected the TPP option, but pursued preferential agreements with each of its members and established a Trade and Technology Council with the EU. Through agreements with smaller circles of friends, states coordinate on a range of economic policies that might otherwise have gone forward under the auspices of the WTO.

Shifting Standards

International relations theories offer contrasting views of the ties that connect states within the international system. The realist portrayal of states as billiard balls that are largely autonomous of each other expects thin relationships based on temporary alliances. Interdependence plays a larger role for liberal theories, where the exchanges among states constrain choices and encourage deeper commitments for cooperation bound by institutions. Constructivist theories emphasize that interaction forms the basis for mutually constituted identities. This book has drawn on aspects of each theoretical perspective. The primacy of security interests in the sequence of cooperation reflects a realist approach, but the drive to create institutions for cooperation emerges as an augmented alliance strategy. States associate with other states within institutions in part because identity and perception are so malleable. Far from anonymous actors forming contracts, states care about *whom* they cooperate with. This book encourages us to think more about the interconnection between institutions and relationships.

International institutions lay the foundation for international society. Hedley Bull saw the central challenge to maintenance of order in the lack of social solidarity (Bull, 1977, p. 65). Primitive societies could cooperate based on cultural homogeneity upholding rules and beliefs, but international society was too diverse. For Bull, the common interest of the European state system arose from its respect for sovereignty and law, which eventually expanded to a global scope. International society evolved out of shared expectations about rules. Without a higher authority, the system remained anarchical. But order was possible because social institutions guided behavior toward a common interest.

On what dimensions do states focus when they try to reduce heterogeneity? The answer has varied across historical periods and regions. Using institutions as discriminatory clubs has allowed states to augment particular identity characteristics that form a common ground among states, but the choice of these characteristics is historically contingent. Early modern Europe witnessed dynastic networks of ties among states in Europe with shared Christian values, and the key disruptor to this *relational institutionalism* came with the Reformation and heterodox religious movements (Nexon, 2009). Order during the early modern period in East Asia, however, centered around Confucianism and Sino-centric tributary relationships, and it was remarkably stable until it collapsed under the pressure of European colonialism (Kang, 2012). Imperial expansion forced conformity to European standards of civilization across many regions, with an order imposed at gunpoint. The period after 1945 that is the focus of this book saw geopolitical alignment replace dynastic, cultural, or imperial ties.

Domestic political processes influence choices over the criteria for membership in international society. At times IGO accession became a topic for political leaders in election campaigns, or featured in the debates inside legislative bodies. Bureaucrats have used IGO accession to expand their jurisdiction. This helps to explain why geopolitical alignment came to the forefront as the dimension that matters for international society today. Whereas the servants of monarchies would have seen lineage and personal networks as important, for leaders and diplomats in constitutional states, alliances and diplomacy are the tools of international relations. Their primary goal is to maximize security for the state, and consolidating security coalitions is part of that mission. This shapes their agenda for all issues, even for questions of membership in technocratic IGOs far from the halls of great power military strategy. Rather than dividing high politics and low politics, one must consider how domestic decision processes switch the track for a policy. In the case of IGO accession, the predilection of diplomats to associate with allies puts more weight on geopolitical alignment.

As a mechanism for connecting states, international organizations offer choices. States can opt in or out of organizations and comply with or ignore rules with far fewer consequences than those trying to resist feudal alliances or colonial diktat. This choice brings power. Those who enter organizations can set the rules and become the gatekeepers. The criteria used to select states as members of international institutions define actors in the system and allocate benefits. They also guide change. Discretion allows states to change their definition of who qualifies to join the club.

The analogy to society opens the comparison to social clubs that motivates this book. States have chosen to design flexible rules for entry that they can use to favor friends and draw boundaries around the desired community. The largest circle is those recognized by universal organizations. The universal organizations confer sovereignty through association in the broadest pursuits of global public goods. Yet society is much more rich in structure.

The lines are constantly changing. Establishing markets and competitive elections or adopting the Anti-Bribery Convention may emerge as preconditions to be eligible for joining an organization. What was good enough to win entry into an organization in the 1950s may no longer be good enough 70 years later. Security has emerged as an important source of affinity for this most recent period. It could be replaced by other features that make states value association in clubs for cooperation. We could one day see pro-environmentalism emerge as a new criterion pulling some states together. Even after the decline of security as a dimension for selection of cooperation partners, states will still discriminate. Choosing whom to associate with is part of being in society.

BIBLIOGRAPHY

Abbott, Kenneth W. and Duncan Snidal. 1998. "Why States Act through Formal International Organizations." *The Journal of Conflict Resolution* 42:3–32.

Abbott, Kenneth W., Jessica F. Green and Robert O. Keohane. 2016. "Organizational Ecology and Institutional Change in Global Governance." *International Organization* 70:247–277.

Abbott, Kenneth W., Philipp Genschel, Duncan Snidal and Bernhard Zangl. 2015. *International Organizations as Orchestrators*. Cambridge: Cambridge University Press.

Abbott, Kenneth W., Robert Keohane, Andrew Moravcsik, Anne-Marie Slaughter and Duncan Snidal. 2000. "The Concept of Legalization." *International Organization* 54:401–419.

Acharya, Amitav. 2012. *The Making of Southeast Asia: International Relations of a Region*. Singapore: Institute of Southeast Asian Studies.

Acharya, Amitav and Alastair Iain Johnston, eds. 2007. *Crafting Cooperation: Regional Institutions in Comparative Perspective*. Cambridge: Cambridge University Press.

Ackerman, Reuben B. 2002. "Japanese Whaling in the Pacific Ocean: Defiance of International Whaling Norms in the Name of 'Scientific Research,' Culture, and Tradition." *Boston College International and Comparative Law Review* 25:323–341.

Aggarwal, Vinod K., ed. 1998. *Institutional Designs for a Complex World: Bargaining, Linkages, and Nesting*. Ithaca: Cornell University Press.

Akaneya, Tatsuo. 1992. *Nihon no gatto kanyū mondai (Japan's GATT Accession Problem)*. Tokyo: Tokyo University Press.

Akerlof, George and Rachel Kranton. 2010. *Identity Economics: How Our Identitites Shape Our Work, Wages, and Well-being*. Princeton, NJ: Princeton University Press.

Akiyama, Takuya. 2015. "Hantai ha ni yoru bōeki jiyūka (Winning Over the Opposition to Free Trade: Negotiation Linkages and the Influence on Opposition Preferences)." Kokusai Kin'yū 1276:46–51.

Allee, Todd L. and Jamie E. Scalera. 2012. "The Divergent Effects of Joining International Organizations: Trade Gains and the Rigors of WTO Accession." *International Organization* 66:243–276.

Alter, Karen. 2014. *The New Terrain of International Law: Courts, Politics, Rights*. Princeton, NJ: Princeton University Press.

Alter, Karen J. and Sophie Meunier. 2009. "The Politics of International Regime Complexity." *Perspectives on Politics* 7:13–24.

Anderson, Benedict. 2016. *Imagined Communities: Reflections on the Origin and Spread of Nationalism*, Rev. ed. London, England: Verso Books.

Anderson, James E. and Eric van Wincoop. 2003. "Gravity with Gravitas: A Solution to the Border Puzzle." *American Economic Review* 93:170–192.

Arase, David, ed. 2005. *Japan's Foreign Aid: Old Continuities and New Directions*. Routledge.

Asian and Pacific Council. 1966. *International Organization* 20:845–845.

Association, Japan ITU. 1996. *ITU nenpyō: Naigai denki tsūshin hōsō kankei 1865–1995 (ITU Yearbook: Telegraph Communications Domestic and International Relations 1865–1995)*. Tokyo: Shin Nihon ITU kyōkai (Japan ITU Association).

Bagwell, Kyle and Robert Staiger. 2002. *The Economics of the World Trading System*. Cambridge: MIT Press.

Bailey, Michael, Anton Strezhnev and Erik Voeten. 2017. "Estimating Dynamic State Preferences from United Nations Voting Data." *Journal of Conflict Resolution* 61:430–456.

Baldwin, Richard. 1995. *Expanding Membership of the European Union*. Cambridge University Press. Chapter: A Domino Theory of Regionalism, p. 25–48.

Barkin, Samuel. 2021. *The Sovereignty Cartel*. Cambridge: Cambridge University Press.

Barton, John, Judith Goldstein, Timothy Josling and Richard Steinberg. 2006. *The Evolution of the Trade Regime: Politics, Law, and Economics of the GATT and the WTO*. Princeton: Princeton University Press.

Bayer, Resat. 2006. *Diplomatic Exchange Data Set (Version 2006.1)*. Correlates of War.

Bearce, David H. and Daniel C. Tirone. 2010. "Foreign Aid Effectiveness and the Strategic Goals of Donor Governments." *The Journal of Politics* 72:837–851.

Bearce, David H. and Stacy Bondanella. 2007. "Intergovernmental Organizations, Socialization, and Member-State Interest Convergence." *International Organization* 61:p. 703–733.

Becker, Gary. 1971. *The Economics of Discrimination*. 2nd ed. Chicago: University of Chicago Press.

Berger, Daniel, William Easterly, Nathan Nunn and Shanker Satyanath. 2013. "Commercial Imperialism? Political Influence and Trade During the Cold War." *American Economic Review* 103:863–896.

Bermeo, Sarah Blodgett. 2018. *Targeted Development: Industrialized Country Strategy in a Globalizing World*. Oxford, England: Oxford University Press.

Beyer, Jessica L. and Stephanie C. Hofmann. 2011. "Varieties of Neutrality: Norm Revision and Decline." *Cooperation and Conflict* 46:285–311.

Bigdeli, Sadeq Z. 2018. "Iran's Accession to the World Trade Organization: An Impediment or a Catalyst for Development?" In *Industrial, Trade, and Employment Policies in Iran*, ed. Pooya Alaedini and Mohamad R. Razavi. Springer p. 177–210.

Bissell, Richard. 1974. "South Africa and International Ostracism." *World Affairs* 137:179–185.

Boehmer, Charles, Erik Gartzke and Timothy Nordstrom. 2004. "Do Intergovernmental Organizations Promote Peace?" *World Politics* 57:1–38.

Borzyskowski, Inken von and Felicity Vabulas. 2019a. "Credible Commitments? Explaining IGO Suspensions to Sanction Political Backsliding." *International Studies Quarterly* 63: 139–152.

Borzyskowski, Inken von and Felicity Vabulas. 2019b. "Hello, Goodbye: When Do States Withdraw from International Organizations?" *The Review of International Organizations* 14:335–366.

Boughton, James. 2016. "The Final Few: Completing the Universal Membership of the IMF." CIGI Papers No. 89. Centre for International Governance Innovation.

Boutton, Andrew and David B. Carter. 2014. "Fair-Weather Allies? Terrorism and the Allocation of US Foreign Aid." *The Journal of Conflict Resolution* 58:1144–1173.

Box-Steffensmeier, Janet and Christopher J. W. Zorn. 2001. "Duration Models and Proportional Hazards in Political Science." *American Journal of Political Science* 45:972–988.

Braddick, C. W. 2006. *Japan, Australia and Asia-Pacific Security*. Routledge. Chapter: Japan, Australia and ASPAC: The Rise and Fall of an Asia-Pacific Cooperative Security Framework.

Breitmeier, Helmut, Arild Underdal and Oran R. Young. 2011. "The Effectiveness of International Environmental Regimes: Comparing and Contrasting Findings from Quantitative Research." *International Studies Review* 13:579–605.

Brooks, Sarah M., Raphael Cunha and Layna Mosley. 2015. "Categories, Creditworthiness, and Contagion: How Investors' Shortcuts Affect Sovereign Debt Markets." *International Studies Quarterly* 59:587–601.

Brunton, Richard Henry. 1991. *Building Japan 1868–1876*. Sandgate, UK: Japan Library Ltd.

Buchanan, James. 1965. "An Economic Theory of Clubs." *Economica* 32:1–14.

Bueno de Mesquita, Bruce and Alastair Smith. 2012. "Domestic Explanations of International Relations." *Annual Review of Political Science* 15:161–181.

Bull, Hedley. 1977. *The Anarchical Society: A Study of Order in World Politics*. Columbia University Press.

Bull, Hedley and Adam Watson, eds. 1984. *The Expansion of International Society*. Oxford: Clarendon Press.

Burak, Akcapar. 2007. *Turkey's New European Era: Foreign Policy on the Road to EU Membership*. Rowman Littlefield Publishers.

Burkman, Thomas. 2008. *Japan and the League of Nations*. Honolulu: University of Hawaii Press.

Buzan, Barry. 2017. "Universal Sovereignty." In *The Globalization of International Society*, ed. Tim Dunne and Christian Reus-Smit. Oxford University Press p. 227–247.

Buzan, Barry and Ole Waever. 2003. "Security Complexes: A Theory of Regional Security." In *Regions and Powers: The Structure of International Security*. Cambridge: Cambridge University Press. p. 40–82.

Calder, Kent E. 1988. "Japanese Economic Policy Formation: Explaining the Reactive State." *World Politics* 40:517–541.

Campbell, John. 1993. *Japan's Foreign Policy*. M. E. Sharpe. Chapter: Japan and the United States: Games That Work, p. 43–61.

Capling, Ann and John Ravenhill. 2012. *The Trans-Pacific Partnership: A Quest for a Twenty-First Century Trade Agreement*. Cambridge: Cambridge University Press. Chapter: The TPP: Multilateralizing Regionalism or the Securitization of Trade Policy?, p. 279–298.

Cardoso, Joao Da Cruz. 2021. "Is Timor-Leste Ready to Join ASEAN?" *The Diplomat*.

Carnegie, Allison. 2014. "States Held Hostage: Political Hold-Up Problems and the Effects of International Institutions." *American Political Science Review* 108:54–70.

Carnegie, Allison. 2015. *Power Plays: How International Institutions Reshape Coercive Diplomacy*. Cambridge: Cambridge University Press.

Carnegie, Allison and Cyrus Samii. 2017. "International Institutions and Political Liberalization: Evidence from the World Bank Loans Program." *British Journal of Political Science*.

Carnegie, Allison and Nikhar Gaikwad. 2022. "Public Opinion on Geopolitics and Trade: Theory and Evidence." *World Politics* 74:167–204.

Carroll, Peter and Aynsley Kellow. 2011. *The OECD: A Study of Organizational Adaptation*. Cheltenham: Edward Elgar.

Carter, David B. and Curtis S. Signorino. 2010. "Back to the Future: Modeling Time Dependence in Binary Data." *Political Analysis* 18:271–292.

Carter, David, Rachel Wellhausen and Paul Huth. 2018. "International Law, Territorial Disputes, and Foreign Direct Investment." *International Studies Quarterly* 63:58–71.

Catalinac, Amy and Gerald Chan. 2005. "Japan, the West, and the Whaling Issue: Understanding the Japanese Side." *Japan Forum* 17:133–163.

Chan, Lai-Ha. 2017. "Soft Balancing against the US 'Pivot to Asia': China's Geostrategic Rationale for Establishing the Asian Infrastructure Investment Bank." *Australian Journal of International Affairs* 71:568–590.

Chang, Pao-Li and Myoung-jae. 2011. "The WTO Trade Effect." *Journal of International Economics* 85:53–71.

Chapman, Terrence, L. 2011. *Securing Approval: Domestic Politics and Multilateral Authorization for War*. Chicago, IL: University of Chicago Press.

Chase, Kerry A. 2003. "Economic Interests and Regional Trading Arrangements: The Case of NAFTA." *International Organization* 57:137–174.

Chen, Jie. 2002. *Foreign Policy of the New Taiwan: Pragmatic Diplomacy in Southeast Asia*. Cheltenham, UK: Edward Elgar.

Chen, Yu-Jie and Jerome A. Cohen. 2020. "Why Does the WHO Exclude Taiwan?" Research Report. Council on Foreign Relations.

Cho, Hui-Wan. 2002. *Taiwan's Application to GATT/WTO: Significance of Multilateralism for an Unrecognized State*. Westport, CT: Praeger Publishers.

Choi, Chong-ki. 1975. "The Korean Question in the United Nations." *Verfassung und Recht in Übersee / Law and Politics in Africa, Asia and Latin America* 8:395–406.

Chow, Daniel C.K. 2013. "Why China Opposes Human Rights in the World Trade Organization." *University Pennsylvania Journal of International Law* 35:61–111.

Claessens, Stijn, Geoffrey Underhill and Xiaoke Zhang. 2008. "The Political Economy of Basle II: The Costs for Poor Countries." *The World Economy*.

Codding, George. 1964. *The Universal Postal Union*. New York: New York University Press.

Coggins, Bridget. 2011. "Friends in High Places: International Politics and the Emergence of States from Secessionism." *International Organization* 65:433–467.

Cook, Kevin, Margaret Levi and Russell Hardin, eds. 2009. *Whom Can We Trust? How Groups, Networks, and Institutions Make Trust Possible*. New York: Russell Sage Foundation.

Copelovitch, Mark and David Ohls. 2012. "Trade, Institutions, and the Timing of GATT/WTO Accession in Post-colonial States." *Review of International Organizations* 7: 81–107.

Cornes, Richard and Todd Sandler. 1996. *The Theory of Externalities, Public Goods, and Club Goods*. 2nd ed. Cambridge: Cambridge University Press.

Correlates of War Project. 2011. "State System Membership List, v2011." Available at: https://correlatesofar.org. Accessed 10 August 2015.

Cortazzi, Hugh, ed. 2015. *The Growing Power of Japan, 1967–1972: Analysis and Assessments from John Pilcher and the British Embassy, Tokyo*. Kent, England: Global Books.

Crawford, James. 2006. *The Creation of States in International Law*. Oxford, England: Oxford University Press.

Cross, Karen Halverson. 2004. "China's WTO Accession: Economic, Legal, and Political Implications." *Boston College International and Comparative Law Review* 27:319–370.

Cyranoski, David. 2003. "Taiwan Left Isolated in Fight against SARS." *Nature* 422.

Dafoe, Allan. 2011. "Statistical Critiques of the Democratic Peace: Caveat Emptor." *American Journal of Political Science* 55:247–262.

Dafoe, Allan, Jonathan Renshon and Paul Huth. 2014. "Reputation and Status as Motives for War." *Annual Review of Political Science* 17:371–393.

Davis, Christina L. 2003. *Food Fights over Free Trade: How International Institutions Promote Agricultural Trade Liberalization*. Princeton: Princeton University Press.

Davis, Christina L. 2004. "International Institutions and Issue Linkage: Building Support for Agricultural Trade." *The American Political Science Review* 98:153–169.

Davis, Christina L. 2008/9. "Linkage Diplomacy: Economic and Security Bargaining in the Anglo-Japanese Alliance, 1902–23." *International Security* 33:143–179.

Davis, Christina L. 2009. "Overlapping Institutions in Trade Policy." *Perspectives on Politics* 7: 25–31.

Davis, Christina L. 2012. *Why Adjudicate? Enforcing Trade Rules in the WTO*. Princeton, NJ: Princeton University Press.

Davis, Christina L. 2019. "Japan: Interest Group Politics, Foreign Policy Linkages, and the TPP." In *Megaregulation Contested: Global Economic Ordering After TPP*, edited by Benedict Kingsbury, David M. Malone, Paul Mertenskötter, Richard B. Stewart, Thomas Streinz, and Atsushi Sunami, p. 573–591. Oxford: Oxford University Press.

Davis, Christina L. and Jennifer Oh. 2007. "Repeal of the Rice Laws in Japan: The Role of International Pressure to Overcome Vested Interests." *Comparative Politics* 40:21–40.

Davis, Christina L. and Meredith Wilf. 2015. *The Political Economy of International Trade*. Oxford University Press. Chapter: WTO Membership.

Davis, Christina L. and Meredith Wilf. 2017. "Joining the Club? Accession to the GATT/WTO." *The Journal of Politics* 79:964–978.

Davis, Christina L. and Sarah Blodgett Bermeo. 2009. "Who Files? Developing Country Participation in WTO Adjudication." *Journal of Politics* 71:1033–1049.

Davis, Christina L. and Tyler Pratt. 2021. "The Forces of Attraction: How Security Interests Shape Membership in Economic Institutions." *The Review of International Organizations* 16:903–929.

Dedman, Martin. 2010. *The Origins and Development of the European Union 1945–2008*. London: Routledge.

Den, Kenjiro. 1970. *Fifty Years of New Japan*. Vol. 1 second ed. New York: Kraus Reprint Co. Chapter: Japanese Communications: The Post, Telegraph, and Telephone, p. 408–423. Compiled by Count Shigenobu Okuma and first published in 1910.

Dent, Christopher. 2008. *East Asian Regionalism*. London: Routledge.

DeSombre, Elizabeth. 2000. *Domestic Sources of International Environmental Policy: Industry, Environmentalists, and U.S. Power*. Cambridge: The MIT Press.

Donno, Daniela, Shawna K. Metzger and Bruce Russett. 2015. "Screening Out Risk: IGOs, Member State Selection, and Interstate Conflict, 1951–2000." *International Studies Quarterly* 59:251–263.

Downs, George and David M. Rocke. 1995. *Optimal Imperfection? Domestic Uncertainty and Institutions in International Relations*. Princeton: Princeton University Press.

Downs, George, David Rocke and Peter Barsoom. 1996. "Is the Good News about Compliance Good News about Cooperation?" *International Organization* 50:379–406.

Downs, George, David Rocke and Peter Barsoom. 1998. "Managing the Evolution of Multilateralism." *International Organization* 52:397–419.

Dreher, Axel and Stefan Voigt. 2011. "Does Membership in International Organizations Increase Governments' Credibility? Testing the Effects of Delegating Powers." *Journal of Comparative Economics* 39:326–348.

Dreher, Axel, Stephan Klasen, James Raymond Vreeland and Eric Werker. 2013. "The Costs of Favoritism: Is Politically Driven Aid Less Effective?" *Economic Development and Cultural Change* 62:157–191.

Dreyer, David R. 2012. "Issue Intractability and the Persistence of International Rivalry." *Conflict Management and Peace Science* 29:471–489.

Drezner, Daniel. 2007. *All Politics Is Global: Explaining International Regulatory Regimes*. Princeton: Princeton University Press.

Dugard, John. 2013. *The Secession of States and Their Recognition in the Wake of Kosovo*. Hague, Netherlands: The Hague Academy of International Law.

Duque, Marina G. 2018. "Recognizing International Status: A Relational Approach." *International Studies Quarterly* 62(3):577–592.

Dutt, Pushan, Ilian Mihov and Timothy Van-Zandt. 2013. "The Effect of WTO on the Extensive and the Intensive Margins of Trade." *Journal of International Economics* 91:204–219.

Duxbury, Alison. 2011. *The Participation of States in International Organisations: The Role of Human Rights and Democracy*. Cambridge: Cambridge University Press.

Eagleton, Clyde. 1957. *International Government*. Third ed. New York: The Ronald Press Company.

Eicher, Theo S. and Christian Henn. 2011. "In Search of WTO Trade Effects: Preferential Trade Agreements Promote Trade Strongly, but Unevenly." *Journal of International Economics* 83:137–153.

Eilstrup-Sangiovanni, Mette. 2020. "Death of International Organizations. The Organizational Ecology of Intergovernmental Organizations, 1815–2015." *The Review of International Organizations* 15:339–370.

Emmons, Cassandra V. 2022. "Designing Suspension Clauses to Defend Democracy: Lessons from Negotiating the OAS's Washington Protocol." *Cambridge Review of International Affairs* 35:698–720.

Evenett, Simon J. and Carlos A. Primo Braga. 2006. "WTO Accession: Moving the Goalposts?" In *Trade, Doha, and Development: A Window into the Issues*. Washington, DC: World Bank, p. 231–243.

Farrell, Henry and Abraham Newman. 2015. "The New Politics of Interdependence: Cross-National Layering in Trans-Atlantic Regulatory Disputes." *Comparative Political Studies* 48:497–526.

Fazal, Tanisha. 2007. *State Death: The Politics and Geography of Conquest, Occupation, and Annexation*. Princeton, NJ: Princeton University Press.

Fearon, James. 1998. "Bargaining, Enforcement, and International Cooperation." *International Organization* 52:269–306.

Fee, Elizabeth, Cueto Marcos and Theodore Brown. 2016. "At the Roots of the World Health Organization's Challenges: Politics and Regionalization." *American Journal of Public Health* 106:1912–1917.

Ferguson, Clyde C. 1981. "The United States, the United Nations and the Struggle against Racial Apartheid." In *The Dynamics of Human Rights in U.S. Foreign Policy*, ed. Natalie Kaufman Hevener. New Brunswick, NJ: Transaction Books, p. 203–213.

Forsberg, Aaron. 2000. *America and the Japanese Miracle: The Cold War Context of Japan's Postwar Economic Revival, 1950–1960.* Chapel Hill: The University of North Carolina Press.

Franck, Thomas. 1990. *The Power of Legitimacy among Nations.* Oxford: Oxford University Press.

Freedman, Lawrence. 2018. "Trump and Brexit." *Survival* 60:7–16.

Freedman, Lawrence. 2020. "The United Kingdom's Search for a Post-Brexit Role." *Foreign Affairs* 100.

Frost, Frank. 2016. *Engaging the Neighbours: Australia and ASEAN since 1974.* Australia: ANU Press.

Fuchs, Andreas and Nils-Hendrik Klann. 2013. "Paying a Visit: The Dalai Lama Effect on International Trade." *Journal of International Economics* 91:164–177.

Fujioka, Masao. 1986. *Ajia Ginkō Sōsai Nikki, Manira e no Satogaeri "Diary of the Asian Development Bank President, The Return to Manila."* Tokyo: Tōyō Keizai Shinpōsha.

Garon, Sheldon. 1987. *The State and Labor in Modern Japan.* Berkeley: University of California Press.

Garrett, Geoffrey and George Tsebelis. 1996. "An Institutional Critique of Intergovernmentalism." *International Organization* 50:269–299.

GATT. 1947. *General Agreement on Tariffs and Trade.* Available at: https://www.wto.org/english /docs_e/legal_e/gatt47_e.pdf. Accessed 10 August 2015.

Ghosn, Faten and Scott Bennett. 2003. "Codebook for the Dyadic Militarized Interstate Incident Data, Version 3.0." Available at: http://correlatesofwar.org.

Gibler, Douglas M. 2009. *International Military Alliances, 1648–2008.* CQ Press.

Gilligan, Michael J. 2004. "Is There a Broader-Deeper Trade-off in International Multilateral Agreements?" *International Organization* 59:459–484.

Gilpin, Robert. 1981. *War and Change in World Politics.* Cambridge: Cambridge University Press.

"Global Economic Prospects: Spillovers amid Weak Growth." 2016. Technical Report. World Bank, Washington D.C.

Goldstein, Judith, Douglas Rivers and Michael Tomz. 2007. "Institutions in International Relations: Understanding the Effects of the GATT and the WTO on World Trade." *International Organization* 61:37–67.

Gowa, Joanne. 1989. "Bipolarity, Multipolarity, and Free Trade." *American Political Science Review* 83:1245–1256.

Gowa, Joanne. 1994. *Allies, Adversaries, and International Trade.* Princeton: Princeton University Press.

Gowa, Joanne. 2010. "Alliances, Market Power, and Postwar Trade: Explaining the GATT/WTO." *World Trade Review* 9:487–504.

Gowa, Joanne and Edward Mansfield. 1993. "Power Politics and International Trade." *American Political Science Review* 87:408–420.

Gowa, Joanne and Edward Mansfield. 2004. "Alliances, Imperfect Markets, and Major-Power Trade." *International Organization* 58:775–805.

Gowa, Joanne and Soo Yeon Kim. 2005. "An Exclusive Country Club: The Effects of GATT 1950–94." *World Politics* 57:453–478.

Grabbe, Heather and Kirsty Hughes. 1998. *Enlarging the EU Eastwards*. London: Pinter.

Gray, Julia. 2009. "International Organization as a Seal of Approval: European Union Accession and Investor Risk." *American Journal of Political Science* 53:931–949.

Gray, Julia. 2013. *The Company States Keep*. Cambridge: Cambridge University Press.

Gray, Julia. 2018. "Life, Death, or Zombie? The Vitality of International Organizations." *International Studies Quarterly* 62:1–13.

Gray, Julia and Raymond P. Hicks. 2014. "Reputations, Perceptions, and International Economic Agreements." *International Interactions* 40:325–349.

Gray, Julia, René Lindstädt and Jonathan B. Slapin. 2017. "The Dynamics of Enlargement in International Organizations." *International Interactions* 43:619–642.

Greenhill, Brian. 2008. "Recognition and Collective Identity Formation in International Politics." *European Journal of International Relations* 14:343–368.

Greenhill, Brian. 2010. "The Company You Keep: International Socialization and the Diffusion of Human Rights Norms." *International Studies Quarterly* 61:127–145.

Greenhill, Brian and Yonatan Lupu. 2017. "Clubs of Clubs: Fragmentation in the Network of Intergovernmental Organizations." *International Studies Quarterly* 54:181–195.

Greenhouse, Carol J. and Christina L. Davis, eds. 2020. *Landscapes of Law Practicing Sovereignty in Transnational Terrain*. Philadelphia: University of Pennsylvania Press.

Grieco, Joseph. 1993. "Anarchy and the Limits of Cooperation: A Realist Critique of the Newest Liberal Institutionalism." In *Neorealism and Neoliberalism*, ed. David Baldwin. New York: Columbia University Press, p. 116–142.

Gross, Eva. 2009. *The Europeanization of National Foreign Policy: Continuity and Change in European Crisis Management*. New York, NY: Palgrave MacMillan.

Gruber, Lloyd. 2000. *Ruling the World: Power Politics and the Rise of Supranational Institutions*. Princeton: Princeton University Press.

Grun, Bettina and Friedrich Leisch. 2008. "FlexMix Version 2: Finite Mixtures with Concomitant Variables and Varying and Constant Parameters." *Journal of Statistical Software* 28:1–35.

Haas, Ernst B. 1958. *The Uniting of Europe: Political, Economic and Social Forces, 1950–57*. Stanford, CA: Stanford University Press.

Hafner-Burton, Emilie M. and Alexander H. Montgomery. 2006. "Power Positions: International Organizations, Social Networks, and Conflict." *Journal of Conflict Resolution* 50: 3–27.

Hafner-Burton, Emilie M., Miles Kahler and Alexander H. Montgomery. 2009. "Network Analysis for International Relations." *International Organization* 63:559–592.

Haftel, Yoram Z. 2007. "Designing for Peace: Regional Integration Arrangements, Institutional Variation, and Militarized Interstate Disputes." *International Organization* 61:217–237.

Haftel, Yoram Z. 2012. *Regional Economic Institutions and Conflict Mitigation: Design, Implementation, and the Promise of Peace*. Ann Arbor: University of Michigan Press.

Haftel, Yoram Z and Stephanie C. Hofmann. 2019. "Rivalry and Overlap: Why Regional Economic Organizations Encroach on Security Organizations." *Journal of Conflict Resolution* 63:2180–2206.

Hammond, John L. and Joao Roberto Martins Filho. 2007. "Introduction: Brazil under Cardoso." *Latin American Perspectives* 34:5–8.

Hansen, Holley E., Sara McLaughlin Mitchell and Stephen C. Nemeth. 2008. "IO Mediation of Interstate Conflicts: Moving beyond the Global versus Regional Dichotomy." *Journal of Conflict Resolution* 52:295–325.

Haus, Leah. 1992. *Globalizing the GATT: The Soviet Union's Successor States, Eastern Europe, and the International Trading System*. The Brookings Institution.

Henke, Marina. 2017. "How the United States Builds Multilateral Military Coalitions: The Politics of Diplomacy." *International Studies Quarterly* 61:410–424.

Henke, Marina. 2019. *Constructing Allied Cooperation: Diplomacy, Payments, and Power in Multilateral Military Coalitions*. Ithaca: Cornell University Press.

Hill, Christopher, Michael Smith and Sophie Vanhoonacker, eds. 2017. *International Relations and the European Union*. Oxford: Oxford University Press.

Hill, Christopher and Reuben Wong. 2011. *National and European Foreign Policies: Towards Europeanization*. London: Routledge.

Hooghe, Liesbet and Gary Marks. 2015. "Delegation and Pooling in International Organizations." *The Review of International Organizations* 10:305–328.

Hooghe, Liesbet, Gary Marks, Tobias Lenz, Jeanine Bezuijen, Besir Ceka and Svet Dverderyan. 2016. *Community, Scale, and Regional Governance: A Postfunctionalist Theory of Governance*. Vol. 2 Oxford, England: Oxford University Press.

Hooghe, Liesbet, Gary Marks, Tobias Lenz, Jeanine Bezuijen, Besir Ceka and Svet Dverderyan. 2017. *Measuring International Authority: A Postfunctionalist Theory of Governance*. Vol. 3 Oxford, England: Oxford University Press.

Hooghe, Liesbet, Tobias Lenz and Gary Marks. 2019. *A Theory of International Organization*. Vol. 4 Oxford, England: Oxford University Press.

Howard-Ellis, Charles. 1929. *The Origin, Structure and Working of the League of Nations*. Boston: Houghton Mifflin Company.

Howland, Douglas. 2014. "Japan and the Universal Postal Union: An Alternative to Internationalism in the 19th Century." *Social Science Japan Journal* 17:23–39.

Hurd, Ian. 1999. "Legitimacy and Authority in International Politics." *International Organization* 53:379–408.

Hurd, Ian. 2021. *International Organizations: Politics, Law, Practice*. Fourth ed. Cambridge: Cambridge University Press.

Hurrell, Andrew. 2004. "Power, Institutions, and the Production of Inequality." In *Power in Global Governance*, ed. Michael Barnett and Raymond Duvall. Cambridge University Press p. 33–58.

Ida, Tetsuji. 2019. "*IWC kara no tettai* (Withdrawal from the IWC)." *Sekai*.

Ikenberry, John. 2001. *After Victory: Institutions, Strategic Restraint, and the Rebuilding of Order after Major Wars*. Princeton, NJ: Princeton University Press.

Ilgaz, Mahir and Ilke Toygu. 2011. "EU-Turkey Accession Negotiations: The State of Play and the Role of the New Turkish Foreign Policy." Working Paper No. 8. Elcano Royal Institute Madrid, Spain.

Imai, Kosuke and Dustin Tingley. 2012. "A Statistical Method for Empirical Testing of Competing Theories." *American Journal of Political Science* 56:218–236.

Ingram, Paul, Jeffrey Robinson and Marc L. Busch. 2005. "The Intergovernmental Network of World Trade: IGO Connectedness, Governance, and Embeddedness." *American Journal of Sociology* 111:824–58.

Ishikawa, Kōichi, Keiichi Umada and Yorizumi Watanabe, eds. 2014. *TPP kōshō no ronten to nihon (Key Issues of TPP Negotiations and Japan)*. Tokyo: Bunshindō. Chapter: TPP Kōshō to nihon no tsūshō senryaku (TPP Negotiations and Japanese Commercial Strategy), p. 215–236.

Ishikawa, Kōichi, Keiichi Umada and Yorizumi Watanabe, eds. 2014. *TPP kōshō no ronten to nihon (Key Issues of TPP Negotiations and Japan)*. Tokyo: Bunshindō. Chapter: TPP to Nōgyō Rikkoku (TPP and the Agricultural Country), p. 19–32.

Iwanaga, Kazuki. 2000. *The Japanese and Europe: Images and Perceptions*. Richmond: Japan Library, Curzon Press. Chapter: Europe in Japan's Foreign Policy, p. 208–235.

Jacoby, Wade. 2004. *The Enlargement of the European Union and NATO*. Cambridge: Cambridge University Press.

Jansen, Marius. 2000. *The Making of Modern Japan*. Cambridge: Harvard University.

Jetschke, Anja. 2017. "What Drives Institutional Reforms in Regional Organisations? Diffusion, Contextual Conditions, and the Modular Design of ASEAN." *Trans-Regional and -National Studies of Southeast Asia* 5:173–196.

Jetschke, Anja and Philomena Murray. 2012. "Diffusing Regional Integration: The EU and Southeast Asia." *West European Politics* 35:174–191.

Jetschke, Anja and Tobias Lenz. 2013. "Does Regionalism Diffuse? A New Research Agenda for the Study of Regional Organizations." *Journal of European Public Policy* 20:626–637.

Johns, Leslie. 2015. *Strengthening International Courts: The Hidden Costs of Legalization*. Ann Arbor: University of Michigan Press.

Johnson, Tana. 2011. "Guilt by Association: The Link between States' Influence and the Legitimacy of Intergovernmental Organizations." *The Review of International Organizations* 6:57–84.

Johnston, Alastair Iain. 2001. "Treating International Institutions as Social Environments." *International Studies Quarterly* 45:487–515.

Johnston, Alastair Iain. 2007. *Social States: China in International Institutions, 1980–2000*. Princeton, NJ: Princeton University Press.

Jones, Kent. 2009. "The Political Economy of WTO Accession." *World Trade Review* 8:279–314.

Jonsson, Gabriel. 2017. *South Korea in the United Nations: Global Governance, Inter-Korean Relations and Peace Building*. London: World Scientific Publishing Europe.

Joo, Seung-ho. 1993. "South Korea's Nordpolitic and the Soviet Union (Russia)." *The Journal of East Asian Affairs* 7:404–450.

Jupille, Joe, Walter Mattli and Duncan Snidal. 2013. *Institutional Choice and Global Commerce*. Oxford: Oxford University Press.

Kahler, Miles. 1992. "Multilateralism with Small and Large Numbers." *International Organization* 46:681–708.

Kalinowski, Thomas and Hyekyung Cho. 2009. "The Political Economy of Financial Liberalization in South Korea: State, Big Business, and Foreign Investors." *Asian Survey* 49:221–242.

Kamiyama, Akiyoshi. 2014. *"Kokusai rōdō kikan to no kyōryoku shūshi kankei shiryō* [Records related to the terminations of cooperative relations with ILO]." *Journal of the Diplomatic Archives* 28:71–83.

Kan, Shirley and Wayne Morrison. 2014. U.S.-Taiwan Relationship: Overview of Policy Issues. Report for Congress. Congressional Research Service.

Kang, David. 2012. *East Asia before the West: Five Centuries of Trade and Tribute.* New York: Columbia University Press.

Kaoutzanis, Christodoulos, Paul Poast and Johannes Urpelainen. 2016. "Not Letting 'Bad Apples' Spoil the Bunch: Democratization and Strict International Organization Accession Rules." *Review of International Organization* 11:399–418.

Kaplan, Stephen S. 1975. "United States Aid to Poland, 1957–1964: Concerns, Objectives and Obstacles." *The Western Political Quarterly* 28:147–166.

Katzenstein, Peter. 2005. *A World of Regions: Asia and Europe in the American Imperium.* Ithaca, NY: Cornell University Press.

Kawasaki, Ken'ichi. 2014.The Relative Significance of EPAs in Asia-Pacific. Technical Report. Research Institute of Economy, Trade, and Industry Tokyo.

Kaya, Ayse and Byungwon Woo. 2021. "China and the Asian Infrastructure Investment Bank (AIIB): Chinese Influence over Membership Shares?" *The Review of International Organizations.* 17(4):781–813.

Kaya, Ayse, Christopher Kilby and Jonathan Kay. 2021. "Asian Infrastructure Investment Bank as an Instrument for Chinese Influence? Supplementary versus Remedial Multilateralism." *World Development* 145.

Keene, Edward. 2007. "A Case Study of the Construction of International Hierarchy: British Treaty-Making Against the Slave Trade in the Early Nineteenth Century." *International Organization* 61:311–339.

Keene, Edward. 2012. "The Treaty-Making Revolution of the Nineteenth Century." *The International History Review* 34:475–500.

Kelley, Judith. 2004. *Ethnic Politics in Europe: The Power of Norms and Incentives.* Princeton, NJ: Princeton University Press.

Kennedy, Kevin. 1987. "The Accession of the Soviet Union to GATT." *Journal of World Trade Law* 21.

Keohane, Robert. 1984. *After Hegemony: Cooperation and Discord in the World Political Economy.* Princeton: Princeton University Press.

Keohane, Robert and Joseph Nye. 1977. *Power and Interdependence.* Boston: Little, Brown, and Co.

Keohane, Robert O. 2010. "The Economy of Esteem and Climate Change." *St Antony's International Review* 5.

Keohane, Robert O. and David G. Victor. 2011. "The Regime Complex for Climate Change." *Perspectives on Politics* 9:7–23.

Keohane, Robert O. and Joseph Nye. 2001. *Efficiency, Equity, and Legitimacy: The Multilateral Trading System at the Millennium.* Washington, DC: Brookings. Chapter: The Club Model of Multilateral Cooperation and Problems of Democratic Legitimacy, p. 264–294.

Keshk, Omar, Rafael Reuveny and Brian Pollins. 2004. "Trade Still Follows the Flag: The Primacy of Politics in a Simultaneous Model of Interdependence and Armed Conflict." *Journal of Politics* 66:1155–1179.

Khong, Yuen Foong and Helen E.S. Nesdaurai. 2007. *Crafting Cooperation: Regional Institutions in Comparative Perspective.* Cambridge University Press. Chapter: Hanging Together, Institutional Design, and Cooperation in Southeast Asia: AFTA and the ARF, p. 32–82.

Kim, Chulsu. 2005. *The World Trade Organization: Legal, Economic and Political Analysis.* Vol. 2 New York: Springer. Chapter: Korea, p. 183–214.

Kim, Soo Yeon. 2010. *Power and the Governance of Global Trade: From the GATT to the WTO.* Ithaca: Cornell University Press.

Kindleberger, Charles P. 1986. *The World in Depression.* Berkeley: University of California Press.

Kinne, Brandon J. 2013a. "IGO Membership, Network Convergence, and Credible Signaling in Militarized Disputes." *Journal of Peace Research* 50:659–676.

Kinne, Brandon J. 2013b. "Network Dynamics and the Evolution of International Cooperation." *American Political Science Review* 107:766–785.

Kinne, Brandon J. 2014. "Dependent Diplomacy: Signaling, Strategy, and Prestige in the Diplomatic Network." *International Studies Quarterly* 58:247–259.

Komatsu, Yugoro. 1963. *Gatto no chishiki (GATT Knowledge).* Tokyo: Nihon Keizai Shimbun.

Kono, Daniel Yuichi. 2008. "Democracy and Trade Discrimination." *The Journal of Politics* 70:942–955.

Koremenos, Barbara. 2005. "Contracting around International Uncertainty." *American Political Science Review* 99:549–565.

Koremenos, Barbara. 2016. *The Continent of International Law: Explaining Agreement Design.* Cambridge: Cambridge University Press.

Koremenos, Barbara, Charles Lipson and Duncan Snidal. 2001. "The Rational Design of International Institutions." *International Organization* 55:761–799.

Krasner, Stephen. 1976. "State Power and the Structure of International Trade." *World Politics* 28:317–347.

Krasner, Stephen. 1983. "Regimes and the Limits of Realism: Regimes as Autonomous Variables." In *International Regimes*, ed. Stephen Krasner. Ithaca, N.Y.: Cornell University Press p. 355–368.

Krasner, Stephen, ed. 1999. *Sovereignty: Organized Hypocrisy.* Princeton: Princeton University Press.

Kucik, Jeffrey and Eric Reinhardt. 2008. "Does Flexibility Promote Cooperation? An Application to the Global Trade Regime." *International Organization* 62:477–505.

Kulakowski, Jan and Leszek Jesień. 2007. *The Accession Story: The EU From 15 to 25 Countries.* Oxford: Oxford University Press. Chapter: The Accession of Poland to the EU, p. 297–317.

Kydd, Andrew. 2001. "Trust Building, Trust Breaking: The Dilemma of NATO Enlargement." *International Organization* 55:801–828.

Lake, David. 2009. *Hierarchy in International Relations.* Ithaca: Cornell University Press.

Landau-Wells, Marika. 2018. "High Stakes and Low Bars: How International Recognition Shapes the Conduct of Civil Wars." *International Security* 43:100–137.

Lascurettes, Kyle M. 2020. *Orders of Exclusion: Great Powers and the Strategic Sources of Foundational Rules in International Relations.* Oxford: Oxford University Press.

Lauterpacht, H. 1944. "Recognition of States in International Law." *The Yale Law Journal* 53: 385–458.

Lechner, Michael. 2011. "The Estimation of Causal Effects by Difference-in-Difference Methods." *Foundations and Trends in Econometrics* 4:165–224.

Lee, James. 2020. "US Grand Strategy and the Origins of the Developmental State." *Journal of Strategic Studies* 43:737–761.

Lee, Yeon-ho. 2000. "The Failure of the Weak State in Economic Liberalization: Liberalization, Democratization and the Financial Crisis in South Korea." *The Pacific Review* 13:115–131.

Lenz, Tobias and Lora Anne Viola. 2017. "Legitimacy and Institutional Change in International Organisations: A Cognitive Approach." *Review of International Studies* 43:939–961.

Levy, Jack S. and William R. Thompson. 2010. "Balancing on Land and at Sea: Do States Ally against the Leading Global Power?" *International Security* 35:7–43.

Li, Chien-pin. 2006. "Taiwan's Participation in Intergovernmental Organizations: An Overview of Its Initiatives." *Asian Survey* 46:597–614.

Libman, Alexander and Anastassia Obydenkova. 2013. "Informal Governance and Participation in Non-democratic International Organizations." *The Review of International Organizations* 8:221–243.

Licht, Amanda A. 2011. "Change Comes with Time: Substantive Interpretation of Nonproportional Hazards in Event History Analysis." *Political Analysis* 19:227–243.

Lien, Chan. 1993. "The Republic of China on Taiwan Belongs in the United Nations." *Orbis* 37:633–641.

Lim, Daniel Yew Mao and James Raymond Vreeland. 2013. "Regional Organizations and International Politics: Japanese Influence over the Asian Development Bank and the UN Security Council." *World Politics* 65:34–72.

Lipscy, Phillip. 2008. *Japan and the World: Japan's Contemporary Geopolitical Challenges*. Yale CEAS Occasional Publications. Chapter: Japan's Shifting Role in International Organizations, p. 133–158.

Lipscy, Phillip Y. 2015. "Explaining Institutional Change: Policy Areas, Outside Options, and the Bretton Woods Institutions." *American Journal of Political Science* 59:341–356.

Lipscy, Phillip Y. 2017. *Renegotiating the World Order*. Cambridge: Cambridge University Press.

Liu, Xuepeng. 2009. "GATT/WTO Promotes Trade Strongly: Sample Selection and Model Specification." *Review of International Economics* 17:428–446.

Long, Andrew and Brett Ashley Leeds. 2006. "Trading for Security: Military Alliances and Economic Agreements." *Journal of Peace Research* 43:433–451.

Maclachlan, Patricia. 2011. *The People's Post Office*. Cambridge: Harvard University Asia Center.

Maggi, Giovanni and Andres Rodriquez-Clare. 1998. "The Value of Trade Agreements in the Presence of Political Pressures." *The Journal of Political Economy* 106:574–601.

Magliveras, Konstantinos D. 1999. *Exclusion from Participation in International Organisations: The Theory and Practice Behind Member States' Expulsion and Suspension of Membership*. The Hague: Kluwer Law International.

Manby, Bronwen. 1992. "South Africa: The Impact of Sanctions." *Journal of International Affairs* 46:193–217.

Manger, Mark. 2009. *Investing in Protection: The Politics of Preferential Trade Agreements between North and South*. Cambridge: Cambridge University Press.

Mansfield, Edward and Brian Pollins, eds. 2003. *Economic Interdependence and International Conflict*. Ann Arbor, MI: University of Michigan Press.

Mansfield, Edward and Eric Reinhardt. 2008. "International Institutions and the Volatility of International Trade." *International Organization* 62:621–52.

Mansfield, Edward and Etel Solingen. 2010. "Regionalism." *Annual Review of Political Science* 13:145–163.

Mansfield, Edward and Helen Milner. 2012. *Votes, Vetoes, and the Political Economy of International Trade Agreements*. Princeton, NJ: Princeton University Press.

Mansfield, Edward and Helen Milner. 2015. *Trade Cooperation: The Purpose, Design and Effects of Preferential Trade Agreements*. Cambridge University Press. Chapter: The Political Economy of Preferential Trade Agreements, p. 56–81.

Mansfield, Edward, Helen Milner and Jon Pevehouse. 2008. "Democracy, Veto Players and the Depth of Regional Integration." *The World Economy* 31:67–96.

Mansfield, Edward and Jon Pevehouse. 2006. "Democratization and International Organizations." *International Organization* 60:137–167.

Mansfield, Edward and Jon Pevehouse. 2009. "Democratization and the Varieties of International Organizations." *Journal of Conflict Resolution* 52:269–294.

Mansfield, Edward and Rachel Bronson. 1997. "Alliances, Preferential Trading Arrangements, and International Trade." *The American Political Science Review* 91:94–107.

March, James and Johan Olsen. 1998. "The Institutional Dynamics of International Political Orders." *International Organization* 52:943–969.

Martin, Lisa. 1992. "Interests, Power, Multilateralism." *International Organization* 46:765–792.

Mastny, Vojtech. 2009. "Eastern Europe and the Early Prospects for EC/EU and NATO Membership." *Cold War History* 9:203–221.

Mattli, Walter. 1999. *The Logic of Regional Integration: Europe and Beyond*. Cambridge: Cambridge University Press.

Mavroidis, Petros C. and Andre Sapir. 2021. *China and the WTO: Why Multilateralism Still Matters*. Princeton, NJ: Princeton University Press.

Mayer, Thierry and Soledad Zignago. 2011. "Notes on CEPII's Distances Measures: The GeoDist Database." CEPII Working Paper No. 2011-25. Available at SSRN: https://ssrn.com/abstract=1994531.

McGrath, Liam F. 2015. "Estimating Onsets of Binary Events in Panel Data." *Political Analysis* 23:534–549.

McMahon, Robert and Jonathan Masters. 2012. "Palestinian Statehood at the UN." Available at: https://www.cfr.org/backgrounder/palestinian-statehood-un. Accessed 30 August 2020.

Mearsheimer, John. 2001. *The Tragedy of Great Power Politics*. New York: W.W. Norton.

Meernik, James, Eric L. Krueger and Steven C. Poe. 1998. "Testing Models of U.S. Foreign Policy: Foreign Aid during and after the Cold War." *The Journal of Politics* 60:63–85.

Michalski, Anna and Ludvig Norman. 2016. "Conceptualizing European Security Cooperation: Competing International Political Orders and Domestic Factors." *European Journal of International Relations* 22:749–772.

Middlebush, Frederick. 1934. "International Affairs: The Effect of the Non-recognition of Manchukuo." *The American Political Science Review* 28:677–683.

Milner, Helen and Dustin Tingley. 2015. *Sailing the Water's Edge: The Domestic Politics of American Foreign Policy*. Princeton, NJ: Princeton University Press.

Milner, Helen and Edward Mansfield. 2012. *Votes, Vetoes, and the Political Ecoomy of International Trade Agreements*. Princeton: Princeton University Press.

Milner, Helen and Edward Mansfield, eds. 1997. *The Political Economy of Regionalism*. New York: Columbia University Press.

Milner, Helen and Keiko Kubota. 2005. "Why the Move to Free Trade? Democracy and Trade Policy in the Developing Countries." *International Organization* 59:107–143.

Mitrany, David. 1965. "The Prospect of Integration: Federal or Functional." *Journal of Common Market Studies* 4:119–149.

Moravcsik, Andrew. 1998. *The Choice for Europe: Social Purpose and State Power from Messina to Maastricht*. Ithaca, New York: Cornell University Press.

Morrow, James. 2000. "Alliances: Why Write Them Down?" *Annual Review of Political Science* 3:63–83.

Morse, Julia C. and Robert O. Keohane. 2014. "Contested Multilateralism." *The Review of International Organizations* 9:385–412.

Nakao, Takehiko. 2022. *The Rise of Asia: Perspectives and Beyond. Memoir of the President of the Asian Development Bank 2013–2020*. Mandaluyong City, Asian Development Bank.

Nakatsuji, Keiji. 2001. "Essence of Trade Negotiation: A Study on China's Entry for WTO." *Ritsumeikan Research Report* 14.

Naoi, Megumi and Arata Kuno. 2012. "Framing Business Interests How Campaigns Affect Firms' Positions on Preferential Trade Agreements." Working Paper.

Naoi, Megumi and Shūjirō Urata. 2013. "Free Trade Agreements and Domestic Politics: The Case of the Trans-Pacific Partnership Agreement." *Asian Economic Policy Review* 8:326–349.

Nelson, Stephen C. 2010. "Does Compliance Matter? Assessing the Relationship between Sovereign Risk and Compliance with International Monetary Law." *Review of International Organizations* 5:107–39.

Neumayer, Eric. 2008. "Distance, Power and Ideology: Diplomatic Representation in a World of Nation-States." *Area* 40:228–236.

Neumayer, Eric. 2013. "Strategic Delaying and Concessions Extraction in Accession Negotiations to the World Trade Organization." *World Trade Review* 12:669–692.

Nexon, Dan. 2009. *The Struggle for Power in Early Modern Europe: Religious Conflict, Dynastic Empires, and International Change*. Princeton: Princeton University Press.

Nishihara, Masashi. 1976. *The Japanese and Sukarno's Indonesia: Tokyo-Jakarta Relations, 1951–1966*. Honolulu: University of Hawaii Press.

Nixon, Richard M. 1967. "Asia After Viet Nam." *Foreign Affairs* 46:111–125.

Nordhaus, William. 2015. "Climate Clubs: Overcoming Free-Riding in International Climate Policy." *American Economic Review* 105:1339–70.

Obydenkova, Anastassia and Alexander Libman. 2019. *Authoritarian Regionalism in the World of International Organizations: Global Perspective and the Eurasian Enigma*. Oxford, England: Oxford University Press.

OECD. 2016. *Agricultural Policy Monitoring and Evaluation 2016*. Paris: OECD Publishing.

Okura, Kimio. 1964. "Ajia kaihatsu ginkō setsuritsu ni kansuru mondaiten 'Problems about the Asia Development Bank.'" *Kokusai Kin'yū (International Finance Journal)* 334:6–9.

O'Rourke, Kevin. 2019. *A Short History of Brexit*. UK: Penguin.

Ortiz Mena, Antonio. 2005. *The World Trade Organization: Legal, Economic and Political Analysis*. Vol. 2 New York: Springer. Chapter: Mexico, p. 217–247.

Ortuoste, Maria. 2019. "Timor-Leste's ASEAN membership limbo." *East Asian Forum*.

Ostrom, Elinor. 2000. "Collective Action and the Evolution of Social Norms." *Journal of Economic Perspectives* 14:137–158.

Pahre, Robert. 2008. *Politics and Trade Cooperation in the Nineteenth Century*. Cambridge: Cambridge University Press.

Pandya, Sonal. 2016. "French Roast: Consumer Response to International Conflict—Evidence from Supermarket Scanner Data." *Review of Economics and Statistics* 98:42–56.

Paul, T. V., Deborah Welch Larson and William C. Wohlforth, eds. 2014. *Status in World Politics*. Cambridge: Cambridge University Press.

Peaslee, Amos and Dorothy Peaslee Xydis. 1979. *International Governmental Organizations, Constitutional Documents*. The Hague: Martinus Nijhoff.

Pelc, Krzysztof. 2011. "Why Do Some Countries Get Better WTO Accession Terms than Others?" *International Organization* 65:639–72.

Peterson, M. J. 1983. "Recognition of Governments Should Not Be Abolished." *The American Journal of International Law* 77:31–50.

Petri, Peter, Michael G. Plummer, Shūjirō Urata and Fan Zhai. 2017. "Going It Alone in the Asia-Pacific: Regional Trade Agreements without the United States." Technical Report No. 10. Peterson Institute for International Economics Washington D.C.

Pevehouse, Jon. 2002. "Democracy from the Outside-In? International Organizations and Democratization." *International Organization* 56:515–50.

Pevehouse, Jon and Bruce Russett. 2006. "Democratic International Governmental Organizations Promote Peace." *International Organization* 60:969–1000.

Pevehouse, Jon C., Timothy Nordstrom and Kevin Warnke. 2004. "The COW-2 International Organizations Dataset Version 2.0." *Conflict Management and Peace Science* 21.

Phillips, Lester H. 1968. "Universality, Expulsion, and South Africa." *Social Science* 43:195–201.

Poast, Paul. 2013. "Can Issue Linkage Improve Treaty Credibility?: Buffer State Alliances as a 'Hard Case.'" *Journal of Conflict Resolution* 57:739–764.

Poast, Paul. 2019. *Arguing about Alliances*. Ithaca, NY: Cornell University Press.

Poast, Paul and Johannes Urpelainen. 2013. "Fit and Feasible: Why Democratizing States Form, Not Join, International Organizations." *International Studies Quarterly* 57:831–841.

Poast, Paul and Johannes Urpelainen. 2015. "How International Organizations Support Democratization: Preventing Authoritarian Reversals or Promoting Consolidation?" *World Politics* 67:72–113.

Poast, Paul and Johannes Urpelainen. 2018. *Organizing Democracy: How International Organizations Assist New Democracies*. Chicago: The University of Chicago Press.

Pollins, Brian. 1989. "Does Trade Still Follow the Flag?" *American Political Science Review* 83:465–480.

Powers, Kathy L. 2004. "Regional Trade Agreements as Military Alliances." *International Interactions* 30:373–395.

Pratt, Tyler. 2021. "Angling for Influence: Institutional Proliferation in Development Banking." *International Studies Quarterly* 65:95–108.

Quinn, Terry. 2011. *From Artefacts to Atoms: The BIPM and the Search for Ultimate Measurement Standards*. Oxford: Oxford University Press.

Recchia, Stefano and Jonathan Chu. 2021. "Validating Threat: IO Approval and Public Support for Joining Military Counterterrorism Coalitions." *International Studies Quarterly* 65:919–928.

Renshon, Jonathan. 2017. *Fighting for Status: Hierarchy and Conflict in World Politics*. Princeton: Princeton University Press.

Reus-Smit, Christian and Tim Dunne. 2017. *The Globalization of International Society*. Oxford University Press. Chapter: The Globalization of International Society, p. 18–40.

Rhamey, Patrick, Kirssa Cline, Nicholas Thorne, Jacob Cramer, Jennifer L. Miller and Thomas J. Volgy. 2013. *The Diplomatic Contacts Data Base (Version 3.0)*. School of Government and Public Policy, University of Arizona.

Roberts, Christopher. 2012. *ASEAN Regionalism: Cooperation, Values, and Institutionalization*. London: Routledge.

Roger, Charles B. and Rowan, Sam S. 2021. "Analyzing International Organizations: How the Concepts We Use Affect the Answers We Get." *The Review of International Organizations* 17(3):597–625.

Rose, Andrew. 2004. "Do We Really Know That the WTO Increases Trade?" *American Economic Review* 94:98–114.

Rose, Andrew. 2005. "Which International Institutions Promote International Trade?" *Review of International Economics* 13:682–698.

Rosendorff, Peter and Helen Milner. 2001. "The Optimal Design of International Trade Institutions: Uncertainty and Escape." *International Organization* 55:829–857.

Rozman, Gilbert. 2004. *Northeast Asia's Stunted Regionalism: Bilateral Distrust in the Shadow of Globalization*. Cambridge: Cambridge University Press.

Russett, Bruce and John Oneal. 2001. *Triangulating Peace: Democracy, Interdependence, and International Organizations*. New York: Norton.

Russett, Bruce, John R. Oneal and David R. Davis. 1998. "The Third Leg of the Kantian Tripod for Peace: International Organizations and Militarized Disputes, 1950–85." *International Organization* 52:441–467.

Sakuyama, Takumi. 2015. *Nihon no TPP kōshō sanka no shinjitsu: Sono seisaku katei no kaimei (The Truth of Japan's Participation in the TPP Negotiations: Revealing Its Policy Process)*. Tokyo: Bunshindō.

Sandler, Todd. 1999. "Alliance Formation, Alliance Expansion, and the Core." *Journal of Conflict Resolution* 43:727–747.

Satō, Seizaburō. "The Foundations of Modern Japanese Foreign Policy." *The Foreign Policy of Modern Japan*, edited by Robert A. Scalapino, Berkeley: University of California Press, 1977, p. 367–390.

Scharpf, Fritz W. 2006. "The Joint-Decision Trap Revisited." *Journal of Common Market Studies* 44:845–864.

Schimmelfennig, Frank. 2001. "The Community Trap: Liberal Norms, Rhetorical Action, and the Eastern Enlargement of the European Union." *International Organization* 55:47–80.

Schneider, Christina. 2009. *Conflict, Negotiation and European Union Enlargement*. Cambridge: Cambridge University Press.

Schneider, Christina J. and Johannes Urpelainen. 2012. "Accession Rules for International Institutions A Legitimacy-Efficacy Trade-off?" *Journal of Conflict Resolution* 56:290–312.

Schoppa, Leonard. 1993. "Two-Level Games and Bargaining Outcomes: Why Gaiatsu Succeeds in Japan in Some Cases but Not Others." *International Organization* 47:353–386.

Schultz, Mark D. 1992. "Austria in the International Arena: Neutrality, European Integration and Consociationalism." *West European Politics* 15:73–99.

Sell, Susan and John Odell. 2006. "Reframing the Issue: The WTO Coalition on Intellectual Property and Public Health, 2001." In *Negotiating Trade: Developing Countries in the WTO and NAFTA*, ed. John Odell. Cambridge: Cambridge University Press.

Shaffer, Gregory and Henry Gao. 2020. "Changing Internally to Engage Externally: China and the WTO Legal System." In *Landscapes of Law: Practicing Sovereignty in Transnational Terrain*, ed. Carol J. Greenhouse and Christina L. Davis. Philadelphia: University of Pennsylvania Press, p. 64–96.

Shimomura, Tetsuo. 1964. *OECD kamei to nihon keizai (OECD) Membership and Japan's Economy*, Tokyo: Keizai.

Shinohara, Hatsue. 1959. *Kokusai renmei: Sekai heiwa e no yume to zasetsu (The League of Nations: Dreams and Disappointment for World Peace)*. Tokyo: Chūō Kōronsha.

Simmons, Beth. 2000. "International Law and State Behavior: Commitment and Compliance in International Monetary Affairs." *American Political Science Review* 94:819–835.

Simmons, Beth. 2005. "Rules over Real Estate." *Journal of Conflict Resolution* 49:823–847.

Simmons, Beth A., Frank Dobbin and Geoffrey Garrett. 2006. "Introduction: The International Diffusion of Liberalism." *International Organization* 60:781–810.

Small, Melvin and J. David Singer. 1973. "The Diplomatic Importance of States, 1816–1970: An Extension and Refinement of the Indicator." *World Politics* 25:577–599.

Snidal, Duncan and Felicity Vabulas. 2022. "ASEAN Way, No Way: Informality and Regional Organizations." Paper presented at the Political Economy of International Organizations Conference.

Solingen, Etel. 1998. *Regional Orders at Century's Dawn: Global and Domestic Influences on Grand Strategy*. Princeton, NJ: Princeton University Press.

Solingen, Etel. 2015. *Comparative Regionalism: Economics and Security*. New York: Routledge.

Solis, Mireya. 2017. *Dilemmas of a Trading Nation: Japan and the United States in the Evolving Asia-Pacific Order*. Washington, D.C.: The Brookings Institution.

Solís, Mireya and Saori N. Katada. 2015. "Unlikely Pivotal States in Competitive Free Trade Agreement Diffusion: The Effect of Japan's Trans-Pacific Partnership Participation on Asia-Pacific Regional Integration." *New Political Economy* 20:155–177.

Stauer, Carsten. 2016. "Ready for Membership? Denmark and Israel's Application for Membership of the United Nations in May 1949." *Danish Foreign Policy Yearbook*.

Stein, Arthur. 1984. "The Hegemon's Dilemma: Great Britain, the United States, and the International Economic Order." *International Organization* 38:355–386.

Steinberg, David A. and Krishan Malhotra. 2014. "The Effect of Authoritarian Regime Type on Exchange Rate Policy." *World Politics* 66:491–529.

Stone, Randall W. 2008. "The Scope of IMF Conditionality." *International Organization* 62:589–620.

Stone, Randall W. 2011. *Controlling Institutions: International Organizations and the Global Economy*. Cambridge: Cambridge University Press.

Stone, Randall W., Branislav Slantchev and Tamar London. 2008. "Choosing How to Cooperate: A Repeated Public-Goods Model of International Relations." *International Studies Quarterly* 52:335–362.

Story, Dale. 1982. "Trade Politics in the Third World: A Case Study of the Mexican GATT Decision." *International Organization* 36:767–794.

Strausz, Michael. 2014. "Executives, Legislatures, and Whales: The Birth of Japan's Scientific Whaling Regime." *International Relations of the Asia-Pacific* 14:455–478.

Subedi, Surya P. 1993. "Neutrality in a Changing World: European Neutral States and the European Community." *The International and Comparative Law Quarterly* 42:238–268.

Subramanian, Arvind and Shang-Jin Wei. 2007. "The WTO Promotes Trade, Strongly but Unevenly." *Journal of International Economics* 72:151–175.

Sullivan, Jonathan and Eliyahu V. Sapir. 2012. "Ma Ying-jeou's Presidential Discourse." *Journal of Current Chinese Affairs* 41:33–68.

Tallberg, Jonas, Thomas Sommerer, Theresa Squatrito and Christer Jonsson. 2013. *The Opening Up of International Organizations: Transnational Access in Global Governance*. Cambridge: Cambridge University Press.

Tallberg, Jonas, and Michael Zürn. 2019. "The Legitimacy and Legitimation of International Organizations: Introduction and Framework." *Review of International Organizations* 14:581–606.

Tan, Yeling. 2021a. *Disaggregating China, Inc*. Ithaca: Cornell University Press.

Tan, Yeling. 2021b. "How the WTO Changed China: The Mixed Legacy of Economic Engagement." *Foreign Affairs* 100.

Tandon, Yash. 1972. "The Organisation of African Unity and the Principle of Universality of Membership." *The African Review: A Journal of African Politics, Development and International Affairs* 1:52–60.

Taras, Ray. 2003. "Poland's Accession into the European Union: Parties, Policies and Paradoxes." *The Polish Review* 48:3–19.

Terada, Takashi. 2015. "The Abe Effect and Domestic Politics." *Asian Perspective* 39:381–403.

Terry, Sarah Meiklejohn. 2000. "Poland's Foreign Policy since 1989: The Challenges of Independence." *Communist and Post-Communist Studies* 33:7–47.

Thacker, Strom C. 1999. "The High Politics of IMF Lending." *World Politics* 52:38–75.

Thomann, Bernard. 2018. "Labor Issues as International Affairs: Japan and the International Labour Organization from 1919 to 1938." *Social Science Japan Journal* 21:329–344.

Thomas, Daniel. 2017. "Beyond Identity: Membership Norms and Regional Organization." *European Journal of International Relations* 23:217–240.

Thompson, Alexander. 2006. "Coercion through IOs: The Security Council and the Logic of Information Transmission." *International Organization* 60:1–34.

Thompson, Alexander and Daniel Verdier. 2014. "Multilateralism, Bilateralism, and Regime Design." *International Studies Quarterly* 58:15–28.

Thompson, William R. 2001. "Identifying Rivals and Rivalries in World Politics." *International Studies Quarterly* 45:557–586.

Thomson, Alex. 2008. *U.S. Foreign Policy towards Apartheid South Africa, 1948–1994*. New York, NY: Palgrave Macmillan.

Tir, Jaroslav and Johannes Karreth. 2018. *Incentivizing Peace: How International Organizations Can Help Prevent Civil Wars in Member Countries*. Oxford University Press.

Tollison, Robert D. and Thomas D. Willett. 1979. "An Economic Theory of Mutually Advantageous Issue Linkages in International Negotiations." *International Organization* 33:425–449.

Trezise, Philip. 1978. "US-Japan Trade: The Bilateral Connection." In *The Politics of Trade: U.S. and Japanese Policymaking for the GATT Negotiations*, ed. Michael Blaker. New York: Columbia University East Asian Institute, p. 1–14.

Tsebelis, George. 2002. *Veto Players: How Political Institutions Work*. Princeton, NJ: Princeton University Press.

Tubilewicz, Czeslaw. 2012. "Friends, Enemies or Frenemies? China-Taiwan Discord in the World Health Organization and Its Significance." *Pacific Affairs* 85:701–22.

Uchida, Hiroshi. 1959. *Gatto: Bunseki to tenbo (GATT: Analysis and Prospects)*. Tokyo: Nihon Kanzei Kyōkai.

"Universal Postal Union." 1966. *International Organization* 20:834–842.

Vabulas, Felicity and Duncan Snidal. 2013. "Organization without Delegation: Informal Intergovernmental Organizations (IIGOs) and the Spectrum of Intergovernmental Arrangements." *The Review of International Organizations* 8:193–220.

Vachudova, Milada Anna. 2005. *Europe Undivided. Democracy, Leverage, and Integration After Communism*. Oxford: Oxford University Press.

Vasilopoulou, Sofia and Liisa Talving. 2019. "British Public Opinion on Brexit: Controversies and Contradictions." *European Political Science* 18:134–42.

Vidmar, Jure. 2013. *Democratic Statehood in International Law: The Emergence of New States in Post-Cold War Practice*. Oxford, England: Hart Publishing;.

Vigevani, Tullo, Marcelo Fernandes de Oliveira and Timothy Thompson. 2007. "Brazilian Foreign Policy in the Cardoso Era: The Search for Autonomy through Integration." *Latin American Perspectives* 34:58–80.

Viola, Lora Anne. 2020. *The Closure of the International System : How Institutions Create Political Equalities and Hierarchies*.Cambridge: Cambridge University Press.

Viola, Lora Anne, Duncan Snidal and Michael Zürn. 2015. "Sovereign (In)equality in the Evolution of the International System." In *The Oxford Handbook of Transformations of the State*, ed. Matthew Lange, Jonah D. Levy, Frank Nullmeier, John D. Stephens, Stephan Leibfried, Evelyne Huber. Oxford: Oxford University Press p. 221–236.

Voeten, Erik. 2000. "Clashes in the Assembly." *International Organization* 54:185–215.

Voeten, Erik. 2013. *Routledge Handbook of International Organization*. New York: Routledge. Chapter: Data and Analyses of Voting in the UN General Assembly, p. 54–66.

Voeten, Erik. 2021. *Ideology and International Institutions*. Princeton, NJ: Princeton University Press.

von Stein, Jana. 2005. "Do Treaties Constrain or Screen? Selection Bias and Treaty Compliance." *American Political Science Review* 99:611–631.

Vreeland, James and Axel Dreher. 2014. *The Political Economy of the United Nations Security Council: Money and Influence*. Cambridge: Cambridge University Press.

Wajner, Daniel F. 2022. "The Populist Way Out: Why Contemporary Populist Leaders Seek Transnational Legitimation." *The British Journal of Politics and International Relations* 24(3), 416–436.

Wallander, Celeste and Robert Keohane. 1999. *Imperfect Unions: Security Institutions over Time and Space*. Oxford: Oxford University Press. Chapter: Risk, Threat, and Security Institutions, p. 21–47.

Walt, Stephen. 1985. "Alliance Formation and the Balance of World Power." *International Security* 9:3–43.

Wan, Ming. 1995. "Japan and the Asian Development Bank." *Pacific Affairs* 68:509–28.

Warren, T. Camber. 2010. "The Geometry of Security: Modeling Interstate Alliances as Evolving Networks." *Journal of Peace Research* 47:697–709.

Watanabe, Takeshi. 1973. *Ajia Ginkō Sōsai Nikki "Diary of the Asian Development Bank President."* Tokyo: Nihon Keizai Shimbunsha.

Weatherbee, Donald E. 1983. "Brunei: The ASEAN Connection." *Asian Survey* 23:723–735.

Weiler, Joseph. 2003. *The Constitution of Europe: "Do the New Clothes Have an Emperor?" and Other Essays on European Integration*. Cambridge: Cambridge University Press.

Wendt, Alexander. 1994. "Collective Identity Formation and the International State." *The American Political Science Review* 88:384–396.

Whalley, John. 1998. *The Regionalization of the World Economy*. Chicago: University of Chicago Press. Chapter: Why Do Countries Seek Regional Trade Agreements?, p. 63–83.

Whitman, Richard G. 2016. "Brexit or Bremain: What Future for the UK's European Diplomatic Strategy?" *International Affairs* 92:509–529.

Winkler, Sigrid. 2012. Taiwan's UN Dilemma: To Be or Not to Be. Technical Report. Brookings. Available at: https://www.brookings.edu/opinions/taiwans-un-dilemma-to-be-or-not-to-be/. Accessed 3 April 2020.

Woodward, Richard. 2009. *The Organisation for Economic Co-operation and Development*. London: Routledge.

Woodward, Richard. 2012. *Debating a Post-American World What Lies Ahead?* Routledge. Chapter: What Lies Ahead for the OECD?

Wu, Mark. 2016. "The 'China, Inc.' Challenge to Global Trade Governance." *Harvard International Law Journal* 57:261–324.

Yamaoka, Tokio. 2013. "Analysis of China's Accession Commitments in the WTO: New Taxonomy of More and Less Stringent Commitments, and the Struggle for Mitigation by China." *Journal of World Trade* 47.

Yasutomo, Dennis. 1983. *Japan and the Asian Development Bank*. New York: Praeger.

Yokoi, Noriko. 2003. *Japan's Postwar Economic Recovery and Anglo-Japanese Relations, 1948–62*. London: Routledge.

Young, Oran. 1999. *The Effectiveness of International Environmental Regimes*. Cambridge, MA: MIT Press.

Zarocostas, John. 2018. "Palestine Not to Seek Full Membership of WHO." *The Lancet* 391:0140–6736.

INDEX

Note: Page numbers in *italics* refer to figures and tables.

Abbas, Mahmoud, 363

Abe, Shinzō, 220, 223, 226, 228, 230, 232, 234–35, 237–39, 242, 245, 250, 252

accession process, 2, 7, 40–41, 43, 73, 78–79, 96; accession review process, *60*, *61*–63, 67, 70, 132–33, 138, 151, 170, 286, 289, 384; and ADB, *67*; and ASEAN, 304–7; costs of entry (*see* "favoring friends" hypothesis; costs of entry/negotiable terms of membership); and EU, 285–87, 289–91; and GATT/WTO, *67*, 98–122 (*see also* GATT/WTO accession); informal practices, 67–70, 153, 304, 384; joint entry of states, 172, 287, 345–46; models of, 42–48 (*see also* club IGOs; hierarchical organizations; meritocratic organizations; universal organizations); and OECD, *67*, 129–32, 149–73; speed of negotiations, 26, 31, 95, 101, 108–11, *110*, 114, *115*, 117–18, 121; time between eligibility and application, 31, 95, 101, 108–10, *110*, 113–14, *115*, *116*, 119, 121; and UPU, 187–88

accession rules. *See* rules for accession and membership

Acharya, Amitav, 301, 303

ADB. *See* Asian Development Bank

Adenauer, Konrad, 284

Afghanistan, 39, 51, *102*, 121

Africa: newly independent states, and ostracism of South Africa, 368–70; and

regional organizations, 274–75, 276, 370. *See also specific states and organizations*

African Union (AU), 56

AIIB. *See* Asian Infrastructure Investment Bank

Akiyama, Takuya, 236–37

Allee, Todd L., 119, *120*

alliances, 24, 26–27, 56, 74, 79n18, 209, 231, 388; absence of alliance requirements for IGO membership, 59; and accession of North and South Korea to UN, 341–47; alliance ties as measure of geopolitical alignment, 26, 72, 75, 77, 95; Anglo-Japanese Alliance, 177, 194; and ASEAN, 300, 302, 308, 309, 311, 387; distinguished from geopolitical alignment, 21–22; effect on economic IGO membership (empirical analysis), 79–85, *80* (*see also* economic organizations); effect on GATT/WTO accession, 99–101, 111, 114, *115*, 117–18; effect on IGO membership in different issue areas, 83–84, *84*; and external threats catalyzing regional cooperation, 264; lack of alliances among states of Southeast Asia, 300, 302; non-NATO allies of the U.S., 142, 168; and OECD membership, 123, *141*, 141–42, *146*, 147–48, *148*; and regional IGOs, 269, *270–71*, 273, *274–75*, 276, *277–78*, 279; and TPP, 231; and universal organizations, 328, 330–31, *333*, *334*, *336*, 341–47; U.S.-Japan alliance,

33, 286–87; and Ukraine, 6, 45; UN voting compared to U.S. and UK, *298*
exclusion from international organizations, 7, 14, 39, 313–81, 392; and analysis of
accession, 330–40, *334*; benefits of exclusion, 3, 12–14, 20, 319–20, 324, 394, 395;
and contested sovereignty, 314–15, 318–
19; delay in China's accession to WTO,
93–94, 104–6, 121; evaluating the conditions for exclusion, 327–28; examples
of excluded states, 314–16 (*see also* Iran;
North Korea; Palestine; Russia; South
Africa; South Korea; Taiwan); exclusion from universal organizations, 313–81
(*see also* universal organizations; *specific states and organizations*); exclusion
mechanisms, 14, 56–61, 68, 266, 328–40,
379 (*see also* compliance with organization mandates; costs of entry/negotiable
terms of membership; dues; eligibility
criteria; member approval requirement;
transparency); exclusion of rivals from
GATT/WTO, 99–100, 108, 122; and
guilt by association, 19; Iran blocked
from WTO, 39, 69, 106–8, 121, 392;
Japan's delayed entry to UN, 203; and
North and South Korea (UN accession
controversy), 34, 341–47; and OECD
membership, 129, 132–33, 144; otherwise qualified states excluded due to
lack of benefits from association, 19; and
Palestine, 34, 360–68; political logic of
exclusion, 316–29; Russia excluded from
IGOs following invasions of Ukraine,
5, 7, 144–45, 175; and South Africa, 34,
368–80, 392; states excluded from UN,
1, 44, 314, 315, 323; and Taiwan, 34, 347–
60; Turkey excluded from EU, 291–94,
311. *See also* expulsion from international
organizations; member approval requirement; pariah states
exit (voluntary) from international organizations, 27, 30, 48–49; Brexit, 2, 4, 50,
51, 294–300, 311; Canada and Iceland's

exit from IWC, 249; and economic
organizations, *80*, 81; foreign policy
affinity reducing likelihood of exit, 8;
and geopolitical rifts, 8; and IGO charters, 49; India's exit from RCEP, 245–46;
infrequency of, 50, 66; Japan's exit from
ILO, 202; Japan's exit from IWC, 180,
246–47, 251–53, 255; Japan's exit from
the League of Nations, 185, 199–200;
reasons for ending membership, 48–
52, *52*; South Africa's exit from IGOs,
370–72, *372*; states' exit from G77 upon
OECD accession, 152, 164; U.S. exit from
TPP, 226, 230, 239, 241; U.S. exits from
UNESCO, 49, 315, 367; U.S. intention
to exit WHO under Trump administration, 8, 49; USSR exit from World Health
Assembly, 8. *See also* expulsion from
international organizations
expulsion from international organizations,
5–6, 7–8, 27, 49–53, 62; and democratic
backsliding, 7; flexibility in exclusion
mechanisms, 69; high threshold for, 52–
53, 64; and IGO charters, 7, 30, 50, 51,
62–65, 373, 396; infrequency of, 7, 8, 30,
50, 53, 68, 70, 315, 368, 385, 395–96; and
loss of recognition of sovereignty, 315;
nonrecognition as de facto expulsion, 51;
and power of small states, 52–53; reasons
for expulsion, 52–53; and regional organizations, 267; and Russia, 5, 7, 64; and
signaling to applicants via specific rules
for eligibility or expulsion based on noncompliance, 384–85; and South Africa, 7,
42, 50, 316, 372–80

FAO. *See* Food and Agriculture Organization
"favoring friends" hypothesis, 26–27, 177,
179, 386–89, 391–92; and effectiveness of
IGOs, 391–92; and EU accession, 289;
and GATT/WTO accession, 92, 99–101,
106, 110–11, 119–22, 209, 384; and OECD
accession, 138–39, 384;

Malik, Adam, 303

Manby, Bronwen, 370

Manchukuo, 200, 325

Mandela, Nelson, 370–71, 378, 379

Mansfield, Edward, 112, 138

March, James, 21

Marks, Gary, 9, 16

Matsuoka, Yōsuke, 200

Mattli, Walter, 262, 284, 394

May, Theresa, 296–97

Ma Ying-jeou, 353, 356

McGrath, Liam F., 81n19

member approval requirement, 30, 39, 57, 59–61, 68, 383; and club IGOs, 46, 67, 70; and economic organizations, 59–60, 69; and EU accession, 286–87, 293; as exclusion mechanism, 57, 68; and GATT/WTO accession, 98, 207–8; geopolitics playing less of a role in IGOs with high approval thresholds, 84, 276; and hierarchical organizations, 67; and OECD accession, 59, 129–30, 170, 172, 173, 213; and regional organizations, 266, 267, 270–71, 274–75, 276, 286–87, 311; and SADC, 266; and security organizations, 59–61; and UN, 323, 342; and UNESCO, 364, 365; and universal organizations, 315–16, 335, 336, 337, 364, 379; and UPU, 187, 373; variation in threshold for approval, 59–60; and WHO, 354

membership in international organizations, benefits of, 2, 17–21; benefits of excluding other states, 3, 12–14, 20, 136, 319–20, 394, 395; conflict reduction, 18, 24, 35, 47, 91, 264–65, 304, 322, 389–91; diplomatic recognition/establishing sovereignty, 17, 186–88, 194, 320–23, 365–66, 395; domestic leverage for policy change, 32, 155, 174, 175, 208, 235; economic benefits, 17–18, 31, 47–48, 134–36, 155, 169, 205, 210, 228–31, 262, 281, 288, 289, 291; enhancing relationships among states, 3, 18, 188–89, 193, 195–96, 213, 231, 239, 254; factors

diminishing the value of association, 368; and gaining a voice in international society and global governance, 195, 196, 197, 208, 210–11, 239, 322; and gains in status by association, 5, 18–19, 46–48, 123, 136–39, 173, 254, 395 (*see also* status; *specific organizations and states*); and learning from practices of other countries, 155, 157, 210–11; network ties as cooperation multiplier, 390; peer effects, 17–18, 48, 137; and signaling shifts in foreign policy direction or regime type, 5, 47, 159, 288; socialization of states in IGOs, 20–21, 35, 128, 151, 390, 392; utility of membership as both provision of goods and association with other states, 2, 21, 29, 368, 383, 384, 388, 391. *See also* specific organizations and states

Menendez, Bob, 358

meritocratic organizations, 42–43, 45, 48, 61–62, 68, 90, 384; accession rules, 40, 43, 45, 61–62, 67, 312; described, 42, 45; EU as a meritocratic IGO, 43, 45, 70, 259, 286, 289, 384; rarity of, 39, 45, 68

Metre Convention, 192, 193

Metzger, Shawna K., 100n10

Mexico: economic impact of OECD membership, 126, 134, 157; exit from G77, 152, 164; financial crisis, 126, 157; and GATT, 4, 94; and NAFTA, 149–51, 163, 174; and OECD, 7, 69, 126, 130, 149–52, 163, 174; and TPP, 227

Middle East: and regional organizations, 275, 276; and South Africa, 371. *See also specific states*

Mishustin, Mikhail, 144

Monnet, Jean, 281, 287

Montevideo Convention on the Rights and Duties of States (1933), 323

Montgomery, Alexander H., 18

Moravcsik, Andrew, 283

Moronuki, Hideki, 250

Myanmar, 51, 302, 303, 307

Myoung Ho-shin, 152, 154–55

United Nations (UN) (*continued*)
and China, 343, 348, 349; and defining
regions, 261; and diplomatic recogni-
tion/establishing sovereignty, 17, 320–23,
342; and East and West Germany, 349; as
hierarchical IGO, 66, 128, 324; and India,
17, 321; and Israel, 361–62; and Japan, 203,
256; and Myanmar, 51; and North and
South Korea, 341–47; and observer status, 10, 362, 367; Palestine excluded from,
1, 44, 314, 362, 368; and Partition Plan
for Palestine and Israel, 360–61; rules
for expulsion, 376; and South Africa,
370, 374, 376, 380; and South Sudan, 320;
states excluded from, 1, 44, 314, 315, 323
(*see also specific states*); Taiwan excluded
from, 1, 44, 314, 349, 380; and transfer of
seats to rebel groups, 322; and Ukraine,
321; and universal organizations, 331–32,
334, 336, 337, 339; UN voting similarity as
measure of geopolitical alignment, 26, 72,
75, 77, 95, 102, 111, 116, 116–19, 120, 123, 142,
143, 147, 148, 268, 270–71, 297
United Nations Educational, Scientific and
Cultural Organization (UNESCO), 49,
56, 314, 315, 324, 341, 364–68, 370–72
United States, 23, 186–87, 191, 202–3, 243–
44, 247, 396; and ADB, 216–17; and
AIIB, 219–20; allies within OECD, 142;
and ASEAN Regional Forum (ARF),
304; and Brazil, 32, 126, 166–67, 172; and
Brexit, 296, 298–99; and China, 167, 252,
348–50; and delaying/blocking other
states' accession to IGOs, 39, 99, 106–8,
343; and embassies and IGO membership, 338; European integration favored
by the U.S., 286, 296; exit from TPP, 226,
230, 239, 241, 396; exits from UNESCO,
49, 315, 367; formal alliances and military
cooperation with TPP members, 231n96;
frequency of exits from IGOs, 50; and
hegemony and differential application of
rules, 12; IGO membership by year compared to membership of Japan, Korea,

and China, *180*; intention to exit WHO
under Trump administration, 8, 49; and
Iran, 39, 106–8, 386; and Israel, 361–62;
and IWC, 248, 251; and the League of
Nations, 194; and leverage from alliance
ties, 209; and Mexico, 4, 94, 152; non-
NATO allies, 142, 168; and North Korea,
343; and Palestine, 360, 362, 363, 365,
367; and Russia, 386; and sharing security interests with states that are not
formal allies, 21–22; and South Africa,
369, 374, 375, 377–78, 380; and South
Korea, 341, 347; sponsorship of applicants to GATT/WTO, 101–3, 121, 179,
387; sponsorship of Japan, 179, 187–88,
203–4, 206–7, 387; and TAIPEI Act, 355;
and Taiwan, 349, 350, 352, 352n33, 352n35,
355–56, 358–60; and TPP, 226, 240–41;
and Treaty of Amity and Cooperation
in Southeast Asia, 304; UK favoring ties
with U.S. over ties to Europe, 283, 297–
99; UN voting compared to UK and
Europe, *298*; and UN voting similarity,
102; U.S.-Japanese alliance, 32, 56, 142, 177,
203–4, 215, 228, 232, 236, 251, 254, 256, 387;
U.S.-UK alliance, 297
universal organizations, 29–30, 33–34, 42–
44, 54, 68, 68, 70, 315–81, 334, 336, 337, 339;
accession rules and restrictions, 43, 43–
44, 57–58, 66–67, 314, 316–18, 327–29, 379;
analysis of factors affecting accession,
330–40, 334, 336, 337, 339; as discriminatory clubs, 33–34, 318, 328–40, 379–80;
and embassies and IGO membership,
338; examples, 58; exclusion from, 313–81
(*see also* exclusion from international
organizations); and free rider problem,
317; and geopolitical alignment, 331, 335,
337, 379; and geopolitical discrimination,
315–18, 335, 340; and inefficiency of collective decision-making in heterogenous
groups, 384; and Japan, 203; legitimacy
of, 44, 317, 327; and North Korea, 34,
341–47; and Palestine, 33, 360–68; and

A NOTE ON THE TYPE

THIS BOOK has been composed in Arno, an Old-style serif typeface in the classic Venetian tradition, designed by Robert Slimbach at Adobe.

GPSR Authorized Representative: Easy Access System Europe - Mustamäe tee
50, 10621 Tallinn, Estonia, gpsr.requests@easproject.com